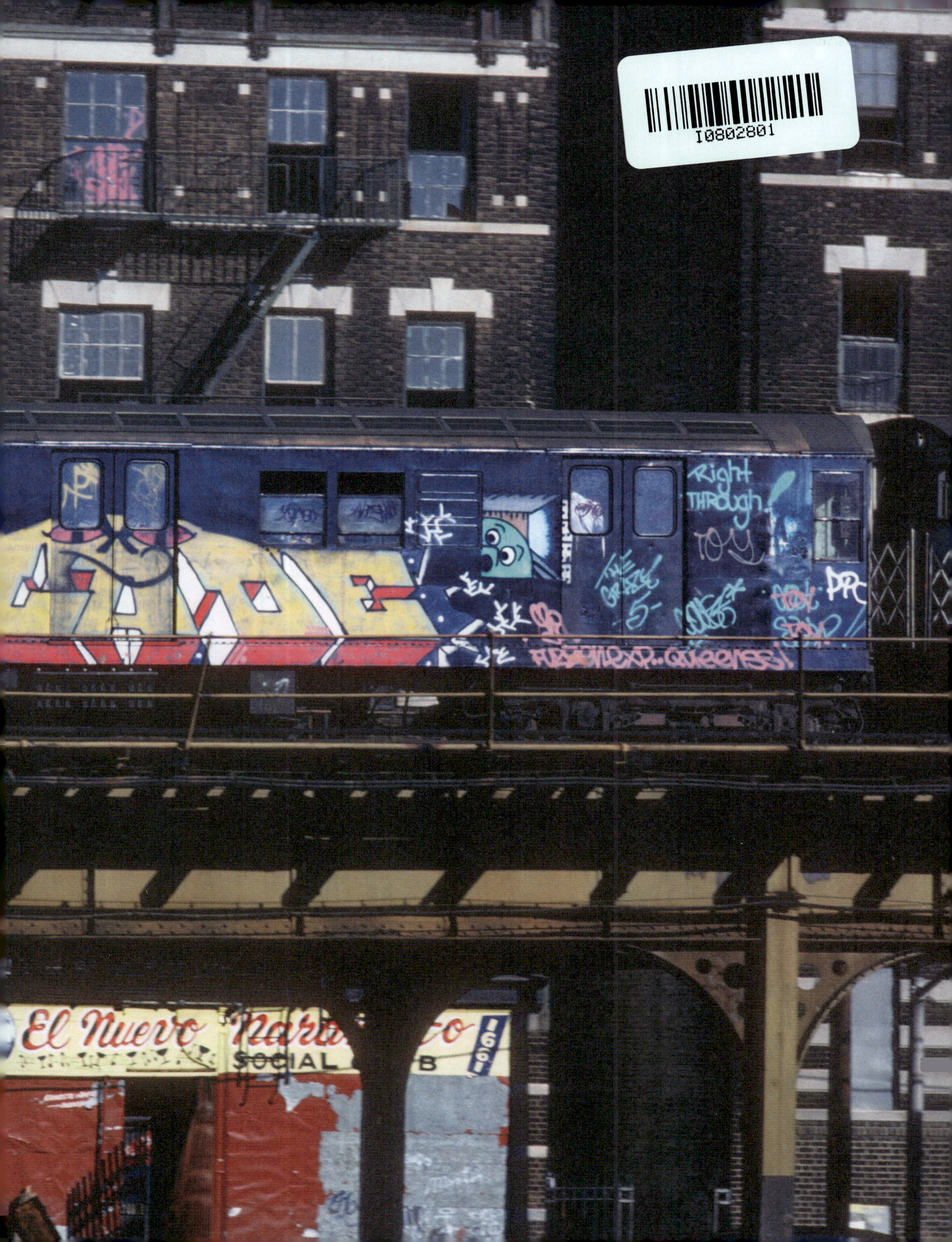
Right
THROUGH
El Nuevo
SOCIAL

BLADE
KING OF GRAFFITI

BLADE with Chris Pape
Roger Gastman, editor

Schiffer Publishing Ltd
4880 Lower Valley Road • Atglen, PA 19310

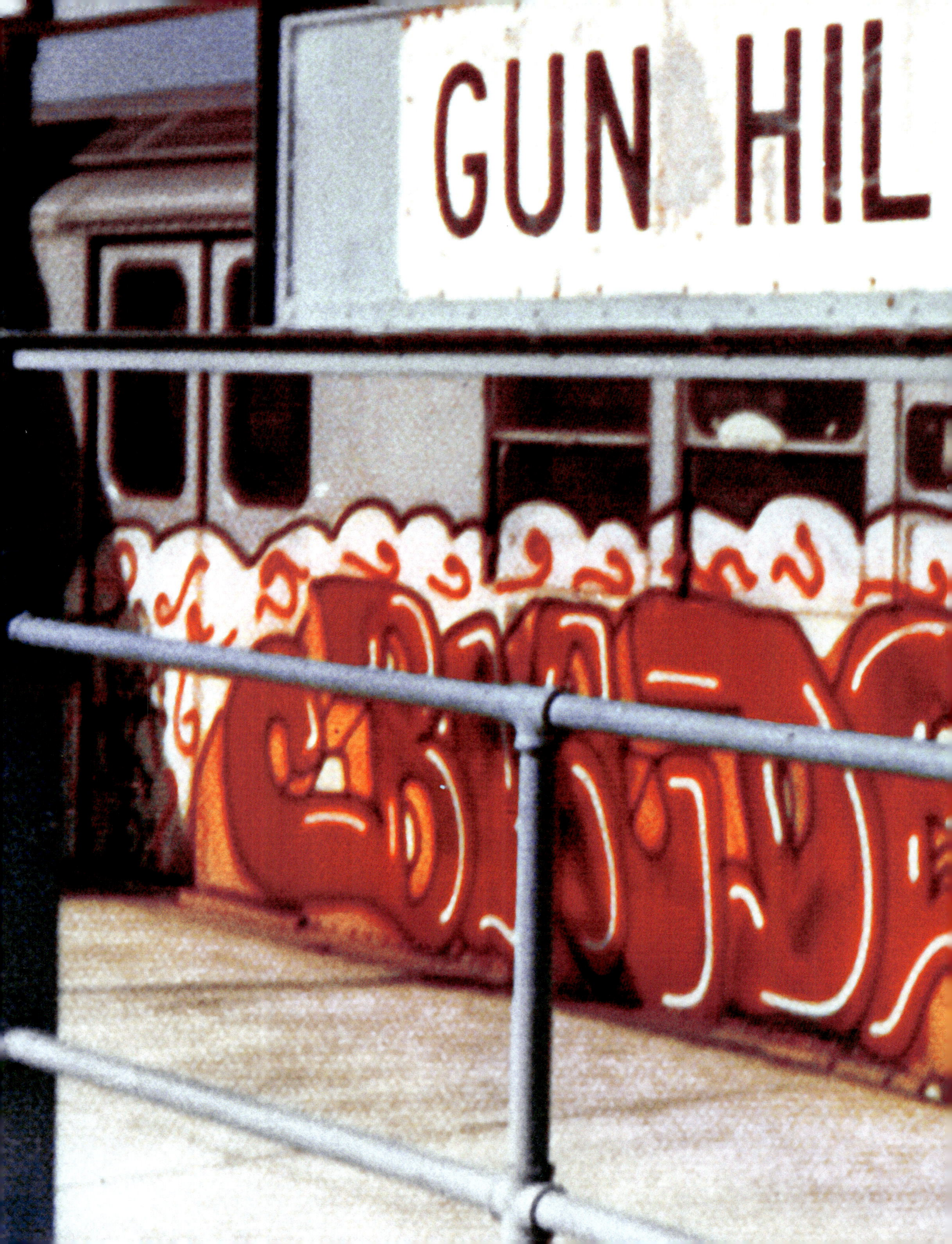
GUN HIL

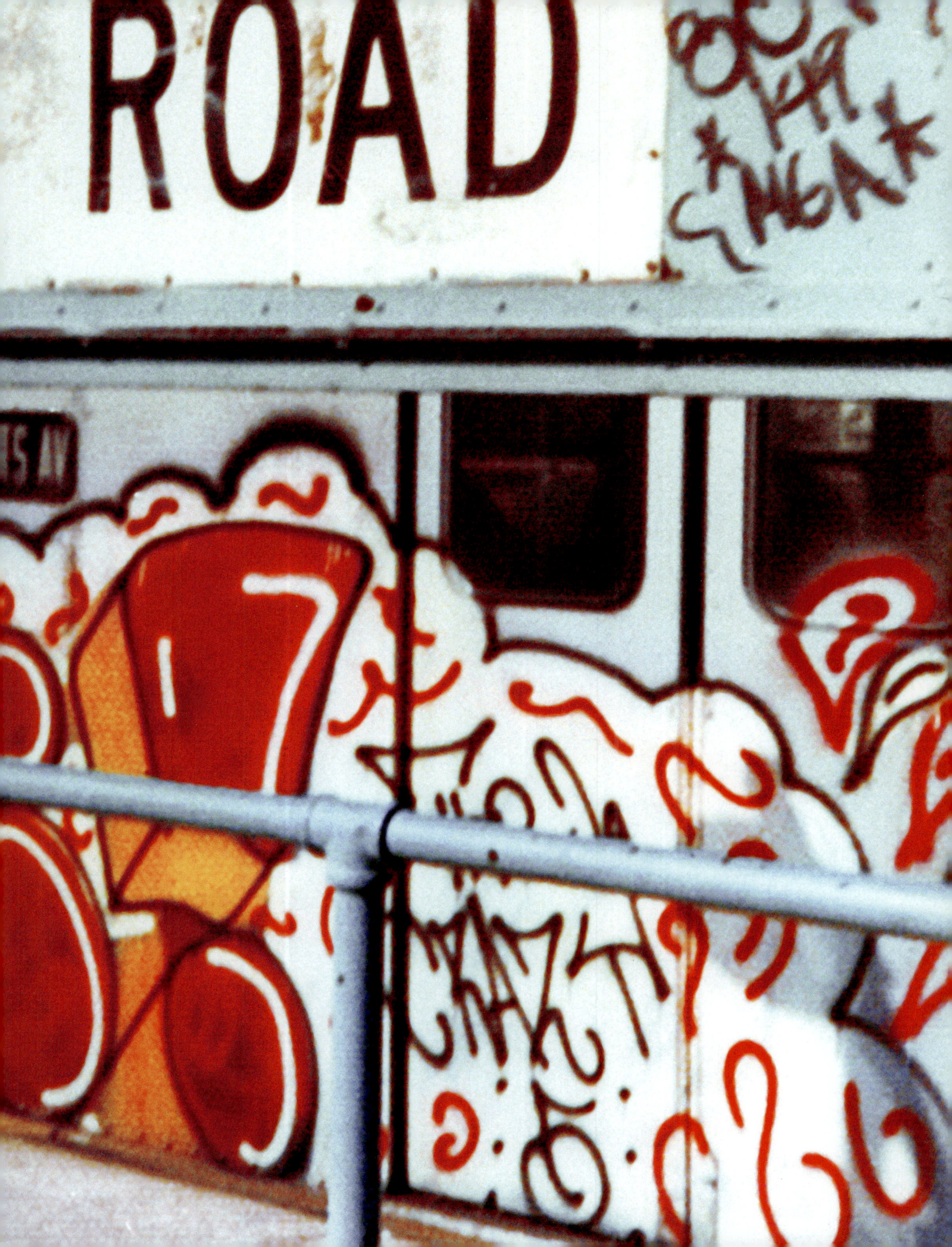
ROAD

Compiled & Edited by: Roger Gastman

Written by: BLADE with Chris Pape

About the Author: Chris Pape was born in 1960. He grew up on the upper west side of Manhattan where he watched the birth of the graffiti movement. In 1980 he started painting in a tunnel that would eventually become known as the Freedom tunnel. He currently lives in Brooklyn with his wife Elsa, and their kids Cora and Dash.

Art Direction by: Michael Delahaut & Leon Gonzalez

Photography by: BLADE, VAMM, CAVS, CRACHEE, DEATH, Martha Cooper, Henry Chalfant, Keith Baugh, Roger Gastman archives, Adam Wallacavage, SEEN, CHEA-OMM CREW The Netherlands, Jack Stewart, Malcolm Jacobson archives, Aileen Middel (Mick La Rock)

Scanning & Production by: Deanna Guzman, Leon Gonzalez, Francesca Quintano, Soraya Espinoza, CAVS, dirtypilot.com

Special Thanks: Henry Chalfant, Martha Cooper, Keith Baugh, Portia, Elsa Ransom, CAVS who tirelessly archived & scanned countless BLADE images, dirtypilot.com DEATH, COMET, CRACHEE, TULL 13, VAMM, GEAR, Caleb Neelon, Amanda Bessette, Nicky & Dracula

http://www.bladekingofgraf.com

Other Schiffer Books on Related Subjects:
New York City Graffiti: The Destiny Children, $50.00
ISBN: 978-0-7643-3720-8
Morris Park Crew: The Official History, $34.99
ISBN: 978-0-7643-4157-1
Don1, The King from Queens: The Life and Photos of a NYC Transit Graffiti Master, $29.99
ISBN: 978-0-7643-4500-5

Cover: Photo © by Martha Cooper
Back Cover: Photo © by Henry Chalfant
Opening spread: BLADE piece with original sketch. 1980. Photo © by Martha Cooper.
Closing spread: BLADE. 1975. Photo ©Keith Baugh.

Library of Congress Control Number: 2014930877

ISBN: 978-0-7643-4661-3
Printed in China
5 4 3 2

Published by Schiffer Publishing Ltd.
4880 Lower Valley Road
Atglen, PA 19310
Phone: (610) 593-1777; Fax (610) 693-2002
E-mail: info@schifferbooks.com

Previous spread: BLADE rolls through the Gun Hill Road station. Circa 1975.
Opposite page: Detail of JOHN 150 and BLADE train. 1975. Photo ©Keith Baugh.

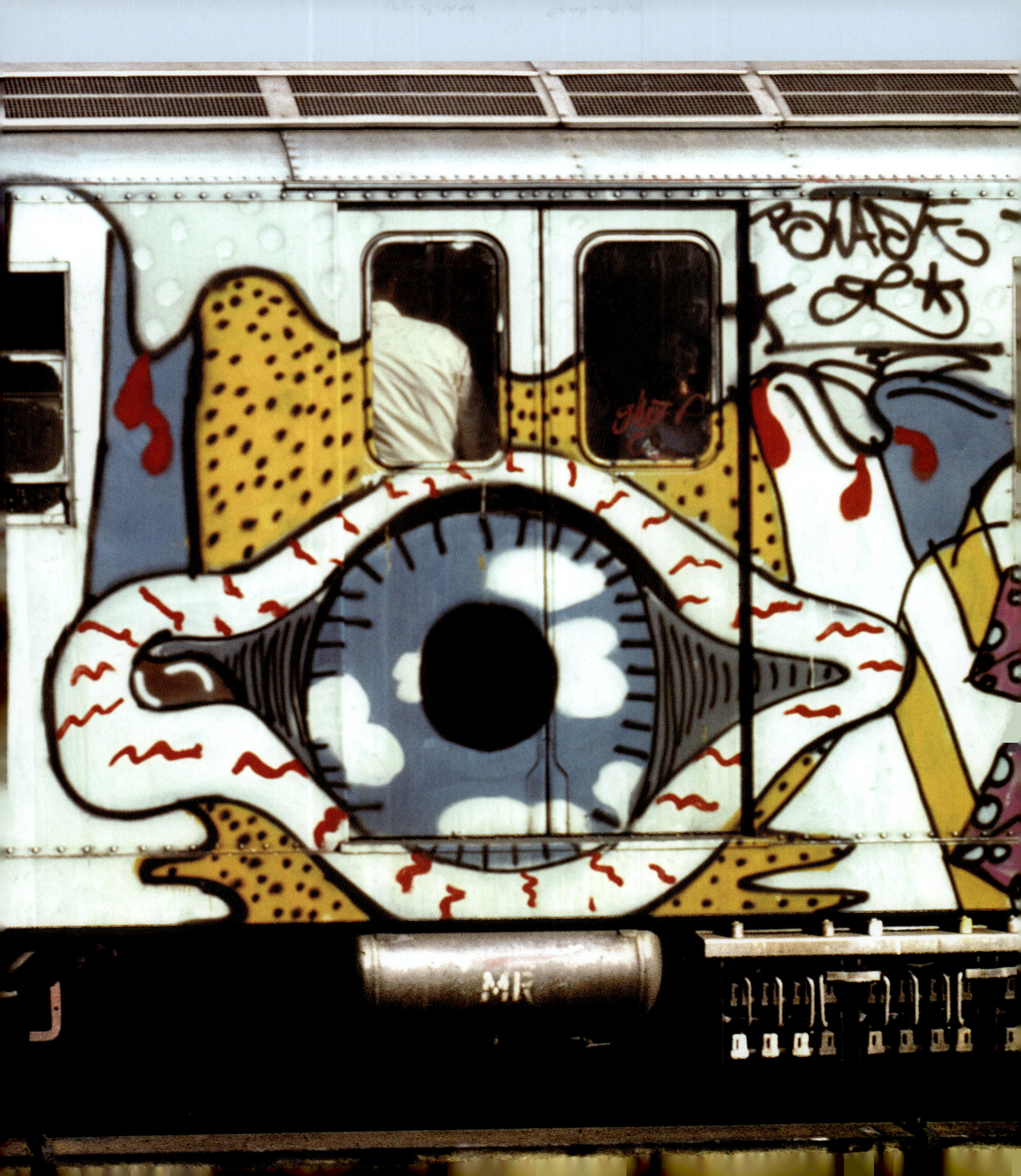
MR

CONTENTS

Opposite page: BLADE with some fresh cans of paint. 1972.
Following spread: BLADE's many boxes of photos. 2012. Photo by Adam Wallacavage.

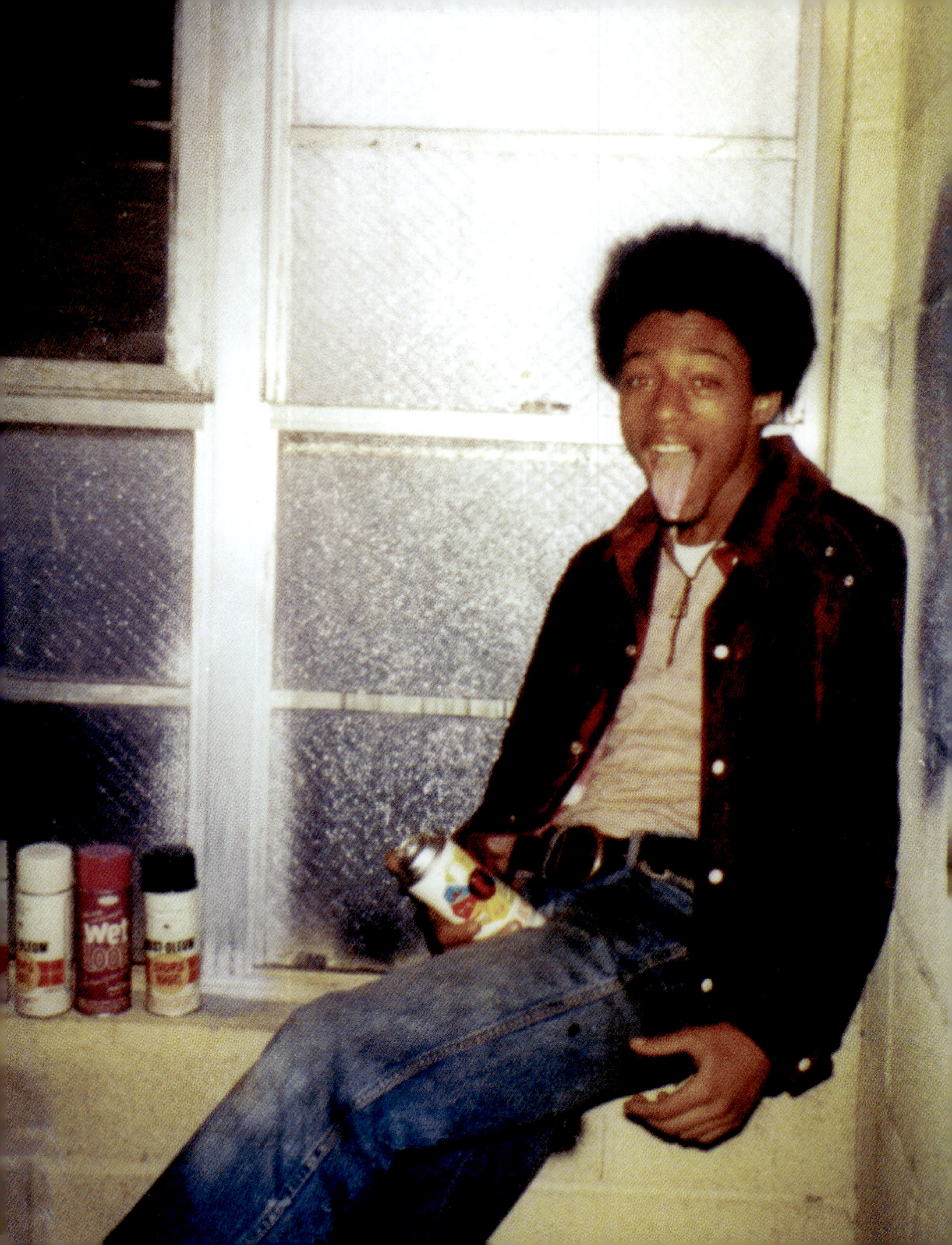
wet

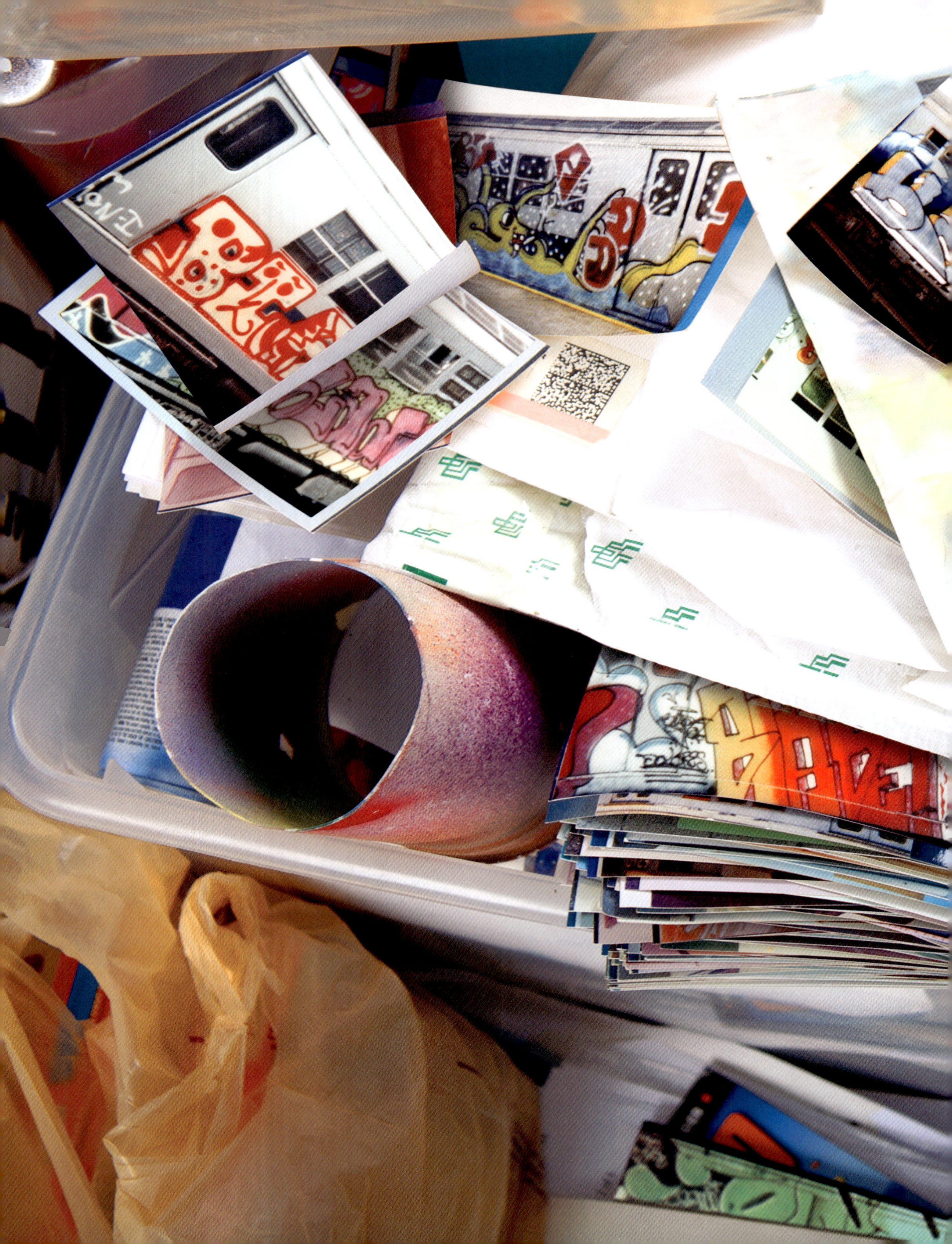

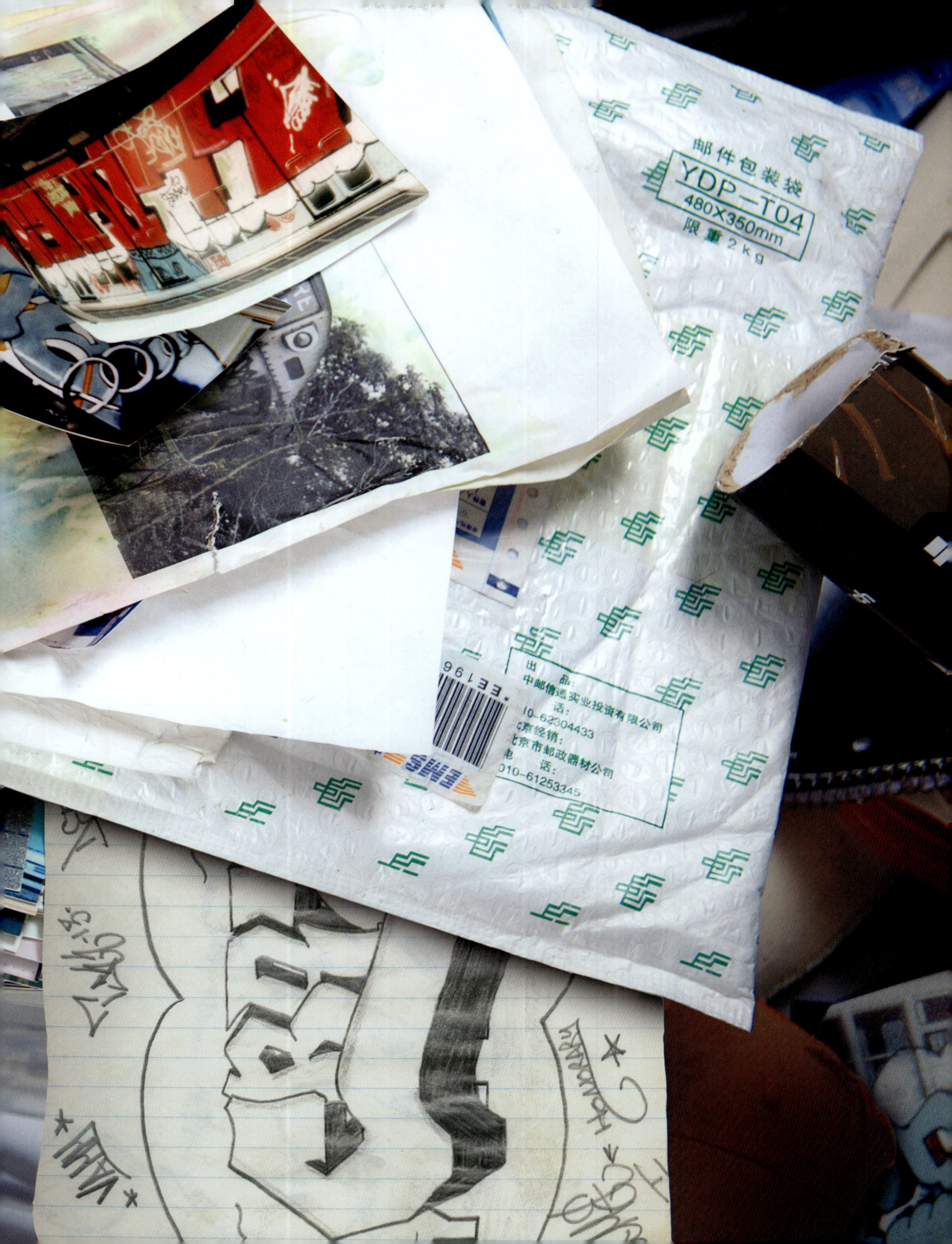
邮件包装袋
YDP—T04
480X350mm
限重2kg
中邮信通实业投资有限公司
10-62304433
北京市邮政器材公司
010-61253345

FOREWORD

Before New York City made graffiti world famous, BLADE was one of the people who made it famous in New York. He made it famous by making it look fun, and when he made it look fun, every kid in New York wanted to have fun too. BLADE's letters are readable, clunky and funky. Unlike most other kids, who were copying comic strip characters, the beasties, ladies and gentlemen that heralded BLADE's pieces were original to him and full of charm. His color palettes were thought out and carefully planned, even though that meant a whole lot of work to maintain a paint stash.

Many dozens of graffiti books have been published in the past fifteen or so years, and BLADE has been in most of them—the story of graffiti without him is wrong. While graffiti writers around the world often visibly trace the lineage of their lettering style to one of BLADE's very few peers in the history of New York subway graffiti, those who follow BLADE seem to do so in spirit, in looseness, and in a sense of freedom and fun. With BLADE's work, it's about that essential freedom of execution, and not the technical bends, breaks, and contours of the design he's rendering. And while it's impossible to measure, we'd guess that BLADE had the most fun of anyone out there.

For all of the—ahem—freedom that BLADE enjoyed in the 1970s, he still has an incredible memory and sat for countless hours with Chris Pape (another kind of FREEDOM) to remember the highs and lows of his storied career. While well spoken and a gentleman, BLADE also held nothing back. His story spans some very difficult years, but he stays remarkably upbeat. It speaks well of BLADE that the dozens of people who were contacted to help with this book all did so with alacrity and were eager to tell a story, help confirm a date or contribute images.

BLADE's influence on the history of graffiti is undeniable, and the number of writers whose output even approaches his on trains and streets of New York is tiny. No one book could ever hold it all, but this one brings us more images of his pieces than have ever been gathered in one place before. A read through this book will show that for reasons of quantity, quality, and perhaps above all for force of sheer spirit, BLADE may well be most graffiti artists' favorite graffiti artist. He's ours.

- Roger Gastman and Caleb Neelon

Opposite page: Various works by BLADE. Circa 1970s.
Following spread: BLADE tribute painted by RIME and designed by FREEDOM for MoCA's Art in the Streets exhibit. 2011.
Photo by Gregory Bojorquez

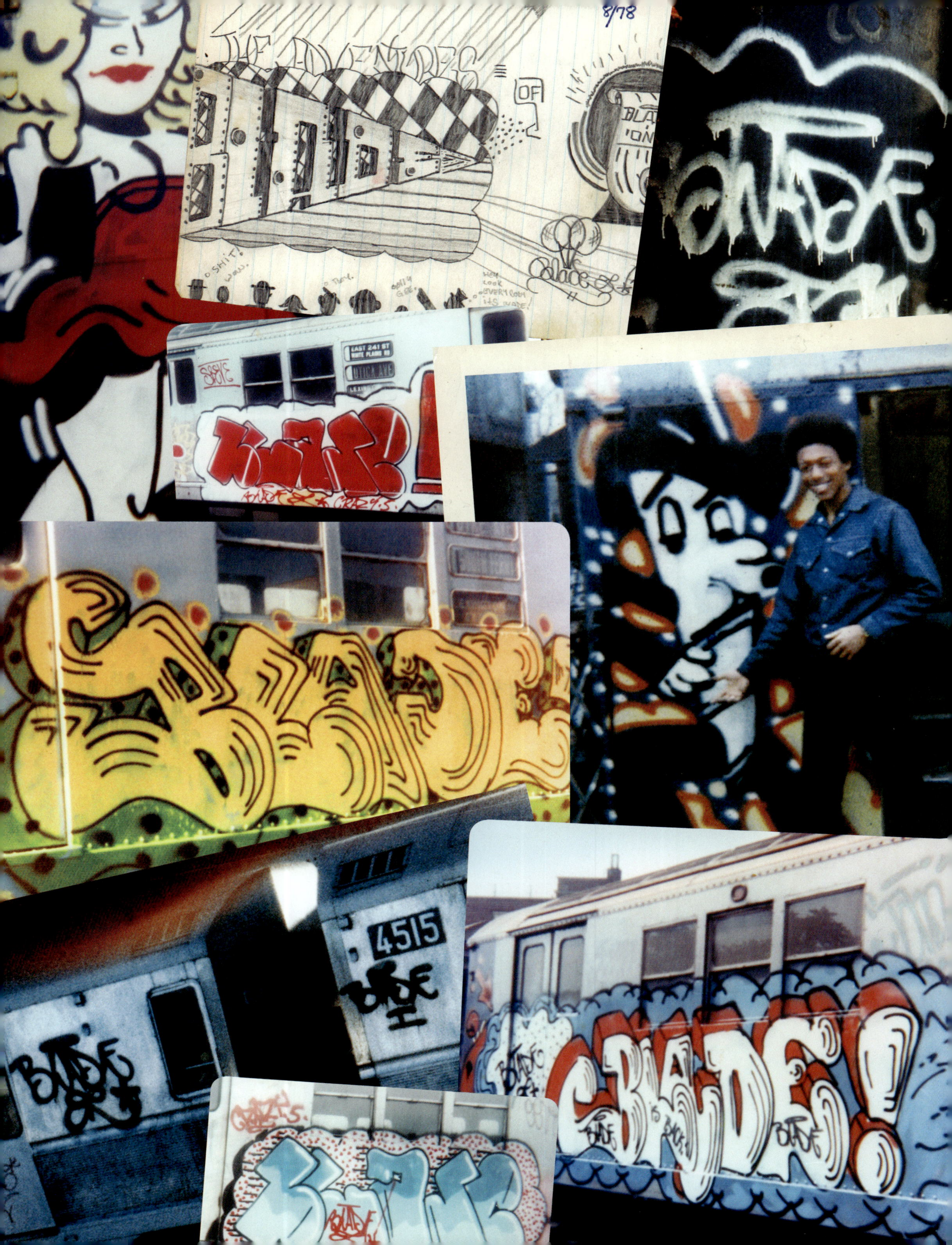
8/78
THE ADVENTURES OF
EAST 241 ST
WHITE PLAINS RD
UTICA AVE
4515

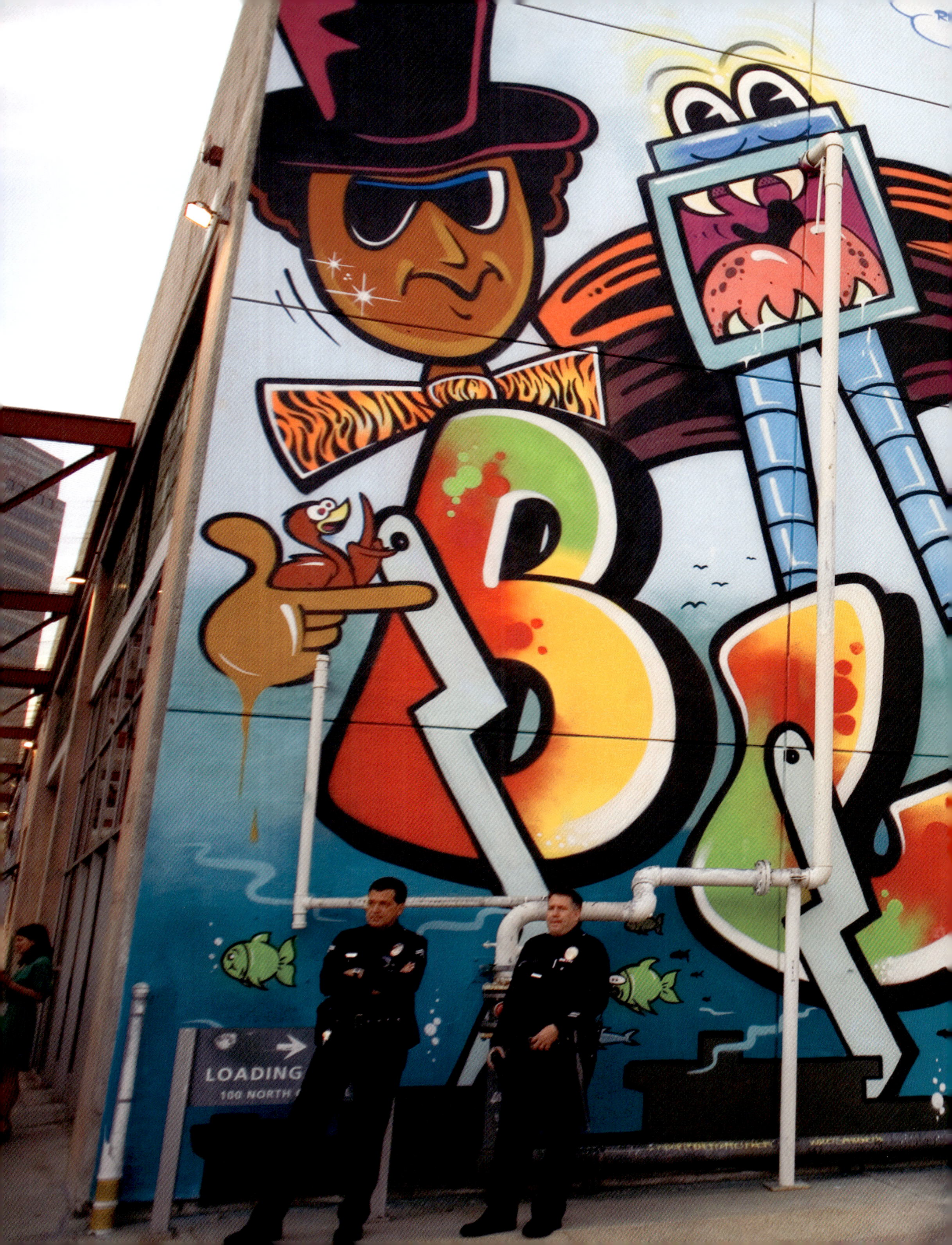
LOADING

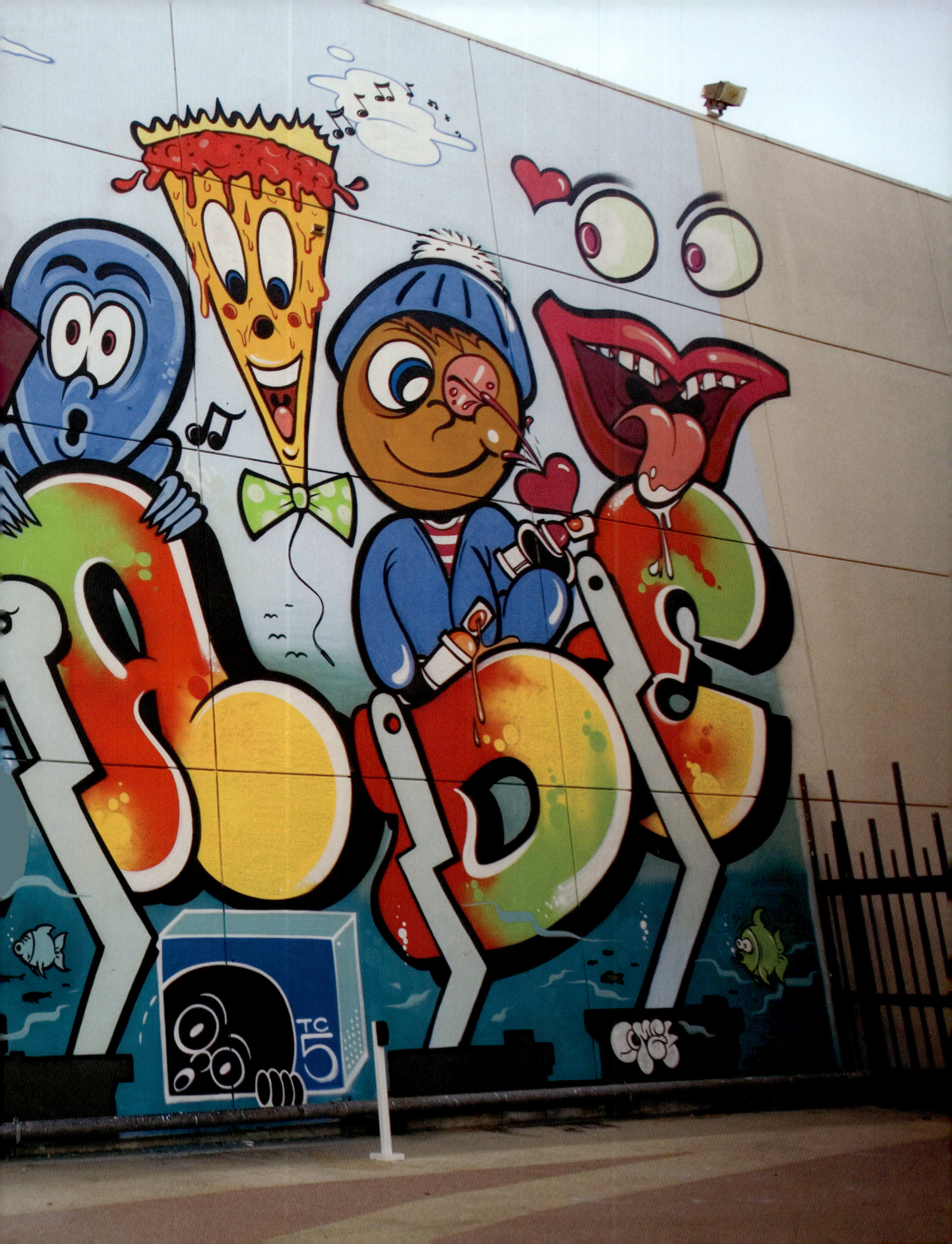
TC
5

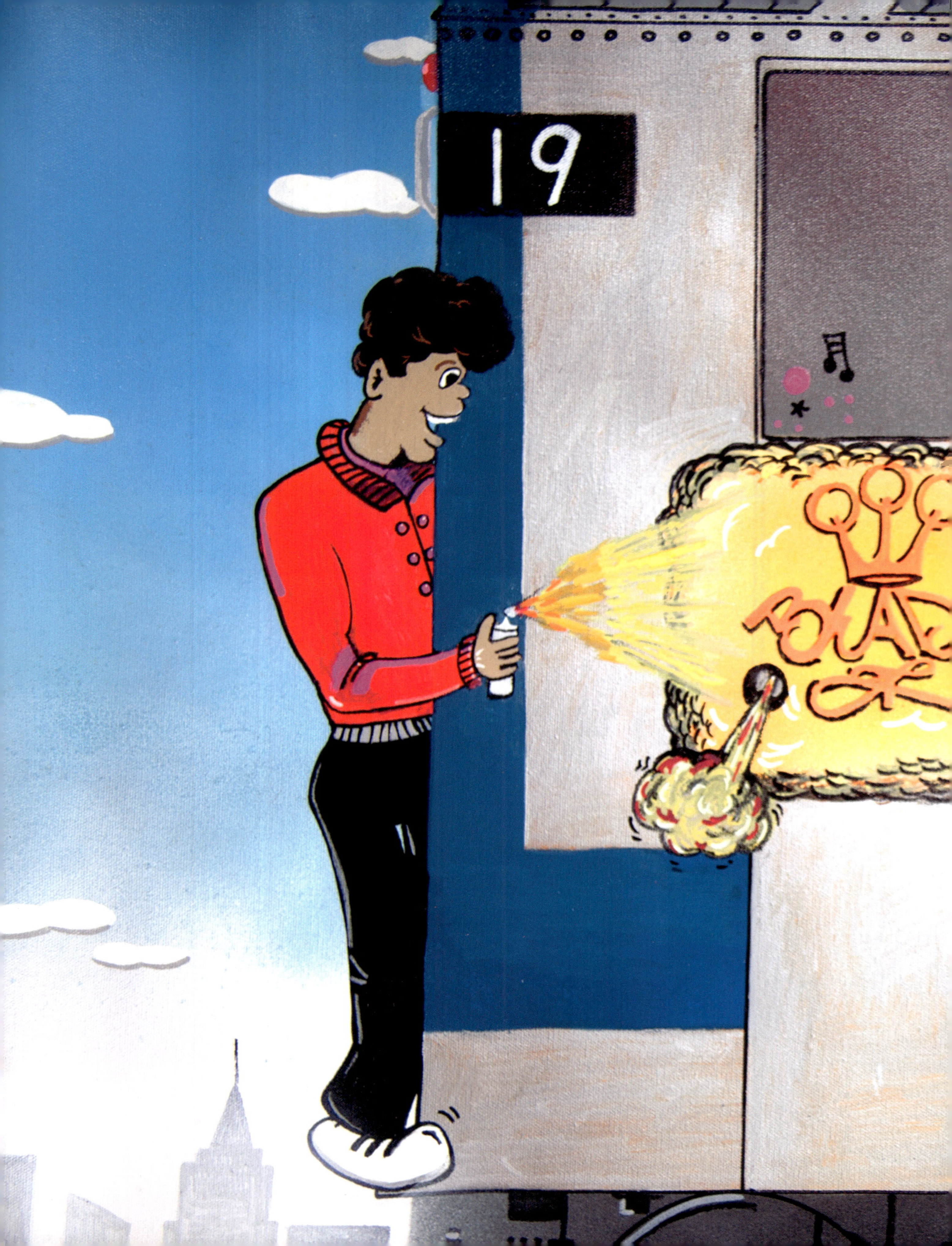
19

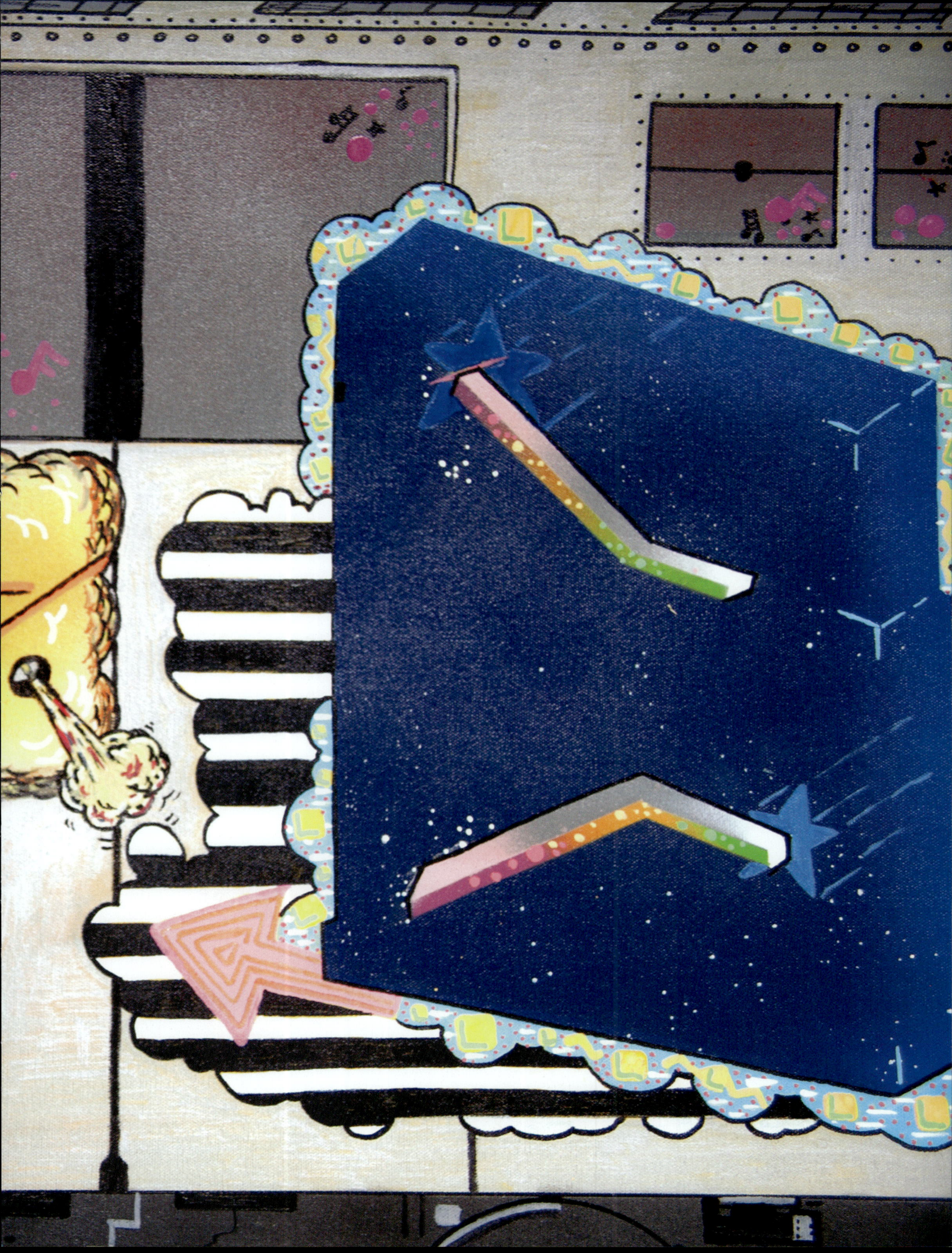

CHAPTER ONE

MY GENERATION:
1957–1968

My name has been BLADE for four decades—forty years. Everyone calls me that, from the casual graffiti fan to my own family. It sometimes feels strange to hear my real name, the one I was born with—Steven Ogburn.

I was born at St. Luke's Hospital on the Upper West Side of Manhattan in 1957. It was a good year for my generation because we just missed the draft for Vietnam. 1956 was the cut-off date. Years later, as a teenager, I thought about the randomness of it all as I watched friends get shipped off to a war they didn't want to fight in.

My dad was a staff sergeant in World War II. As a black man he saw racism at its ugliest. I'm sure the fact that he couldn't become an officer in the same army in which he trained men bothered him. After the war, my dad really wanted a career as a bus driver. He learned how to drive all sorts of trucks in the military, and so he wanted to work for Greyhound, drive a bus, and live in Levittown (the suburban idyll built on Long Island). Neither of those dreams was attainable because of his race, and that bothered him for a long time.

He and my mom settled on the Upper West Side and lived there throughout the 1950s. While my dad saved up to buy a house in the suburbs, they took advantage of the proximity of Harlem and all of the great jazz bands. My Uncle George was a drummer for a lot of the great bands at the time, including Duke Ellington and Count Basie, so he was able to get my parents into the gigs for free. My dad worked tough jobs during the day and became an excellent mamba dancer at night. It may have been their happiest time. And then I was born.

My parents didn't start a family right after the war, because they wanted to hold out until they could live in the suburbs. Parkside Houses in the North Bronx was one of hundreds of projects built for blue-collar families in New York after World War II. That was the suburbs for us. The projects housed laborers who worked at all of the various factories, my dad included. That part of the Bronx was primarily Jewish and Italian, but we seemed to have everybody at Parkside, although we were one of the few black families.

Previous spread: Self portrait detail of a BLADE painting. 2008. Photo by Adam Wallacavage.
Opposite page: Top: Baby BLADE. 1957. Bottom: BLADE (fourth from left, standing) and his family. Circa 1962.

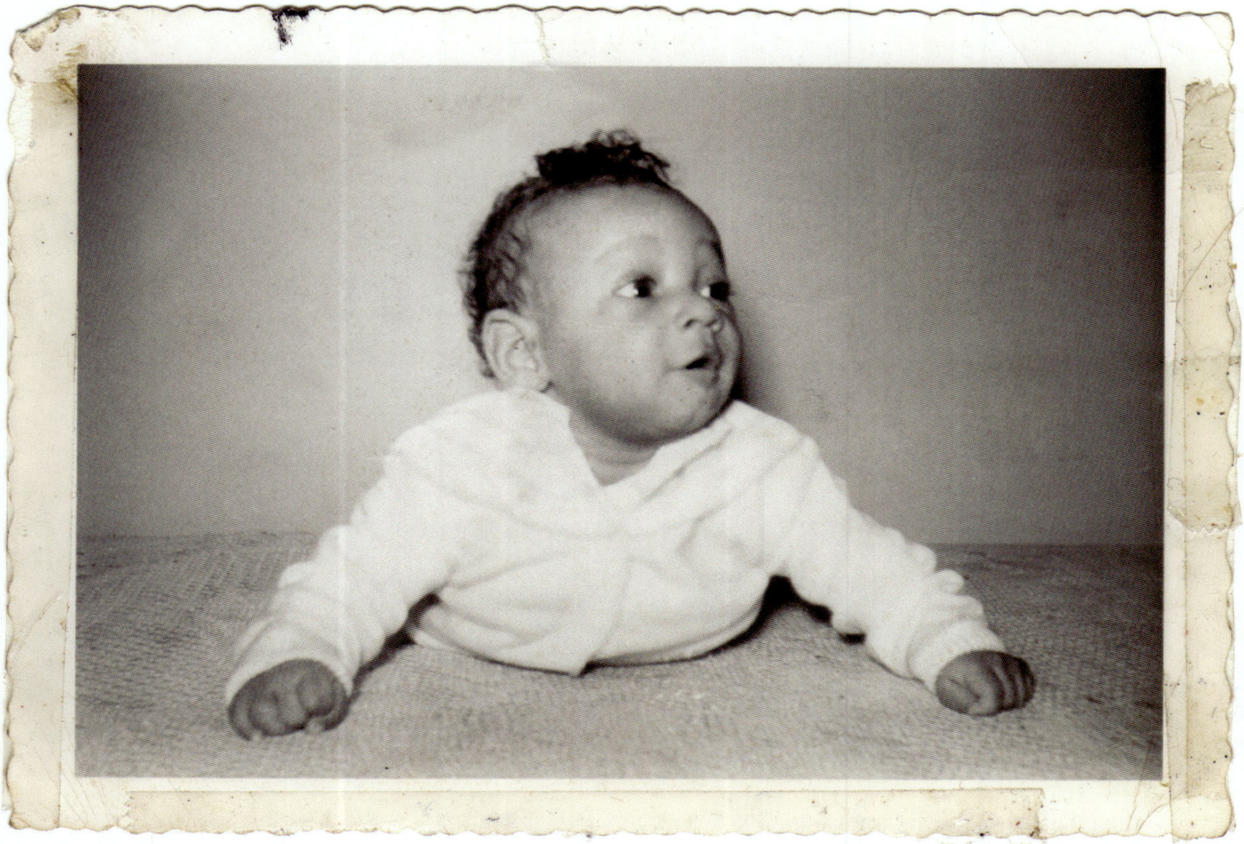

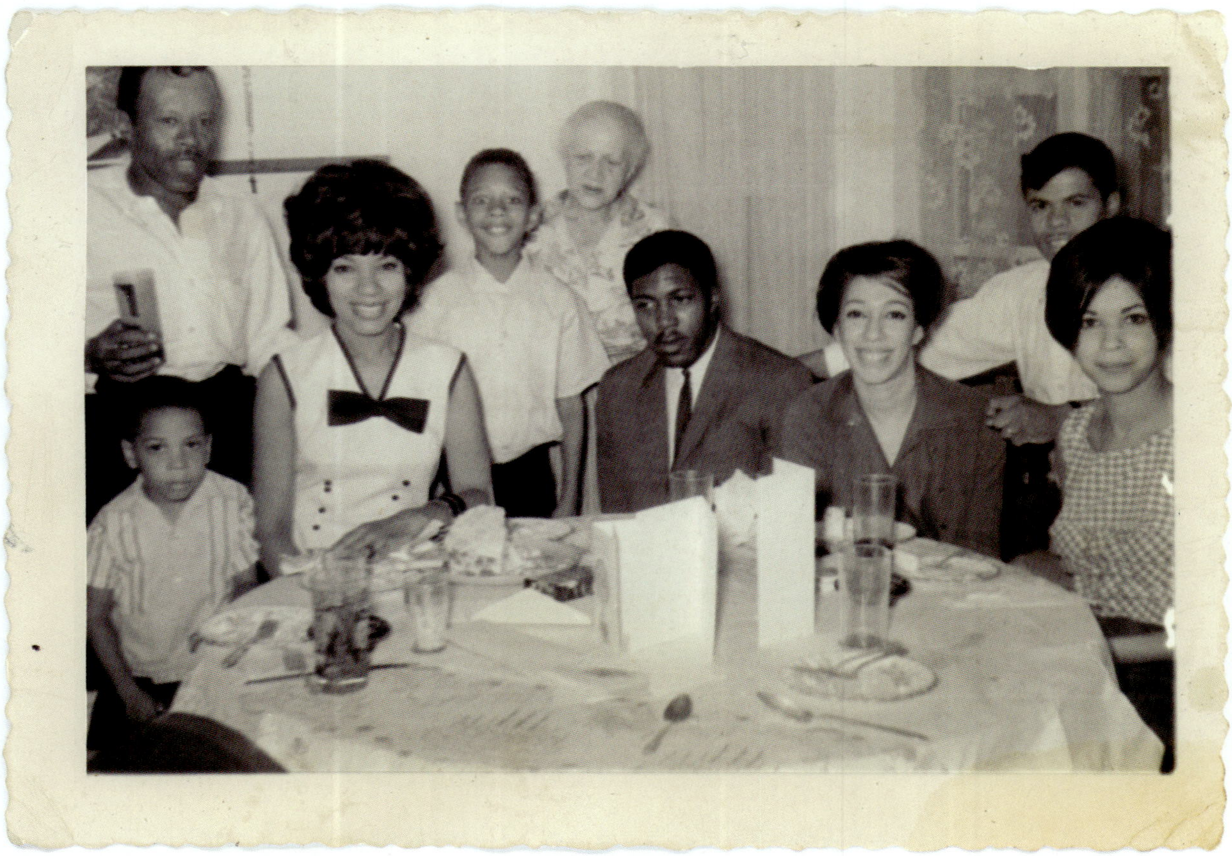

The Bronx was a fractured borough. The Italians fought the Irish and the Irish fought the Jews. At Parkside people were forced to live with each other, and for the most part it worked. If you viewed the projects from the sky they took up three city blocks. There were ten buildings in all, with dense foliage to make it feel more rural. Running along the perimeter of Parkside was the number 2 train. The tracks stretched right past my windows. As a kid I watched as the tenants of Parkside made the long commute into Manhattan.

I had many friends. We all went to the same school and hung out in the same playground, so it was almost impossible to not know the other kids your age. Michael Visvader was Italian; Mitch Weiss was Jewish. Mitch lived below me on the first floor of our building; Michael lived next door. Years later we would go on incredible adventures, but in the mid-1960s we were limited to the playground at Parkside. Our biggest goal at that age was to wrestle the playground away from the older kids so we could shoot hoops.

Our other hangout was a little candy store across the street called Izzy and Phil's. We'd go in and get egg creams for a dime or we'd stretch deep into the soda cooler (with the ice floating by) and pick out a Coke. Izzy and Phil's had everything a kid could want: baseball cards, comics, spinning tops, and Spaldeens. If you needed it, Izzy and Phil's had it. There was an old school phone booth made of wood. Older guys would sit inside it, smoking cigarettes and calling their bookies. I learned a lot of my early curse words from that phone booth, as losing bettors smashed the phone into the receiver. But the egg cream was the big draw. Nobody made an egg cream like Izzy and Phil's.

In the mid-1960s the projects had no locks on them so you could play Project Tag all night and hope to catch your girlfriend in the staircase and grab a kiss. Usually we'd come home from school, watch Speed Racer, The 8th Man, and Officer Joe Bolton then head out to play. My parents might go out on a weekend night. Theirs was the first generation that had any disposable income and they wanted to experience things. Sometimes I had a babysitter; sometimes not; it didn't really matter. We weren't afraid and our parents weren't afraid. It was completely different than today when every time you turn on the TV you see an Amber alert.

New York was still a factory town—although not by much—so you could see the factories right across from Parkside Houses. My father worked in a belt factory until the mid-1960s, stamping holes in leather until the day it closed. My friend Jody, who lived in our building, had a mom who also worked in a factory until they closed. I thought it must have been awful work, so I was glad when my dad became a Fuller Brush man. It was a time when people were happy to see a "negro" man at the front door with the latest vacuum cleaner. My dad's sales pitch broke up the monotony of the day. All of that's lost on this generation, where you can buy everything at Walmart or on the computer.

Every night I watched Batman on ABC. On Sunday nights the family gathered around to watch The Ed Sullivan Show. We watched him mostly for the music acts, because he had some cool bands on. The Flip Wilson Show of the early 1970s amazed me. This black guy had his own variety show with great acts like James Brown and The Jackson Five. It seemed like everything came to us through the TV, all of the major historical events, and it was really vivid.

I was six years old and in Catholic school when John F. Kennedy was assassinated in 1963. I remember it so well. When we got home from school my parents were crushed and my mother was crying. All those assassinations seemed to happen back-to-back, from JFK to Malcolm to King and then Robert Kennedy. Kill 'em, kill 'em, kill 'em! It was like an assault. It especially hurt when Robert Kennedy died because he was trying to end the war and we really thought he'd do it. All of those events came to us through the TV.

A few years earlier I may not have cared about the political process. But in 1968 everybody was thinking about the war and everyone knew someone who came back from it. Kennedy's death was a big awakening. His death left a numbness that was different than the King assassination. When King died there were anger and riots, whereas with Robert Kennedy there was more of a sense of resignation. Either way, for the first time we were aware of things outside our neighborhood.

The last of the old street gangs were just going through the motions by 1965. A lot of them died from heroin. Others went to Vietnam—not by choice. It was usually one felony too many, because back then it was jail or the army. Either way, the gangs didn't care about us, so they left us alone. It wasn't until years later that violent gangs like The Black Spades, The Savage Nomads, and the Golden Guineas came out in the Bronx.

The greasers and the gangs from the 1950s gave way to the hippies in the 1960s. Glaze and Stewie were some of the first hippies in the neighborhood. They had long hair, smoked weed openly, and we could always find them at the playground. We later learned they were dealing pot and hash, something we took advantage of once we heard. The greasers were fading away and the British invasion took hold. Groups like The Beatles and The Stones all had long hair. A car show was the only place you'd still see greasers and Doo-wop. By the mid-1960s long hair was worn by blacks and whites alike, so all of my friends had long hair growing up.

Glaze was a few years older than the rest of us, so he got to see the tail end of the gangs. One time, some guys from Parkside asked him if he wanted to go "skulling" with them. Glaze asked what "skulling" was and they said they'd get their baseball bats and find some niggers to hit over the head with them. Glaze was quizzical: "What did they do to you? Did they rob you? Did they spit on you?" They didn't have an answer, so he told them it was the stupidest thing he had ever heard and then walked away. Although there were some violent guys like this, mostly people got along.

By 1968, I wasn't a very good student. I was eleven years old, I went to Immaculate Conception on Gun Hill Road, and my dad—the former staff sergeant in World War II—didn't know what to make of me. My brother Craig, five years younger than me, seemed perfect because he did everything according to my father's expectations. I was different. Not only did my dad and I battle over school on a daily basis, but also bringing home my report card was cause for a beating. I don't blame my dad for the spankings, because that was the way his generation parented. All of my friends got spankings and we'd compare notes. Mine went like this: I'd walk into the house, my dad would point to my bedroom door, and that was it. I'd go in, wait five or ten minutes—the wait was sometimes more painful than the spankings—and then he'd appear with a belt and the whipping would begin.

While I don't blame my dad for that part of the situation, his final solution for my bad grades wasn't forgiven for a long time. I wasn't a bad kid. At eleven years old I was too young to be a bad kid. My only sin—I say that because I went to Catholic school—was that I couldn't get good grades. But my dad's solution was to buy me a one-way ticket to Saratoga Springs in upstate New York to live with my grandmother and my uncle. I was heartbroken. My parents put me on the bus all by myself for that long trip. Although I've cried a half dozen times since that day, I refused to cry that afternoon when my days at Parkside came to an end.

CHAPTER TWO

SARATOGA AND CO-OP CITY: 1968–1970

My Uncle George was my dad's brother-in-law and they were completely different. At the time, my uncle was fifty years old. We kind of looked alike. He was a drummer with Duke Ellington and had been around jazz clubs his whole life, which made him cool and very mellow. He made me want to get into music, because he allowed me to explore my artistic side—something that wasn't going to happen at Parkside Houses, since my mom, dad, and brother didn't have an artistic side. I grew to love my grandmother and uncle very much in the two years I spent in Saratoga.

Uncle George was doing jazz sessions in Saratoga by the racetrack. At eleven, I thought that was great. I called my Uncle George 'Dad' one day by accident—a deep moment for me. I had great respect for my uncle so I tried hard to do well in school. My grandmother was also important during that period because she provided a maternal touch. Granny was eighty years old when I lived with her. She was born on St. Patrick's Day in 1891 and took a shot of brandy every day of her adult life.

My first few months in Saratoga Springs were tough and I cried a great deal. I didn't understand why my father sent me there and so I thought of it as punishment for not doing well in school. It was a painful experience, but it got better. In fact, I grew to like it. My parents even visited a few times, which lead to me feeling like I had a shot at moving back to the Bronx.

I slept upstairs in a small room. I had the same experiences most small town kids did, whether it be fishing in a stream or catching frogs. Sometimes I walked to school; sometimes I rode my bike. We'd all leave our stingray bikes on the lawn outside of school. You'd never have seen that in the Bronx, so this was a new thing for me. In fact, everything I saw in Saratoga was new. From the horses in the stables to the clouds in the sky, everything seemed less busy, which I liked.

I made friends easily. My two best friends were Jimmy Dory and Billy Code. I remember we spent months building one go-cart, after school and weekends. We were obsessed. Uncle George supplied the tools and Granny tipped us off to where we could find stray planks of wood.

Opposite page:
BLADE plays with friends at his grandmother's house in Saratoga Springs. Circa 1969.

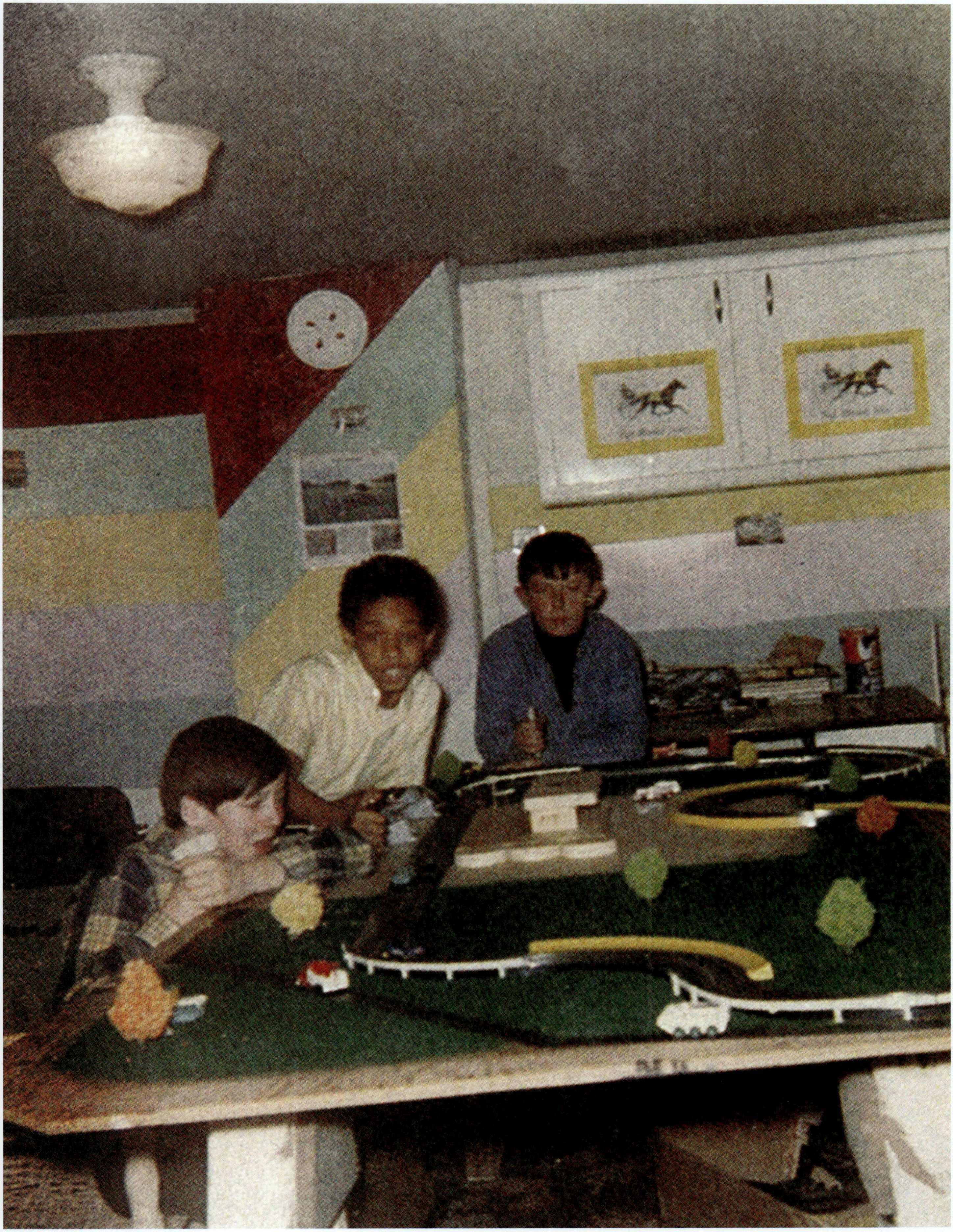

“I RAN ACROSS THE HIGHWAY AND CLIMBED THE FENCE WITH MY SUITCASE...”

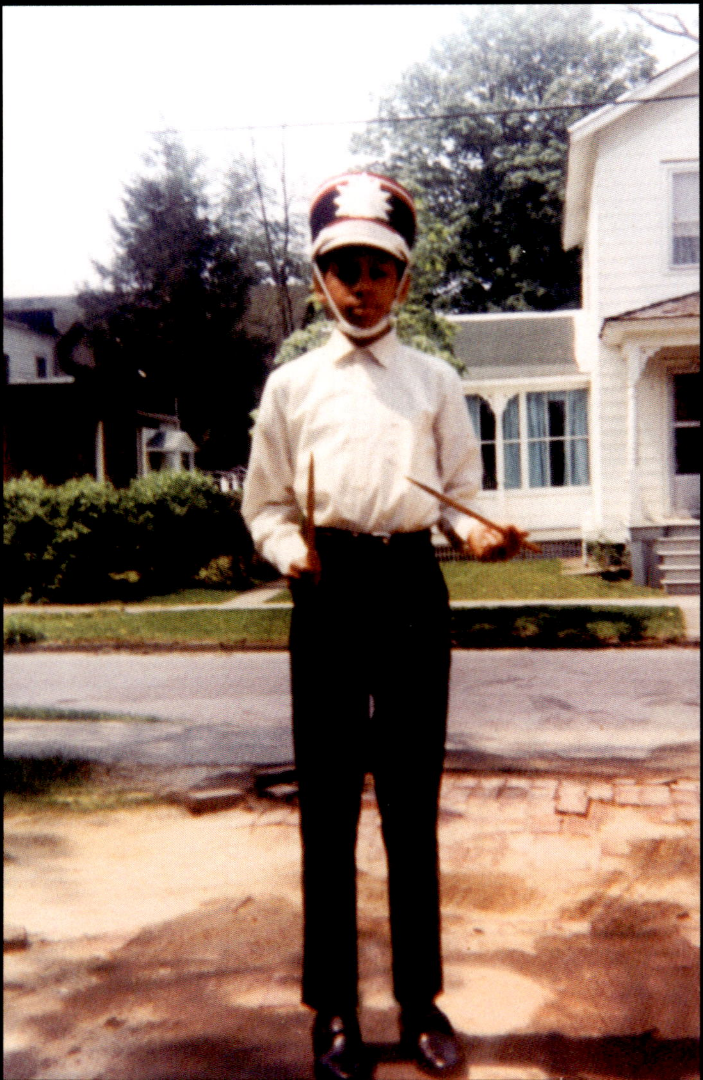

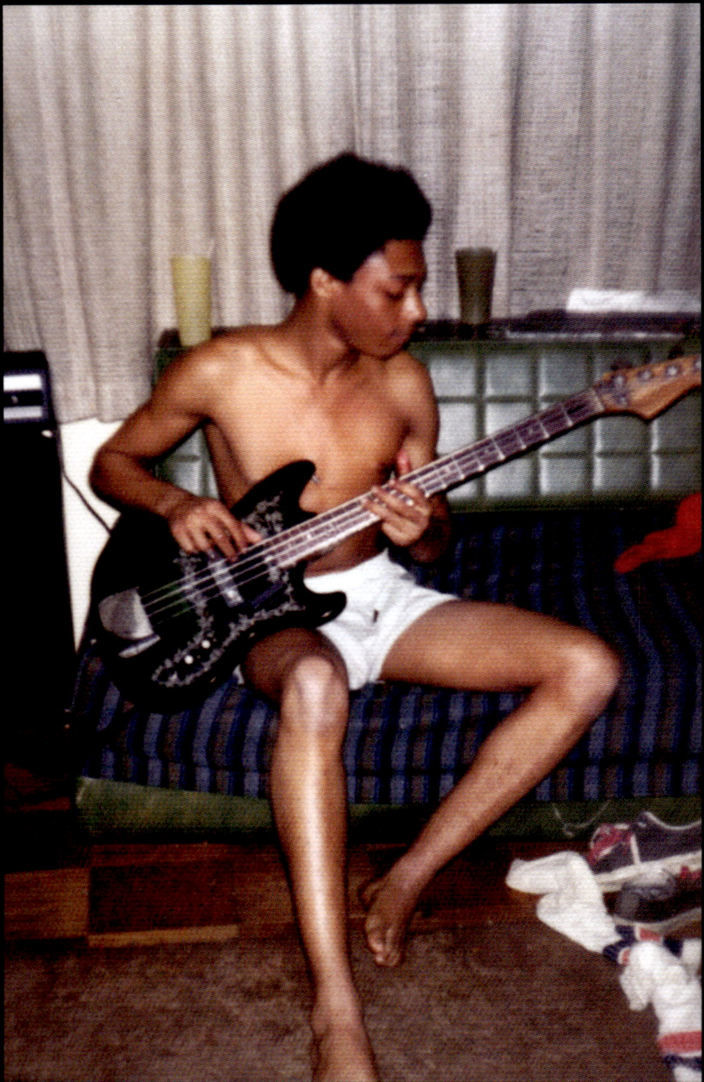

I was in Saratoga Springs for the moon landing. I'll always remember that. But Woodstock was a much bigger deal. All of my friends from Saratoga Springs went to Woodstock. It was attainable; the moon wasn't. At twelve years old, I asked my grandmother for permission to go to Woodstock. Her answer was "I was born in 1891 and you're not going." End of discussion.

When my parents finally did call for me, there was a side of me that didn't want to go back to the Bronx. I came back to New York in July of 1970 on a Trailways bus with my luggage and a pair of Converse sneakers. Nobody was there to pick me up at the Port Authority, so I took the train all the way up to the Baychester station in the Bronx. My parents moved while I was in Saratoga Springs, so I walked from the bus station to a home I had never seen in Co-op City. I ran across the highway and climbed the fence with my suitcase. There were only two buildings completed at the time, with construction started on dozens more. When I found our address, I rang the buzzer and my parents let me in. They had no idea I was coming and apologized for the mix up.

The new apartment was much nicer than Parkside. It was clean and new, as though the paint were still wet. With the new apartment the family seemed happy. I remember feeling as though I intruded upon their newly found happiness. Craig and I shared a room. Since my family had moved without me, he was already comfortable. There was a side of me that always wondered when I would be shipped away again. I resented my father for having that power over me, but it was something we never really talked about.

Co-op City was built on the former site of Freedomland U.S.A, a disused amusement park. It was at a time in the Bronx when the blacks and Hispanics were taking over the Grand Concourse. Co-op City was an oasis for Jews looking to get out of the South Bronx. Freedomland U.S.A wasn't making any money and all of this land was a swamp, so there was the question of what to do with the land. As the blacks moved further north into the Parkside Houses, the

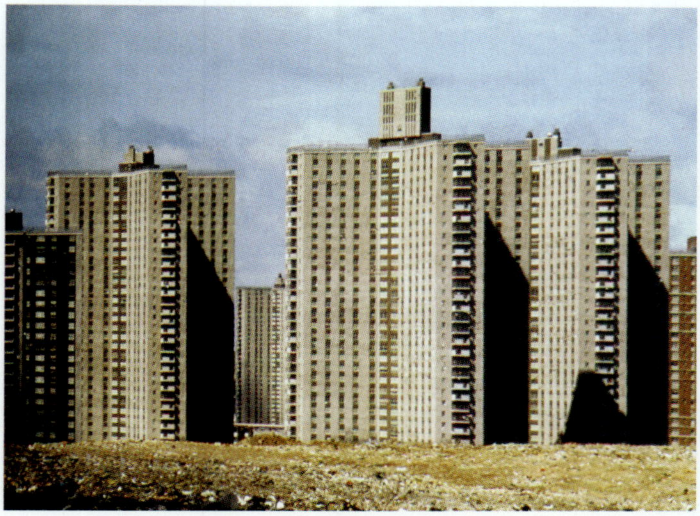

families that could afford it moved further up the rung to Co-op City. My mother was the head of the Department of Buildings, so if you wanted an apartment at Co-op City hers was the final signature necessary to get it. That's how my family got one of the first places.

My dad left his Fuller Brush Man job and started driving a taxi. He eventually saved enough money to buy his own taxi medallion. Back then, it cost around $20,000 and you could purchase it from the Taxi and Limousine Commission. The medallion meant you were the real thing, rather than being some gypsy cab driver who roamed the outer boroughs. My dad sold that taxi medallion in the early eighties for $106,000 and turned a nice profit.

During my time in Saratoga Springs, I had become a better student. My improved grades helped diffuse some of the tension between my dad and me. Of course, my brother Craig always did well in school, went along with the program, and never made waves. Today he's a top broker on Wall Street.

CHAPTER THREE

A MOVEMENT BEGINS:
1970–1973

Upon returning home to the Bronx in the fall of 1970, I started to notice graffiti. I would see single hits on buses and trains—little marker tags. On the streets, writers were bolder and hit them with spray paint. Two names I remember from back then are STAFF 161 and TUROK 161. I would find out later that TUROK 161 was a Manhattan writer, and not from the Bronx, which added to the mystery element of graffiti: What was TUROK 161 doing in my neighborhood? Graffiti seemed like such a secret world with three major questions: Who did it? When did they do it? And where did they do it? I figured I would find the answers to my questions once I started writing. But first I needed a name—a very cool name.

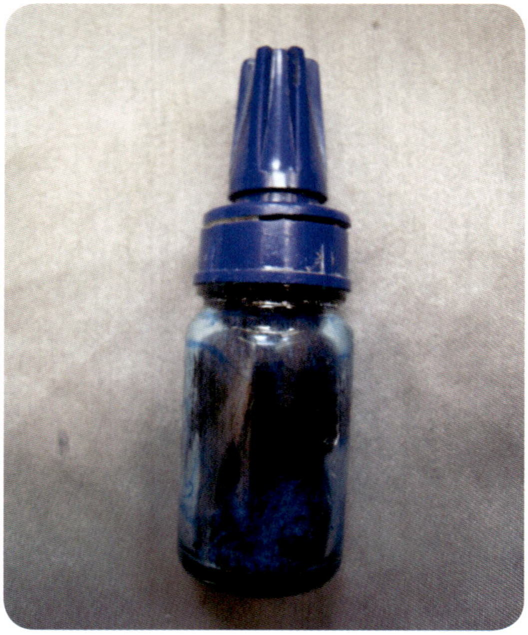

In 1971, I was working at a Pathmark supermarket in Co-op City. Part of my job was breaking down boxes with a box cutter, which I usually carried with me. Thinking about how I wanted to write on buses and first needed a name, I reached into my pocket and took out the box cutter. I pushed the lever back and forth with my thumb and stared down at the sharp razor—hmmmm. I went upstairs and borrowed a magic marker from a friend of mine. I wrote the name BLADE 1 on as many old boxes as I could. By the time I was done, every box in the basement had my name on it and the style of my hit was taking form. I immediately loved the name. Now, I just had to get it around.

Having a name and getting it up were separate things, and this is where a lot of graffiti careers ended. My first few single hits were done with a Dri Mark, a small marker that fit easily into the hand and was easy to steal from stores. I wrote the name BLADE 1 on the inside of buses. The easiest spots for kids to hit were the backs of the last seats. Even while the bus was moving, you could crouch down and quickly hit your name. The seat you were tagging blocked you from just about everyone, including the bus driver. I had no illusions that I was becoming a great writer; in fact, it made me wonder even more how the more famous writers hit the outsides with spray paint.

This page: Dri Mark marker courtesy of SPAR.
Opposite page: One of BLADE's earliest tags. Circa 1973.

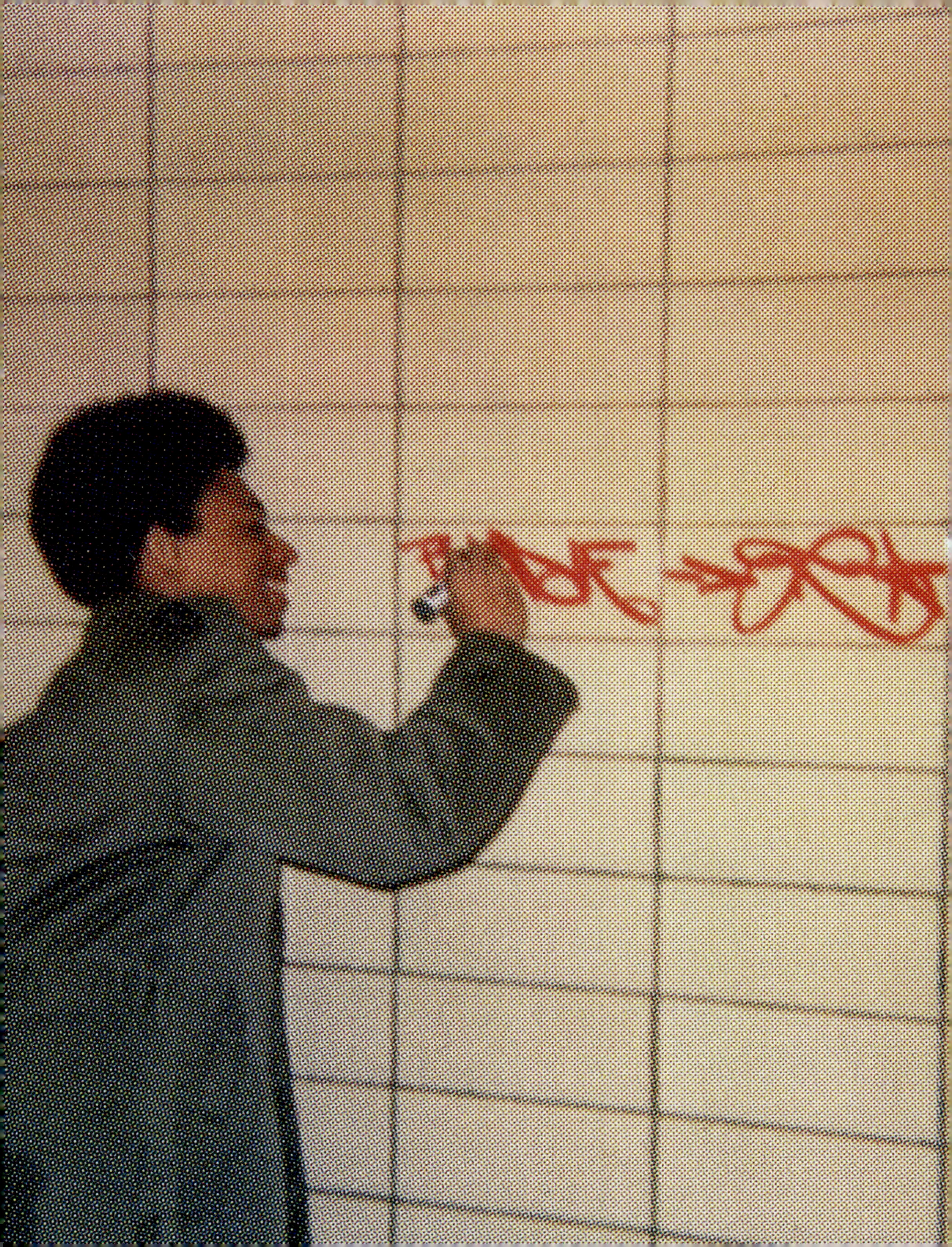

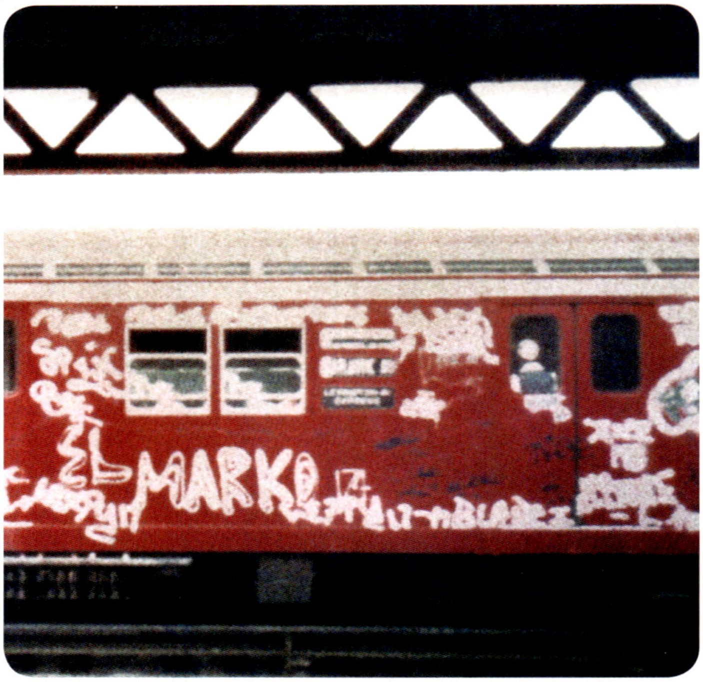

"I WANTED TO LOOK JUST LIKE THEM, SO FOR CHRISTMAS MY PARENTS GOT ME A VINYL JACKET..."

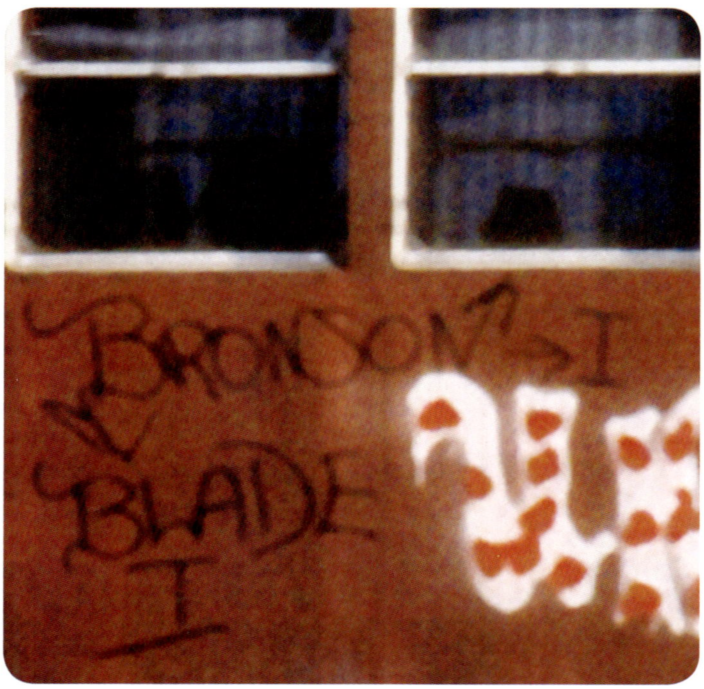

There were some famous bus writers in 1971 and 1972: THE BIG 0 116, OTTO, K-GEE 9, SUPERKOOL 223, JAMBU 2, SPEC 1-229 and CAT 2233 (the 2233 really meant 226th street). NEAL 182 was a writer who gained a lot of respect by doing a top-to-bottom piece on the side of a bus; we were amazed when we saw that. PUFF 167 and TUZO 1 were writing partners and they were up on all of the Bronx lines; they loved buses so much that they never moved on to the trains. They started to move out to other boroughs to hit the buses when TUZO 1 was in an awful accident. He was writing in a bus depot in Brooklyn where all of the buses were parked closely together. He was working his way in between two of them when the driver started it up, the bus lurched forward and crushed him, killing him instantly.

Those writers had a huge amount of respect and a lot of them went to my school. They hit the outsides of buses with marker and spray paint while I tried to summon up the courage to get a single hit on the insides with a Dri-Mark. I don't count that as writing. Everybody has their own definition of what writing is; to me a writer had to get to the trains and hit them regularly—period. That's why I say I started writing in 1972, not 1971. I don't count my bus days.

During the time I was hitting buses, I was also hitting the post office trucks. In late 1971/early 1972, I was still too afraid to hit the trains, but I really wanted to write. The post office trucks were laid up about eight blocks from my house. I'd go there at night with another local writer named CHINO 1. Today the truck depot is fenced off with barbed wire, but back then you could just walk in. During the winter, at around 10:30pm, there was no one around for blocks, so we'd hit the trucks at will. We had no expectations other than trying to write our names. However, two things happened: the first was that we learned to use spray paint on metal; the second was that, although we never really thought of the impact of the trucks, as it turned out they traveled far and wide, so other writers began seeing our names. The buses and trucks proved to be a great training ground for me.

In 1972 I began racking paint. It wasn't difficult at all because hardware stores didn't connect one missing can of paint with the new graffiti movement. It was still okay for teenagers to roam around a hardware store and most of

This page: Early BLADE marker tags on the outside of redbird trains. Top photo © Jack Stewart 1972.
Opposite page: HONDO 1. 1972. Photo ©Keith Baugh

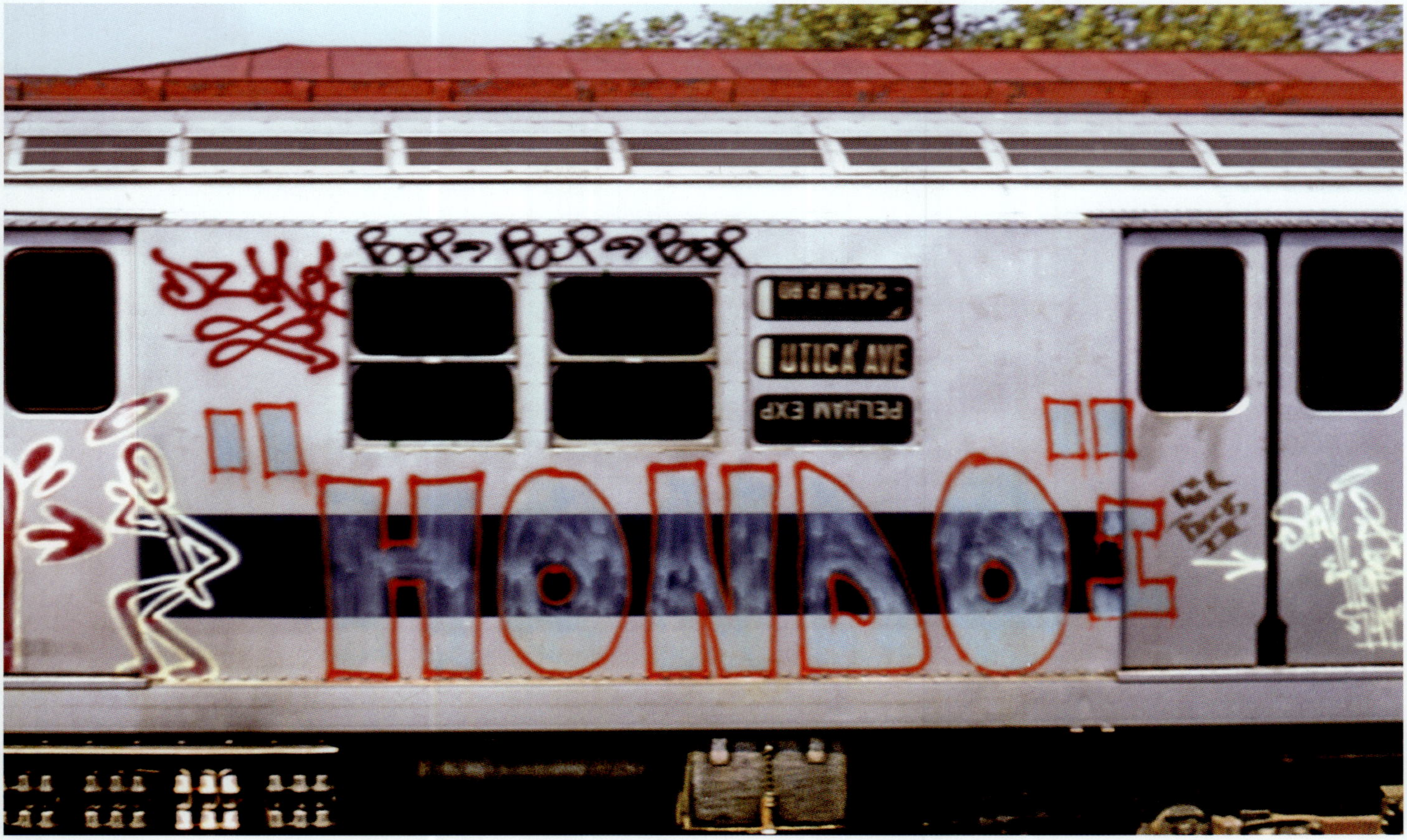

the stores kept the paint right on the shelf out in the open. That would all change by 1974 when writers needed at least four cans of paint for a piece. The stores I hit were Lou's Hardware and Andy's Variety Store, both on Burke Avenue. Soon after, I'd have a long list of stores to rack from.

In the fall of 1971, I met HONDO 1, who was the king of the trains. He was a tough guy, short and stocky like Joe Frazier, with wide shoulders and bowlegs. He'd beat up anyone. At the time, we all hung out at Cappy's candy store in Co-op City. We didn't know each other personally but we all knew the faces in the room. People would point to HONDO as though he was a celebrity. And to me, he was. There were other writers hanging out as well, including CAMARO 170, RICAN 120, DR. SEX 1, and FRESCO 1. Later on we'd get pushed together onto the same school bus. That's when we became friends. Those guys—HONDO 1 and his writing partner FRESCO 1—wore long leather jackets and Playboy shoes, which was the look back then. I wanted to look just like them, so for Christmas my parents got me a vinyl jacket. I became the moron kid on the bus wearing the fake leather.

In the early 1970s, the gangs reemerged. I was able to avoid them, because I had no relationship with any of the street gangs, although I did have a fistfight with DOC JSA of the Black Spades in the tenth grade. The fight was over my jacket. He was a light-skinned guy, lighter than me, with a huge Afro. Because I was wearing a fake leather jacket, he thought he could pick on me. He was wrong. We got into a huge fight in the hallway, right in front of the Black Spades. I kicked his ass in front of all of them. My fighting style back then was more of a windmill style of boxing, trying desperately to throw as many blows as possible. It made no sense, but it didn't matter because DOC JSA couldn't fight at all. After that, all of the kids in the school respected me. When you're a kid, your peers care a lot less about style and more about heart. I stood up to the bully and won. How I did it was irrelevant.

I was going to school at Evander Childs High School. The district created a whole new bus line just to take us there from Co-op City. I did most of my hitting on the bus. Evander had big-name writers, such as GUN 229, SPEK 229, and MOE TR from the Edenwald Projects, who were hitting the trains a lot. I remember looking out the window of my classroom and seeing a GUN 229 top-to-bottom passing by on the 3rd Avenue El. It was red with no outline. The whole class raced over to the window to see it. Anytime something new flew by our window all of the boys jumped up to see what it was and offer a critique. The teacher would yell at us, but we didn't listen.

That year at Evander seemed like the longest one of my life, because the other writers called me a DGA, which stood for "Don't Get Around." Hitting the insides of buses wasn't giving me the credibility I needed. Believe me, I wanted more, I just didn't know how to get it. One night at Cappy's, HONDO 1 asked me if I wanted to go painting with him to show me the ropes. He had more pieces riding at the time than any other writer. HONDO's pieces were simple, created with stick letters. Since they were painted quickly, he could do five in a night. In my two years back from Saratoga, I had been a pretty good kid, but that was about to change.

At one o'clock in the morning, I snuck out of my house and met up with HONDO and the others. We crossed the highway, leaving the safety of Co-op City, and walked to the Baychester lay-up, the home of the 5 trains.

Graffiti writers painted in train yards and lay-ups. Train yards were enormous lots at the end of each subway line, where the MTA would park the trains at night. The problem with train yards was that cops knew about them too, so the Vandal Squad could bring four people to the yard in a night, sit on the yard, and wait for writers to show up. As the writers started to paint, losing their concentration, the cops would pounce on them. With four cops, they'd have all four sides of the yard covered, leaving nowhere to run. I hated train yards. A lay-up was usually a spot along the line with extra tracks in the middle to accommodate a few trains overnight. There were usually a few lay-ups along each train line. Lay-ups weren't a definite thing, cops didn't raid them as frequently, and there were usually more ways out of a lay-up. The Baychester lay-up was highly desirable because it was up a steep hill, which meant you could keep an eye on anyone coming after you.

As we arrived at Baychester, HONDO pushed toward the front of the group, climbed the hill, and scoped out the lay-up. There were two ten-car trains parked in the center tracks with the lights off; there were no track bums or cops anywhere. This was as simple as it got. The rest of us climbed up the hill and went through a small hole in the fence. The track bed was made of gravel. The only noise we heard was the crunching sound beneath our feet.

We had one can of paint for the five of us: HONDO, FRESCO, DR.SEX, RICAN 120, and me. The red trains were parked in a row on the right, with a few black ones as well. We walked down the lane and put a single hit on each train—the one on the right and the one on the left. It was amazing. I had never stood on train tracks before, and now I was being told to stand on the third rail to get more height. Of course, a wooden plank guarded the top of the third rail, as with most of the transit system. When it's not covered, the MTA lets you know. A surge of fear ran through me, which turned into adrenaline. I was really into it. I remember the humming of the generators—all of the sounds seemed amplified. When the can was empty we headed back to Co-op City and I went home.

In the summer of 1972, I had the chance to do my first masterpiece. PROBE 2 and I went to the Baychester lay-up expecting to hit the red cars there. It was nighttime and I had a can of both Red Devil white and red paint. I was using the white paint to get single hits as we went down the tracks. As we came to the end of the train, I saw a brand new silver car with a blue stripe. I knew I had to do a masterpiece! I quickly did a stick letter BLADE piece in red. I outlined it with the white paint and added some stars in it. When that train came by school the next day, everybody raced to the windows to see it. My reputation got a huge boost, as did my ego.

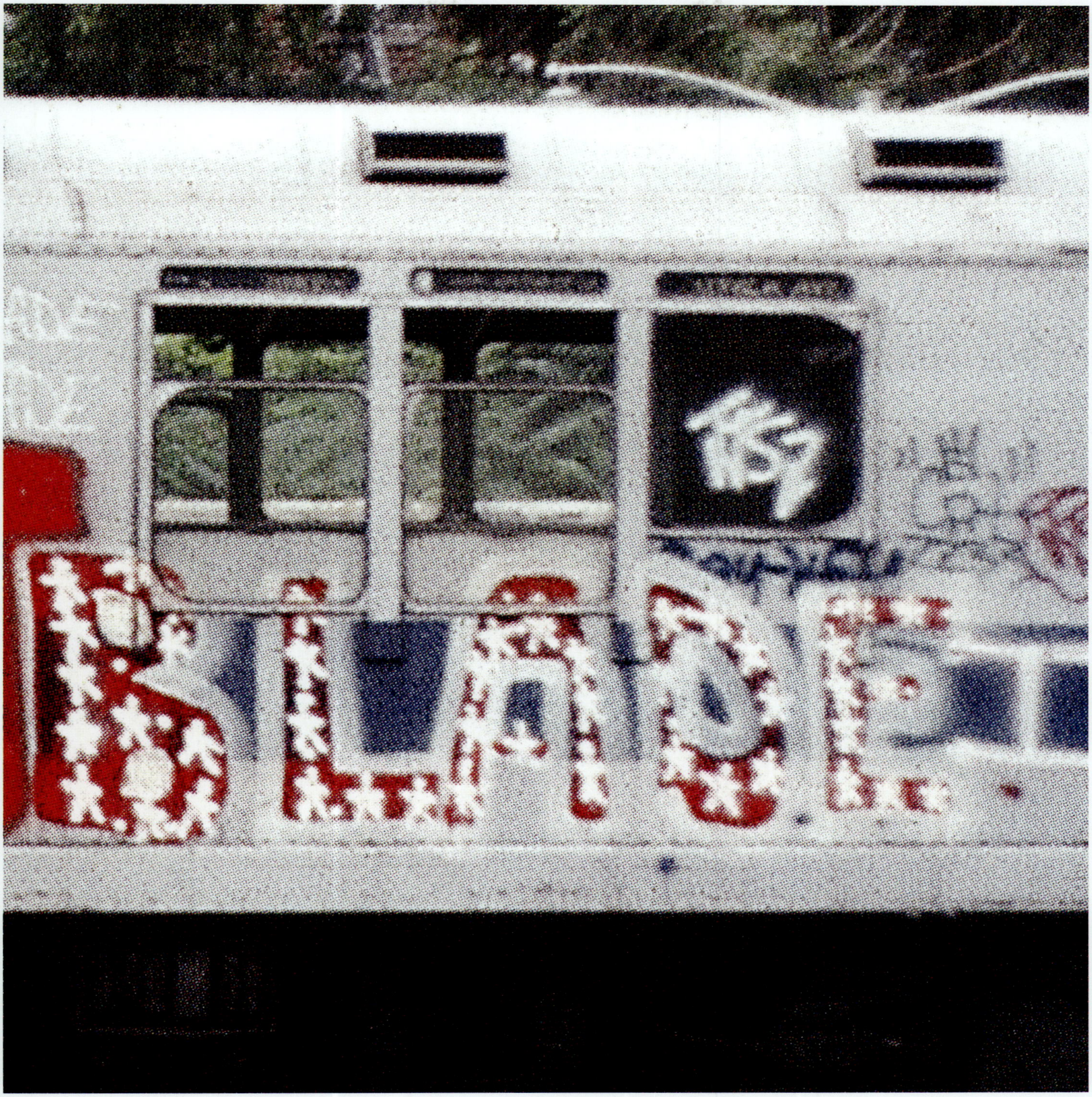

This page:
BLADE's first piece. 1972. Photo ©Jack Stewart.

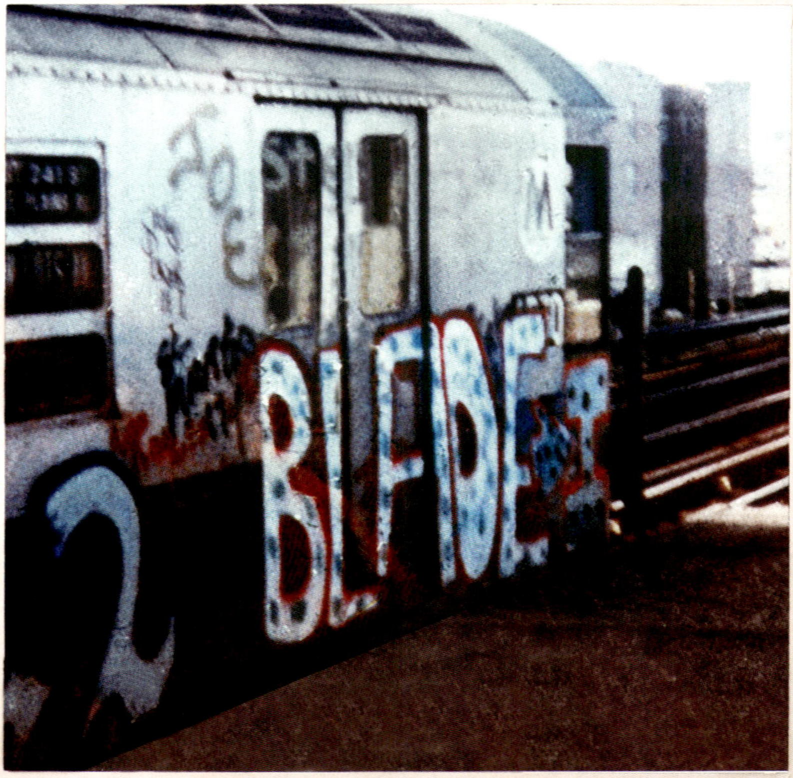
BLADE

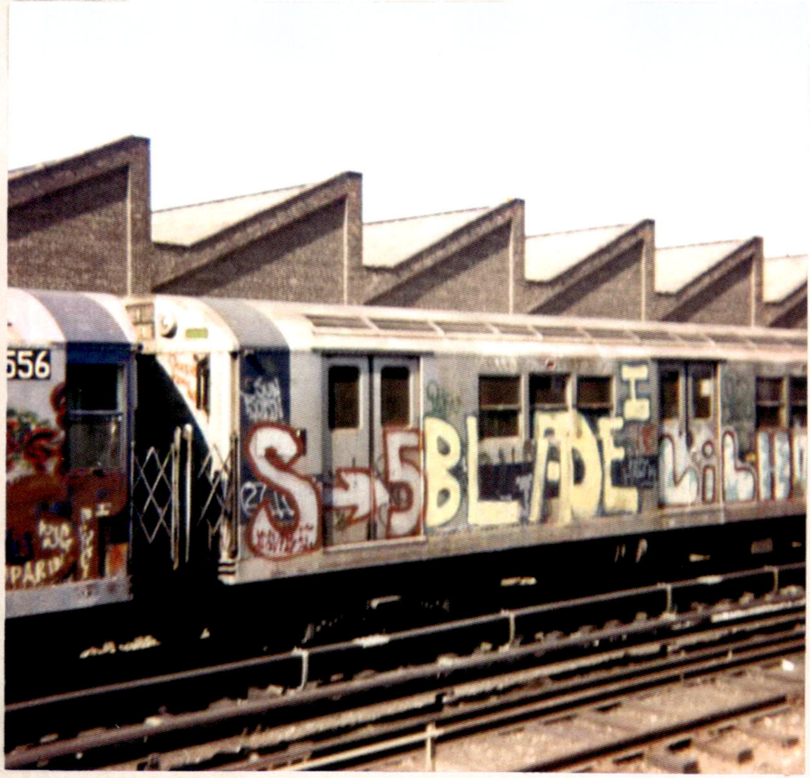
556
BLADE

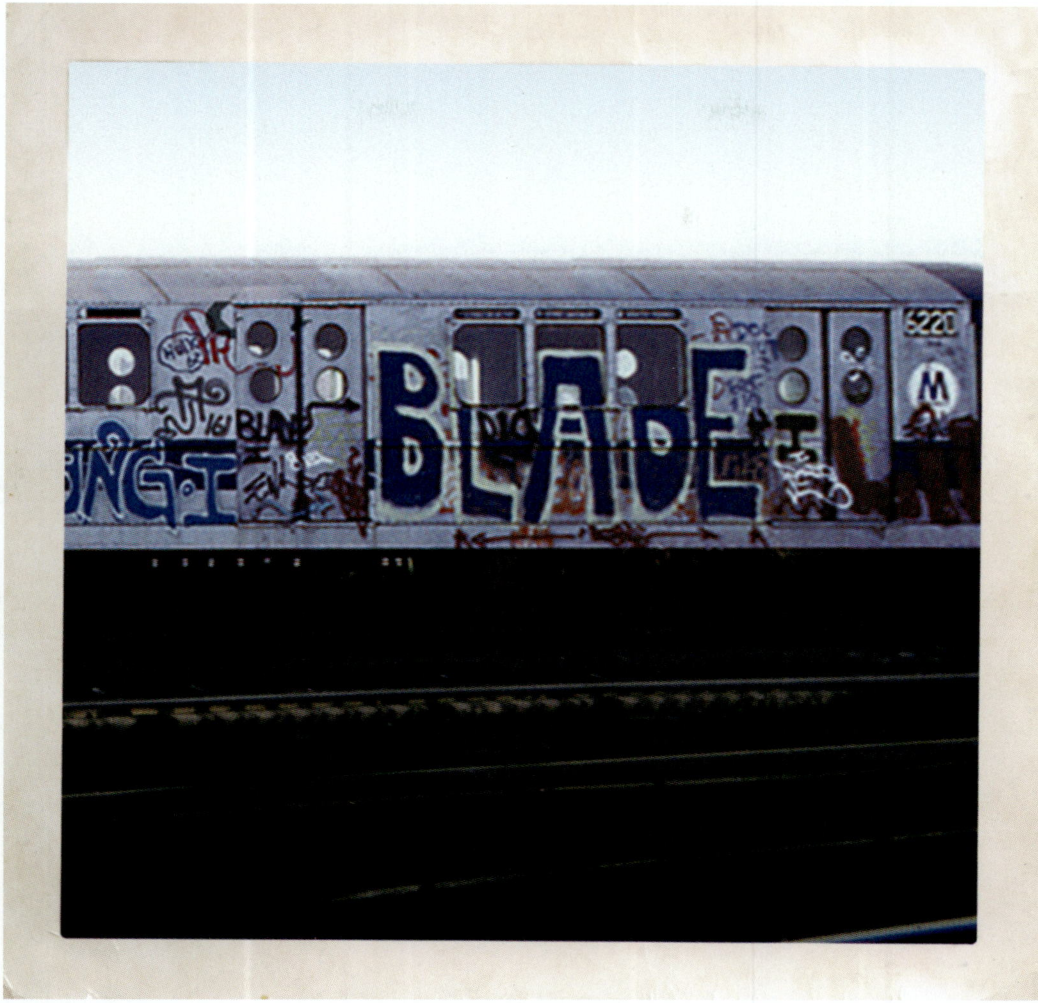

What HONDO 1, FRESCO 1, and DR. SEX 1 were doing with stick letters was great. I quickly learned that you had to have a very confident line, because the precision of it was difficult. The guy who was the best at it was THE MAN 550. His letters were perfect and a little wider than the rest. By the end of 1972, I had done ten to twenty pieces while HONDO 1 did hundreds of them.

In 1973, HONDO, CAMARO 170, FRESCO, and DR. SEX were gone. Once they turned eighteen, they either got shipped off to Vietnam or simply moved on to adulthood.

People today have no idea what it's like living with a war hanging over your head. I missed the draft by twenty-three days, but I remember it well. I watched the first draft on TV at my uncle's house in Saratoga Springs. There was a guy with all 365 days of the year placed in a large bowl. He pulled them out one by one. If your birthday was one of the earlier dates picked off, then you went to war. If your name was picked toward the end, then you probably wouldn't have to go. There were no dramatic farewells with the writers I hung out with. People just disappeared and you no longer saw them at Cappy's. Some went to Vietnam, some to jail, and others just moved away; but without them I might never have started my writing career. They both inspired me and taught me well. Now it was time for me to move on.

This spread: Top: Early BLADE piece with a JOE 182 tag on the train. 1972.
Bottom: Early BLADE panel piece. 1972.Following spread: Various BLADE pieces. circa 1973.

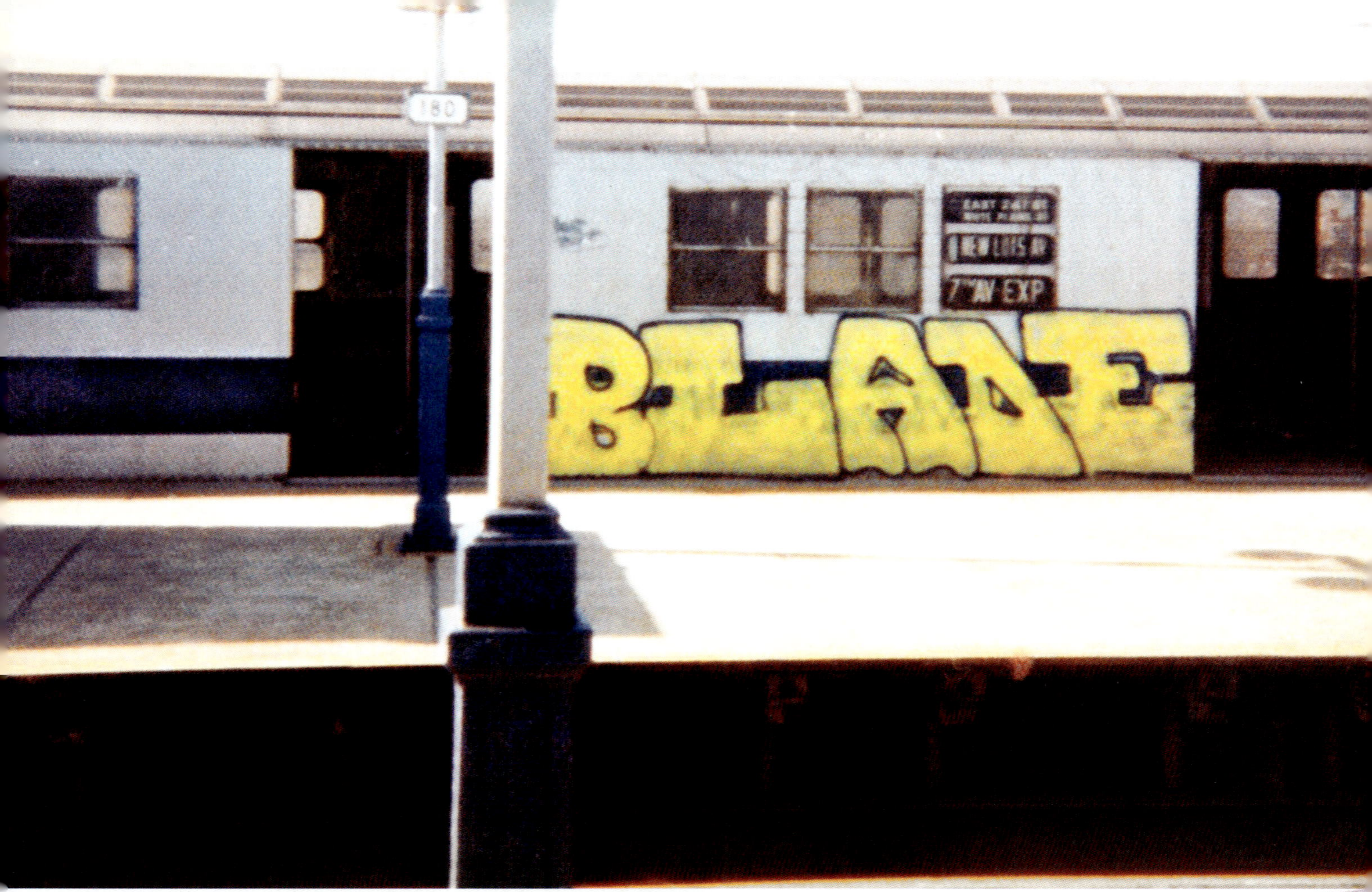
180
NEW LOTS AV
7TH AV EXP
BLADE

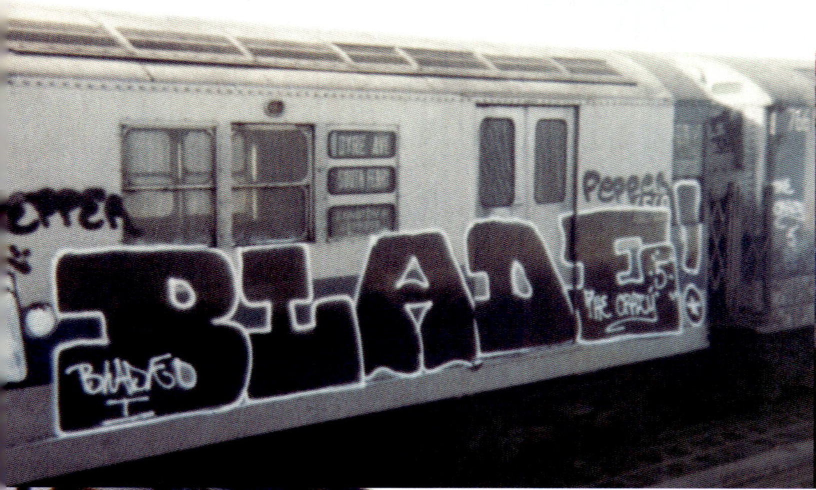
DYRE AV
SOUTH FERRY
BLADE

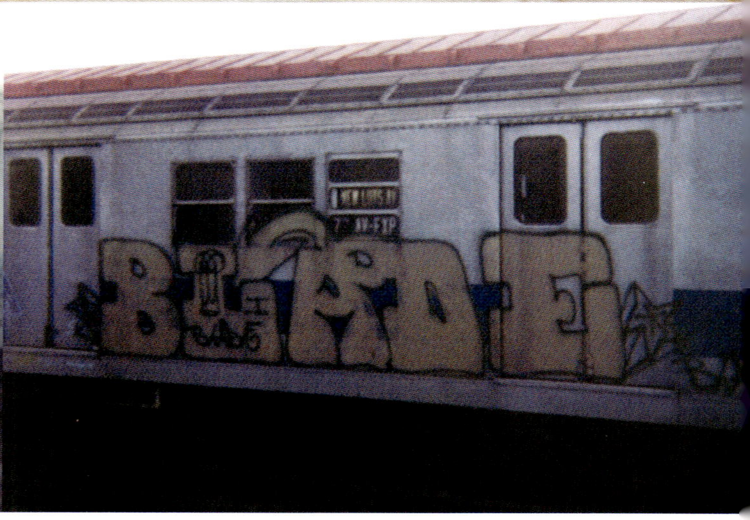
NEW LOTS AV
7TH AV EXP
BLADE

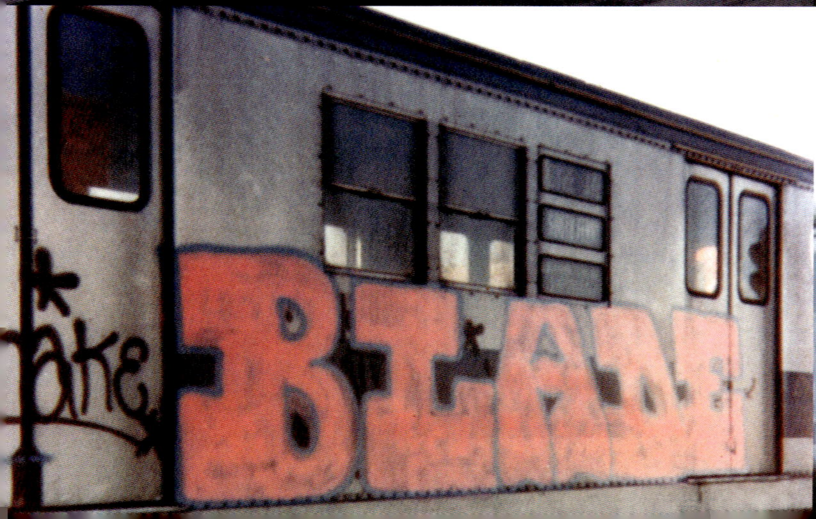
BLADE

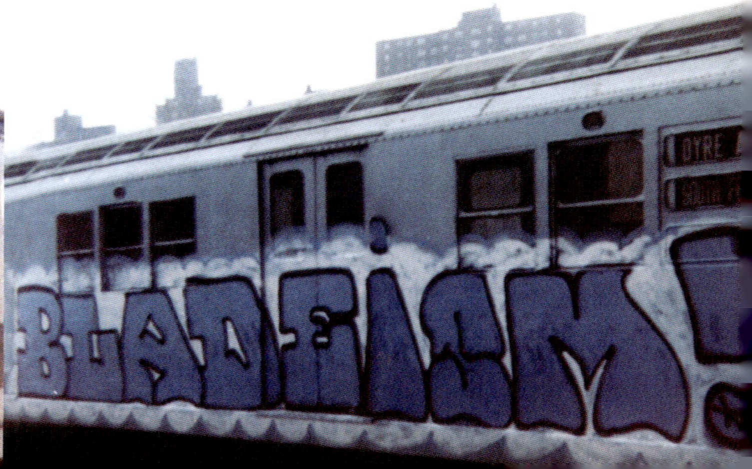
DYRE
BLADEISM

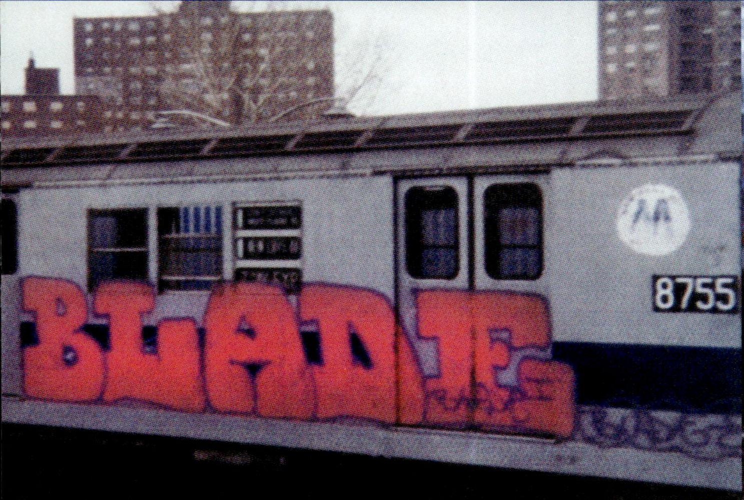
BLADE
8755

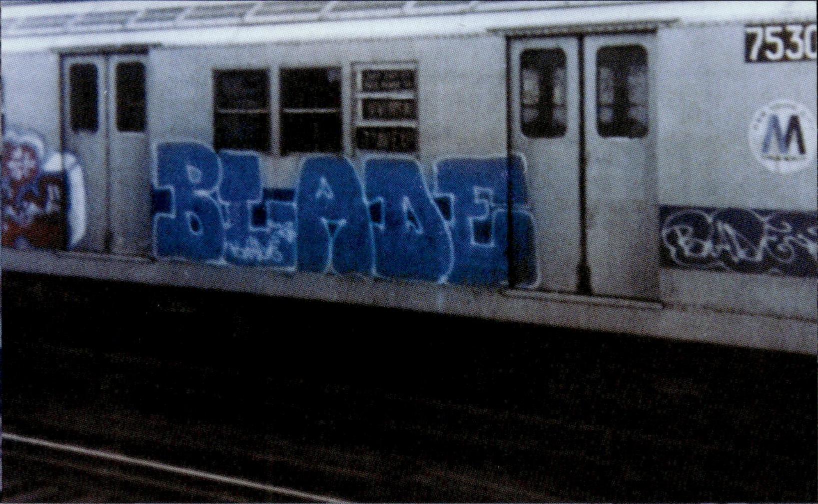
BLADE
7530

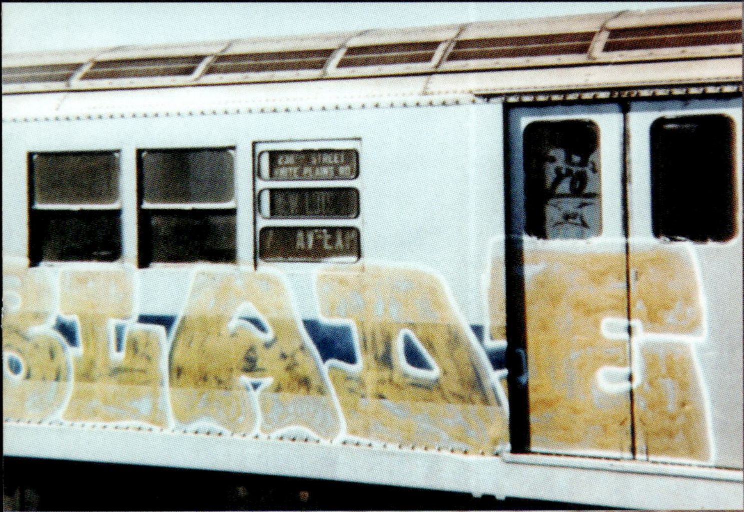

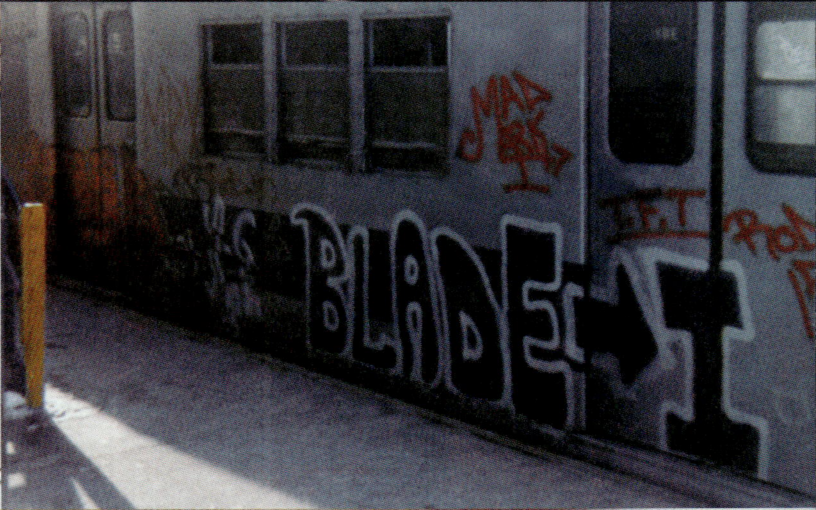
BLADE

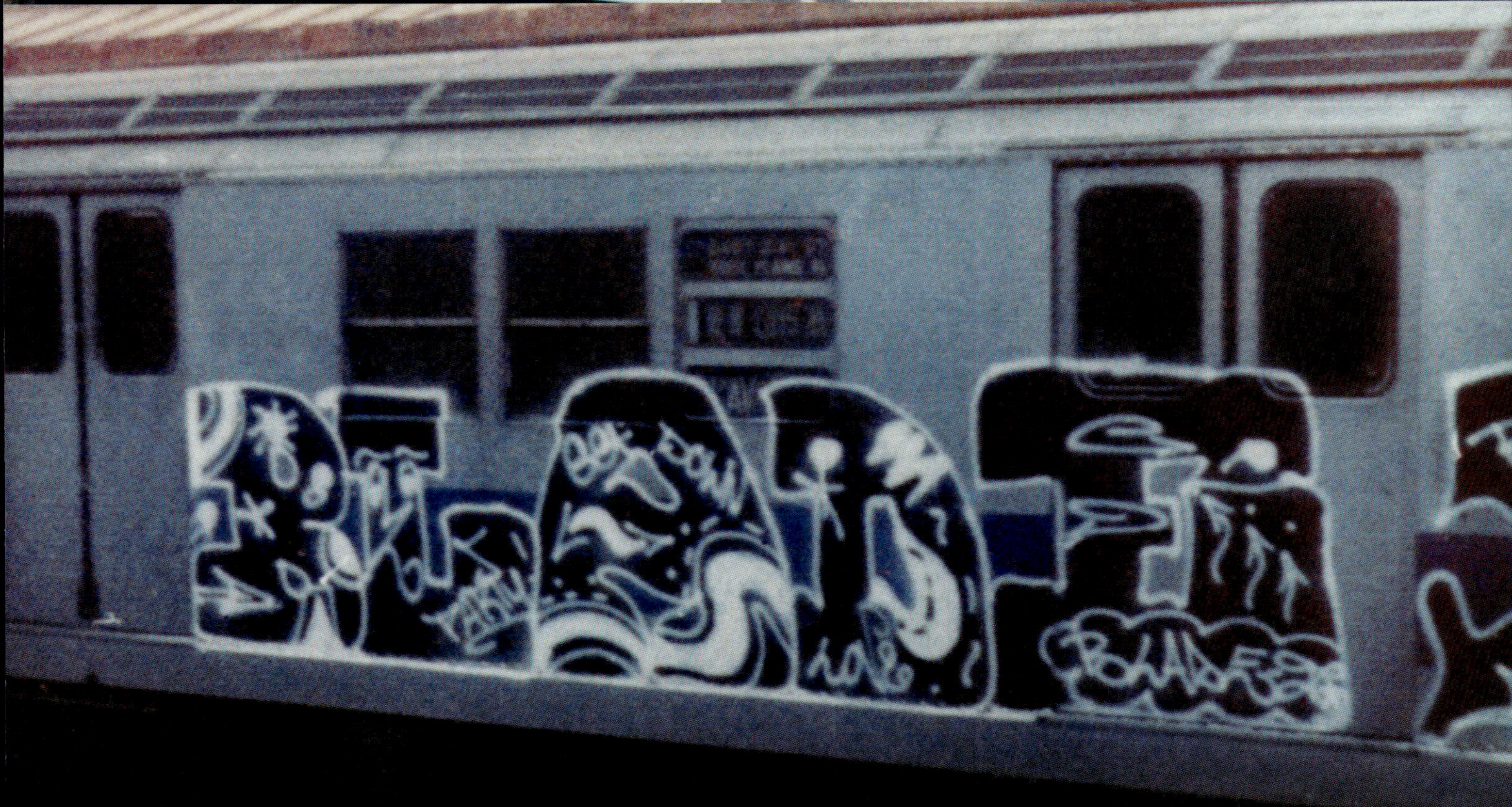

CHAPTER FOUR

THIS IS PARKSIDE:

1974

New York City was really bad in the 1970s. As the factories closed, jobs became tough to find, so a lot of people were unemployed and went on welfare. A lot of writers point to that as the reason graffiti started, since the lack of money coming into the city meant cuts in the city services, including the police department. Think about it: today, we have twice as many cops on the street as we did back then.

But for me, the hippie culture and the rebellion against the government was a bigger factor in graffiti than the economy. People returning from Vietnam brought back the best drugs in the world. In those days, you could spend fifty bucks on an ounce of some of the best pot around—great shit.

There was also a sense of "freedom of expression" in the sixties. For the first time, people could do what they wanted to—even something as simple as growing your hair long, smoking a joint, or writing on a wall. We weren't jocks, we weren't in gangs, but we had the balls to write. That was our claim to fame, even though graffiti was still primitive and mostly written on mailboxes and buses. The fact that there was a smaller police force with bigger crimes to worry about might've enabled the movement, but it didn't start it.

Graffiti began to break down racial barriers. The Bronx was stuck in the 1950s: different communities desperately clung to their turfs; everyone was so afraid of change. You'd walk down the street through one ten-block neighborhood of Irish kids and you'd have to watch your back; then you'd hit a ten-block stretch of Albanians and it was the same thing; then the Jews; then the Italians. The Parkside Houses proved that the Bronx didn't have to be that way. We all had different backgrounds and we all got along together. I felt the same way about graffiti. Although there were some incidents that tested my faith along the way, for the most part kids from different races got along. Maybe this was just something happening through the country as a whole. If it was, I didn't notice it.

Opposite page:
BLADE plays Nok Hockey with friends at Parkside. Circa 1973.

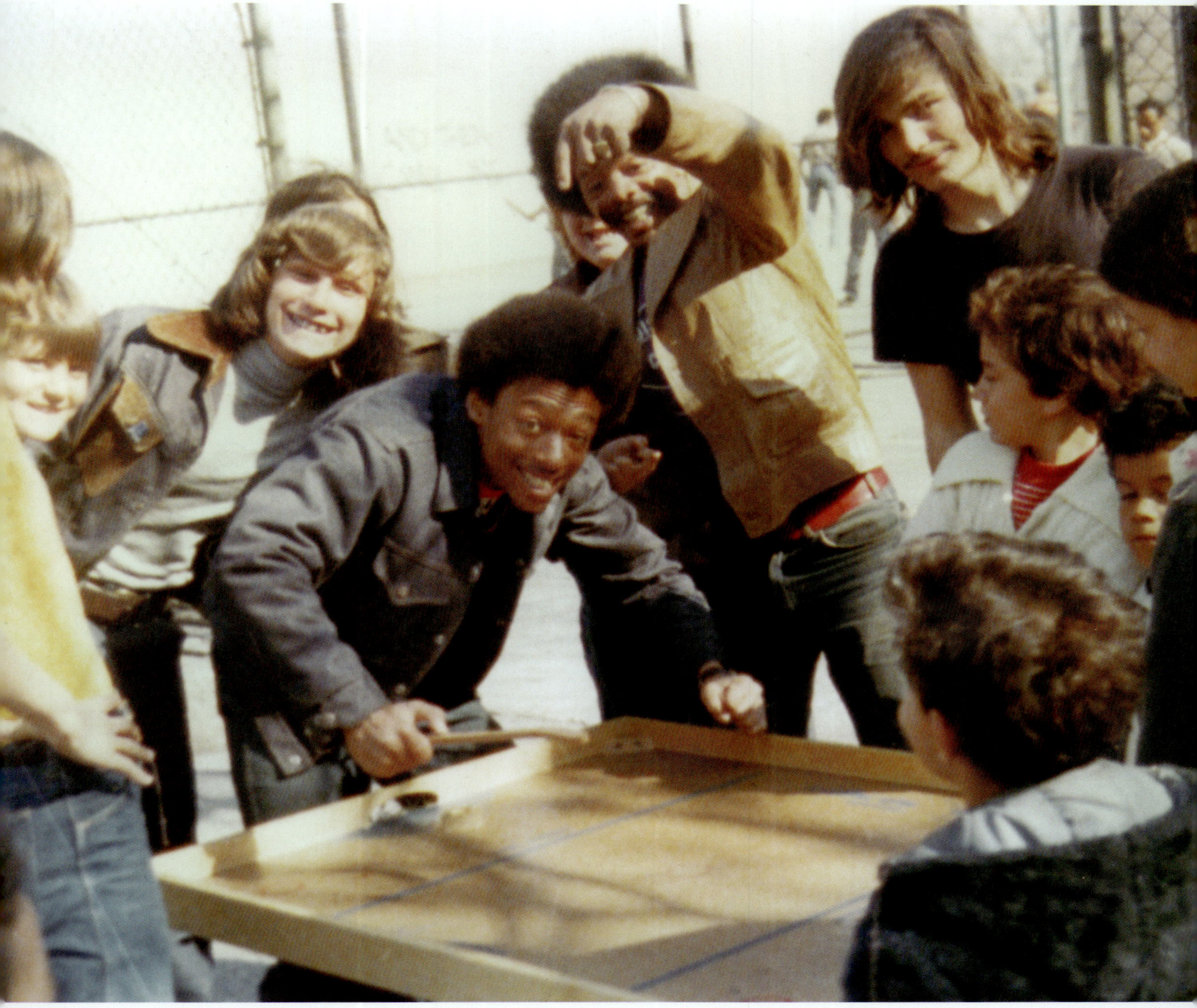

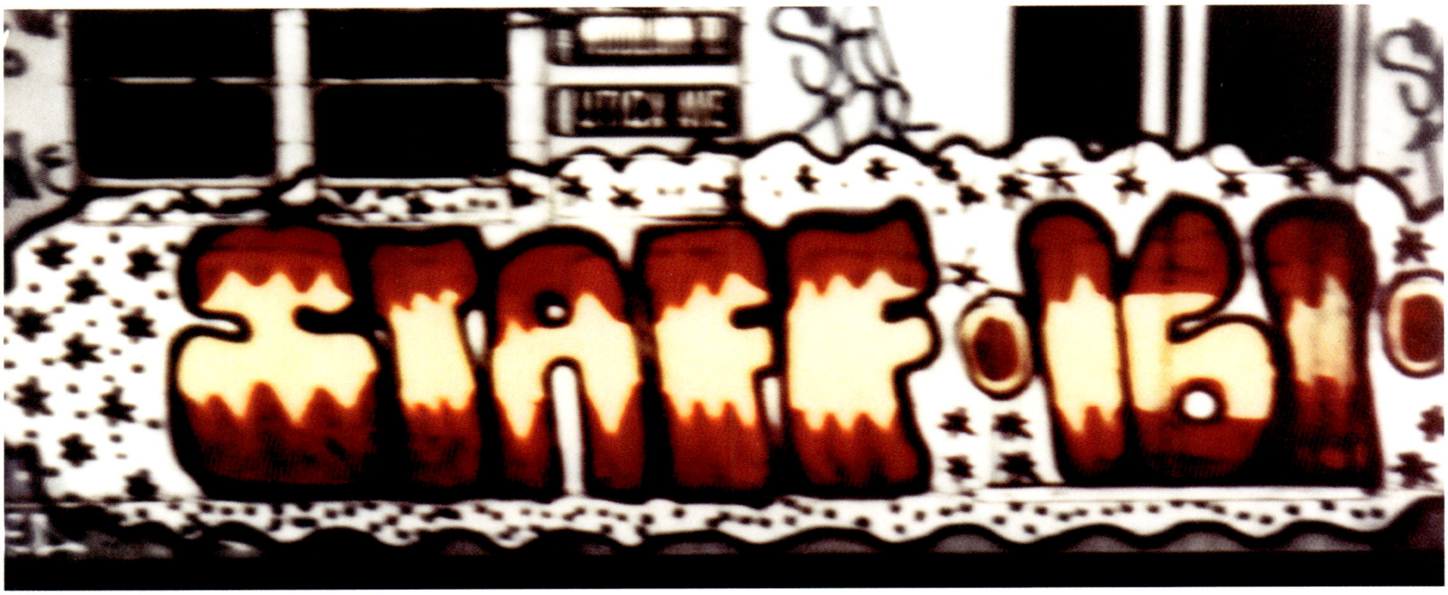

Pieces on trains started appearing right around the time of the changing of the guard from Mayor Lindsey to Mayor Beame. When Beame took over in January of 1973, the trains went from being red, flat black, and green (the green looked like surplus World War II paint) to being painted silver with a blue stripe. The buses were also painted silver with a blue stripe. Of course, it didn't take long before thousands of hits were added to the newly painted trains.

All of the original guys, like PHASE 2 and SUPERKOOL 223, began to fade away because they were bombing the red trains, and the thing to do now was hit the silver ones; and to do masterpieces rather than single hits. Guys like COOLCLIFF 120, who had been around from the beginning, gave up on graffiti. For him, it was about hanging out with chicks, smoking, drinking, and doing single hits to get his name out there; and if you went through one can of paint a day, that was a lot. The idea of turning writing into a job must have seemed insane to the pioneers of the movement. But more and more, that's what graffiti was becoming: a twenty-four-hour-a-day job with no pension plan.

I watched as graffiti moved forward from stick letter pieces to whole-cars with 3-Ds. Some of the early writers to go beyond stick letter pieces were STAFF 161, DOC COOL, JIVE 3, SUPERKOOL 223, and THE MAN 550. Whereas stick pieces were skinny letters with designs inside—dots, stars, and candy cane stripes—those five writers widened their letters and gave them weight. That was the beginning of style.

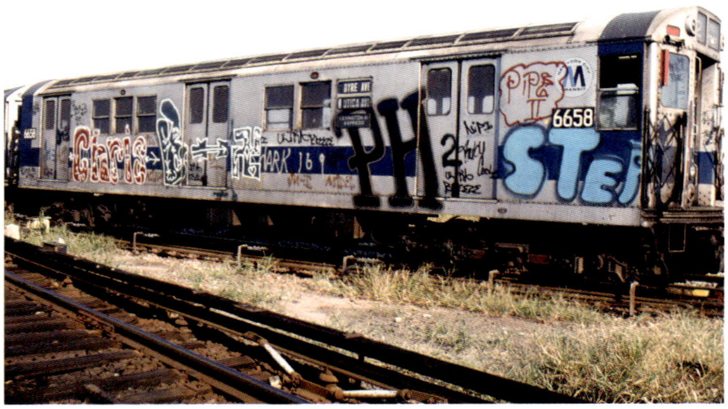

In the summer of 1972, SUPER KOOL 223 painted his name with a fat-cap. We couldn't believe it, because it seemed so large to us and we couldn't figure out how he did it. Word got around that he took a cap off of an oven cleaner, which sprayed a larger arc, and put it on his can of spray paint. Pretty soon everyone was stealing fat-caps (our name for the new nozzles) from their local supermarkets. We soon realized that no one remembered the single hits on the train or the stick pieces—it was as though they were all mixed in together—but everyone remembered the SUPERKOOL 223 piece. Bigger was better!

This page:
Top: STAFF 161. Circa 1973. Bottom: PHASE 2 and others. 1972.
Opposite page: SUPER KOOL 223. 1972.

"WORD GOT AROUND THAT HE TOOK A CAP OFF AN OVEN CLEANER... PRETTY SOON, EVERYONE WAS STEALING FAT-CAPS..."

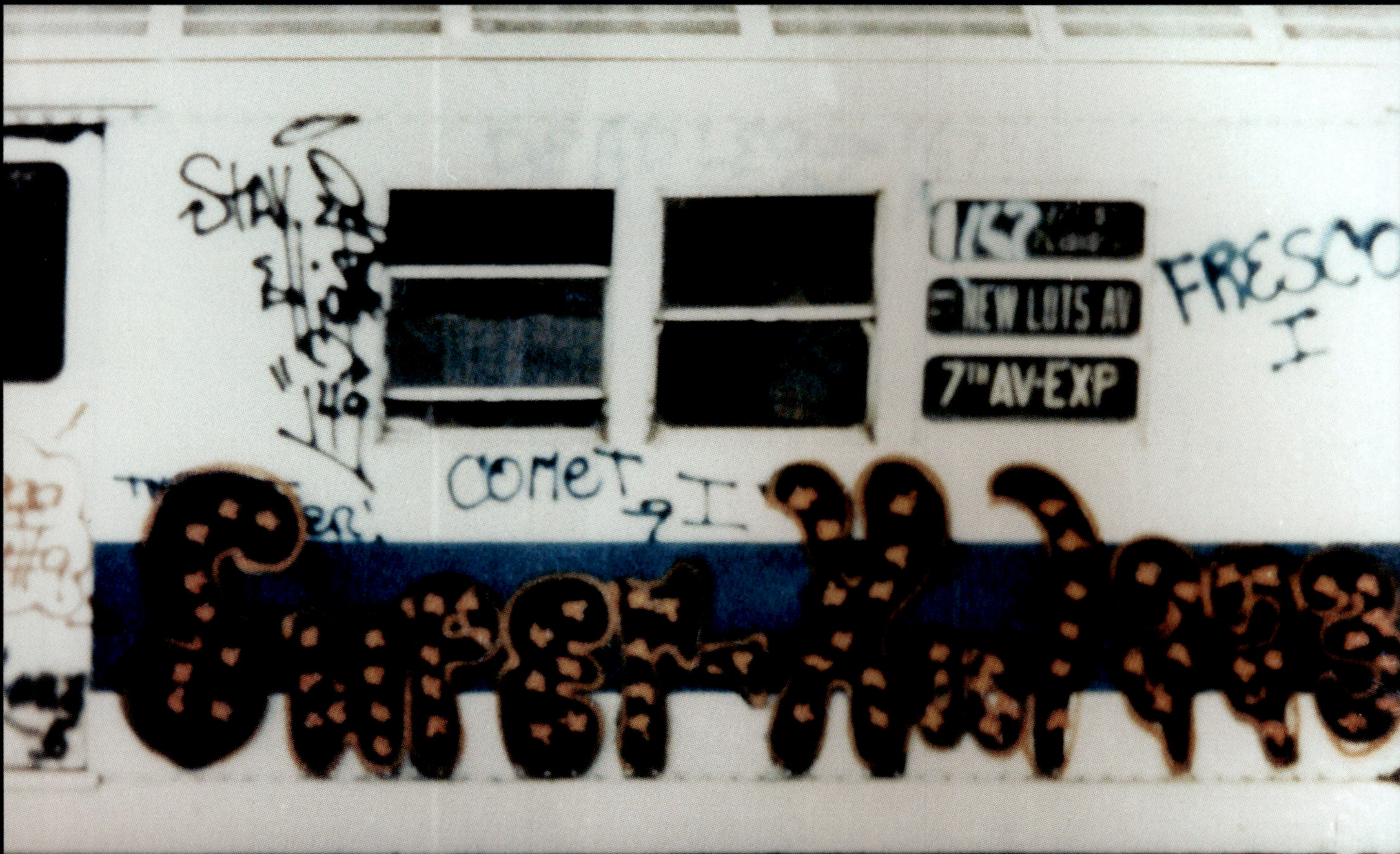

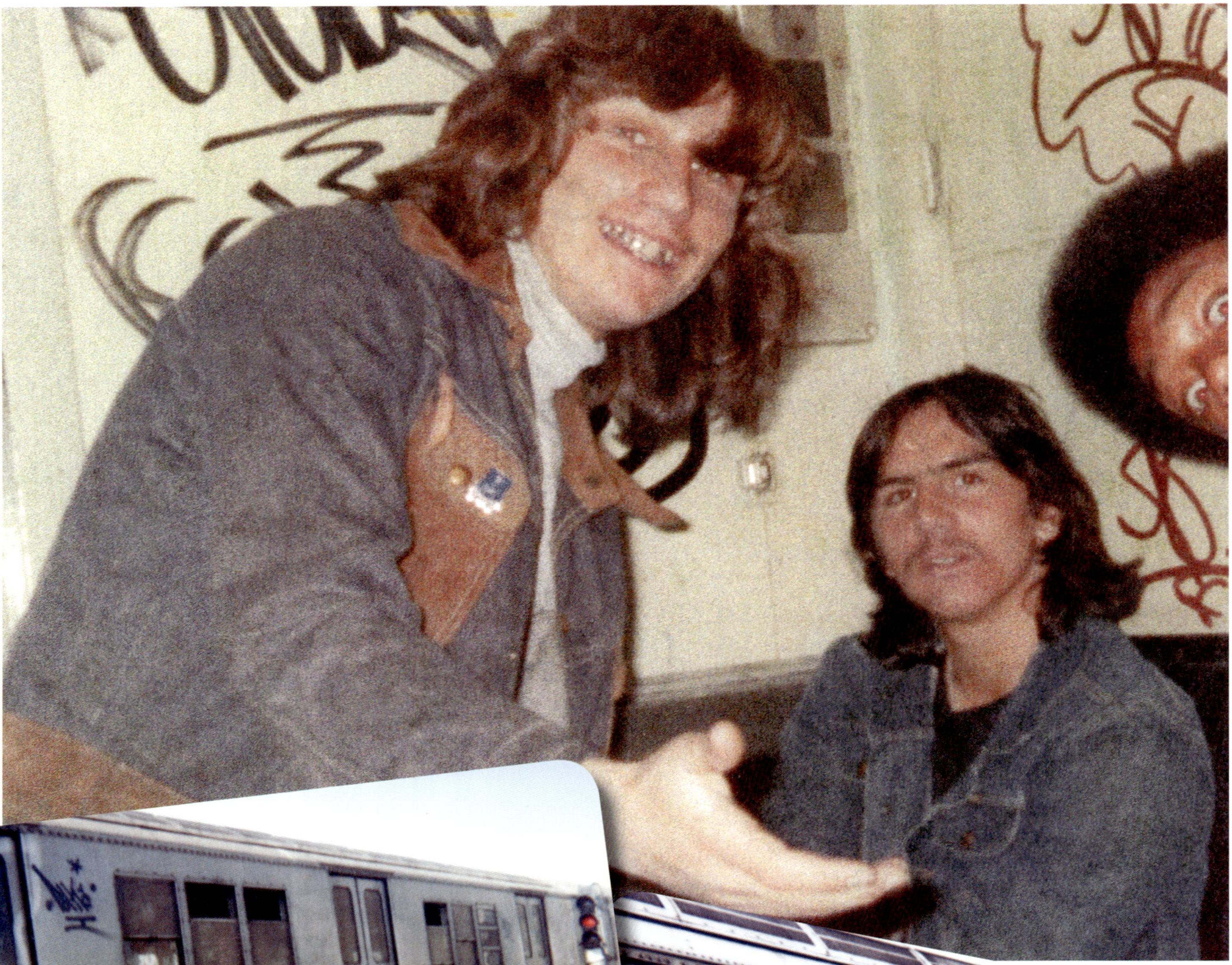

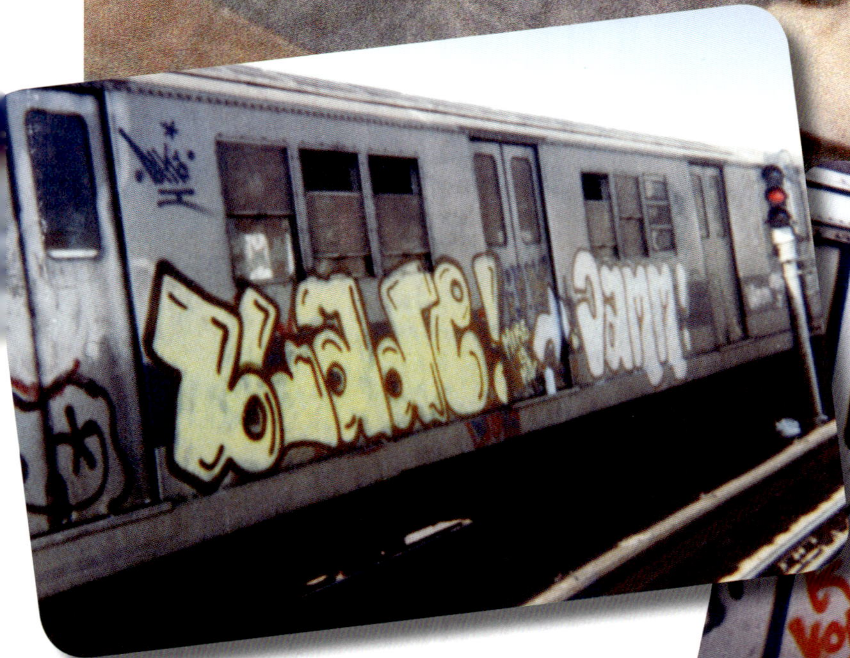

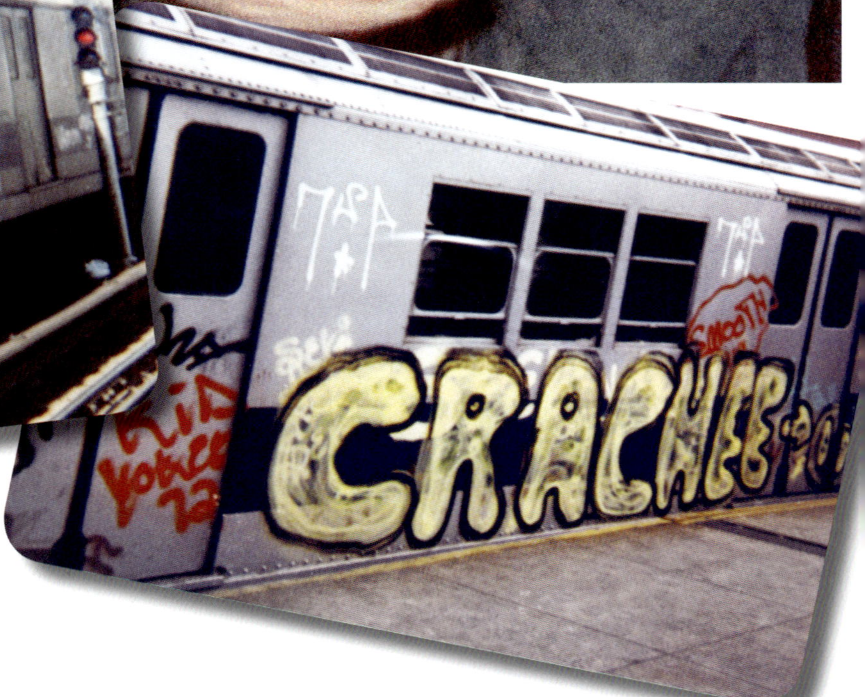

After I did my first pieces in the summer of 1972, I went back to Parkside Houses and hooked up with Michael and Mitch, my childhood friends. No one had heard from me in years, although word got around that I was BLADE. I knew Mitch was CRACHEE and Michael was VAMM. I had been following them both on the 2 line, watching their pieces and wondering what had become of my childhood friends. My first pieces were bigger than theirs, because I was taller than they were. CRACHEE was doing small signature pieces, which were called floaters because they arrived at eye level. Both writers were up on the trains more than I was at the time.

My father always considered Co-op City a huge step up from Parkside. I thought about that as I crossed the highway and headed over to the playground I had grown up in. Finding Mitch and Michael was easy, because they were still waiting for their turn to run the playground. They were fifteen years old and just beginning to get some respect from the older guys. The three of us shot some hoops, testing each other's skills, and talked trash. The sun was out and our shirts were off. We were all so rail thin that if a huge gust of wind came through the playground, we would've blown away. Two other writers entered the game: Gillen, who wrote DEATH, and Mario, who wrote TULL 13. They didn't live in Parkside but they hung out with CRACHEE and VAMM. When we were finished, we walked over to Izzy and Phil's and drank some egg creams while talking about writing late into the night. With HONDO and FRESCO retired, my future was in Parkside with a group that later became THE CRAZY 5.

People today think of graffiti as stylized pieces with images attached. If you look at it that way, then graffiti really began in 1973, because that's when all of the innovations occurred. As the letters were getting thicker, writers did other things to make their names stand out. PRIEST 167 added a shadow to his name, which made it look like his name was jumping off the train. PISTOL 1, from Brooklyn, took that a step further by adding a thick, wide bottom and side 3-D. PHASE 2 came up with the arrow, which was important to style writers. PHASE 2 claims he created bubble letters, or softies, but COMET and JESTER really popularized them and COMET certainly had rounded letters running in 1973. Another big thing to come out of 1973 was the idea of back-grounding your piece so the writers you went over wouldn't get mad. This set the stage for the next year, when writers would do three pieces on a car with a uniform look and a cloud.

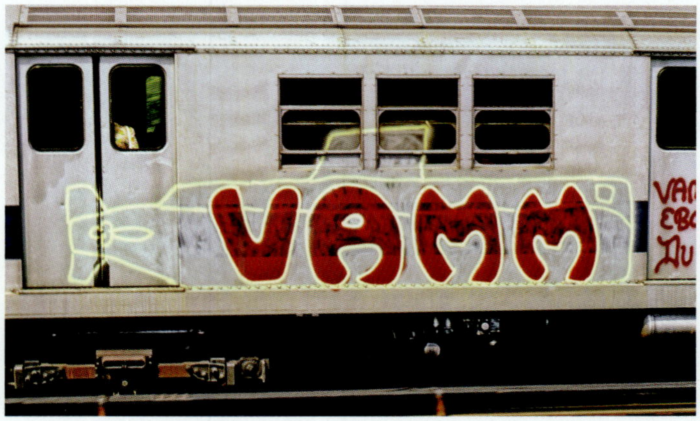

Some of the top trains done in 1973 were the PISTOL 3-D and the VAMM Submarine. While I didn't think much of KING KOOL 156's style I loved the flames he painted, which jumped off his name. Other writers tried to do drawings on trains. Usually they did a profile of a smiling black kid that looked like Michael Jackson from The Jackson 5 cartoon. Unlike VAMM's submarine, which was fully painted in, writers never filled in the profiles, which were done with scrap paint. In early 1974, STAFF 161 painted his famous Grim Reaper train. It featured his name with a 3-D, a grim reaper character to the left, and a hand coming out of a grave and a can of spray paint on the right. It was a revelation to me, which showed an entirely new way to paint on a train. To me, it was the first conceptual car ever done and it inspired me to do characters.

Opposite page: Top: CRACHEE, VAMM and BLADE. Circa 1974. Bottom left: BLADE and VAMM. Circa 1973. Bottom right: CRACHEE. 1973. This page: VAMM's submarine car. 1973. Photo ©Keith Baugh. Following spread: Various pieces by TULL 13, VAMM, BLADE and CRACHEE. 1973.

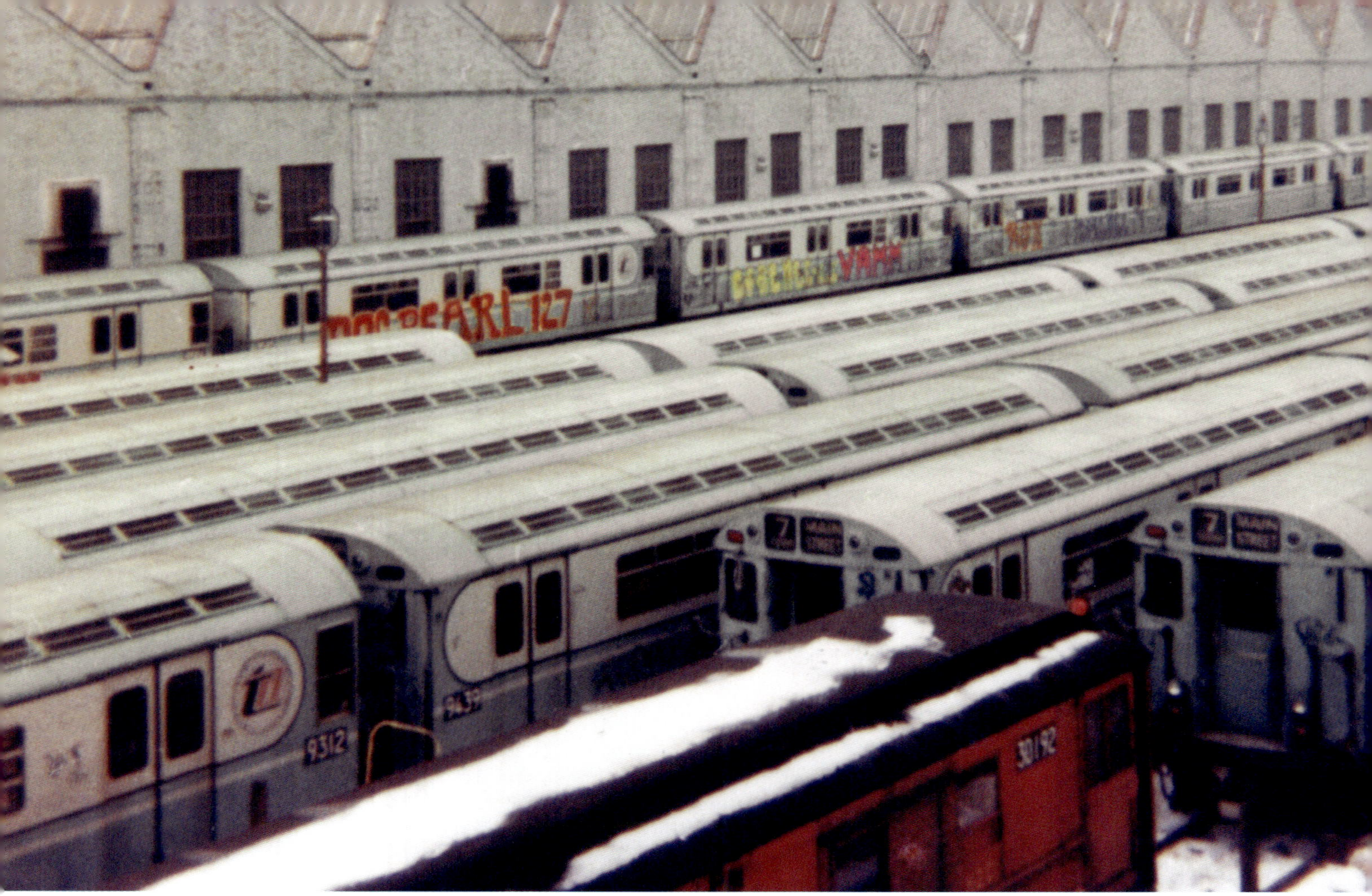
9312
30192

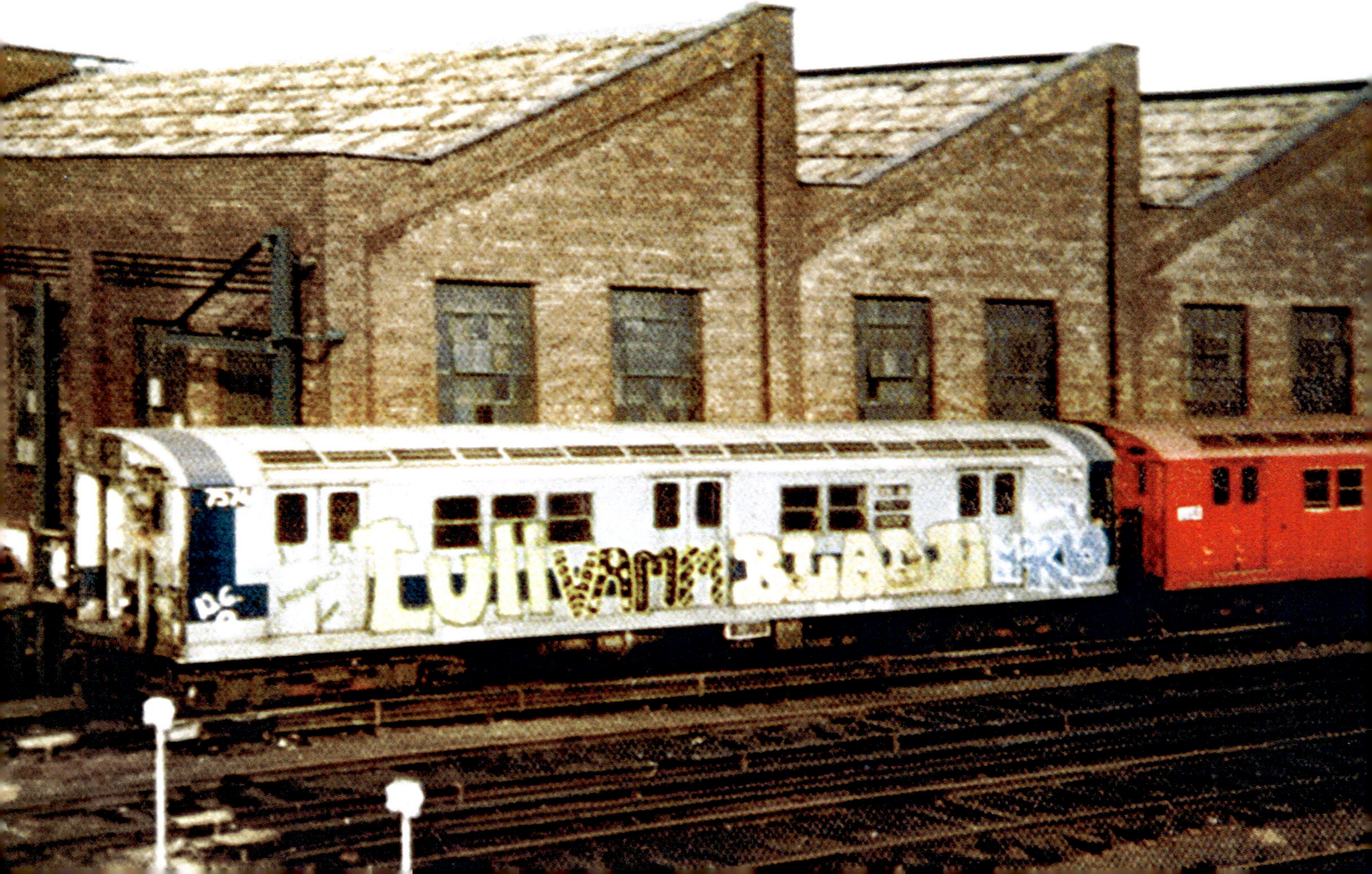

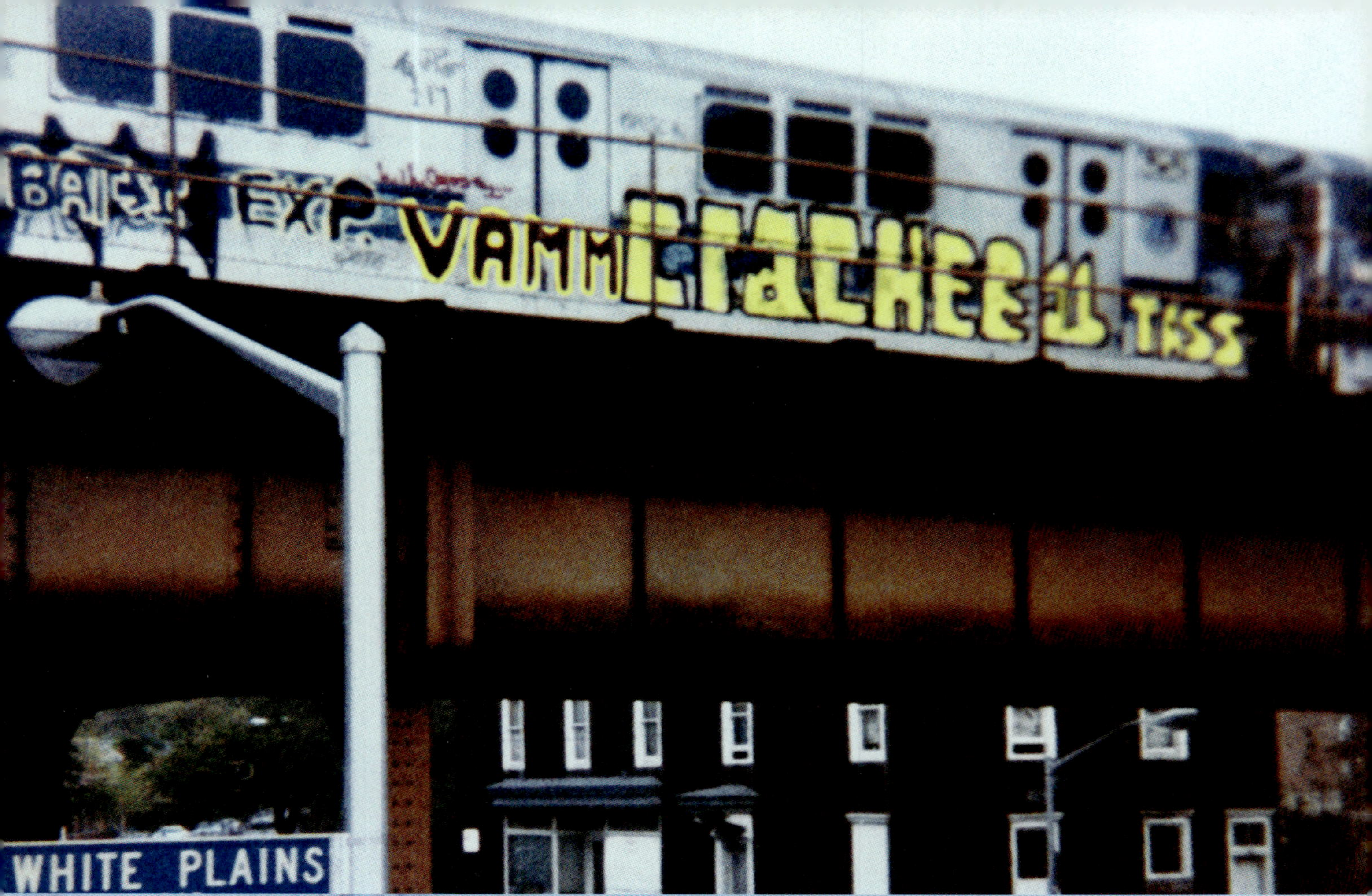
WHITE PLAINS

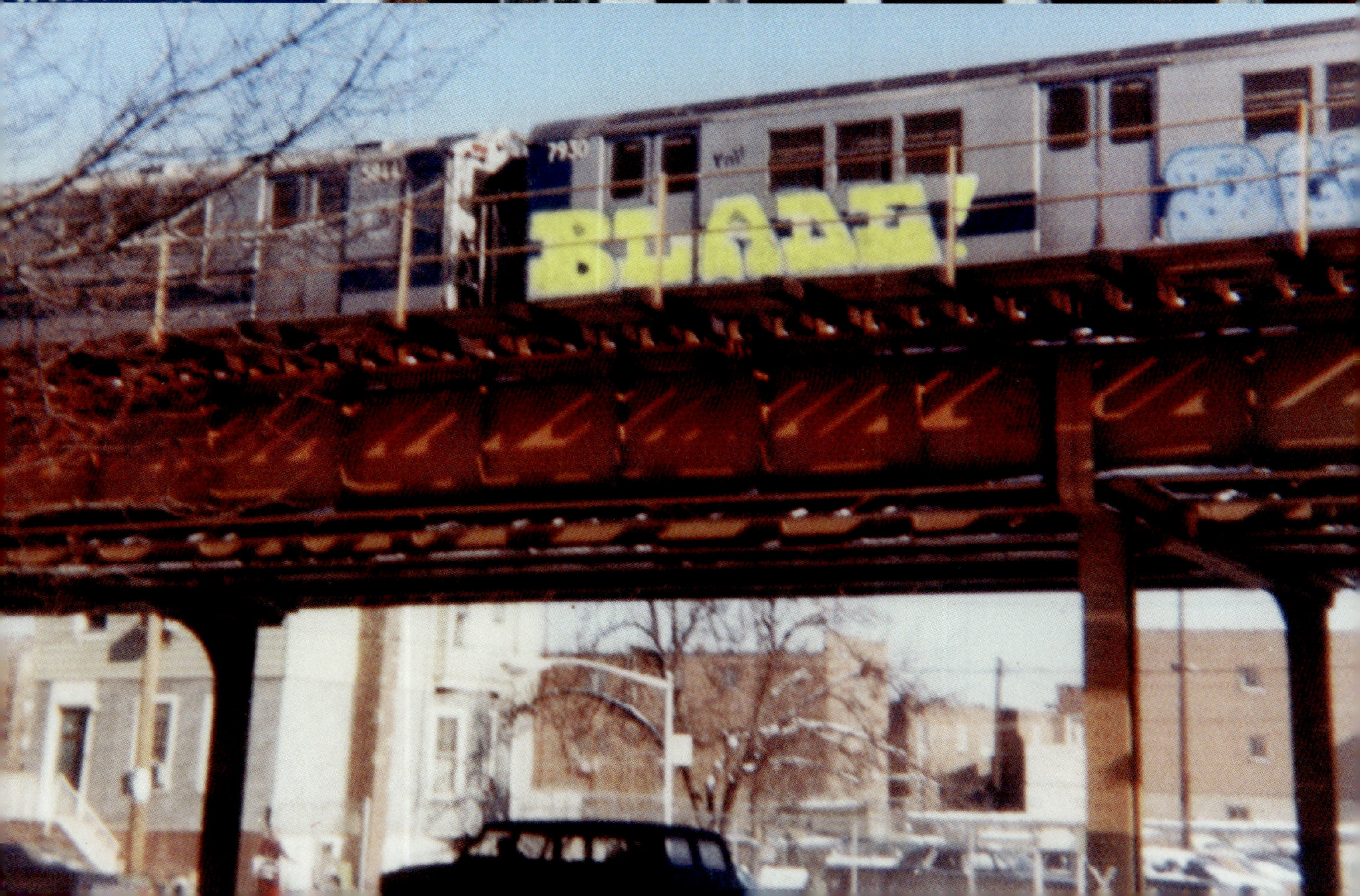

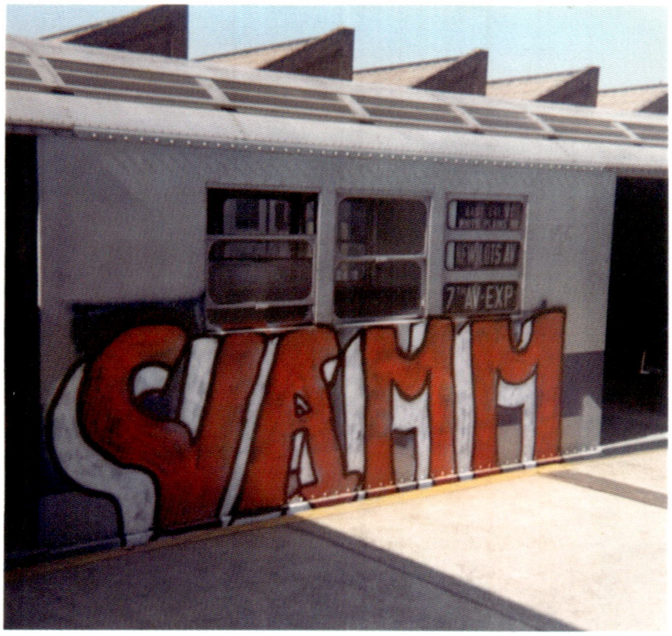
NEW LOTS AV
7th AV-EXP
VAMM

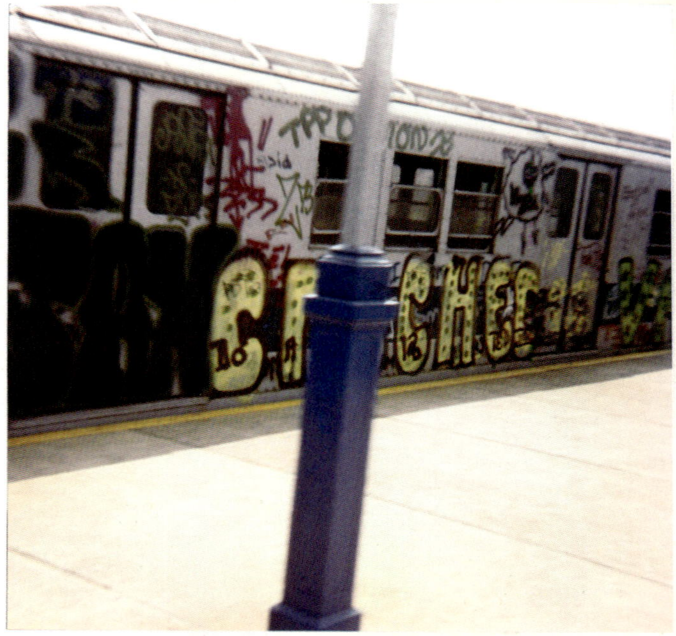

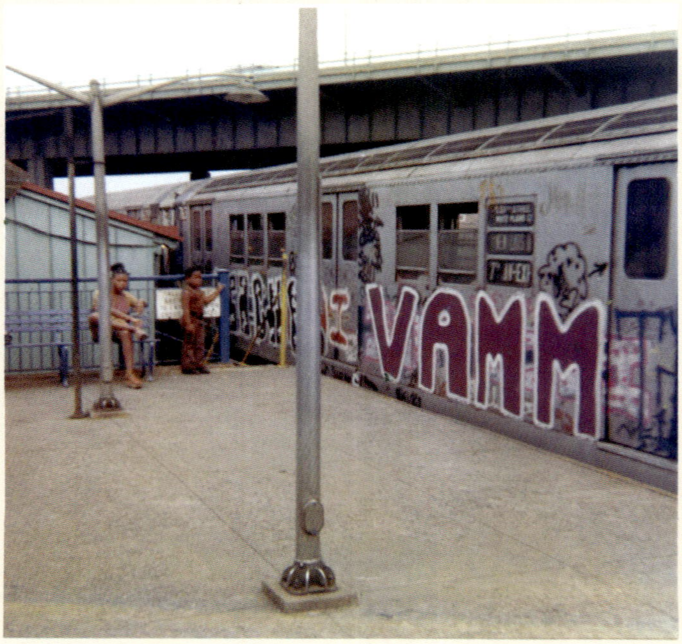
VAMM

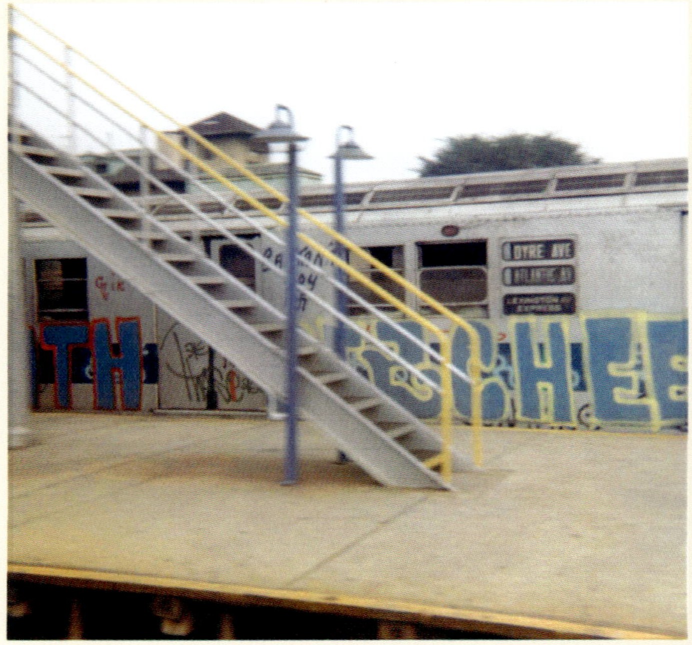
DYRE AVE
ATLANTIC AV

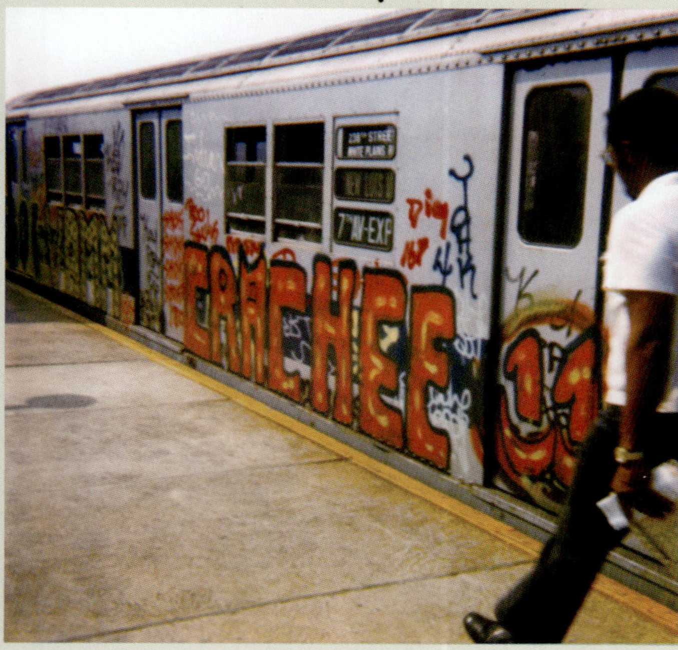

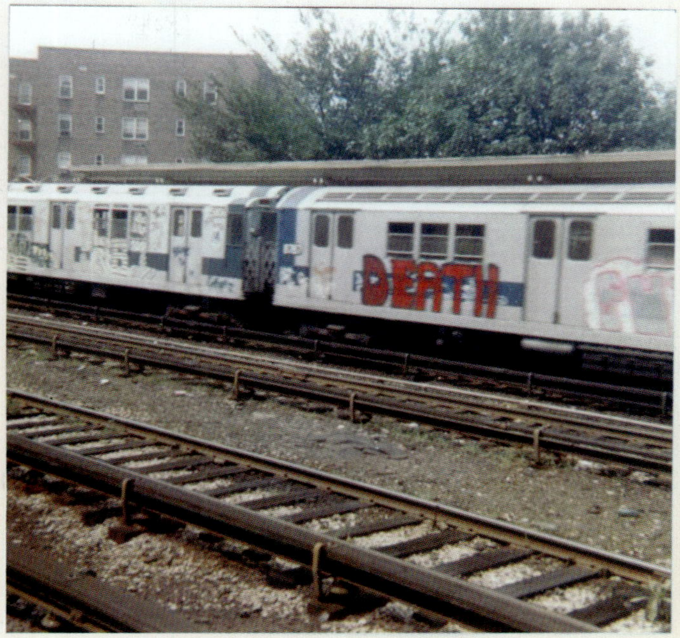

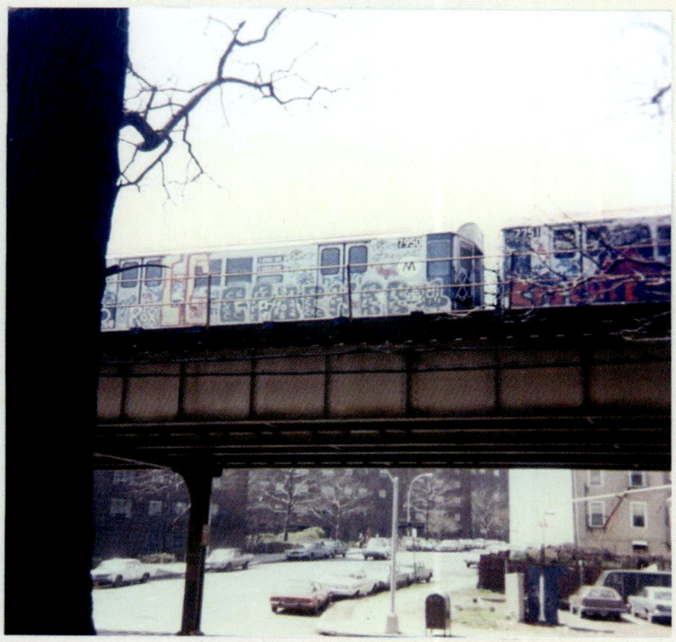

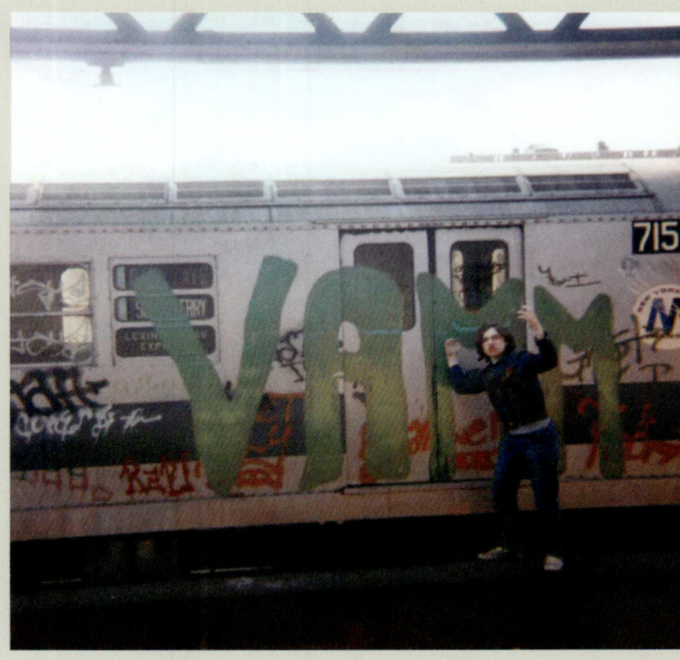

This spread: Panel pieces by VAMM, CRACHEE and DEATH. 1973.
Following two spreads: various panel pieces by the original members of THE CRAZY FIVE – BLADE, DEATH, VAMM, CRACHEE and TULL. Circa 1973.

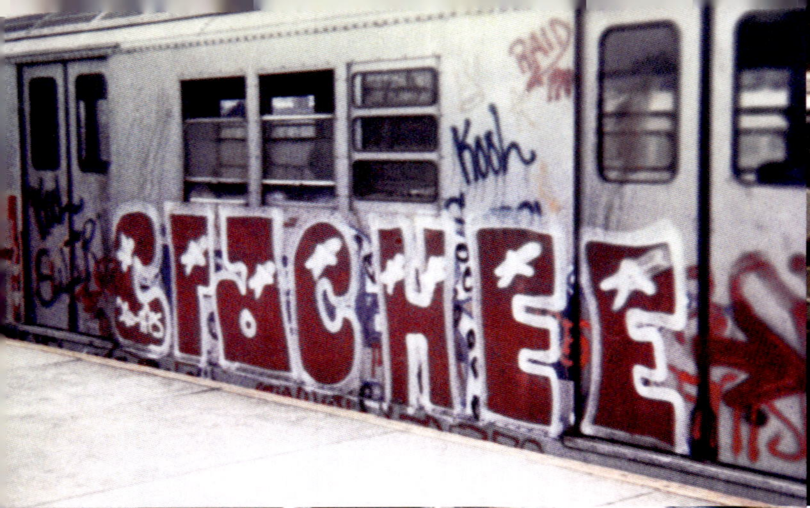

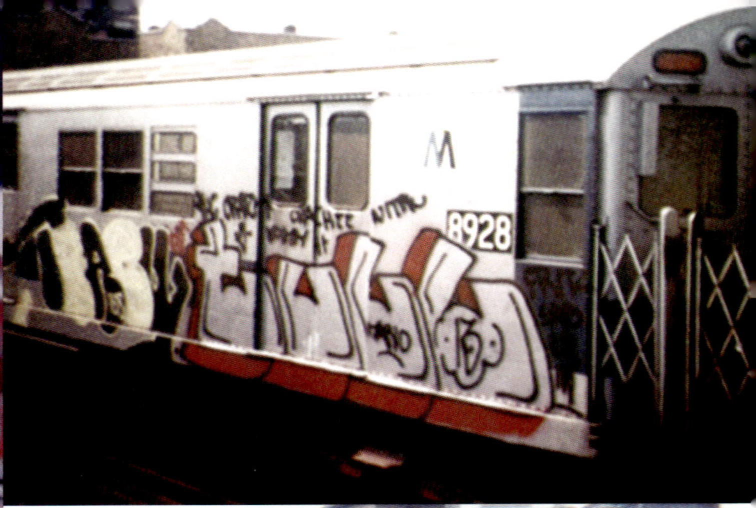
8928

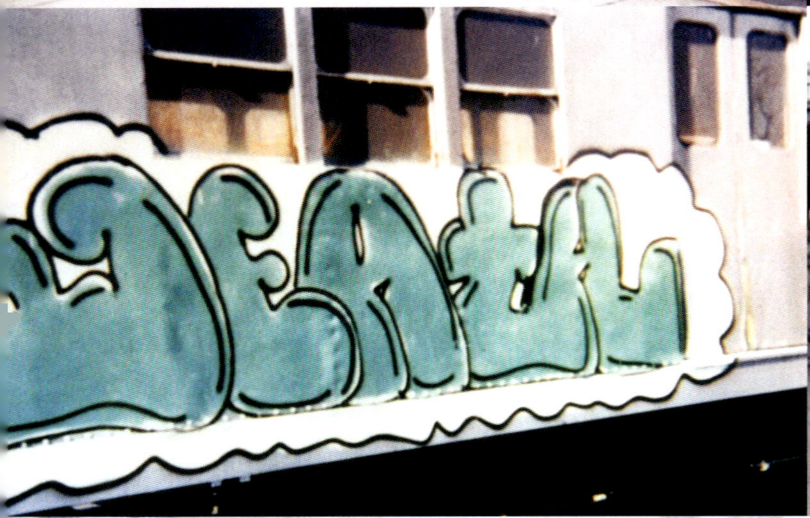

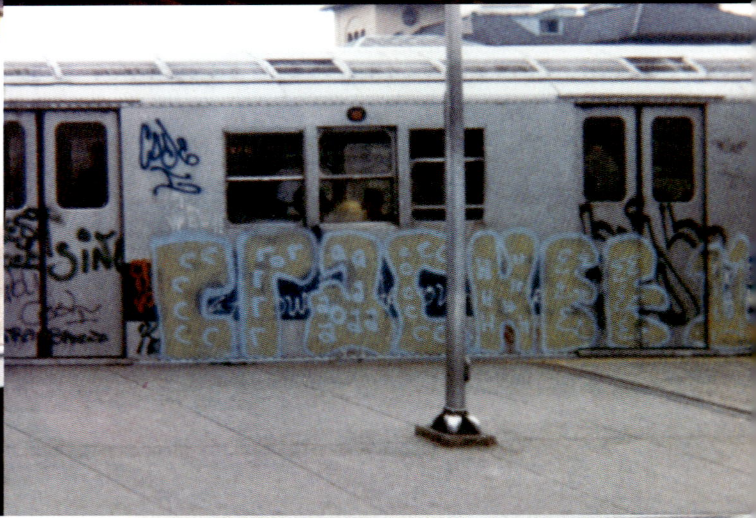

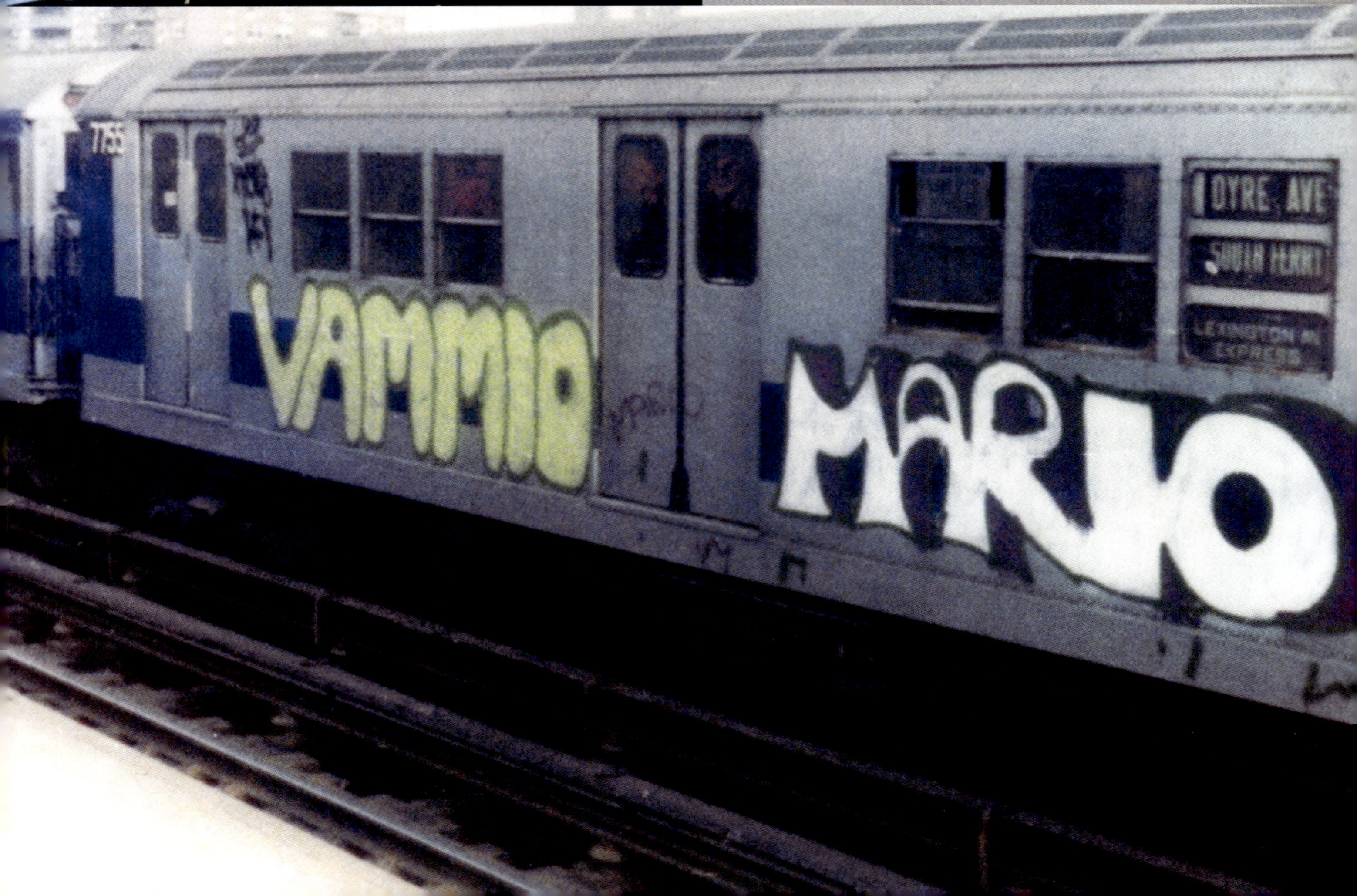
7755
DYRE AVE
LEXINGTON AV
EXPRESS

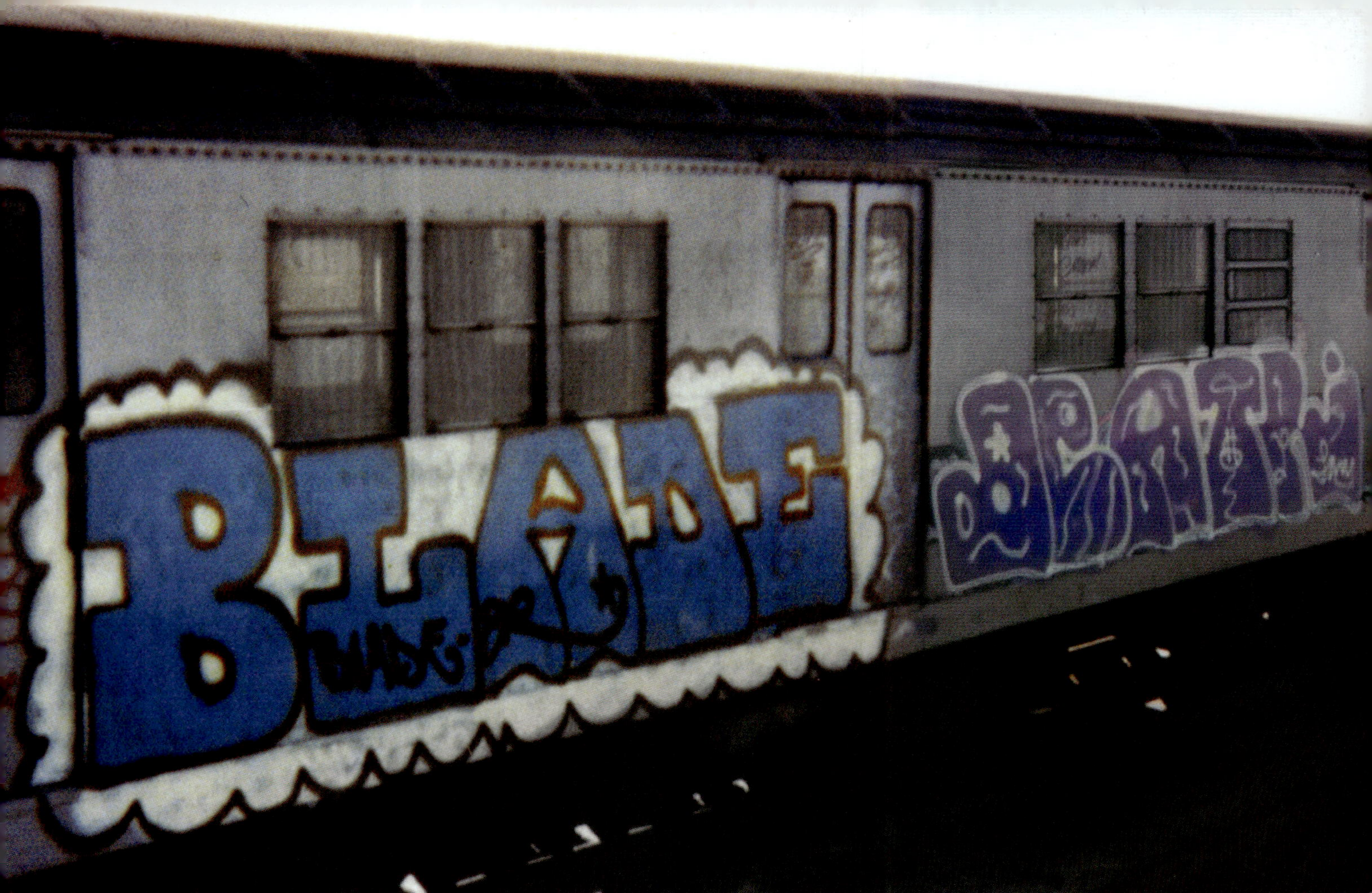
BLADE

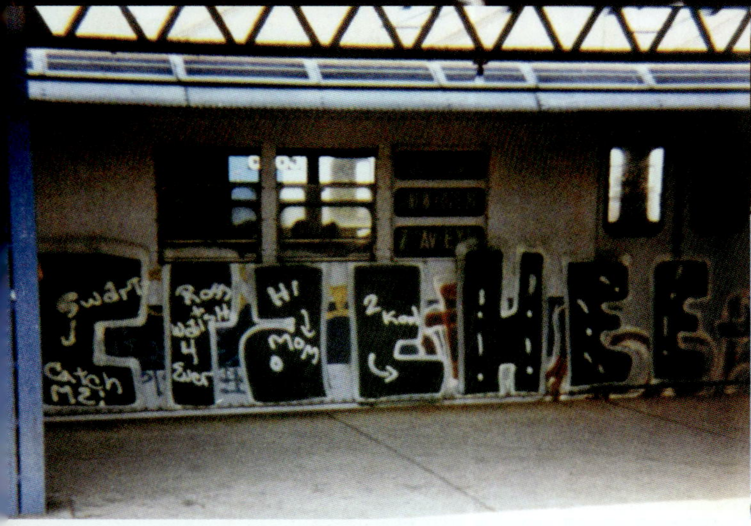

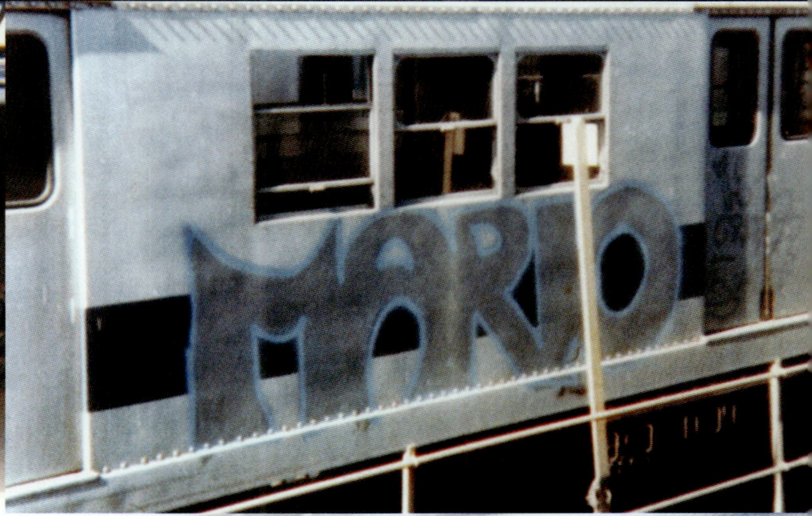
MARIO

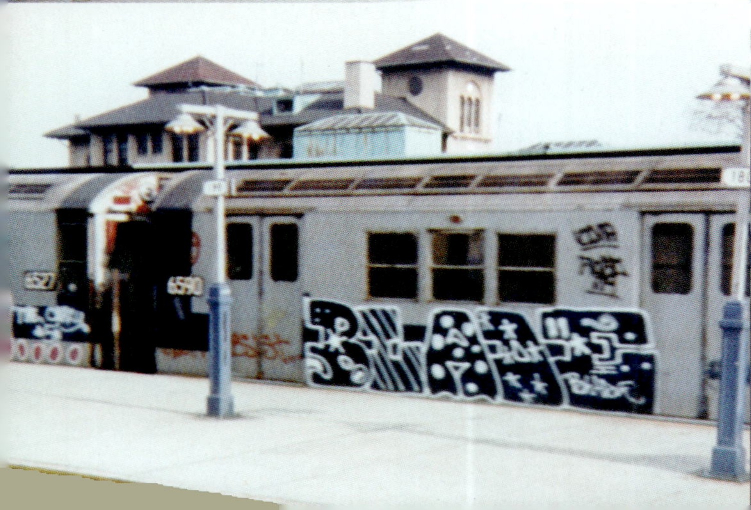

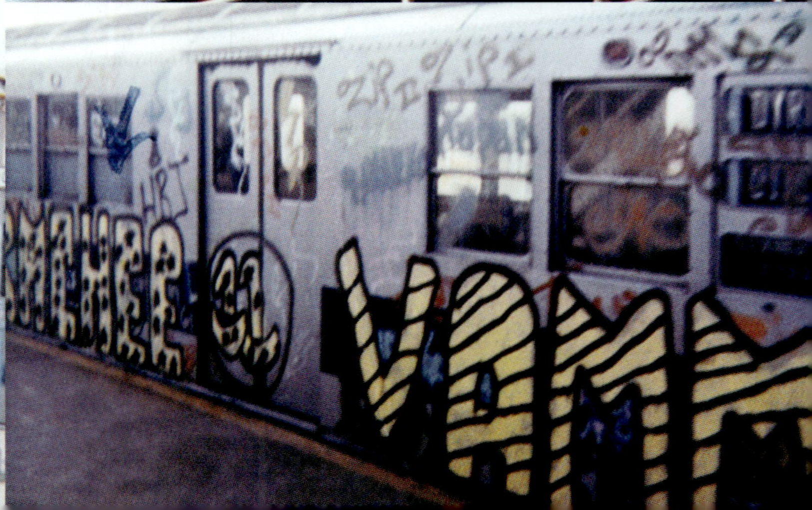

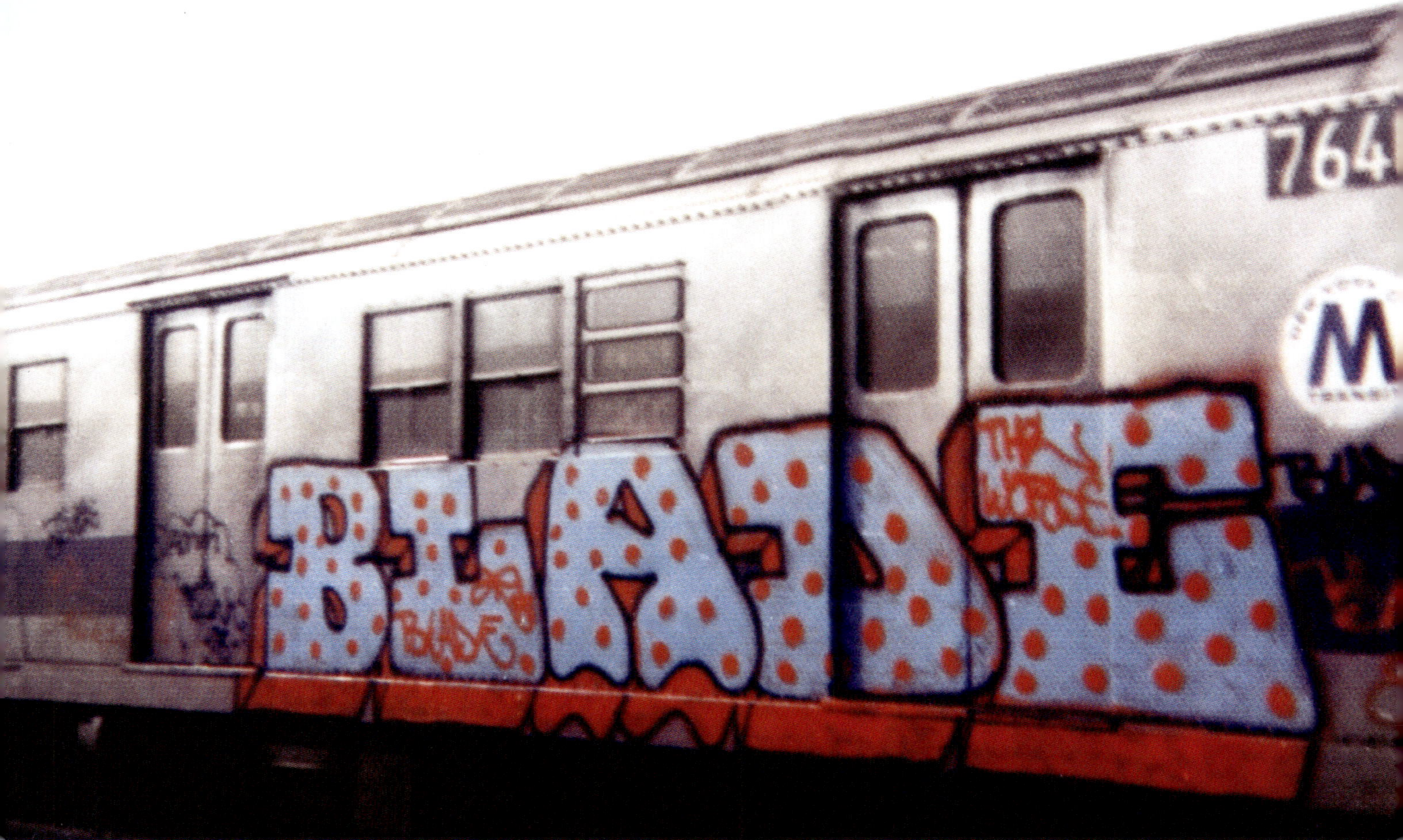
764
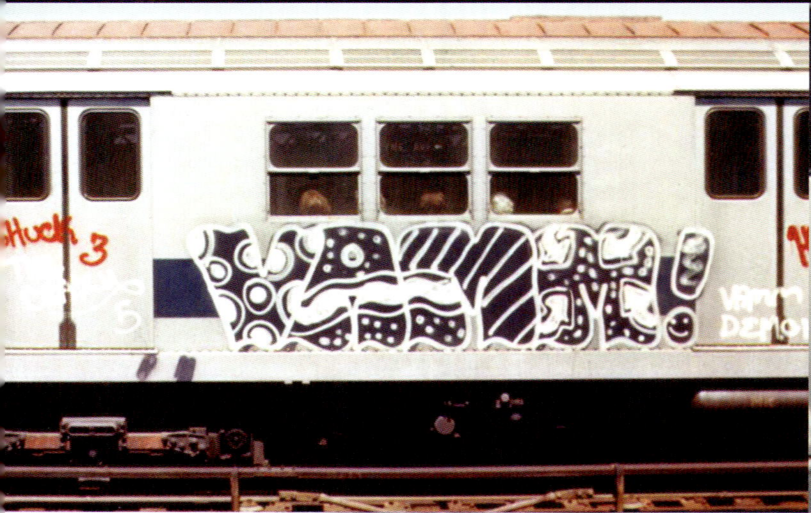
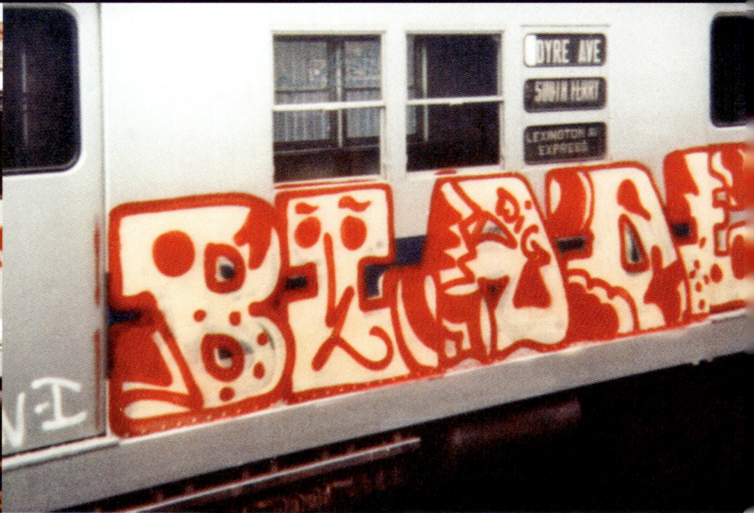
DYRE AVE
SOUTH FERRY
LEXINGTON AV EXPRESS
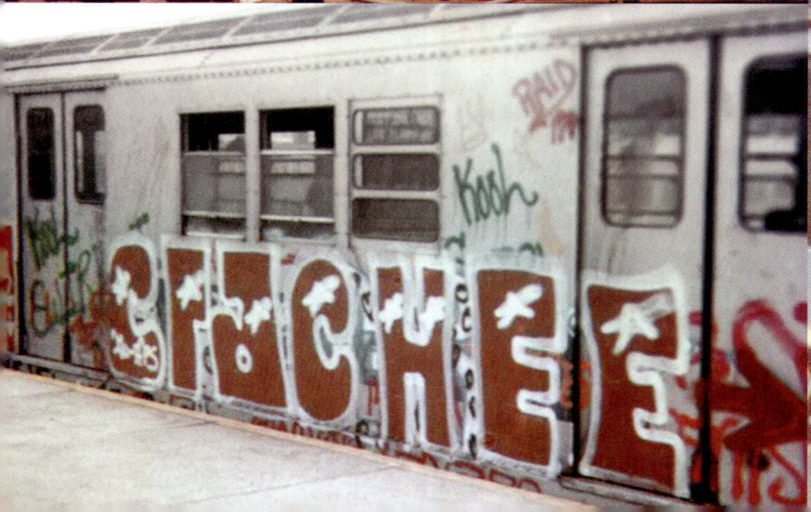
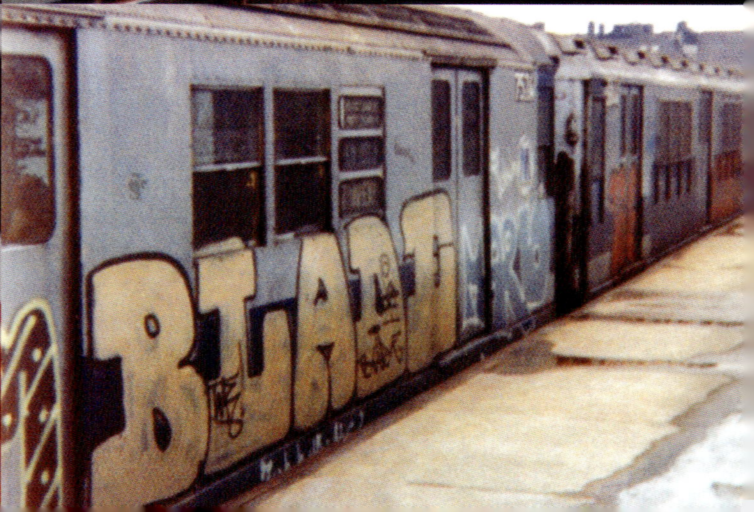

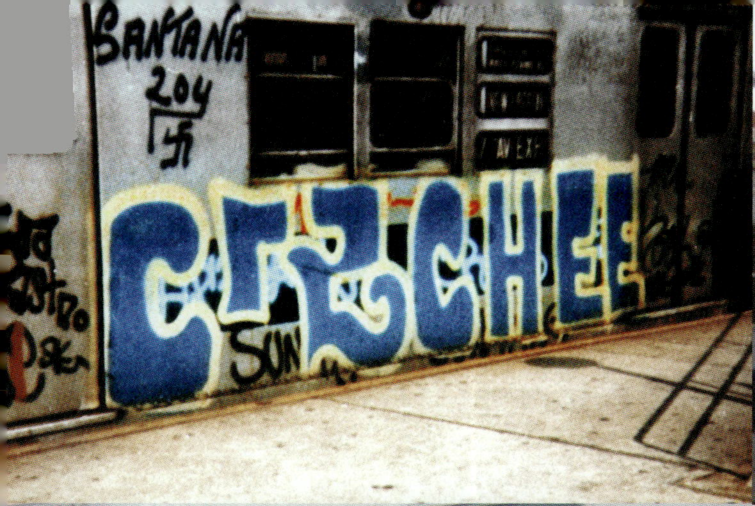

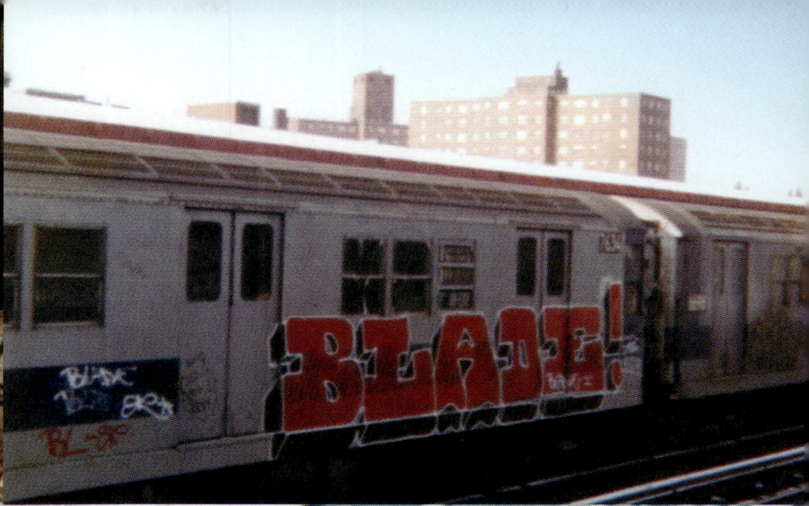

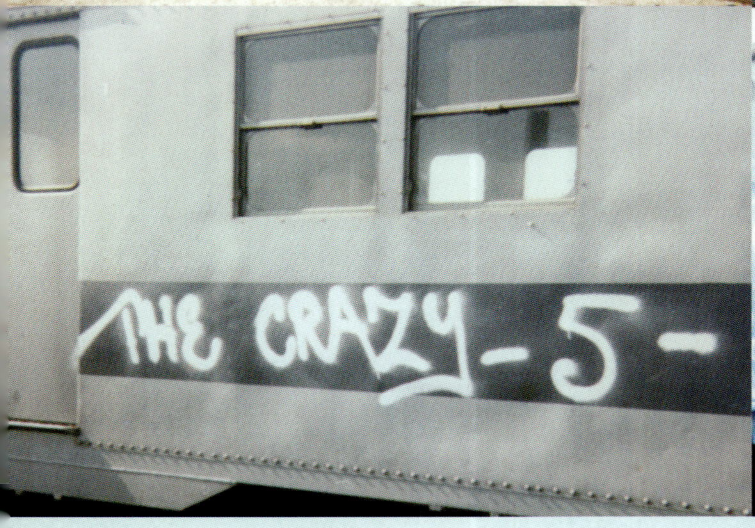
THE CRAZY - 5 -

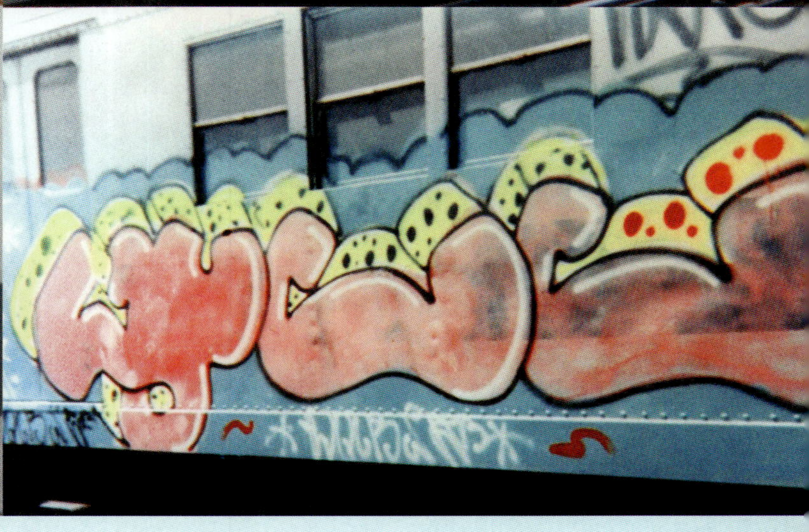

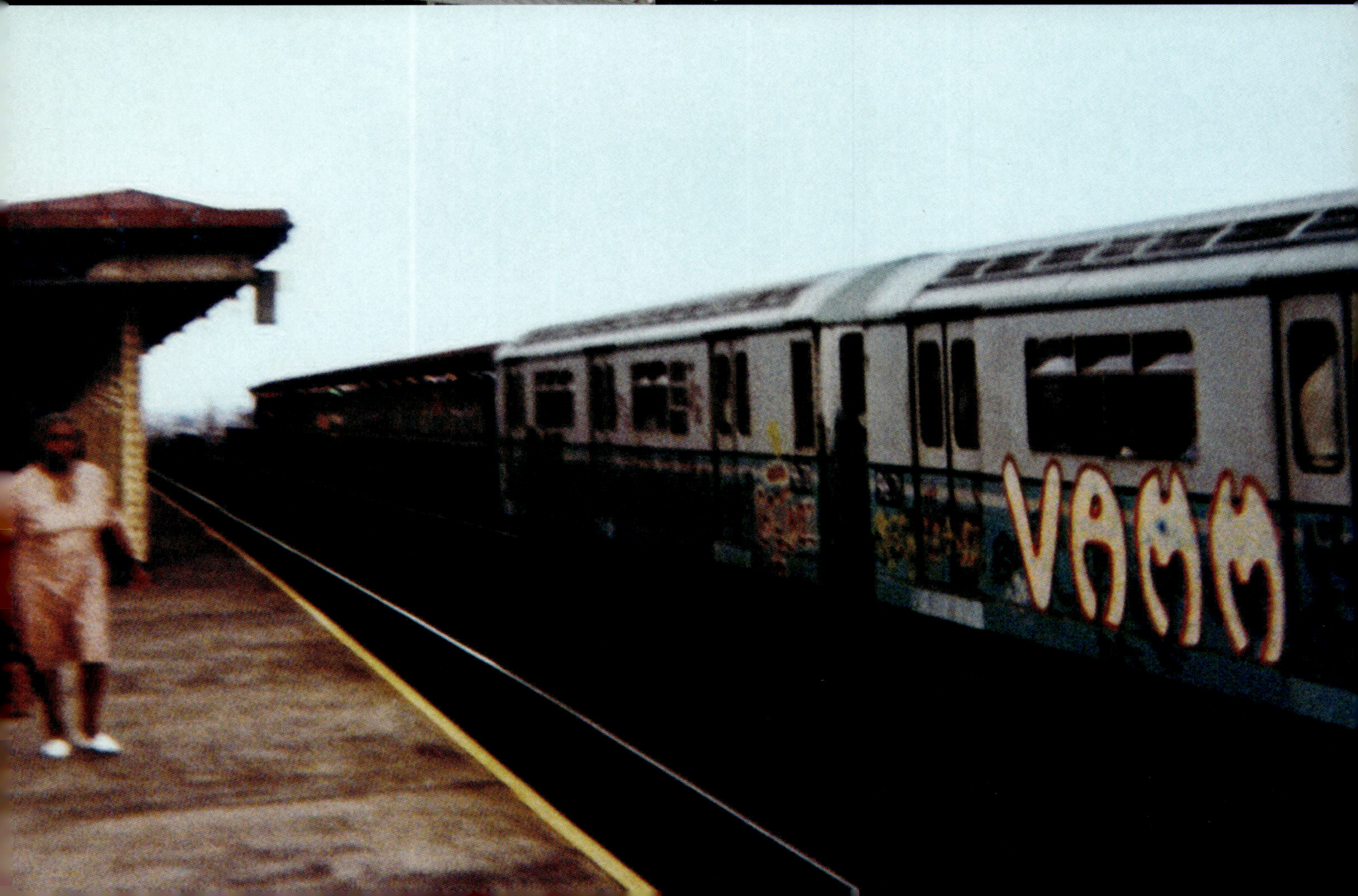

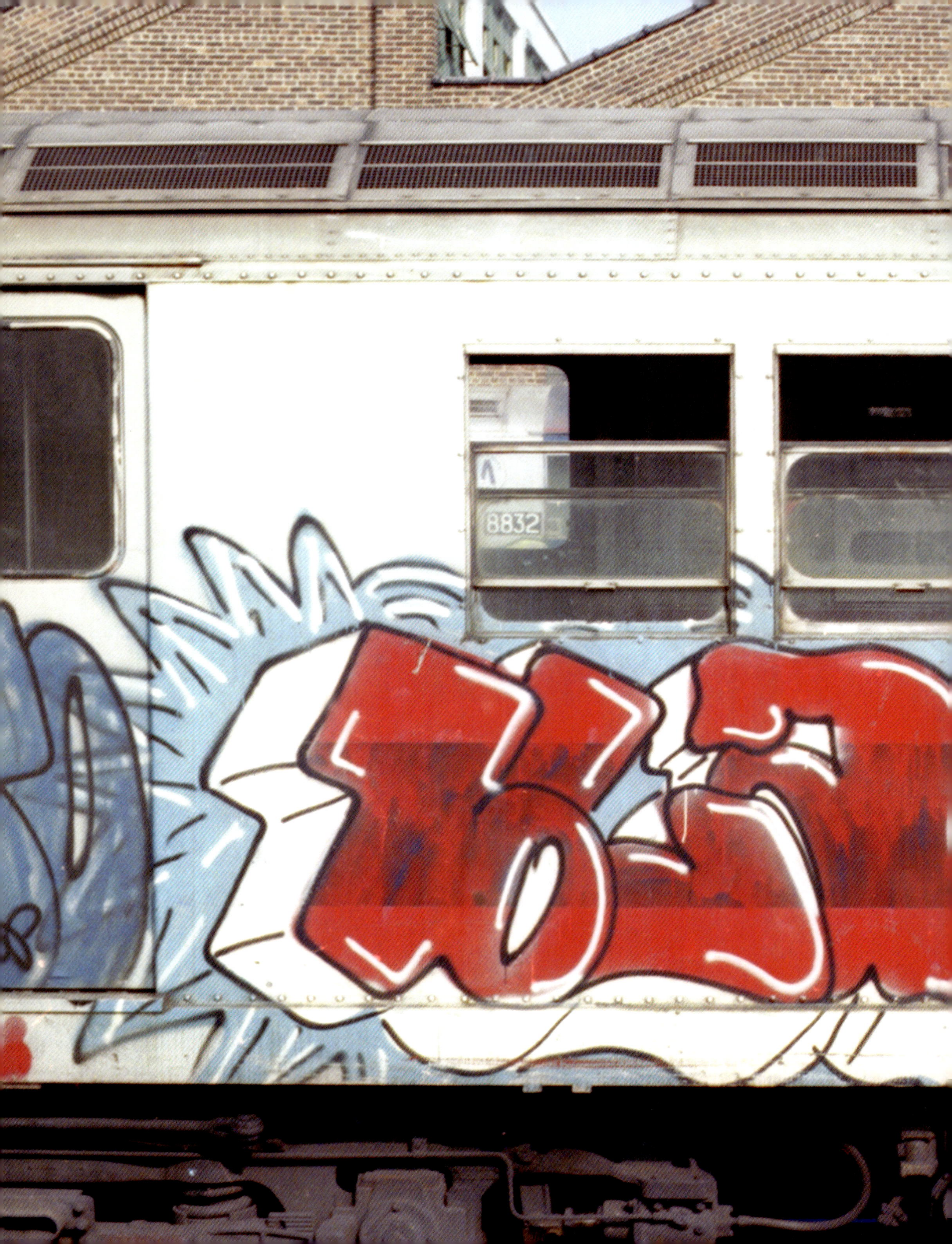
8832

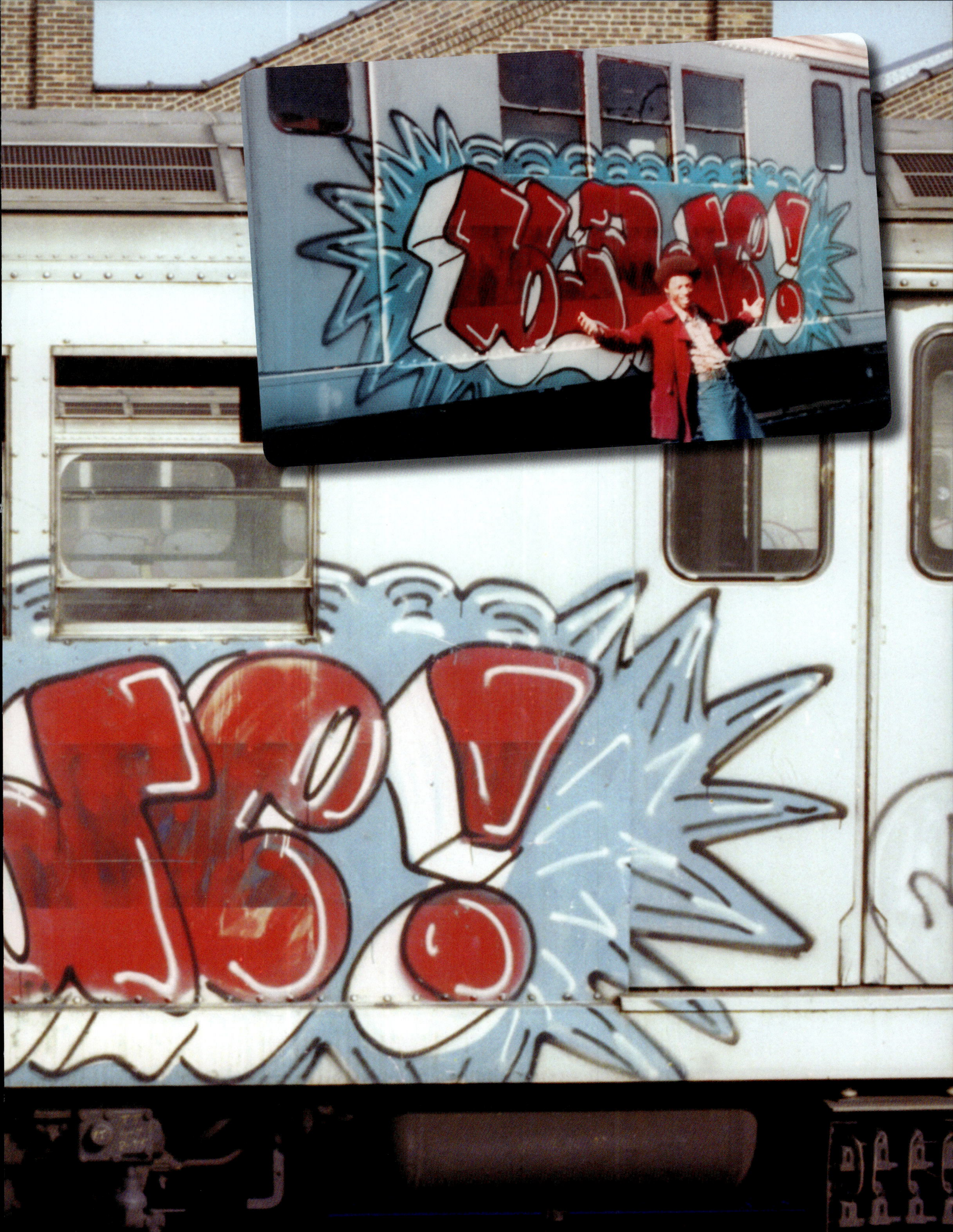

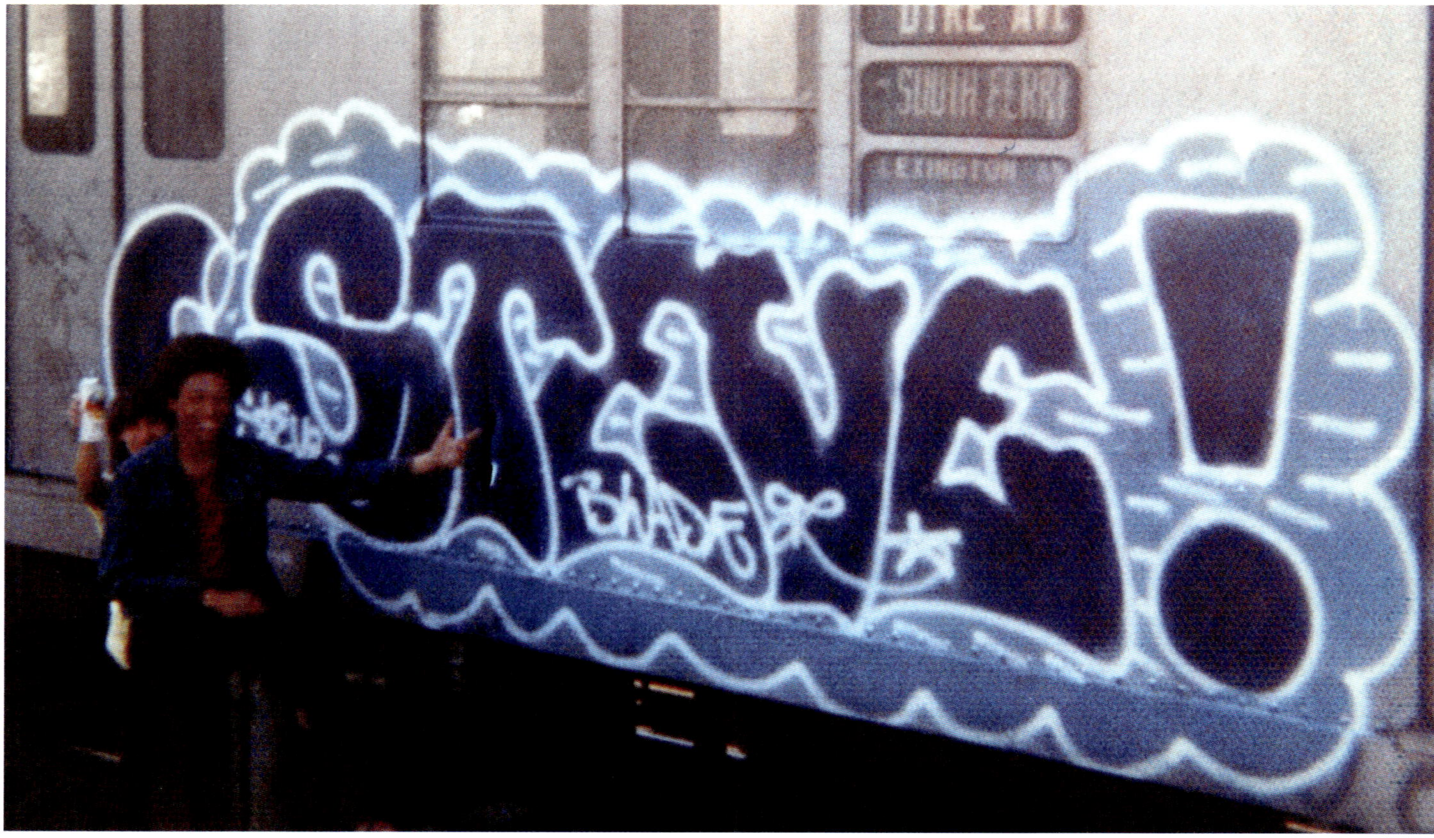

Writers started drawing their names in school to get better and come up with new ideas. I remember doing STEVE pieces in art class and adding cartoons as part of the design. We'd take those outlines with us to the lay-up to use as blueprints for our pieces. As styles evolved, so did color schemes. The early writers just stole whatever paint they could get their hands on, but by 1973 we were beginning to rack up the colors we needed. AJAX was the first guy I remember who was into racking specific colors. Sometimes, he'd even leave a store empty-handed if they didn't have what he wanted.

AJAX was one of a whole new group of writers hanging around the Parkside Houses with us. Everybody came to see us at Parkside to shoot hoops, smoke some hash, and talk about writing. Guys like COMET 1, SILVERTIPS, DEVIL 1, and AJAX came from uptown where they were known as The Boulevard Boys. BILLY 167, HIPPIE 44, and SHORTY 5 came from further downtown. Since we were right in the middle, everybody gravitated to us. The other writers continued to hit their lay-ups as well as our home base. Although we were protective of our home base, they were our friends. We could spend hours every day sitting on the park benches drawing new designs to go on the trains. This fostered a great sense of competition, which we all benefited from.

I met my first girlfriend, Karen, at the Parkside playground in 1974. She used to come by and hang out and get drunk with us. We were both black, so it seemed like a perfect fit. There was always a group of girls in our playground, such as SUEKI and POONI, and Z-73, and they all wrote. Some of these girls wrote before me, hitting the red trains in 1971.

Karen lived in a group home just a few blocks away, although she spent most of her time at Parkside. Her full name was Karen Hunt. She had no family, because her parents abandoned her and her distant relatives didn't want her. The first group home Karen lived in was off Holland Avenue. This was when I got to know her. In 1975 she moved to a new home on Givens Avenue. The Givens Avenue home had guards, so I would climb up her fire escape and enter through her window. Then, we'd make out all night. Since we hung out with female writers, Karen always asked me to do a piece with our names, which I did reluctantly. Since graffiti was about getting your name up, with the Karen pieces I used the name Steve.

Previous spread: BLADE. Photo by Henry Chalfant in 1982, Subway Art, *25th Anniversary Edition, Thames and Hudson, Ltd. London 2009. Inset: BLADE posing after he painted the train. 1975. This page: STEVE by BLADE. circa 1975. Opposite page: Top STEVE by BLADE and KAREN whole-car. Circa 1975. Bottom: Various KAREN pieces by BLADE. Circa 1975.*

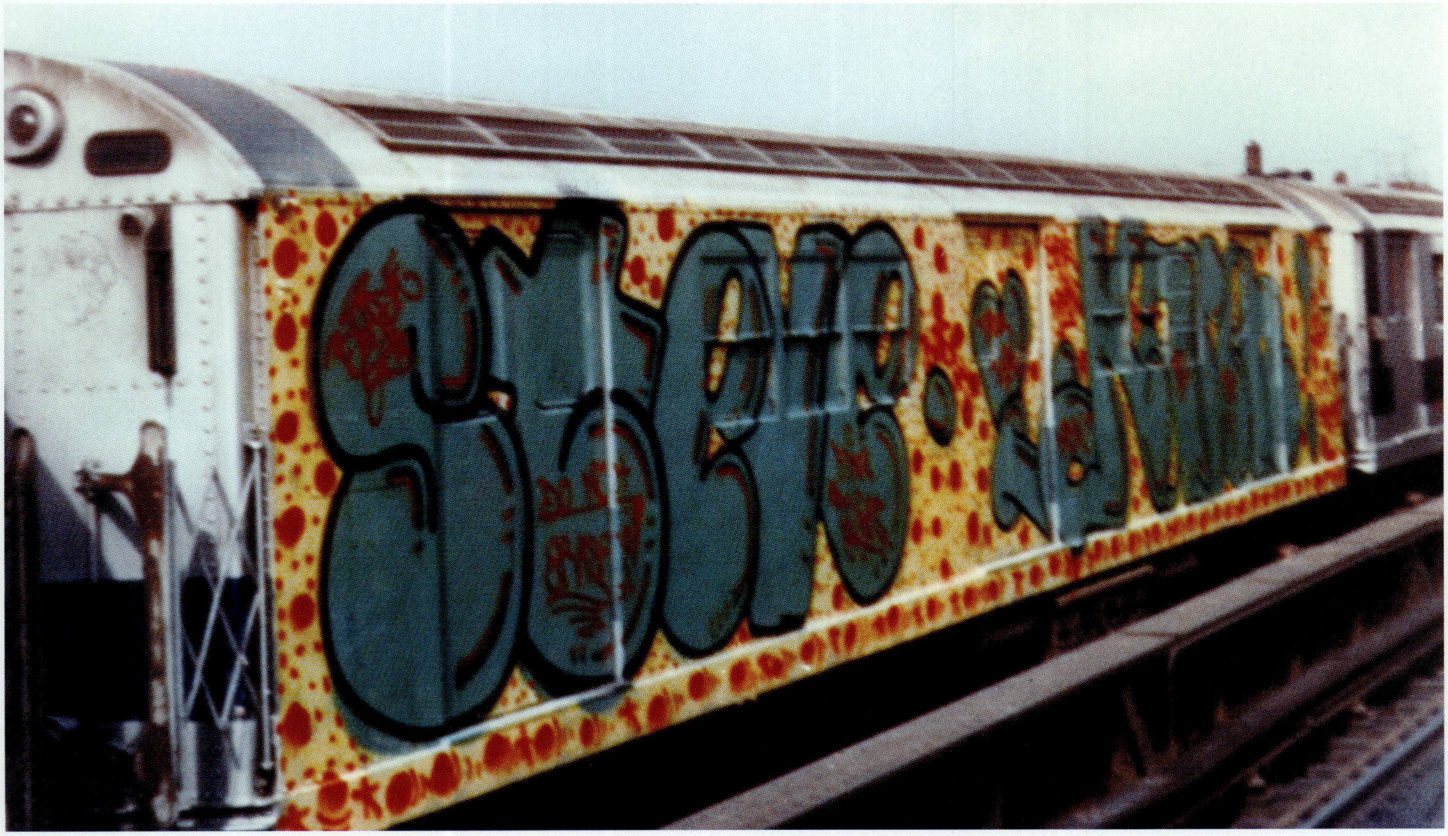

“I MET MY FIRST GIRLFRIEND, KAREN, AT THE PARK-SIDE PLAYGROUND IN 1974. SHE USED TO COME BY AND HANG OUT AND GET DRUNK WITH US...”

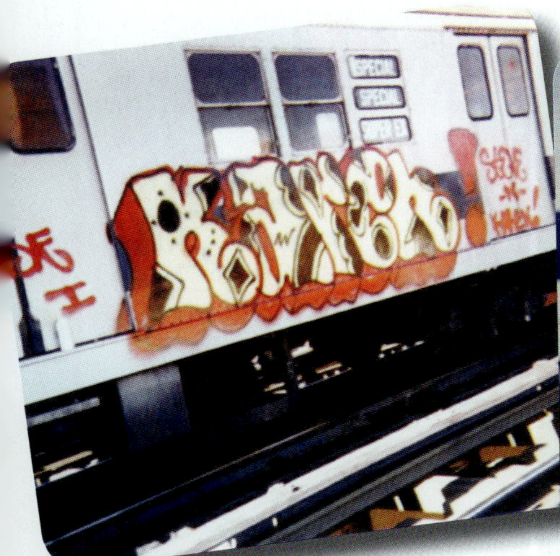

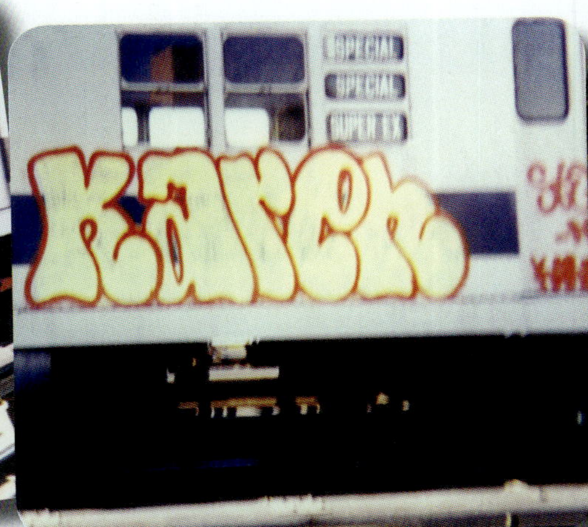

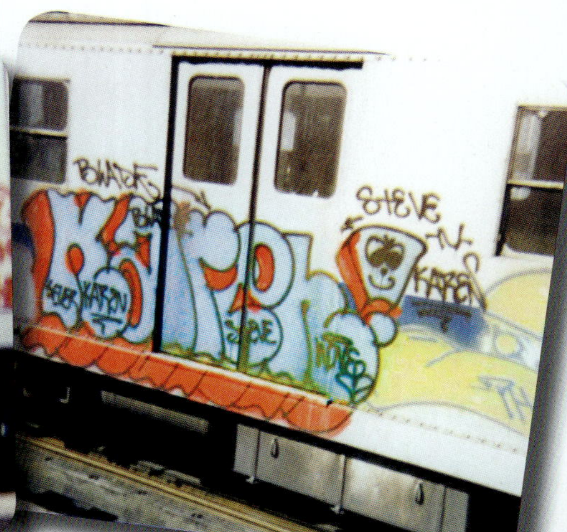

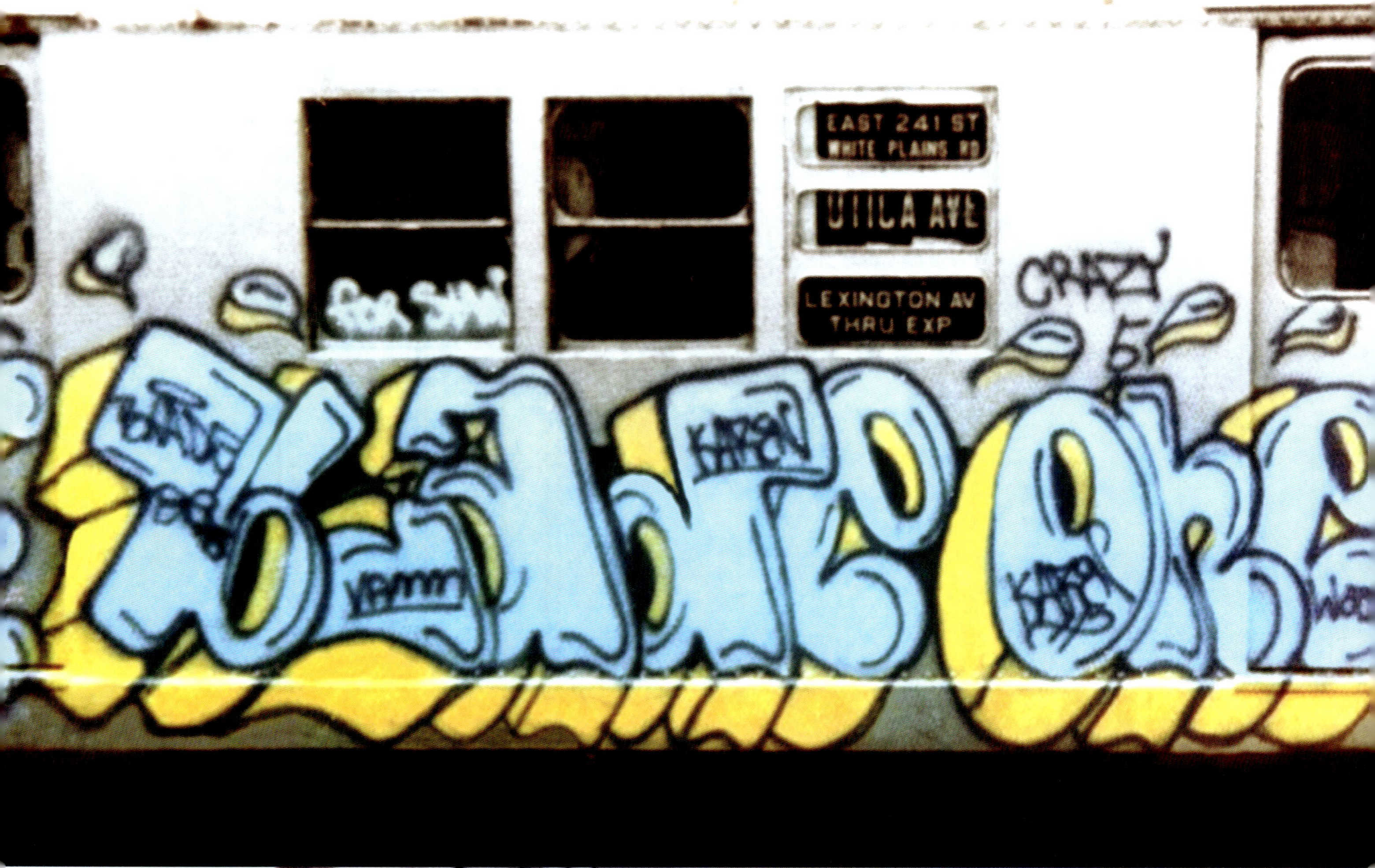
EAST 241 ST
WHITE PLAINS RD
UTICA AVE
LEXINGTON AV
THRU EXP
CRAZY 5

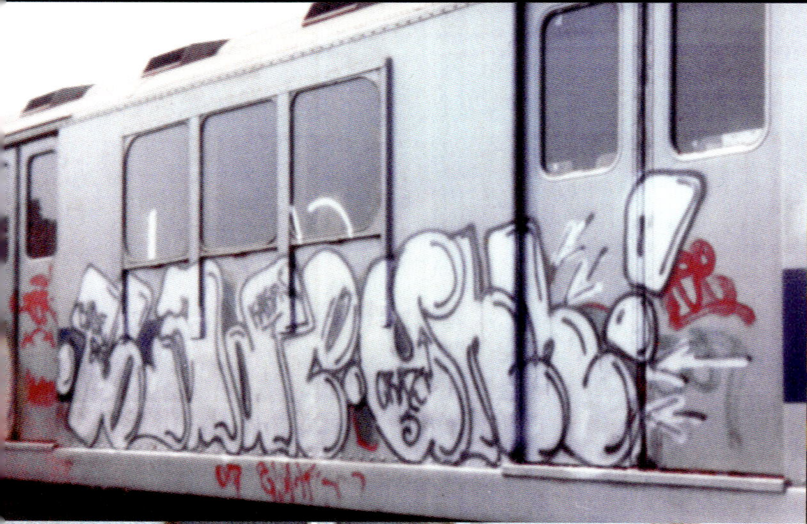

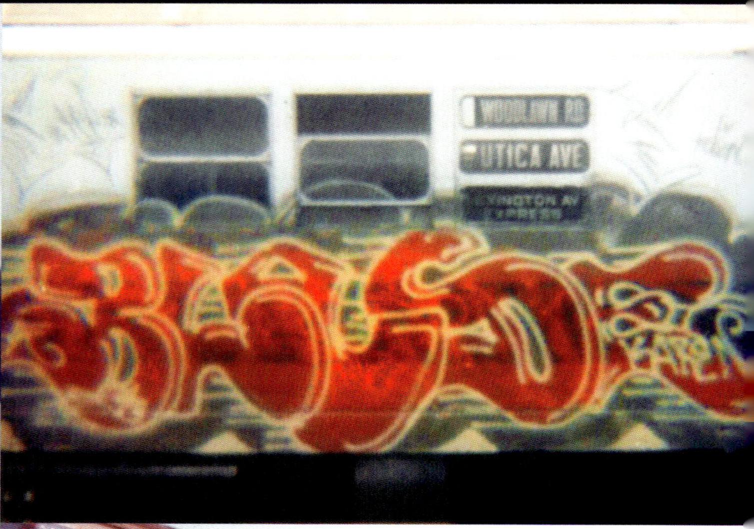
WOODLAWN RD
UTICA AVE

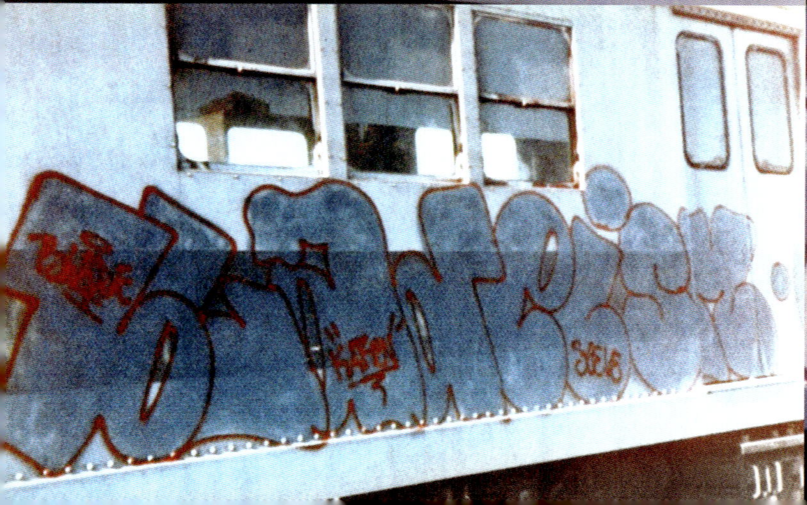

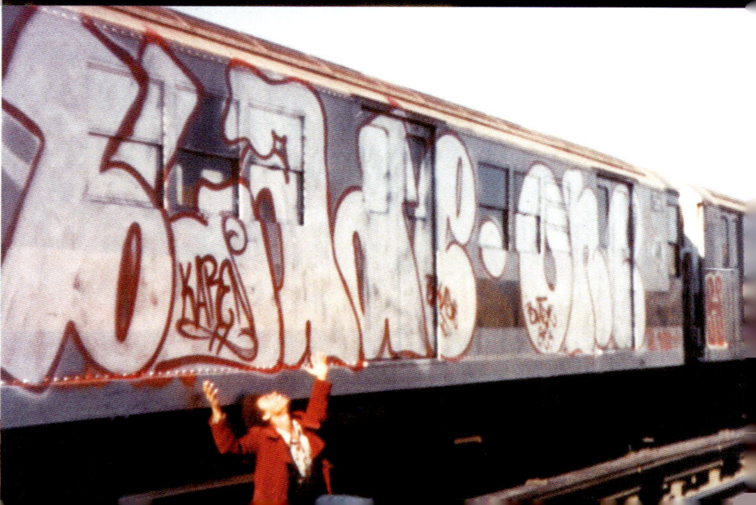

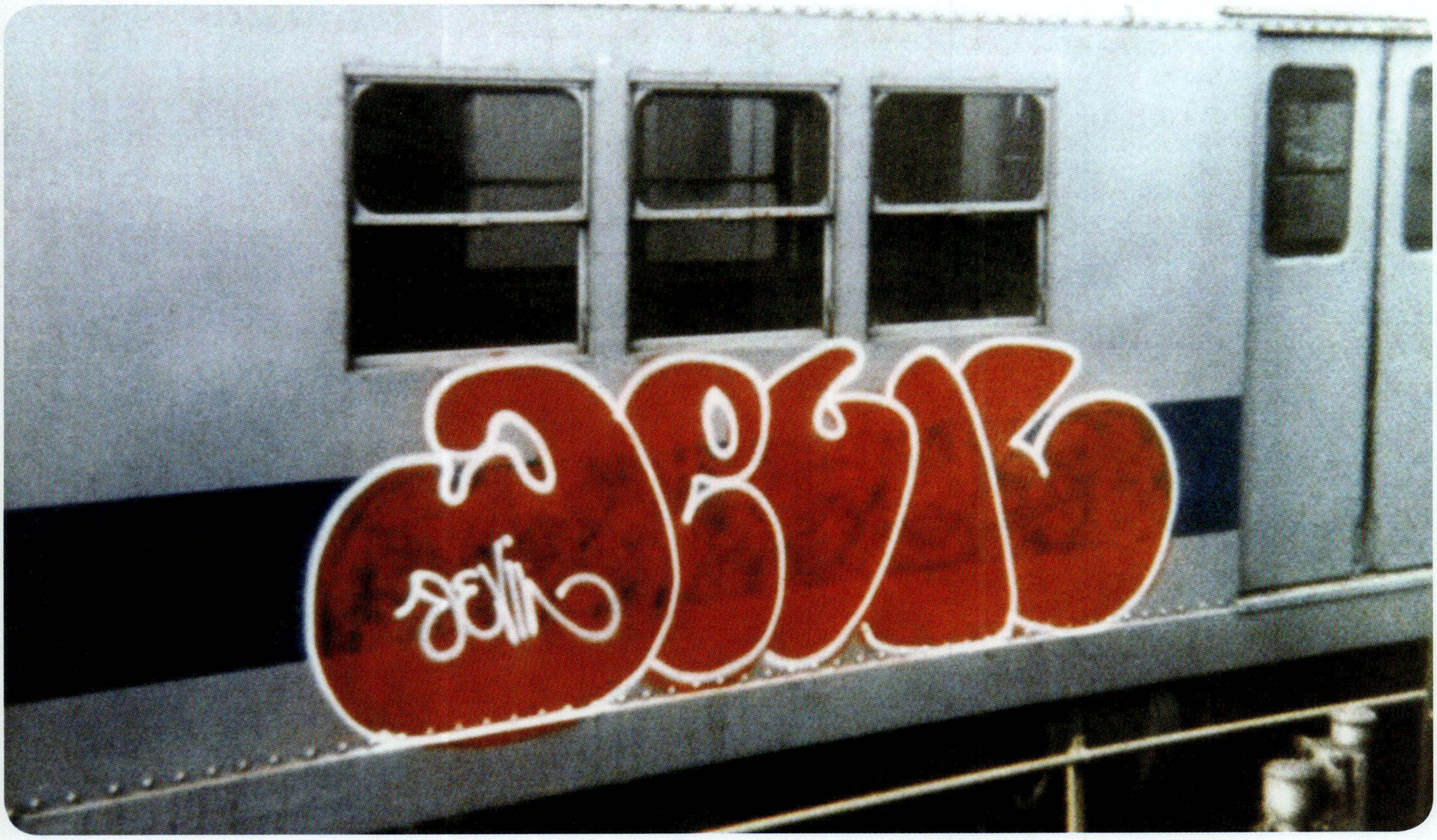

I met Karen when I was sixteen years old and I thought I was in love with her. Most kids who dated at that age went to movies and school events, but that didn't interest either of us. Our relationship was based around Parkside, where we hung out with a crowd that could roll twenty deep, getting drunk, shooting hoops, and trying to get laid. Karen was all right with that; she was right in the mix.

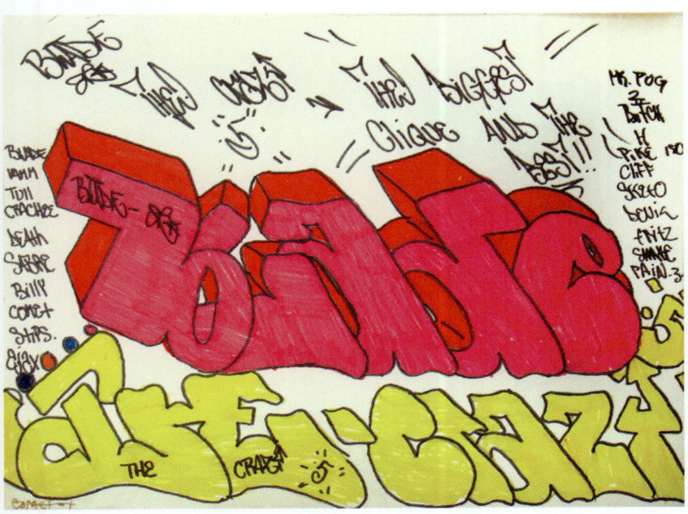

By the end of 1973, the days of straight letter pieces were over. I knew I was going to need a style to at least keep up with the others. Finding a style was tough, because you didn't have a copy of *Subway Art* to steal your style from back then.

In January of 1974, I was at the Parkside playground, just hanging out and doing sketches. It was so cold out that DEVIL and I were the only two in the playground. DEVIL was sitting next to me on a bench, drawing in his notebook. He turned to me and said, "I think I've got something." He tore the page out and handed it to me without looking up. It was a BLADE outline, which I really liked because the letters were round and simple. I painted it a few days later at the Burke lay-up. Although it was freezing cold that night, I finished the piece. The next day, when I saw it riding, I dubbed the style "bubble" letters. I went on to do a thousand more like it.

Opposite page: Various pieces by BLADE where he puts up KAREN. Circa 1975. This page: Top: DEVIL. 1974. Bottom: BLADE black book sketch. Circa 1974. Following spread: BLADE bubble letter pieces. 1974.

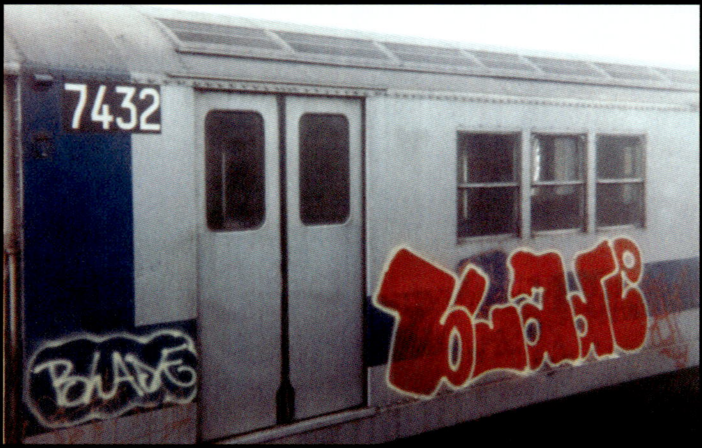
7432

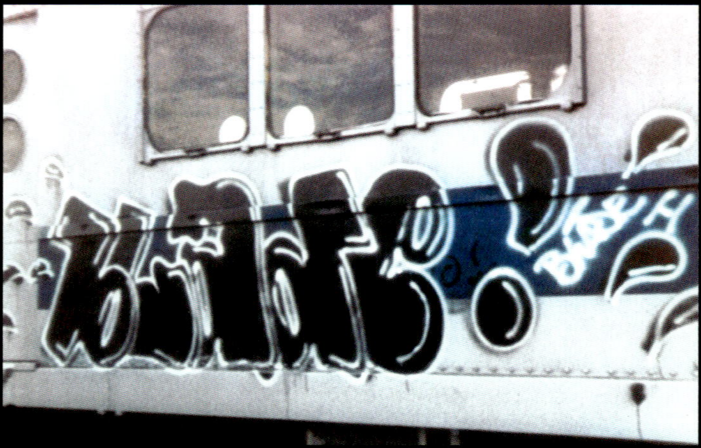

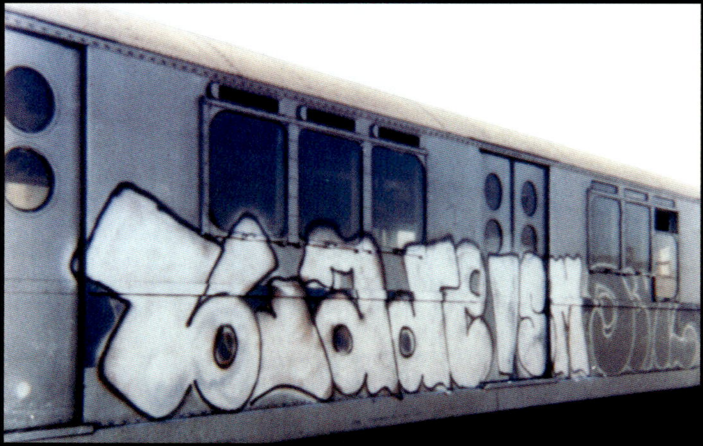

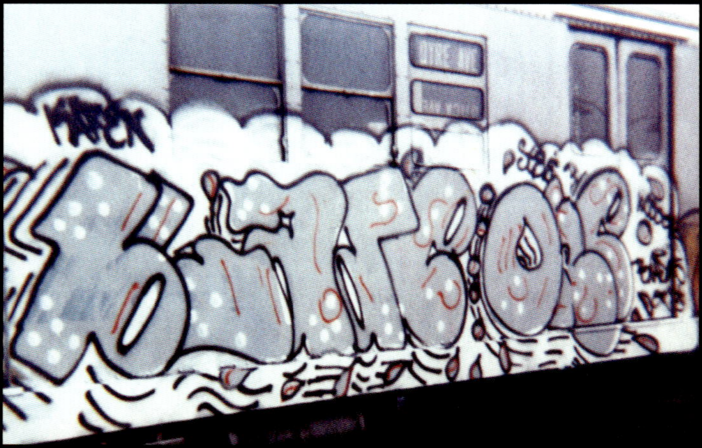

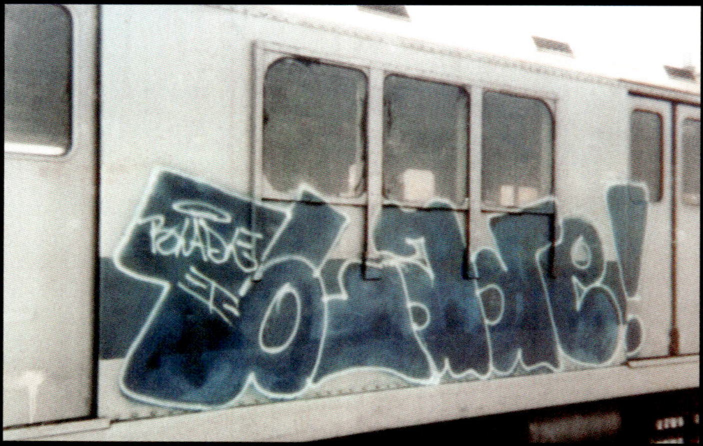

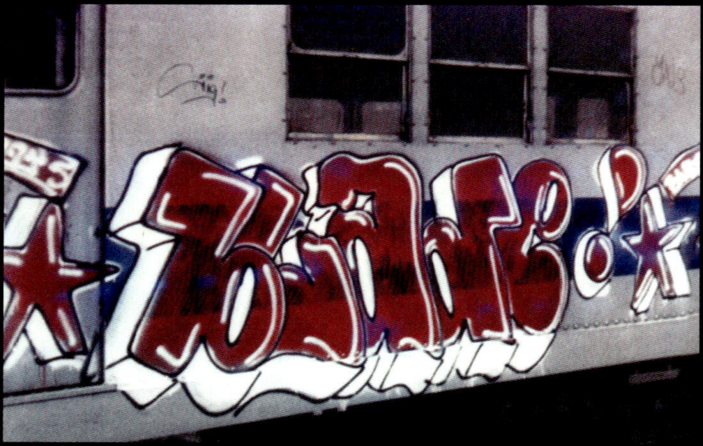

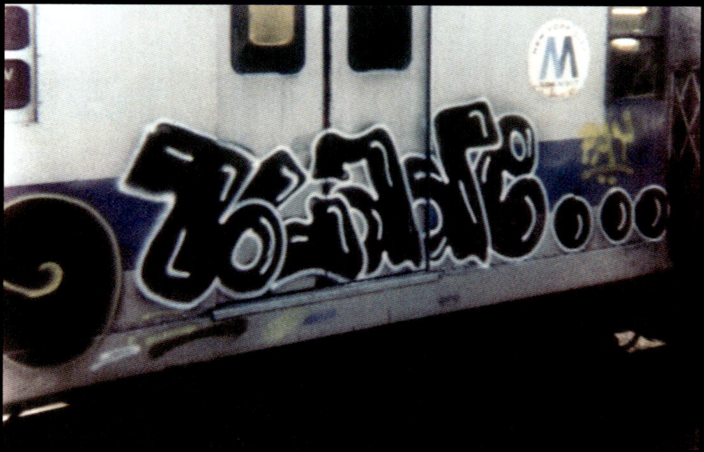

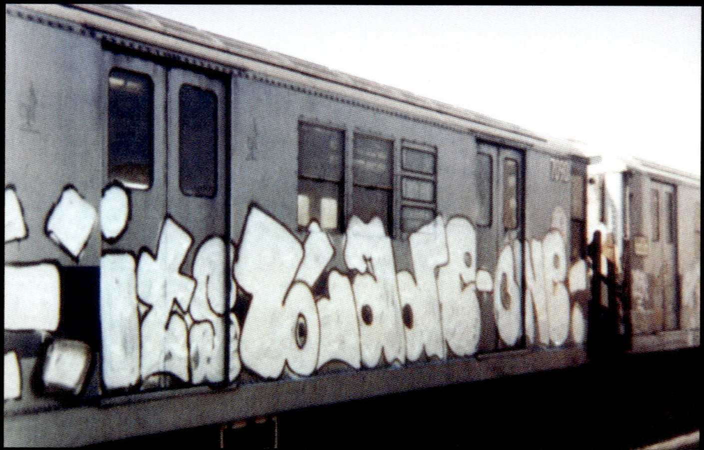

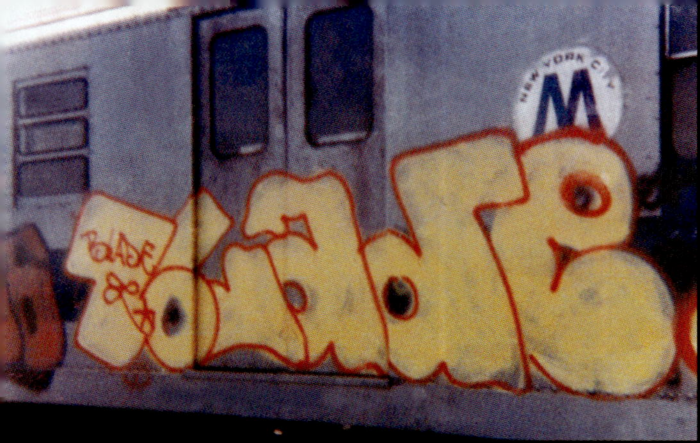
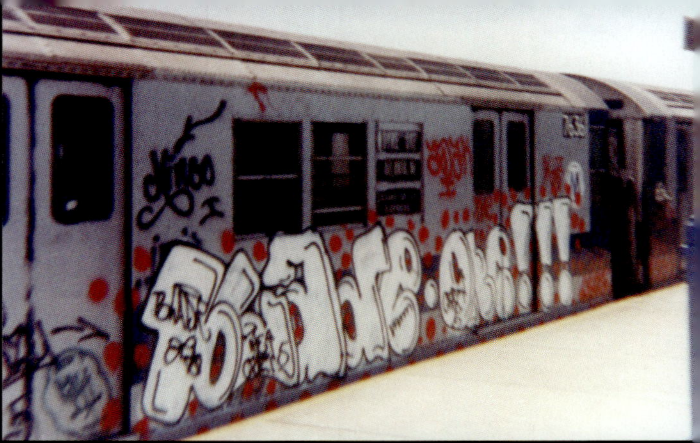
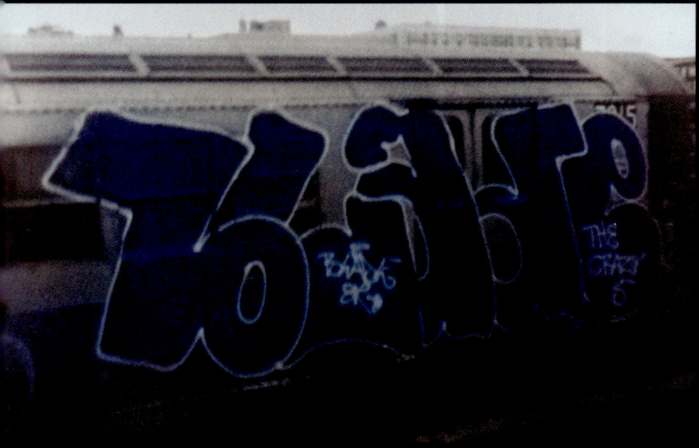
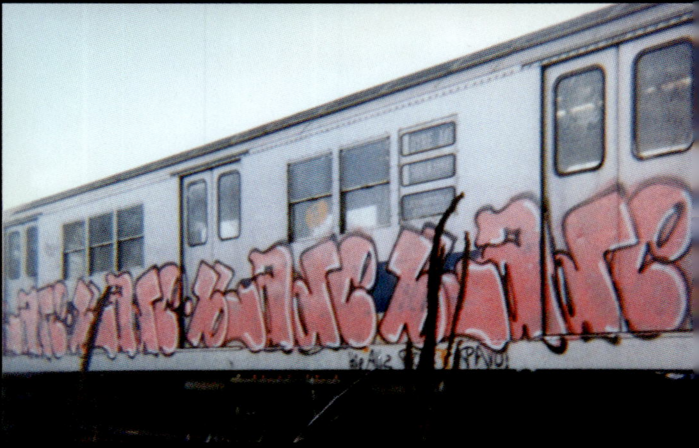
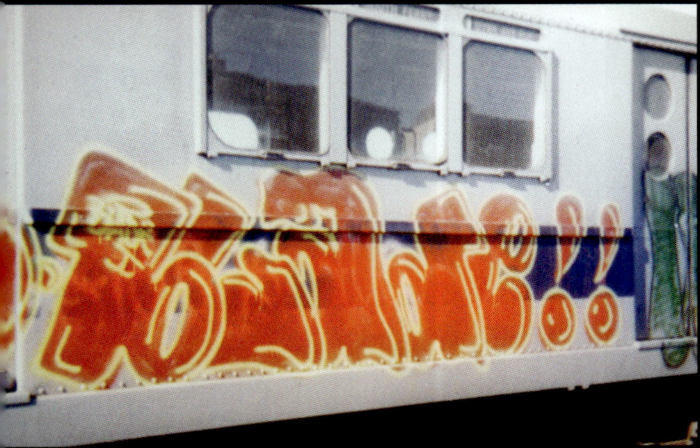
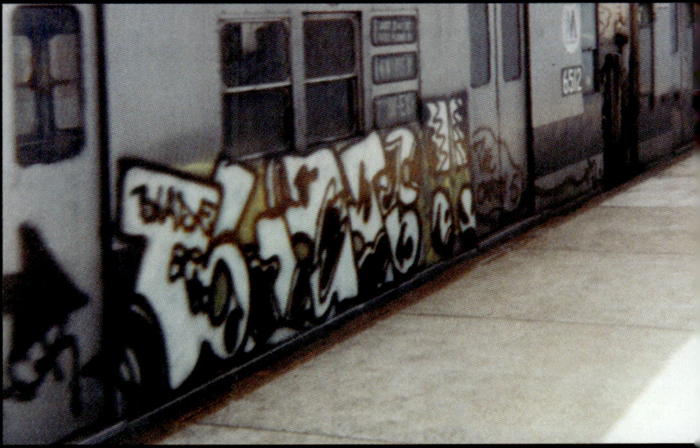
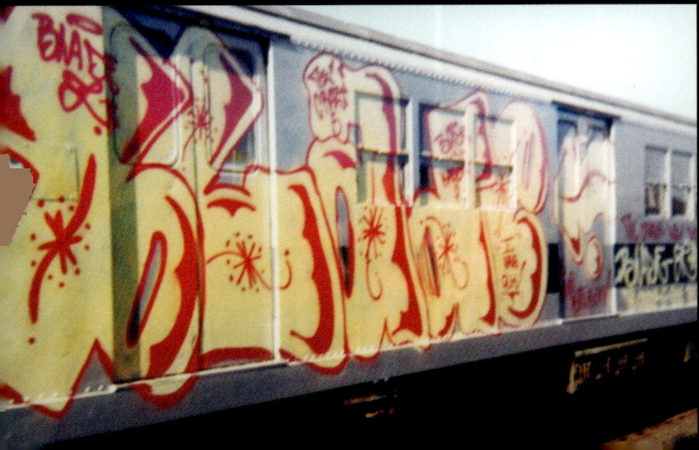
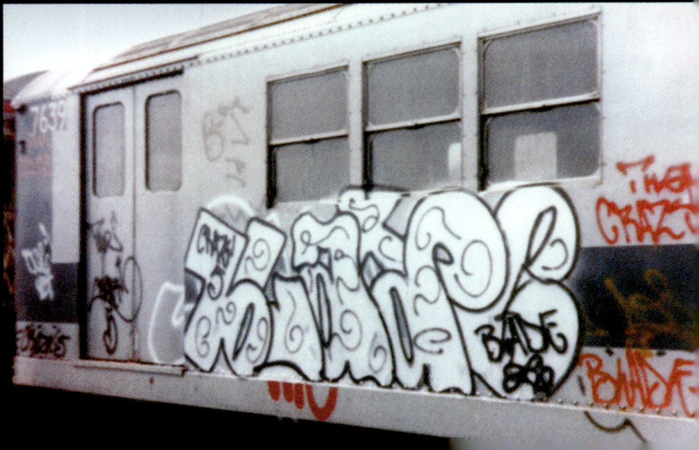

CHAPTER FIVE

THE CRAZY 5:

1974–1975

I was down with a lot of graffiti crews, or gangs, including THE EBONY DUKES, who came out of the Hewitt Place projects in the South Bronx. They started as a street gang and switched to a writing gang in 1972. They had members in the Bronx, Brooklyn, and even Queens, a borough that barely had graffiti. The gang was formed by STAFF 161 and featured some of the best writers around, including his younger brother Adam, who wrote ALL JIVE 161, as well as KING KOOL 156 and DOC COOL and TE KOOL, the writers who invented marshmallow letters.

We all had stories about how we became members of the DUKES. CRACHEE and VAMM bumped into DYNAMITE 161 on a train. He invited them to meet STAFF 161 at the writer's bench at 149th Street. That day they hung out and watched the trains go by. As CRACHEE and VAMM were leaving, STAFF 161 told them to come by the next day and he would give them their membership cards, which were beautiful because STAFF 161 drew each one by hand. CRACHEE and VAMM were to become the first two white members of THE EBONY DUKES. I was put in a week later while watching trains at the 180th Street station.

CRACHEE and VAMM had a good relationship with the DUKES. They even went racking with them in the notorious South Bronx. VAMM returned the favor by taking them on a racking mission to Westchester, where STAFF 161 was shocked to find spray paint still openly displayed. I didn't hang out at the writer's bench that much, because there were black writers who couldn't understand why I was writing with white boys and I didn't feel it needed an explanation. I wrote with whomever I wanted to write with.

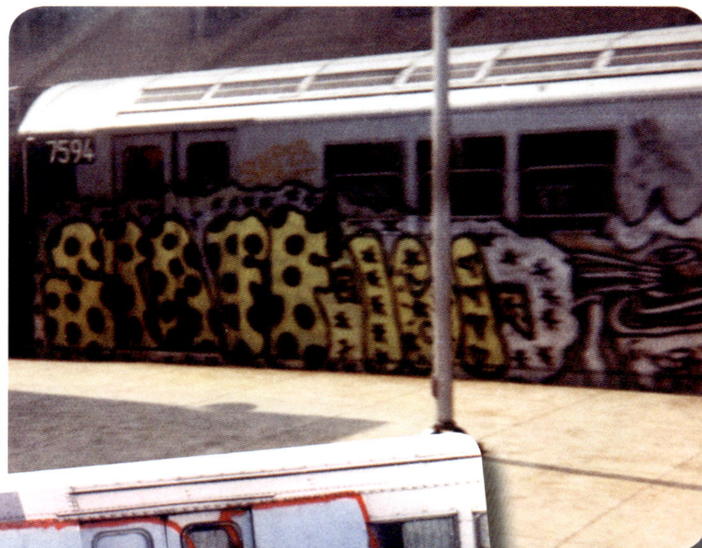

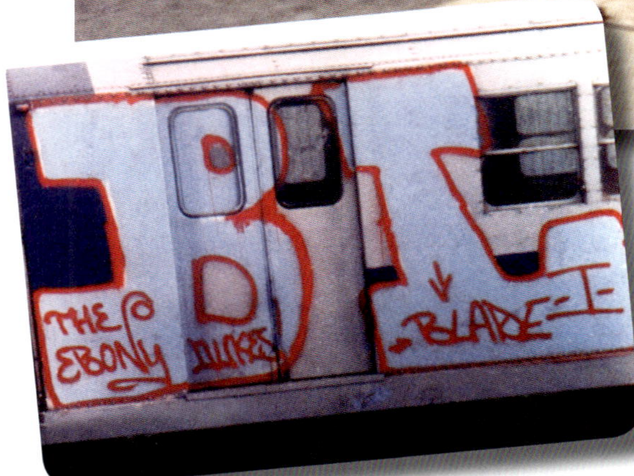

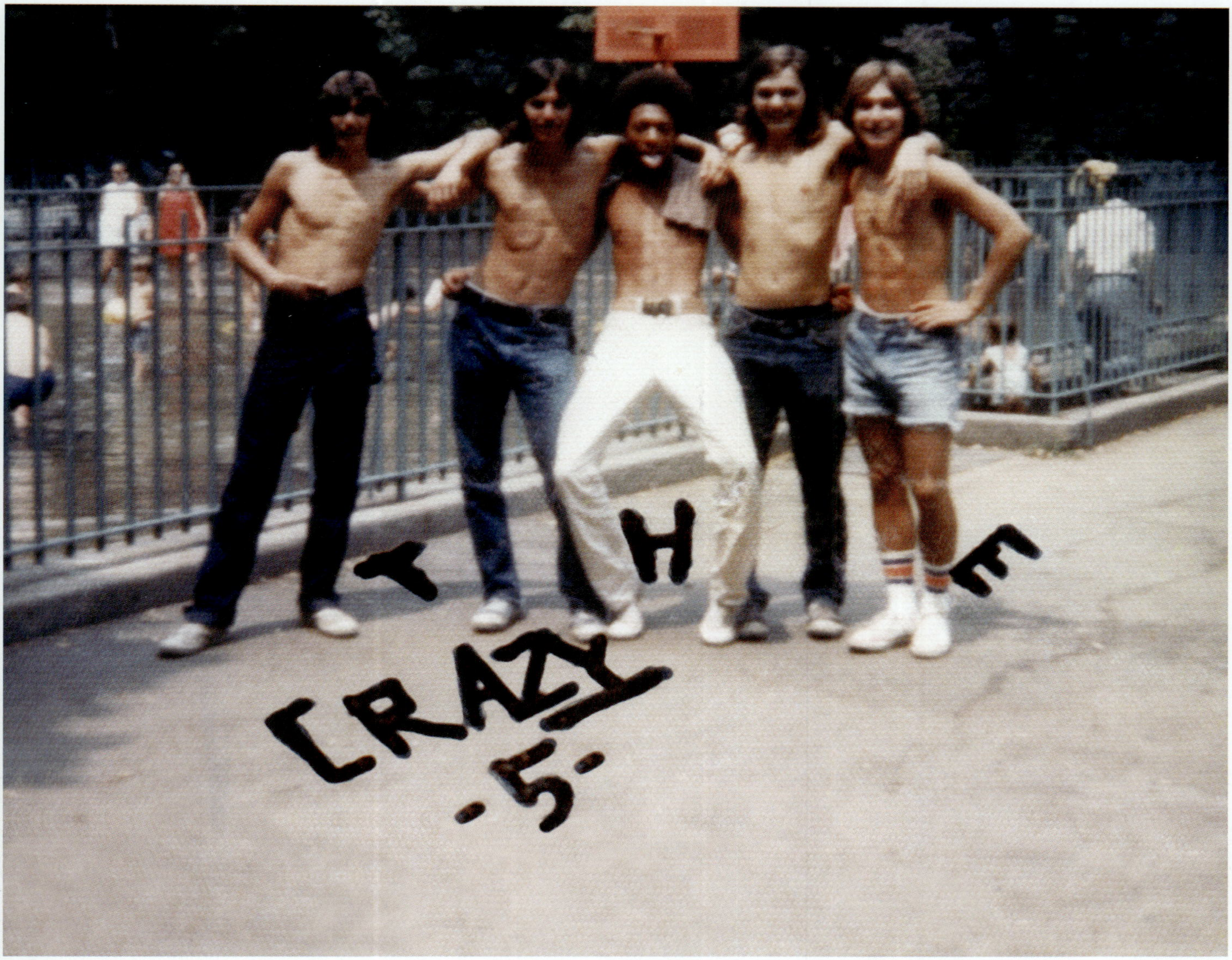

Opposite page: Top: STAFF 161 of THE EBONY DUKES. 1973. Bottom: Early BL by BLADE where he puts up THE EBONY DUKES. 1973. This Page: The original members of THE CRAZY FIVE. 1974.

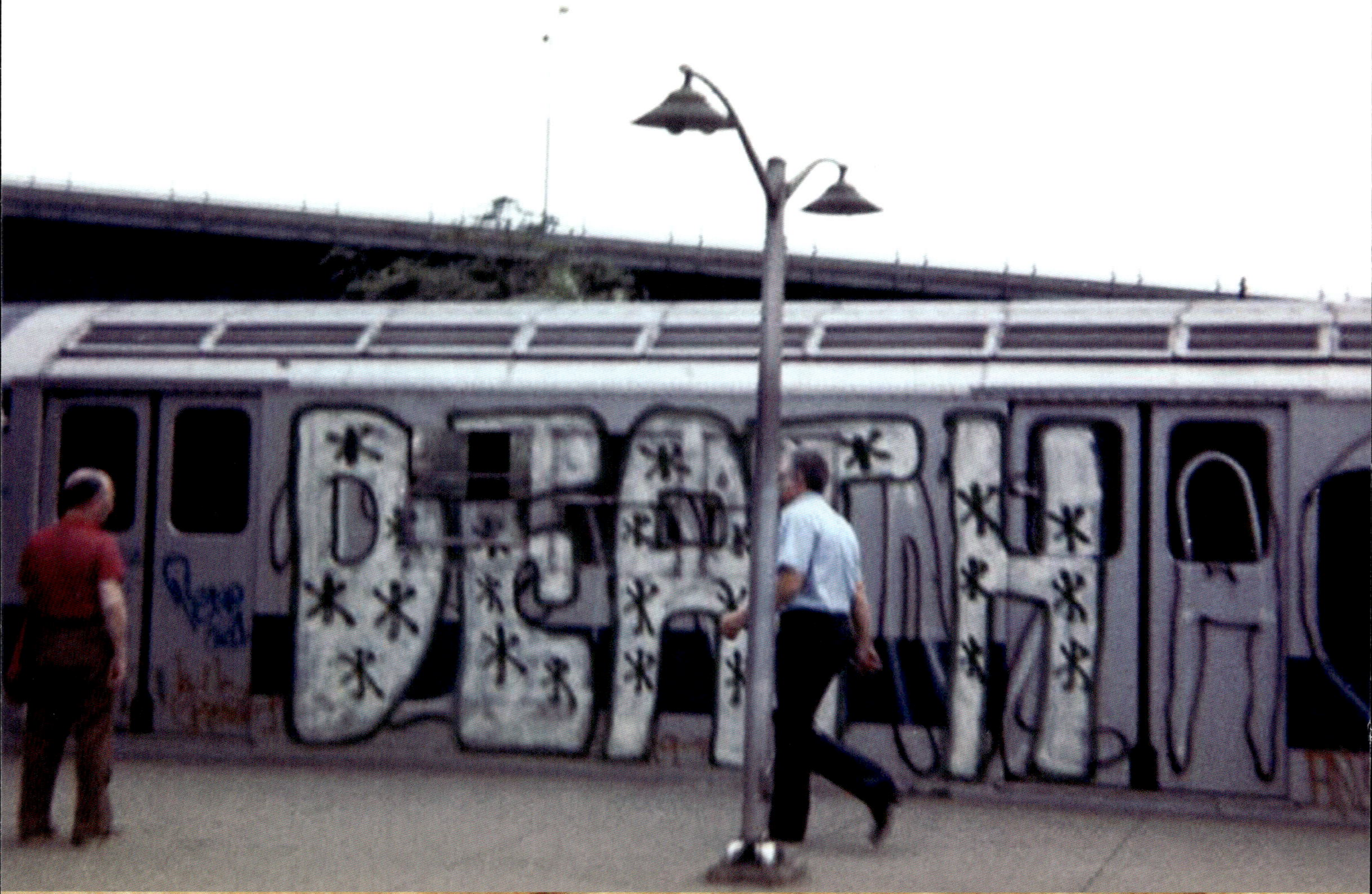

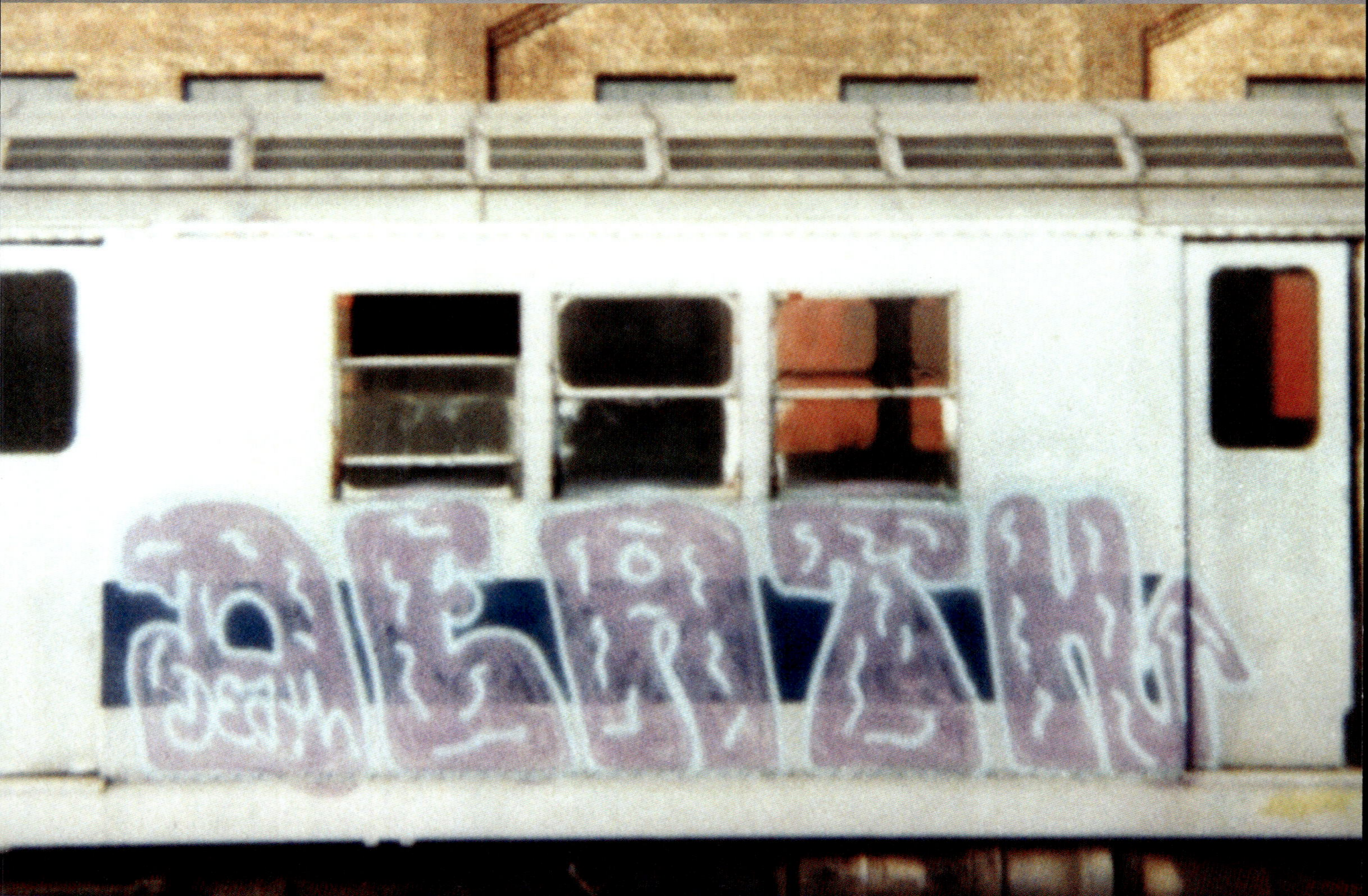

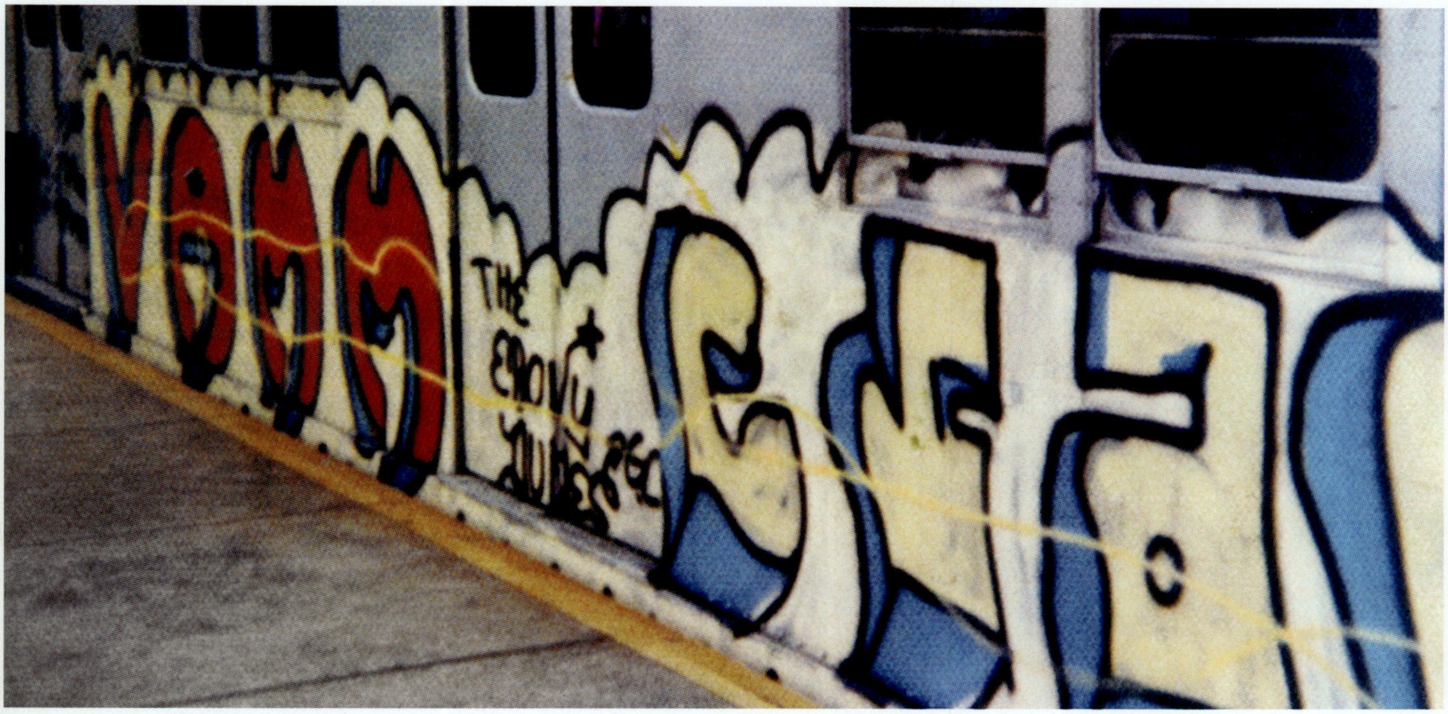

We were proud members of the DUKES, so we were surprised when they started crossing out a lot of our pieces. They claimed our friend DEATH had gone over a STAFF 161 piece, which is possible. Things happened in lay-ups late at night when it was hard to see and DEATH had a reputation for going over other writers. However, the piece wasn't just any piece. DEATH had the nerve to go over one of STAFF's greatest pieces ever. It was called the Cannon piece. For it, STAFF borrowed STAYHIGH 149's stick figure and painted him lighting a cannon on the side of a train. The cannon shot fire, which turned into a cloud featuring STAFF161's name. We heard the DUKES were looking for us and it wasn't a comfortable feeling, even though they were really looking for DEATH, who was the culprit in the whole mess. Apparently, there were long discussions at the writer's bench over what to do with us for weeks before STAFF 161 gathered the group together and headed uptown.

The DUKES took the train up to Parkside and spread out along the basketball court. It was a scary sight, because blacks just didn't come to the North Bronx. There were older guys playing ball in the Parkside playground—some of them Vietnam vets, some of them aging greasers. They were stunned by the appearance of the group, dressed in sharkskin pants and playboy shoes, looking badass. Apparently, some of the DUKES wanted to beat up DEATH and they talked about it on the train ride up, so by the time they arrived they were looking for a fight. I couldn't tell you who threw the first punch, but the whole fight lasted just a few minutes, since the older guys asked the DUKES to leave. Back then, you really didn't argue with vets because they had seen things you hadn't seen and done things you wouldn't do, so the DUKES walked away. They made their point, and at the end of the day, they were right.

I never allowed that incident to cloud my vision of what the graffiti community was all about. DEATH had fucked with the wrong people and that was the payback; it wasn't about race. The one time my vision of racial harmony was called into question was when JIVE 3 and STICK 1 came to Parkside to fight DEATH and me. They called him a "honky" and me an "Oreo". They were both older and there was no reason for it. Although the reason they gave was that I wasn't doing the outline given to me by PHASE 2 correctly, really they were just looking for an excuse to fight. STICK 1 punched me in the face really hard and then they left. I remember, it was like a firecracker going off in my face as my whole face stung. It took me a while to sort the whole thing out in my head. I didn't want to think that this was part of the graffiti movement I loved so much— the movement in which the races hung out together. As time went on, I realized this was an isolated incident. And when THE CRAZY 5 formed, my ideas about the racial composition of writing were reinforced.

Opposite page: DEATH circa 1973.
This page: VAMM and CRACHEE crossed out by THE EBONY DUKES, 1973.

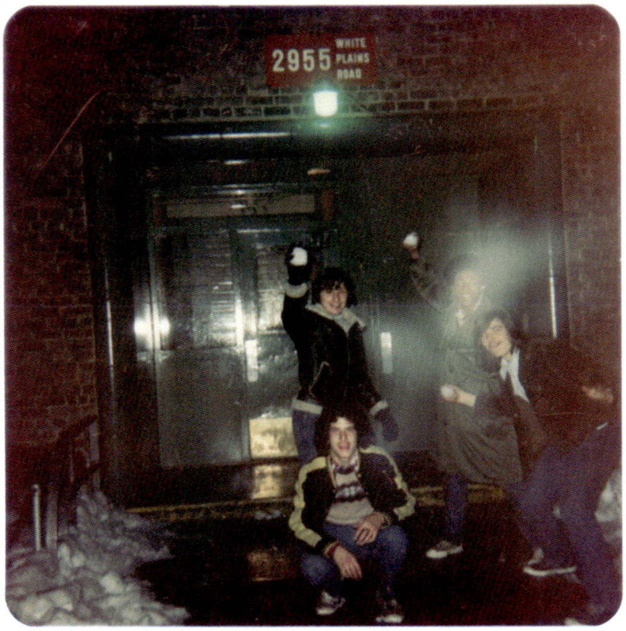

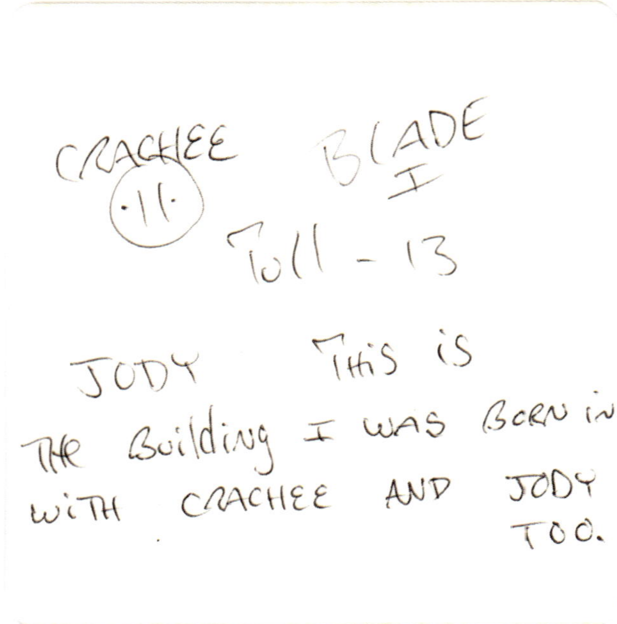

THE CRAZY 5 started in 1974. We had all been writing for a while. Gillen (DEATH) started in 1971; Mitch (CRACHEE 11), Michael (VAMM), and I began in 1972; MARIO (TULL 13) started in 1973. We hung out together with a larger group that nicknamed itself The MOB. It wasn't really a graffiti crew; it was just a bunch of kids that wrote together. In the winter of 1974, the five members of The MOB would morph into a more serious graffiti crew called THE CRAZY 5. Like all good stories, this one began with us looking to get high.

It was a cold day in January, so cold that even basketball was out of the question. Luckily for us, the Parkside projects had countless staircases without locks and with heat—a perfect place to get stoned and be with your friends. We marched over to the PS 41 schoolyard looking for Glaze. We trusted Glaze the most with purchasing weed, and when purchasing weed, trust was an important ingredient. Glaze wasn't there, but some of the 41 boys were and they'd have to do. We put together a small amount of money to buy some hash, each of us chipping in. The walk back was quiet. We settled in the back staircase at 666, one of the buildings on Olinville Avenue. The staircase was nice and warm. As VAMM put a new screen in the hash pipe, he looked at the four of us, and the conversation started.

"What are we doing in the EBONY DUKES? Don't get me wrong, I was honored like the rest of you when I first got down with them, but now they're still crossing me out. It's fucked up."

I looked up from the step below him. I could see VAMM's knees. Gillen passed on the hash, handed it down to me, and cut right to the chase. "What are you gonna do about it?"

VAMM looked at Gillen. I took a long toke from the pipe and said, "I'll fight those guys, I'm not afraid of them, fuck the DUKES."

Gillen smiled. No one was fighting the DUKES. That was suicide. And then Gillen set the trap for VAMM. "And then what? What happens after you beat up a hundred EBONY DUKES?"

Now we were all smiling except VAMM. "What happens is that we all get crossed out forever. I'm not afraid of the DUKES either and you know I've got your back. But we can either be the idiots on the line who are always crossed out or ... we can be kings."

This page: CRACHEE, BLADE, TULL 13 and Jody in front of the building BLADE was born in. Circa 1973. Opposite page: BLADE and other members of THE CRAZY FIVE have too much fun. Circa 1975.

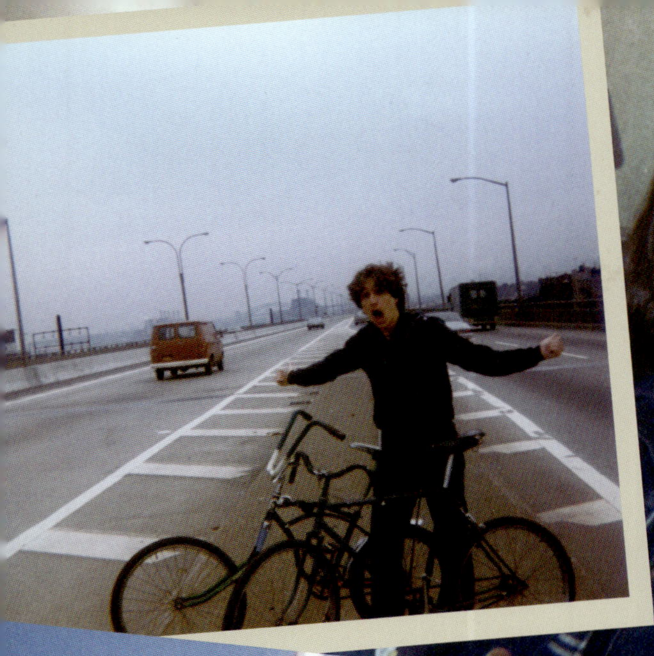

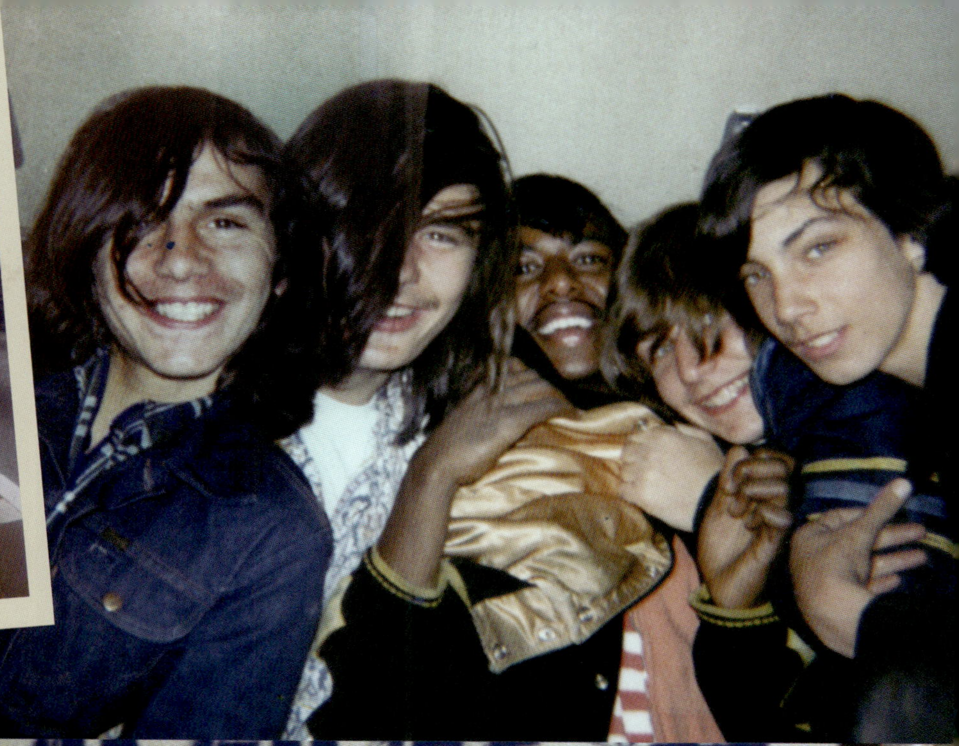

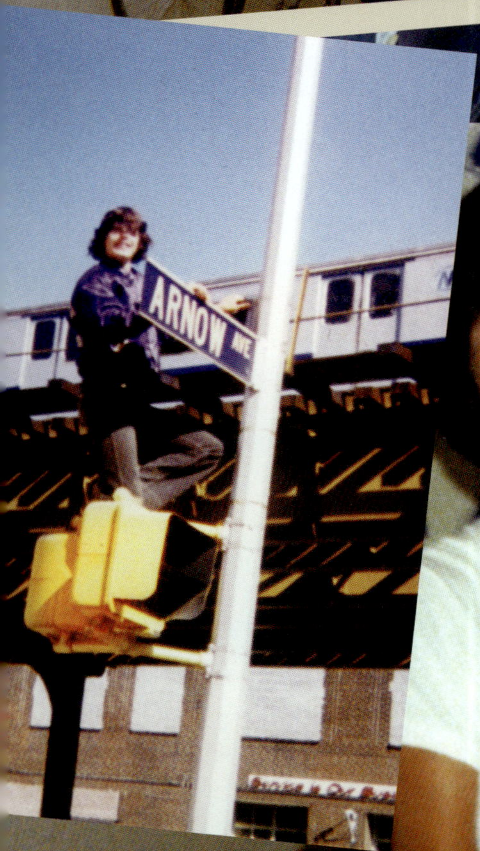
ARNOW
AVE

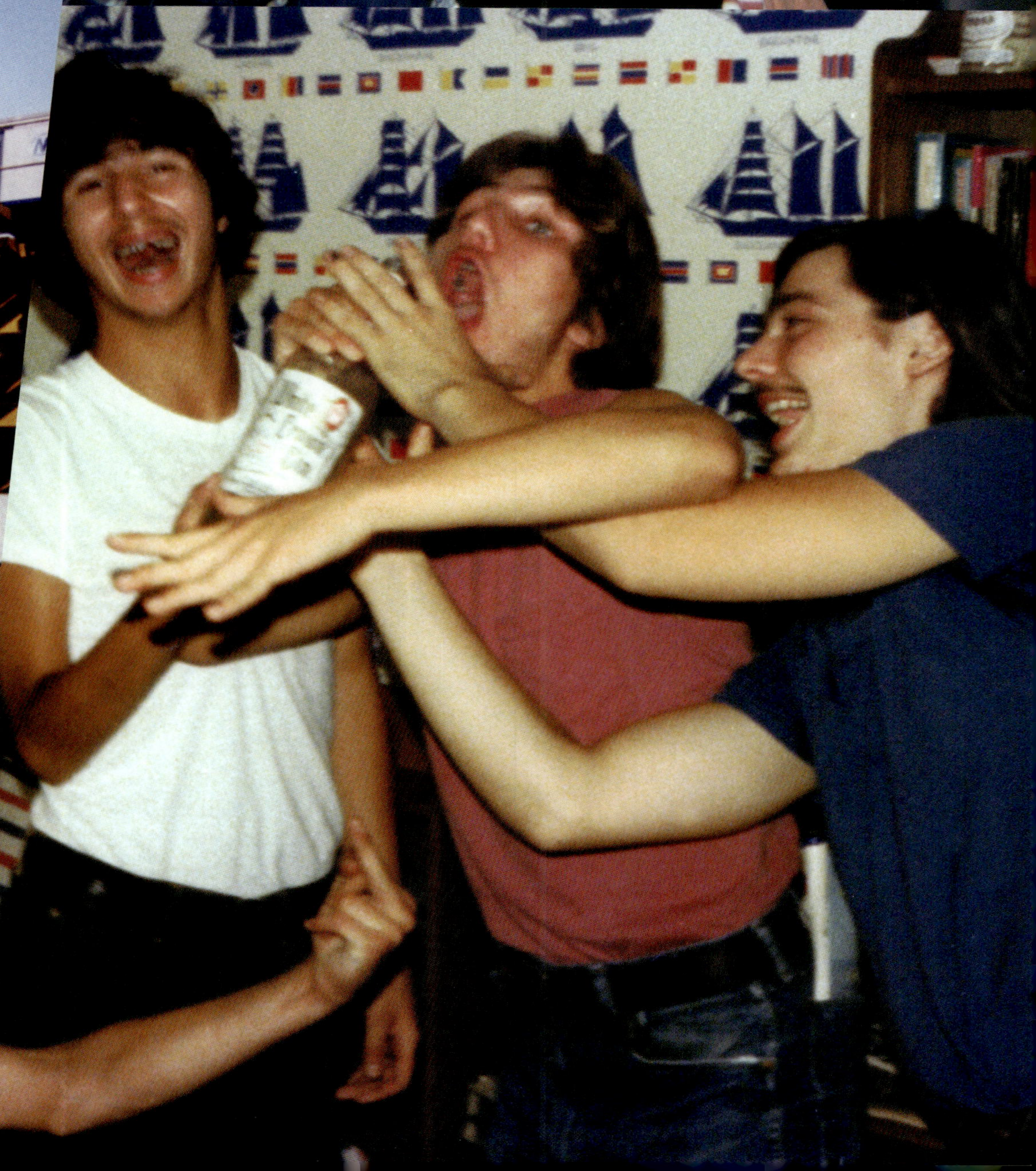

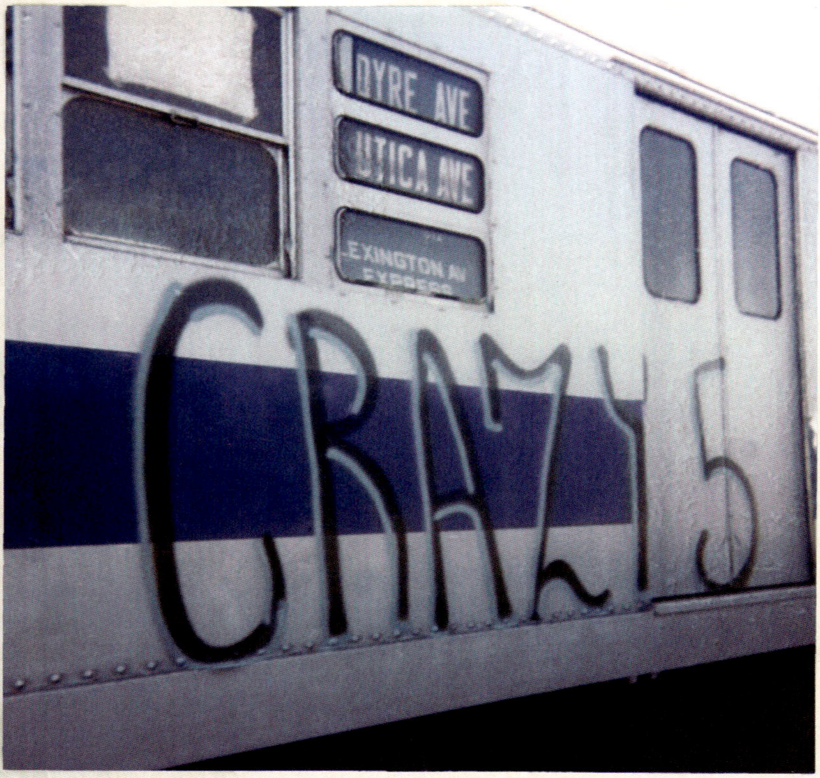
DYRE AVE
UTICA AVE
LEXINGTON AV
CRAZY 5

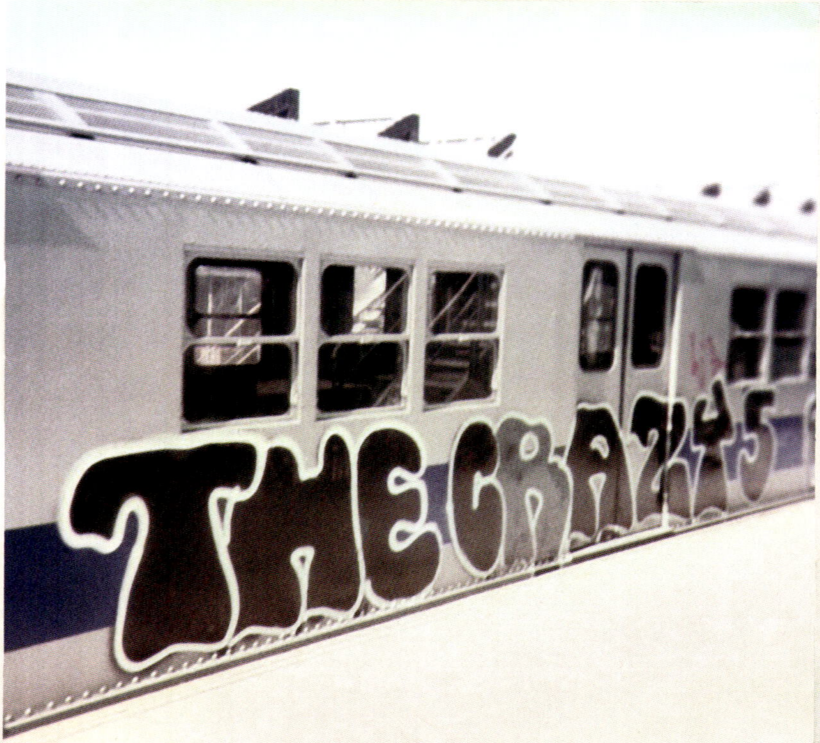
THE CRAZY 5

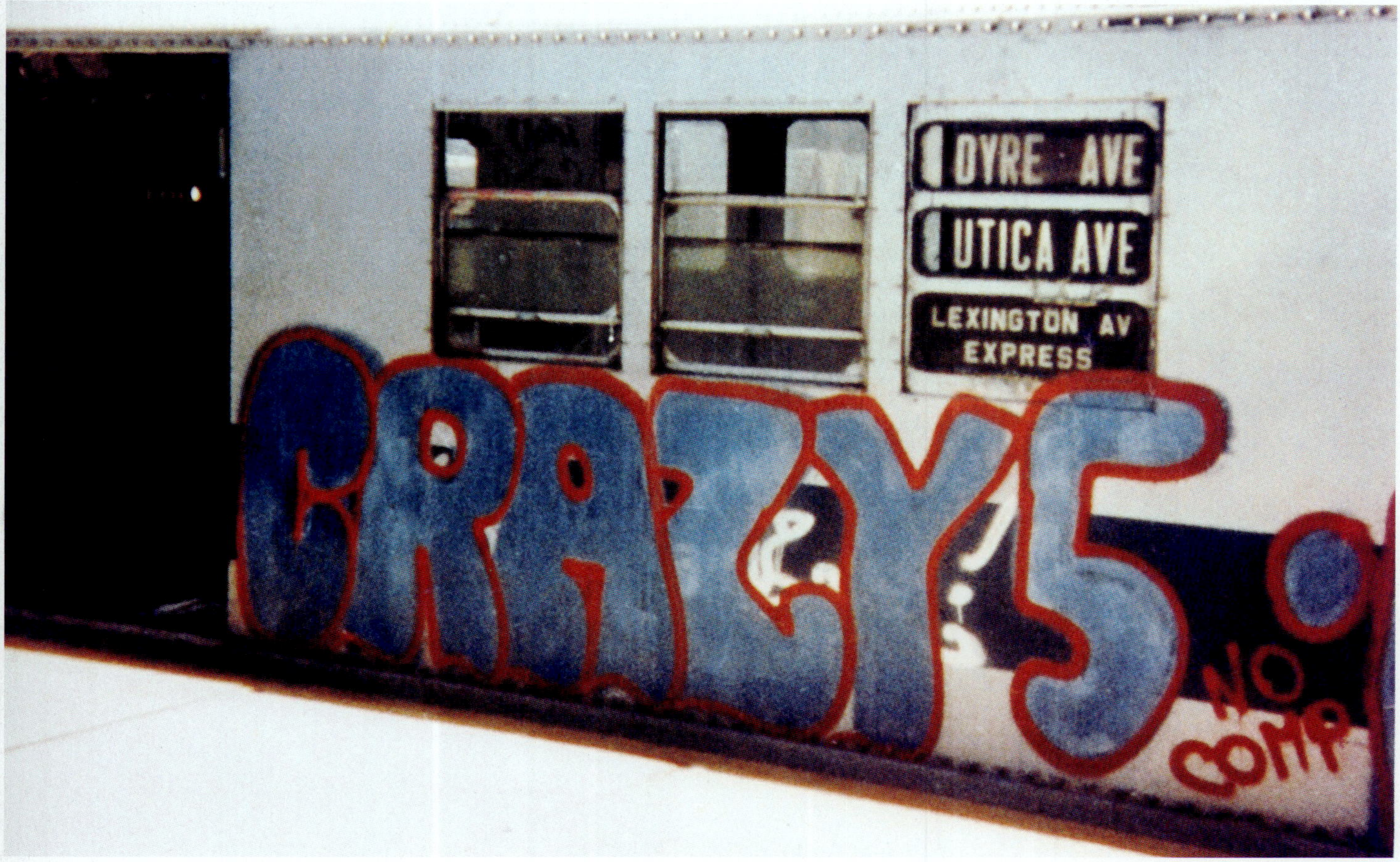

Mitch took a big hit from the pipe and started coughing. All five of us started to laugh. Gillen was on the top step. We all looked up at where he was sitting as he said, "As a crew, the five of us could beat the DUKES and king the line ... and that's the whole point of this, isn't it?"

It wasn't exactly what VAMM wanted to hear, but he liked it. We all liked it. Then there was a round of names tossed out, all of them bad. Gillen looked down at us and smiled, "THE CRAZY 5." We spent the rest of the night talking about being kings as THE CRAZY 5. Fuck the DUKES.

Names were important. THE EBONY DUKES was a great name, although we rarely hit it up after forming our own gang. THE CRAZY 5 was also good. Our own graffiti names meant something to us. Gillen wrote DEATH, as well as ROX, CLUE, and ZELLO; he changed his name every time his parents caught him and gave him a beating.

VAMM came up with his name by combining his initials with his girlfriends. His mom could actually see the lay-up from her window, so she'd see him hitting the trains and then he'd come home to a beating. CRACHEE got his name because he was crazy for cheese. MARIO wrote his given name and the more inspired TULL 13; the 13 was Wilt Chamberlain's number.

If THE CRAZY 5 were crazy, then there was no one more insane then Gillen (DEATH). He was the first one to start writing. In 1971 he had a paper route and started hitting lampposts in the early morning. If you were in that part of the Bronx at 5:00 am, you could write on anything. In 1972, he found the lay-up with all of the trains stashed there overnight, because it was on his paper route. He'd hit the trains for a half-hour before starting his paper route and then continue on his way. He began to get up and quickly moved on to doing pieces—all before school started.

Opposite page: Top: CRAZY 5 by VAMM. Circa 1974.
Bottom: THE CRAZY 5 by BLADE. Circa 1974.
This page: CRAZY 5 by VAMM. Circa 1974.

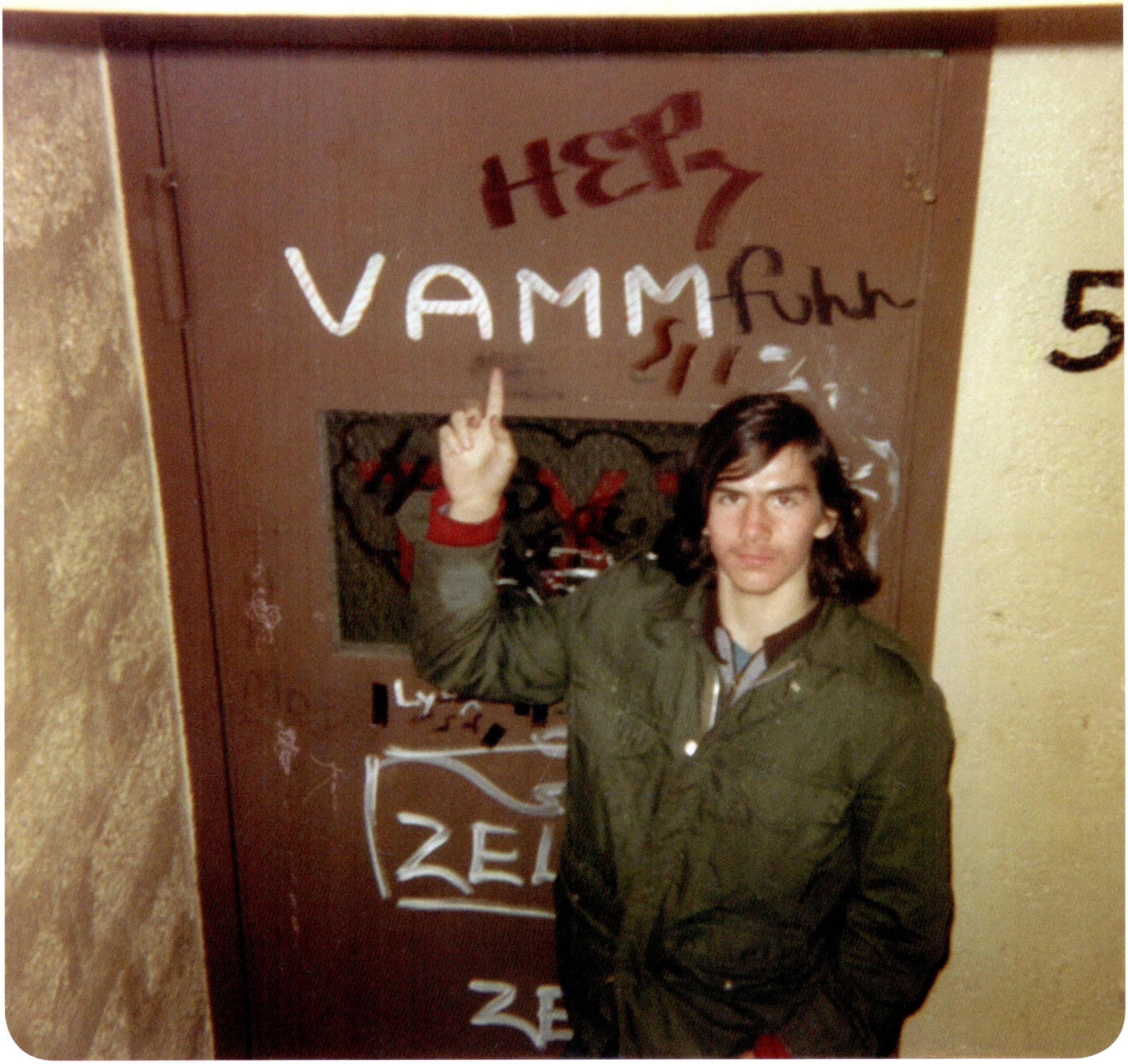
HEP7
VAMM
5

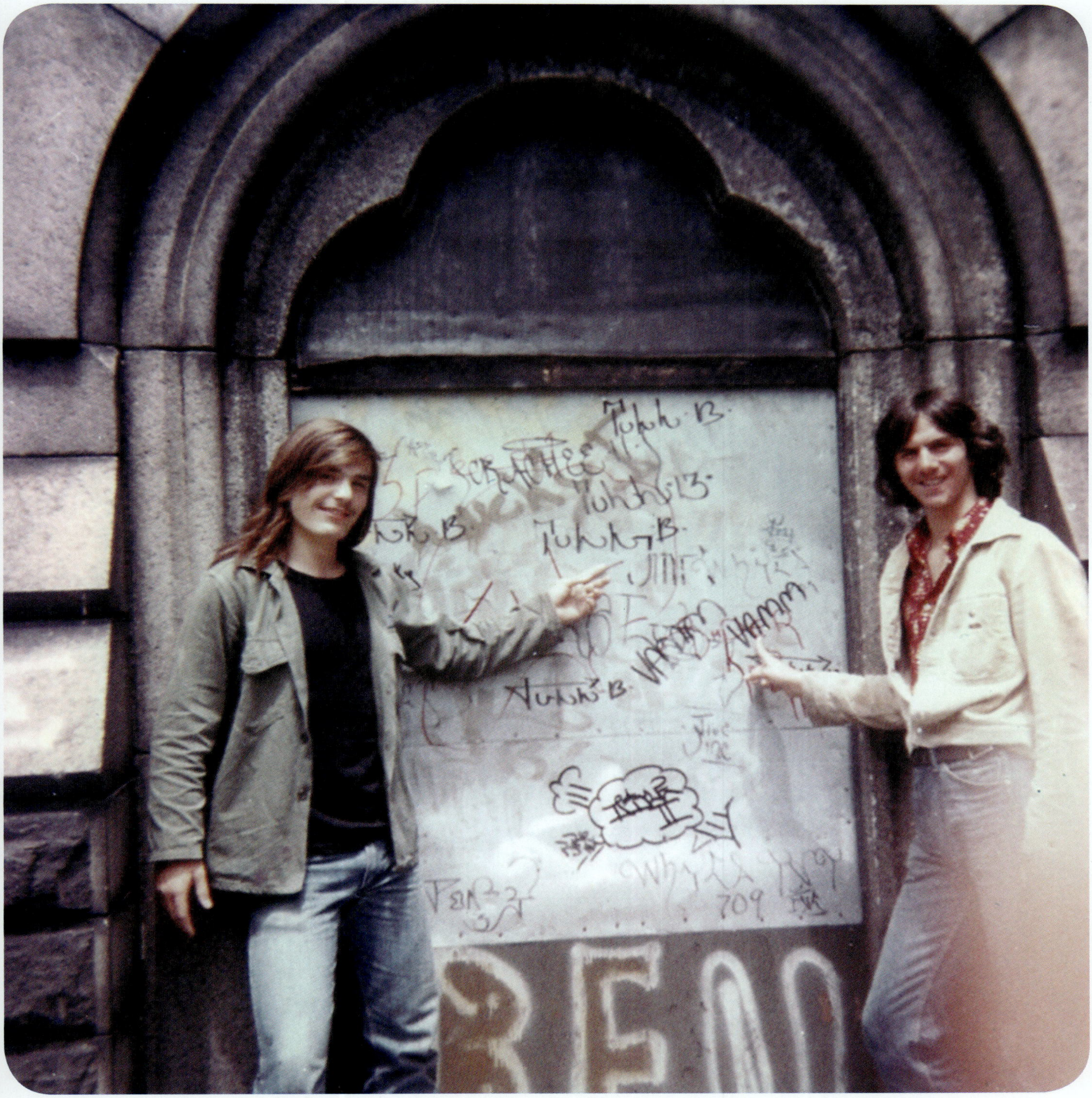

Opposite page: VAMM. 1973.
This page: TULL 13 and VAMM. 1974.

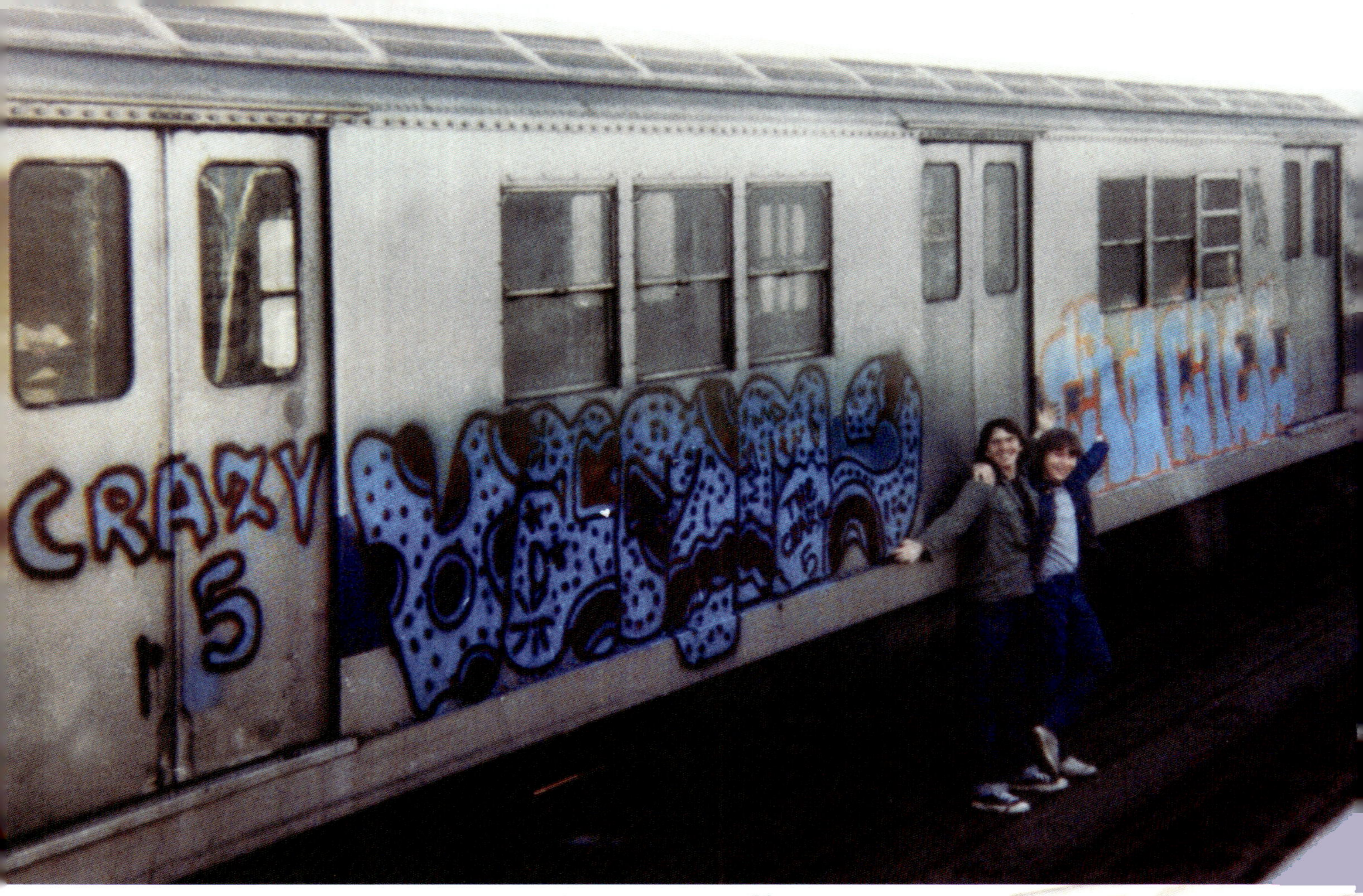
CRAZY
5

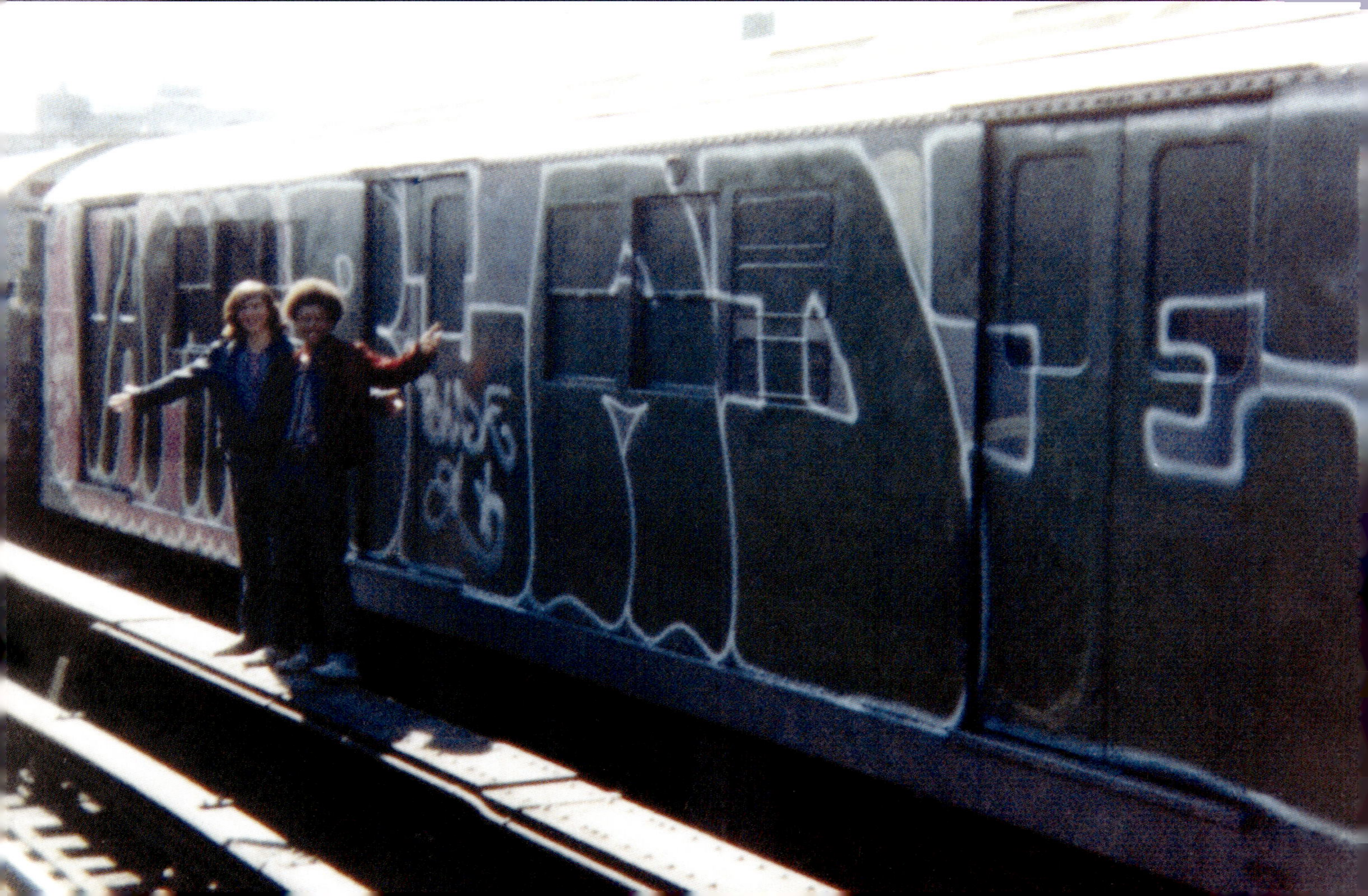

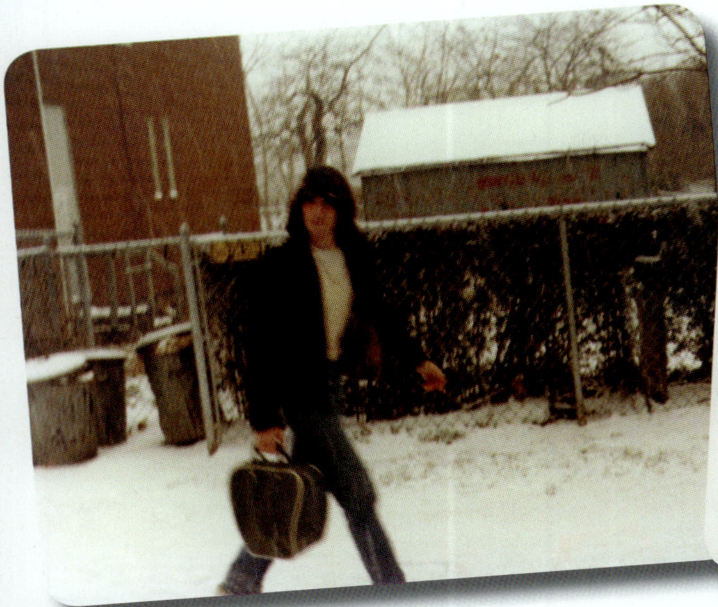

By 1973, at the age of fifteen, DEATH was completely out of control, so his parents kicked him out. Every night he had a new place to sleep; a lot of times it was the back seat of someone's car or one of the rooftops. To make money he'd do smash and grabs about once a month. For the rest of the group it was about stealing paint, but Gillen needed money to survive, and robbing cash registers was a way to do it. He'd stake a place out for a few days, usually in the neighborhood, a local store on a quiet street. Gillen would come back at 3:00am and hurl a garbage can through the window. He'd race inside, open the register, scoop up the cash, then look for cigarettes or anything else he could sell. By the time the cops got there he was long gone. He did about fifteen of these robberies and developed quite a reputation for it.

The robberies were the talk of Parkside, because they didn't always go so smoothly. One night Gillen jumped fifteen feet from the ceiling of a hardware store, scooped the money out of the cash register, and then realized there was no way out. Since he couldn't go back up and the store had a gate on the front window, Gillen spent the next forty minutes trying to squeeze beneath a gate that was only inches from the ground, which left his body scraped raw. When we heard about it, we went to the store to check it out. We all looked at the gate and couldn't figure out how he did it. It was seemingly impossible. Gillen was crazy.

Opposite page: Top: VAMM and CRACHEE in front of their masterpieces, circa 1973. Bottom: VAMM and BLADE pose in front of a whole-car top to bottom, circa 1973. This page: DEATH on his way to the yards with a bowling bag full of paint, 1974.

CRACHEE and VAMM started out as writing partners in 1972. When I came back to Parkside as a writer, I thought Mitch and I would be partners, because we had always gotten along so well. But then he got busted by his parents and had to give up writing for a while. Meanwhile, VAMM was dating Puppy and I was dating Karen. The two girls got along well, which brought VAMM and me closer together. As THE CRAZY 5 came together as a crew, VAMM became my first writing partner.

THE CRAZY 5 had no official leader, though some people pointed to DEATH as the leader, because he came up with the name and because he was highly manipulative. The rest of us respected the rules of writing too much to allow DEATH to be our leader. He was, after all, the one who went over STAFF 161. As bright as CRACHEE was, he didn't fit the bill because he had stopped writing for a while. MARIO didn't have the writing credentials to lead a graffiti crew; he was the last one of us to start writing and he did it just to hang out, although he was a great artist. VAMM, as it turned out, had a lot of ideas. A good example of VAMM's leadership abilities is when the Golden Guineas at the 2 yard beat up COMET. VAMM was able to get word to them that we wouldn't hit the 2 yard anymore and that we would respect their turf if they gave us a free pass elsewhere—and they did. From then on we never worried about the Golden Guineas.

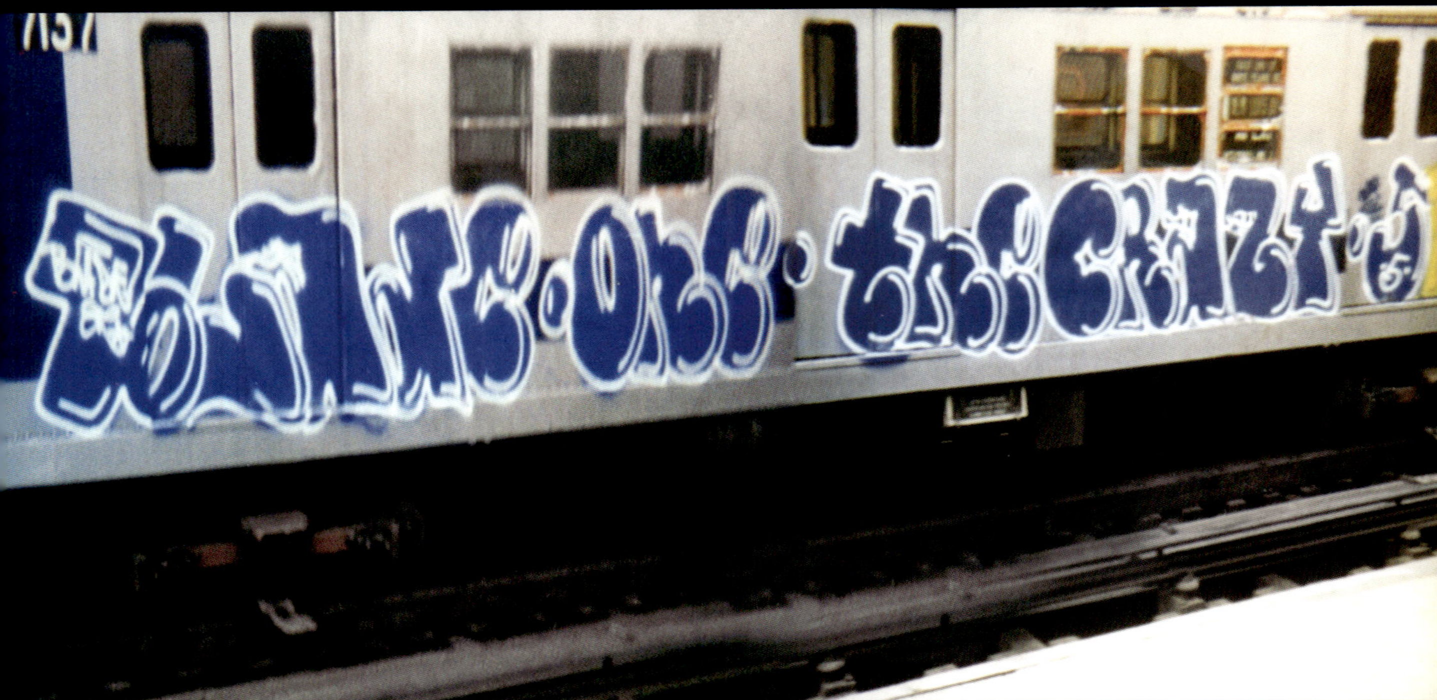

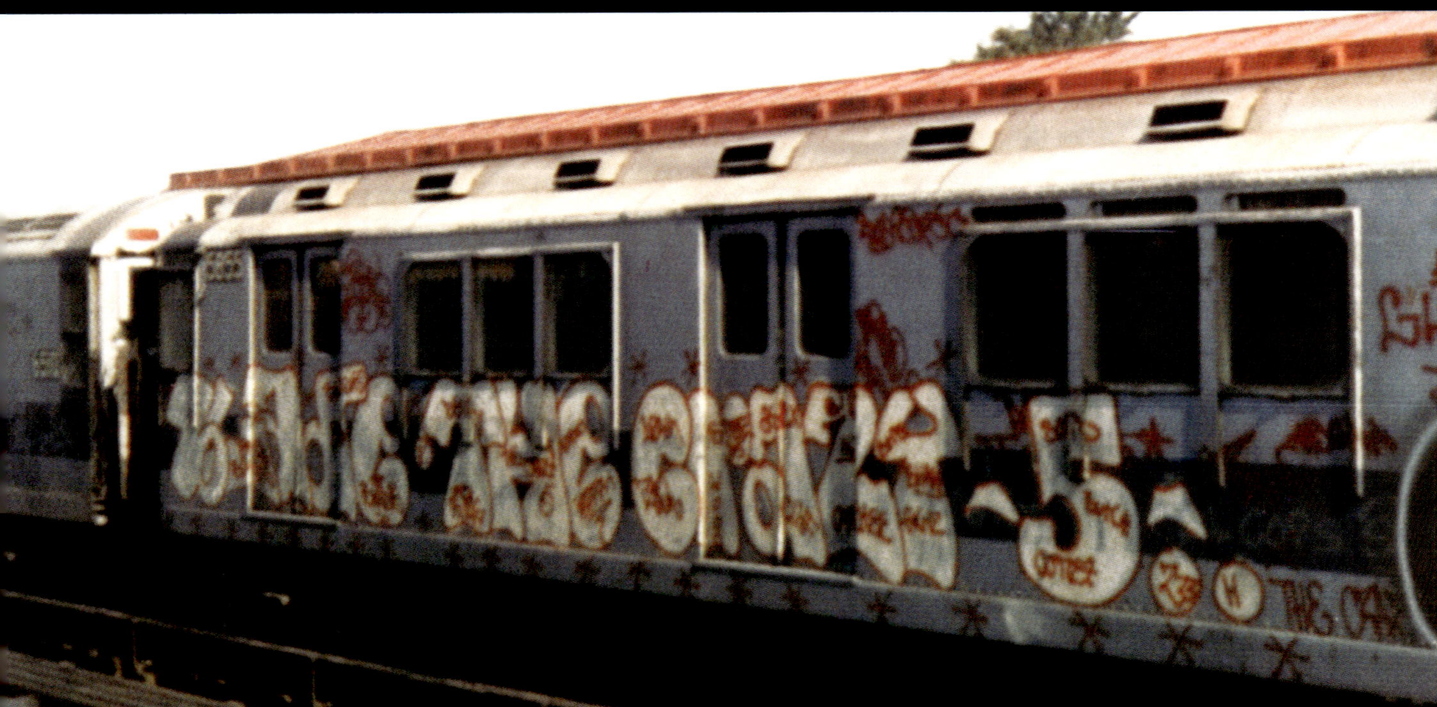

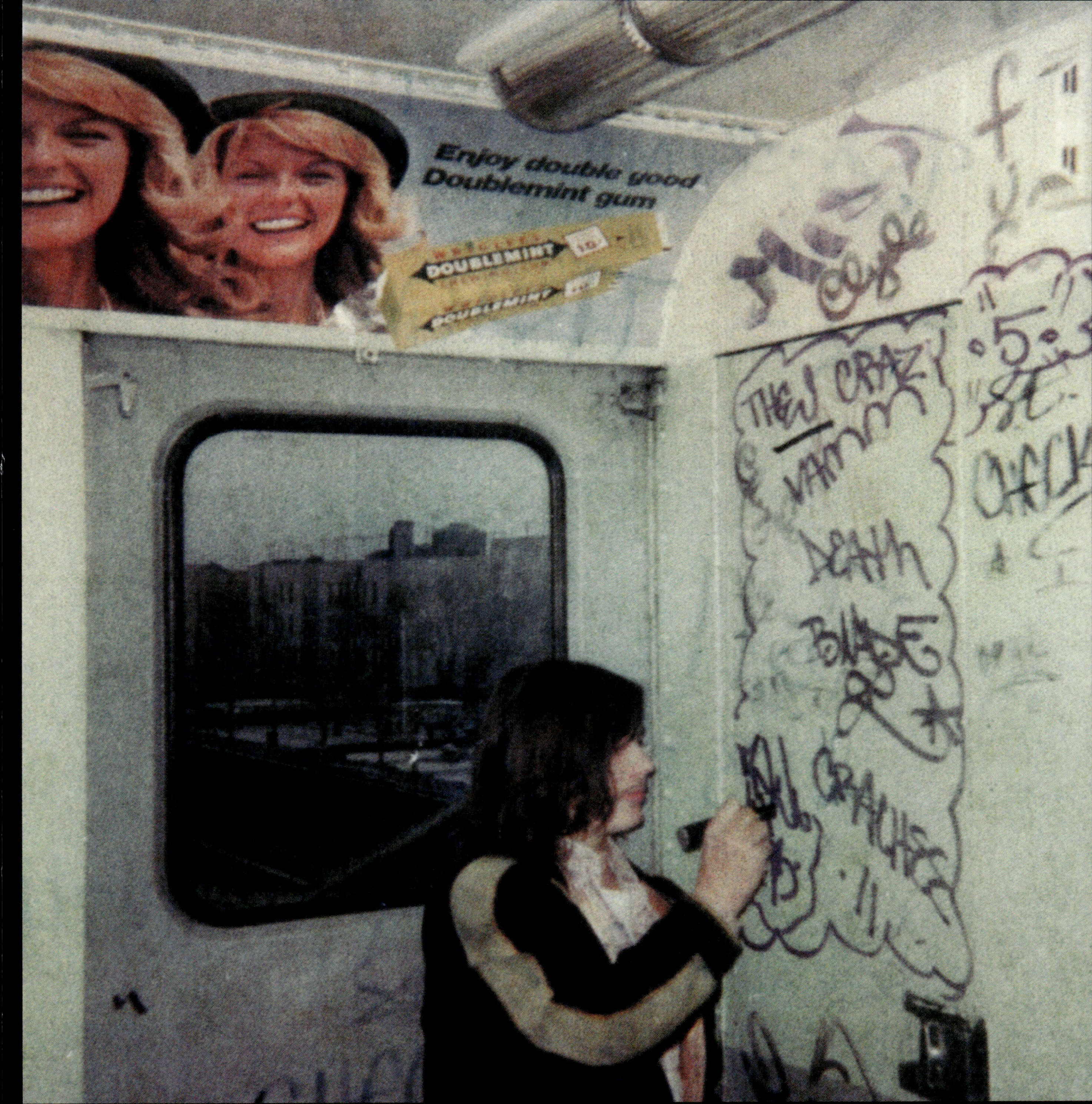
Enjoy double good
Doublemint gum
DOUBLEMINT

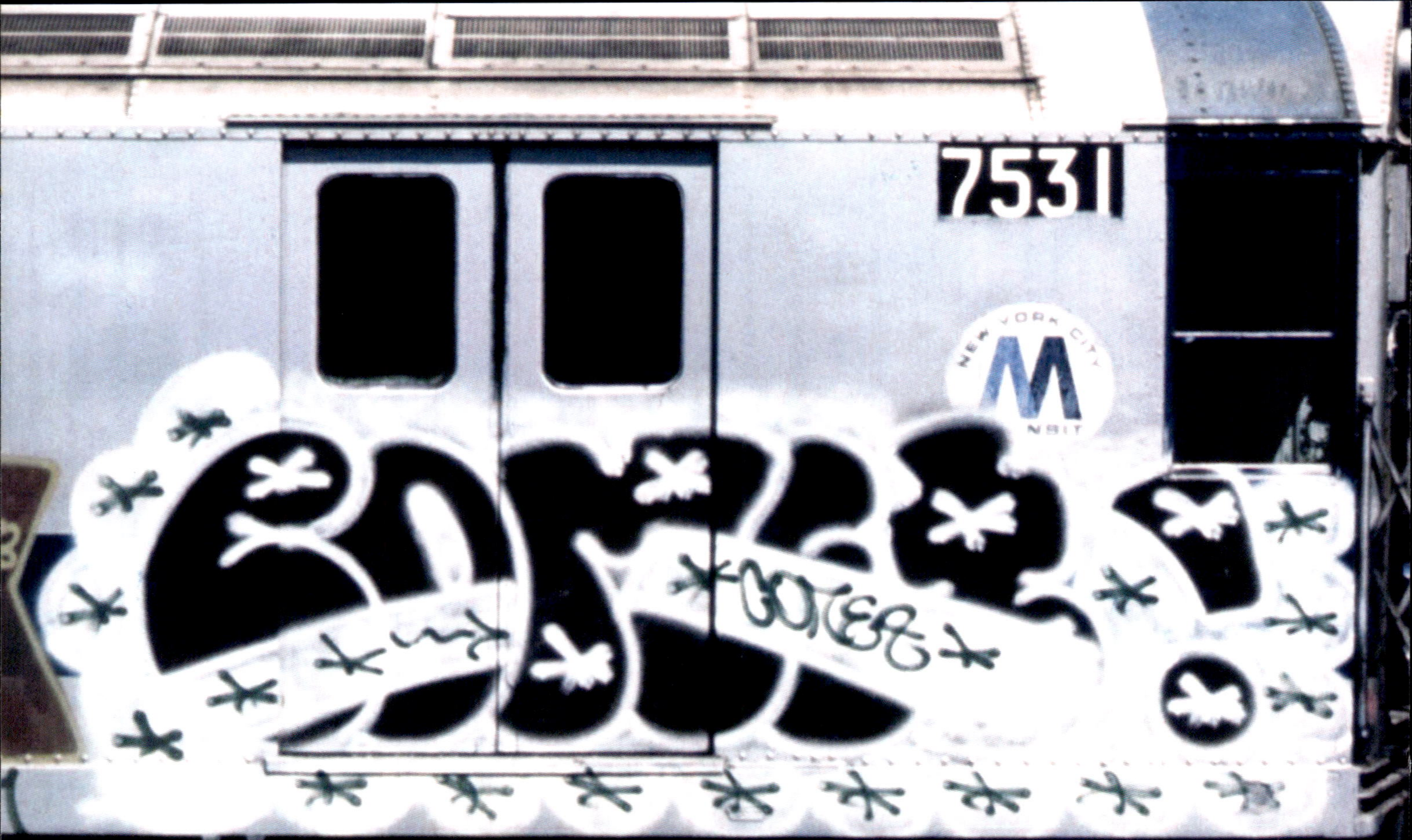
7531

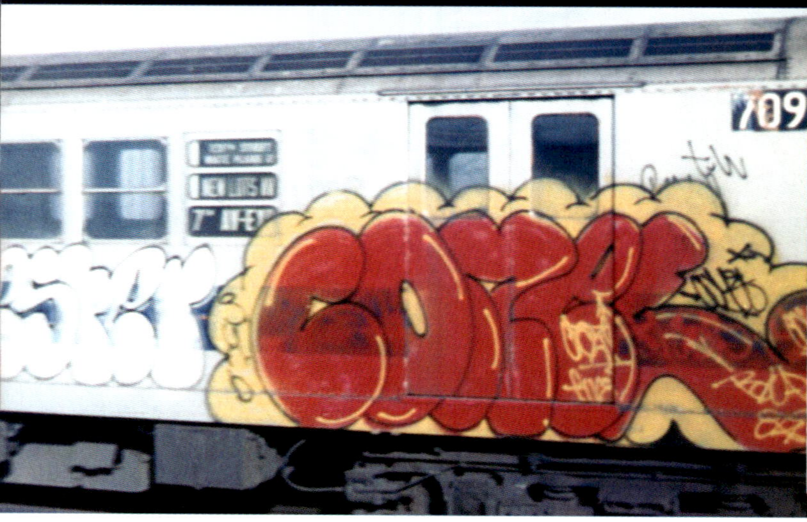
709

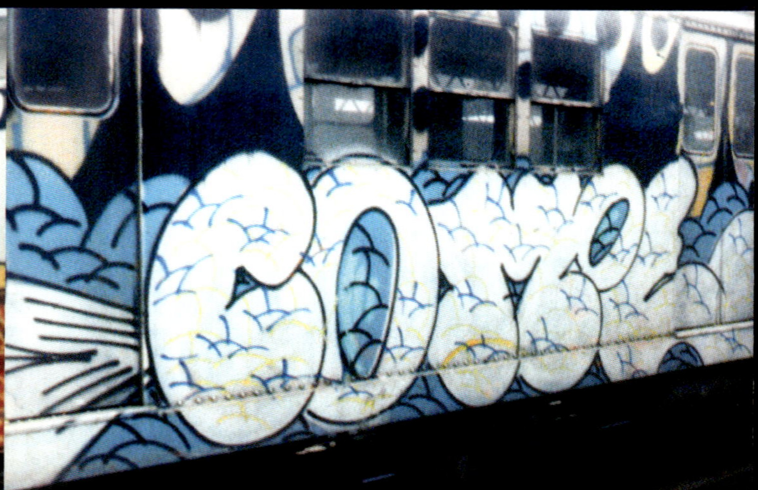

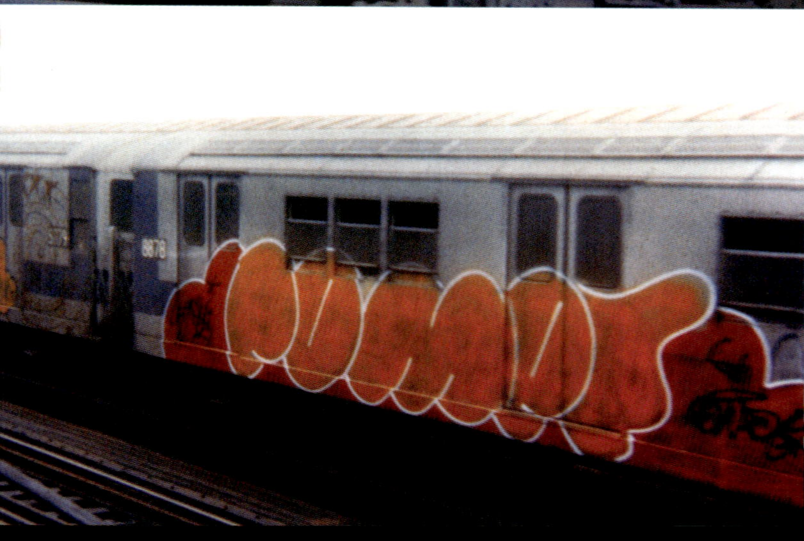

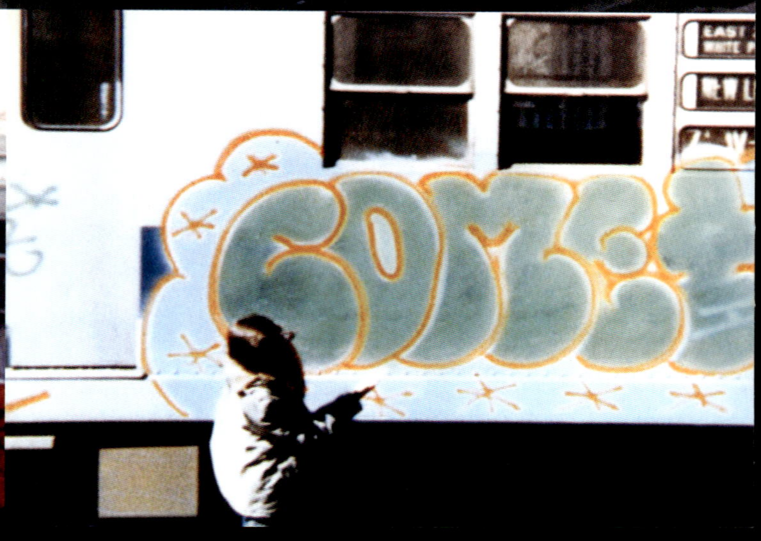

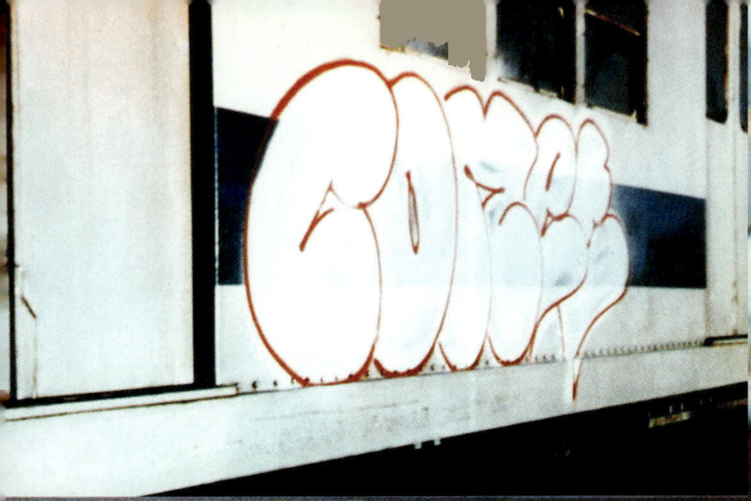
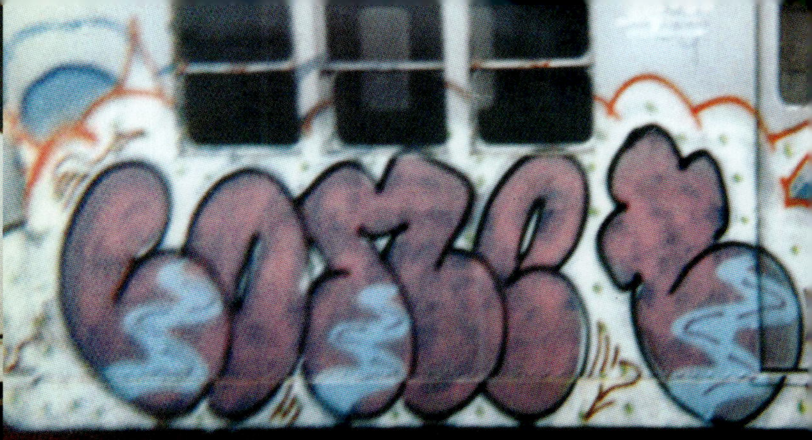
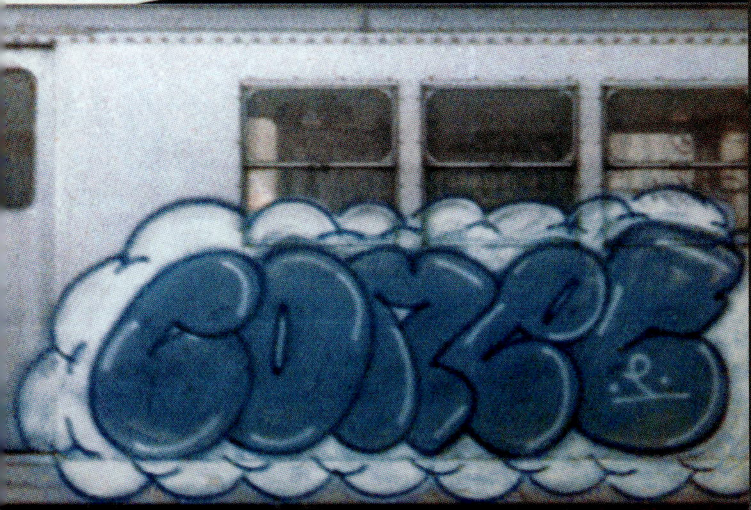
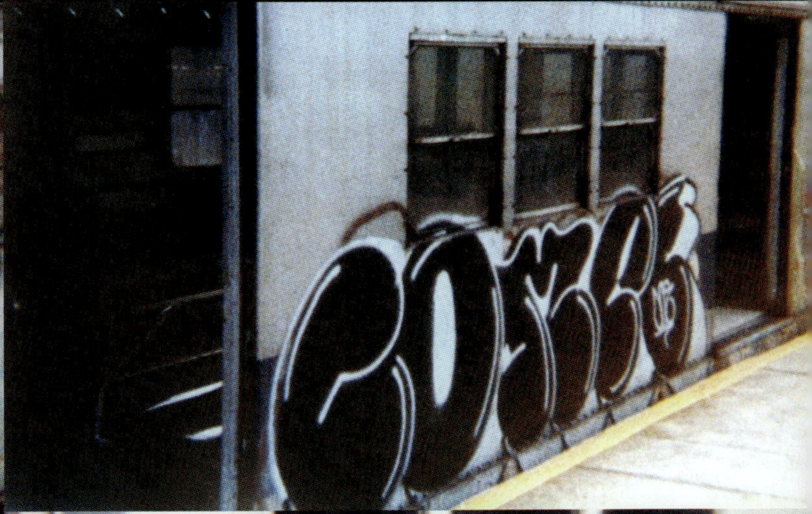
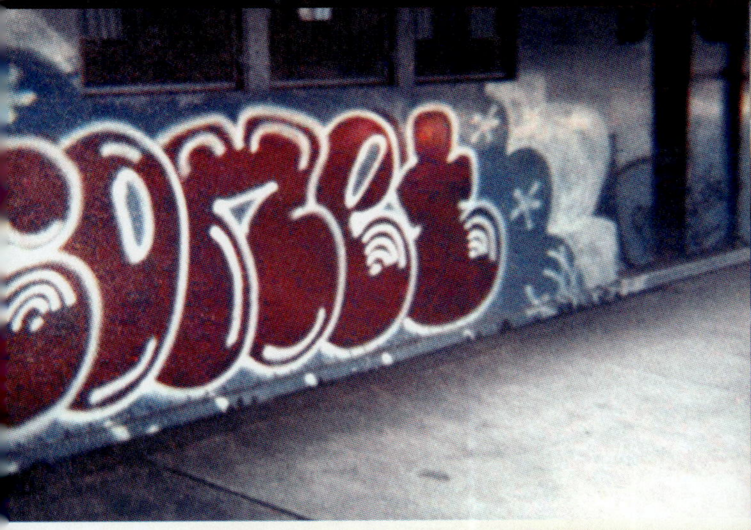
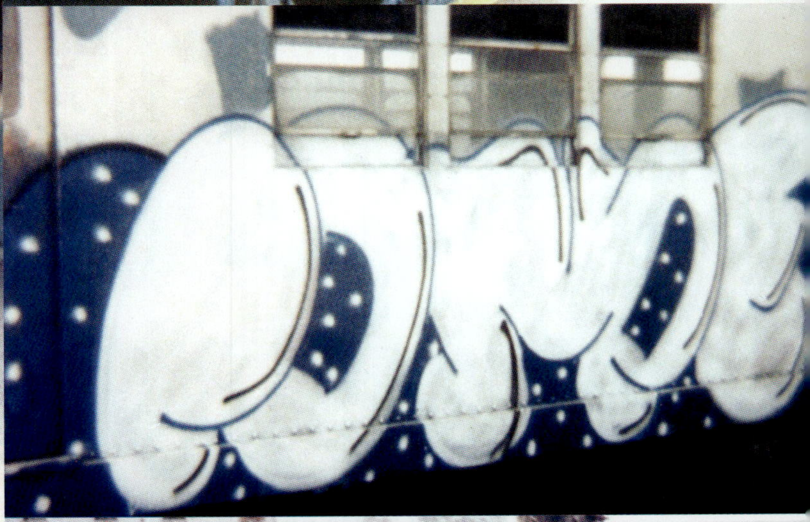
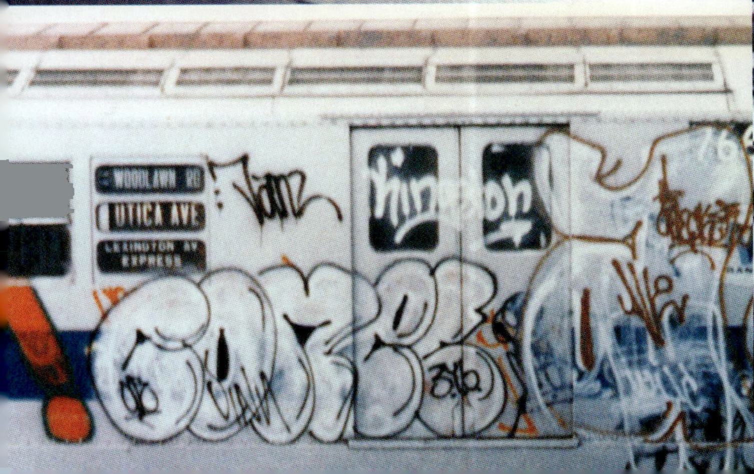
WOODLAWN RD
UTICA AVE
LEXINGTON AV EXPRESS
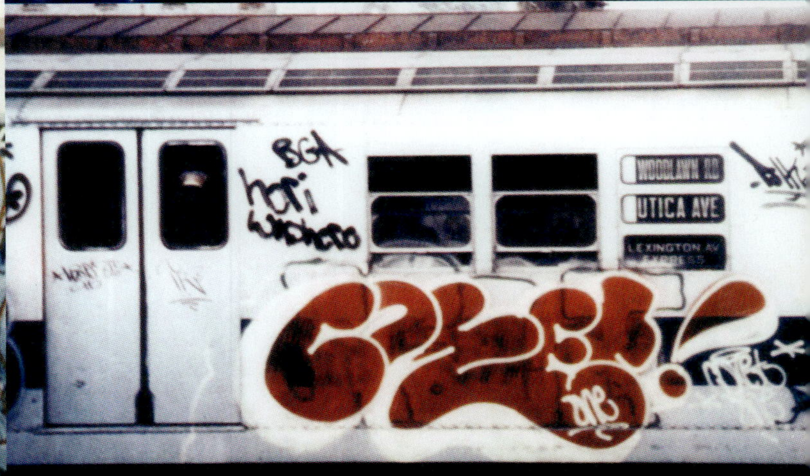
WOODLAWN RD
UTICA AVE
LEXINGTON AV EXPRESS

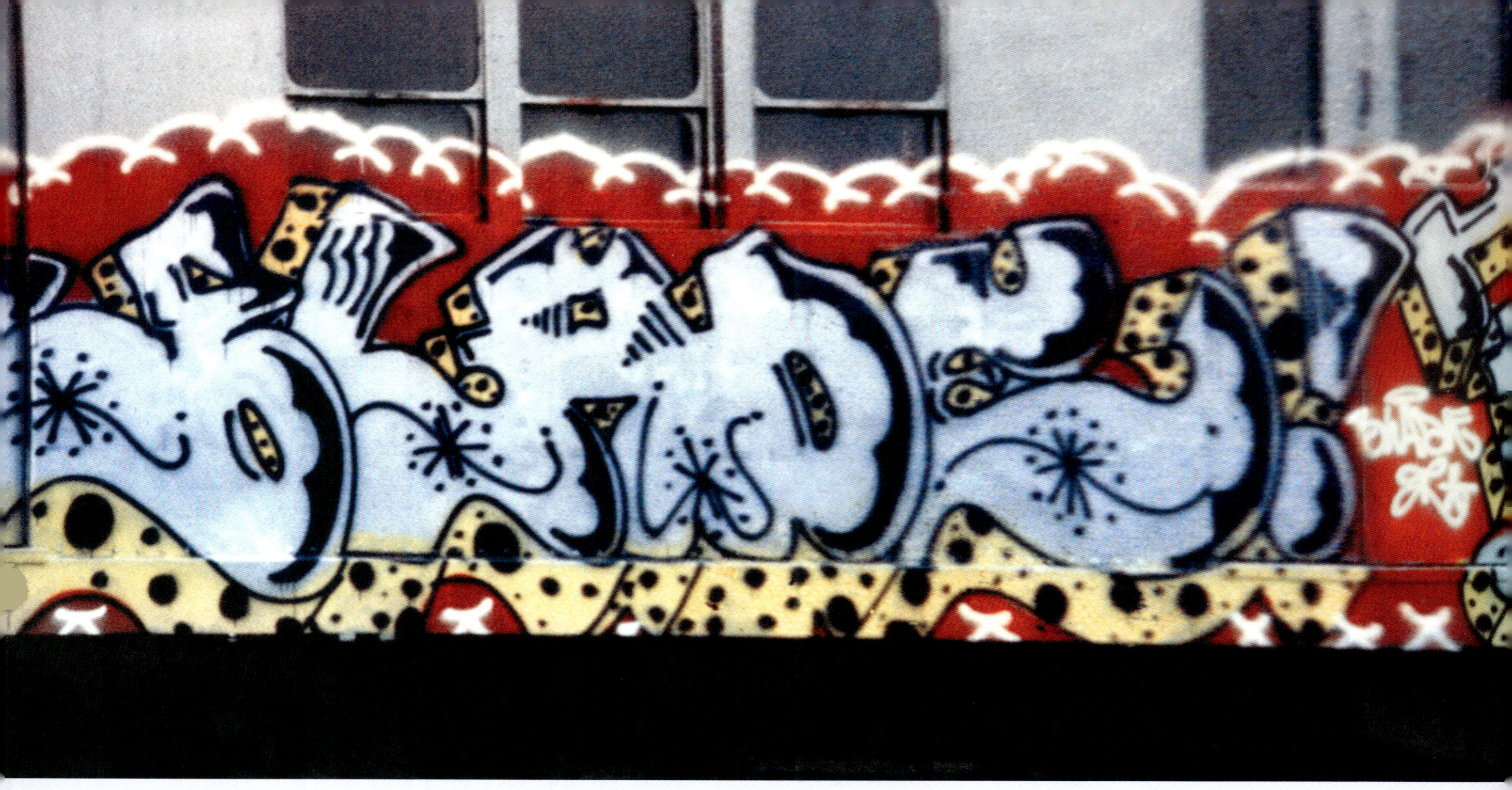

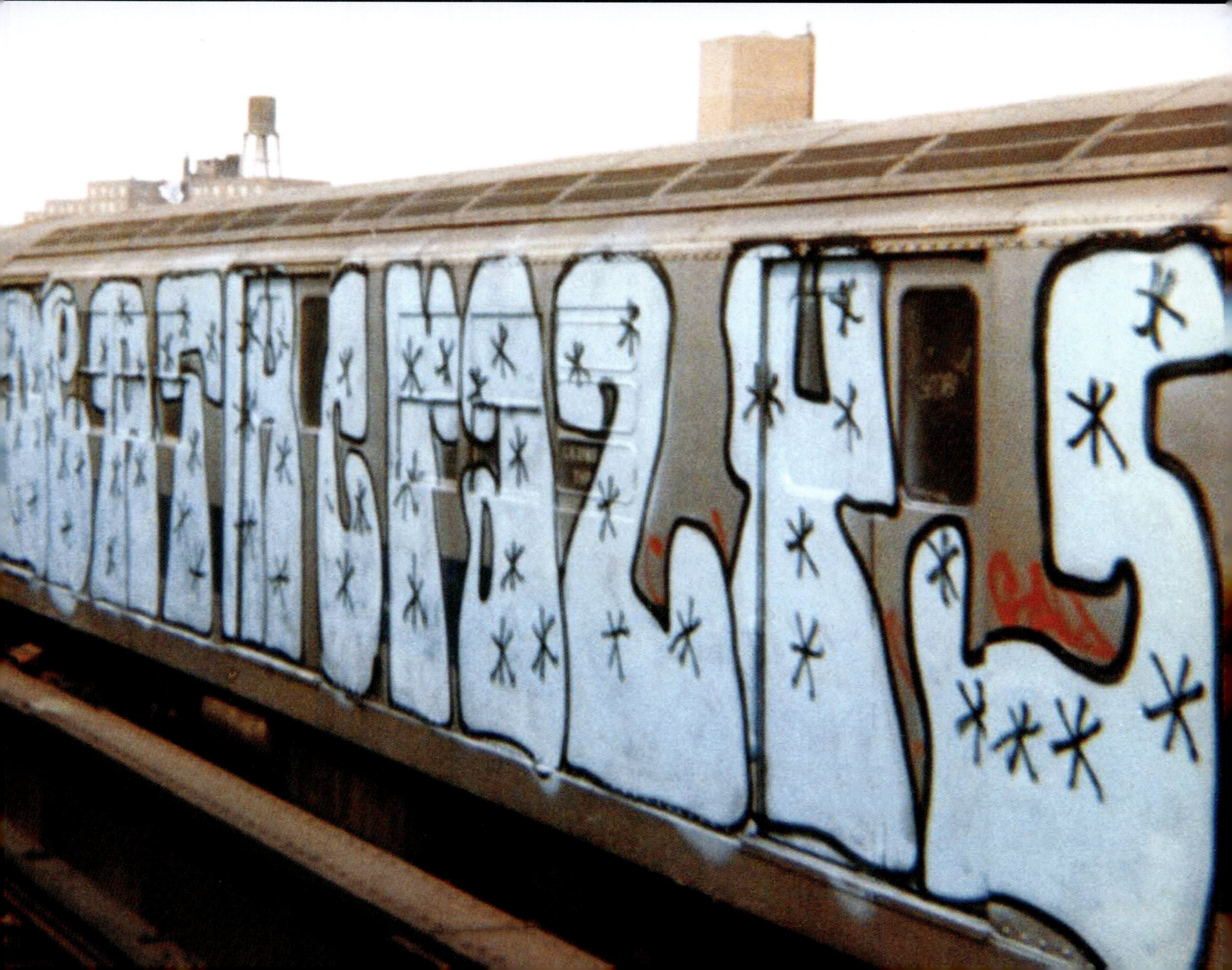

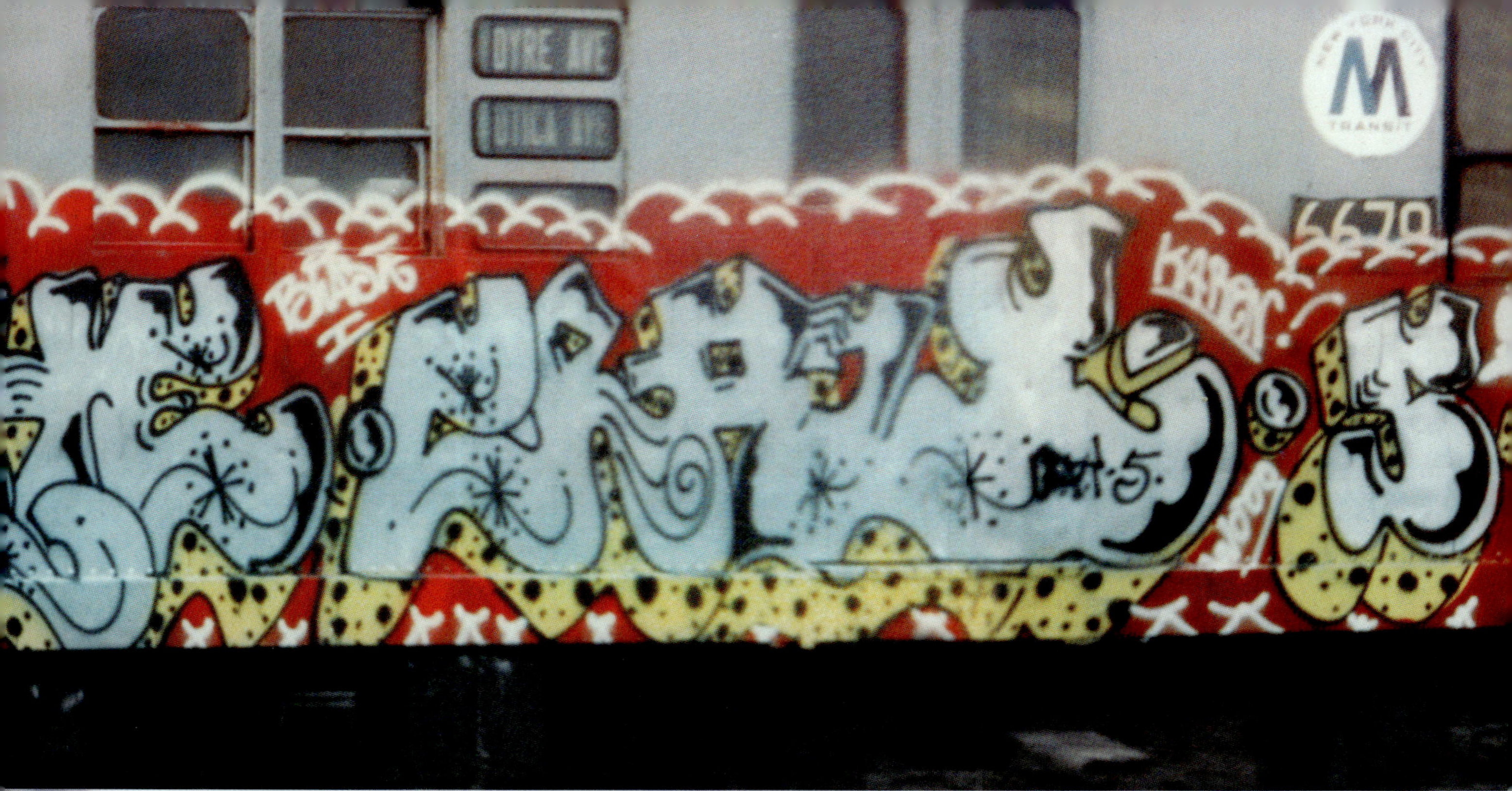
DYRE AVE
UTICA AVE
6670

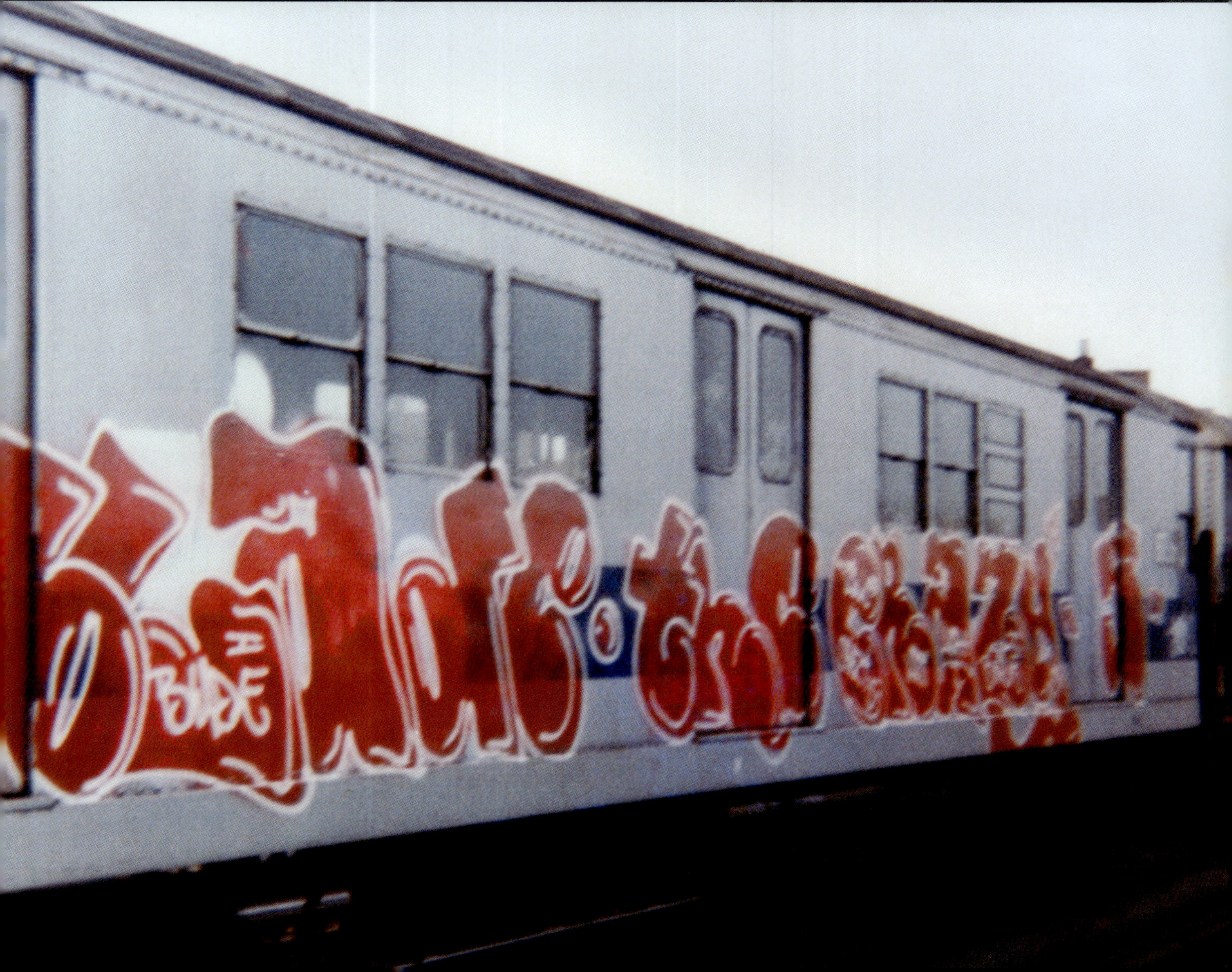

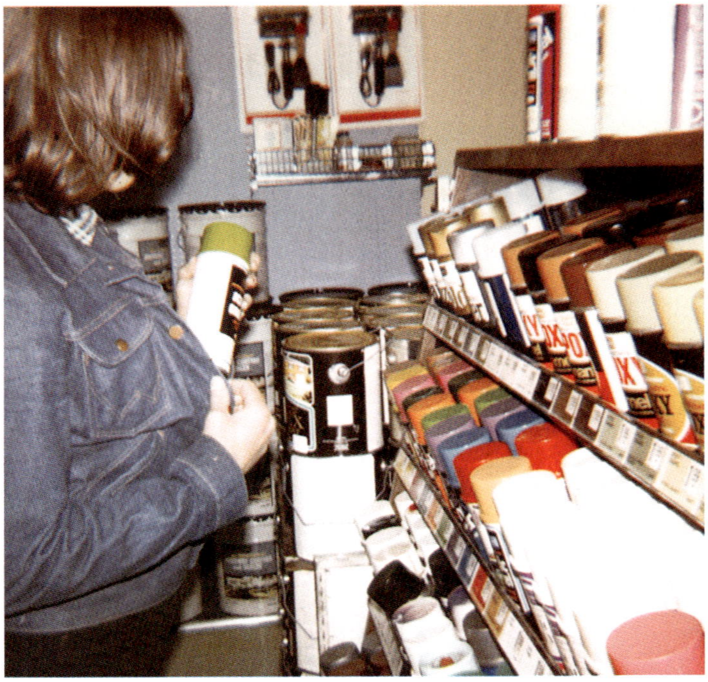

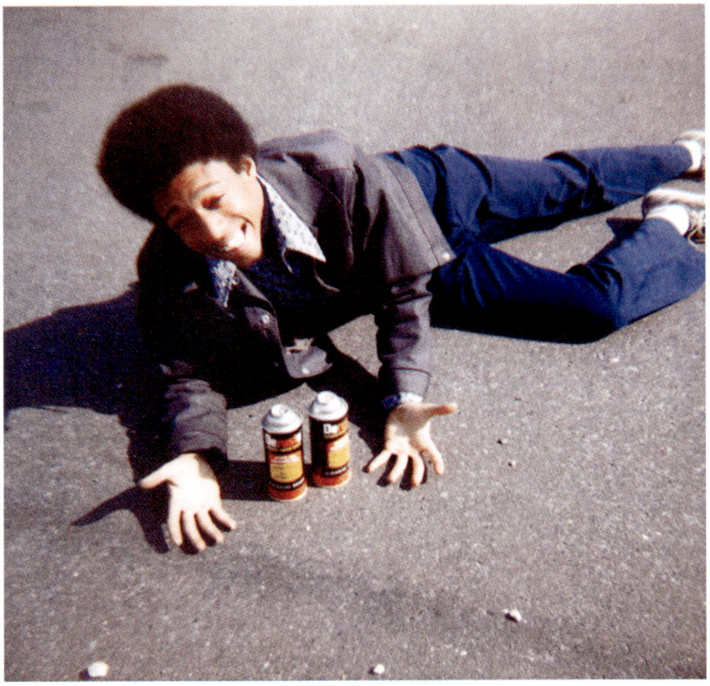

"...WHEN AN OPPORTUNITY LIKE THAT COMES ALONG YOU HAVE TO TAKE IT—YOU CAN ALWAYS RACK MORE PAINT."

VAMM's greatest asset was his racking ability. VAMM was the one who almost singlehandedly burned all of the neighborhood racks. We'd spend our days riding the trains, looking for good spots to rack up paint. A number of times we went to Far Rockaway in Queens, which took about two hours. Places like that had heard of graffiti, but hadn't really made the connection that kids had to be stealing spray paint from hardware stores. In our own neighborhood you could barely get in a hardware store. Other days we'd take the PATH train to New Jersey where they hadn't heard of the graffiti menace at all.

Racking came easy to us. We'd walk into a store with our jean jackets over our shoulders—the sleeves closed off with safety pins—then fill up our jackets with cans. If the store was really cool, we might hit it again on the way back to the train after stashing our paint.

During this one visit we noticed there was a lay-up for the RR trains about three stops into Queens. We decided to check it out on the way back. We racked up about twenty cans each at Robert Hall Village and then scoped out the lay-up as we slowly passed it in the train. It was the middle of the day, so no one was there. When we got to the station, we quickly jumped off the platform and walked down the tracks to the two sets of trains. We did pieces on almost every car there, and returned to the Bronx with no paint. Normally we wouldn't care about a line like the RRs. It was a small line that ran through Queens, a borough without a graffiti track record. But when an opportunity like that comes along you have to take it—you can always rack more paint.

Previous spread: Top: BLADE THE CRAZY 5. Circa 1975.
Bottom left: Whole-car by DEATH that reads DEATH CRAZY 5.Circa 1974.
Bottom right: BLADE THE CRAZY 5. Circa 1974.
This page: Left: VAMM racks up supplies.
Right: BLADE shows off his cans from racking. Circa 1974.
Opposite page: VAMM and BLADE. Circa 1974.

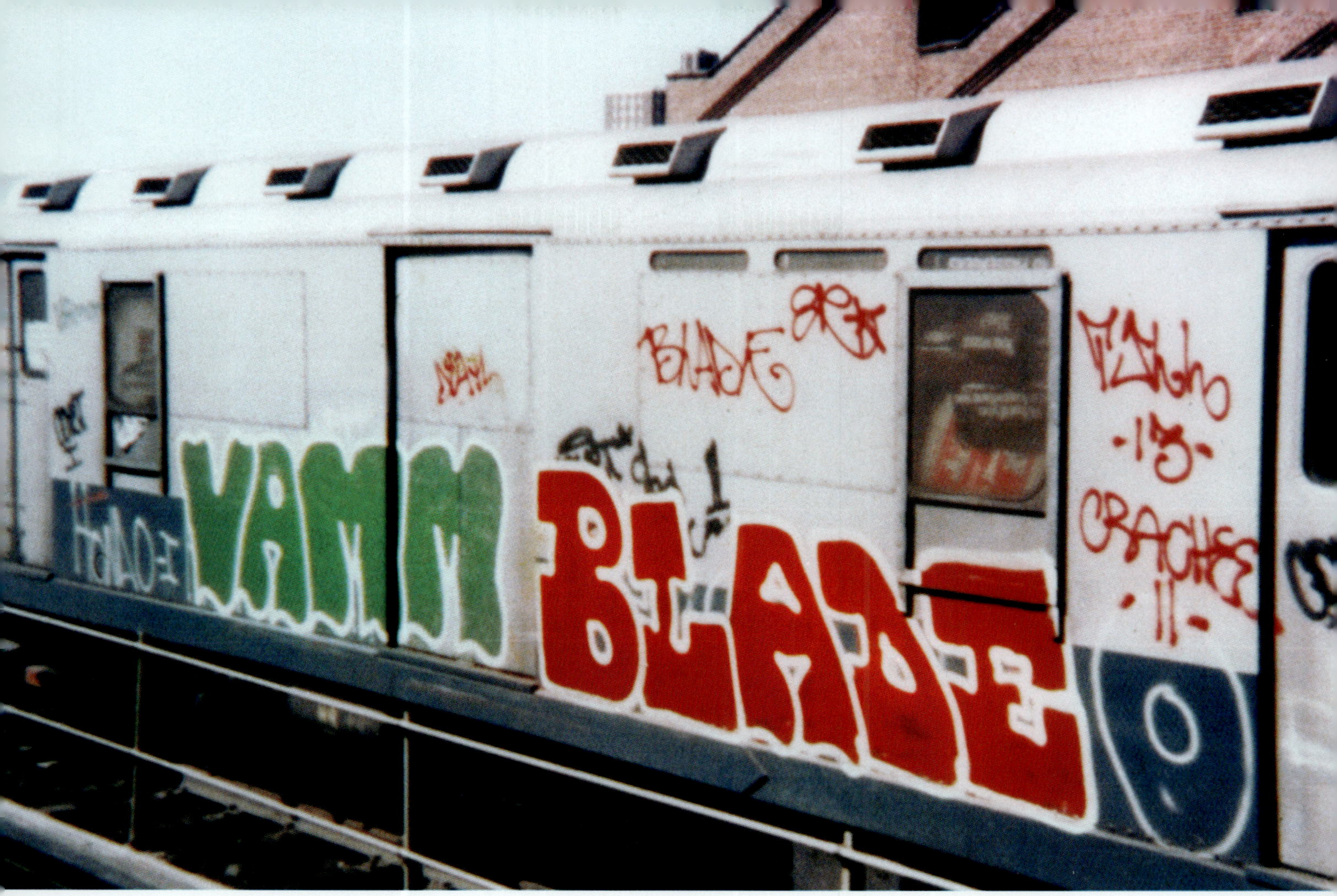

Not long after hitting the RRs, VAMM and I decided to go to the 7 yard. It was his idea; he loved the fact that the cars were painted aqua turquoise and that some of them still had the names of the states painted on them for the World's Fair. The trip to Flushing was long, so we broke it up by stopping in Astoria to rack more paint. When we arrived at the yard we had about twenty-five cans each. VAMM and I walked over a bridge and dropped down toward the fence, which wasn't more than a few feet high and was there to keep stray dogs out. We stepped over the fence and headed straight toward the trains settling on a lane that seemed out of view. We did two-color pieces on each car; one piece would be yellow with a red outline and the next would be red with a yellow outline. They were quick pieces and we were able to do twenty each, which gave us a presence on the line for a long time. When we told everyone at Parkside what we had done, many of them they headed out there the next weekend.

Racking changed in 1974. Prior to that, you only needed a few cans and a few colors: glossy white was great for the redbirds; black and silver were also good. By 1974, the pieces started to get more colorful and writers would look for specific colors. If you had a choice between one can of De Rusto glacier blue or fifteen cans of hunter green, you'd take the glacier blue every time. What would you ever paint with hunter green? Sometimes a lesser brand like Krylon would have a great color that writers searched for, such as hot raspberry or icy grape, two favorites considered a good score.

The most popular brand of paint was Red Devil. It had two advantages: the first was that it was everywhere (Woolworth's even sold it as Home Cote. Other brands were only in certain stores.); second, the quality was greatly enhanced by the lead in the paint, which left it on the trains a lot longer. In 1976, they took the lead out, and writers gave up on the brand. Other brands we racked up were Krylon, Rustoleum, Wet Look, Utilac, and Epoxy.

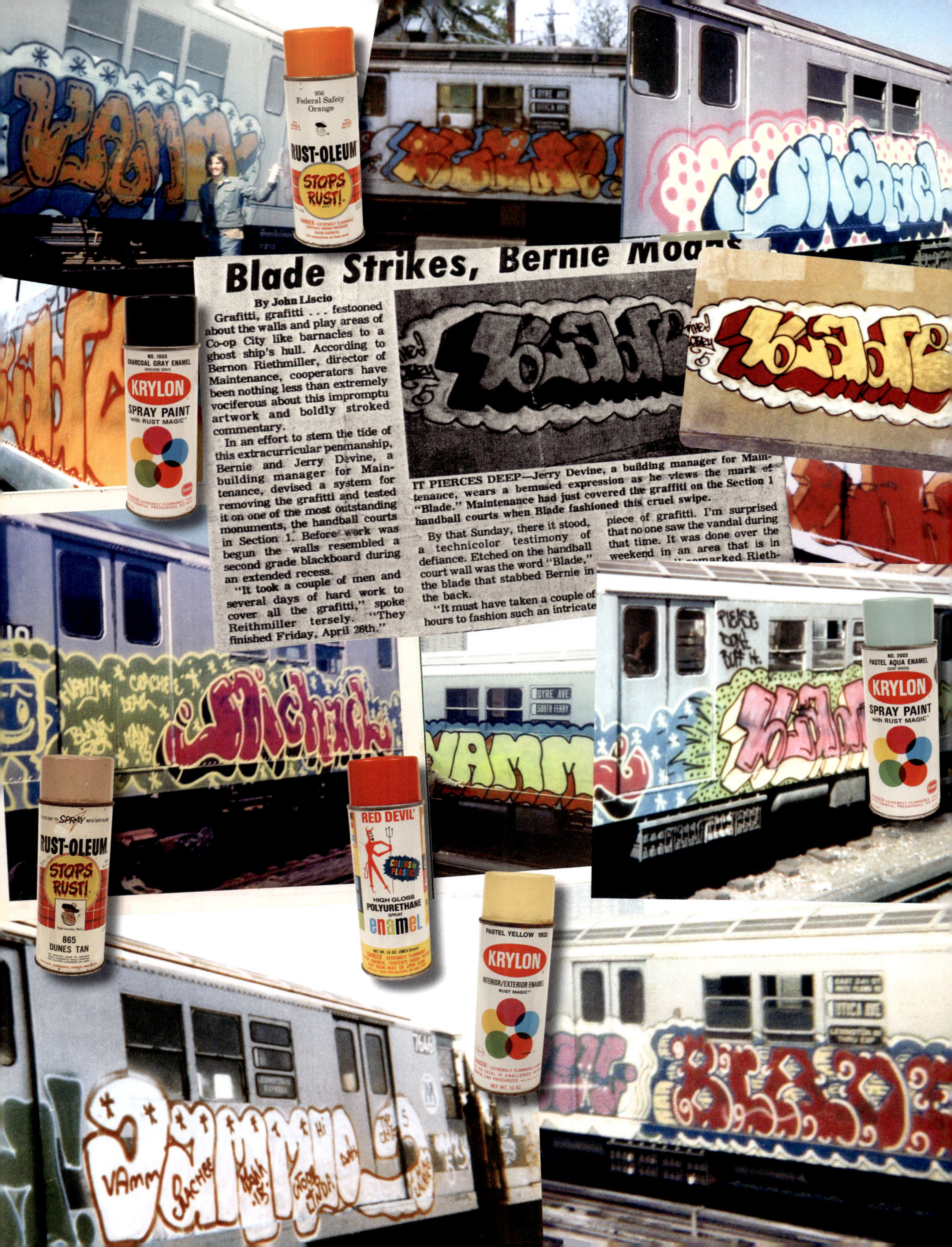

Blade Strikes, Bernie Moans

By John Liscio

Grafitti, grafitti . . . festooned about the walls and play areas of Co-op City like barnacles to a ghost ship's hull. According to Bernon Riethmiller, director of Maintenance, cooperators have been nothing less than extremely vociferous about this impromptu artwork and boldly stroked commentary.

In an effort to stem the tide of this extracurricular penmanship, Bernie and Jerry Devine, a building manager for Maintenance, devised a system for removing the grafitti and tested it on one of the most outstanding monuments, the handball courts in Section 1. Before work was begun the walls resembled a second grade blackboard during an extended recess.

"It took a couple of men and several days of hard work to cover all the grafitti," spoke Reithmiller tersely. "They finished Friday, April 26th."

IT PIERCES DEEP—Jerry Devine, a building manager for Maintenance, wears a bemused expression as he views the mark of "Blade." Maintenance had just covered the graffiti on the Section 1 handball courts when Blade fashioned this cruel swipe.

By that Sunday, there it stood, a technicolor testimony of defiance. Etched on the handball court wall was the word "Blade," the blade that stabbed Bernie in the back.

"It must have taken a couple of hours to fashion such an intricate piece of grafitti. I'm surprised that no one saw the vandal during that time. It was done over the weekend in an area that is in [illegible] remarked Rieth-

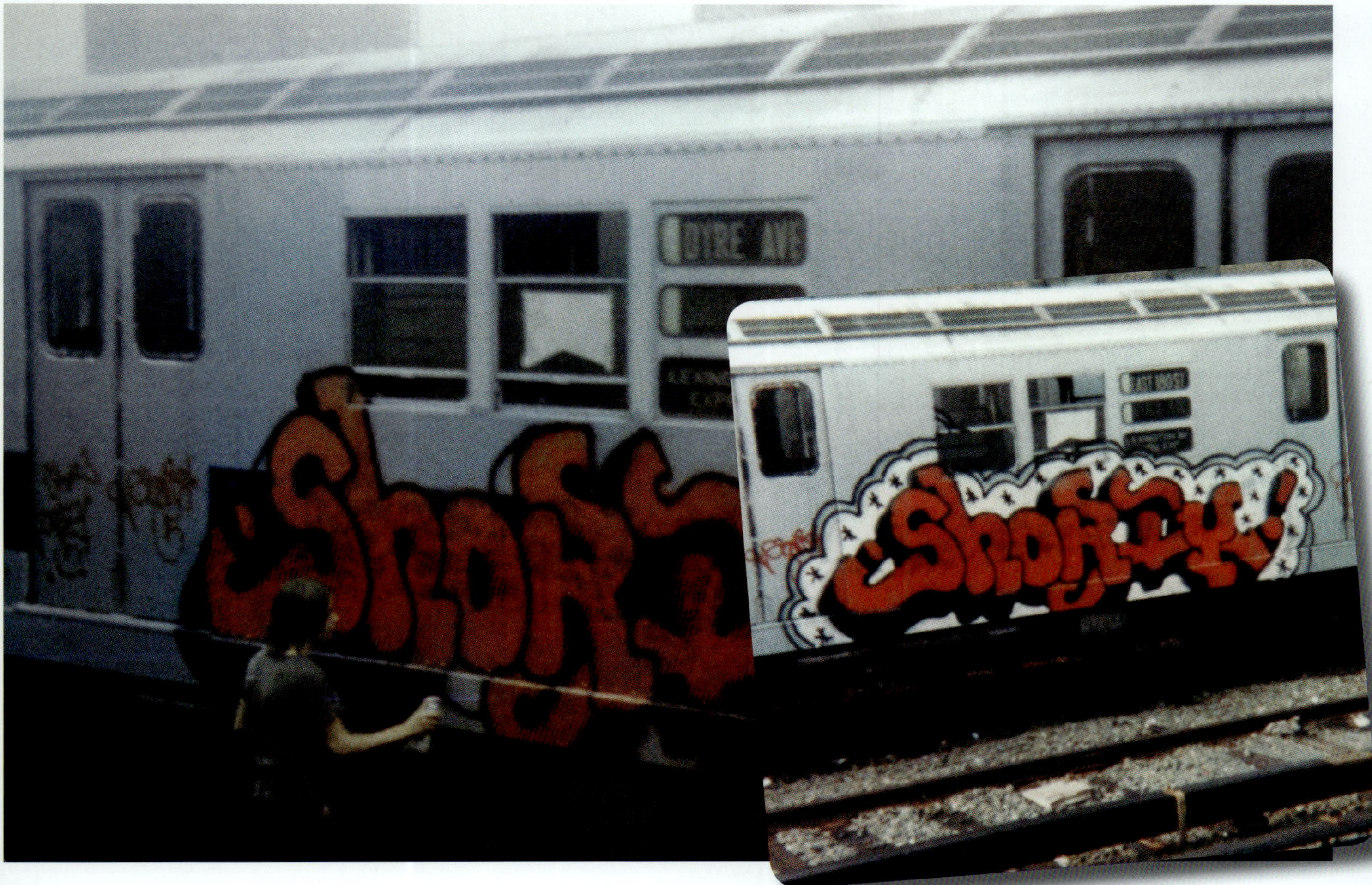

One time, VAMM stole three hundred cans of paint. He hid them in an abandoned lot a few blocks from Parkside—buried underneath piles of brick and debris. Of course, the problem was that he couldn't really tell anyone, because they would've stolen it. But it was such a big score! Finally, he caved in and told Glazer about it. Even though Glaze was older and didn't write, he was amazed by all of the cans. I'm sure some of it was handed down to us by VAMM, but we were still envious. That was a lot of paint, even by our standards.

Some of the writers in the Bronx were also burglars: professional criminals who robbed paint factories and warehouses. Of course, most of them are in jail now. I liked the idea of waking up in the morning to roam the city looking for great colors, although even I could be seduced by the right crime. In 1975, SHORTY 5 came to me with a plan to rob a lumber store in his neighborhood where they had a great display of the best Red Devil colors. It was a two-story climb (which I guess made us second-story men) to the roof of the store. We were able to open a small window on the roof and squeeze through it. Once inside, I ran right to the paint and started filling it into bags and boxes. After about five minutes, I started to wonder where SHORTY 5 was. And then I saw his silhouette over by the cash register, where he was grabbing the money. He asked me if I wanted any and I said no. I was no thief. We snuck back out and I never did a burglary again.

To me, there was a reason to steal paint, and when you're young you can rationalize anything. Stealing paint helped me make art, so it was a necessary evil, but stealing someone's hard-earned money was wrong. The same thing with drugs. Glaze was one of my closest friends because he only sold acceptable drugs, like pot and hash. If he had started dealing heroin, our friendship would've ended. I was just developing my moral compass at the time, and if there's one thing I learned it's that everyone drew the line in the sand somewhere. SHORTY 5 might've robbed a few stores as a teenager, but he would never hurt anyone. That's where he drew the line. And that was fine with me.

Opposite page: Collage of trains by VAMM and his alias MICHAEL, BLADE and vintage cans of spray paint. Circa 1974. This page: SHORTY 5 in action. 1975.

CHAPTER SIX

THE GOLDEN YEARS:

1974–1976

To us, THE CRAZY 5 was just as much about hanging out at Parkside Houses as it was about painting trains. Nobody imagined that forty years later, writers from that period would be traveling the world as artists, lecturing about the movement, and selling their canvases. You were dodging trains to make art. What's amazing is that guys like CRACHEE and VAMM had the foresight to document their works with the old 126 cameras. They had a cube on top that rotated to create a flash ... click, click, click. I also started documenting my pieces. We didn't care about anything materialistic, but the trains meant something to us—something you couldn't put a price on. By 1974, writers were trading photographs like baseball cards and the graffiti movement was blowing up.

We had two hangouts away from the playground. The first was an old garage a few blocks away, across from PS 41. Somehow we got permission to hang out there. We decorated it with a couch from the street and anything else we could find to make it look cool. That was where we went to make out with our girls. There could be twenty or thirty teenagers a night, all begging for a little bit of privacy. When we weren't hanging out there, we had a brand new Burger King to go to. Originally, the manager didn't like us, but one weekend VAMM did a painting of the Burger King character on a train. We showed pictures of the train to the manager; after that, he fell in love with us. We could spend hours at the Burger King, bragging about what went on in the garage. Of course, most of the stories were embellished, as they usually are at that age. We were still seventeen and riding Stingray bikes. The real men had cars.

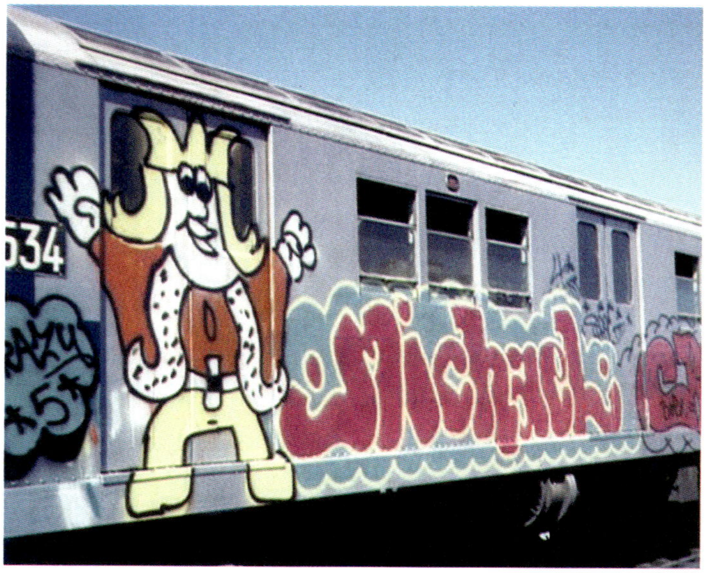

This page: MICHAEL by VAMM. 1974.
Opposite page: Members of THE CRAZY FIVE and friends make a pyramid outside of Burger King. 1974.

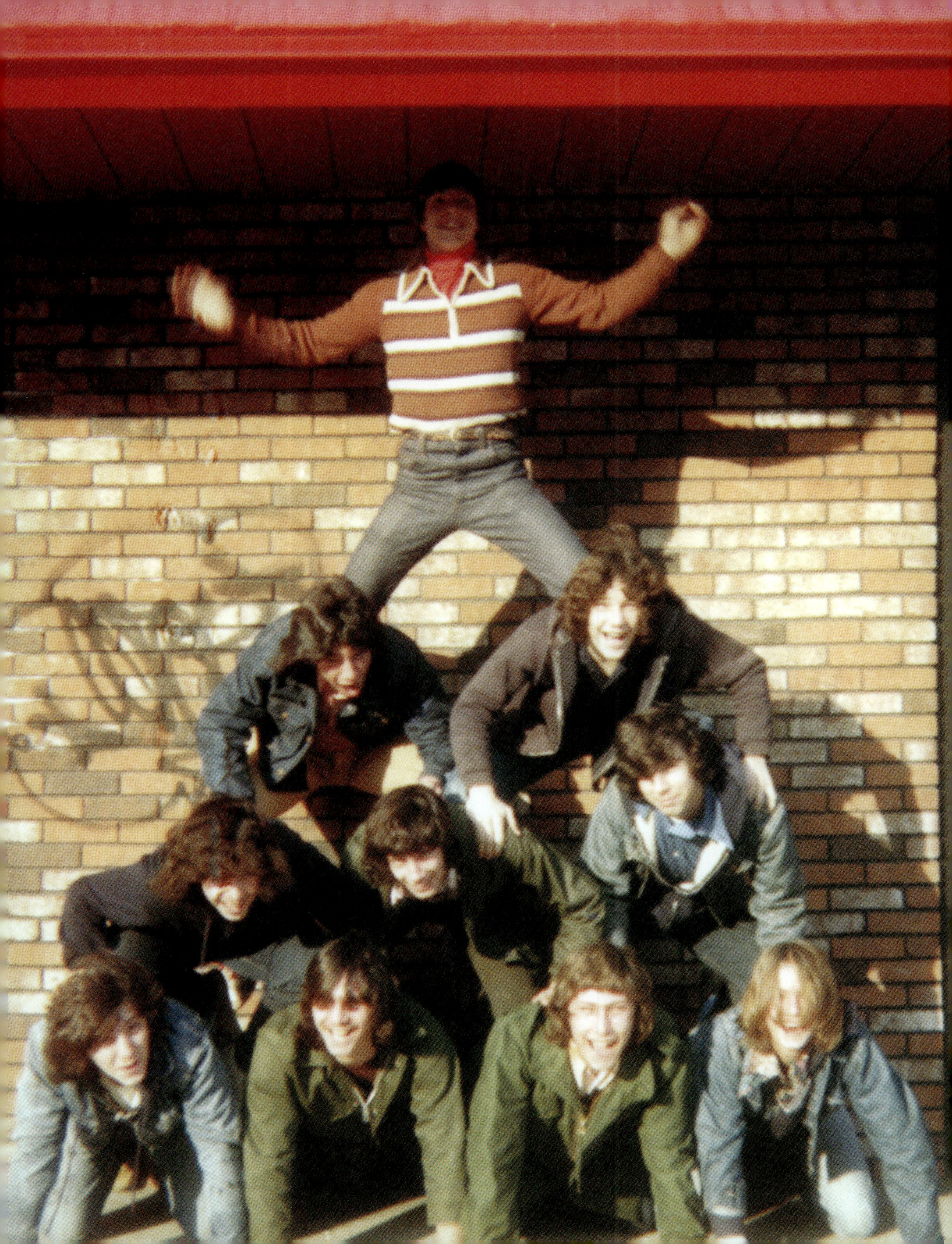

One of the advantages of hanging out at Parkside was that we had a train lay-up running right through it. The elevated 2 line rose above us as we played basketball and rapped to the girls. We would hit the trains seemingly at will. For some of THE CRAZY 5, getting to the lay-up was simple. For CRACHEE, it was just a matter of opening a door, since he lived on the first floor of one of the buildings in Parkside. I had to walk for forty-five minutes from Co-op City and dodge cars, while crossing a major highway and carrying my bags of paint. Early on, we just wanted to get up, and that's how we did it.

In July of 1974, ten of us from the Parkside playground went up to the lay-up, including a couple of the girl writers, KIVU and Z-73, and Karen. We were all drunk off our asses. We walked up the steps to the Burke Avenue station and jumped right over the turnstile while giving the token clerk the finger. We couldn't be stopped. We jumped off the platform and hit cars with tags and pieces. We stumbled back and forth, bumping into each other and laughing under the summer moon. I pulled the bumpers of the two trains apart, lifted the chain that held them together, and helped Karen climb in between cars. She looked so fine. I opened the train door and we crawled into the car. The door shut behind us. It was exciting and Karen started to kiss me. I kissed her back hard and then ran my hand under her halter-top. Karen took off her top and I kissed her breasts.

The two of us huddled under the windows of the subway door so no one would see us—for once, a little privacy in the Bronx. CRACHEE noticed three undercover cops headed our way. He yelled out "DTs!" and we watched as everybody scrambled back toward the station. But there were also cops on the platform coming down the tracks to greet the group. Karen threw her top on and we joined the group. Together we ducked underneath the train and crawled by the cops. We hit the platform and we were gone.

The chase was an amazing one, and we talked about it for weeks, but unfortunately it burned the lay-up. The following weekend, the police placed cops in both the Burke and Allerton stations, denying us access. We were discouraged for a while, until DEATH came up with a revolutionary strategy. If we couldn't go through the stations, then we would climb up to the tracks from the street. From what I've been told (I wasn't there), his first attempt at climbing the girders leading to the tracks absolutely stunned the UPS employees who worked across the street. Some of them shouted and called him a monkey, didn't faze him at all. Before long we were all doing it. If we got chased, we climbed back down the same way. The climb itself was simple. There were hundreds of rivets in the beams, which you could put your toes on. And if you leaned back from the beam, extending your arms, you barely felt your own weight. DEATH also figured out the best way to bring paint up: in a plastic bag held in your teeth.

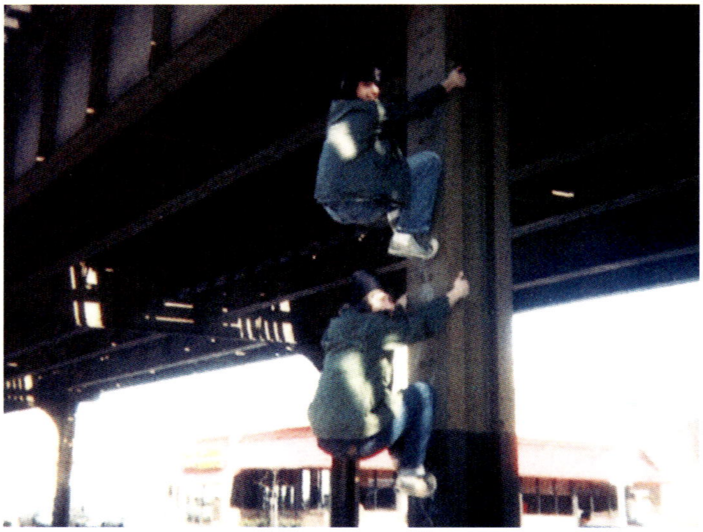

There were still chases at the Burke lay-up because we were there so often, not always to paint. Sometimes we went up there at night just to make out with girls. On occasion, cop cars would pass by and the cops would get out and shine their flashlights at us. About an hour later, a black and white Transit car would come by shining spotlights up at the lay-up. The housing cops would come by in orange and blue cruisers, but they didn't really care about us writing on the trains. In fact, right after painting the BLADEISM, VAMM car, we climbed down the pillar into the waiting hands of one Officer Leon of the Housing Police. It turned out that Officer Leon was a fan, so I took a photo of him and VAMM together and we went on our way.

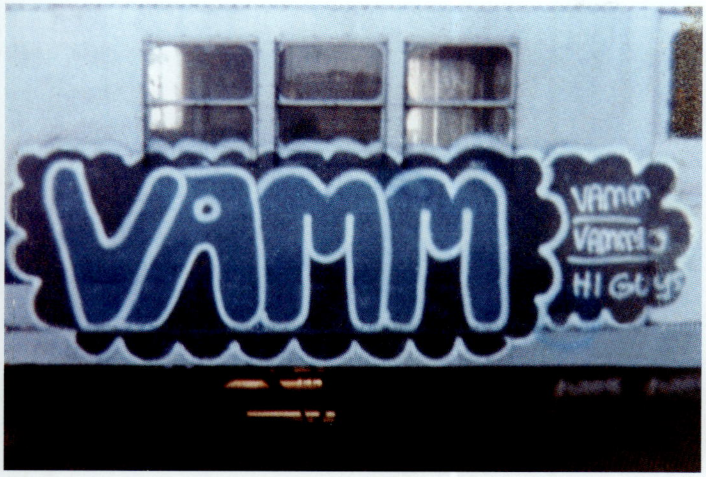

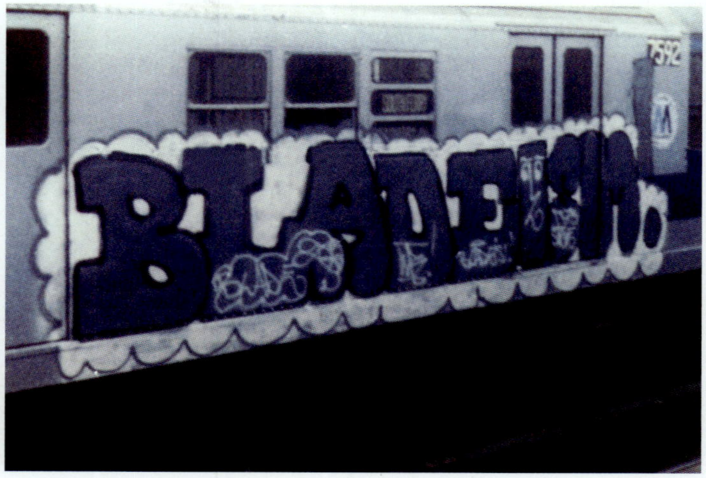

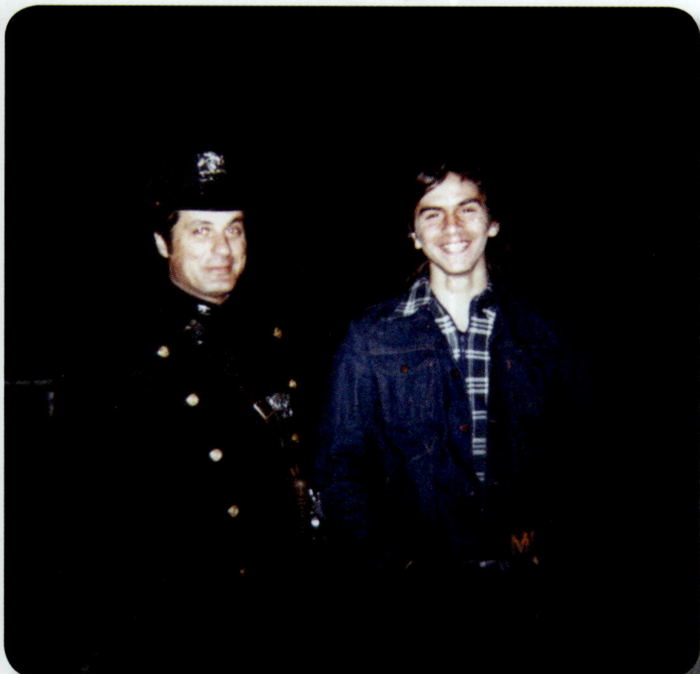

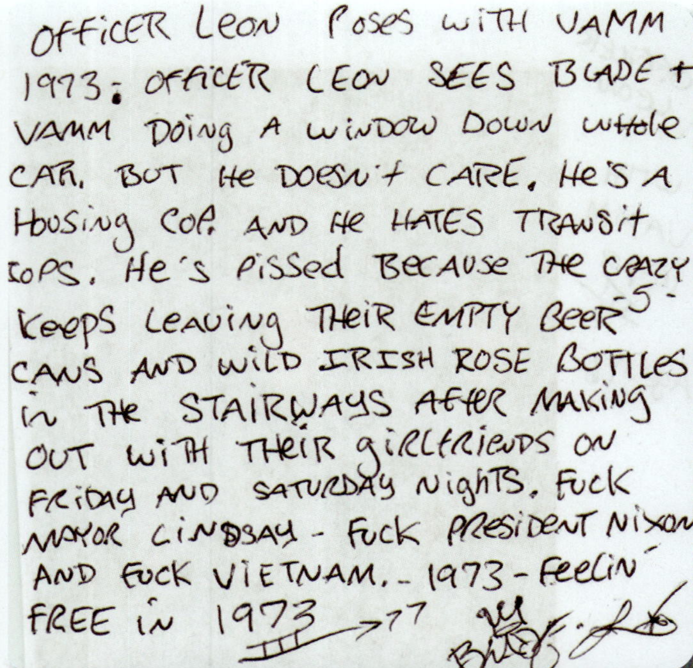
OFFICER LEON POSES WITH VAMM 1973. OFFICER LEON SEES BLADE + VAMM DOING A WINDOW DOWN WHOLE CAR. BUT HE DOESN'T CARE. HE'S A HOUSING COP. AND HE HATES TRANSIT COPS. HE'S PISSED BECAUSE THE CRAZY -5- KEEPS LEAVING THEIR EMPTY BEER CANS AND WILD IRISH ROSE BOTTLES IN THE STAIRWAYS AFTER MAKING OUT WITH THEIR GIRLFRIENDS ON FRIDAY AND SATURDAY NIGHTS. FUCK MAYOR LINDSAY - FUCK PRESIDENT NIXON AND FUCK VIETNAM. - 1973 - FEELIN' FREE IN 1973 →77

Opposite page: *DEATH and VAMM climb up the girders. 1973.*
This page: Top: VAMM and BLADEISM train finished right before being stopped by the Transit police. 1973. Bottom: Officer Leon and VAMM. 1973.

While we painted together in 1973 and 1974, we each had a different method that suited us. DEATH liked to paint alone, so, after we climbed up the pillars, he was gone. He had a lot of worries on his mind, some of it was family related, some of it was the neighborhood. He liked to be alone with his thoughts while he painted. Sometimes we didn't know what he painted until the next day. CRACHEE and VAMM were partners in 1973 and they'd hit a car together, but in 1974 I was usually painting with VAMM. When VAMM wrote with CRACHEE, they did stick letter pieces, but by the time VAMM and I partnered it was important to be able to collaborate and unify the two names. TULL 13 (MARIO) painted right along side us.

VAMM could get intense when he painted, which led to one of the few confrontations that ever took place at our lay-up. VAMM had just broken up with his girlfriend, so he was getting no ass at all, and he was angry about it. Anything could set him off. One night we were painting at the lay-up and KINDU (a notorious writer from the 6 line) was there. KINDU was the darkest guy you'll ever meet, a tough guy who loved to fight. They started a conversation that couldn't have possibly ended well. While painting, VAMM yelled out, "You can't even have your own lay-up anymore!" KINDU stared at me and said, "You better talk to your boy, BLADE." Normally KINDU would have won that fight, but the way VAMM was feeling that day—not getting laid and all—he could've won. I told KINDU the story about VAMM not getting any lovin'. As it turns out, KINDU had a heart after all and he actually felt bad for VAMM, so they didn't fight. The more VAMM bitched, the more KINDU just smiled.

CRACHEE and VAMM had a good run on the 2 line in 1973. Whether they kinged it or not is still debatable. But in 1974, VAMM and I took it over—undisputed kings. Being king of a line in 1974 was a big deal because the competition had expanded tremendously and the new writers coming up had the advantage of copying the latest styles, so a lot of them got good fast. In 1973, THE EBONY DUKES and WAR were the two big crews; everyone envied them and the pieces they did. One of the things about the evolution of graffiti is that the next group to come along would have to double the number of pieces painted by the earlier generations and improve upon the earlier styles.

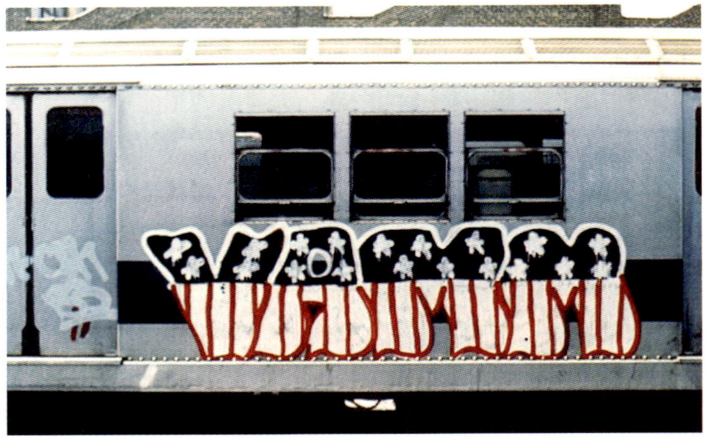

The pieces by THE CRAZY 5 were much different in 1974 than they were in 1973; they had a more polished look. The only one in the group who didn't care about style was DEATH, since he was painting trains for other reasons—mostly to get up and king the line. CRACHEE began to expand on his first pieces, coming up with square letters that had nice 3-Ds. MARIO's best pieces were his TULL 13 whole-cars. The four letters would only take up half the train, but the bottom of the two Ls would shoot across to the end of the car. VAMM was innovative; he celebrated April Fool's Day by painting his name upside down. Another time, he painted the American flag inside the letters of his name—something a lot of writers copied later. In 1975, he painted a VAMMTASTIC piece, which started even more copying, including a PAZTASTIC piece by CLIFF 159.

Bringing new writers into the group was easy because they all hung out with us. In fact, that was one of the rules of THE CRAZY 5—you had to hang out at Parkside. Since we didn't really have a president, someone would mention a name and we'd take an informal vote. It usually worked out. Sometimes a big-name writer didn't get in because they didn't hang out with us. In the end, we probably could've been called THE CRAZY 25.

This page: VAMM gets patriotic. 1974.
Opposite page: Top: A VAMMTASTIC EXP! that was heavily copied. 1975. Bottom: BLADE and VAMM painted upside down and backwards on April Fools Day. 1974.
Following spread: Various members of TC5. Circa 1974.

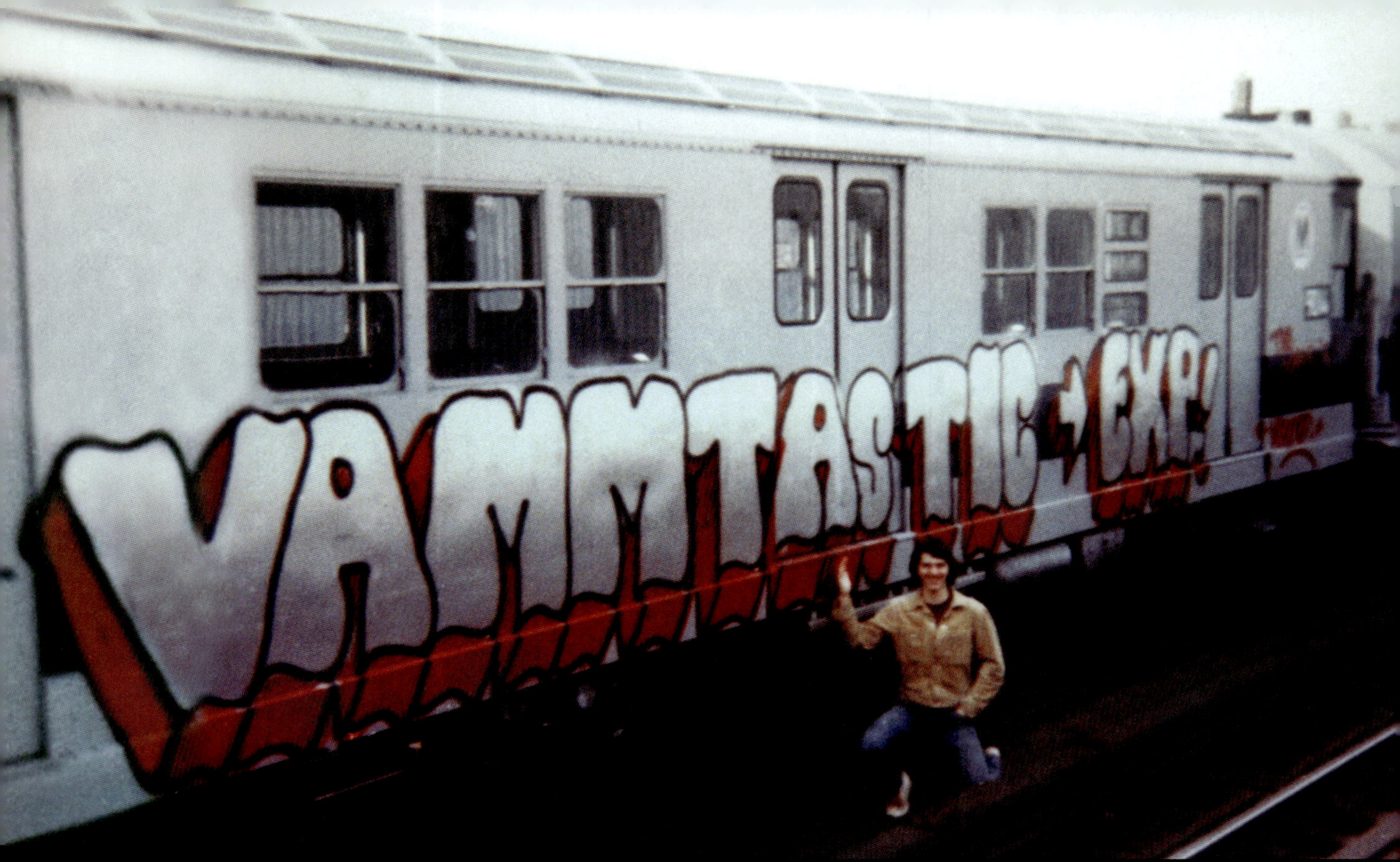

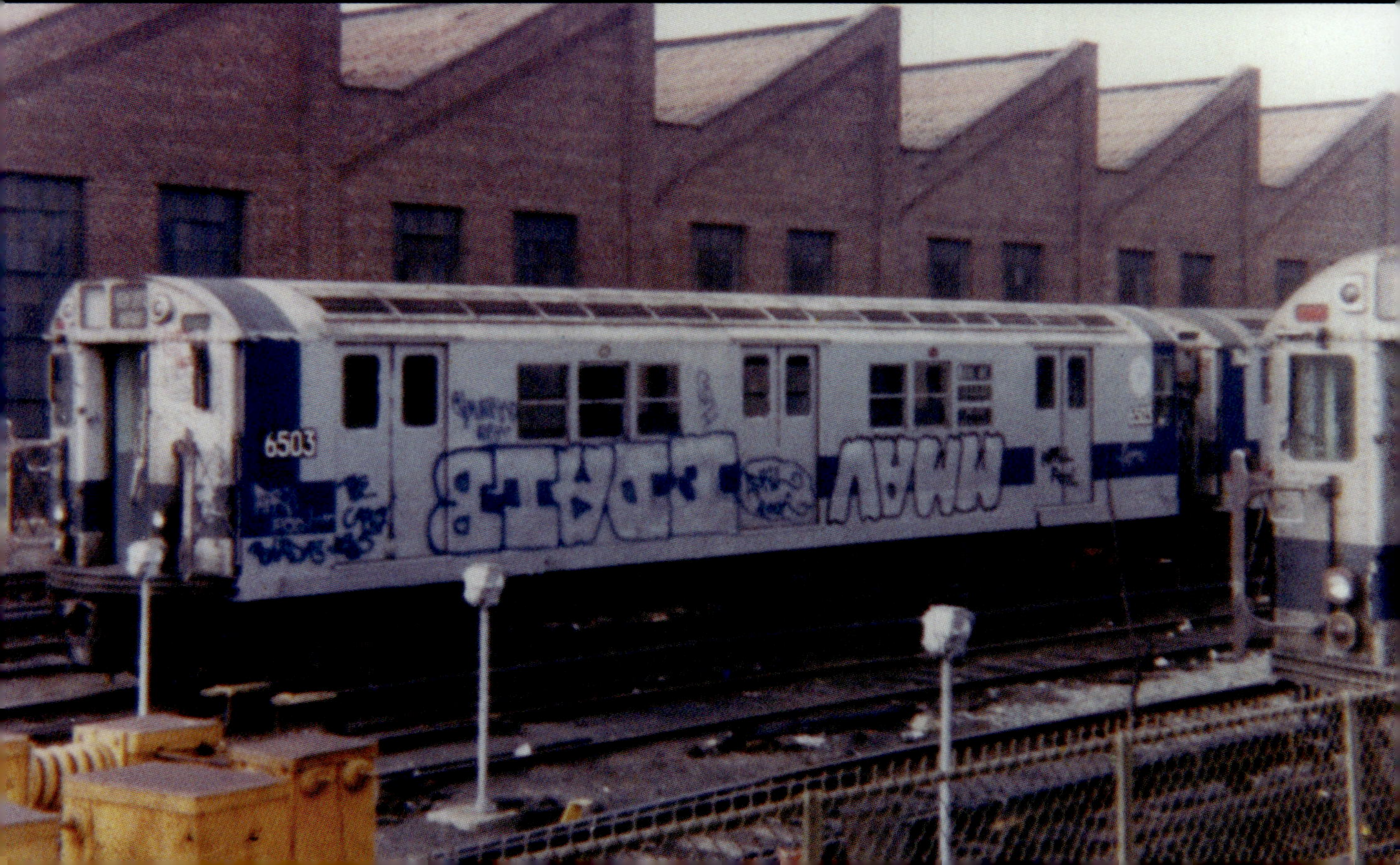
6503

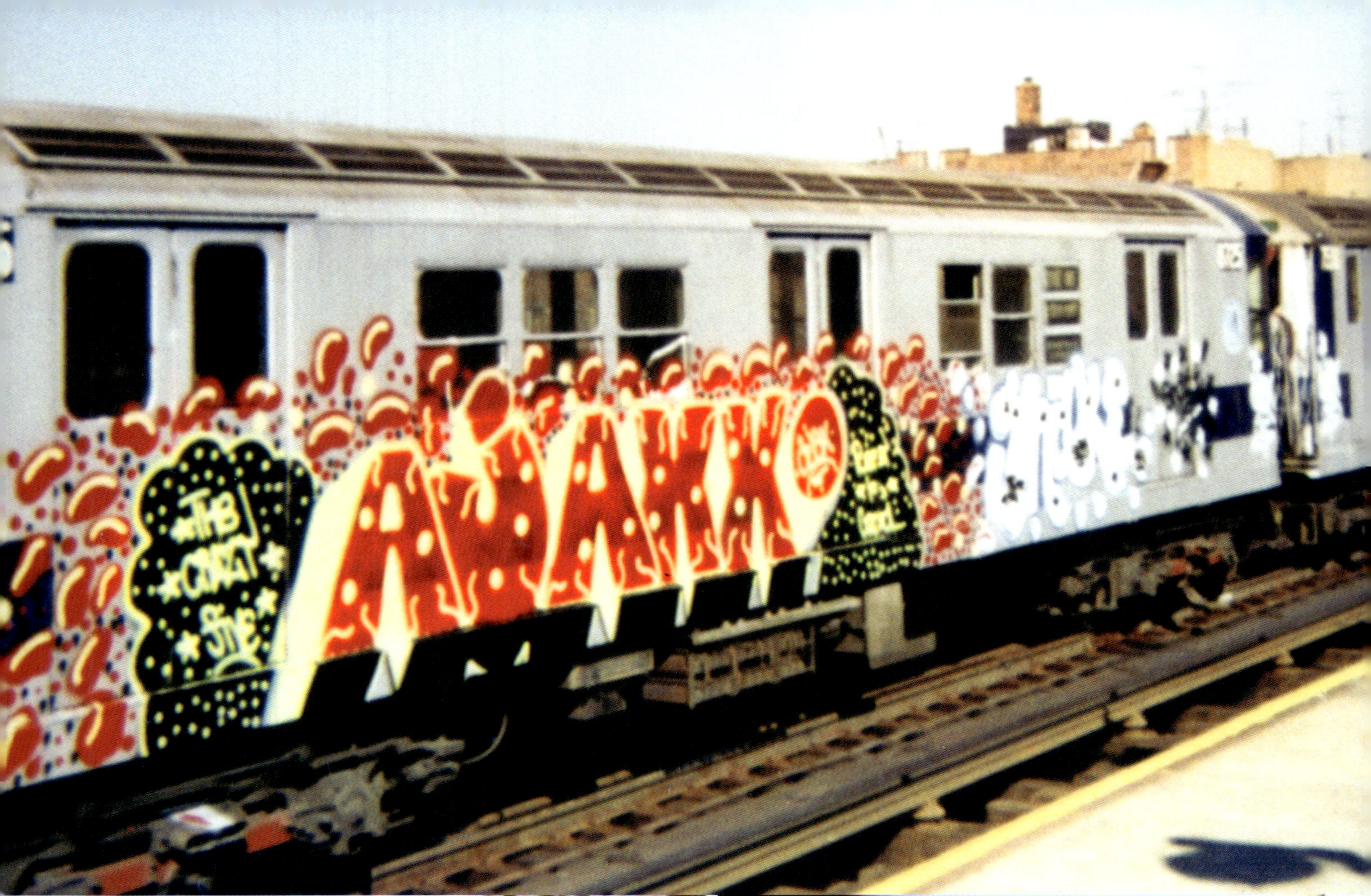

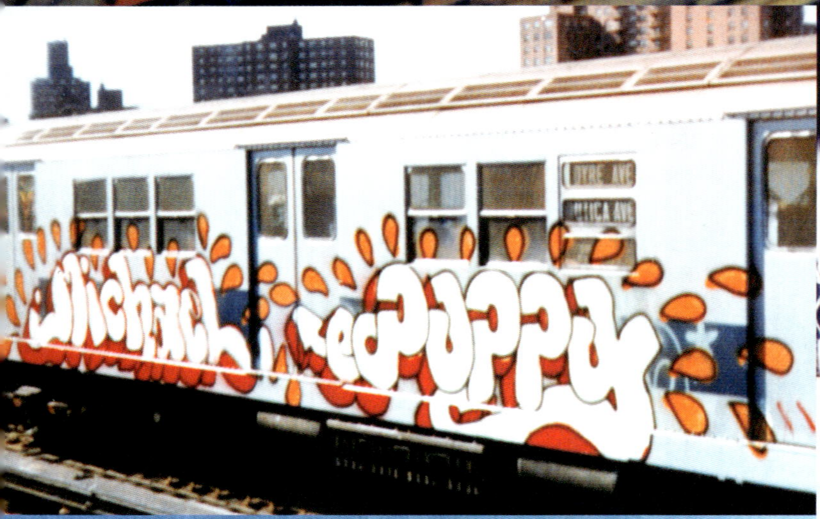

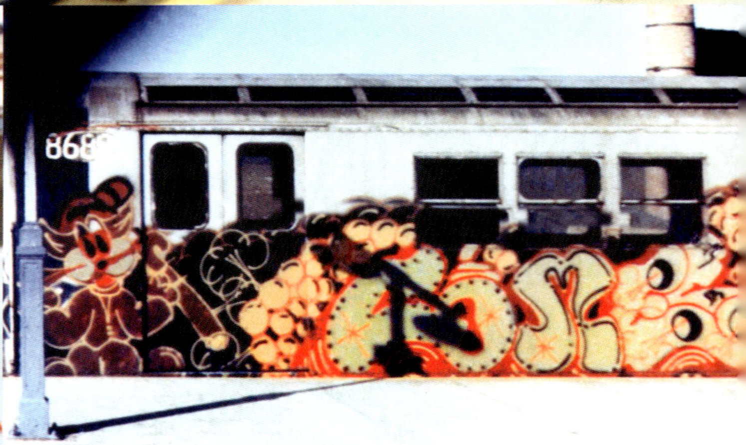

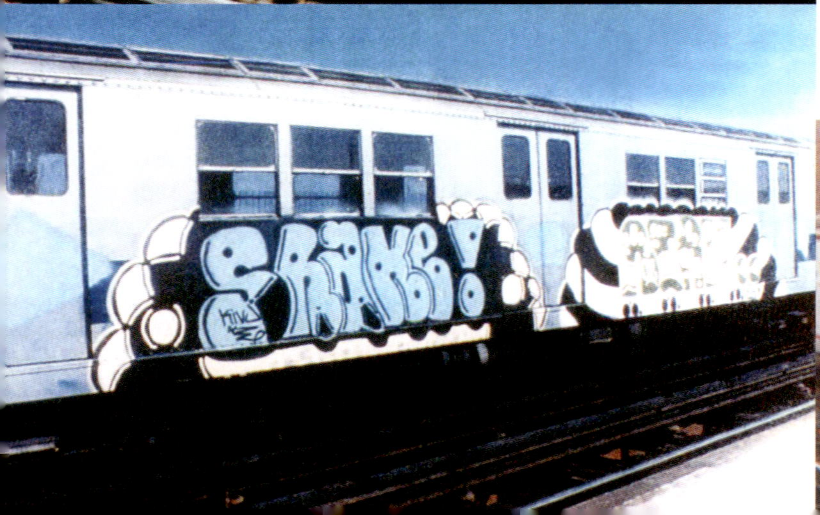

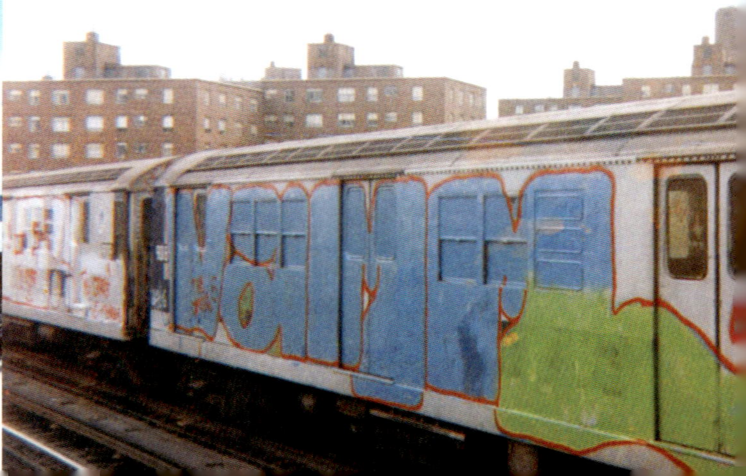

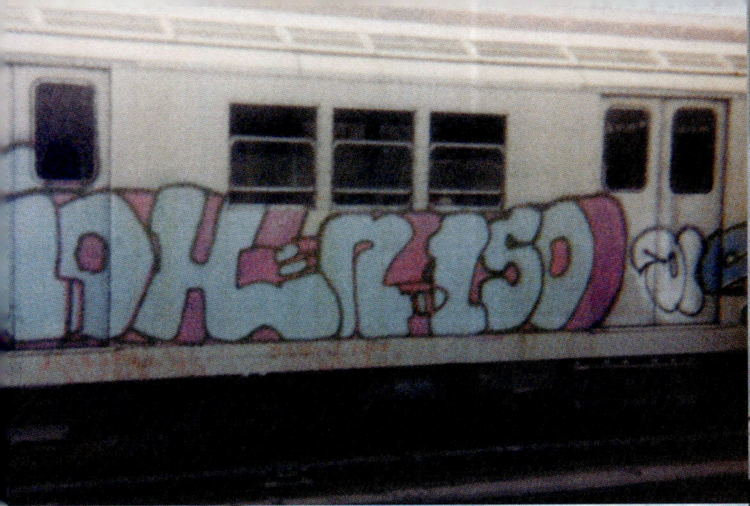
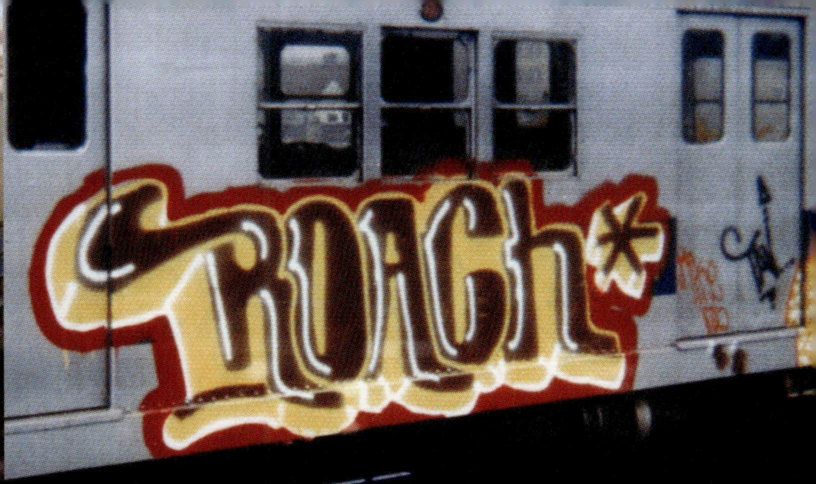
ROACH*
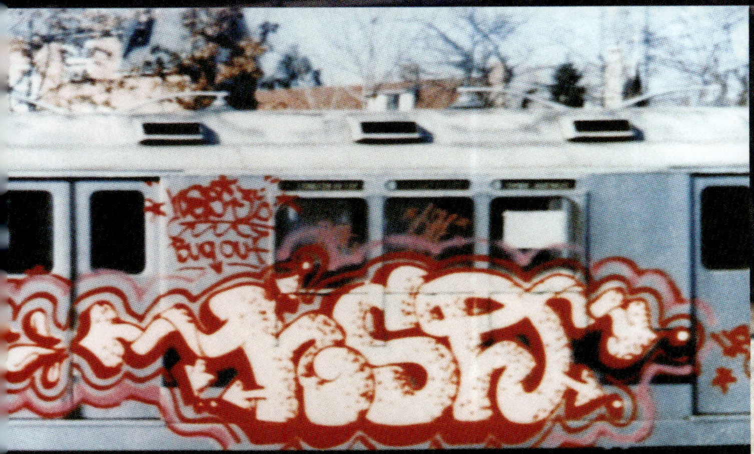
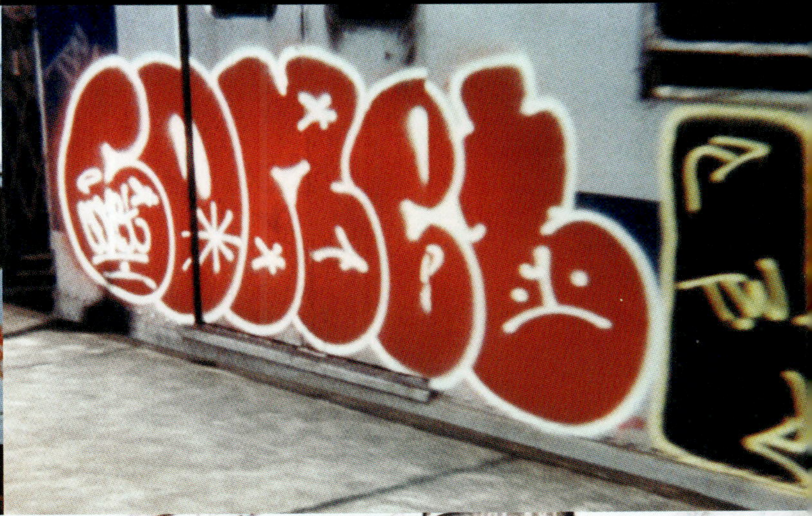
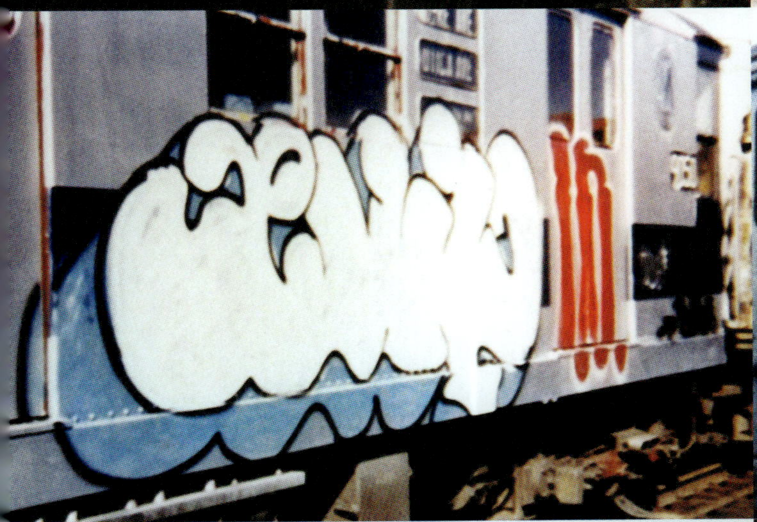
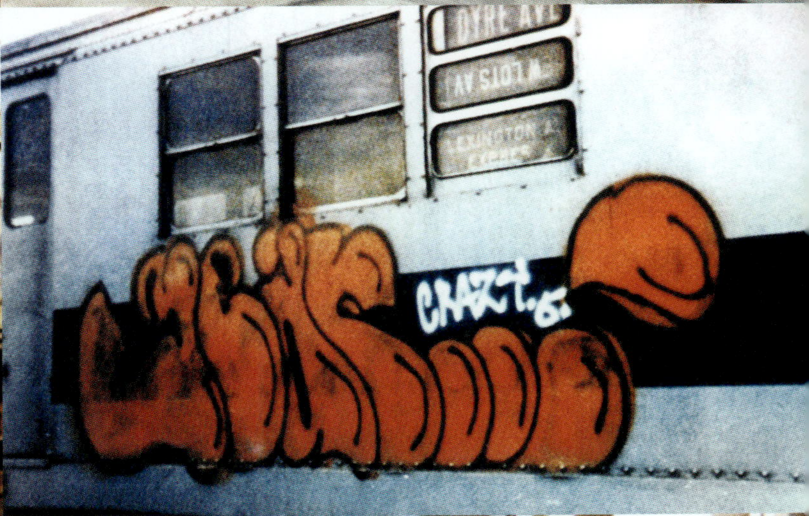
DYRE AVE
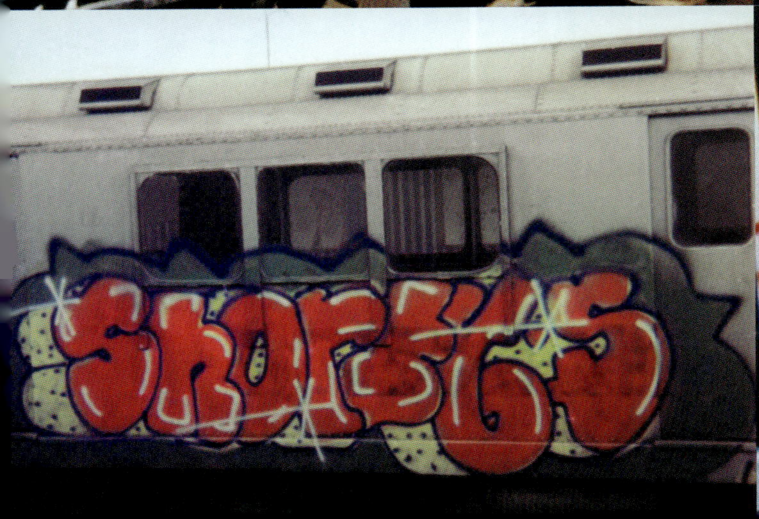
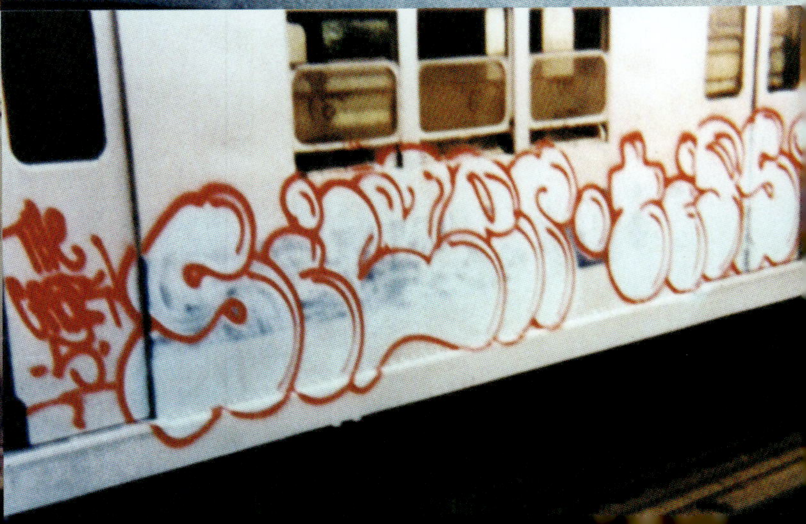

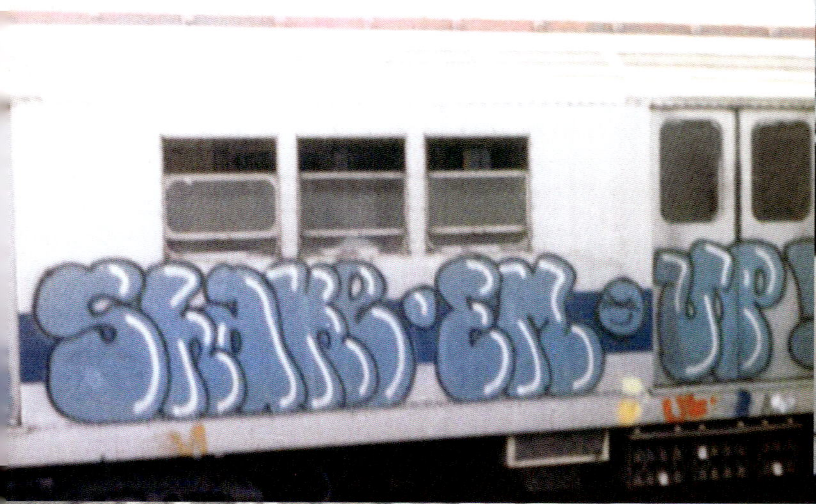

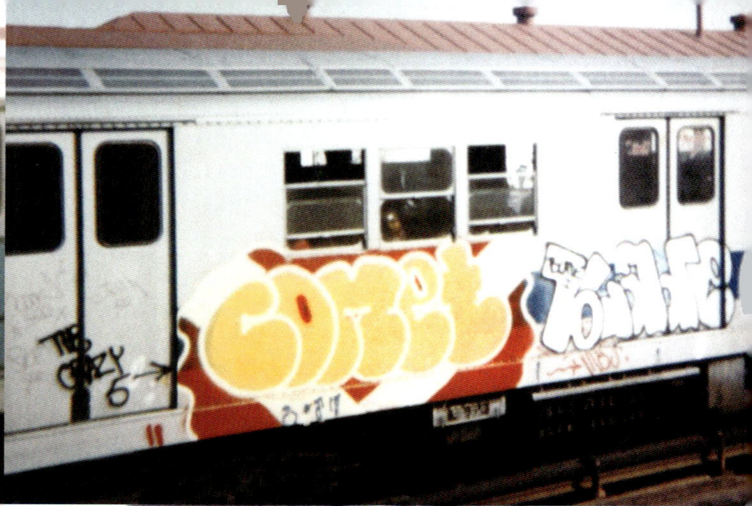

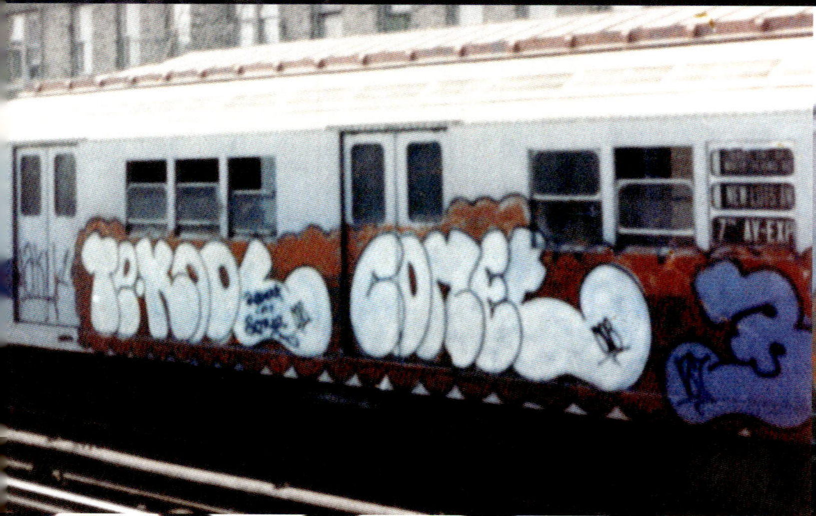
7th AV-EXP

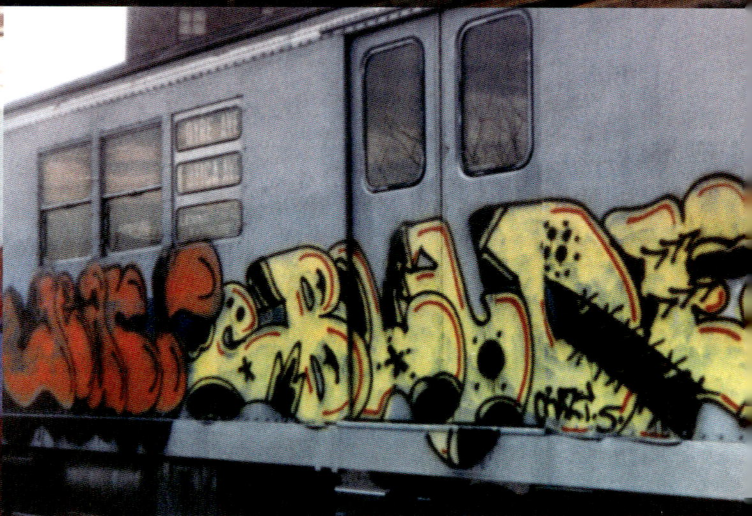

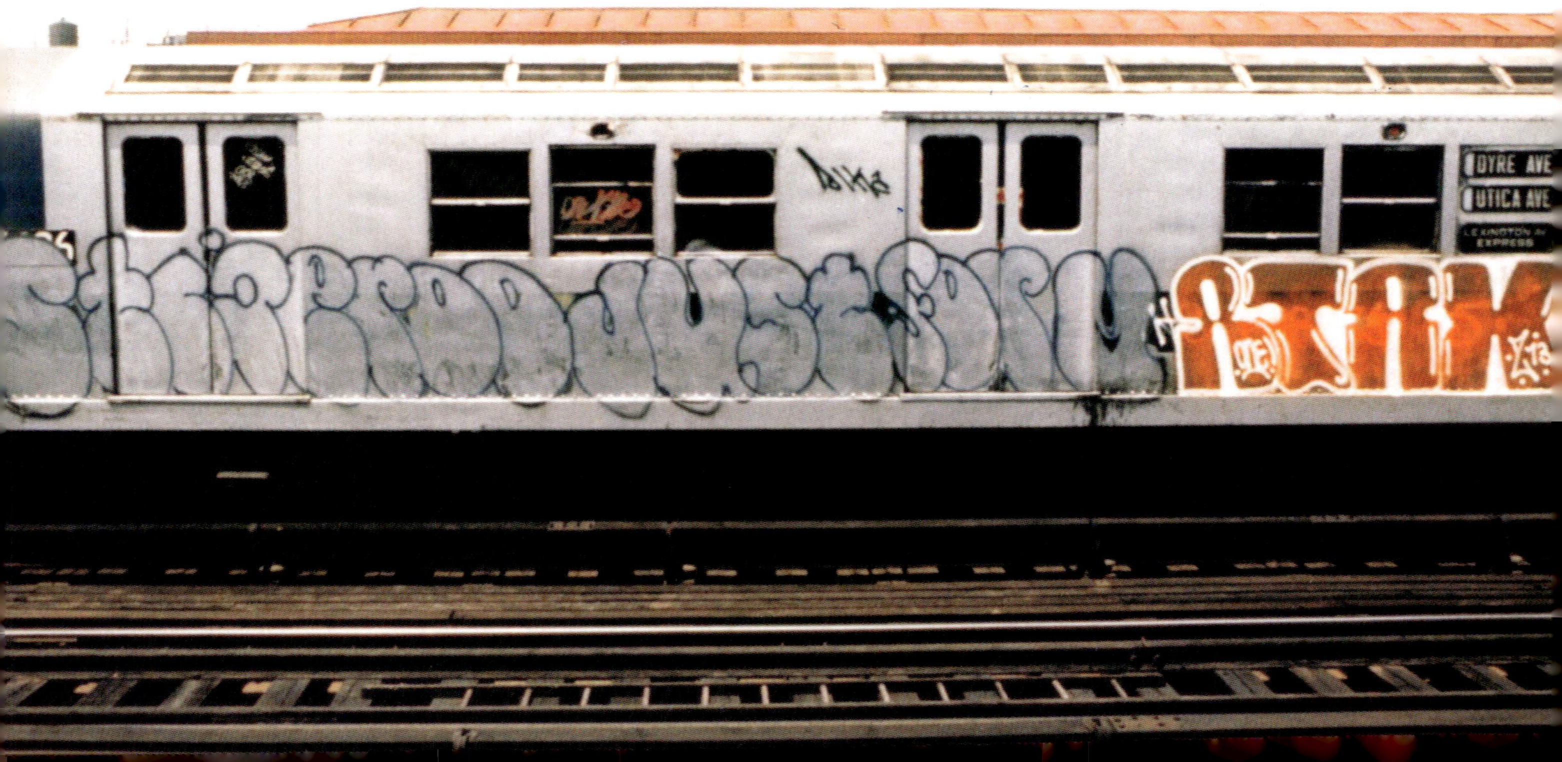
DYRE AVE
UTICA AVE
LEXINGTON AV
EXPRESS

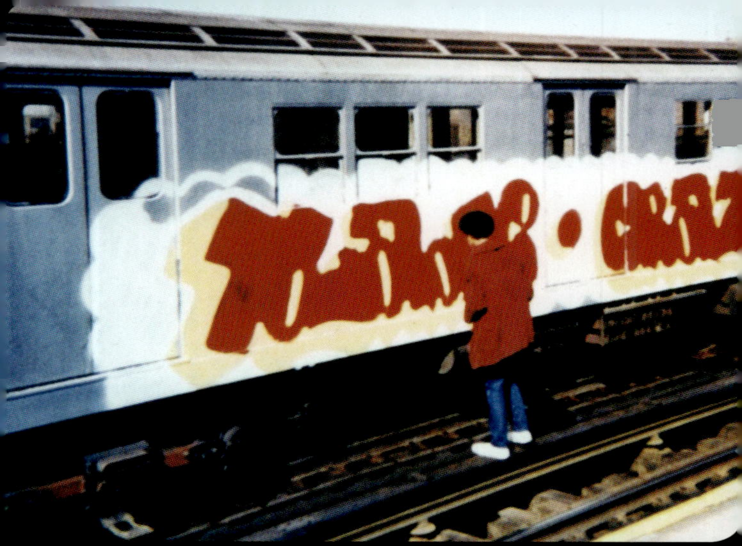

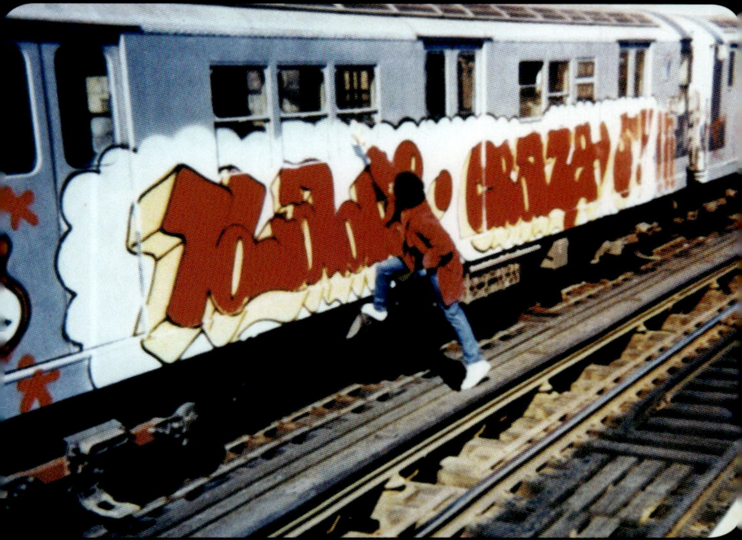

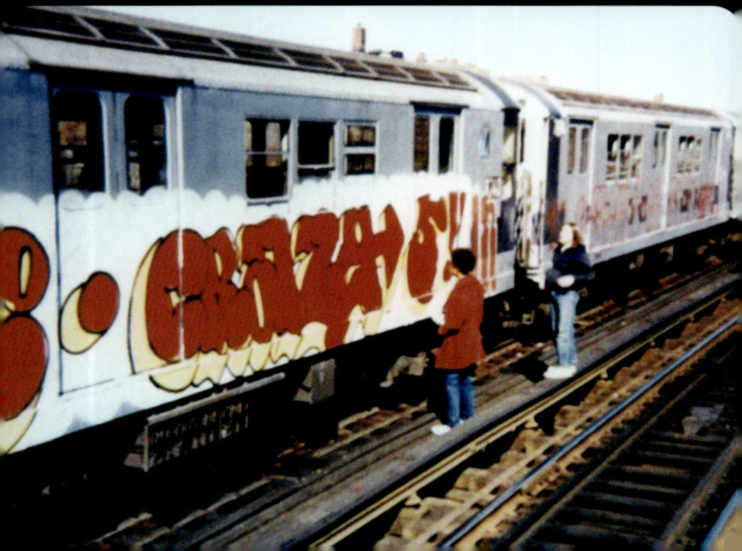

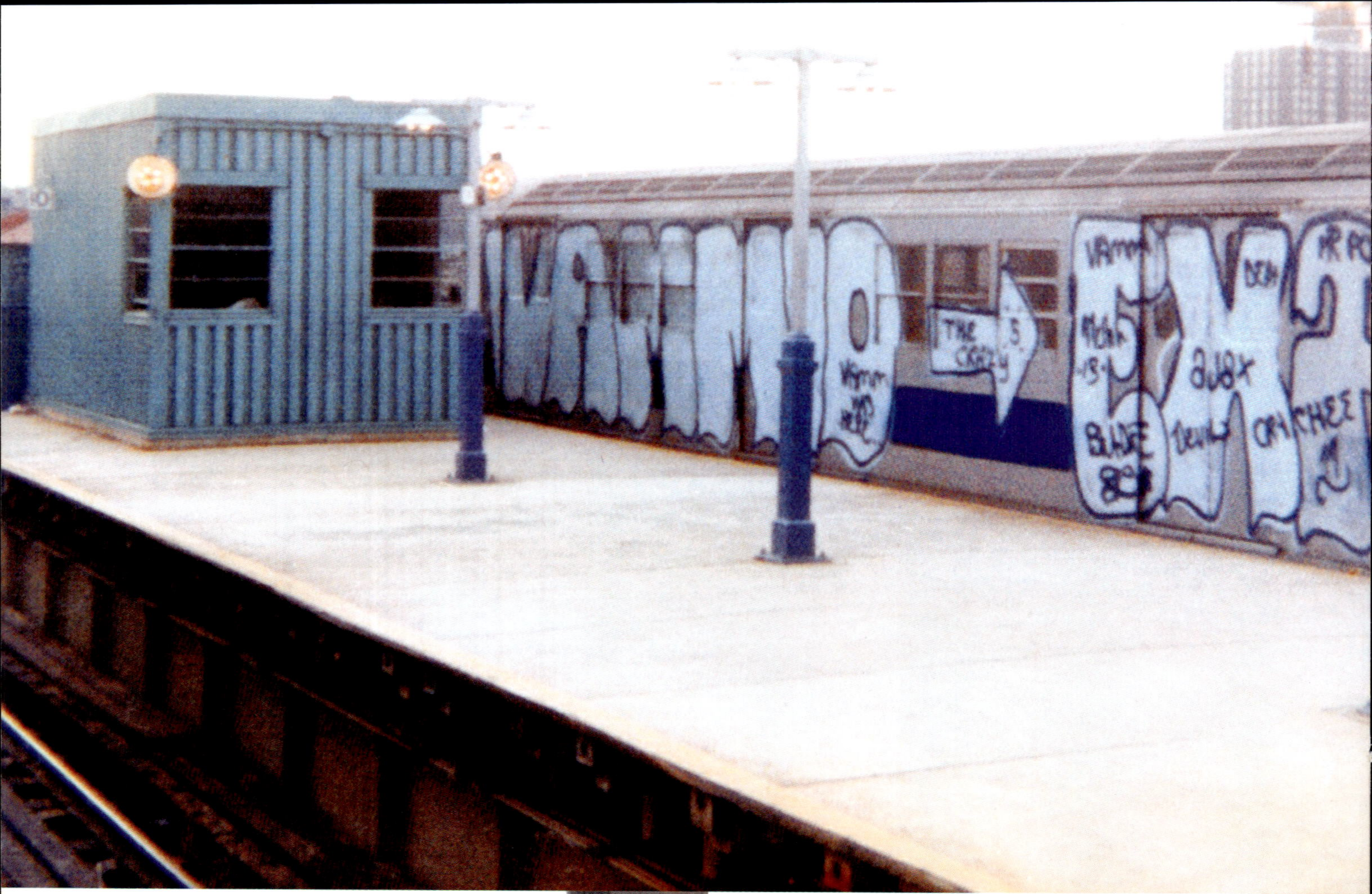
THE CRAZY 5

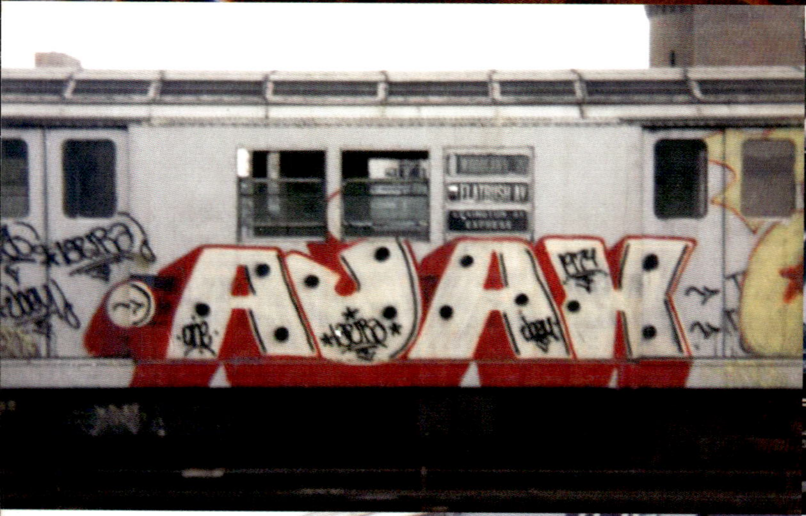

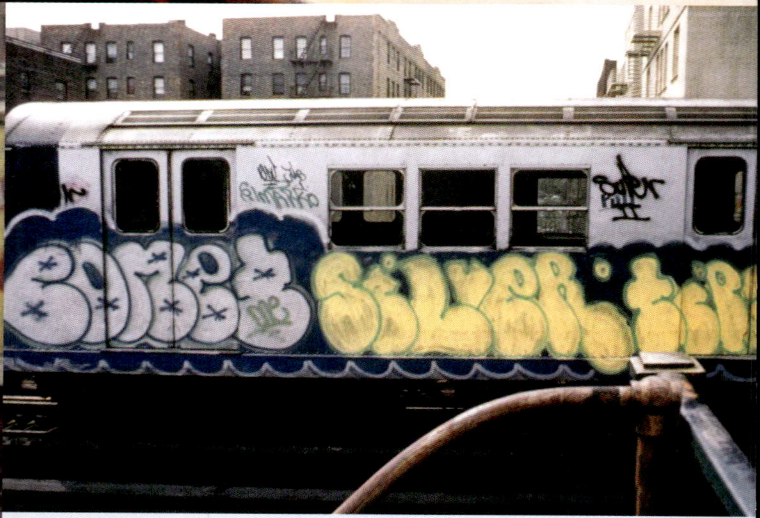

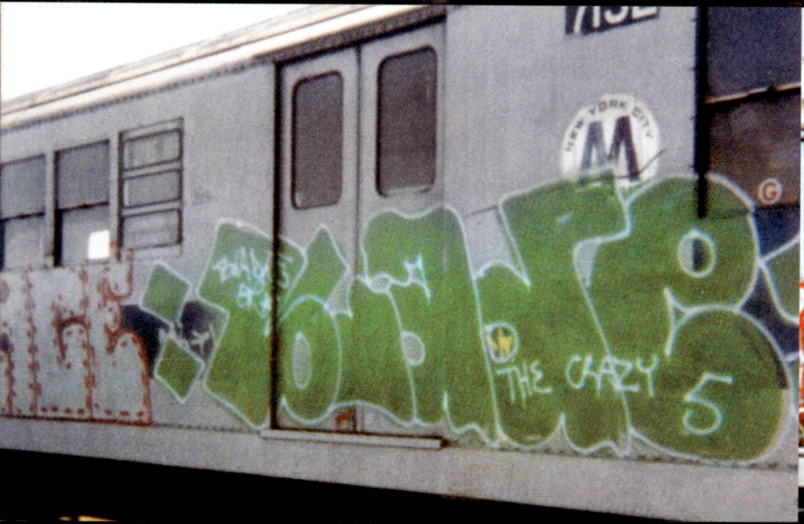
NEW YORK CITY
THE CRAZY 5

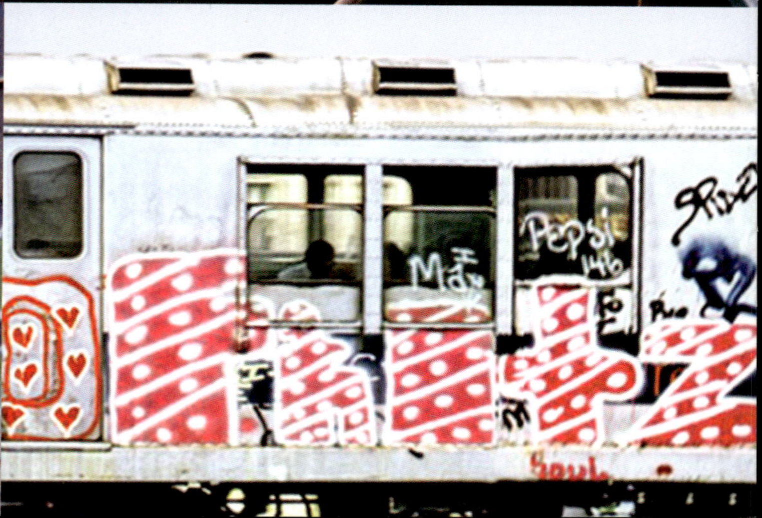

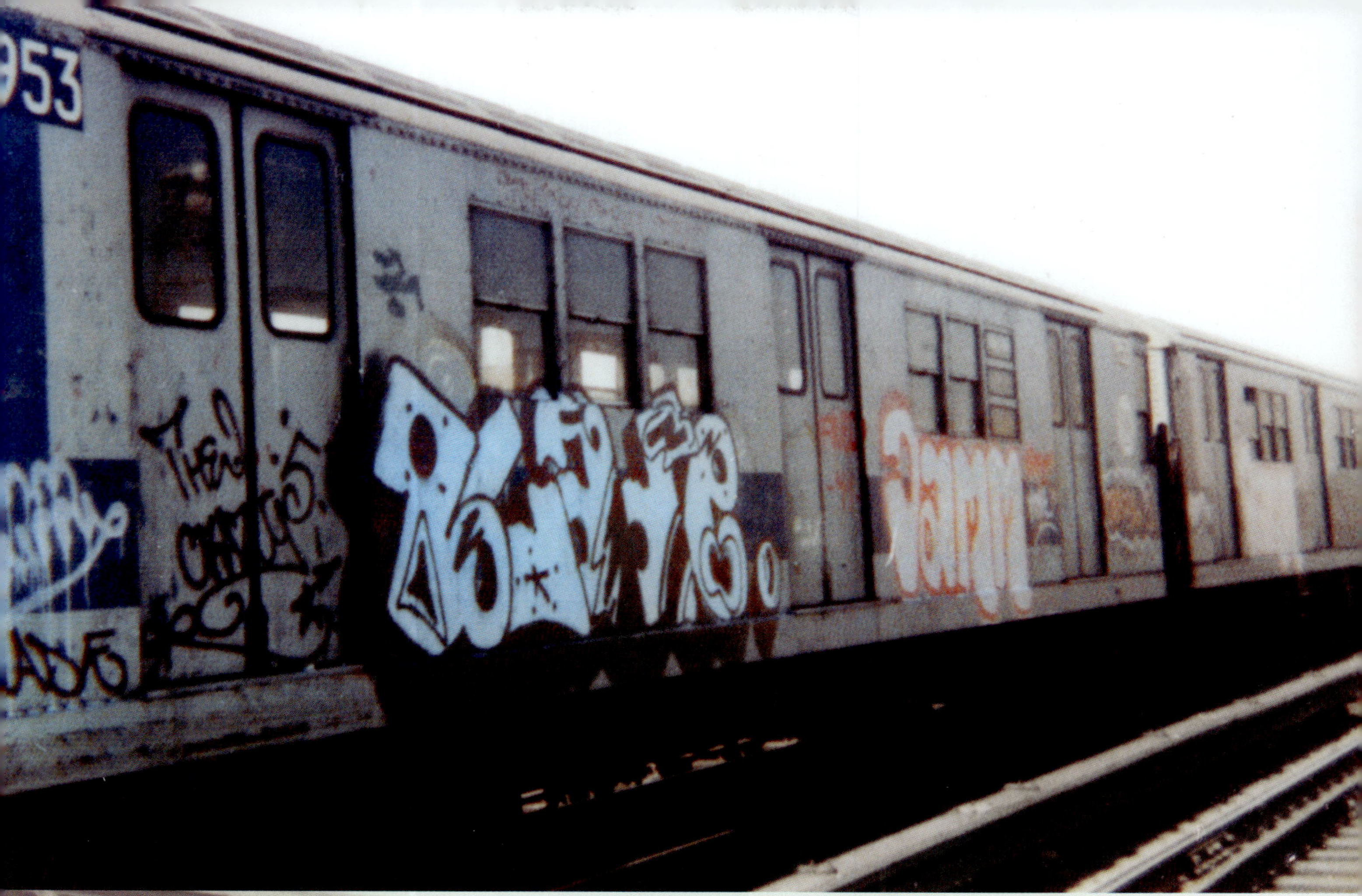
953

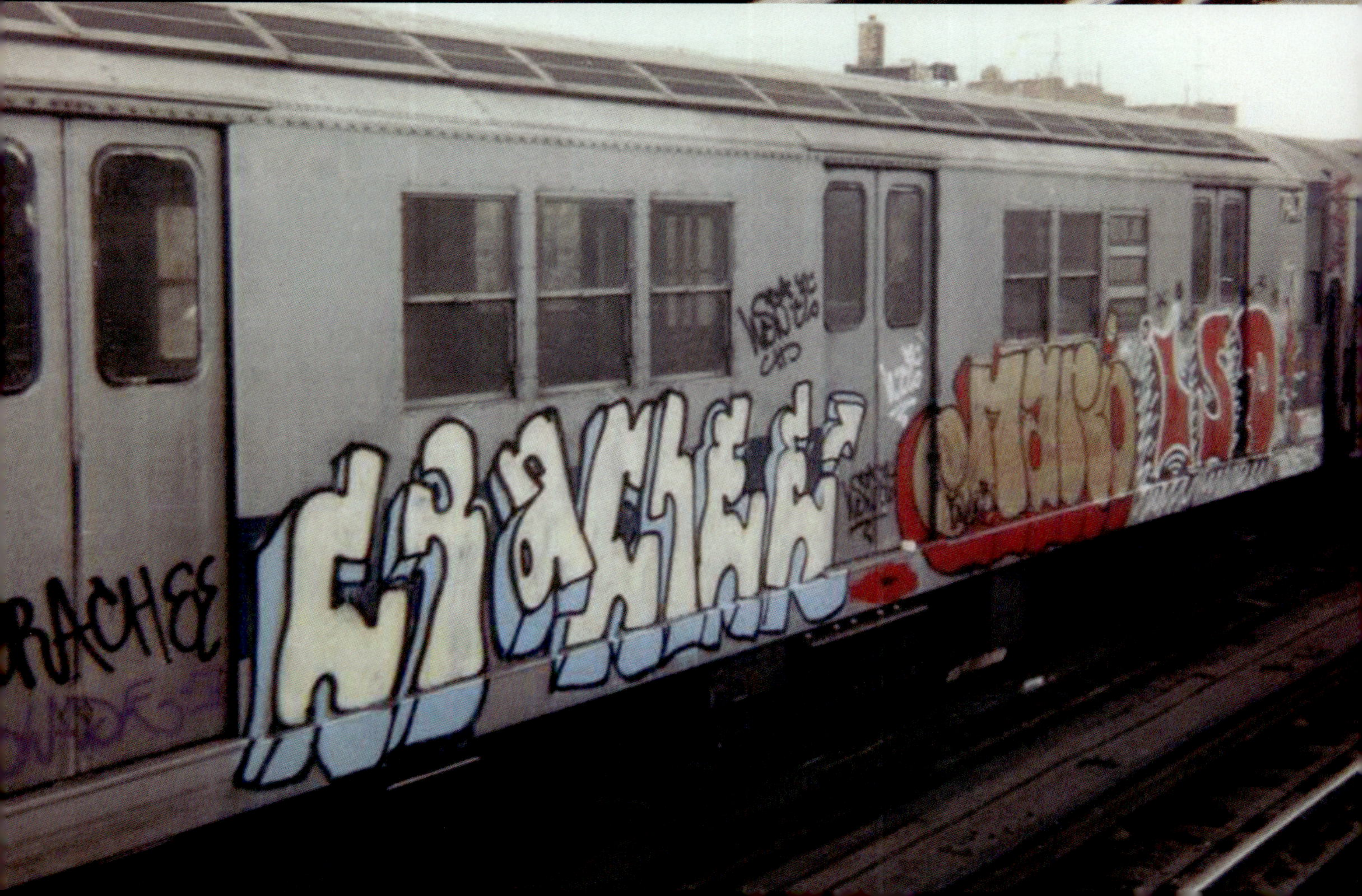

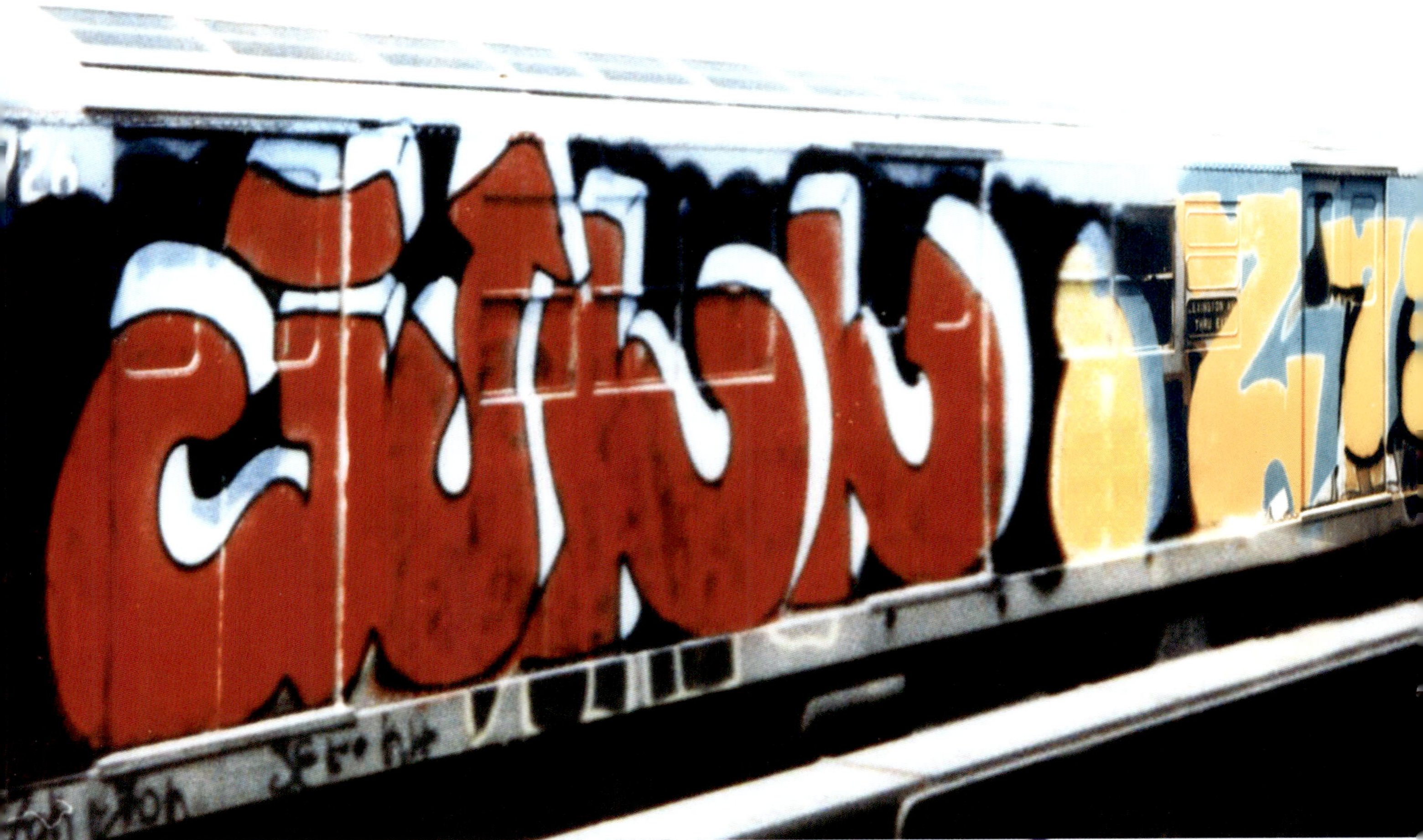

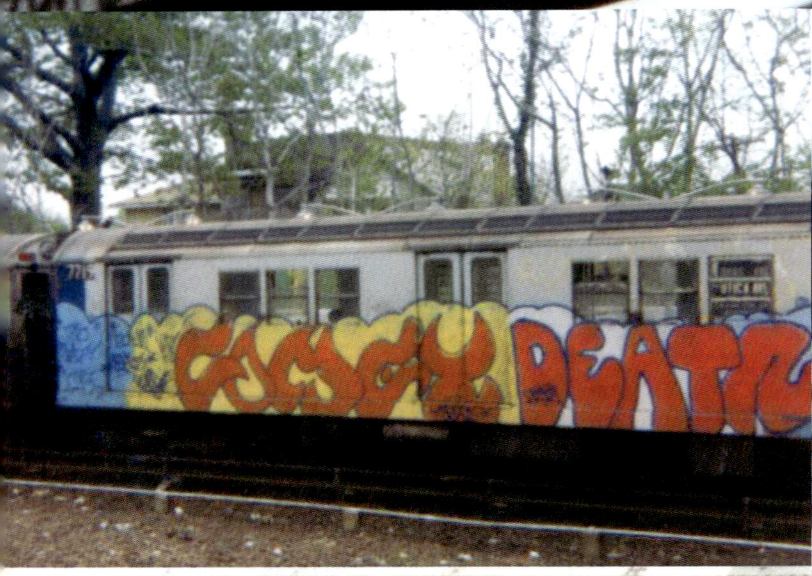

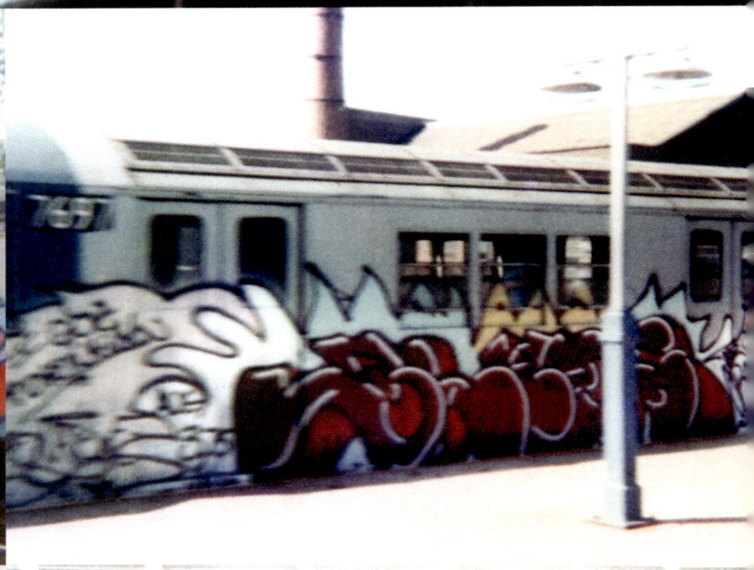

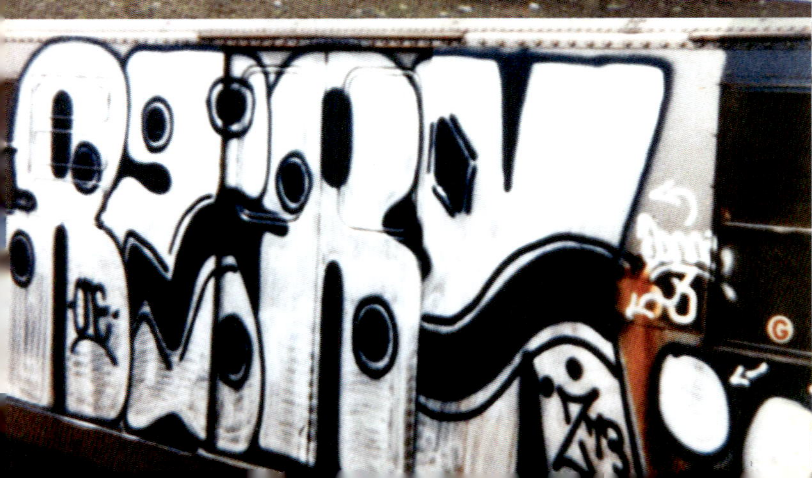

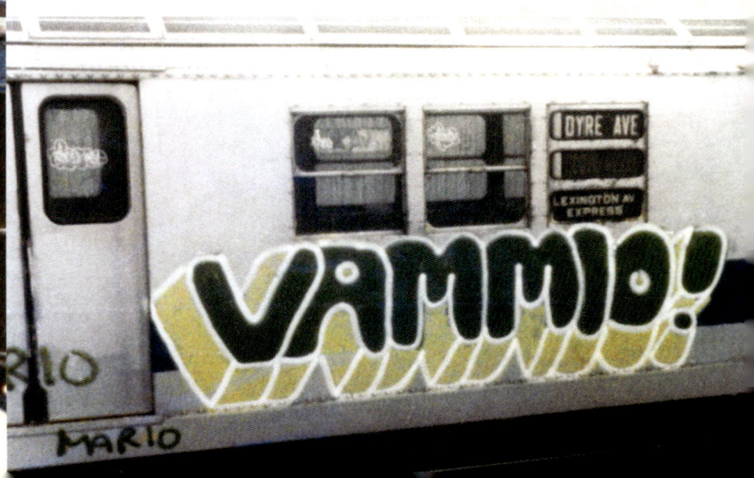
DYRE AVE
LEXINGTON AV
EXPRESS
VAMMIO!
MARIO

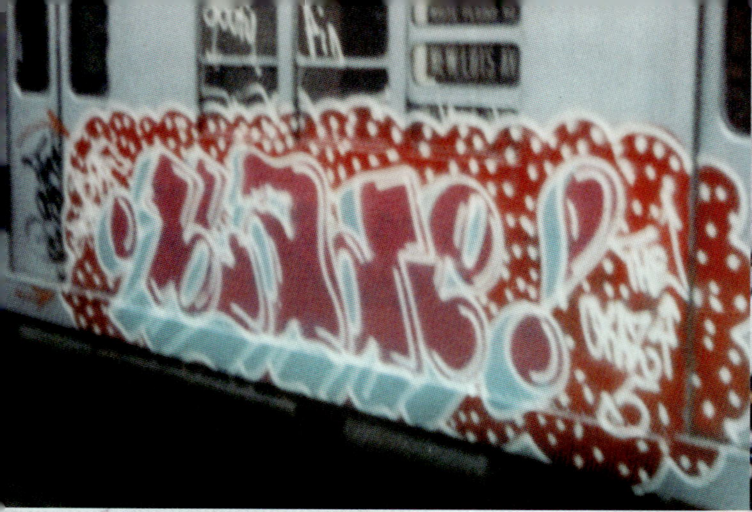

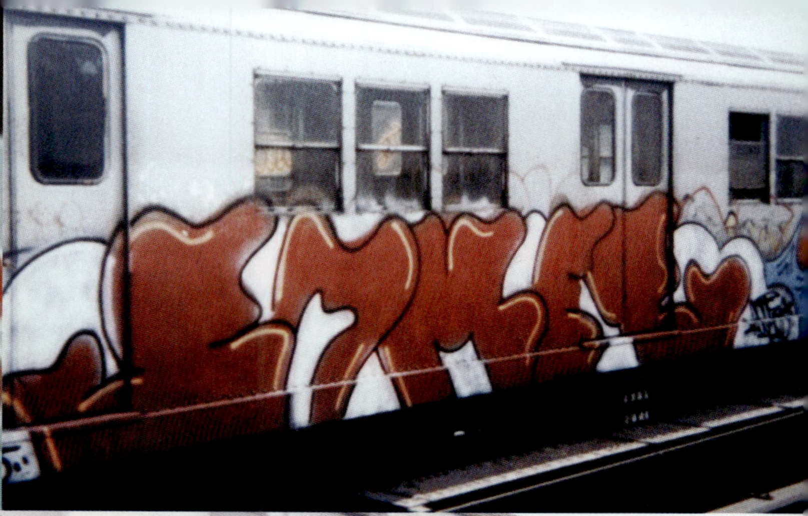

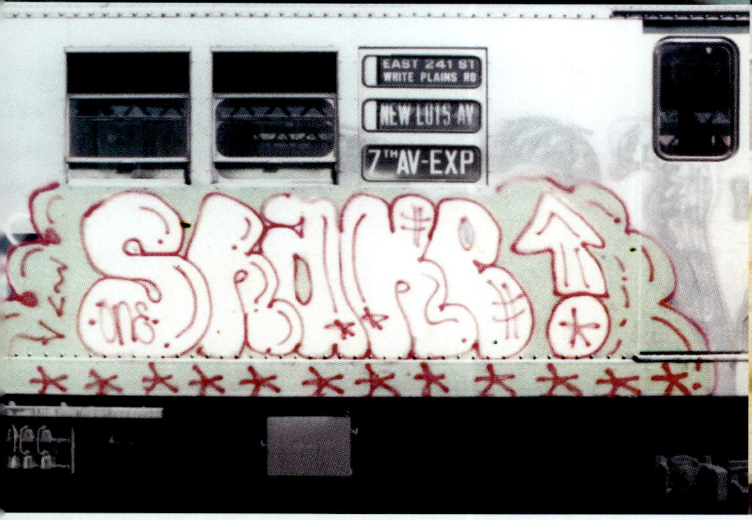
EAST 241 St
WHITE PLAINS RD
NEW LOTS AV
7TH AV-EXP

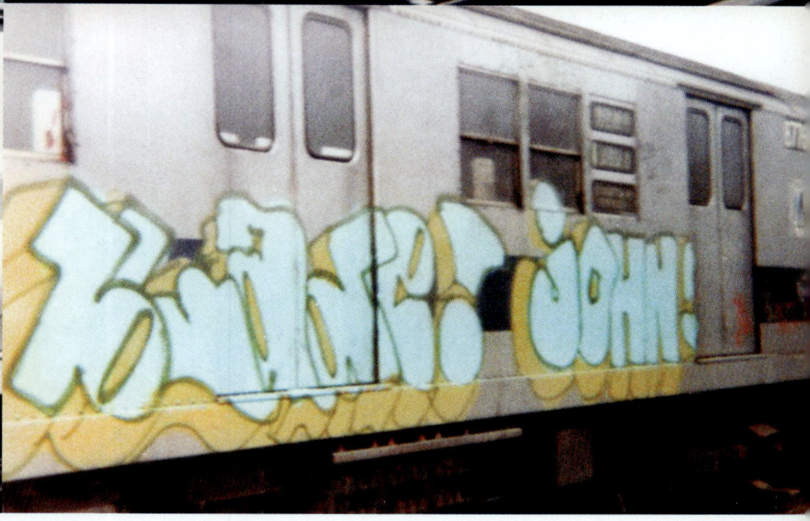

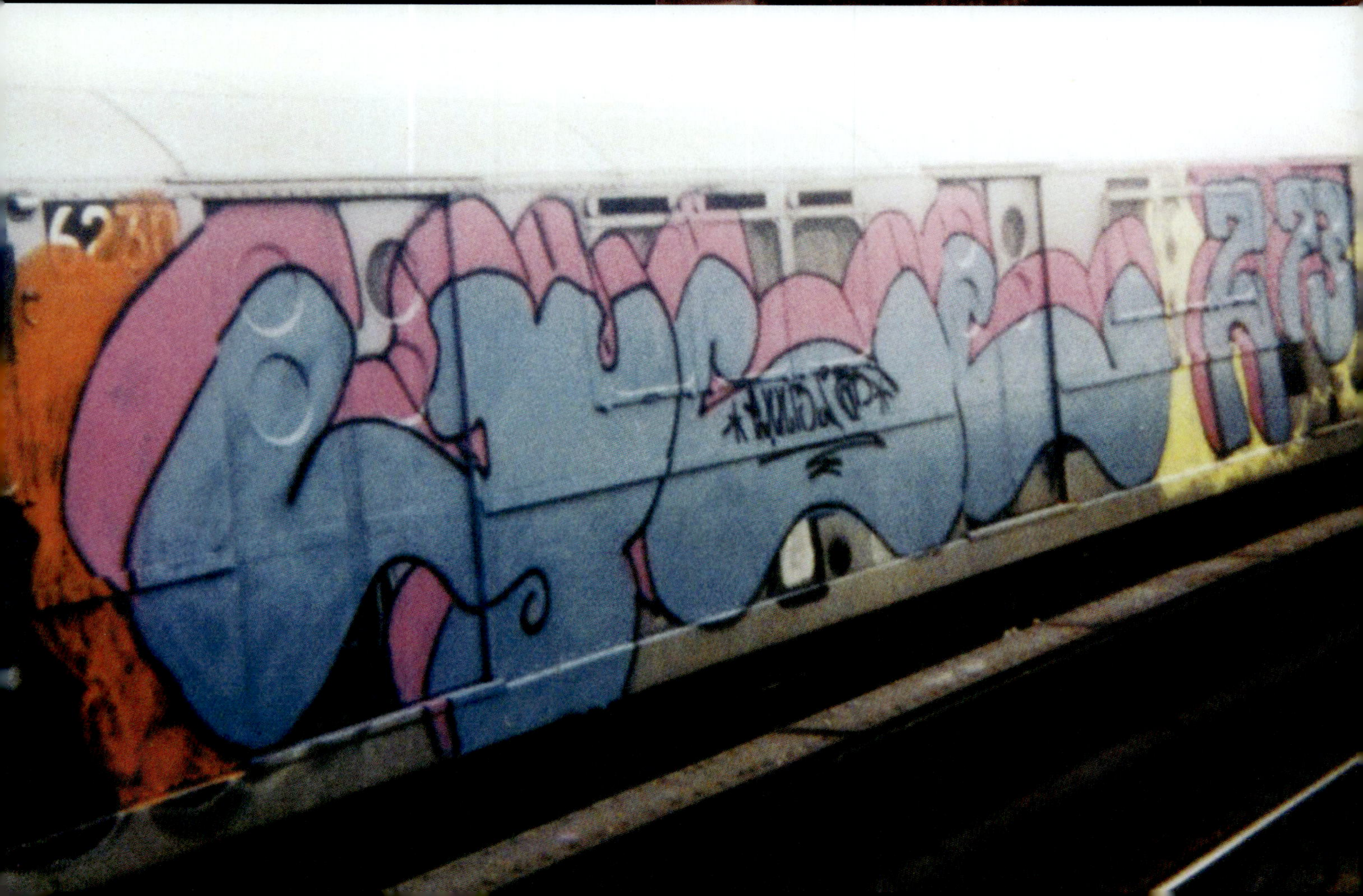

"THERE WERE VERY FEW WHOLE-CAR SPECIALISTS AT THE TIME, WHICH MADE CLIFF 159 MY MAIN COMPETITION."

With WAR and THE EBONY DUKES fading out, there were two crews we were competing with in 1974: WANTED and the INDs. In 1975, the THREE YARD BOYS (3YB) started getting up on all of the lines and so they were added to the mix. The WANTED crew was probably our biggest competition. They had better style than we did and a lineup that included TRACY 168, CHI-CHI133, KING 2, PNUT 2, ALL 2, and SONNY 107, who were all great. They would do three name cars with a unified cloud, which we couldn't compete with. Our solution was to do at least one whole-car for their three name cars. It wasn't that different from what SUPERKOOL 223 had done just two years earlier. But in the end, everyone remembered: bigger is better.

TRACY 168 was a major writer in the movement, and not a big fan of mine. We had different artistic philosophies. For TRACY, painting Yosemite Sam (which he did extremely well) and placing it next to his name was the peak of what a writer could do. It looked great and it was innovative, but I wanted to do my own characters—ones that I created.

I always felt that KING 2 and PNUT 2 had more style than TRACY 168, but it was TRACY 168 that held that crew together. One thing only a few writers knew back then was that TRACY would do pieces for other members of the crew when they weren't there. Also, since he was usually the first one done painting, he had the responsibility of doing the cloud around the names to make the crew look better than it was.The INDs belonged to PHASE 2. Their lineup included RIFF 170, BILLY 167, PEL, and BOT 707. A lot of writers looked up to PHASE 2 and called him a king. He became a graffiti star by hanging out at the bench and giving out styles. He even gave me a style, which I used regularly. We battled the INDs the same way we battled the WANTED crew, with top-to-bottoms, and not just our individual names. We did CRAZY 5 pieces all of the time; some of them top-to-bottoms, which you never saw with the other crews. A problem with the INDs was that they should've worked more like the WANTED crew. RIFF 170 did a lot of great pieces by himself, but they were solo shots and didn't have the power of three names in a color-coordinated cloud. As a fan of the movement, I would've loved to see some PHASE 2, RIFF 170, BILLY 167 cars painted by all of them together.

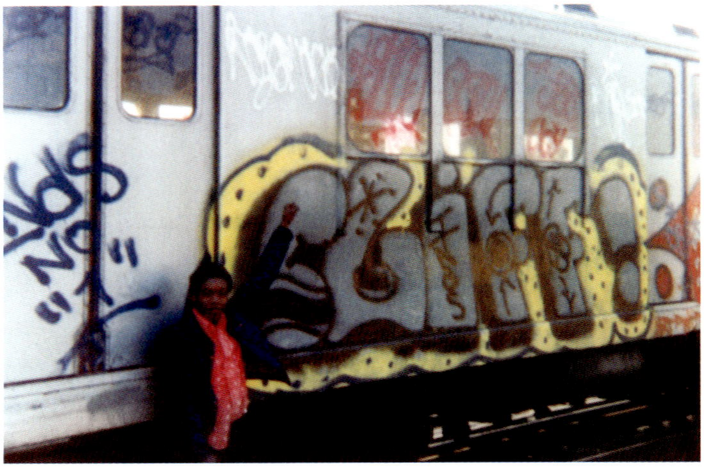

CLIFF 159 had been around forever. He grew up in Harlem right above the 3 yards, a line he owned for years. There's no other way to put it, CLIFF 159 was an improbable king. He hadn't really shown much style until 1974, when TRACY 168 started to teach him some things. Then in 1975, CLIFF 159 started to take off, doing one whole-car after another—and they were good. He surrounded himself with talented writers such as COMET, JESTER, TRACY 168, and PEACE 108, but his main writing partner was IN. IN was the inventor of the throw-up, a two-letter piece done in under a minute. IN was so fast that he painted with both hands. But they were ugly.

This page: CLIFF poses in front of his piece. 1974.
Opposite page: CLIFF paints Beetle Bailey. 1974. Photo ©Keith Baugh.

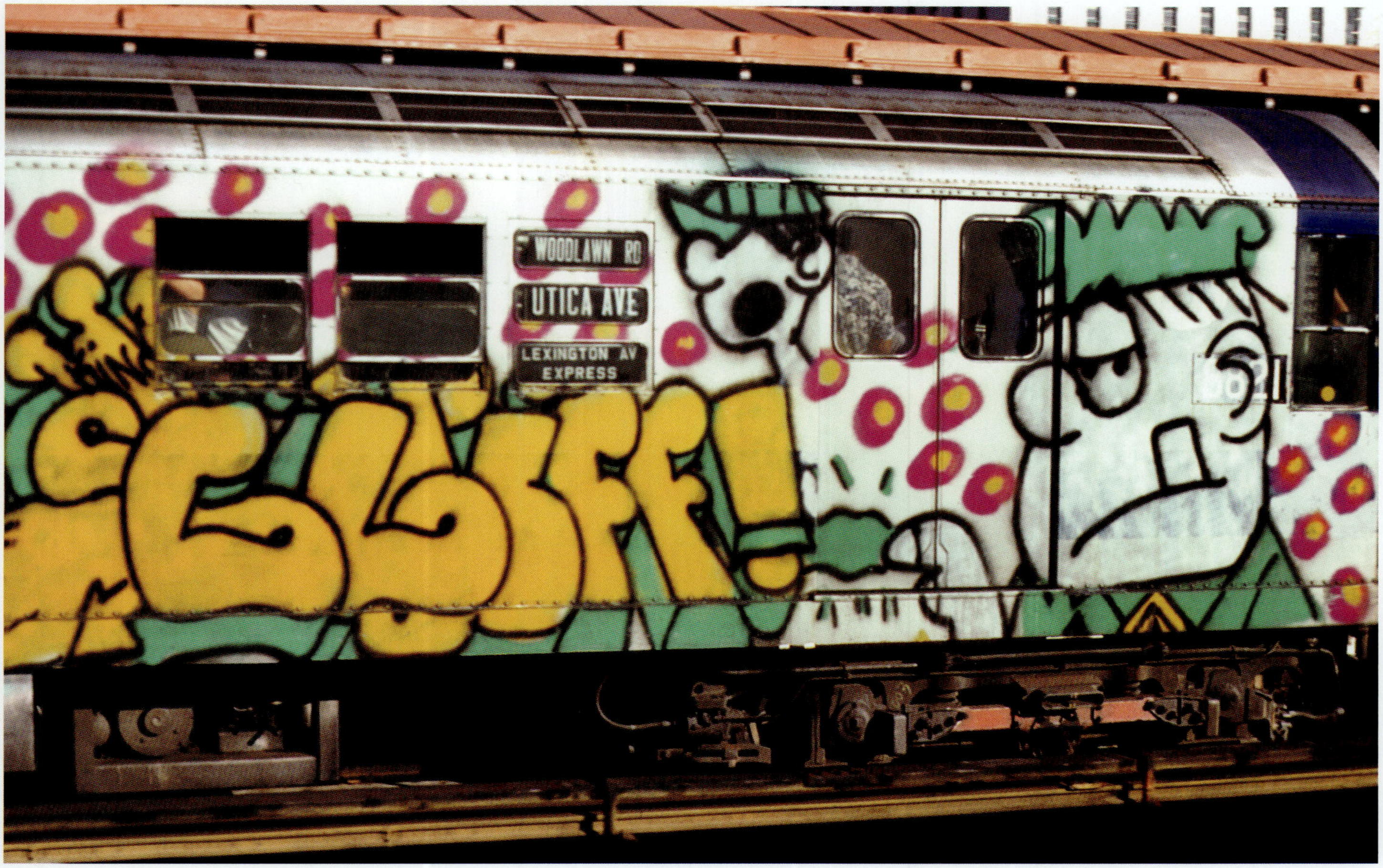

IN came up to see us at Parkside. He tried to be down with THE CRAZY 5, but we said no. That's when he took on the new name of KILL 3 and started to do some style pieces. I did a BLADE THE CRAZY 5, end to end, that took up 95% of the subway car. It took a lot of time and a lot of paint. At the very tip of it, IN had an ugly throw-up, which I went over. He had the balls to cross me out for it. I told him, "You've got these things everywhere that took less than a minute to do, and we're trying to do whole-cars. Are you kidding me?" He wanted respect for doing his throw-up with both hands—they were that fast and that sloppy. It didn't work that way.

CLIFF 159 was the leader of 3YB (THREE YARD BOYS). They were big in 1975, because CLIFF 159 was going to other boroughs and putting down writers he barely knew. A lot of times, he was also getting paint from them. Even though they got up a lot more, you didn't know half the names. THE CRAZY 5 consisted of fifteen or twenty people that hung out together daily at the same spot, smoking weed and shooting hoops. Most of us had known each other since childhood, although we did put in LSD OM, which was odd because he was from the Bronx. A lot of the WANTED crew guys came through to hang out and talk graffiti. I was surprised when PNUT 2 asked to be in THE CRAZY 5. He was a great writer, but he was also in WANTED. Since those were his boys, so we said no. You really had to hang with us to be in THE CRAZY 5.

CLIFF 159 was definitely up in 1974 and 1975, but I'm sure I had more pieces than he did. There were very few whole-car specialists at the time, which made CLIFF 159 my main competition. His influence came directly from TRACY 168, whose influence came directly from comic books, which made me critical of his work, even though it probably helped him in the long run. His work was simple to figure out: Dick Tracy on the side of a train, Beetle Bailey on the side of a train. Kids loved it; I didn't. I felt the works weren't turned into anything new; he was just copying what he saw. He did have a few bright moments though. His Silver Surfer car was a classic. It looked like he was flying right off the car. To me, there was a concept behind this particular painting. His painting of The Thing was nicely animated, which was CLIFF 159 at his best. He also competed with COMET in doing a lot of throw-ups, and the two of them wrote together sometimes.

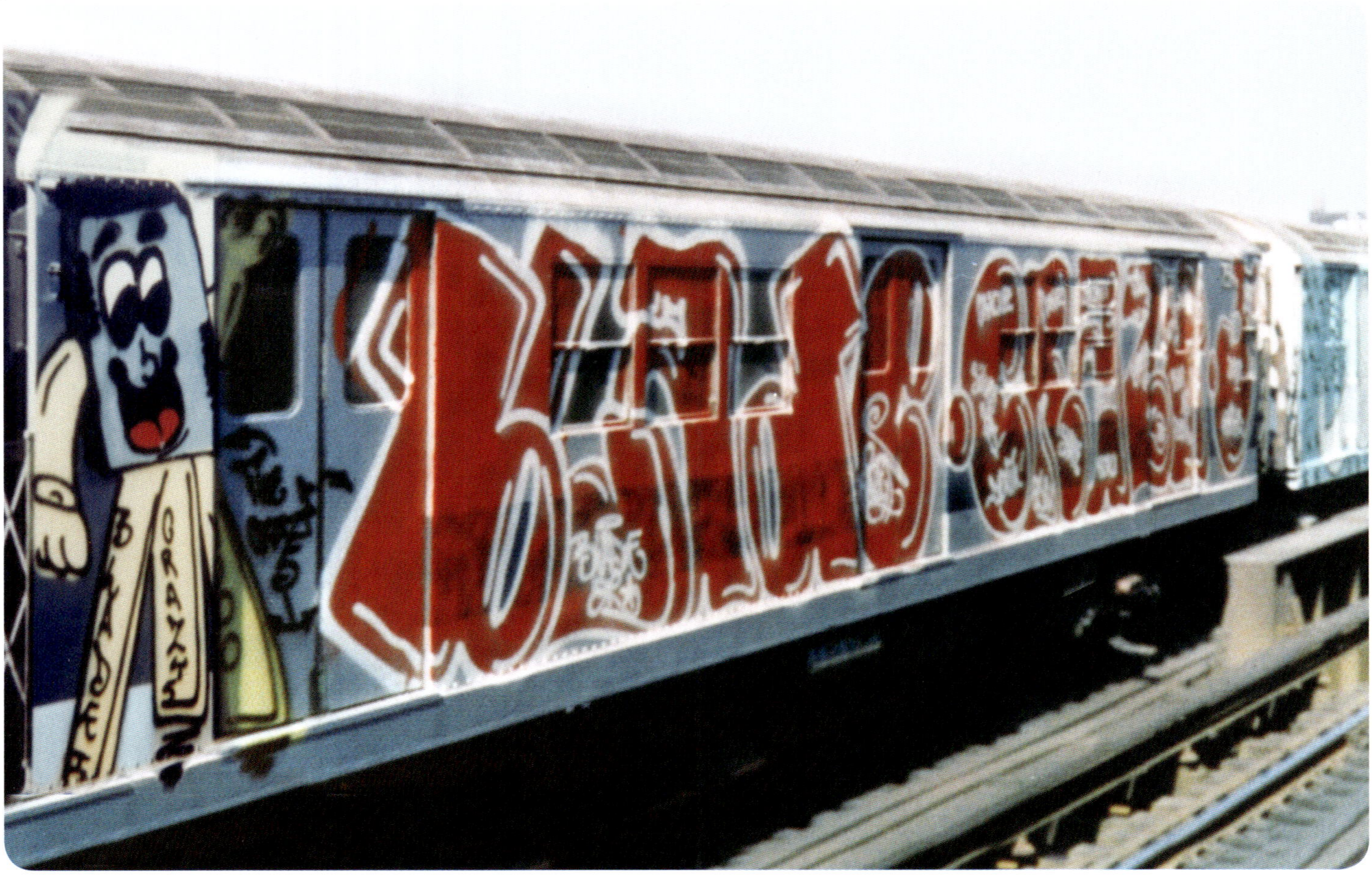

I did three character pieces in 1974, which preceded CLIFF 159's whole-cars. The first was done from a sketch I had drawn in art class of an easel with a head; there was a long CRAZY 5 piece next to it in red paint. If you look at it today, it seems primitive, and certainly not something to be proud of, but in 1974, very few characters had been drawn on trains.

The other guys loved it, and so I was inspired to do more. In November 1974, I painted a snowman; I called it my Merry Christmas piece. This one was a lot better. I remember it was a beautiful night to paint, nice and quiet with no one else at the lay-up. The sketch I did for it placed it nicely on the car and integrated well with the BLADE piece. I was so proud of the Christmas car that I tried hard to think of something to follow it up with. That December I painted an octopus with the letters of my name in its tentacles on the train. I was really stoned, so I spelled my name with two D's. I was just beginning to use the train as a canvas at that time.

While CLIFF 159 and I were battling each other with whole-cars, he was emerging as king of the 1 and 3 lines and I was already king of the 2s and 5s. I was fine with CLIFF 159 owning the 1 line. As LEE once said, "I'd never paint on the 1 trains. They're too dirty." He was right. The early graffiti stars were from the 1 line in Manhattan: TAKI 183, JUNIOR 161 and CAY 161, SNAKE 1 and STITCH 1, PIPER 1 and JACE 2, and MOSES 147. They all hit the 1 line so hard that we knew their names in the Bronx. In 1971 and 1972, being a king of Broadway meant something. But after those guys faded out, the movement took hold in the Bronx, which is where piecing really took off. By the mid-1970s, the 1 line was mostly for throw-ups. In a strange twist of fate, I found myself working near the 1 tunnel at 137th Street and Broadway on weekends. On my lunch break I would go in there and paint one or two trains. I didn't want the 1 line trains. I was looking for cars transferred over from the 7 line, which had long horizontal windows. Those were the ones I hit. I never wanted to make that long trip back to the 7 yard.

This page: BLADE's first concept car with a character. 1974.
Opposite page: Top: BLADE brings in December! 1974.
Bottom: BLADE's octopus smoking weed car.
BLADE was so stoned when he painted it he painted two D's. 1974.

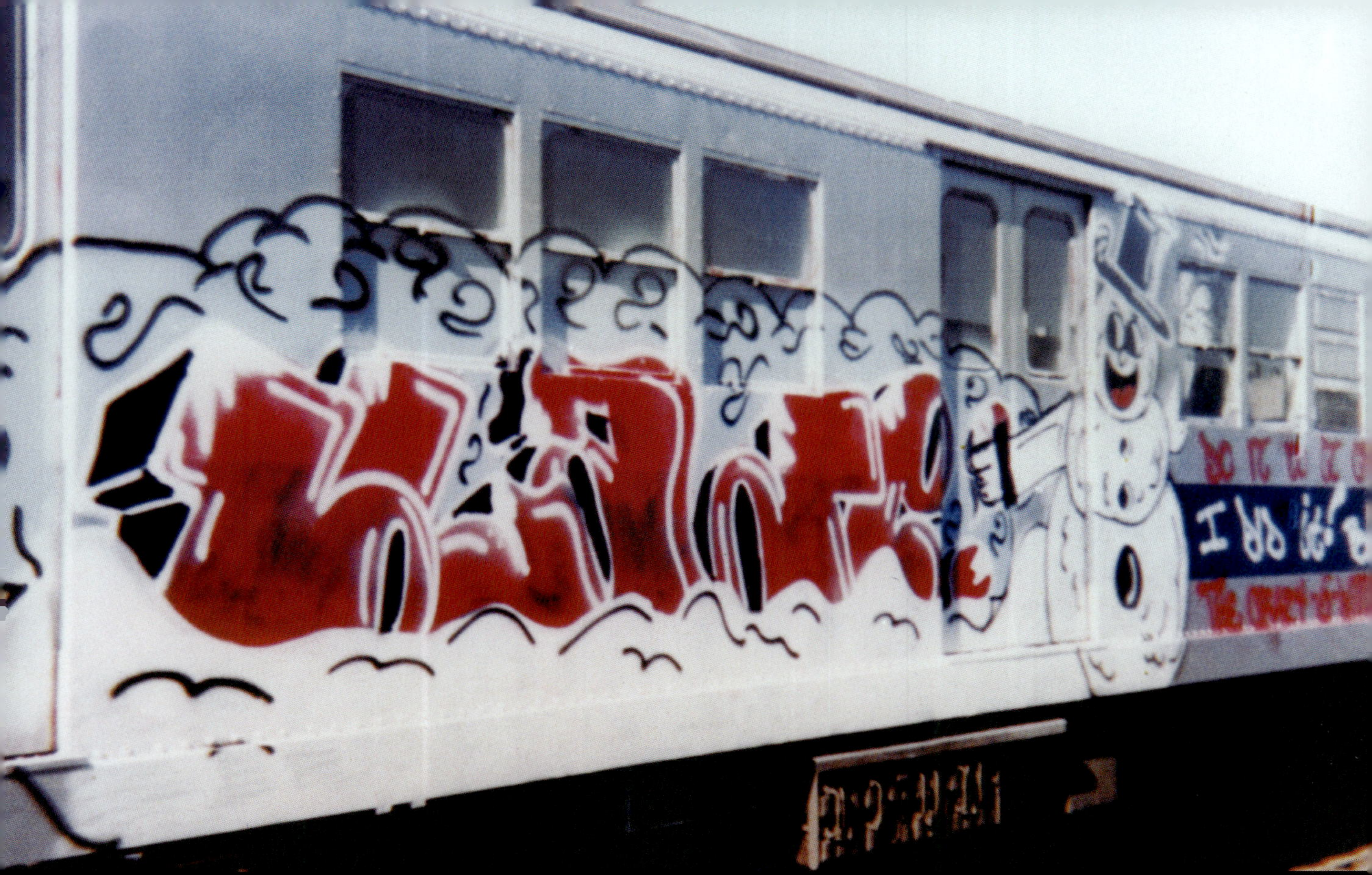

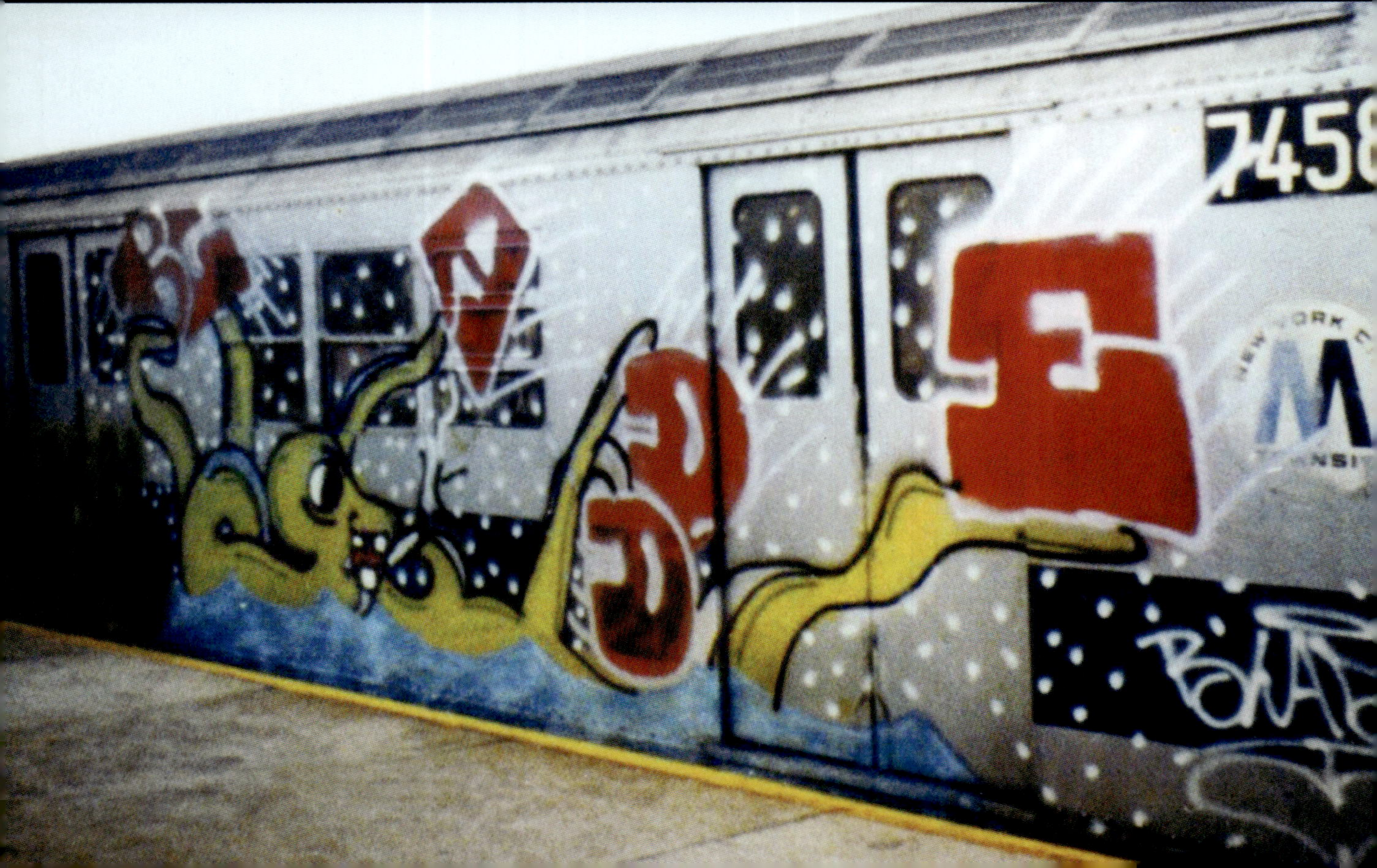
7458

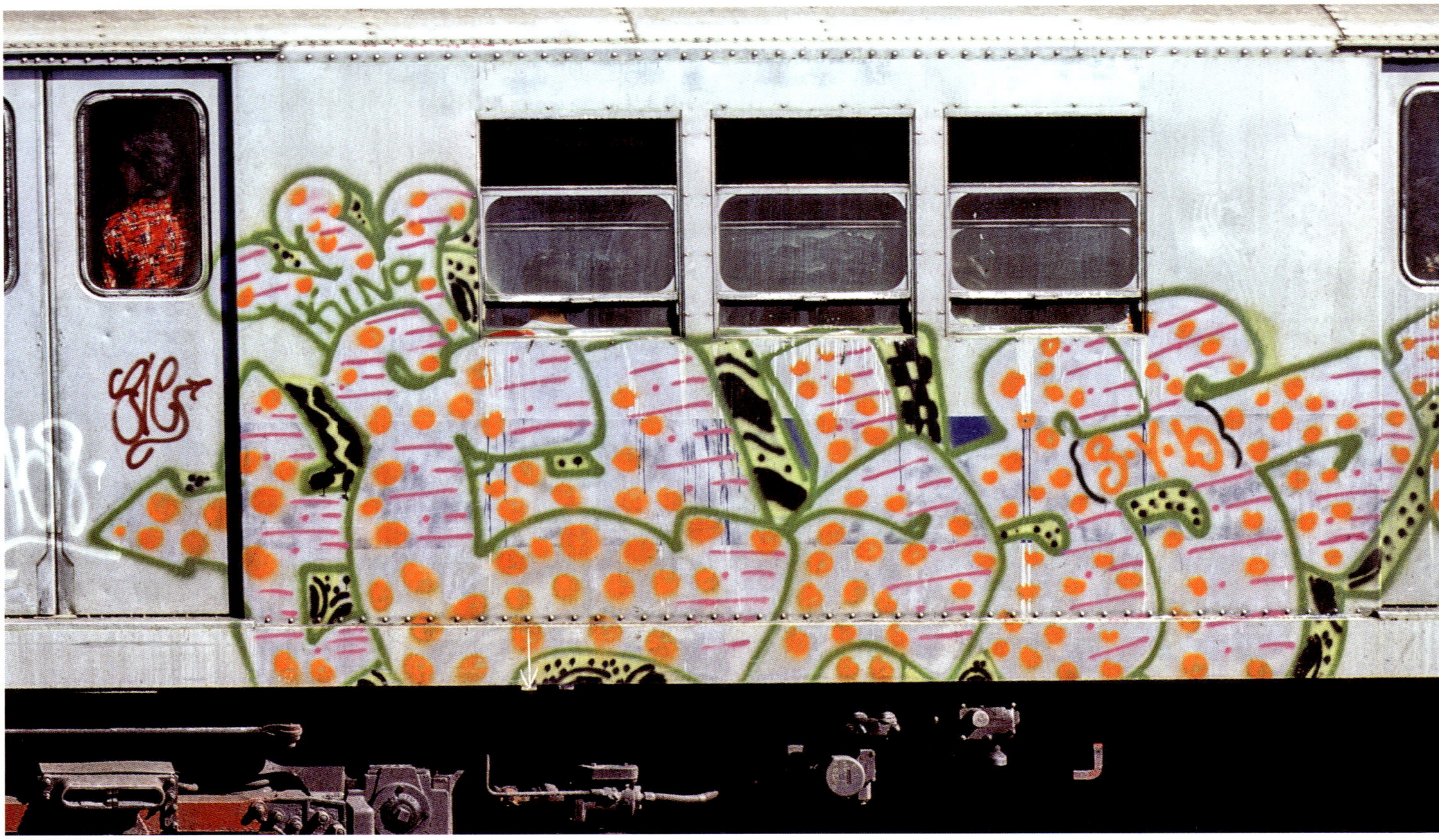

"FOR THE RECORD, I CONSIDER MYSELF TO BE ONE OF THE FASTEST WRITERS OUT THERE."

CLIFF 159 and I painted together a few times. The most memorable one was when we painted our names as kings. CLIFF 159 stopped by Parkside to hang out in the summer of 1975 and we talked about doing a car together. We left the playground, went off to rack some paint, and made plans to meet at 1:00am at the Baychester lay-up, which put CLIFF 159 in my territory. One of the problems with meeting other writers late at night was that you never knew if they were going to show up. In fact, you never even knew if the train was going to be there.

When I got to Baychester, CLIFF 159 had already climbed the hill and he was looking for the hole in the fence. This gave me a chance to study him for a moment. CLIFF 159 looked old. Even though we were the same age, it looked as though his life was going by faster than mine. In my life, you robbed hardware stores for paint to do pieces with. CLIFF 159 was well beyond that, and he was getting busted constantly. That night he wore his famous denim jacket with the studs on the back, which looked like he lived in it—and he probably did. CLIFF 159 certainly wasn't the first writer to sleep in train stations. I climbed up the hill and we said our hellos.

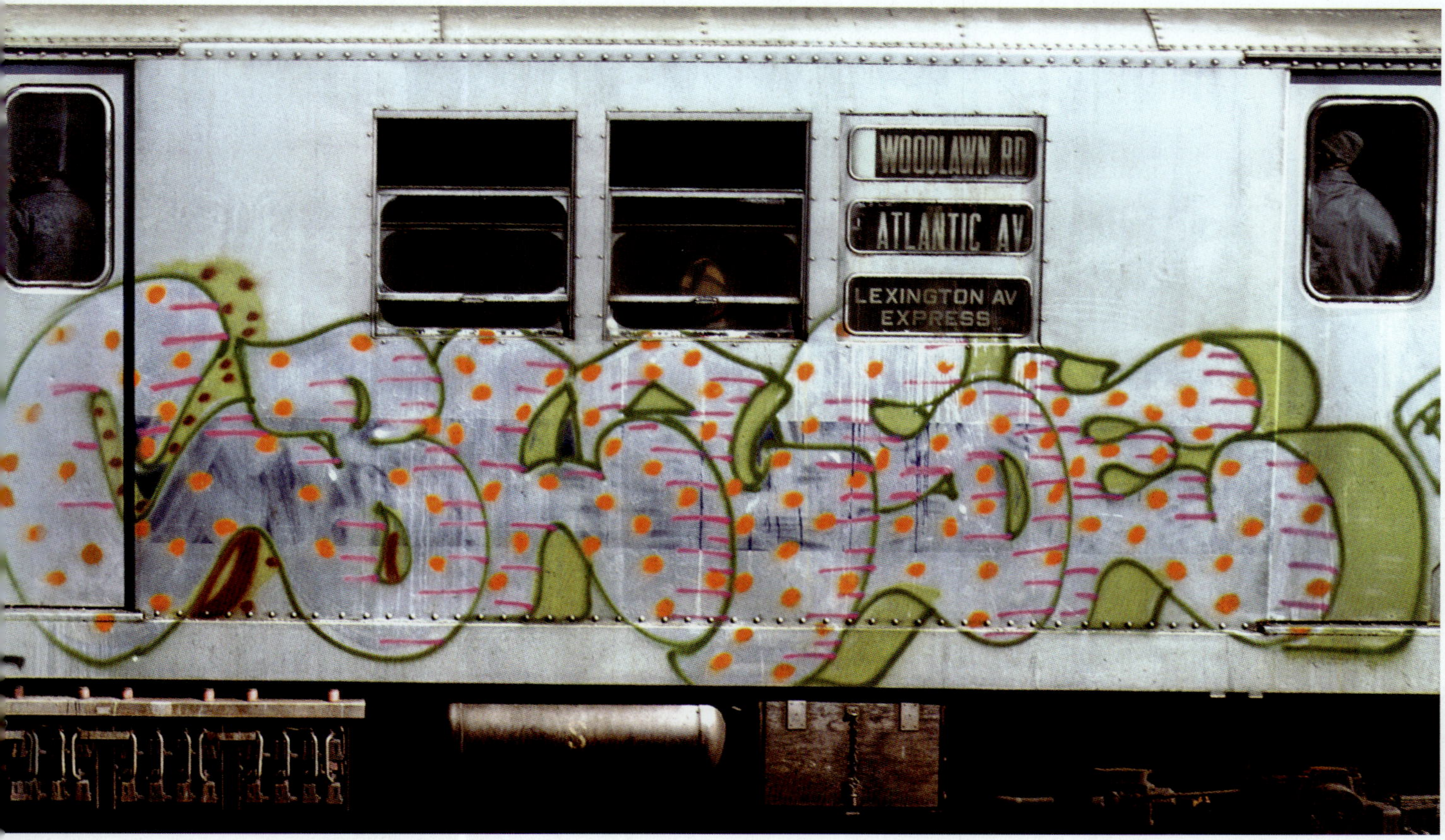

We settled on a car in the middle lane. The car had some ugly throw-ups on it; I was happy to be going over them. CLIFF 159 started his piece almost immediately, sketching in his outline with a can of silver. By the time I was done with my outline, CLIFF 159 was finished with his fill-in. While painting, he was intense; I don't recall him saying a word. I was told that TRACY 168 painted the same way: attack the train, get the piece done, and get the hell out of there. I liked the fact that both writers were so certain of their line. For the record, I consider myself to be one of the fastest writers out there.

CLIFF 159 finished his piece and started to walk toward me. I still had to do the crown on my piece, the most important element of the painting—one for each of the two kings painting together. As we started talking, he looked at my sketch and asked if there was anything he could do. There really wasn't, since I just had a few things left. He turned and looked down the hill of the lay-up, seeming a lot more relaxed now that his piece was done. As he looked over the fence, I could hear a quick humming sound that meant only one thing: in a few seconds the train would be active and the lights would come on. Why? Who knew? These things happened, and when they did, it they usually meant a conductor or motorman was heading our way. CLIFF 159 looked at me hard. This was my playground and he expected me to make the right call. Although I wanted to finish the crown, it was time to bail. We left the few scraps of paint behind, climbed through the hole, and took off into the night. That was the last time we painted together. CLIFF 159 was done painting by the end of 1976.

The piece with CLIFF 159 was done in the summer of 1975, a time when some of THE CRAZY 5 was slowing down. VAMM was my partner, but now he was painting only once a month. When the summer came around, I was left wondering if THE CRAZY 5 was over.

This spread: CLIFF and BLADE's unfinished piece missing part of the outline and a crown. 1975. Photo ©Keith Baugh.

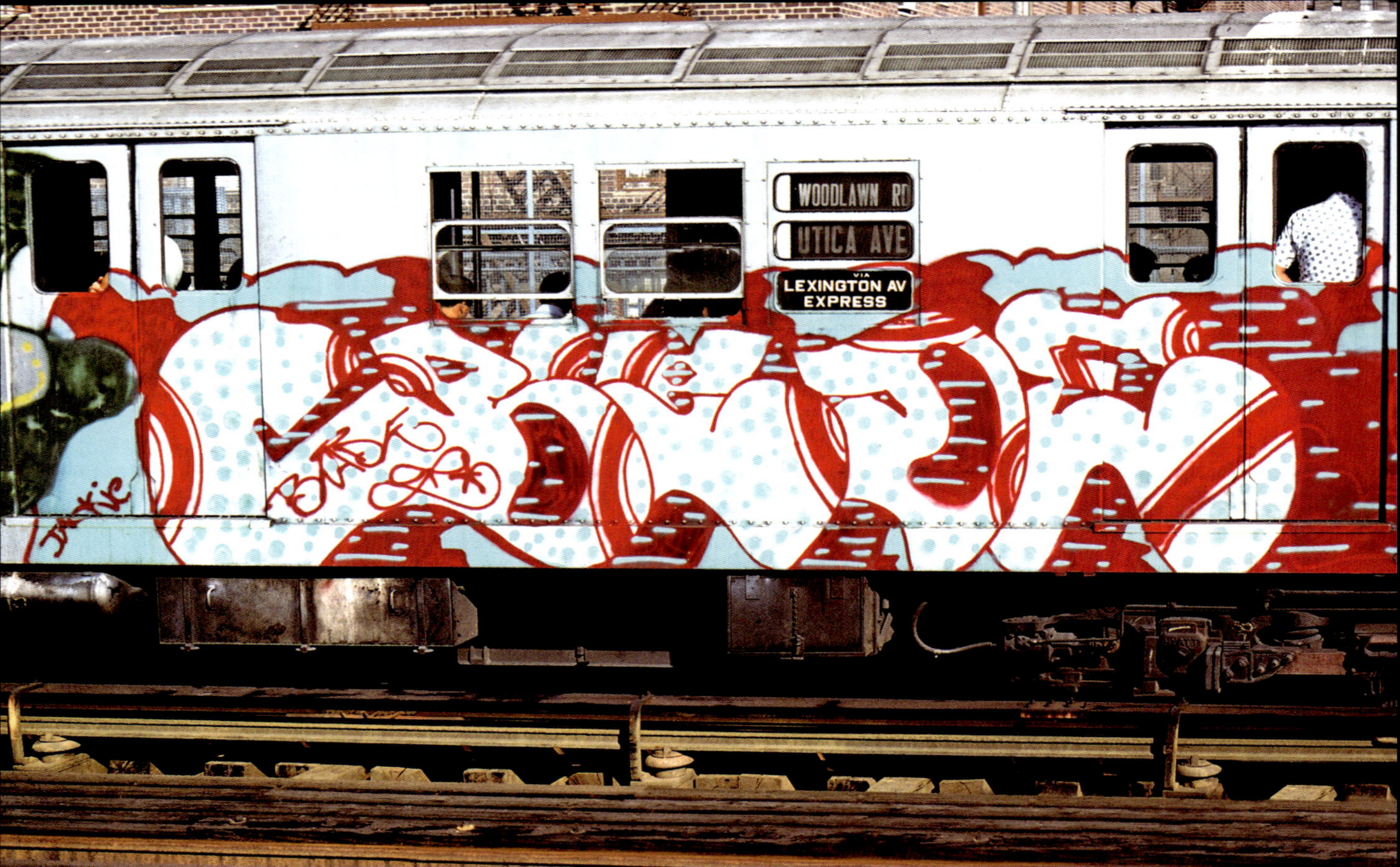
WOODLAWN RD
UTICA AVE
VIA
LEXINGTON AV
EXPRESS

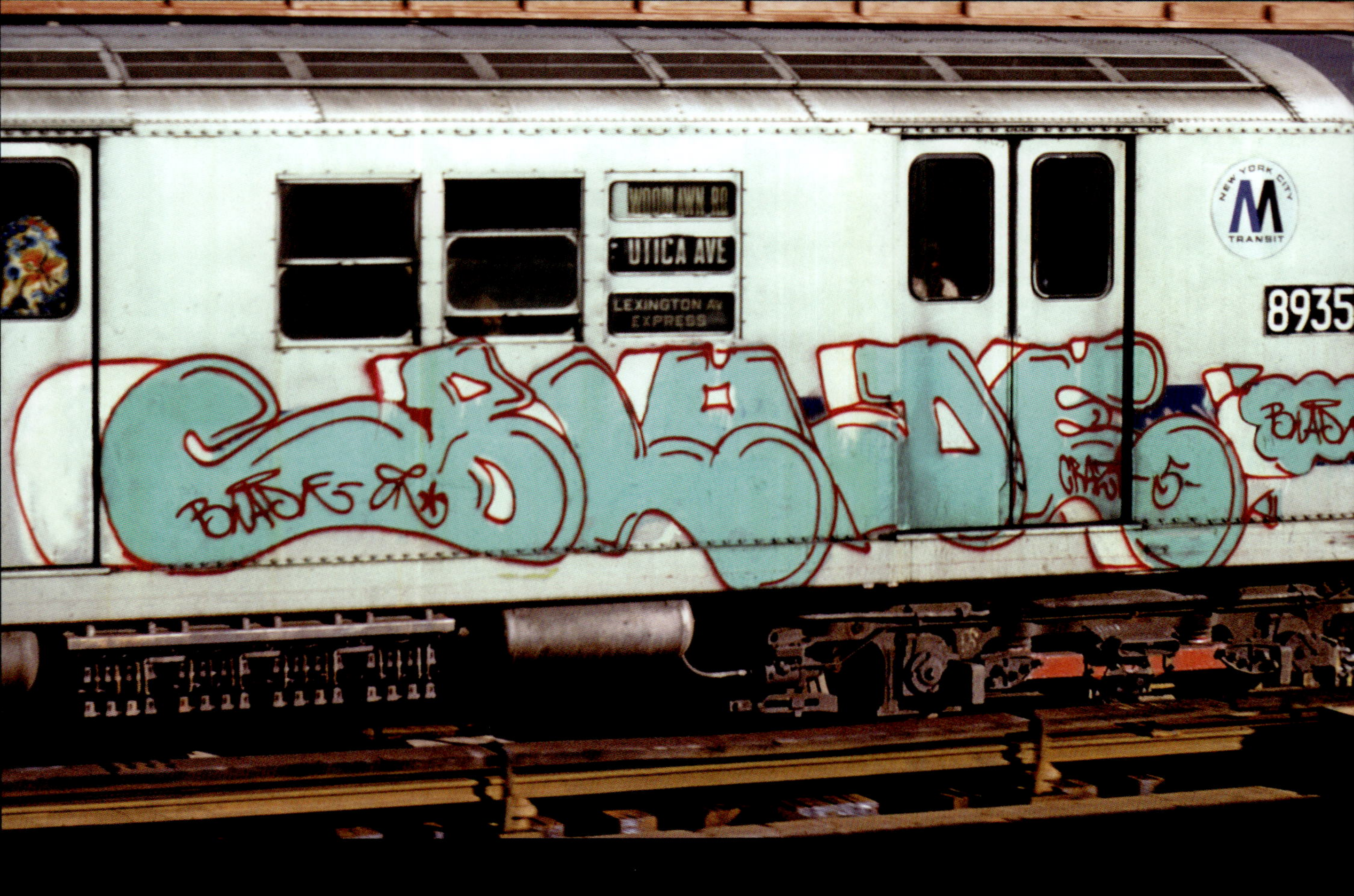
WOODLAWN RD
UTICA AVE
LEXINGTON Av
EXPRESS
NEW YORK CITY
M
TRANSIT
8935

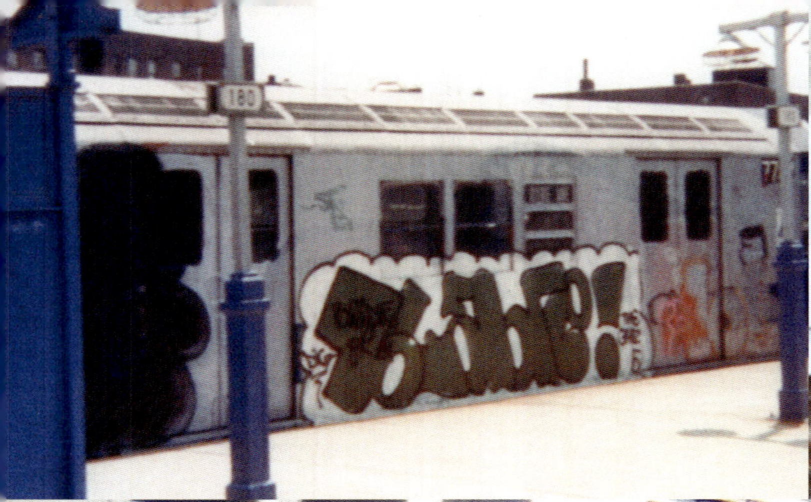
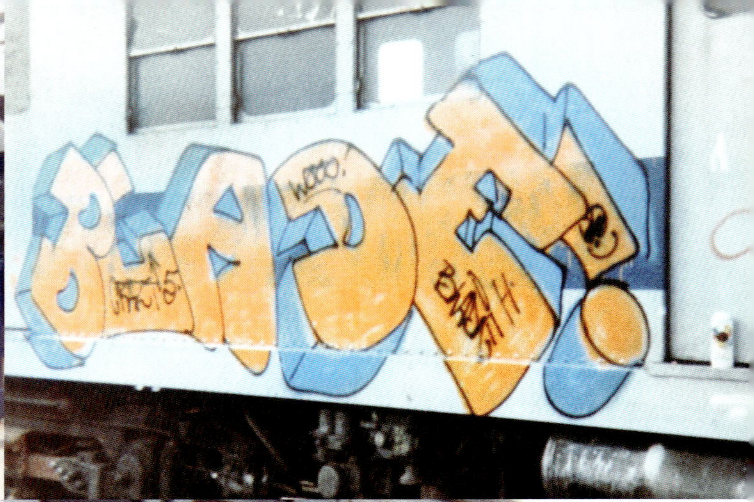
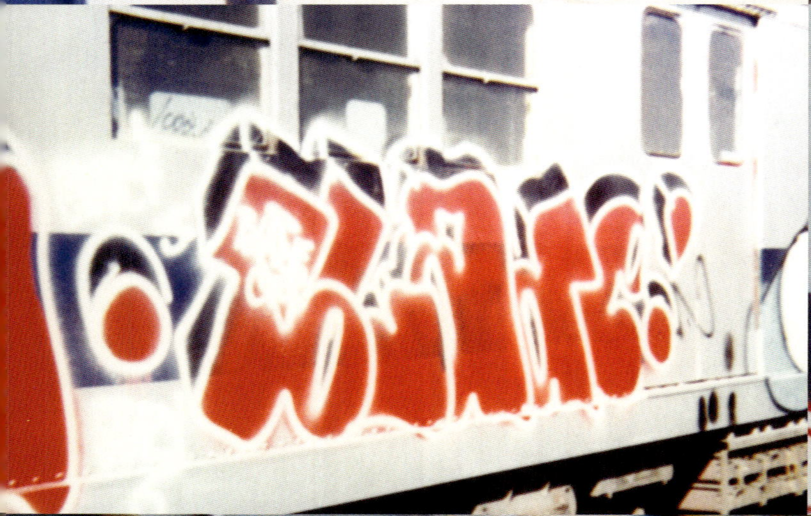
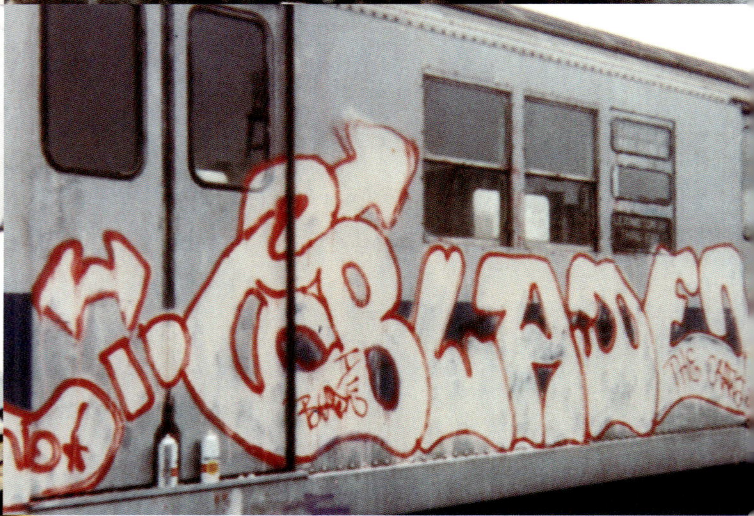
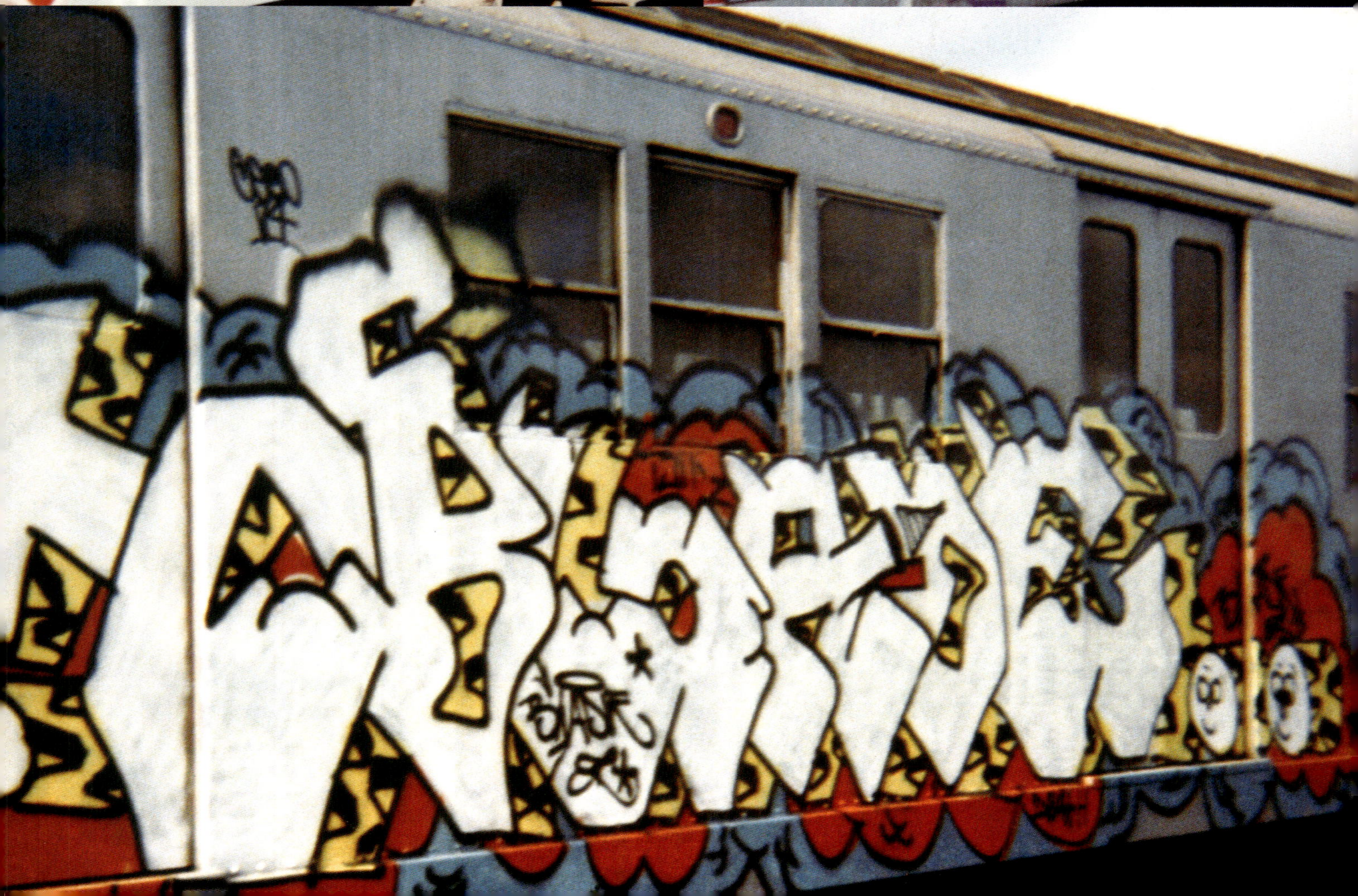

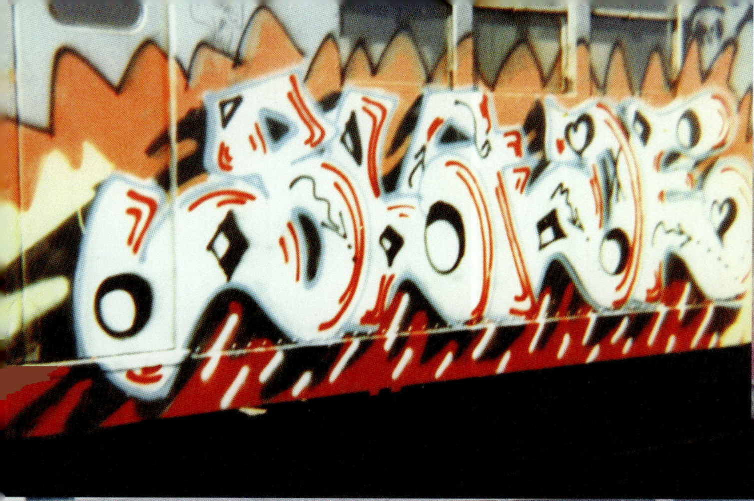

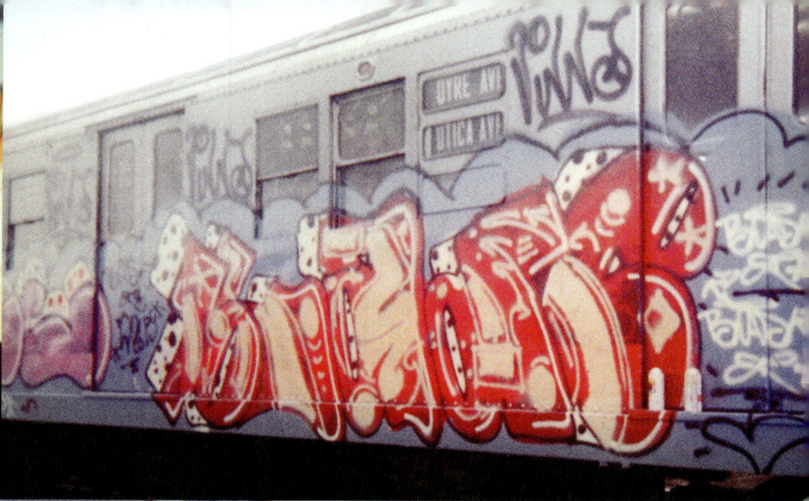
DYRE AV
UTICA AV

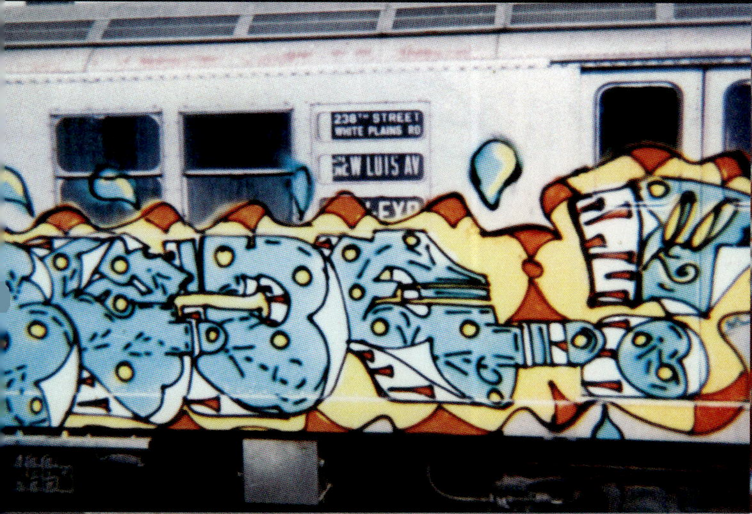
238TH STREET
WHITE PLAINS RD

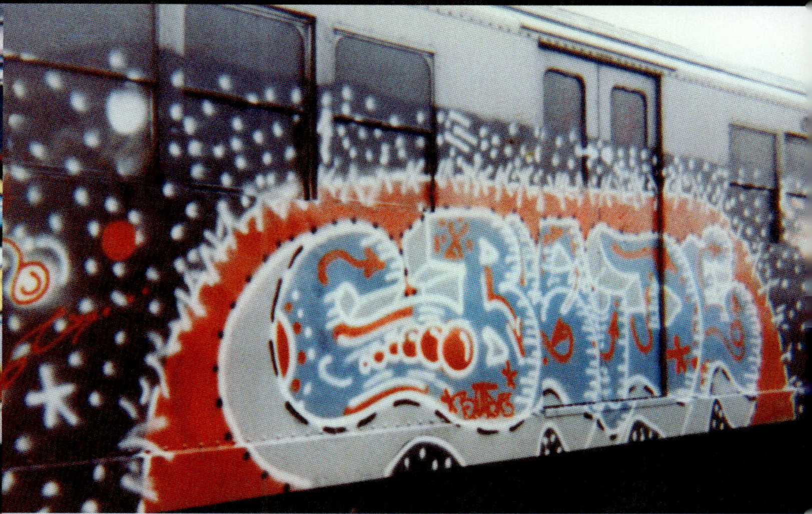

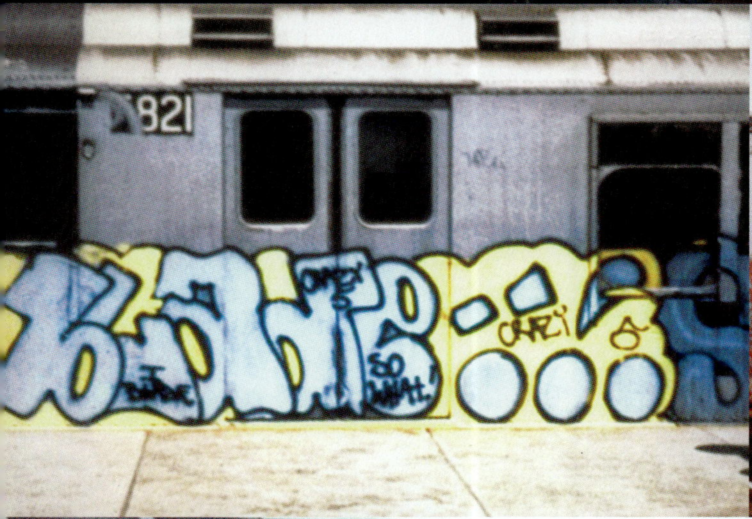
821

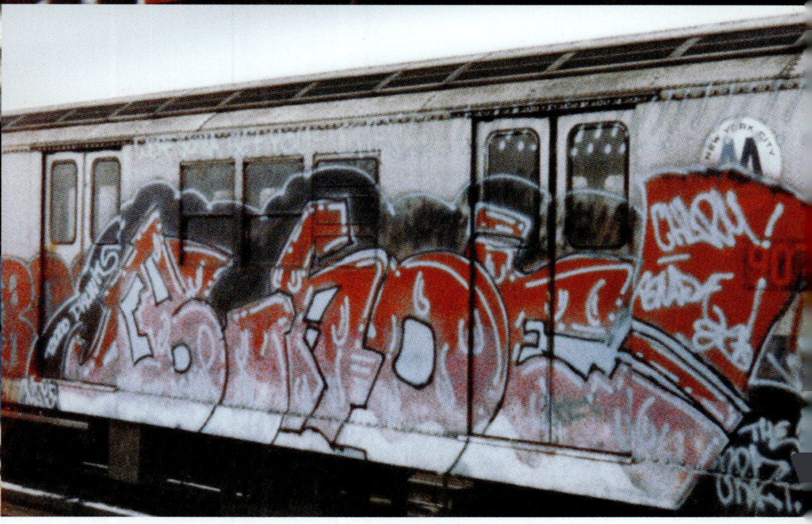

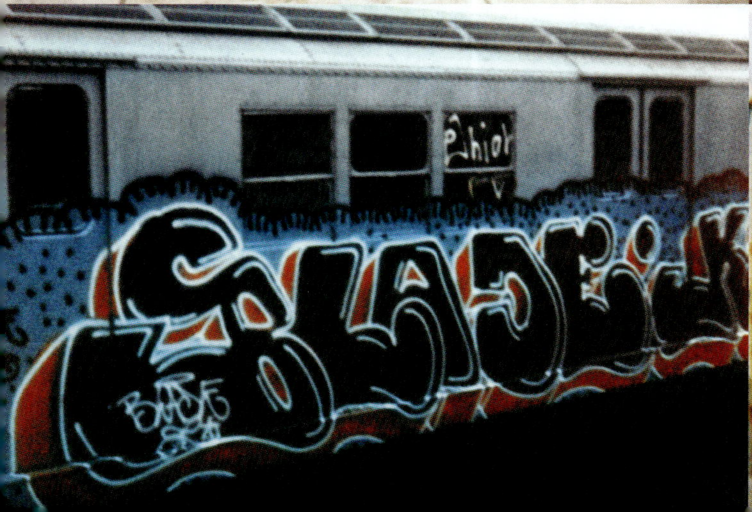

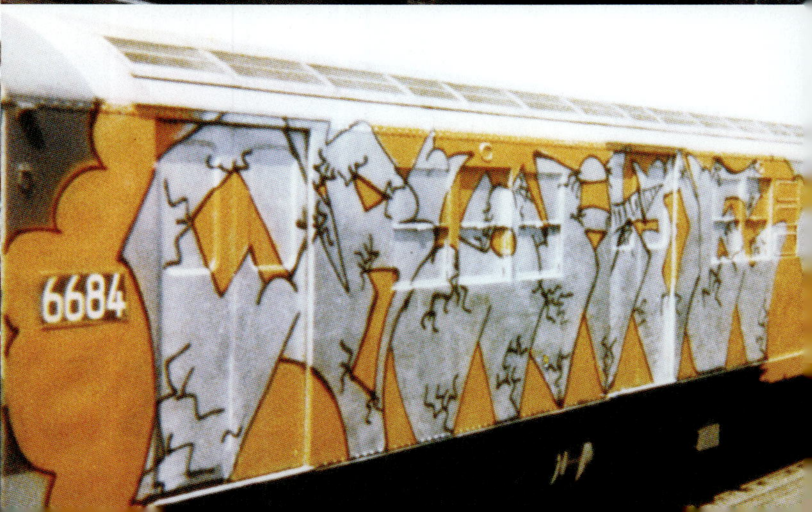
6684

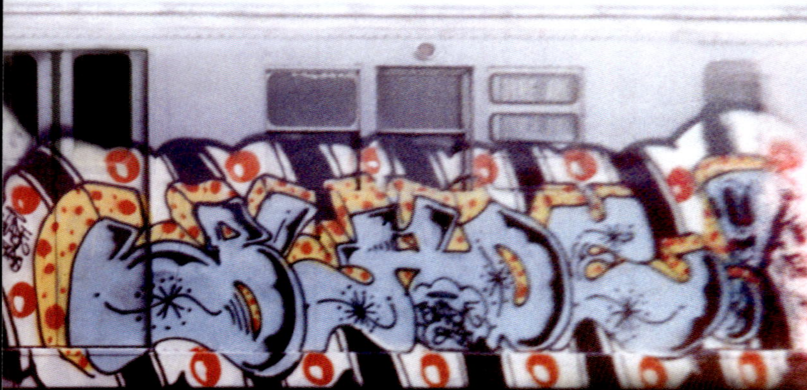

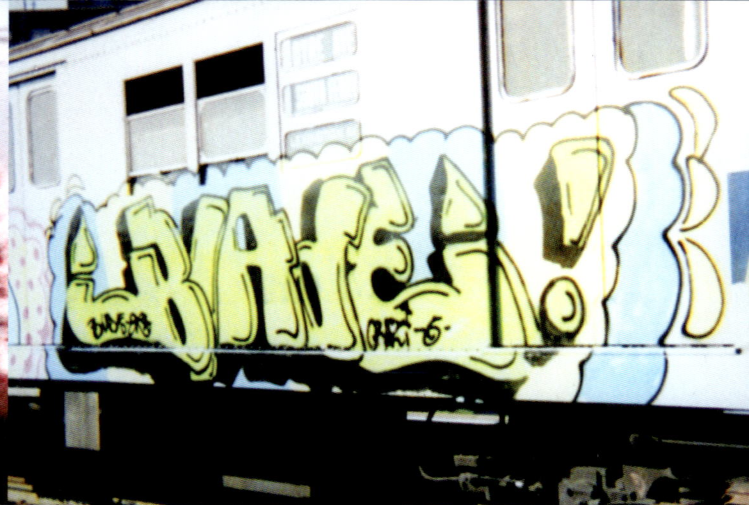

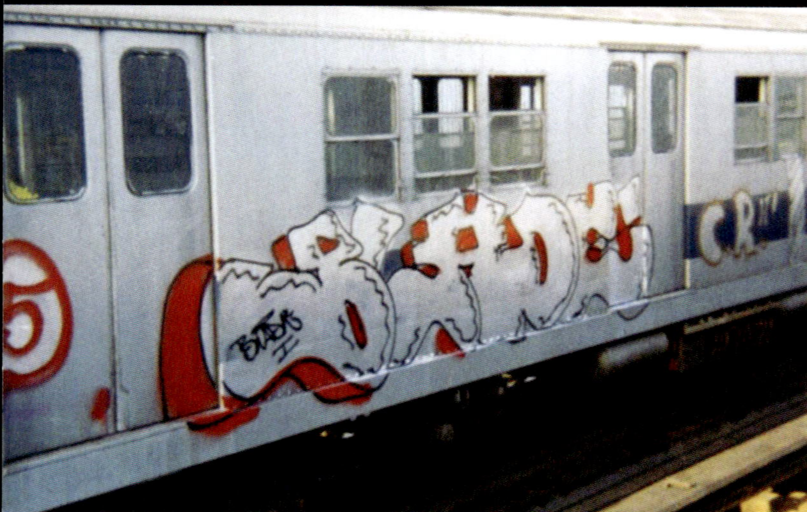

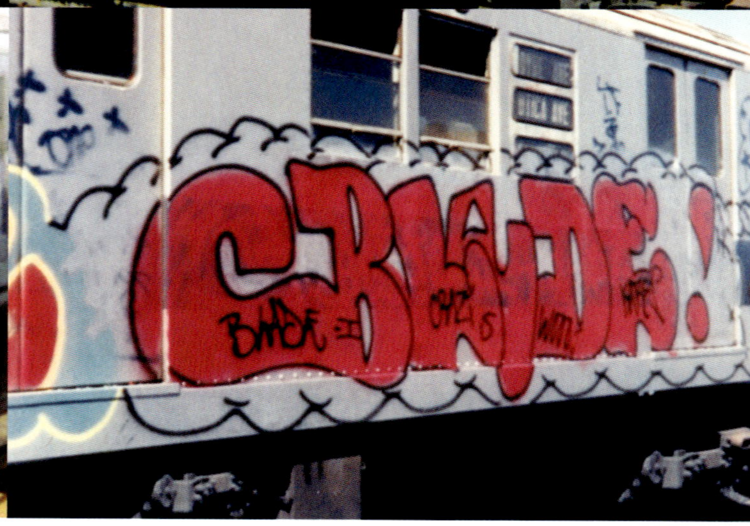

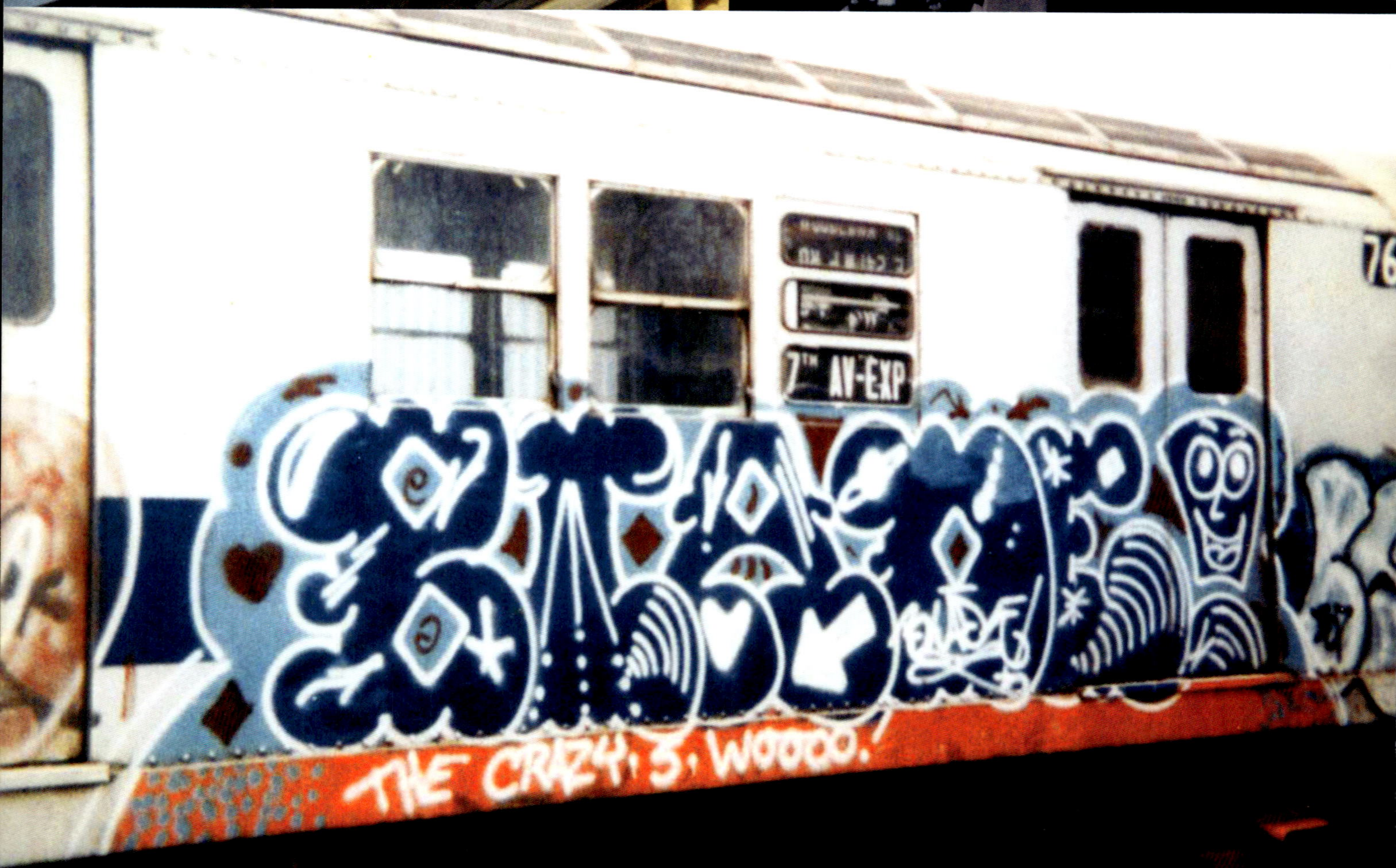
7TH AV-EXP
THE CRAZY, 5, WOOOO!

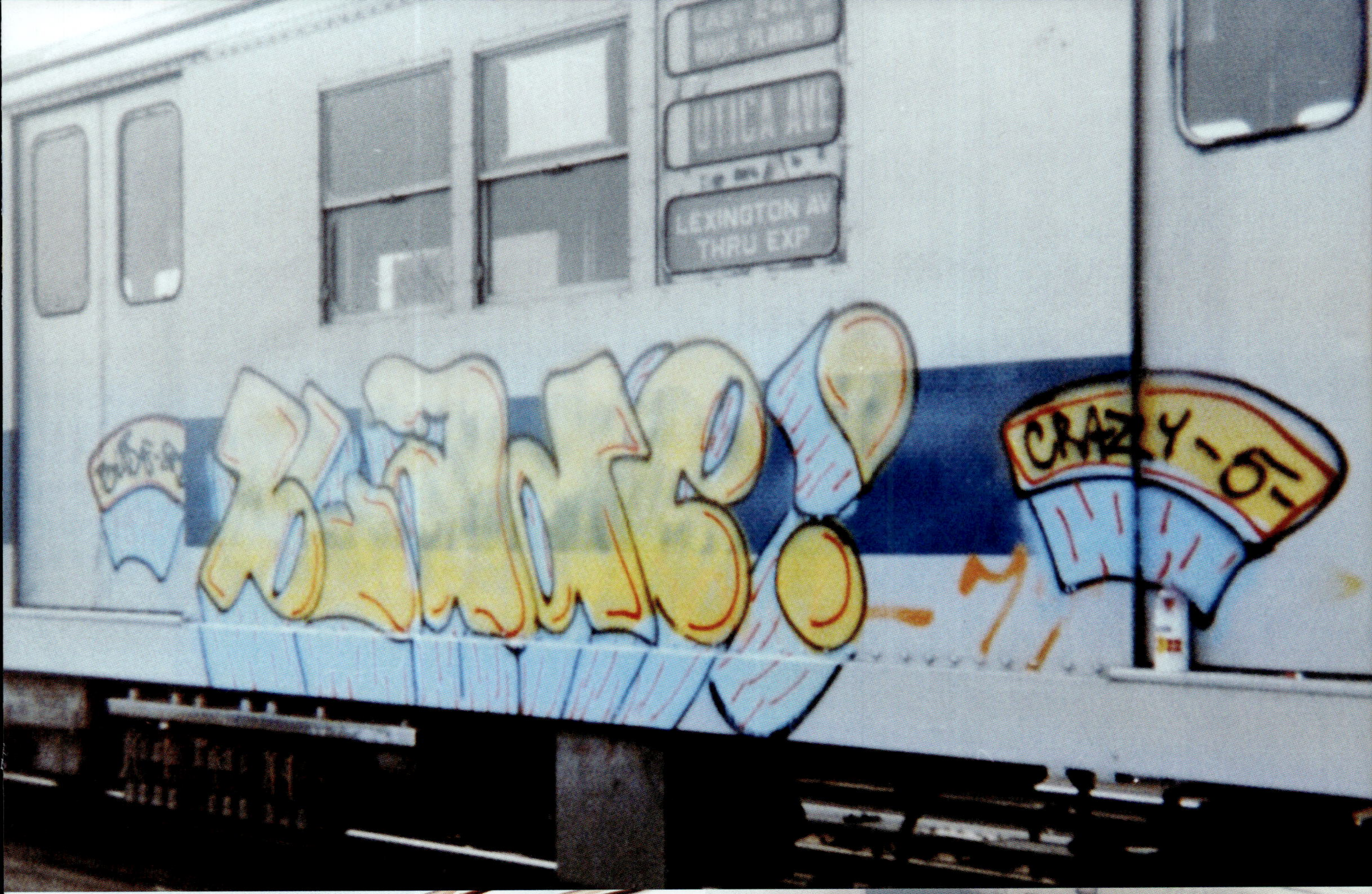
UTICA AVE
LEXINGTON AV
THRU EXP
CRAZY-5-

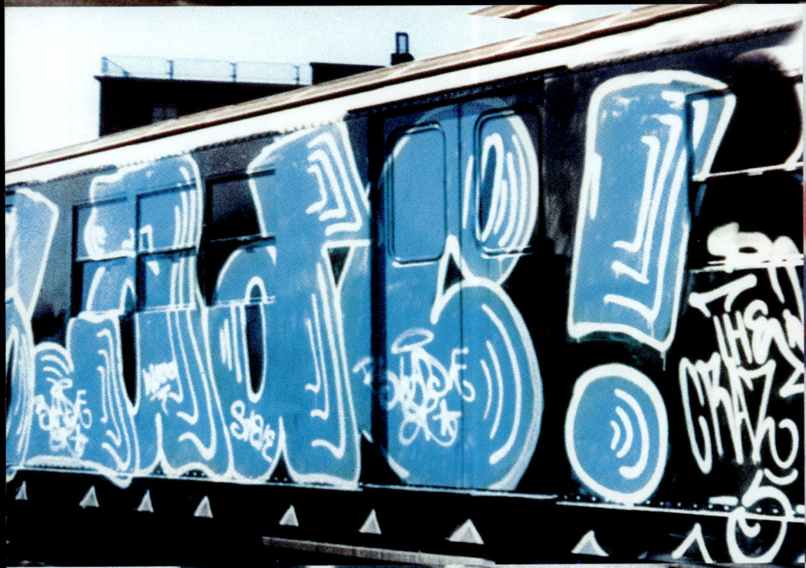

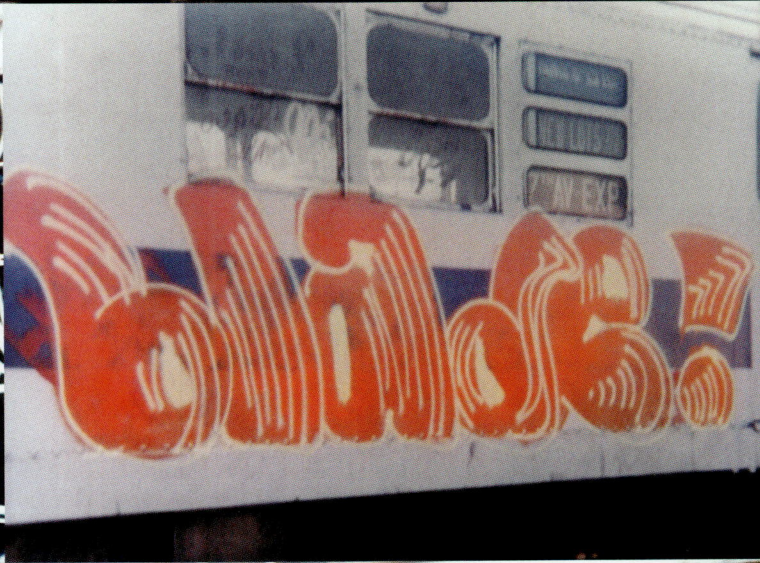

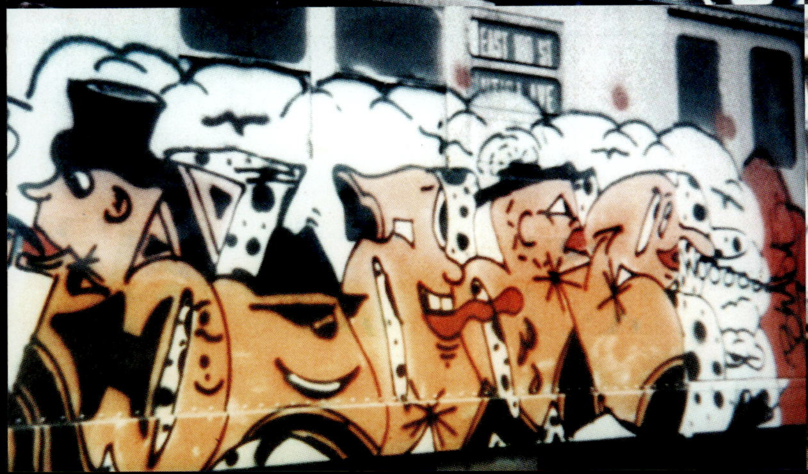

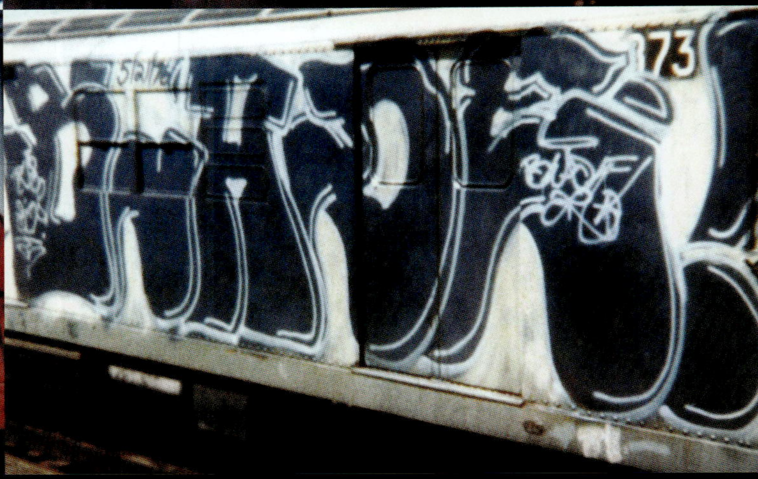
73

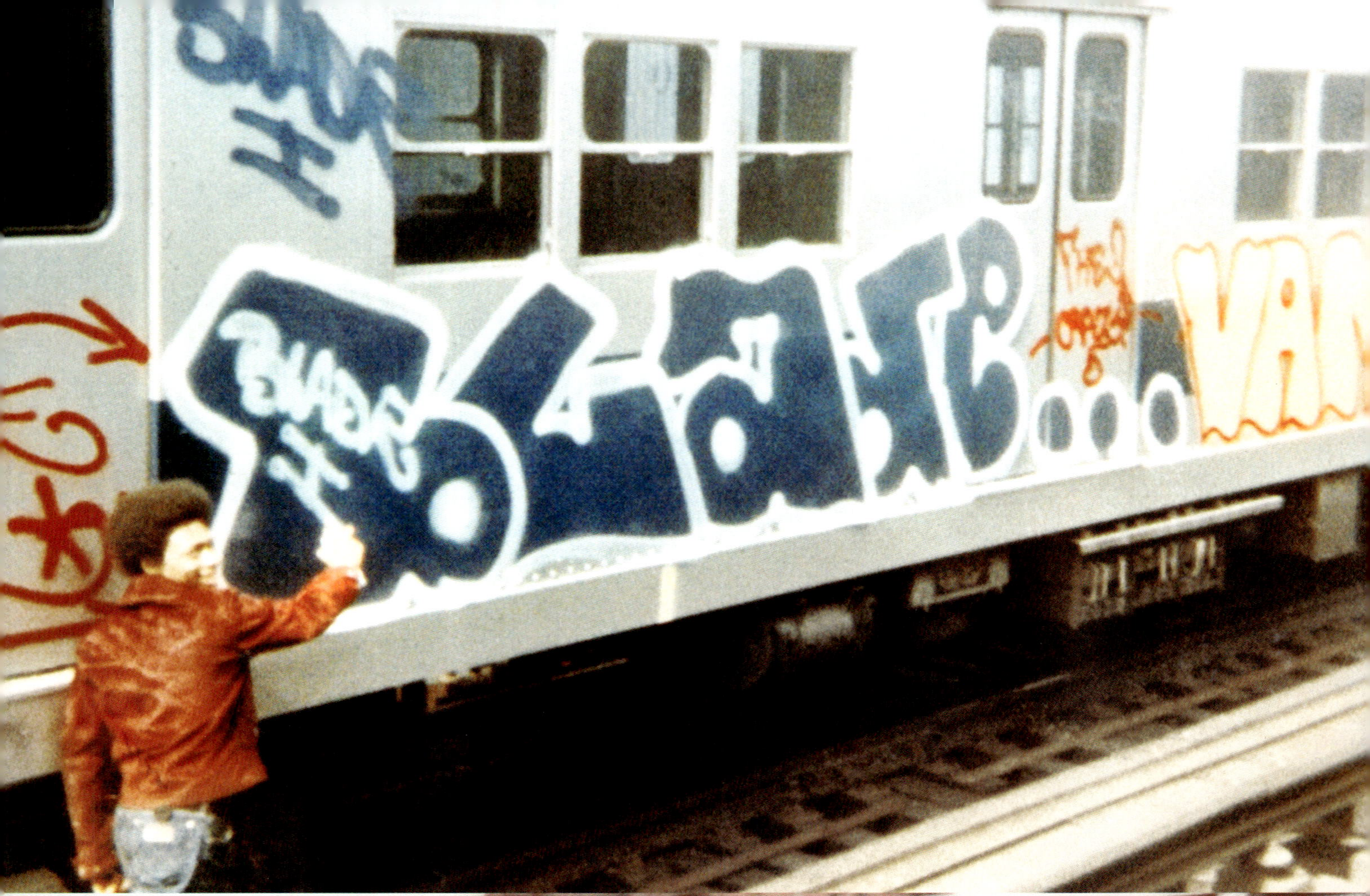

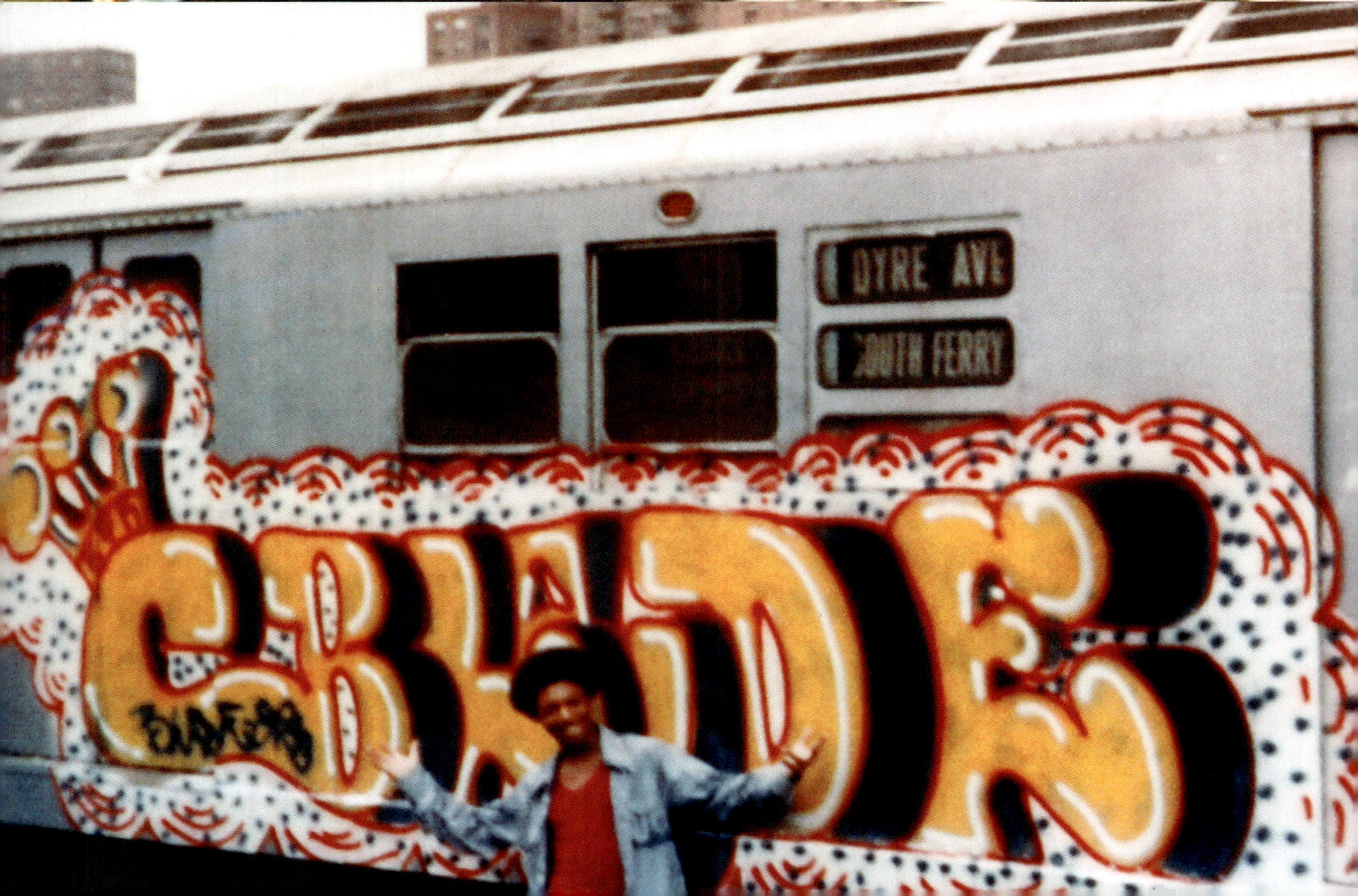
DYRE AVE
OUTH FERRY

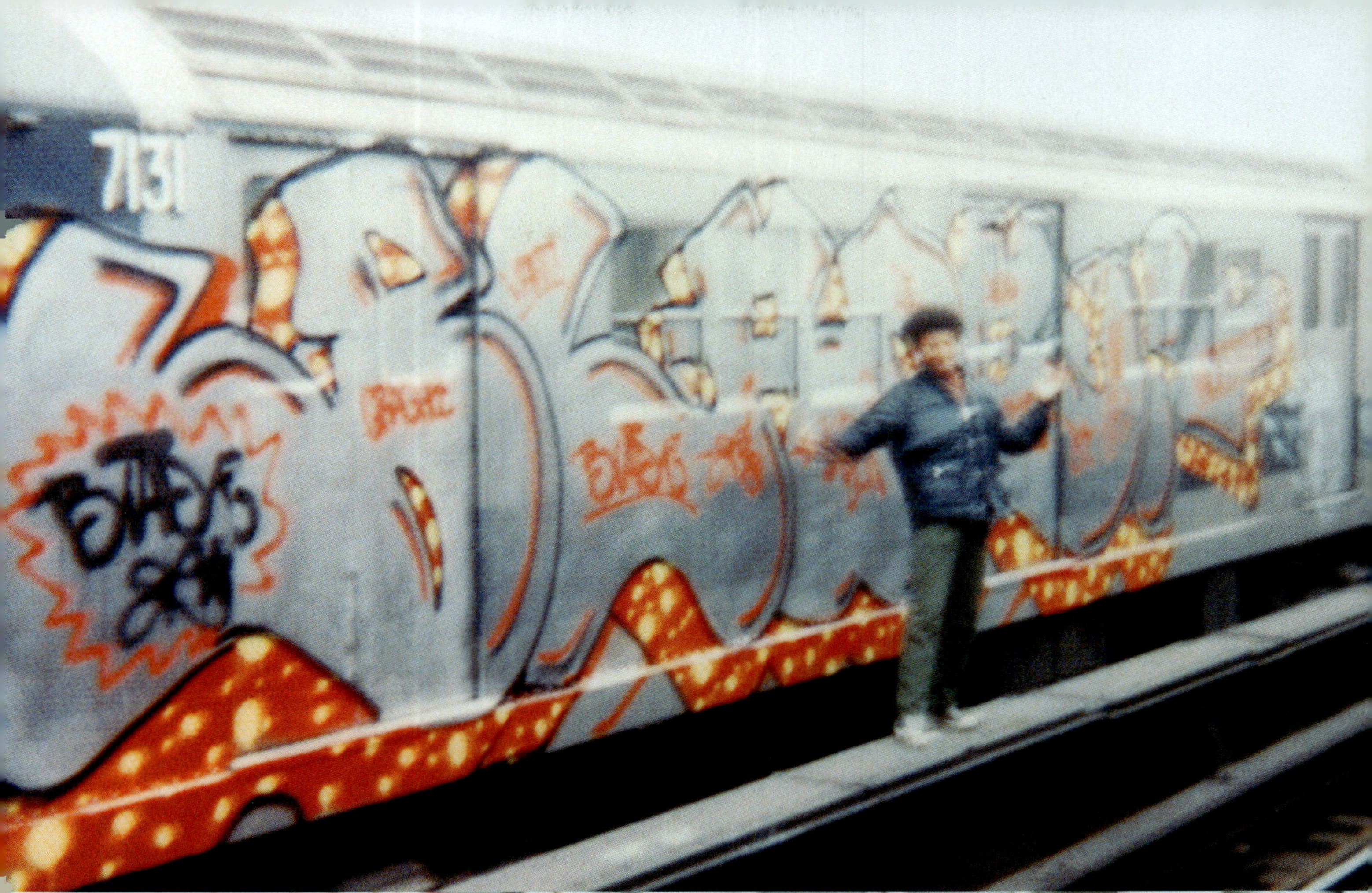
7131

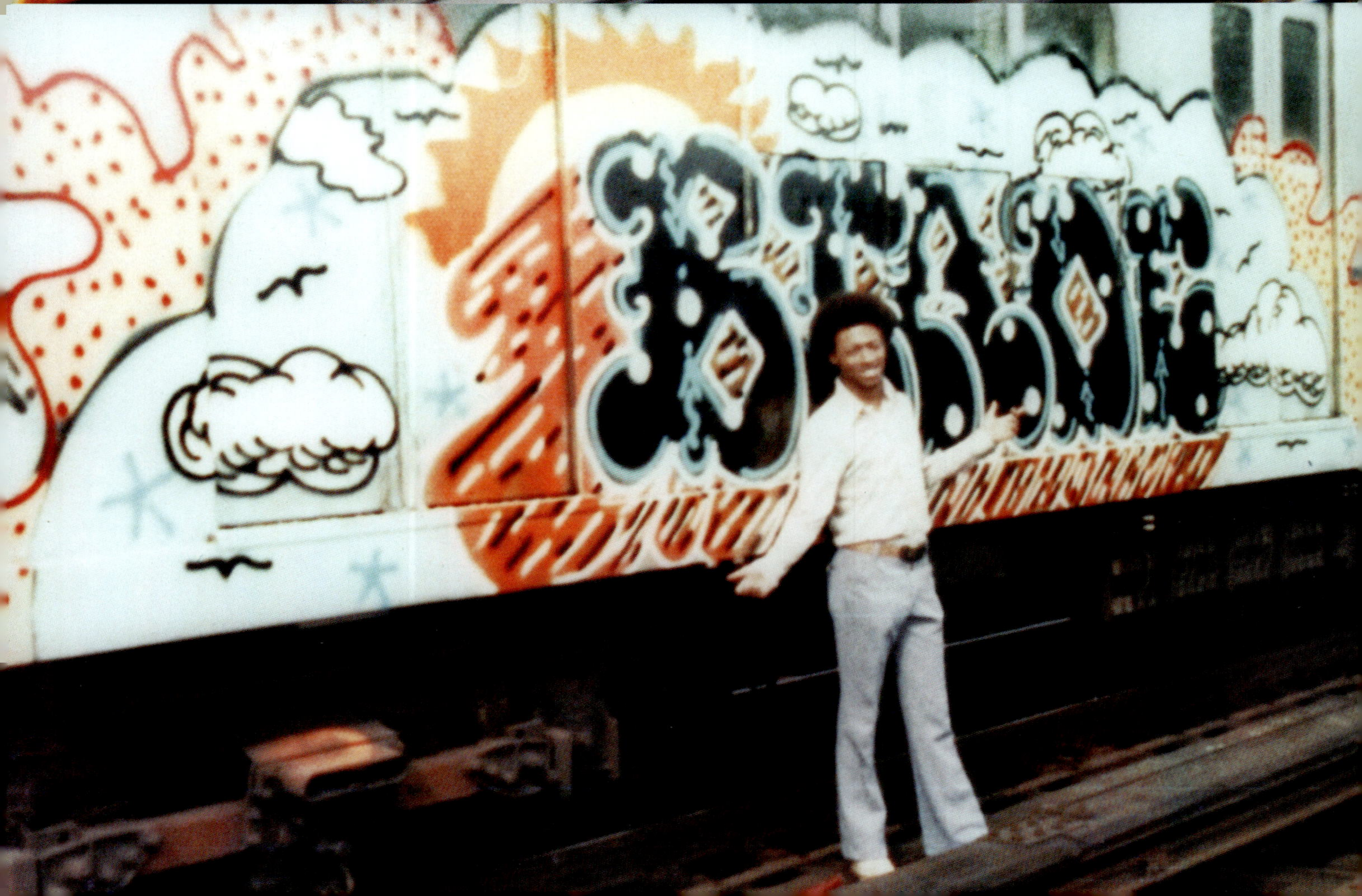

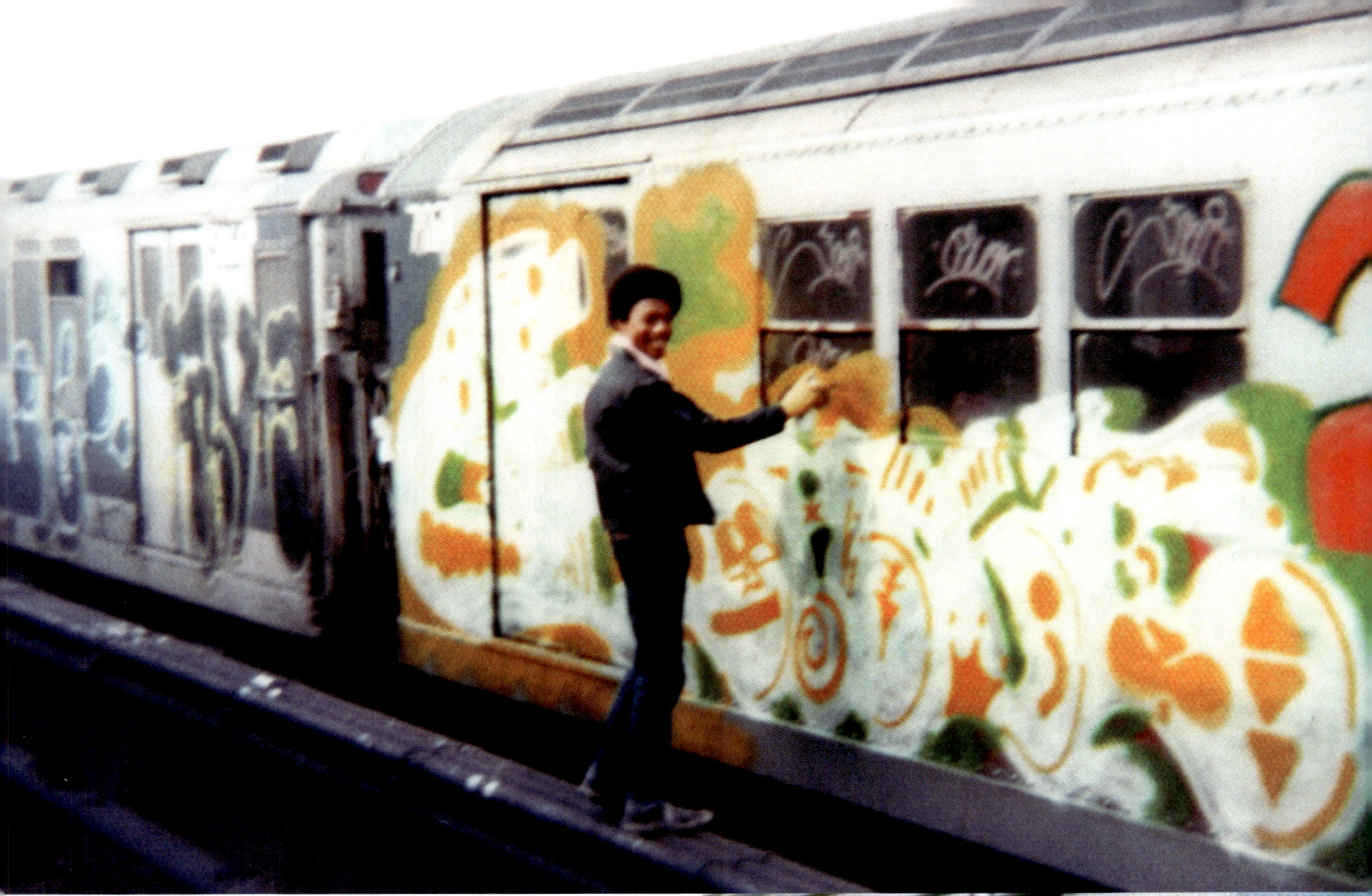

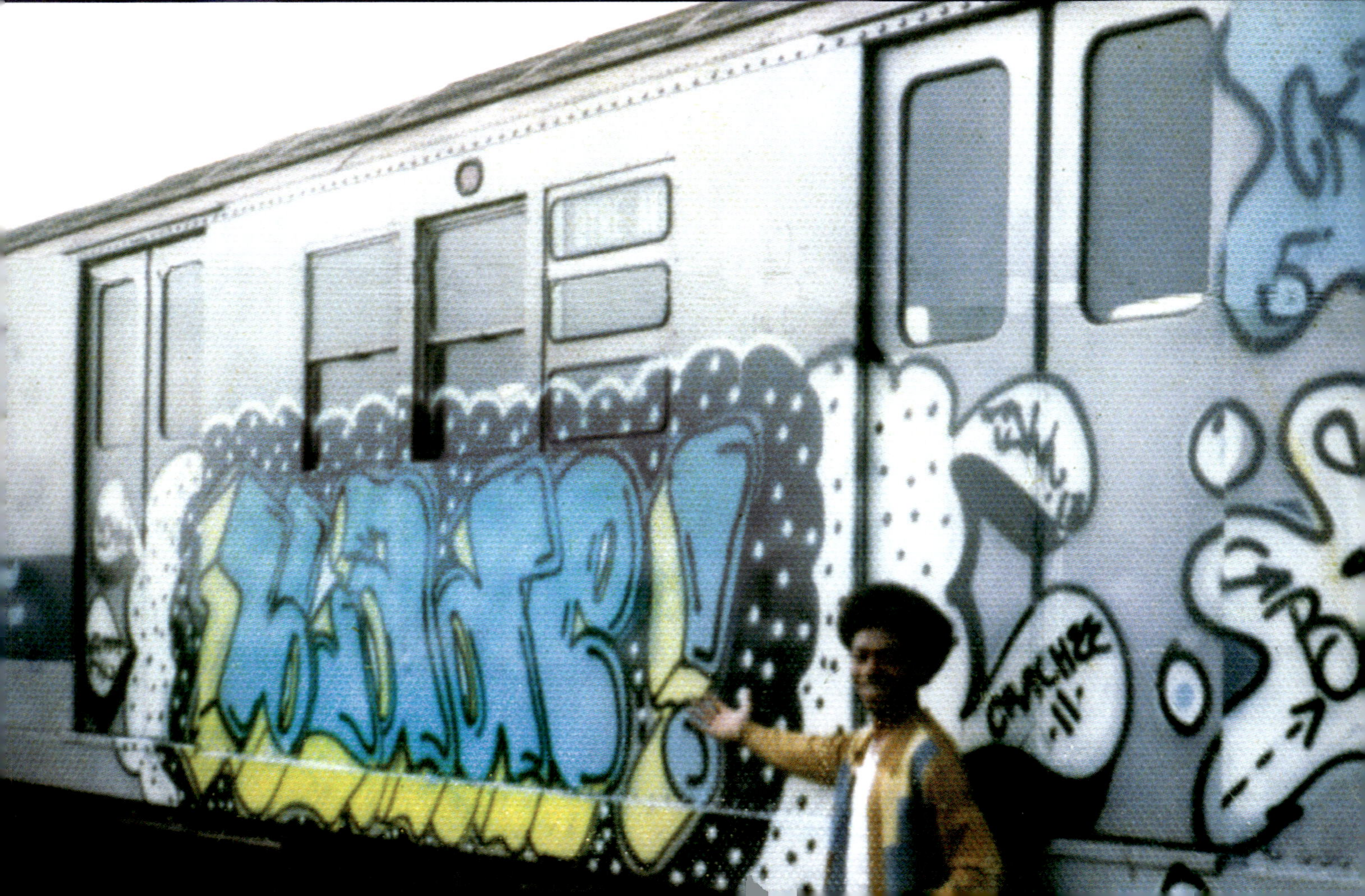

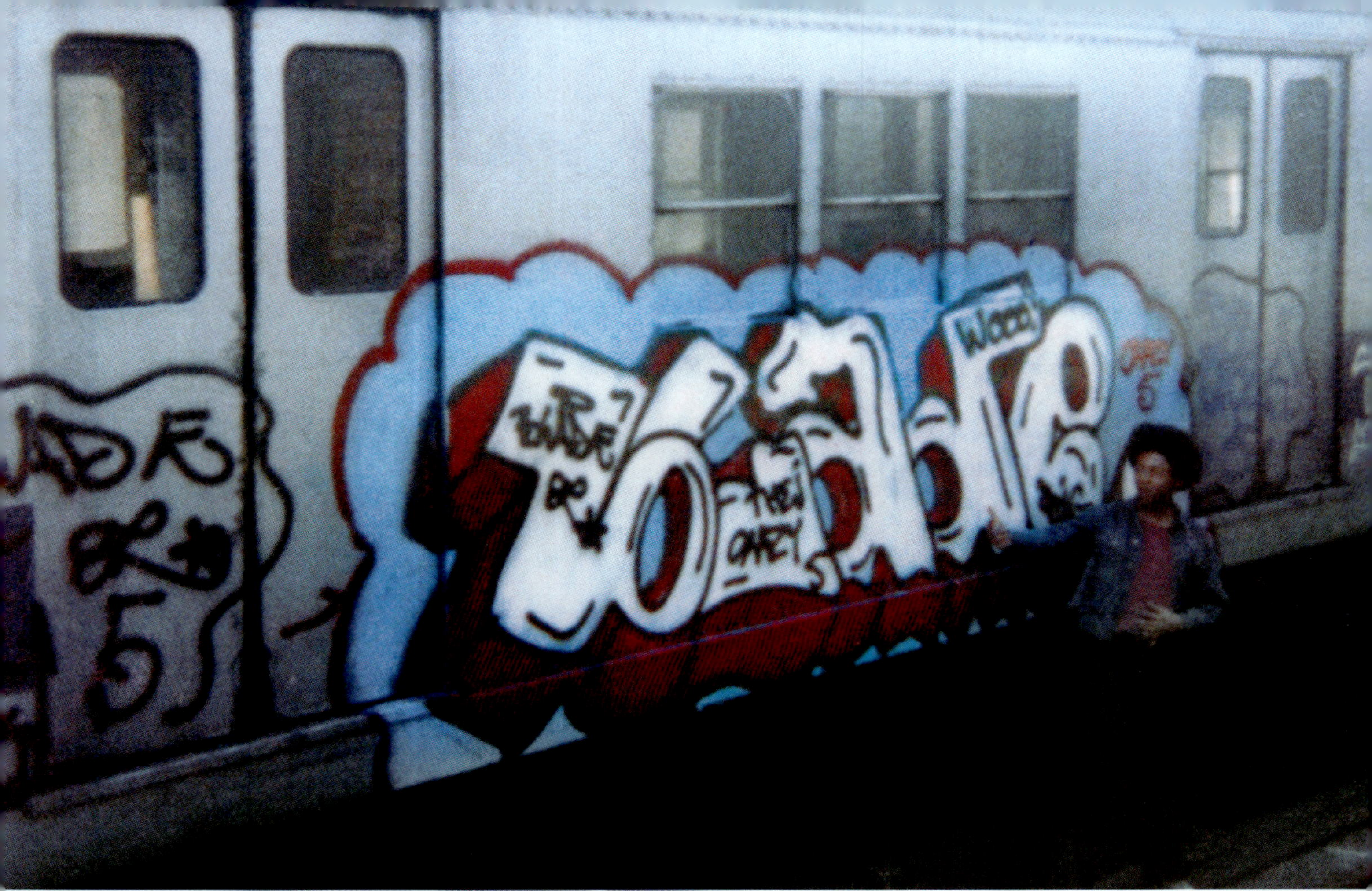

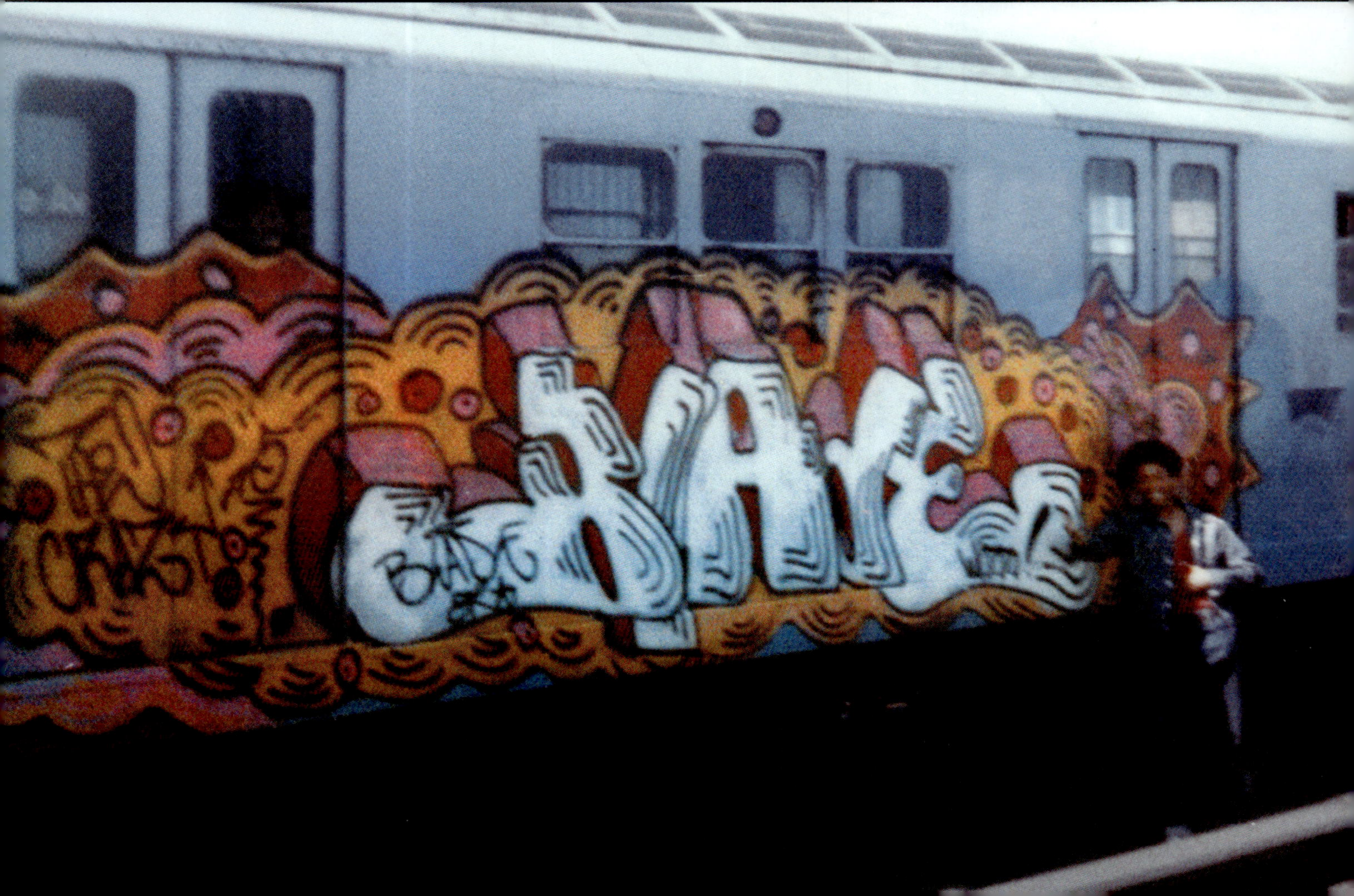

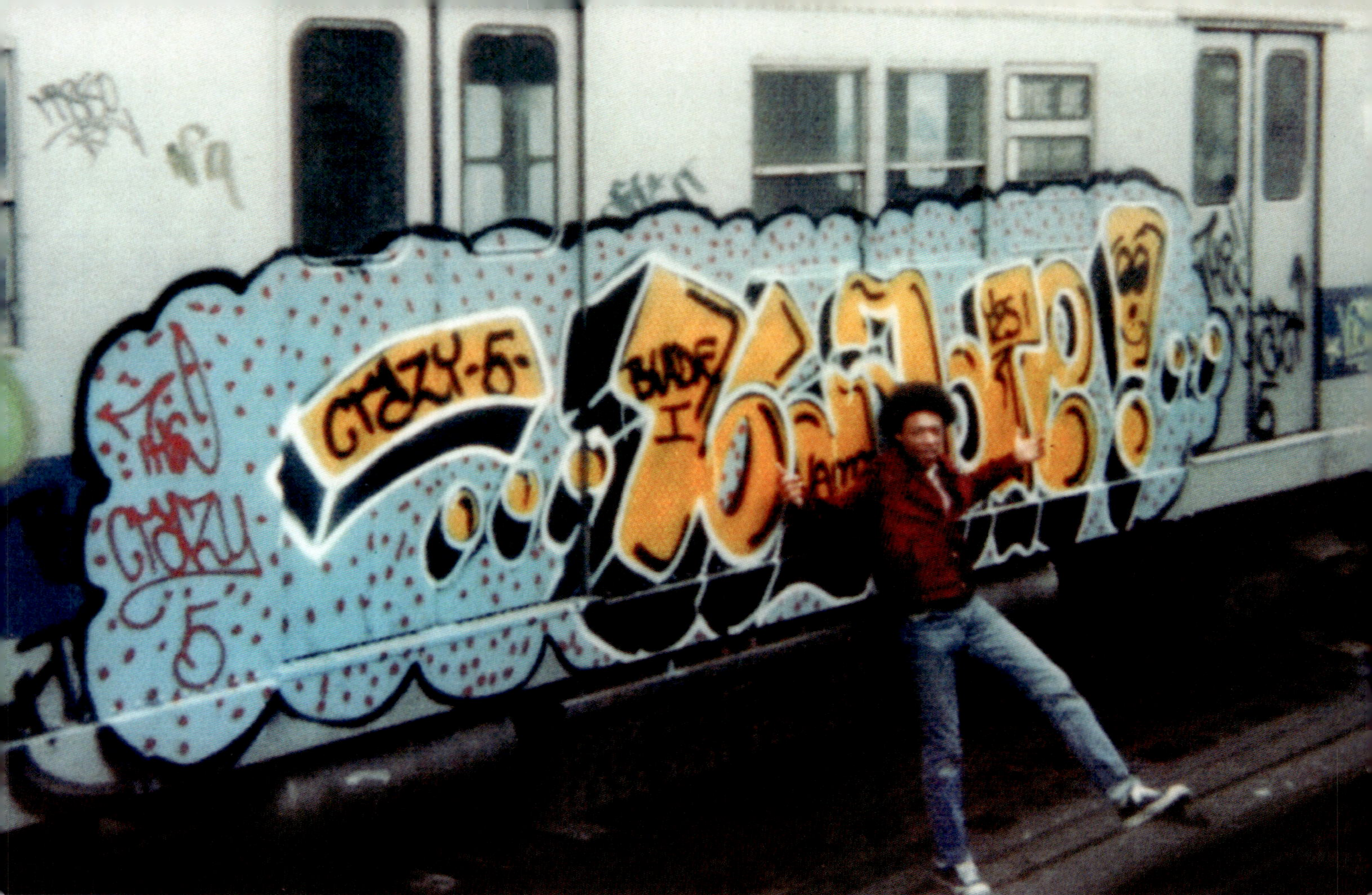
CRAZY-5-
BLADE I

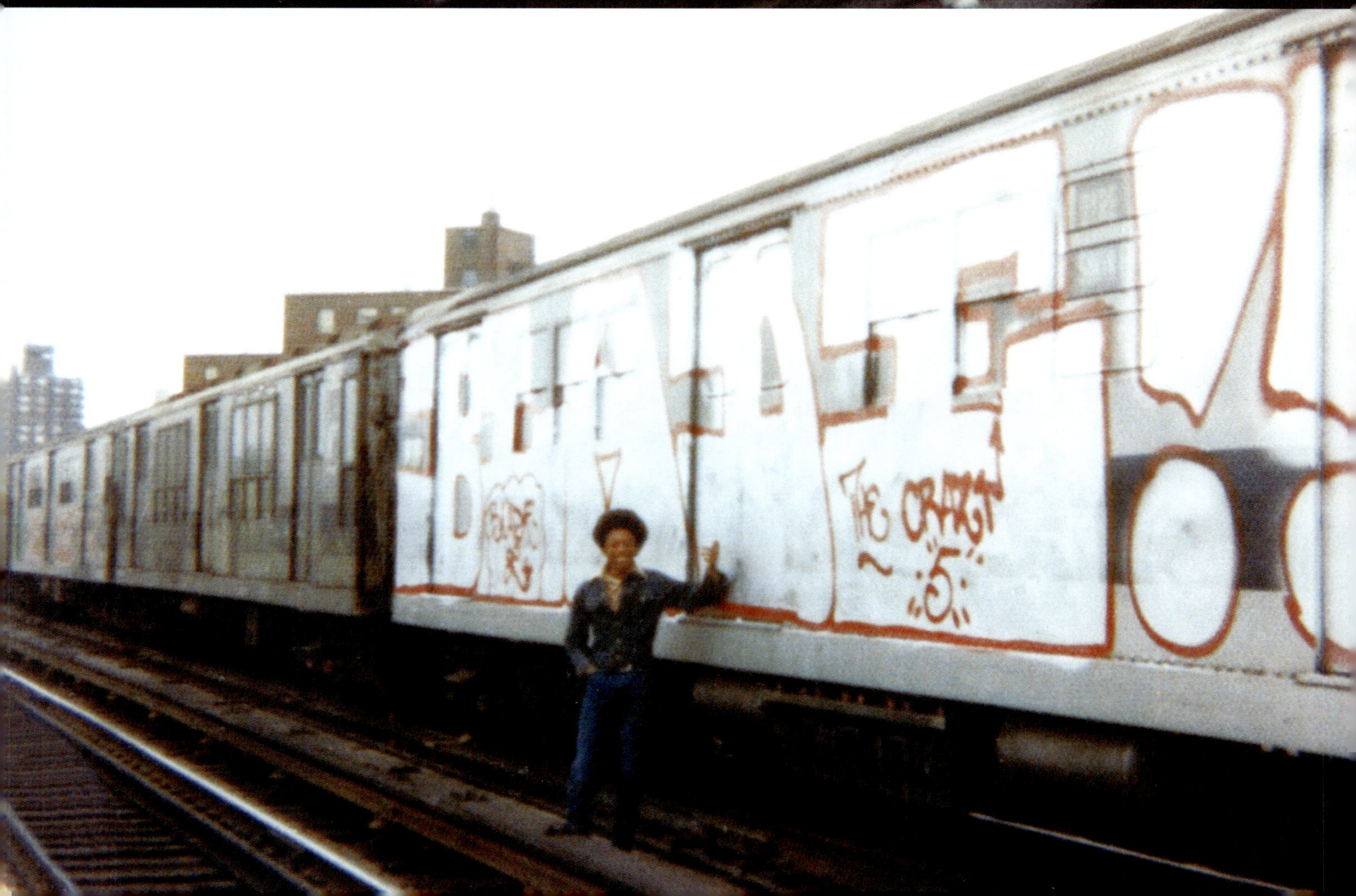
THE CRAZY 5

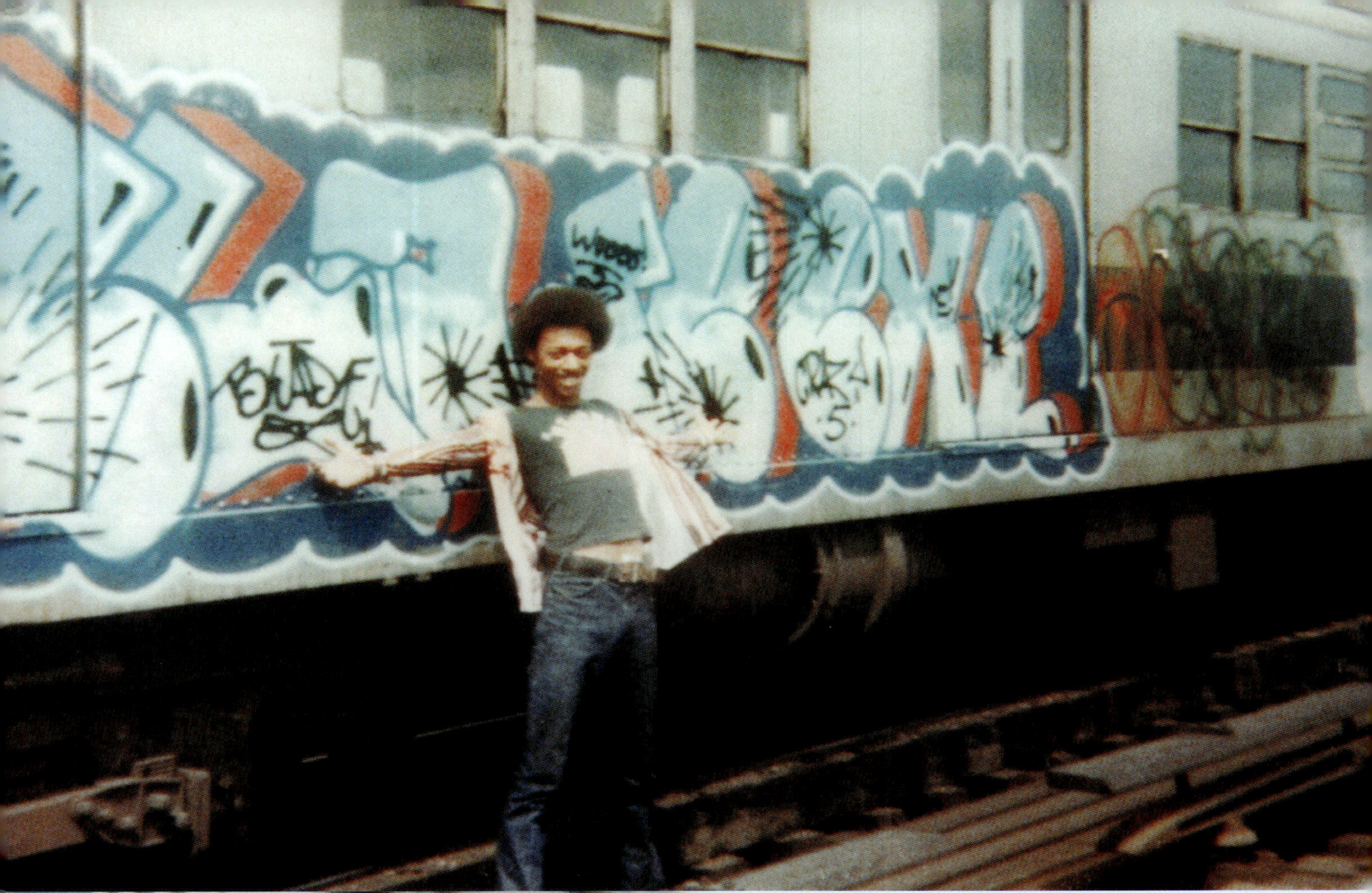

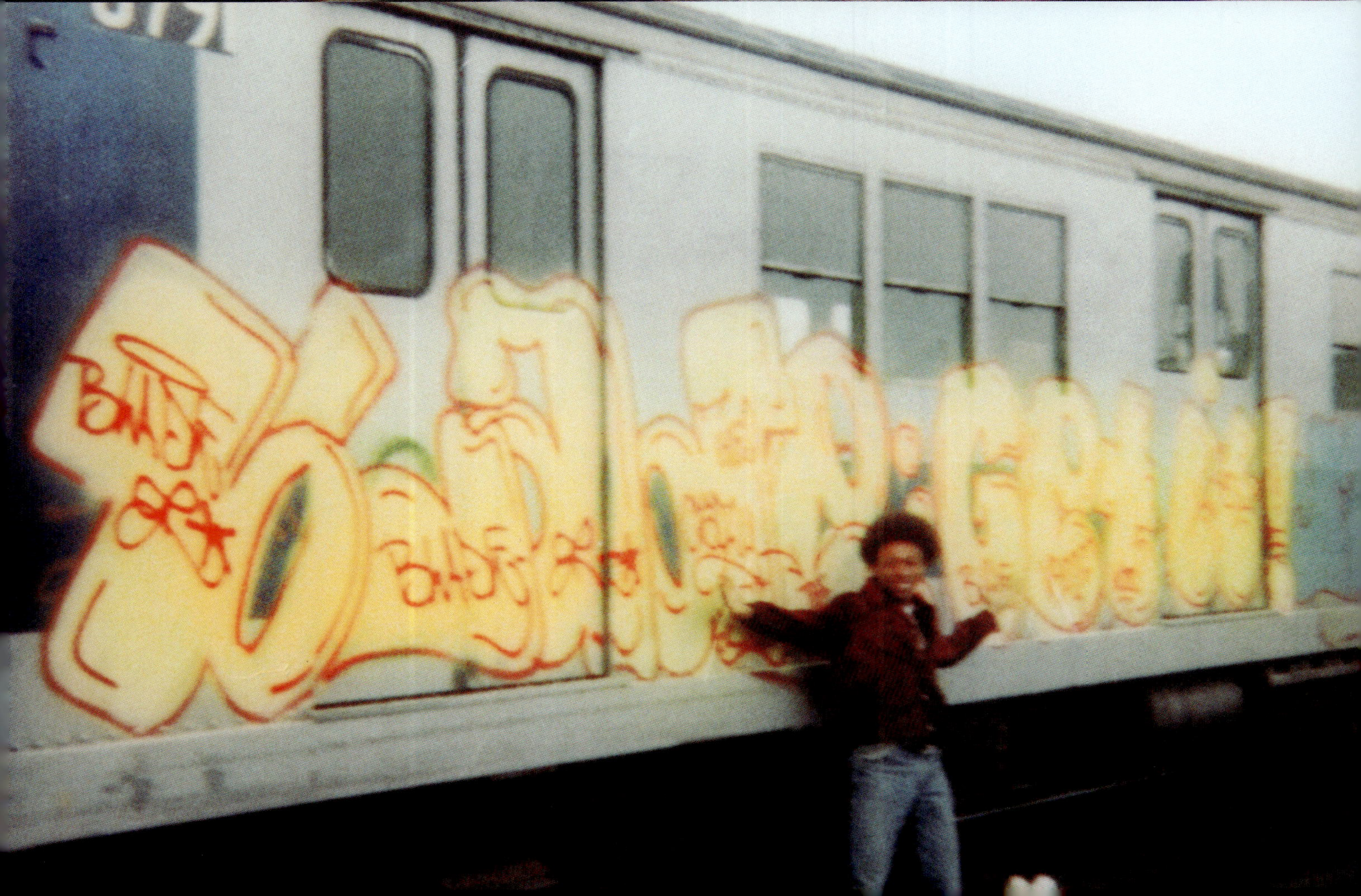

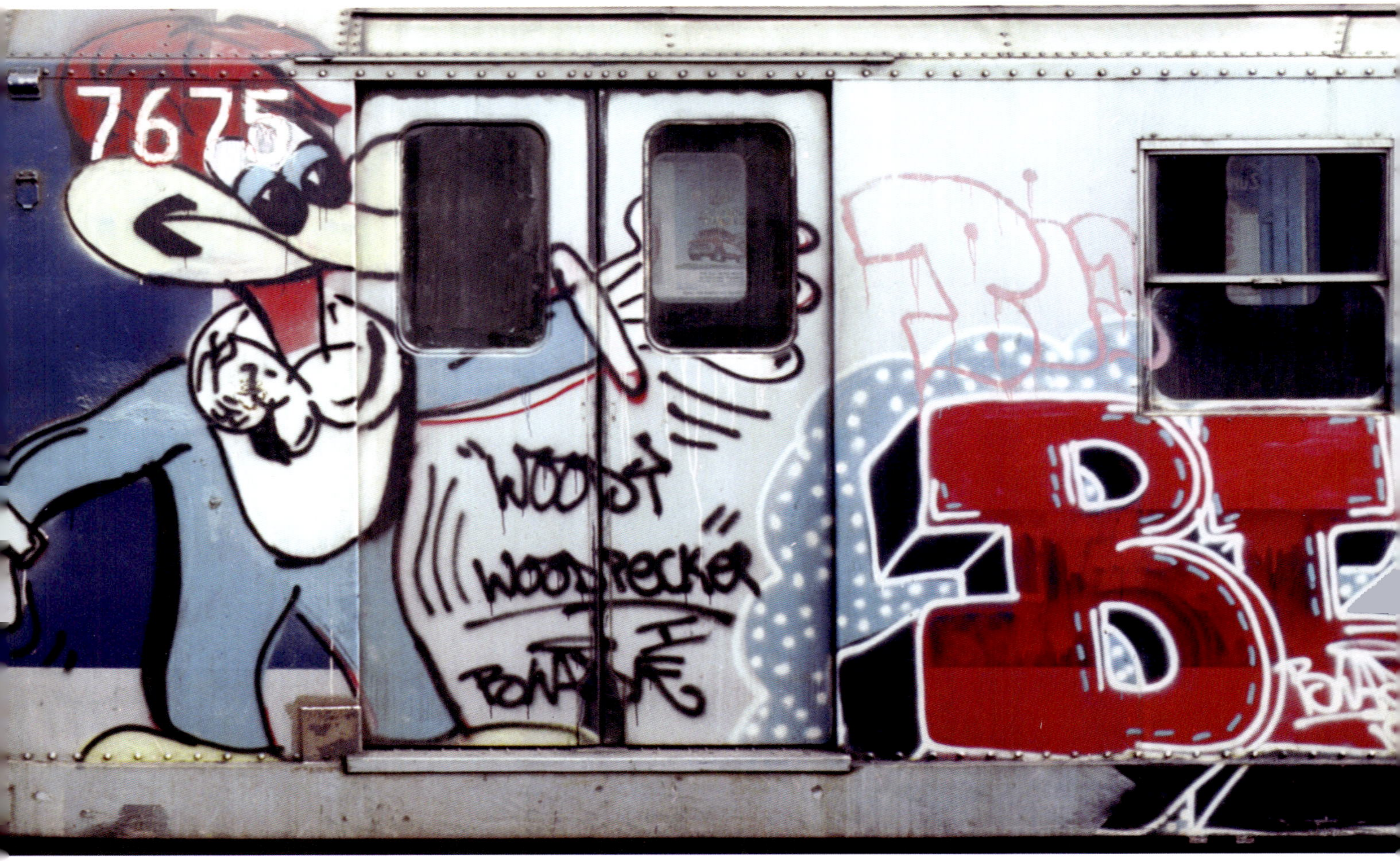

This spread: BLADE and Woody Woodpecker. Photo by Henry Chalfant.
Following spread: BLADE, tick tock style. 1975.

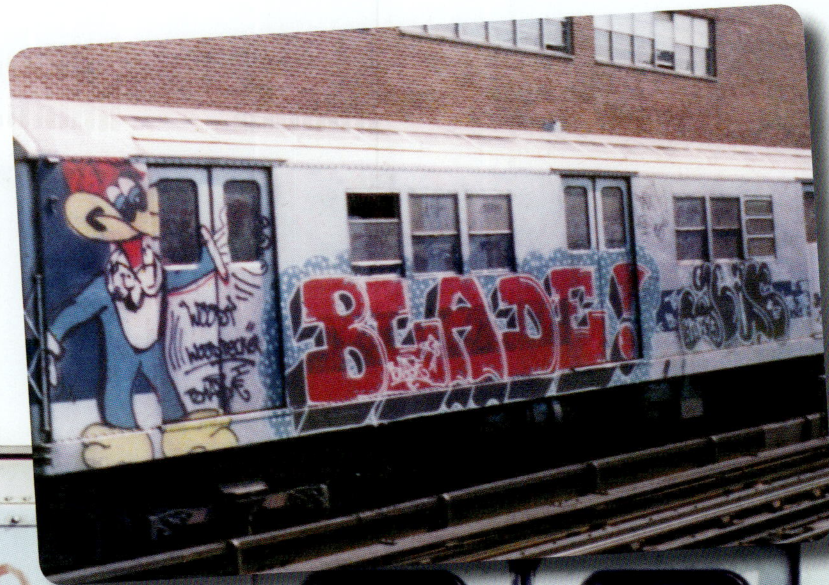
BLADE!

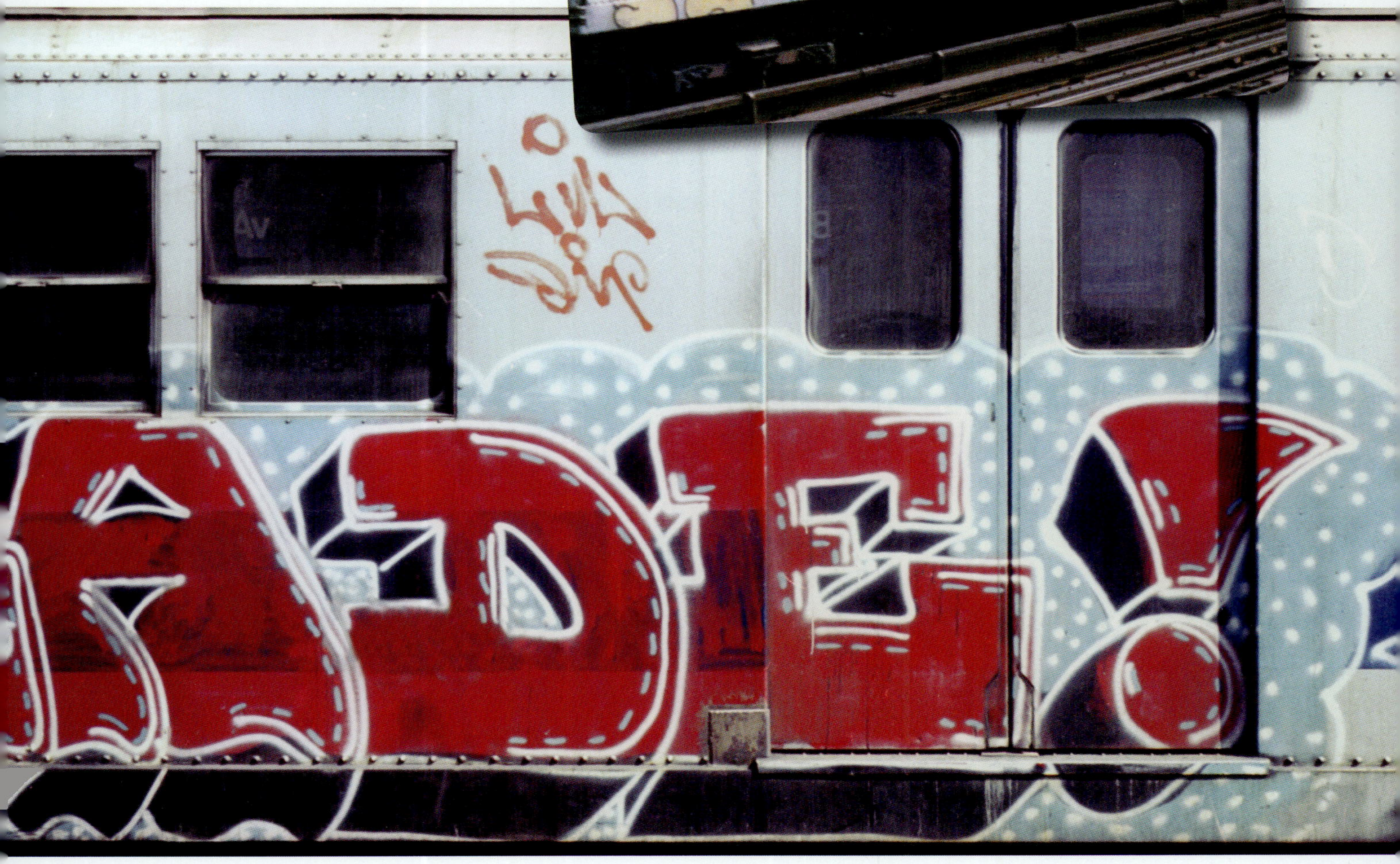

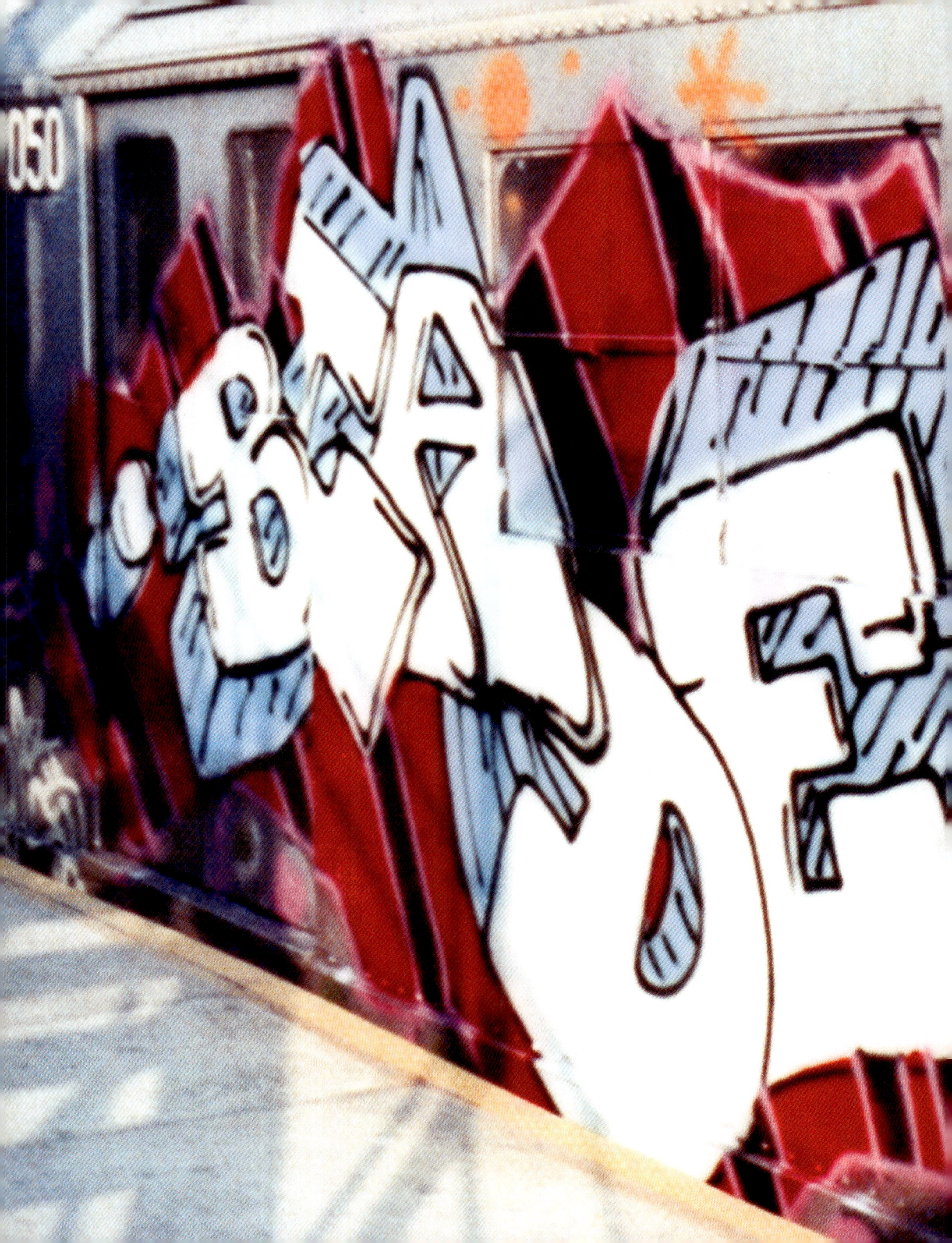
050

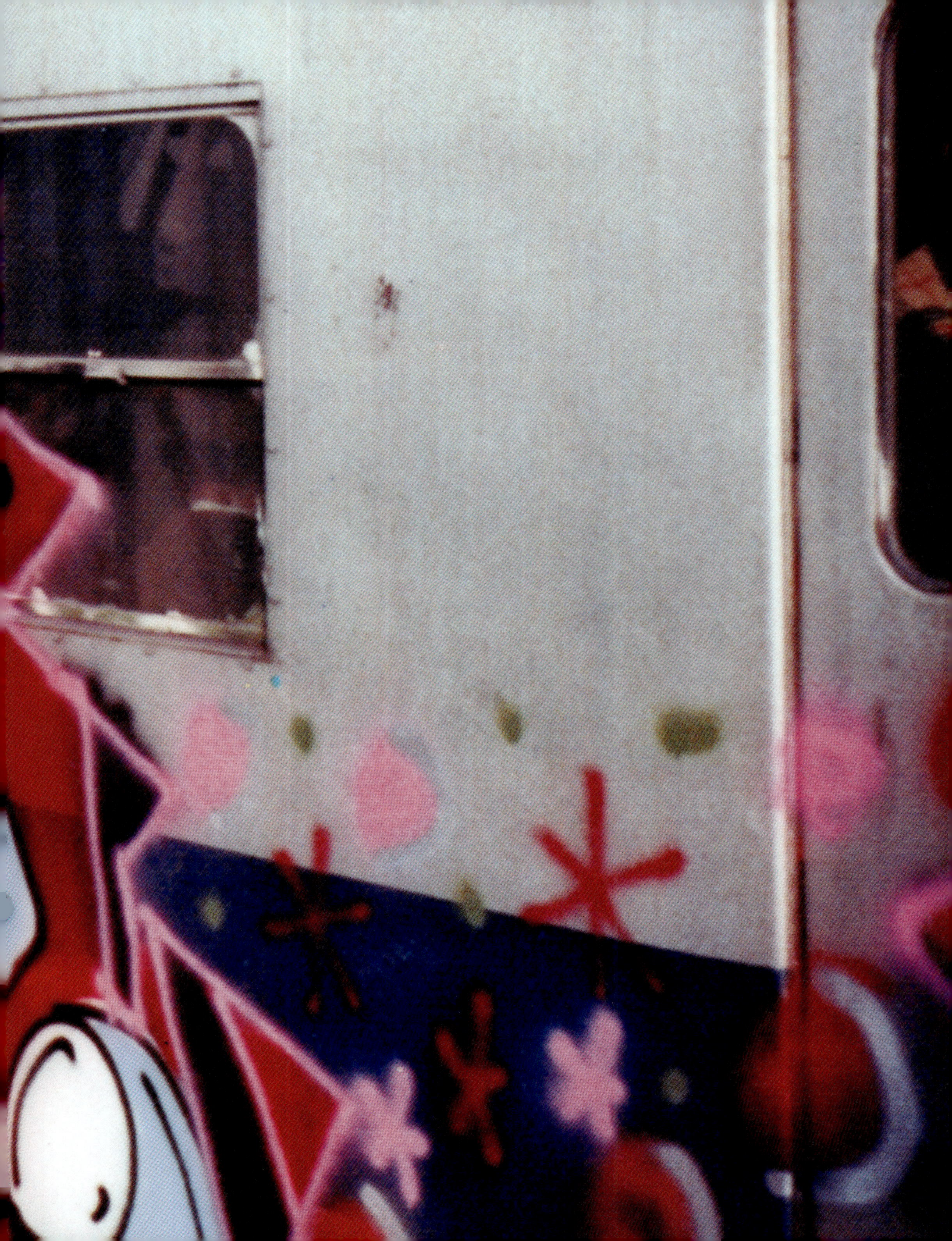

CHAPTER SEVEN

COMET:

1975–1976

COMET 1 was from the Boulevard Boys, just north of Parkside. He got his name when AJAX turned him on to writing. They plucked their names right from the supermarket shelf. COMET started writing in 1971 by hitting the 3rd Avenue El. The El came out of Gun Hill Road, made the curve right in front of his parents' house, then went on to Fordham Road. It was the most rickety train you'd ever ride and it went out of service in 1973. There was another COMET at the time, COMET 163. COMET walked up to him, told him he was taking the name, and then he did. COMET was a badass. It certainly helped that he weighed twenty-five pounds more than the rest of us. In Junior High School, COMET was the biggest kid in the school. He had broad shoulders and he already looked like an adult. And he wasn't done growing.

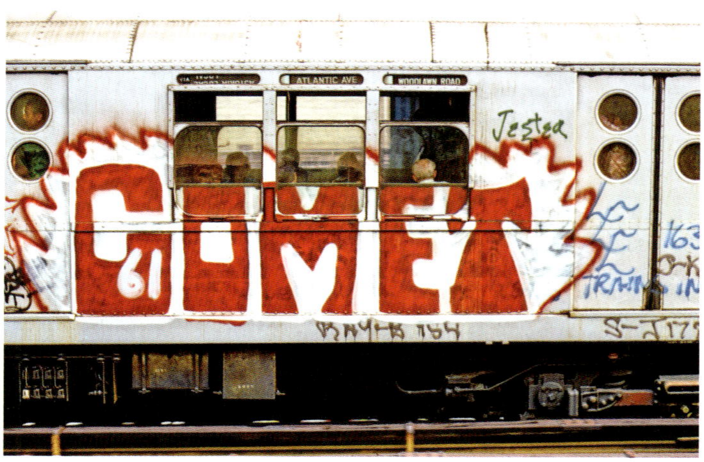

In his early years of writing, COMET dodged a bullet after doing a piece he placed right in the middle of a train wall papered by HONDO 1. "Wall papering" started on the 1 line in Manhattan. It didn't last long but it made a hell of a statement. If a writer came across a clean train, he or she could do as many as fifty tags on it. And they owned that train! The tags looked like a pattern, which is where the term "wall papering" came from. It was so big and excessive it had the same impact as a whole-car before whole-cars were even done. Lucky for COMET, at 1973 HONDO 1 was fading from the scene.

COMET hung out with SHAKE and SILVERTIPS, who went on to form The MOB, which was one of the first crews I was in. They hung out at 216th street where they played basketball with the NOD SQUAD, a crew featuring KITU 1, SAKU 1, and TAKU 1. When they weren't hanging on 216th street, COMET would come to Parkside to pick up girls. He had a number of writing partners over the years, including SILVERTIPS, AJAX, BILLY 167, and finally CLIFF 159. He abandoned his first three partners because they couldn't keep up with him. COMET wanted to bomb full-time, so when he painted with CLIFF 159 in 1974, he found his equal. However, CLIFF 159 wanted to go all-city, whereas COMET wanted the opportunity to king the 2 line. And so we got together.

This page: COMET. 1973. Photo ©Keith Baugh.
Opposite page: COMET. 1975.

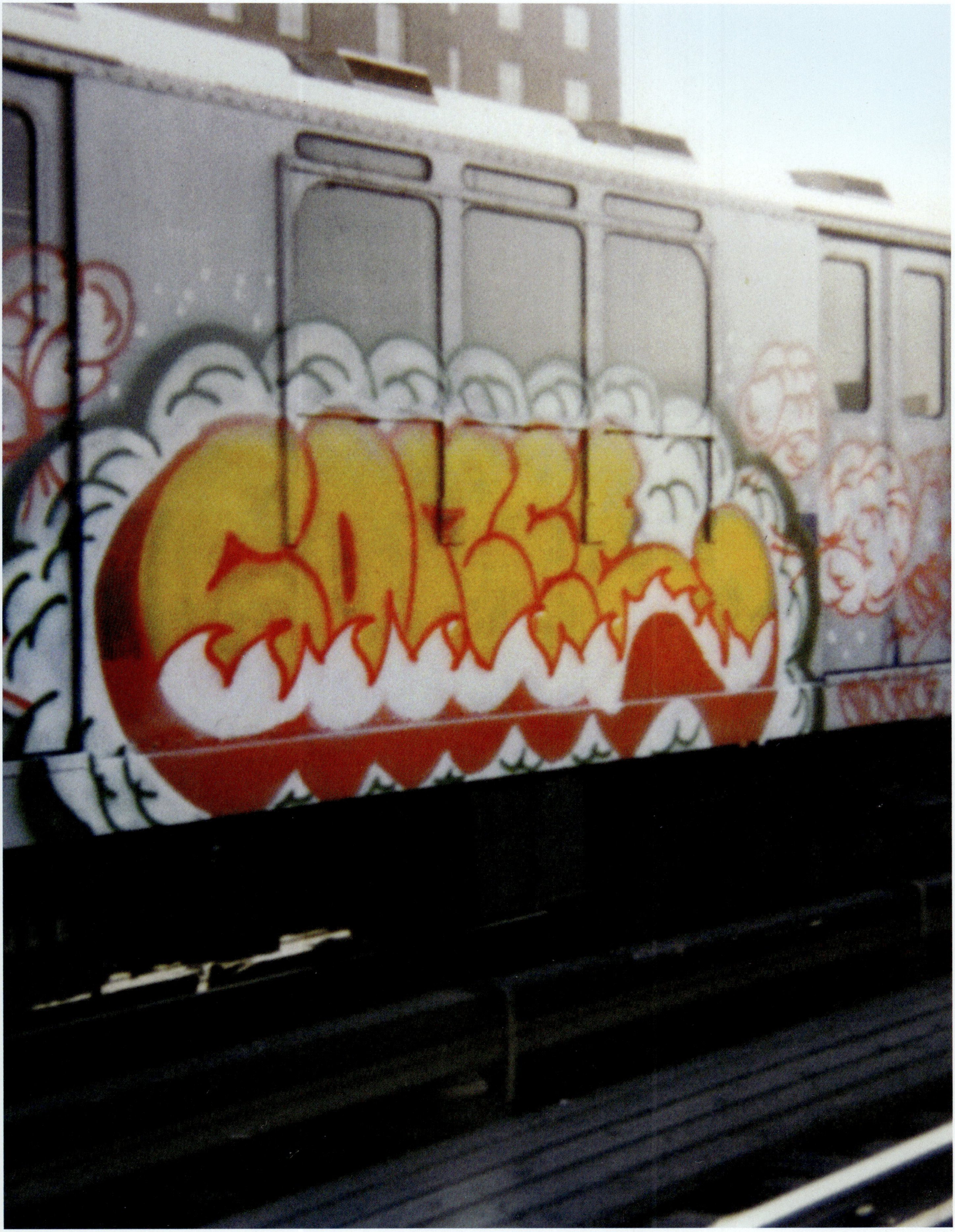

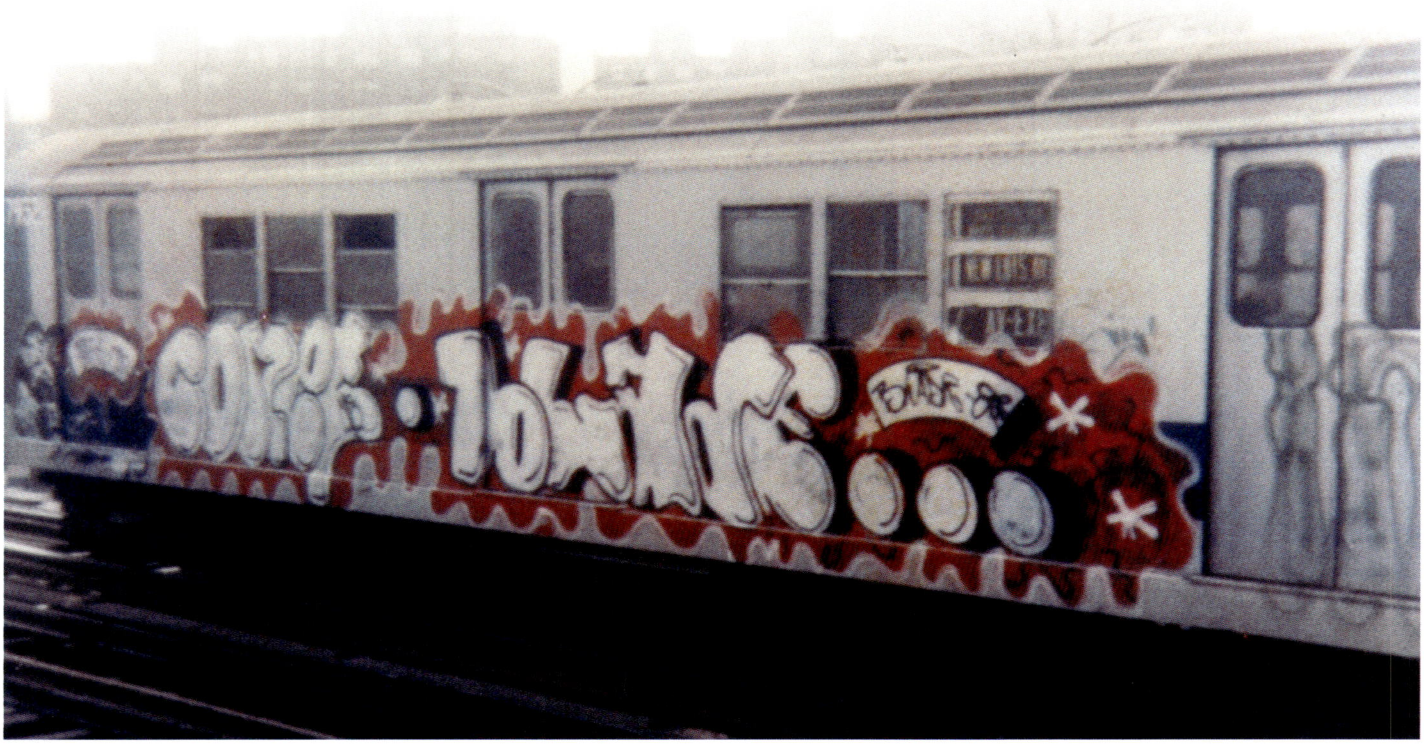

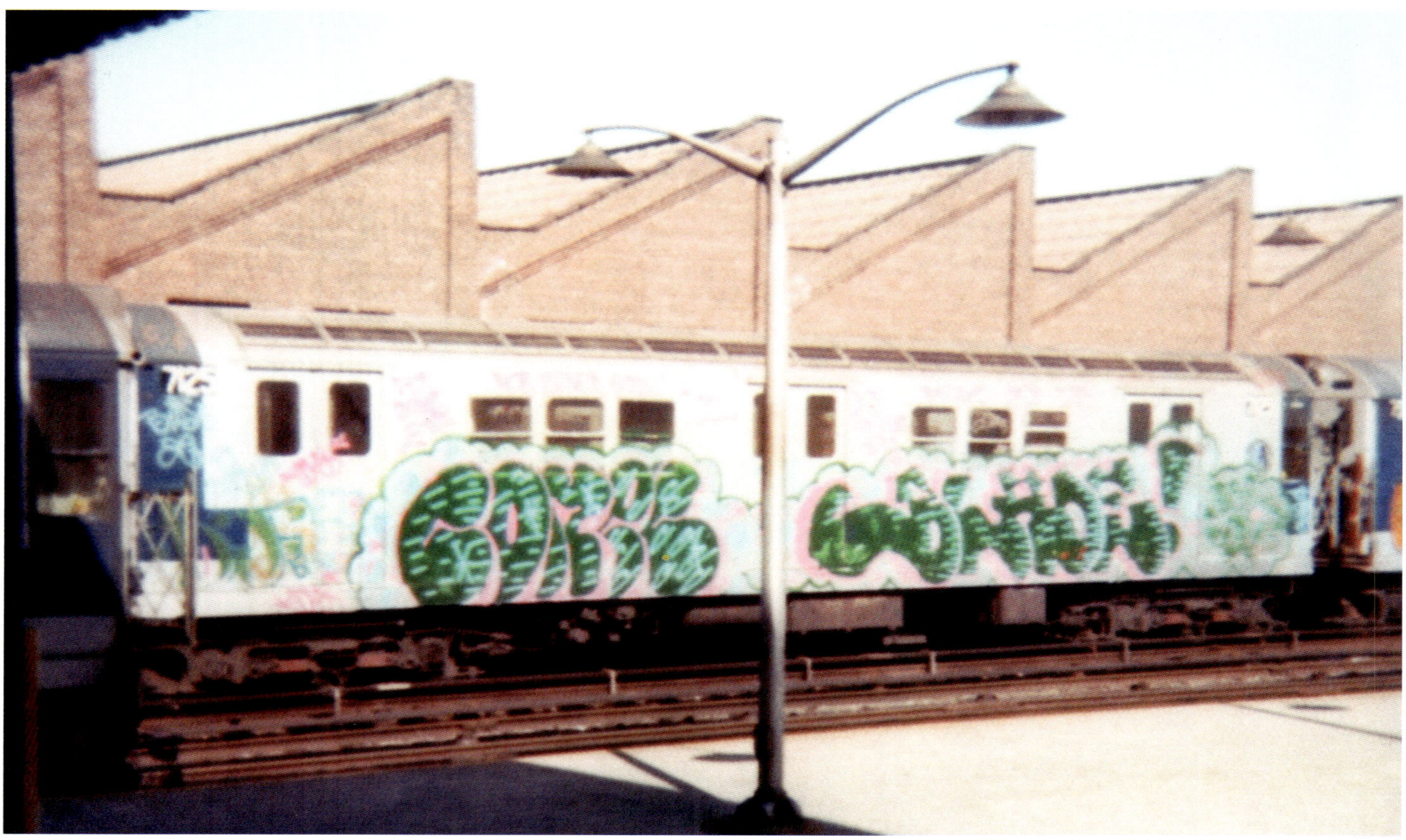

This page: COMET and BLADE window-down cars. Circa 1975.
Opposite page: BLADE AND COMET sit on a rock in Central Park plotting. 1975.
Following spread: Members of TC5 goofing off in Central Park. 1975.

In 1975, VAMM wasn't painting much. He didn't want to piece anymore and he was still dating PUPPY, who wasn't giving it up, so he was distracted. CRACHEE and TULL 13 were near the end of their graffiti careers, because both writers had started college that fall. Both COMET and I just wanted to be out all night bombing. I didn't want to go home because my old man was pissed off about my grades and my not measuring up to his expectations. When I finally dropped out of school, I began living on the rooftop of my old building in Parkside. I slept there a few times the previous year, but in 1975 it became my official address.

The first time I slept there was in May of 1974. Co-op City had built a nice handball court that year, which I did a BLADE piece on. There was an article on the piece in the newspaper, which my parents saw. My dad took one look at my loose-leaf binder with all of my tags and put two and two together. That night, when I came home, he was standing there with the belt again and I caught another beating. As an adult, I understand the position he was in—my parents could've lost their apartment—but as a teenager, I was done getting hit. When everything quieted down, I snuck out the door and ran back to Parkside.

The doors at Parkside were always open—even to the roof. The area I slept in was at the top of the top-floor stairs; the little alcove before you got to the rooftop door. If I slept close to the door, the guards who checked the staircases weren't able to see me. Mitch, Jody, and the others looked out for me, bringing me food and other things.

Usually, I had some cardboard boxes to sleep on and some blankets to keep me warm, so all I needed was a pack of Kools to get through the night. I'd go home for a week until the next argument would break out, then it was back to Parkside. In the morning, I'd wake up and go to the supermarket, where I'd rack up breakfast. I was able to finish a large package of Oscar Mayer bologna and a pint of orange juice before leaving the store. That was my morning ritual.

One summer day in 1975, the whole CRAZY 5 went to Central Park together. At the boat lake, we stole a rowboat, took our clothes off, and then jumped in to the warm water in nothing but our underwear. We swam around the lake most of the day, until COMET and I split from the others. We ended up on a rock, drying off in the sun. COMET started a discussion right out of the Godfather.

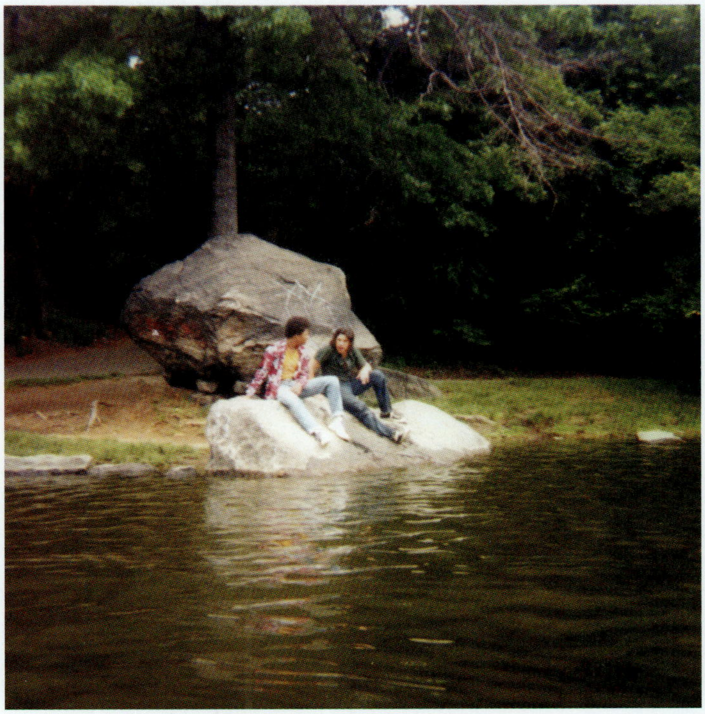

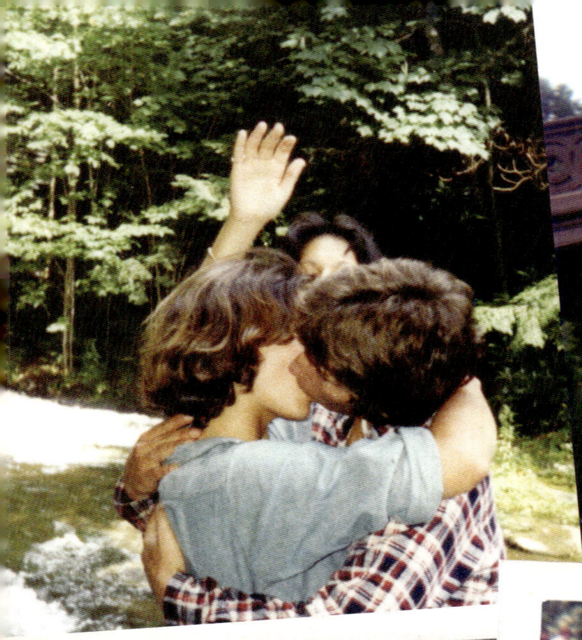
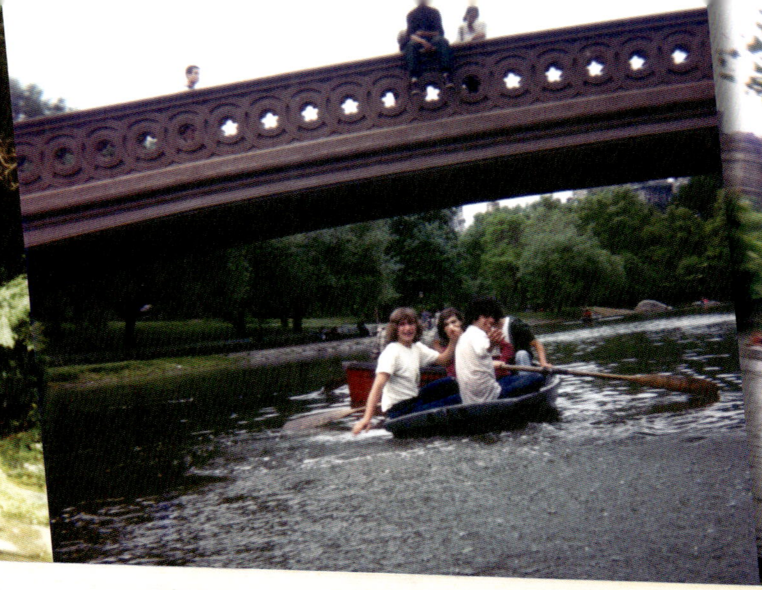
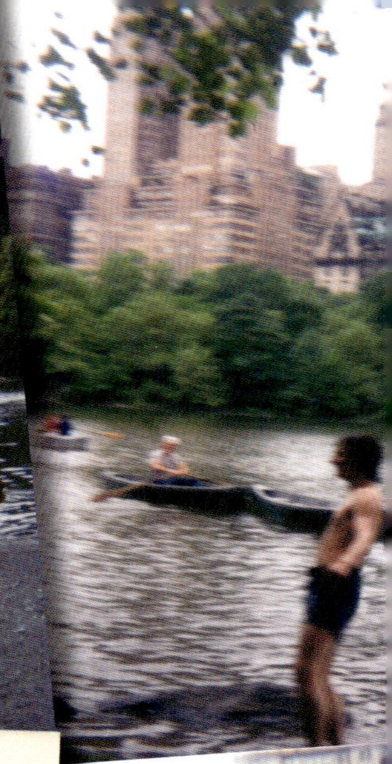
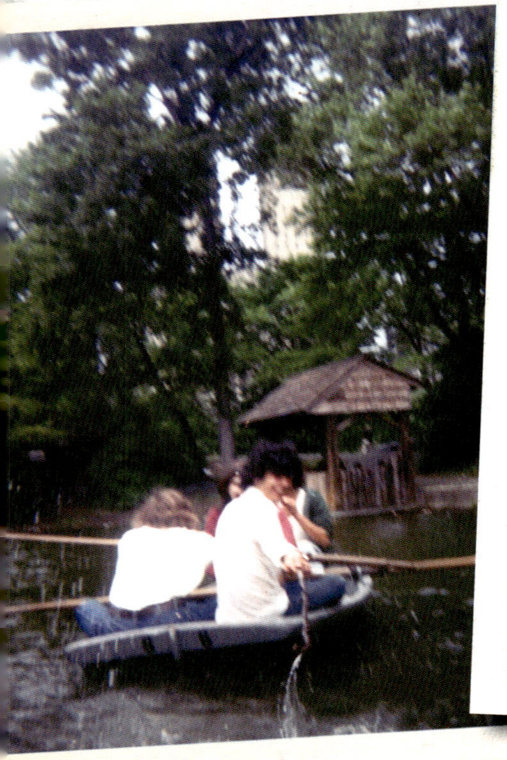
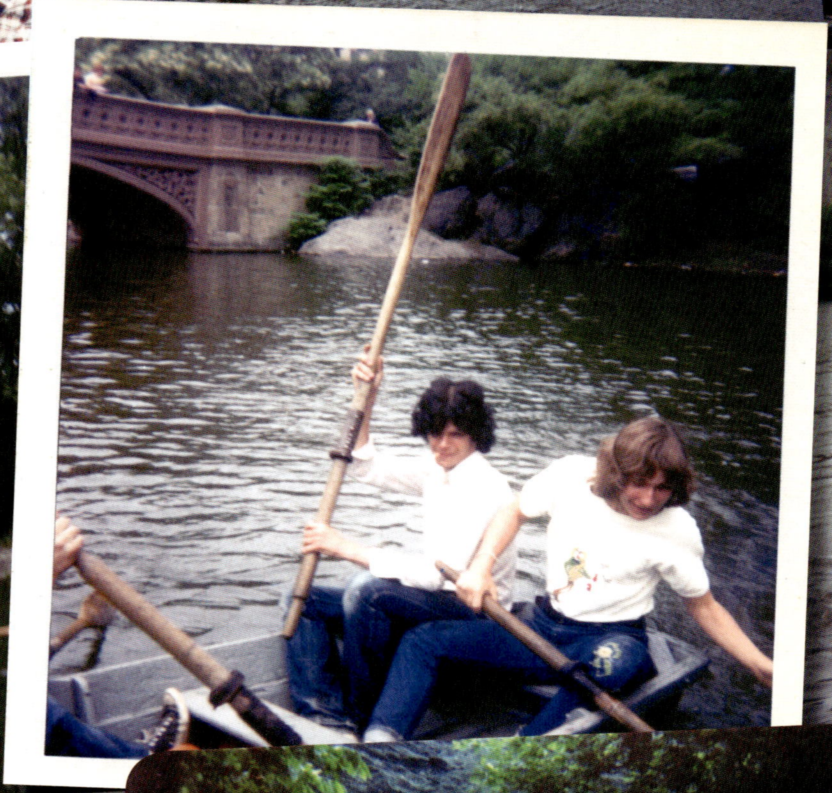
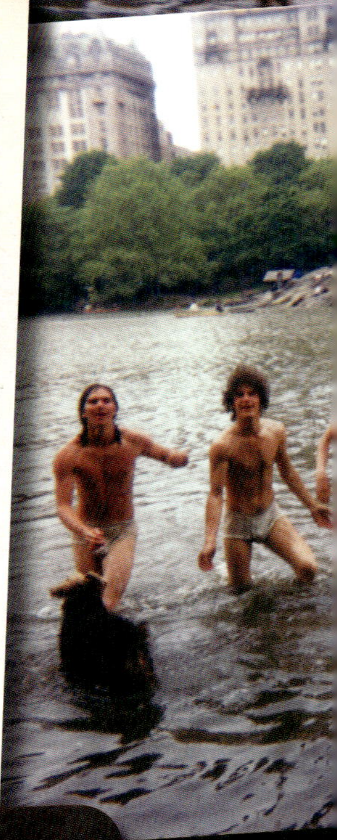
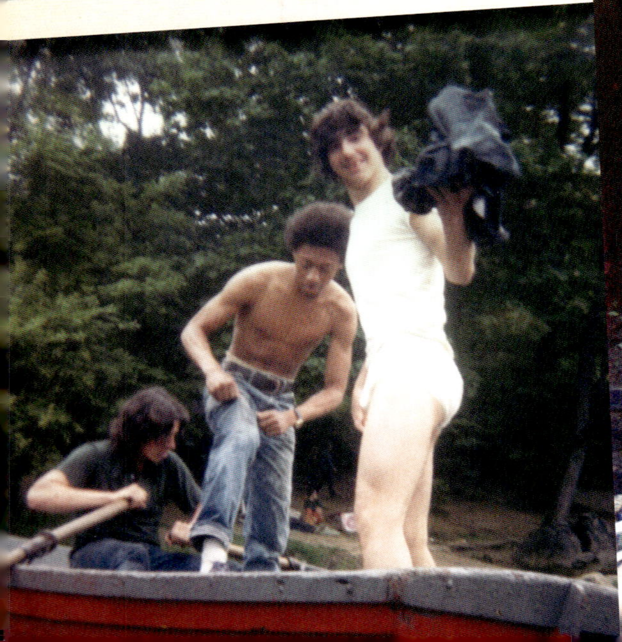
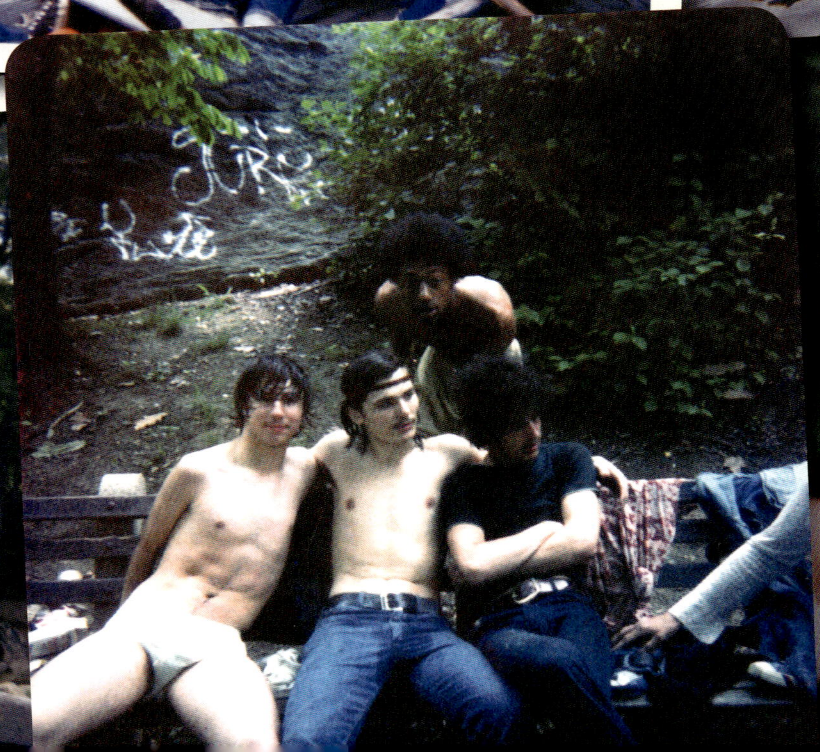
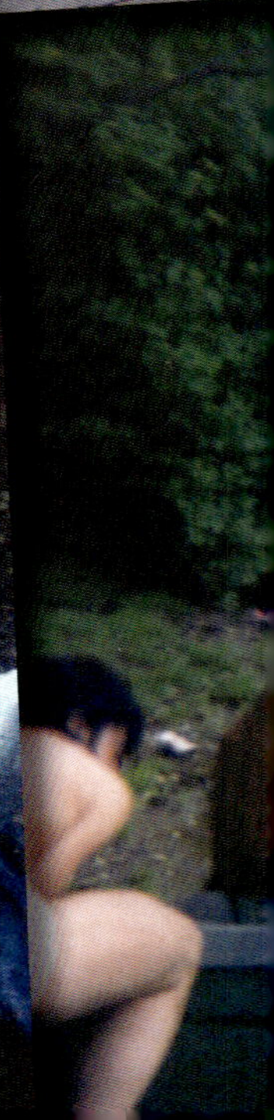

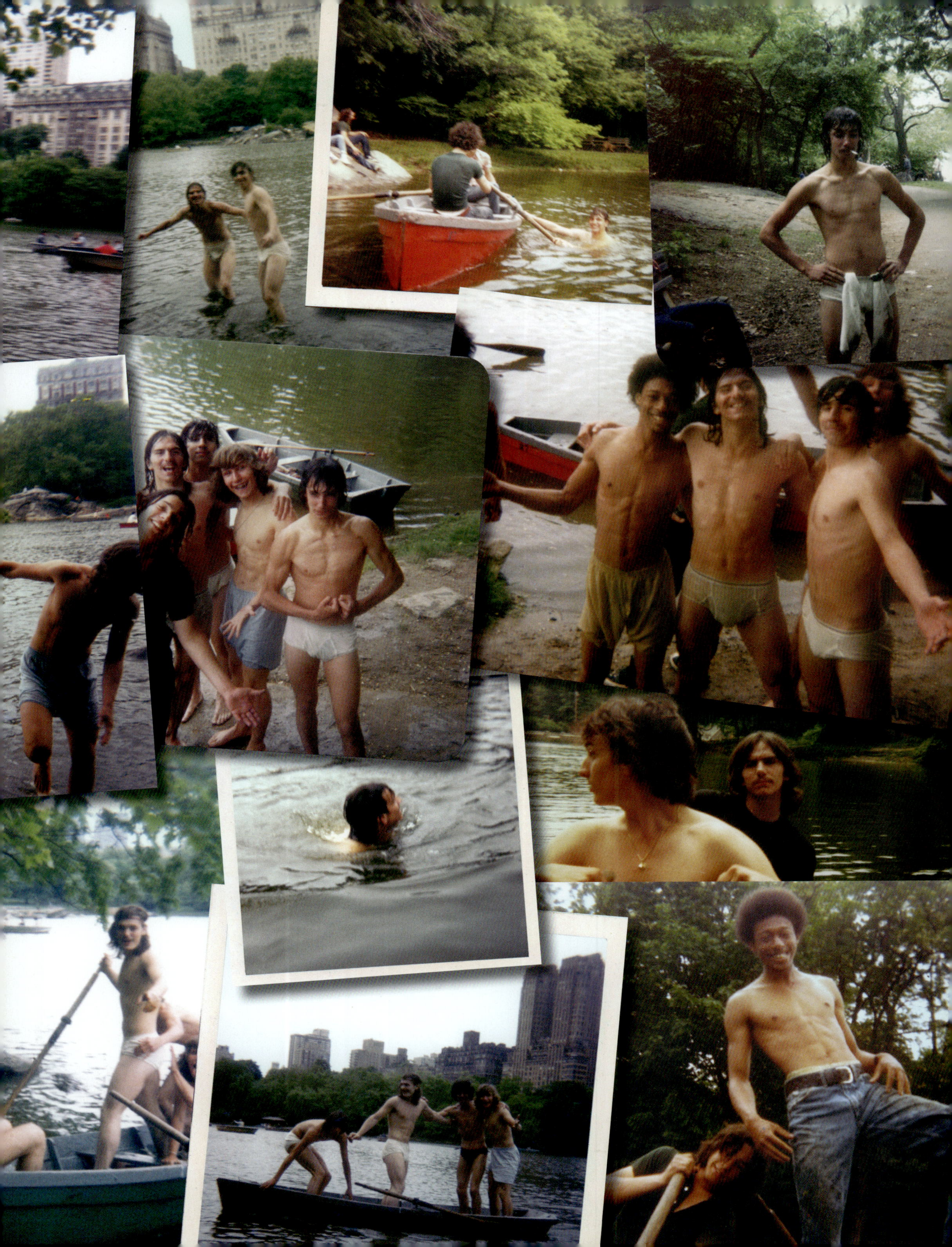

"You know, you and I could take over the 2, 4, and 5 lines together."

"I thought you were writing with CLIFF 159."

"Fuck CLIFF. He can't stay on one line long enough to truly be king. He wants a little piece of every line. I say we take the 2s and 5s together."

"How much paint do you have?"

"Hah! Are you kidding me? I'm white, I'm rolling in spray paint."

"You white boys have it too easy."

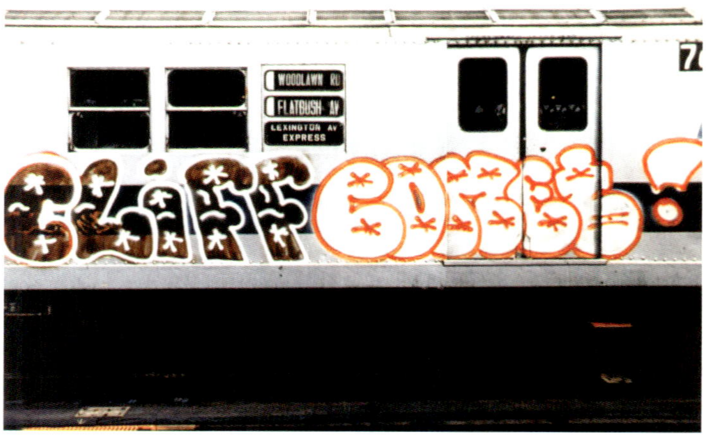

"I'll tell you something else about CLIFF 159. He writes with everybody. I've seen him up with IN, TRACY 168, PNUT 2, TEE, STIM 1, DIABLO, and all of those Brooklyn guys. He's wasting paint!"

"Yeah, he should be sticking to the IRTs. There's nothing in Brooklyn."

"I like CLIFF. I've been to his house and met his mom. I've bought him dinner at least a dozen times 'cause they've got no money. But he's not a writing partner. ... What's up with VAMM?"

"VAMM is cool but he's slowing down. THE CRAZY 5's slowing down. We're all getting old."

"Fuck that. I'm bombing forever!"

That was it. Those were the words: "I'm bombing forever." That's exactly how I felt. I hadn't really thought about the direction of my career or about being king. But obviously COMET had.

"You know, if we king the 2s ... I mean really king the line ... half of those cars will wind up on the 5 line because they switch them with each other."

"We can get the ones we miss at Esplanade."

"Just what I was thinking. If we get the 5s at Esplanade, it's the same thing. Those will get transferred to the 4 line at Kingston."

"That will give us the three biggest lines in the city."

"Can't get more famous than that."

"Fuck no."

By the end of the day we were writing partners. Together, we would hold down the 2 and 5 line from 1975 to 1982.

We started hitting the Burke Avenue lay-up. If that was hot, we'd go to the Gun Hill curve or 225th Street, which was tougher, because if one can fell from the tracks, you were fucked, because you'd have to climb down the elevated pole and then climb back up without anyone seeing you. He was always able to find me when we painted together because I was doing multi-color pieces, so there was always a big cloud of aerosol paint around me. He worked differently. COMET would have eighteen or twenty cans, doing throw-ups down the line. He could walk five cars down and still see me because I was still in the same spot painting my piece. I was never distracted by COMET being nearby, although sometimes I'd hear noises and I'd just have to look. Although I knew it was probably him, I still had to look.

"I'M BOMBING FOREVER!"

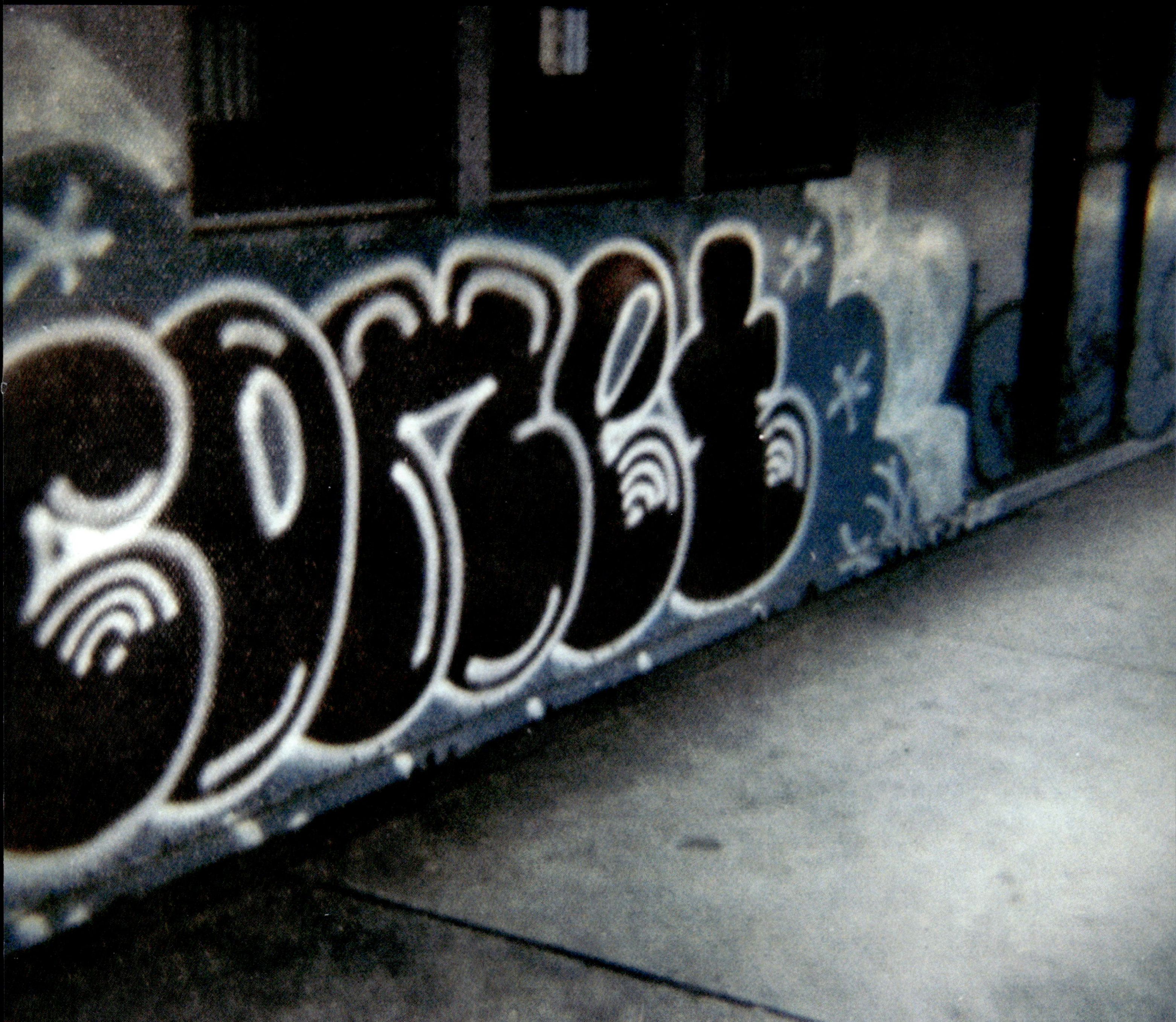

Opposite page: CLIFF and COMET. Circa 1974.
This page: COMET with his classic bubble letters. 1974.
Following spread: Various cars by BLADE and COMET. Circa 1975 -80.

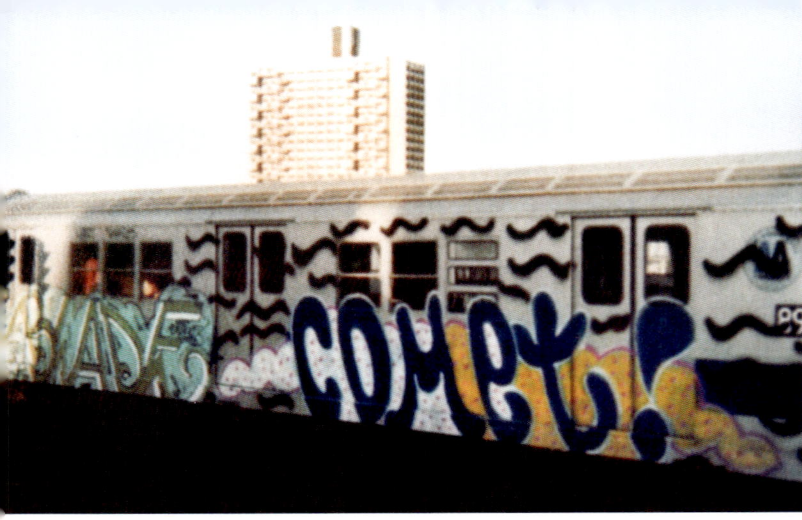
COMET!

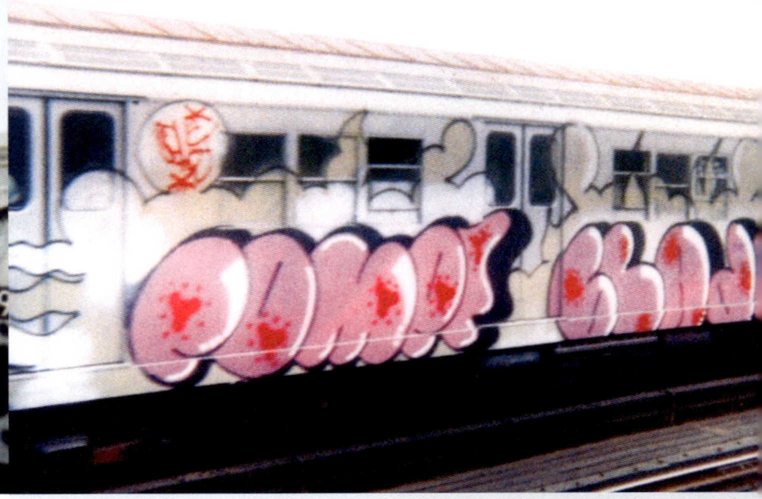

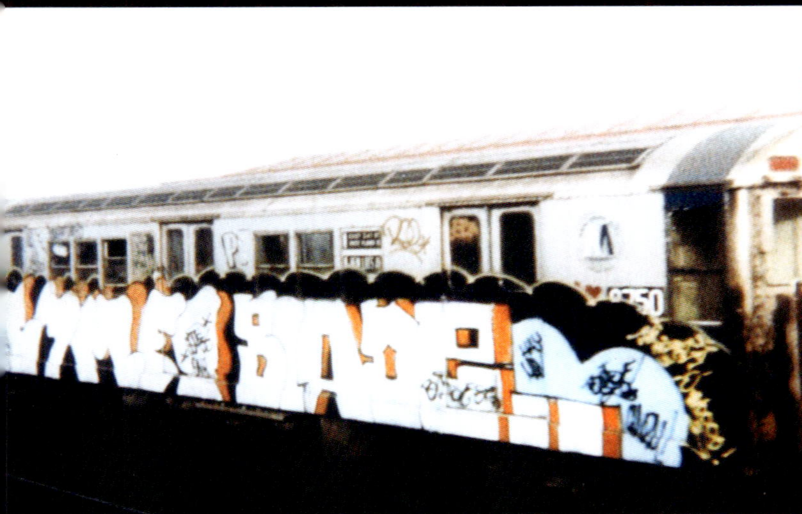

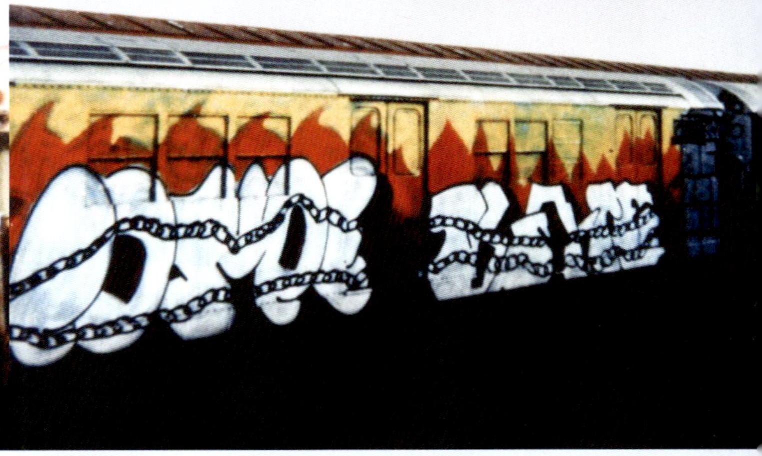

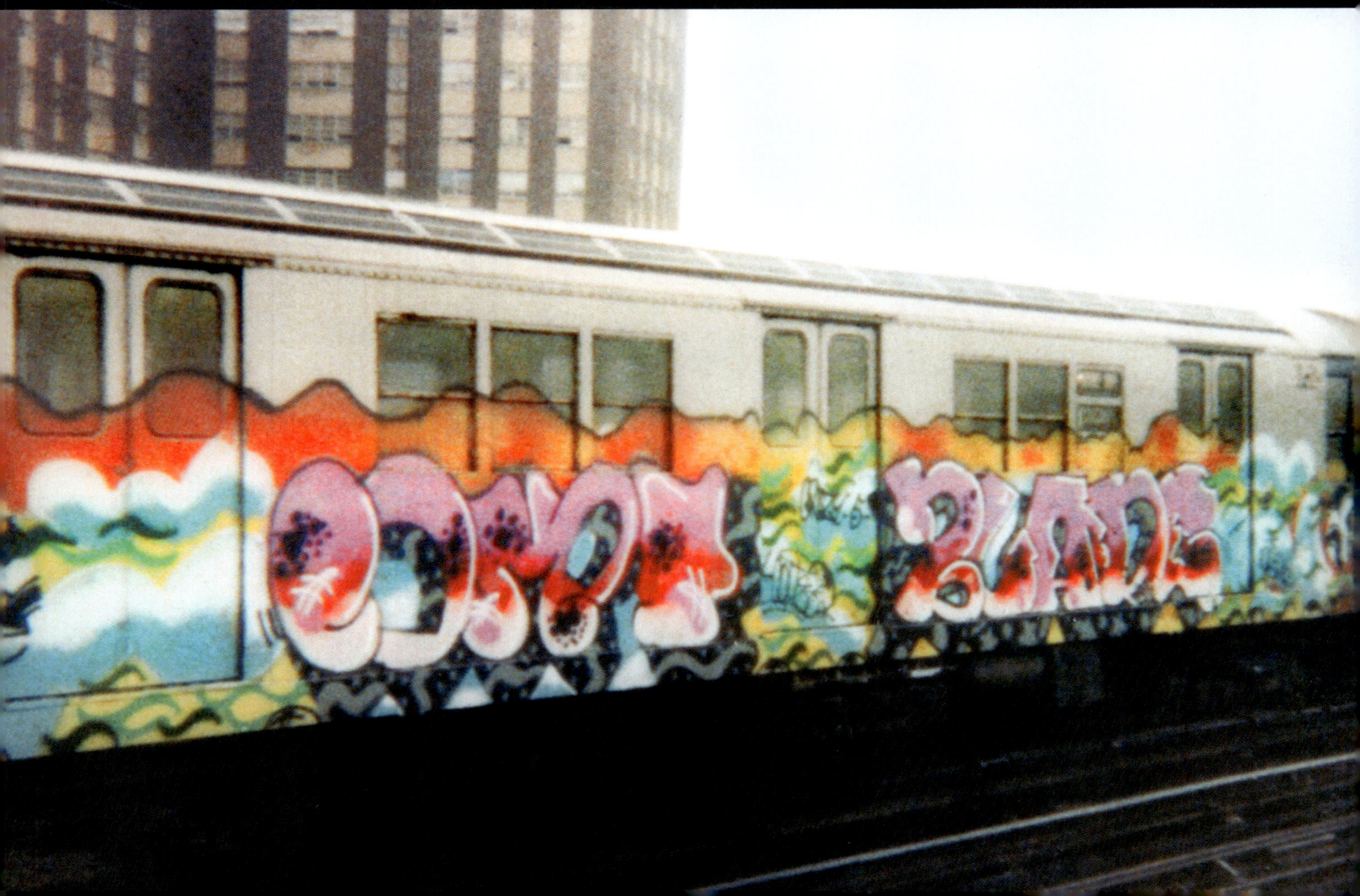

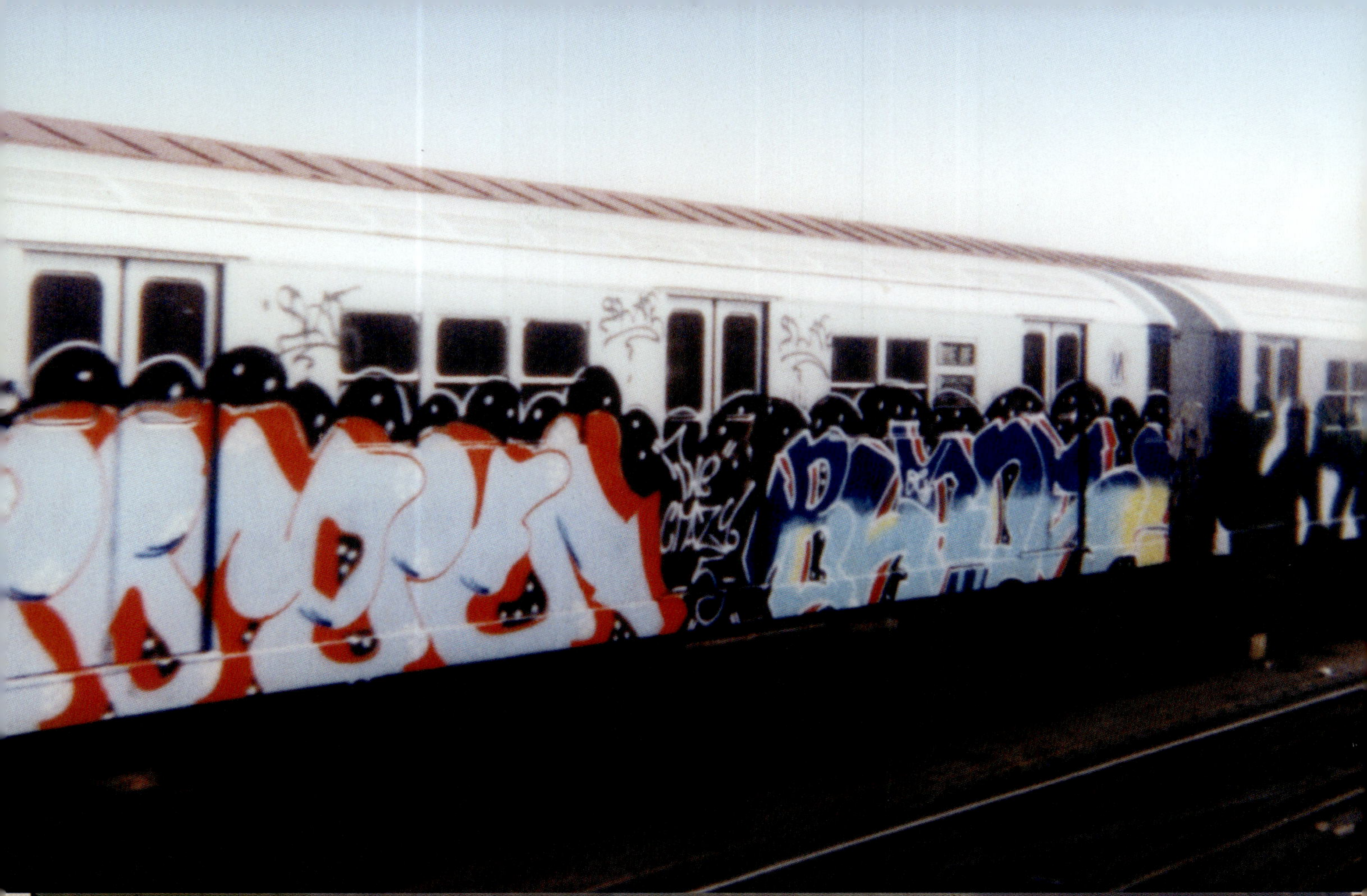

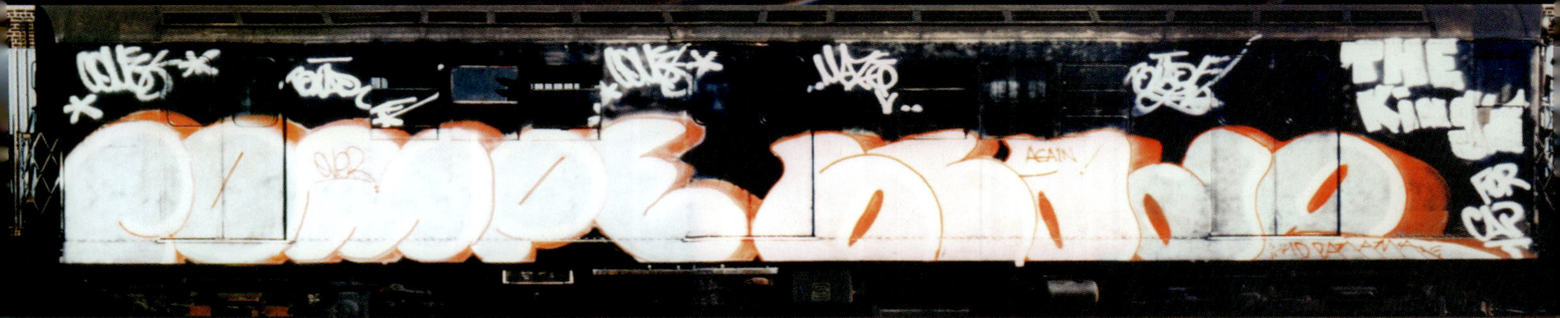

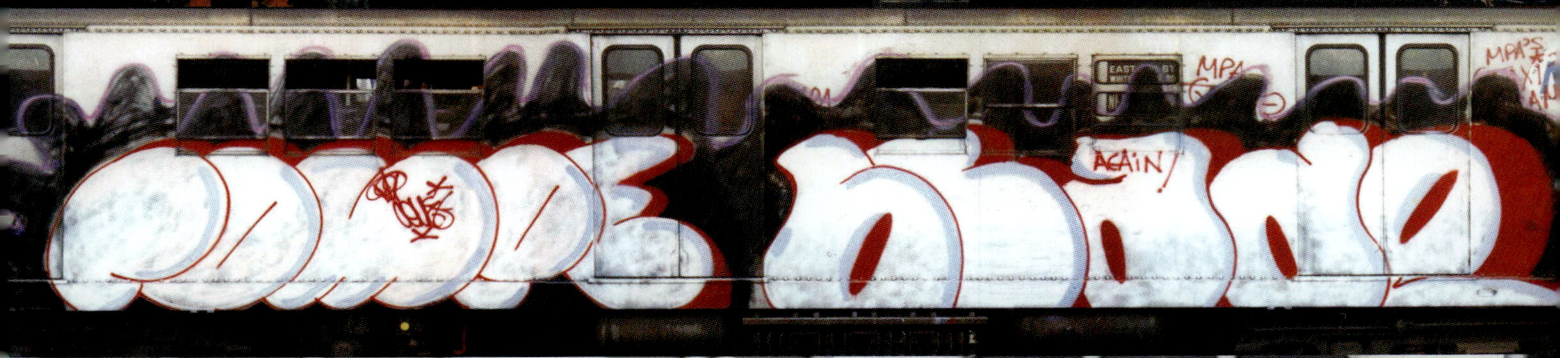

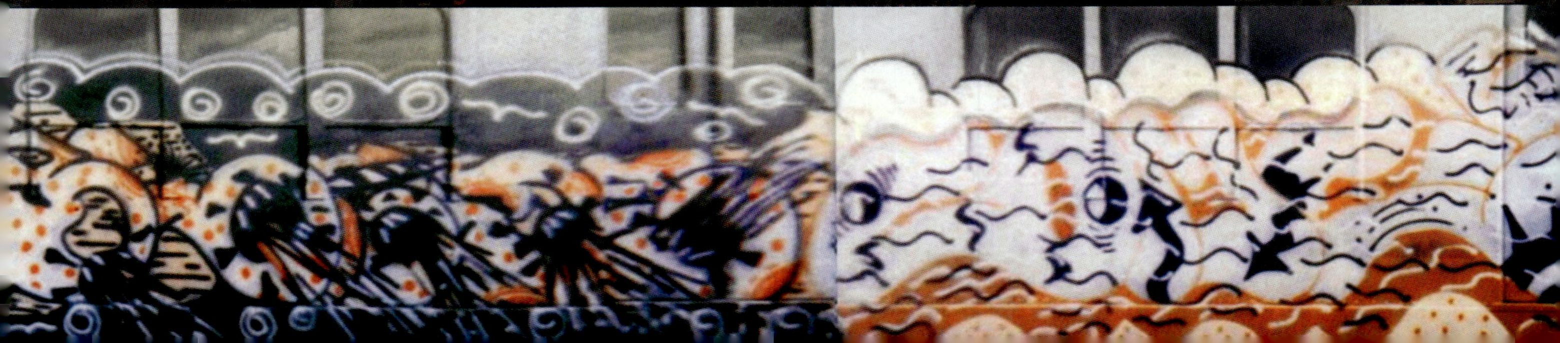

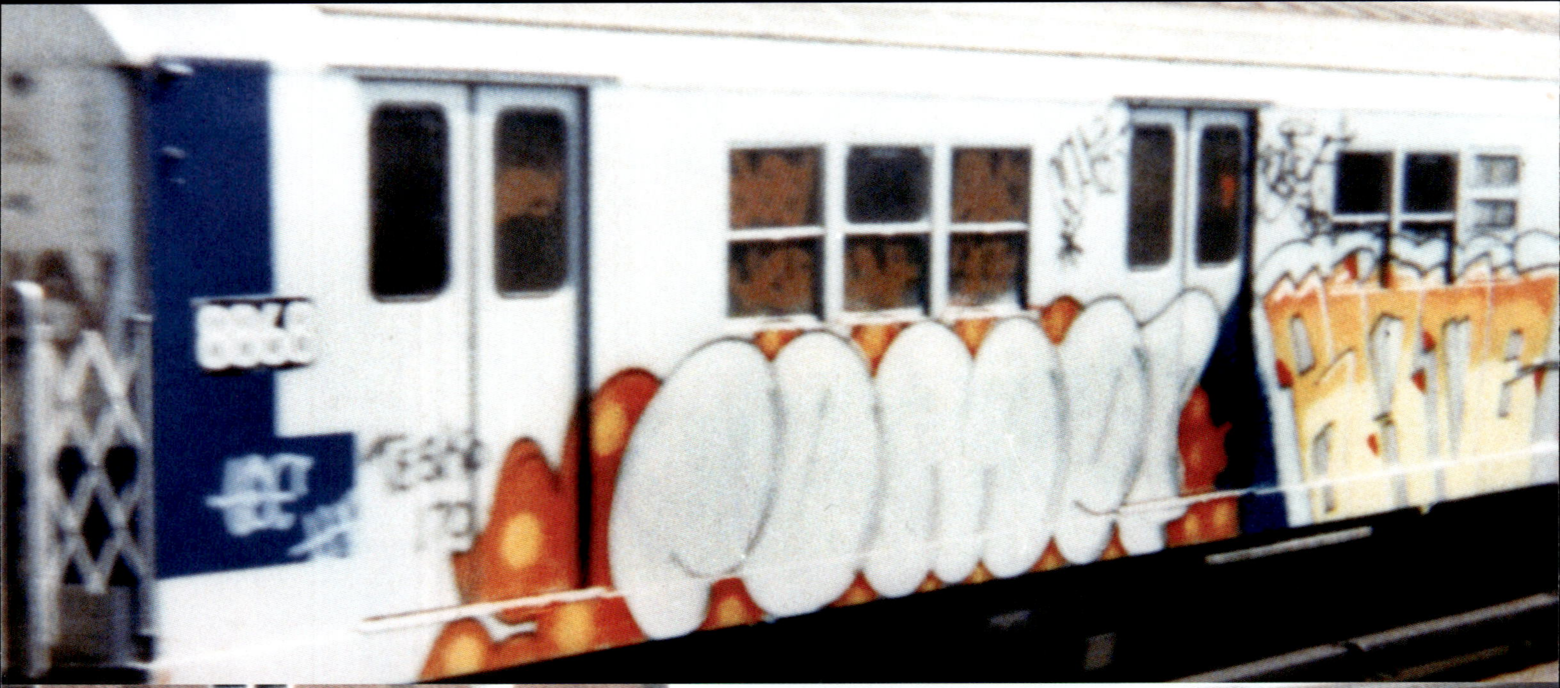

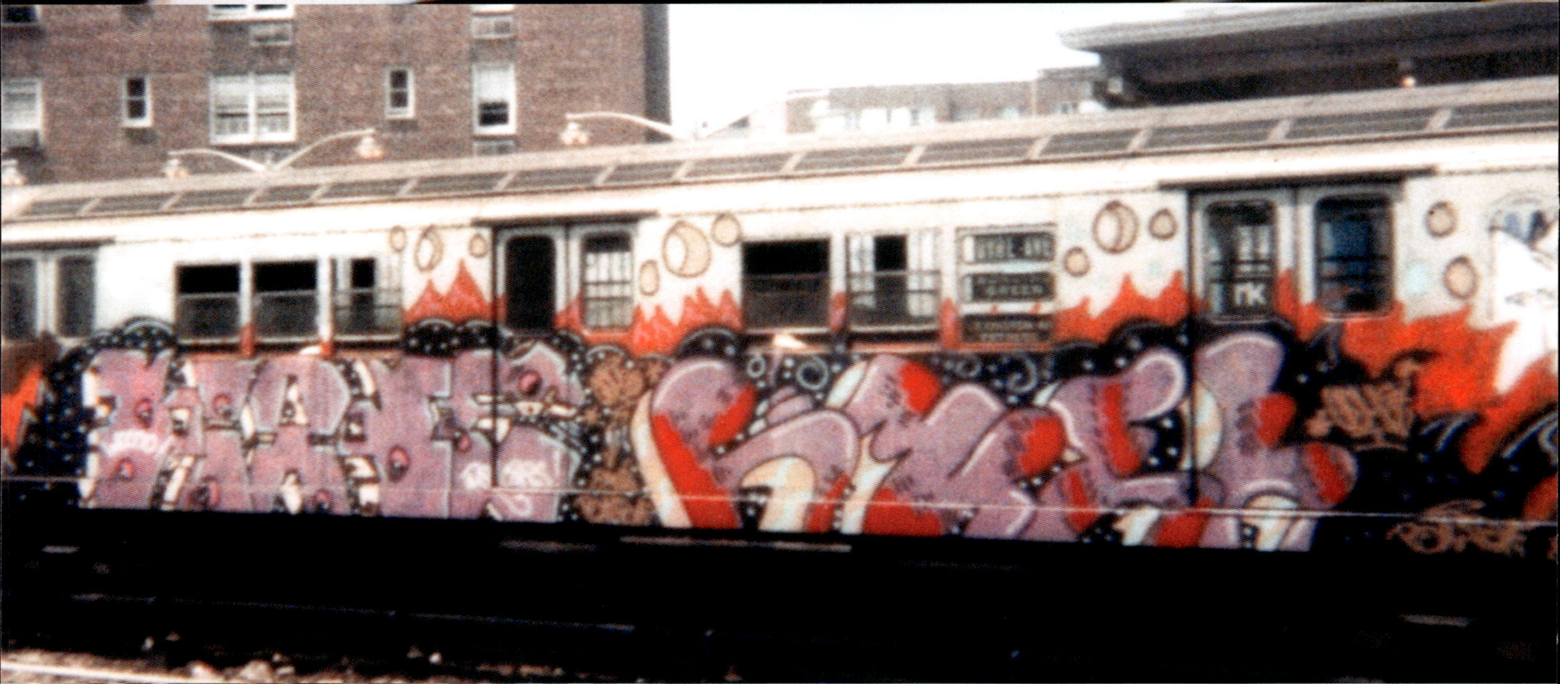

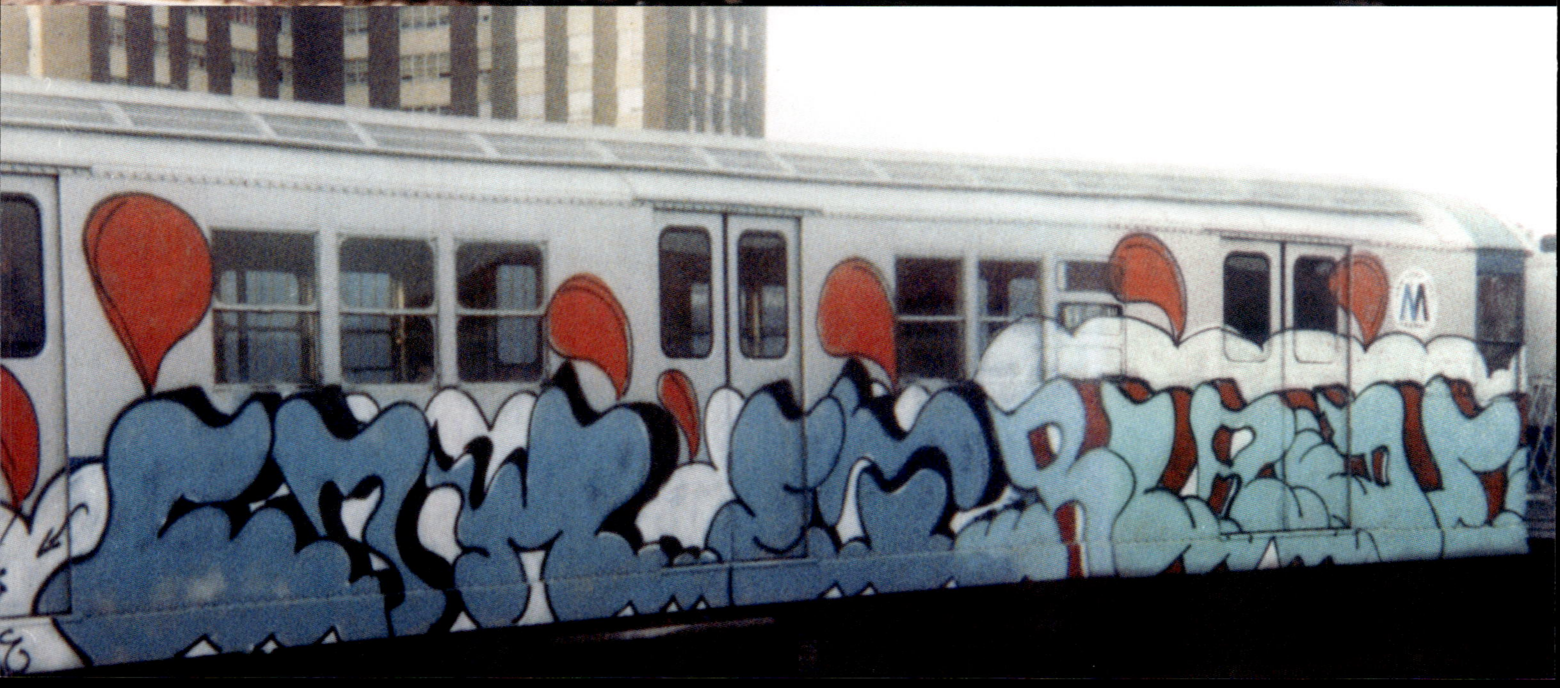

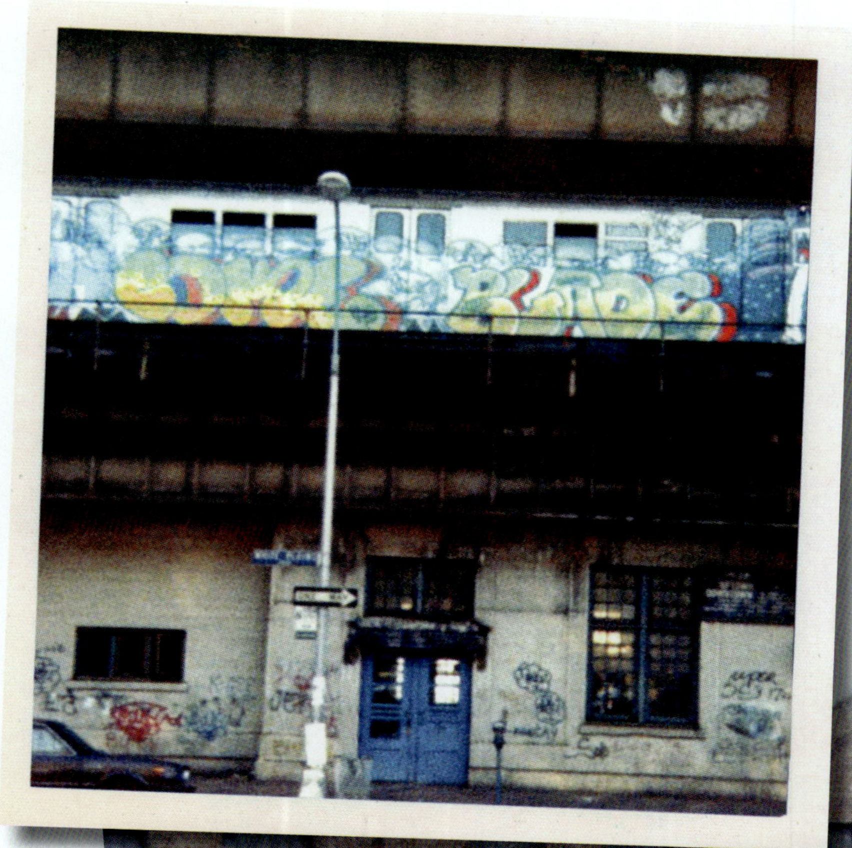

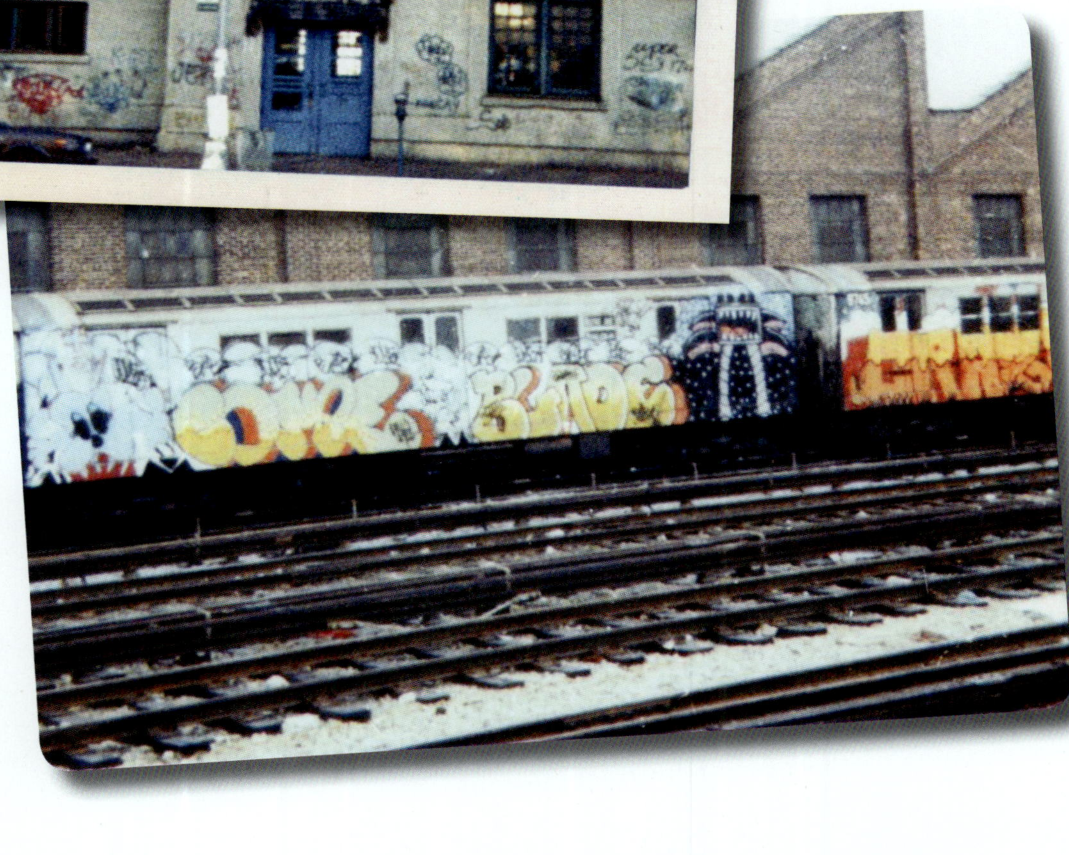

This spread:
COMET and BLADE trains. Circa 1975.

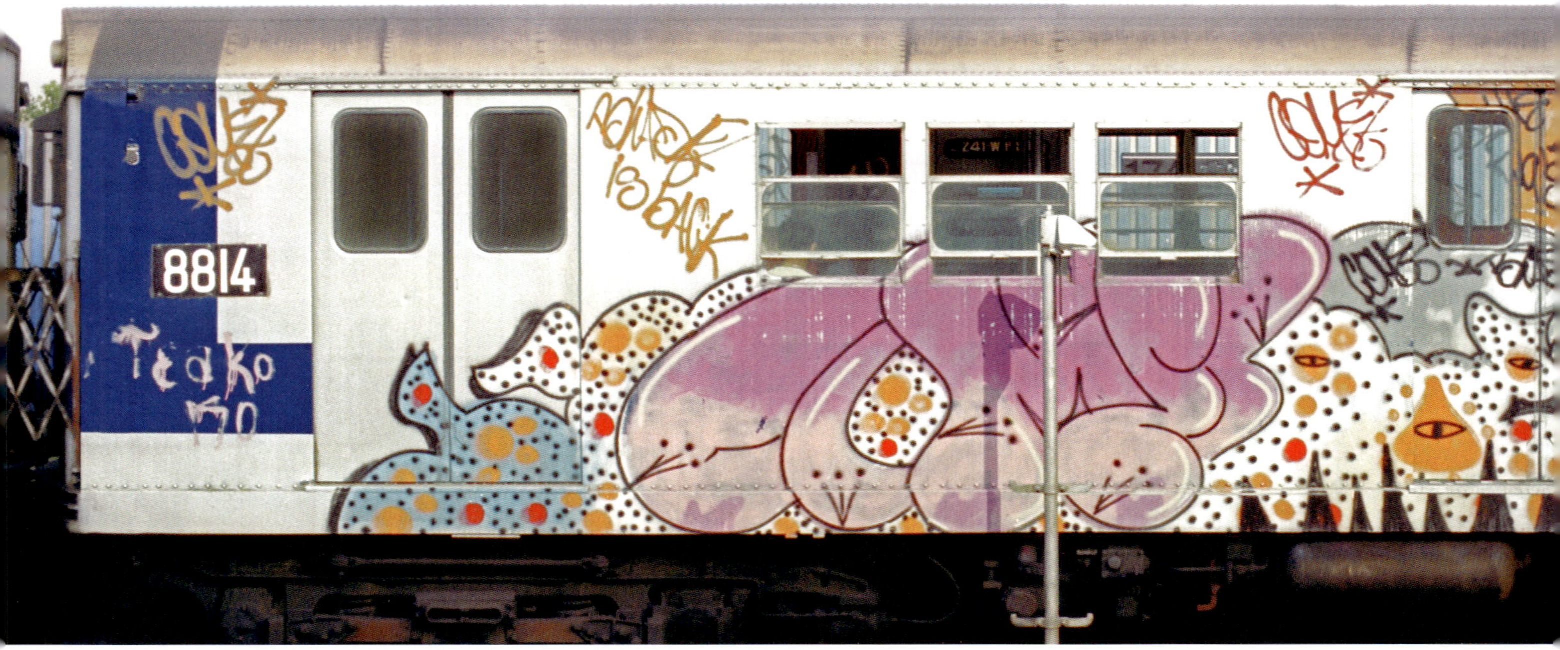

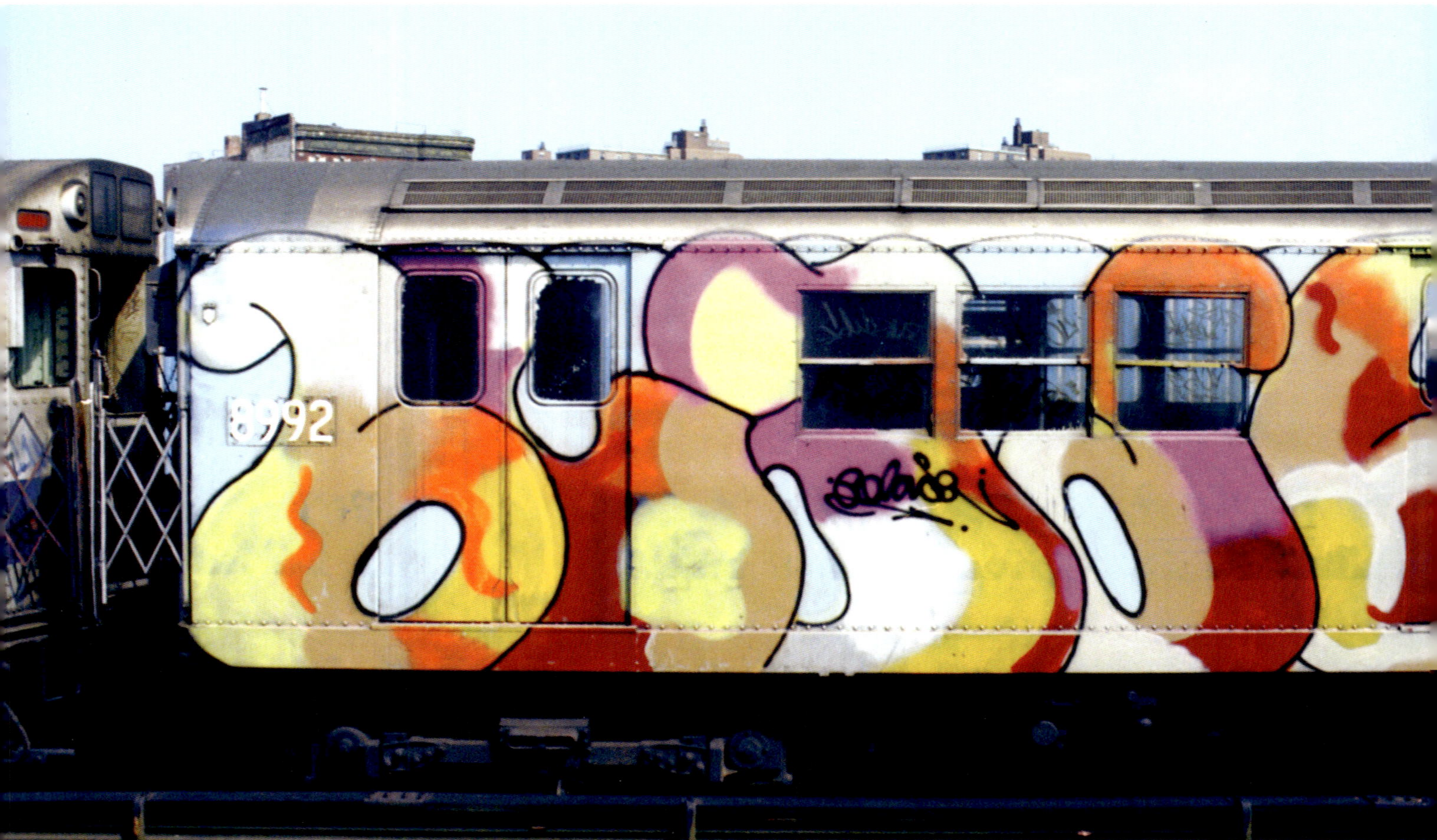

This spread:
COMET and BLADE. Circa 1979. Photos by Henry Chalfant.

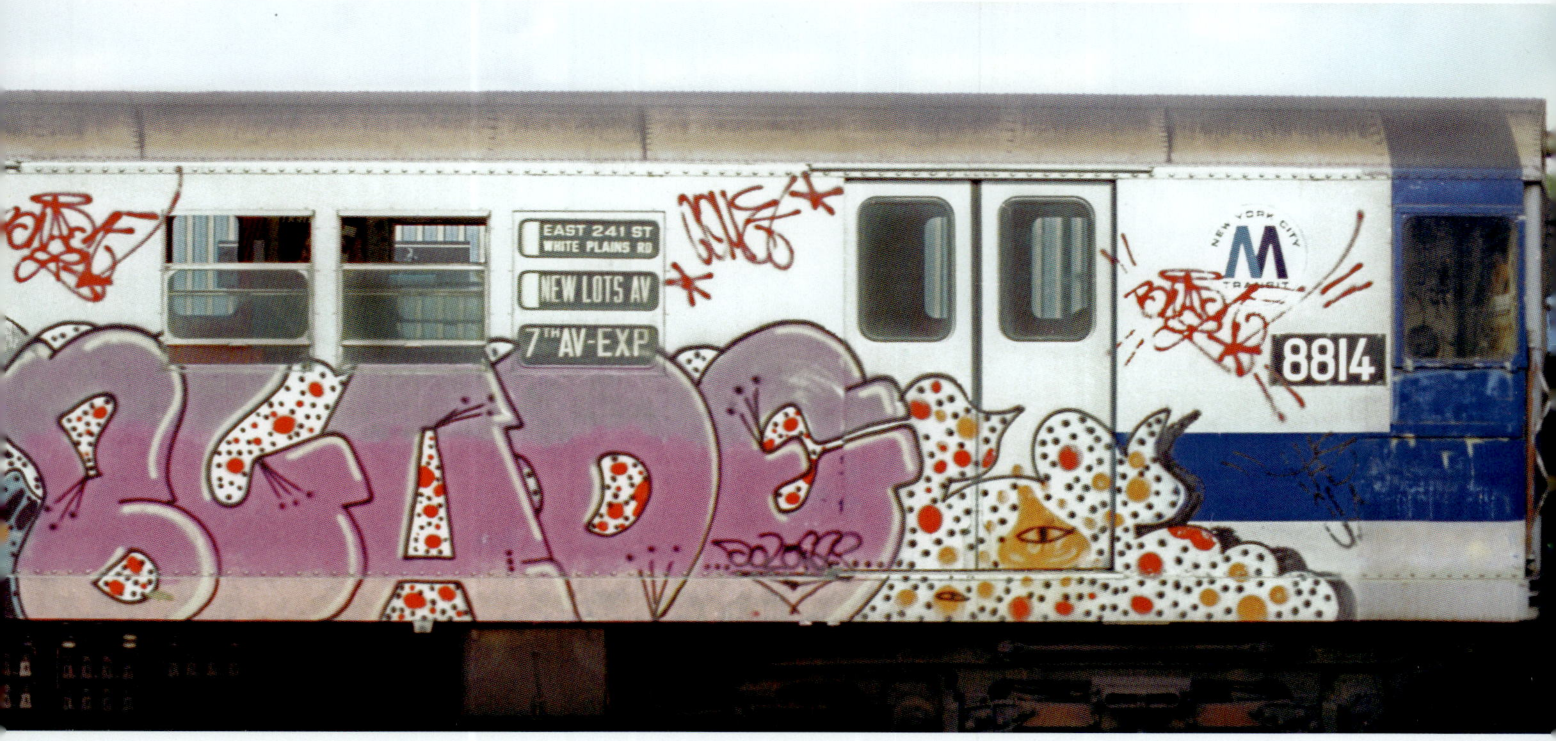
EAST 241 ST
WHITE PLAINS RD
NEW LOTS AV
7TH AV-EXP
8814

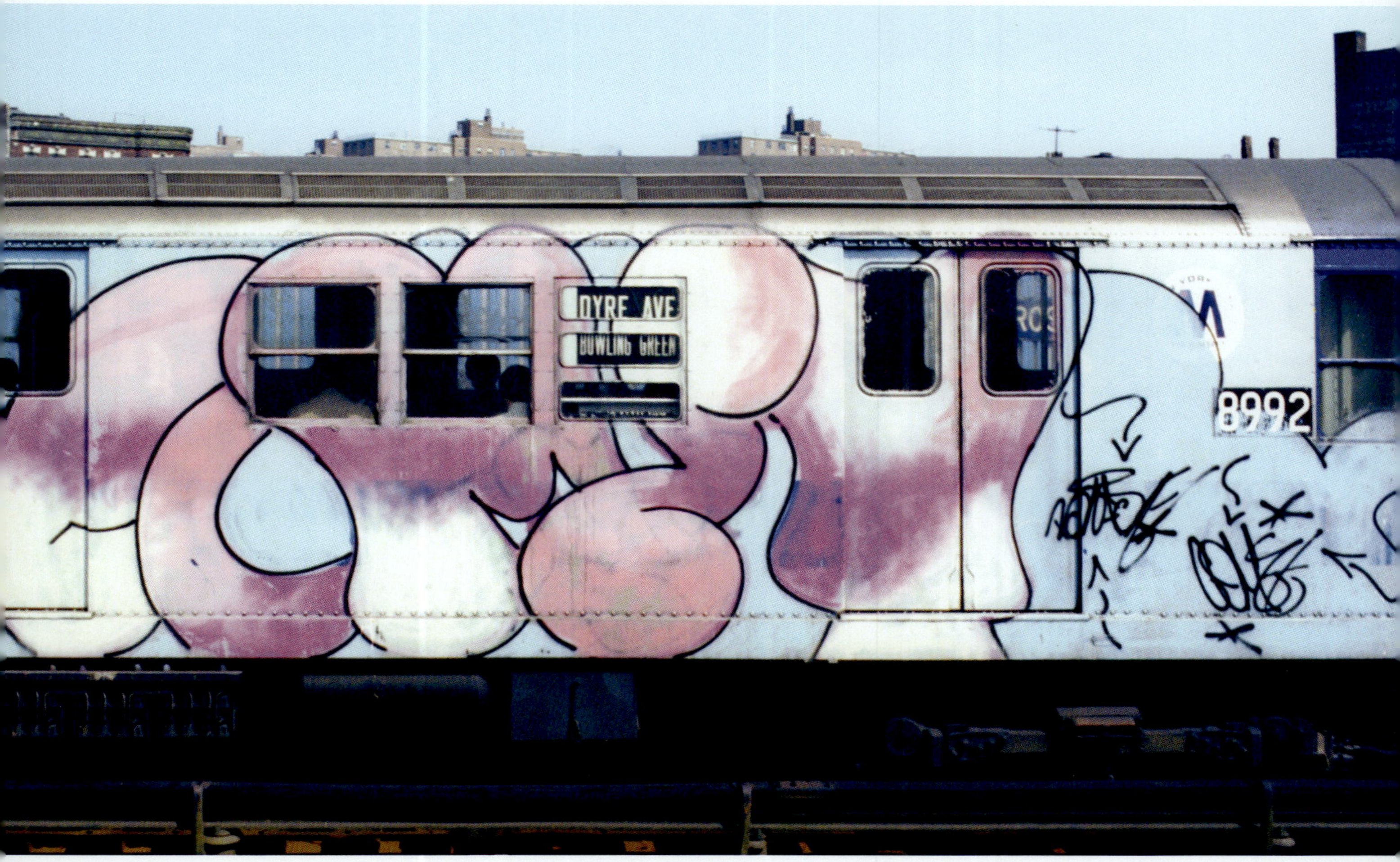
DYRE AVE
BOWLING GREEN
8992

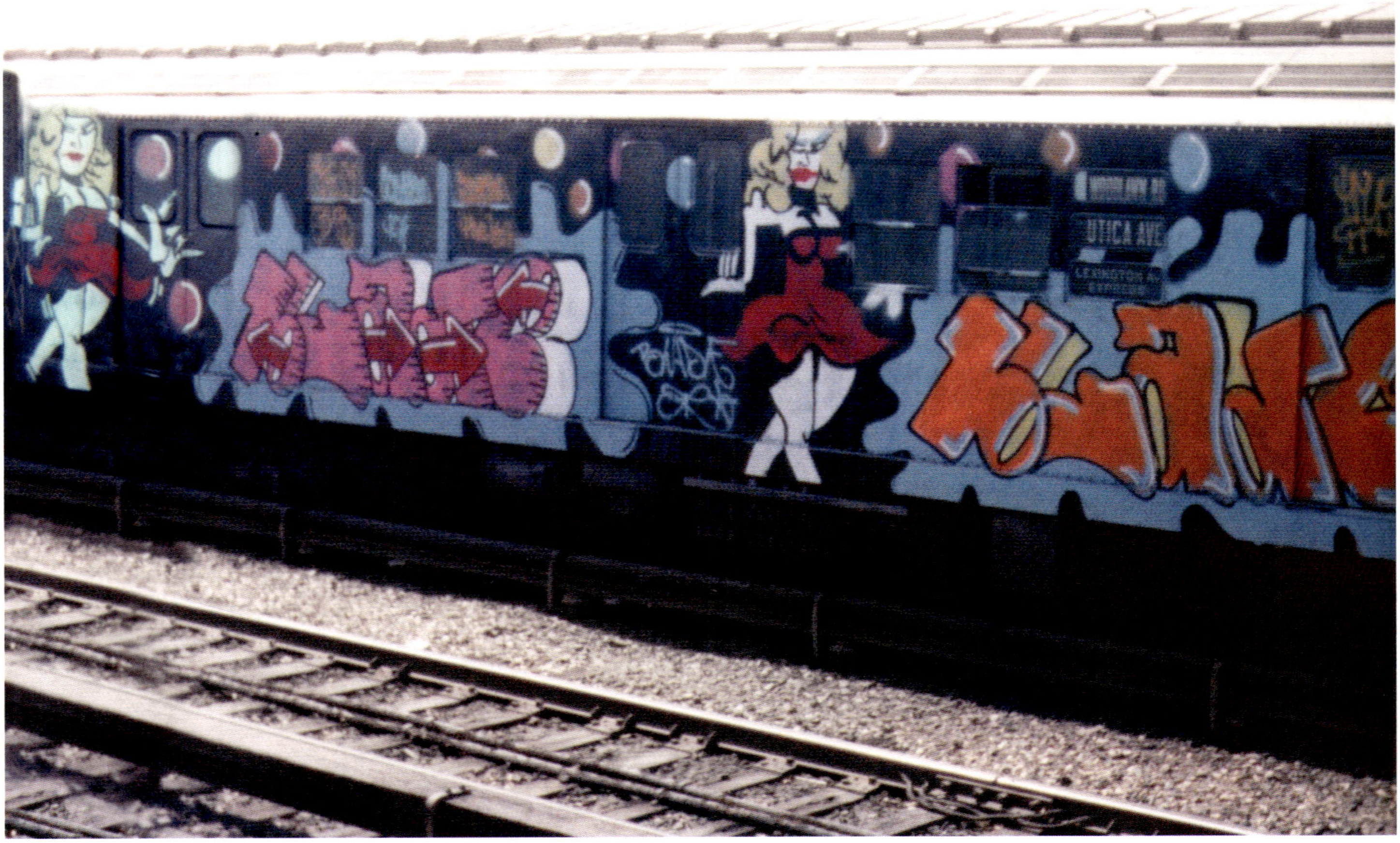

When we got to the 5 trains in Esplanade, it was better because we got to paint pieces together, such as Galaxy Gangster. We did the second version of him as a two-man whole-car. We also did three Joint Men as a two-man whole-car. But in the beginning, COMET just wanted to bomb. He'd say, "Gotta get around, gotta get around." And I'd say, "We're already around! We have no competition, do something creative!"

The most famous car I did, in 1975, was the Dancing Girls whole-car at Esplanade. The train featured two BLADE pieces done in a very rare color known as Sears pink. The pieces were outlined in Krylon hot raspberry. There were dancing girls on the sides of the pieces, which were done realistically. Other writers bugged out when they saw them. It was important for me to challenge guys like CLIFF 159 who were getting famous off of images they were copying from the comics. All of my cartoons came out of my brain.

In 1975 COMET and I worked hard to become kings of the trains—the kings of graffiti. There were other great writers that year, such as TRACY 168, CLIFF 159, and JESTER—all hard-working writers with style. But we worked harder. If we weren't racking paint, we were writing. The cops wanted us and we knew it. One cop chased THE CRAZY 5 for years. He was mad because DEATH pissed on him from an elevated platform— just one of the reasons why the cops hated us. With our crew slowing down in 1975, the cops were looking hard at COMET and I 'cause we kept going.

This page: BLADE's "Dancing Girls" whole-car. 1975.
Opposite page: BLADE and COMET Joint Men car and BLADE's galaxy gangster. 1975.

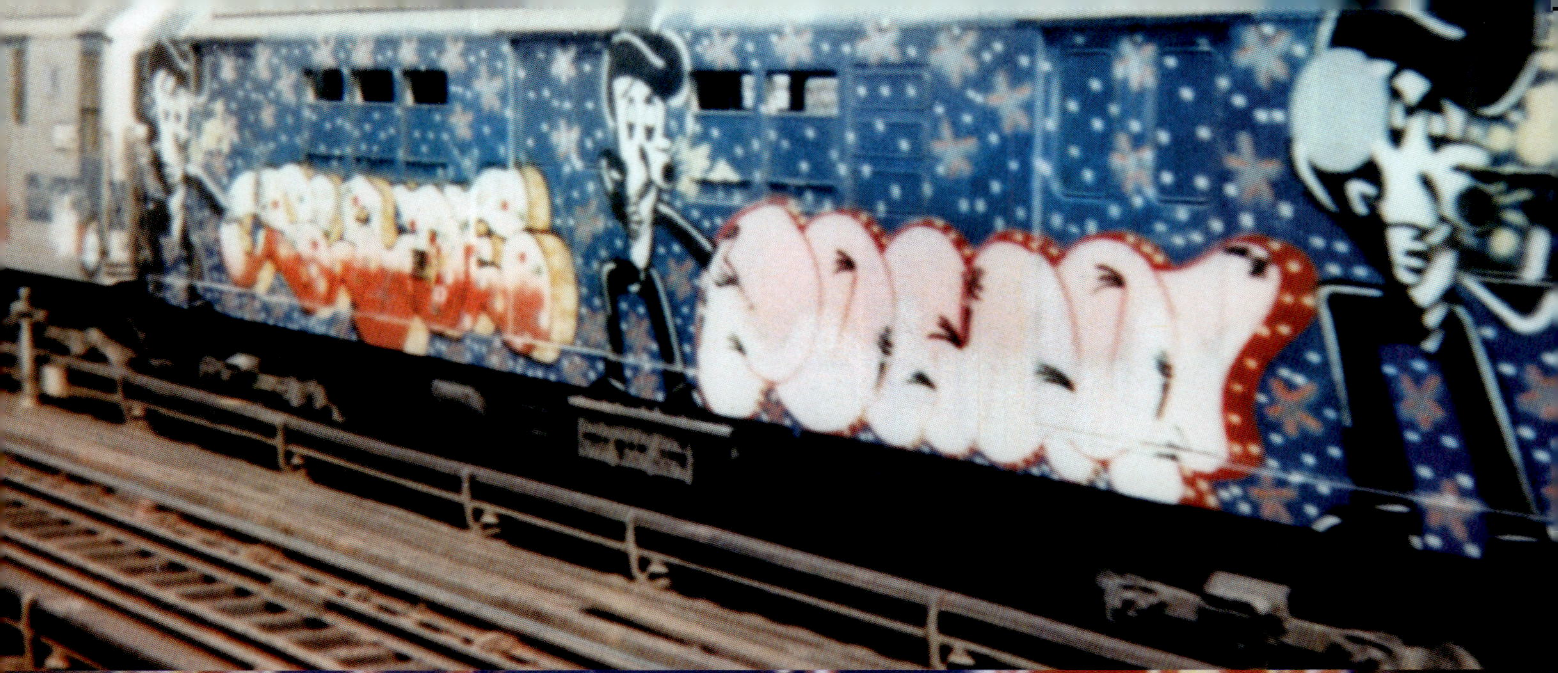

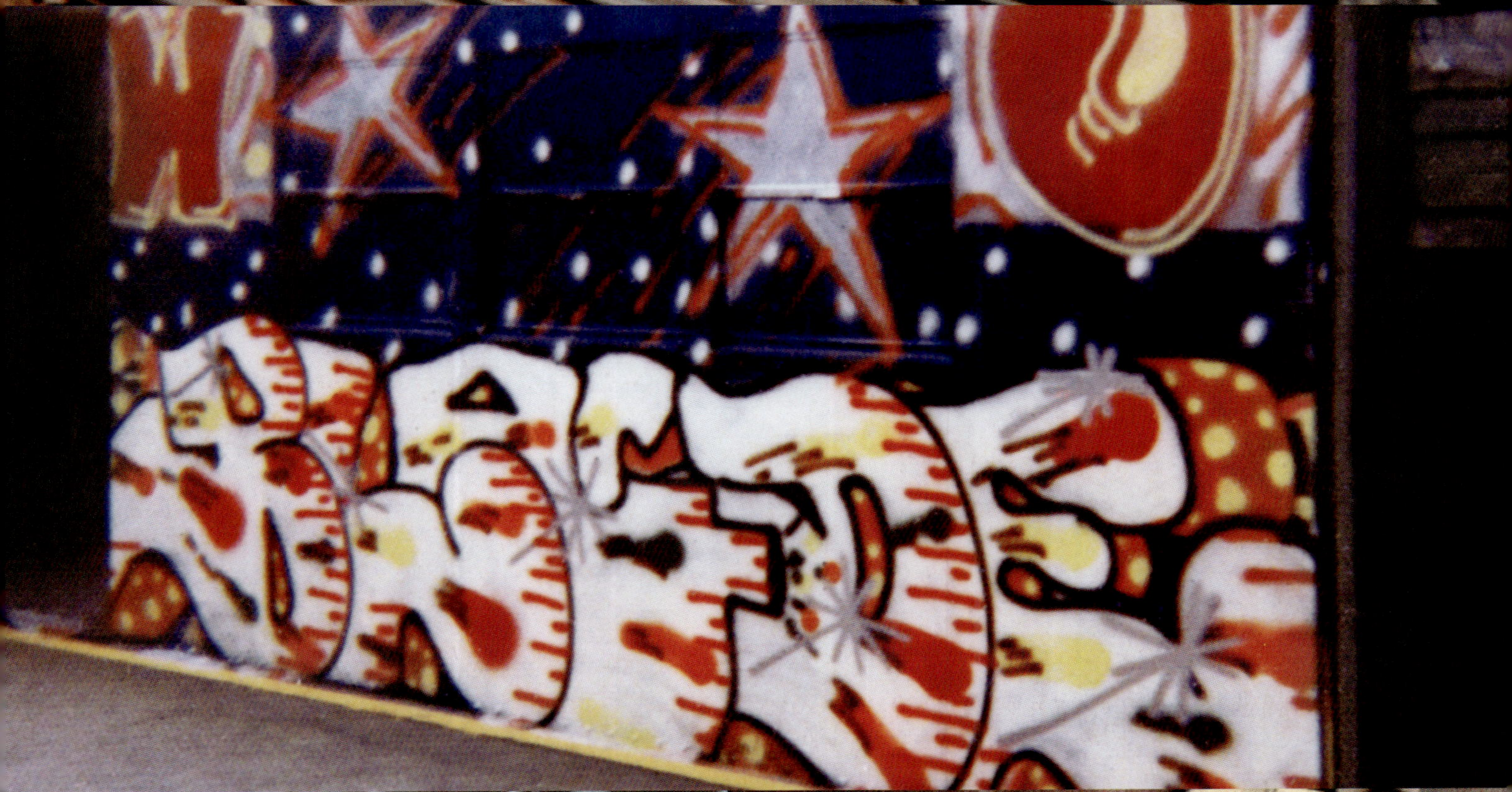

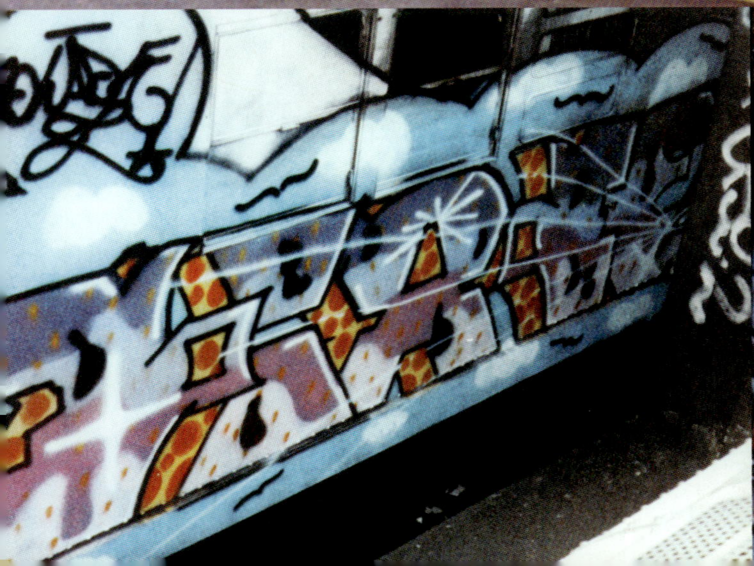

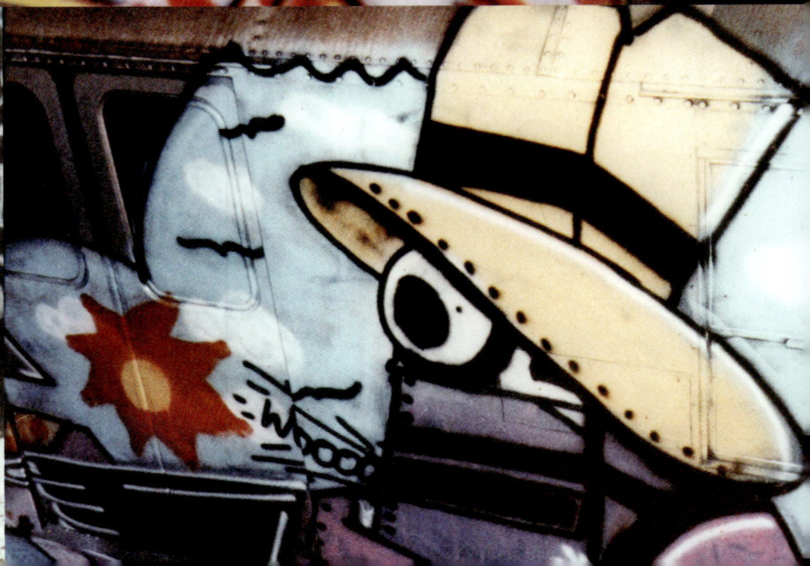

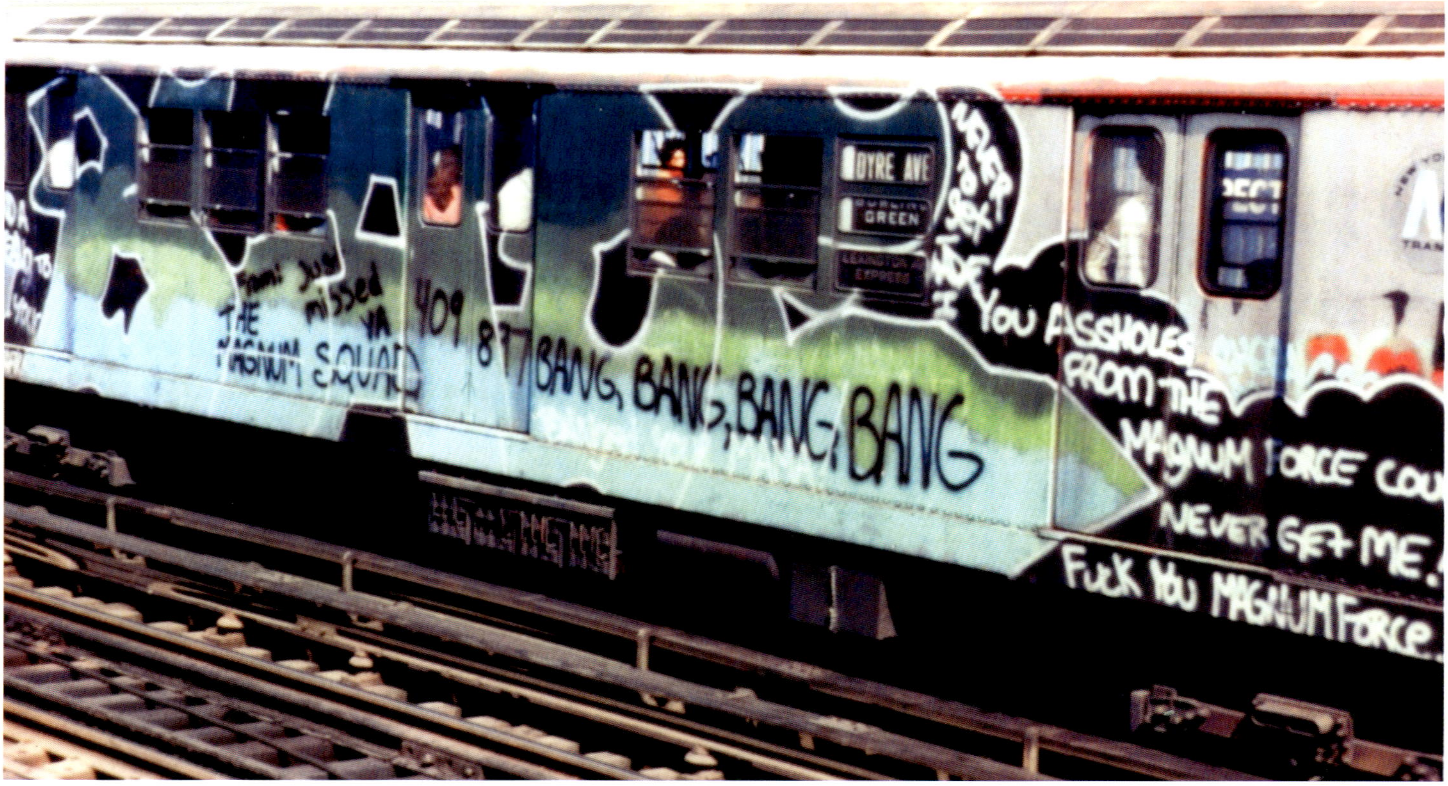

One summer night, after watching Don Kirschner's Rock Concert, COMET and I walked from my house in Co-op City to the Esplanade train station. It was a beautiful night with a spectacular moon out. We barely spoke during the long walk, and when we did, it was with grunts and sighs.

"How can you put Kool and the Gang on with Gilbert O'Sullivan? What the fuck is that?"

"Sheeeeet..."

"Kool and the Gang is one of the greatest funk bands ever."

"So fucked up."

"I've got a great buzz going and Kool and the Gang is kicking ass jamming on 'Funky Stuff' and I'm all ready to paint and then they drop that Gilbert O'Sullivan shit on me."

"Can't even believe it."

COMET and I each had shopping bags full of paint in our hands. Our cigarettes dangling from our lips, how we knew what each other was saying is a mystery to me. But we did. It's one of those funny things writing partners have, a kind of verbal shorthand.

The token booth clerk was awake, so we paid our fare and entered the station—no sense in blowing up the spot. We walked down the stairs and leaned out over the platform looking for trains. A number 4 subway was laid up in the tunnel. We casually climbed off the platform, jumped on the tracks, and walked toward the train as we had done almost every Saturday night for the last year.

I broke out the paint and we quickly sketched our outlines. Then we started with the fill-ins. We were graffiti machines; we had done this a million times and we were fearless. There were many nights at Esplanade when I'd bring my transistor radio with me to listen to music. I can remember doing pieces while listening to President Nixon break in with a speech about committing more troops in Vietnam or talking about a particularly important bombing mission.

That was the early 1970s.

Later that night, I saw two silhouettes climbing off the platform about twenty feet from me and a bunch of voices started shouting at once.

"Freeze! Freeze now! Don't make a fucking move!"
"You're under arrest, assholes!"

That was our cue to leave, so we hauled ass and left our paint behind. Fuck the paint—there was always more paint to rack. I spun around for one last look and there stood Artie and Freddie—two DTs from the vandal squad—with their guns drawn. Pop, pop, pop! They fired their weapons. Now I was afraid. I'll never know if they were shooting at us or up in the air. I made it out of the tunnel and hid behind the old blockhouse, trying to make my six-foot frame even more slender than it was.

I watched the train in the background, half in the tunnel and half out. COMET climbed to the top of the train to figure out which way to go, and then he raced toward me. When he reached the last car he jumped high into the night. From where I was hiding it was as though COMET became a superhero: a black flash flying through the air. He landed on the rocks below and stumbled. Artie was right there pointing his gun at him. COMET ran again and dove over a fence as Artie holstered his gun. We both took off into the Bronx night. We spent the next two hours hiding in a tall field of grass as squad cars circled our location. Then we left. We were 'wanted' all right.

The next day, we met up at Parkside where it was business as usual: smoke some hash, shoot hoops, and flirt with the girls. What we didn't know was that Freddie and Artie weren't done with us. They drove up to Parkside and took us out in handcuffs. We weren't under arrest, which meant I was probably in trouble, but COMET might catch a pass because he was white. This was the last generation of old school Irish cops; if they couldn't catch you at the scene of the crime, an ass kicking the following day would do just fine.

Freddie and Artie drove us around in the back of their unmarked car. Our final destination was the old tombs underneath the 3rd Avenue El. The place was decrepit and it stunk; water seeped out of the walls and rats walked right over your shoes. They put us in separate cells and started what they called their 'interrogation.'

I heard them talking to COMET, but I don't think they beat him. Then it was my turn. The first hit was just a wake up call. SMACK!

"You guys know each other?"

"No officer, I was just shooting hoops and he came into the playground and we started playing 21."

"Just tell us that you and COMET were there the other night. We'll give you a D.A.T (Desk Appearance Ticket). But don't fucking lie to me."

"Officer, I don't know the white guy. It was just a game of 21."

Then came the heavy hitting. PUNCH. This went on for hours. The same shit. I could've taken a beating all day because there was no way I was going to rat on COMET or anyone else for that matter. Unwritten rule in graffiti: you never fucking rat! After they were done beating on me, they marched us both through the hallways and tossed us out the front door. I was messed up for days afterward, with lumps sticking out of my head. That was 1975—when we were kings.

Opposite page: BLADE dissed by the Vandal Squad. Circa 1978. Photo ©Jack Stewart.

CHAPTER EIGHT

THE BAZAY BAND AND MOVING OUT:

1975–1976

I've had a love affair with music since I was a kid listening to my transistor radio. The first pop songs I remember are by The Temptations and the Motown sound. The first record I owned was "Honky Tonk Woman" by The Stones. I remember playing "Wipeout" on my school desk and getting whacked by the nuns. WWRL was the station we all listened to. They played the top-twenty format all day long. 45s were 69 cents. We thought that was funny, even though we didn't know what it meant.

There was always music in our house growing up, usually swing bands, jazz, and standards from the 1940s and 1950s, which my dad was into. One of the best things to come out of my stay in Saratoga was watching Uncle George work his craft. On Friday and Saturday nights, he'd take me to the different clubs he played in and prop me up on a barstool. The cokes were on the house and I'd sit there mesmerized as my uncle played for hours. I became passionate about music, and before long I was in the school band and the town band playing the drums.

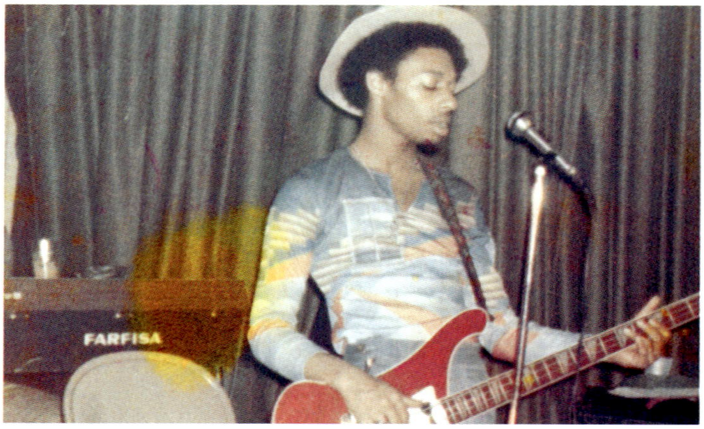

As great as my uncle was on the drums, it simply wasn't my thing. The instrument I really wanted to play was the bass guitar. That desire was fulfilled when my Aunt Constance took me to Jamesway for my eleventh birthday, where she bought me a bass guitar, which she purchased outright for thirty-eight dollars—a lot of money in those days. I don't think anyone in the house saw me for a month as I taught myself chords and figured out how to play along with what was on the radio. The first song I learned was "Stone Free" by Jimi Hendrix—taught it to myself in a week. By the time I got back to Co-op City in 1970, I was pretty good. Then I got side tracked as the graffiti movement started to develop.

When I started hanging out at Parkside again in 1972 it turned out that everyone was into music, at least the people I wanted to hang out with. We would take the old 3rd Avenue El to Fordham Road and walk from the bottom of the hill to the top, hitting all of the stores. Me, CRACHEE, and VAMM—there was a whole group of us stealing records. We targeted bands we liked: Hendrix, Janis Joplin, The Doors, and especially Chicago. We had every Chicago album. They were a big influence on the band we'd later start.

This page: BLADE on bass. Circa 1975.
Opposite page: Whole-car by CRACHEE and BLADE for their Bazay Band. 1975.

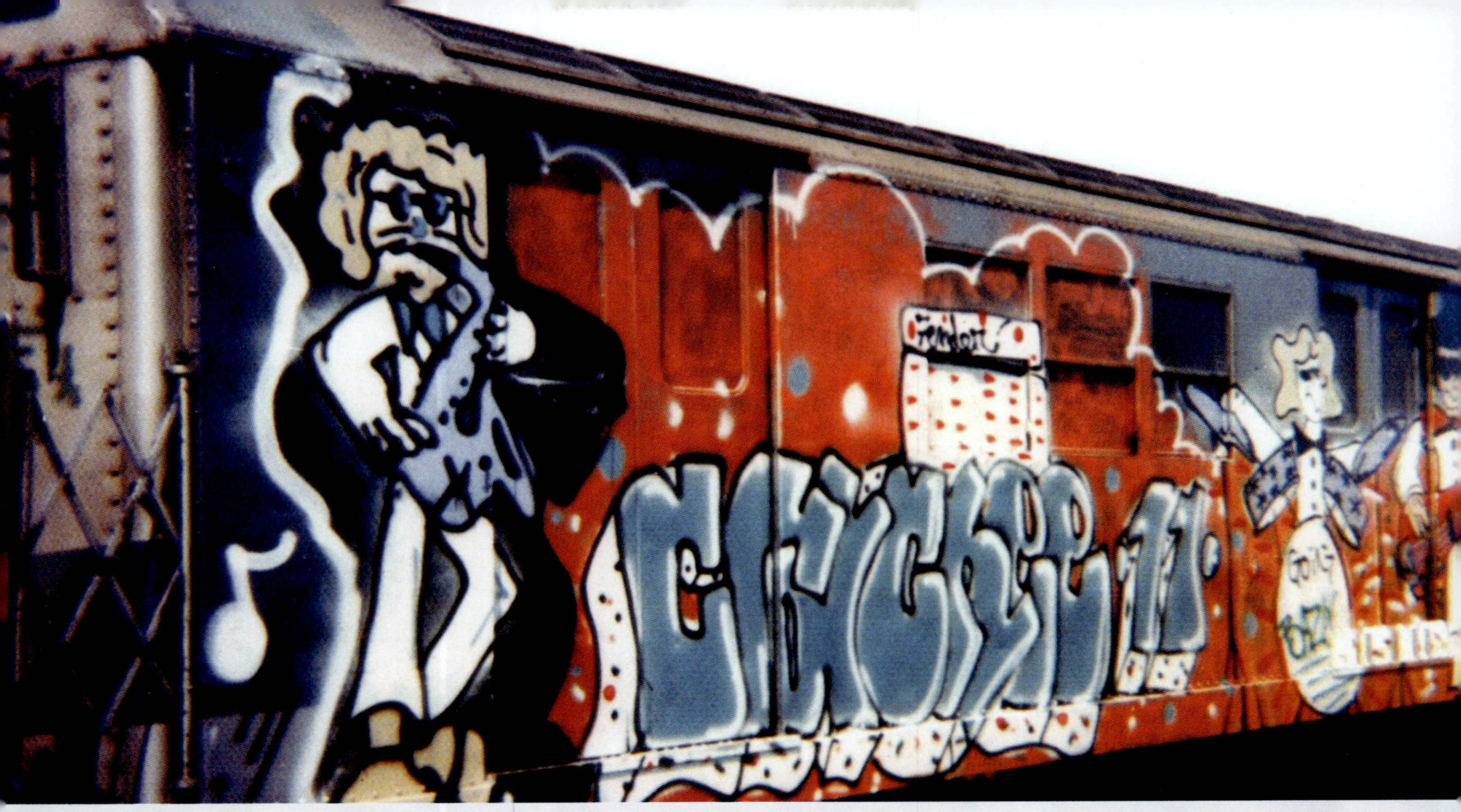

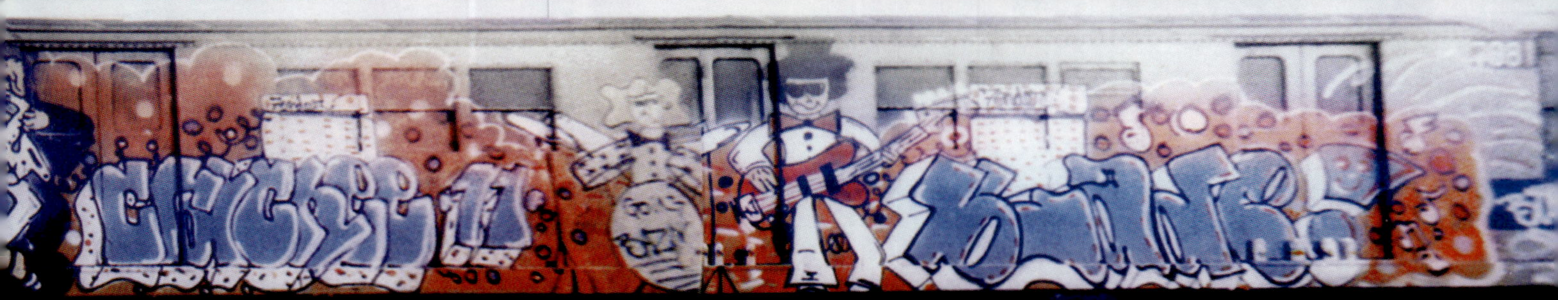

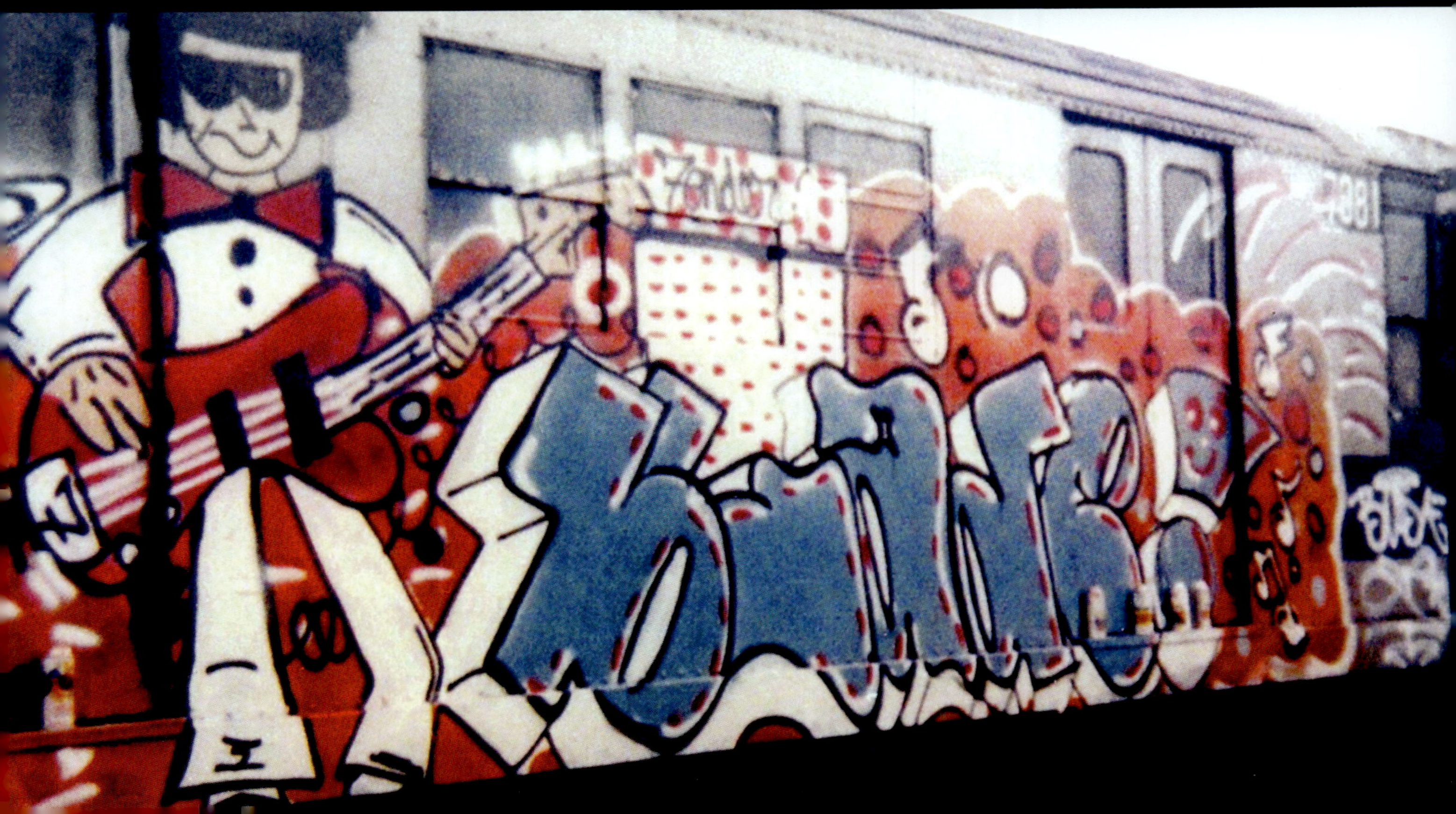

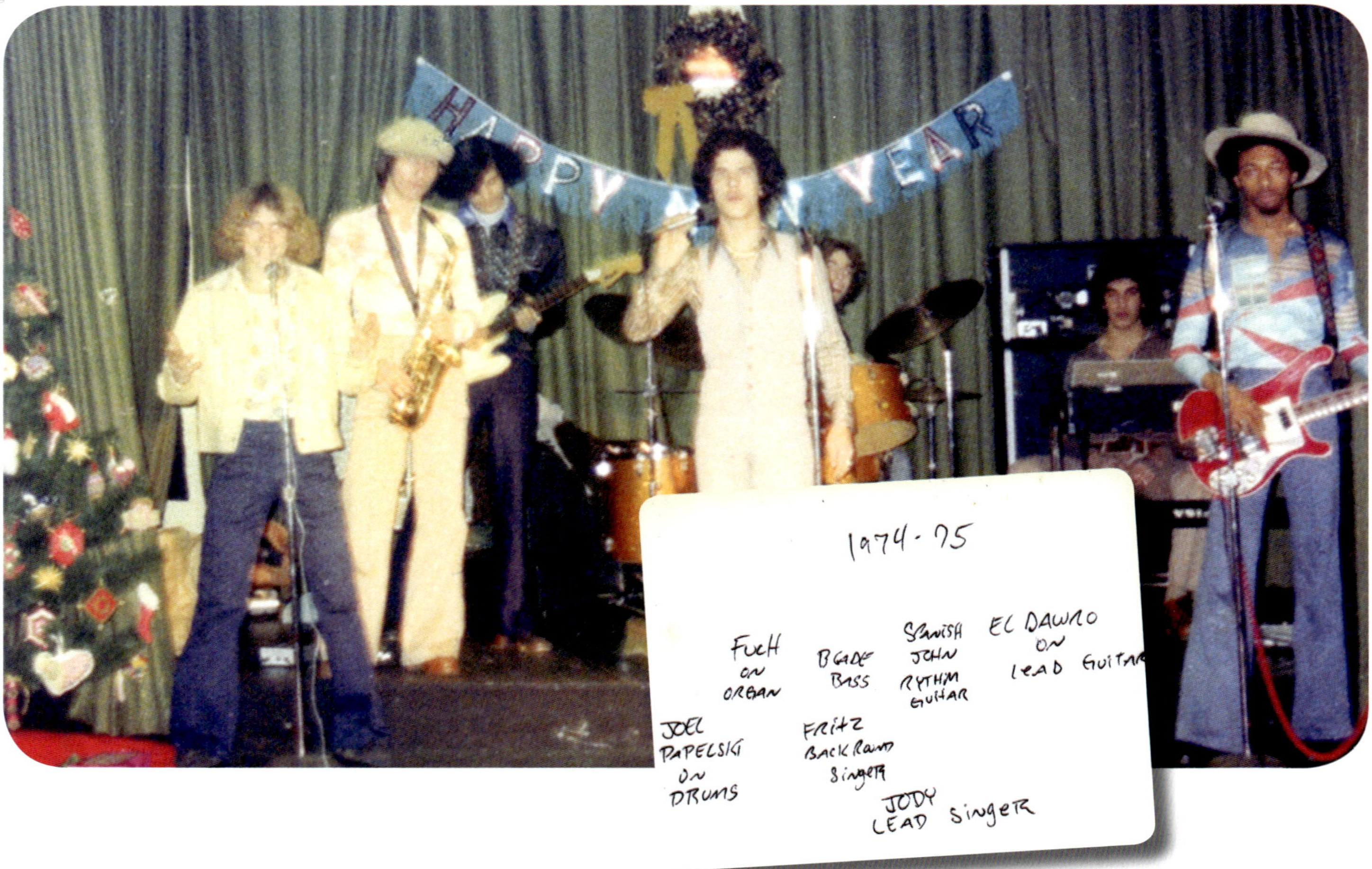

CRACHEE played tenor sax in a band formed by my friend Jody. The band was a hard rock band, which didn't interest me. Jody had some problems booking a hard rock band, so they became more flexible by adding R&B and disco. I signed on. I liked the idea of being in a band. What teenager wouldn't? As a fearless teenager, the idea of performing in front of hundreds of people was great—even when we failed, which rarely happened because our audiences were usually fifteen to twenty-five year olds who didn't mind if you missed a chord.

While my parents didn't know I wrote graffiti at the time, they were smart enough to understand that my life wasn't going in the direction they'd hoped it would go. My father, in particular, was tough about this. We had endless arguments about me spending time at Parkside and the lifestyle he felt our family had outgrown by moving to Co-op City. Add to that the fact that I was now committing more time to rehearsing with the band in CRACHEE's apartment at Parkside—playing a form of music he couldn't relate to—and the arguments increased.

Like a lot of bands, in order to get work we had to do a set featuring current pop hits. We wanted to play some serious funk, and somehow we were able to put together a set-list that merged the two. Our band was able to move seamlessly from the Bread ballad "I Want to Make it with You" to Sly and the Family Stone's "Dance to the Music." Each set was tailored for the client, whether it was a bar owner, a club, or a school dance. We were getting paid to play music and so we gave the customer what they wanted. This ensured we had constant work.

In the winter of 1975, KC and the Sunshine Band released their first album featuring two big hits, "That's the Way I Like It" and "Get Down Tonight." This was huge for us, because it worked for a large disco audience as well as the funk crowd. The music was also linear and easy to learn, so we could play it beautifully. In 1976, disco was sweeping the nation and everyone was climbing on board. For us, that meant more money and a booking in the Catskills.

This spread:
BLADE on bass for the Bazay Band. Circa 1975.

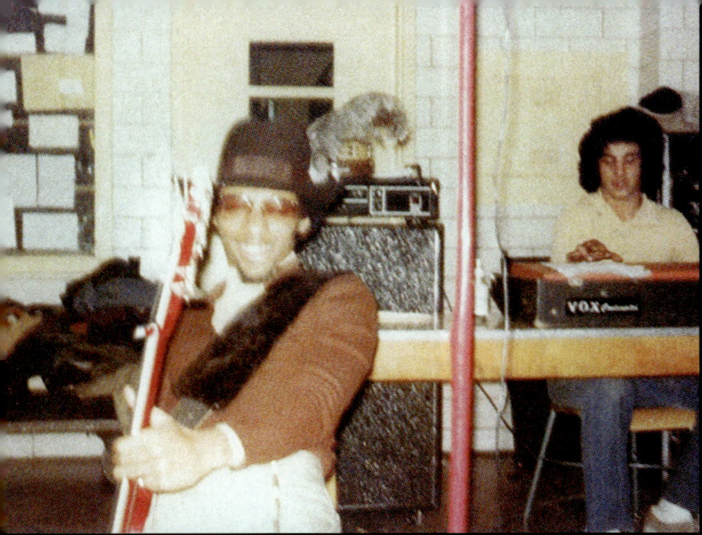
VOX

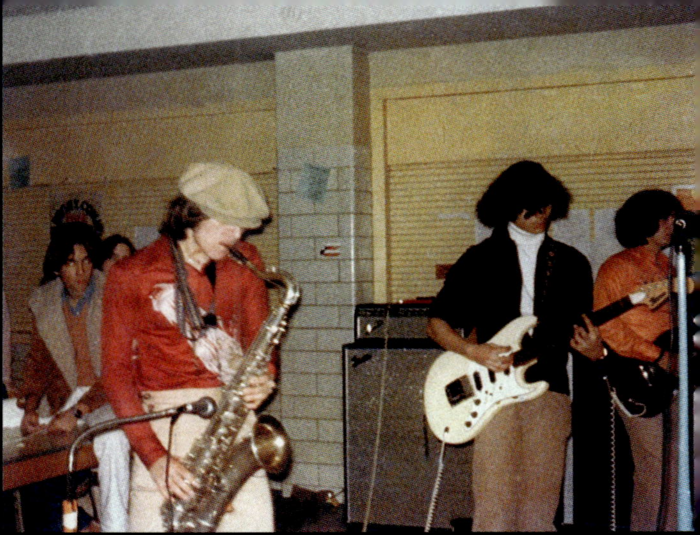

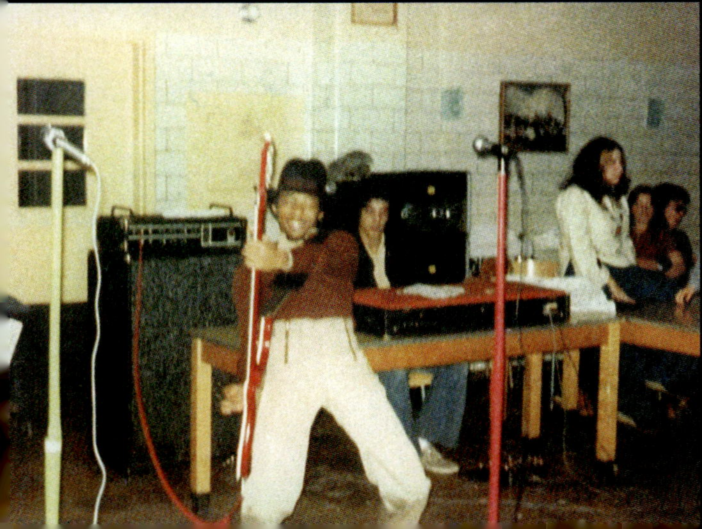

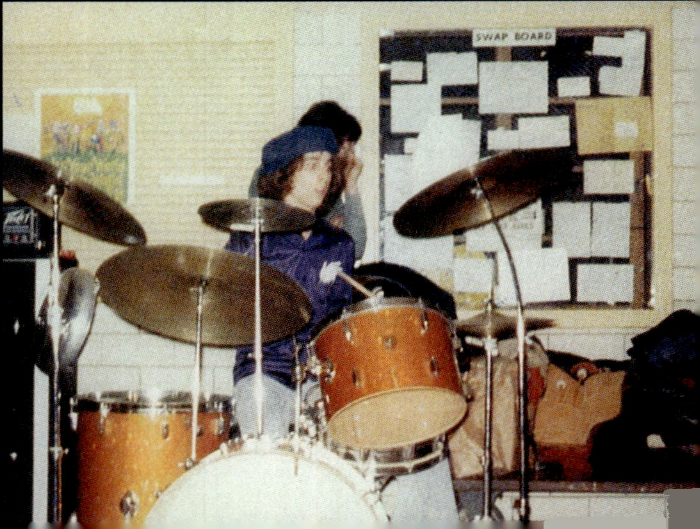
SWAP BOARD

Welcome

Tamarack is always ready with the makings of a sparkling vacation. Here you'll find 400 acres of fun facilities. For unexcelled comfort, you will enjoy the sunny, spacious rooms in the Main Lodge, Cabins, and the adjacent buildings. Most rooms have private or semi-private showers. During the day you'll thrill in the participation of sports on Tamarack's championship fields. After the sun goes down, the lights go up and activities center around Tamarack's playtorium.

On stage you'll see your favorite stars of stage, screen, radio and television. After show time there's always dancing to two name bands.

For a snack or a drink, meet in the air conditioned Sportsman's Lounge or Televue Terrace, where hilarity and good fellowship reigns supreme.

Produced in Magicolor by
Nat Steingart Assoc., So. Fallsburg, N. Y.

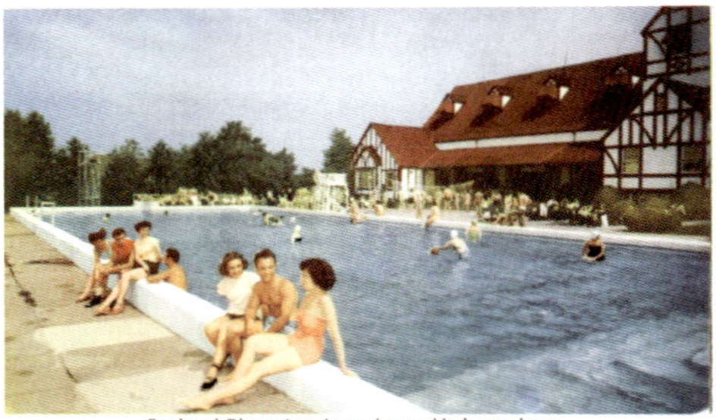

Pool and Playtorium for unforgetable happy hours

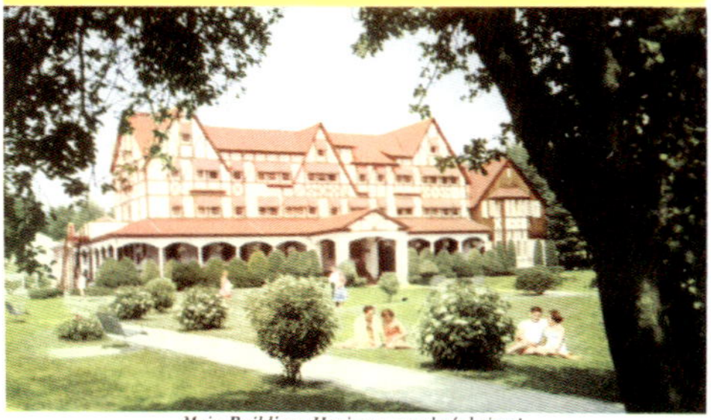

Main Building—Having a wonderful time!

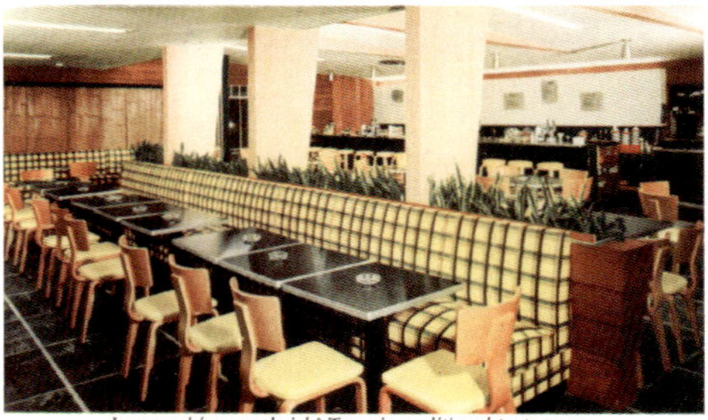

In a mood for a sandwich? Two air conditioned party rooms

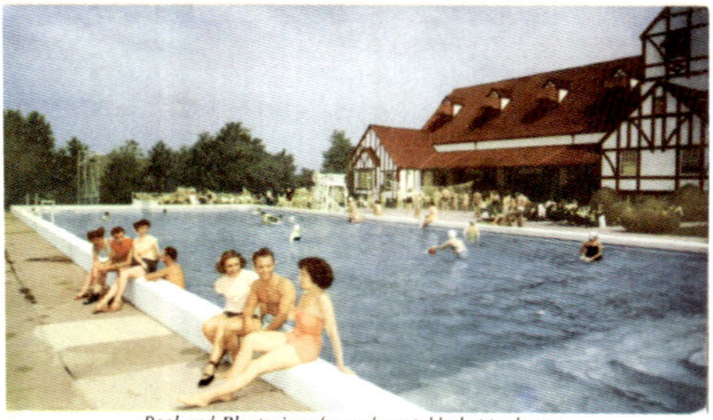

Pool and Playtorium for unforgetable happy hours

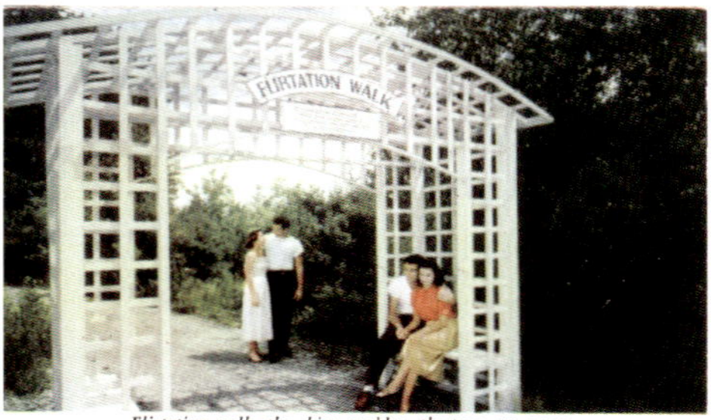

Flirtation walk—the skies are blue, the trees are green

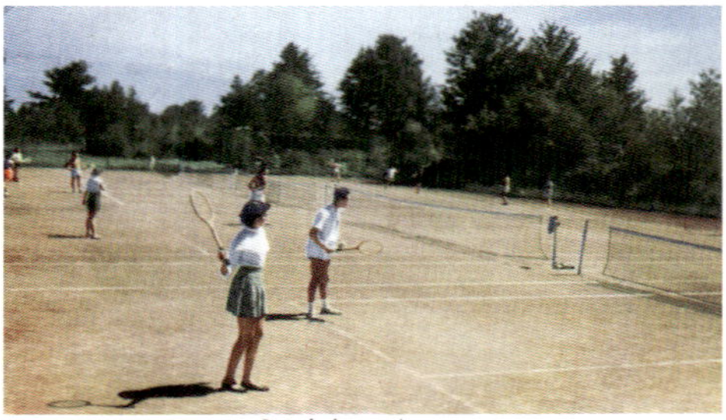

Superb clay tennis courts

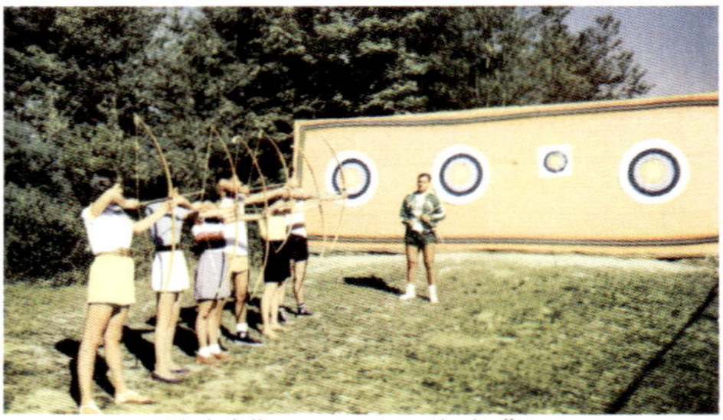

Hit the bull's eye—expert instruction in all sports

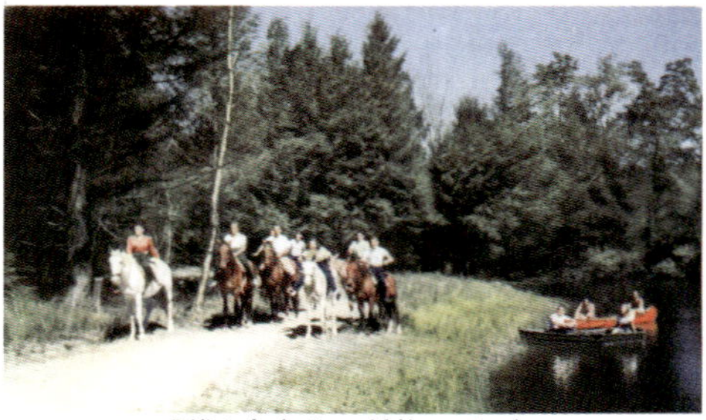

Bridle paths—boating and fishing—on premises

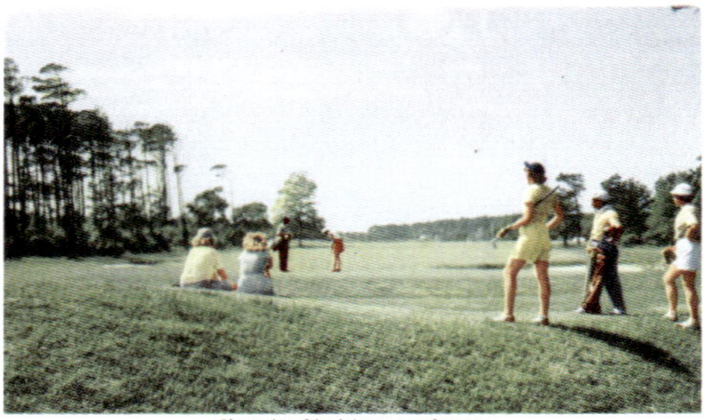

Championship fairways and greens

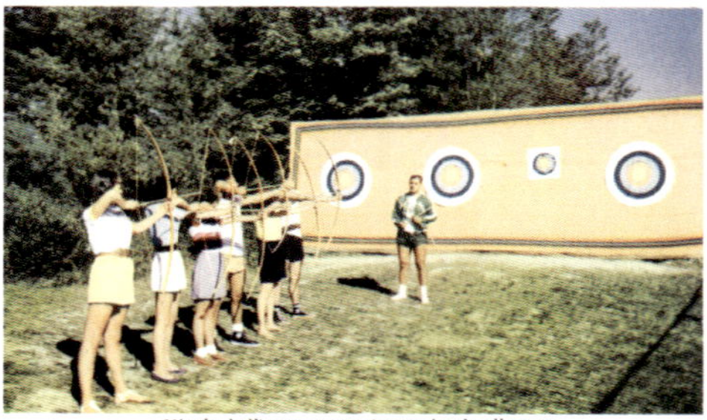

Hit the bull's eye—expert instruction in all sports

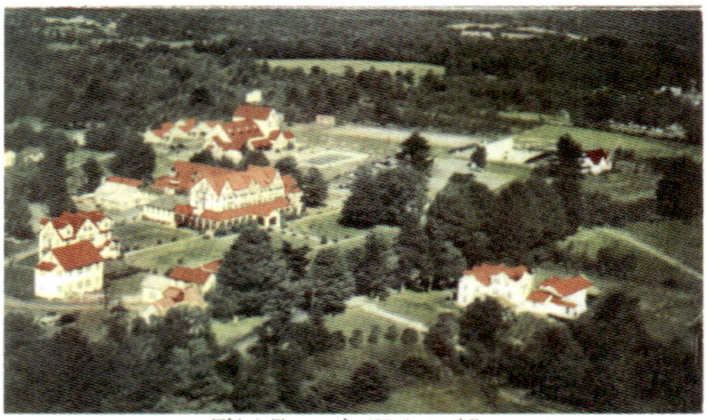

This is Tamarack—400 Acres of Fun

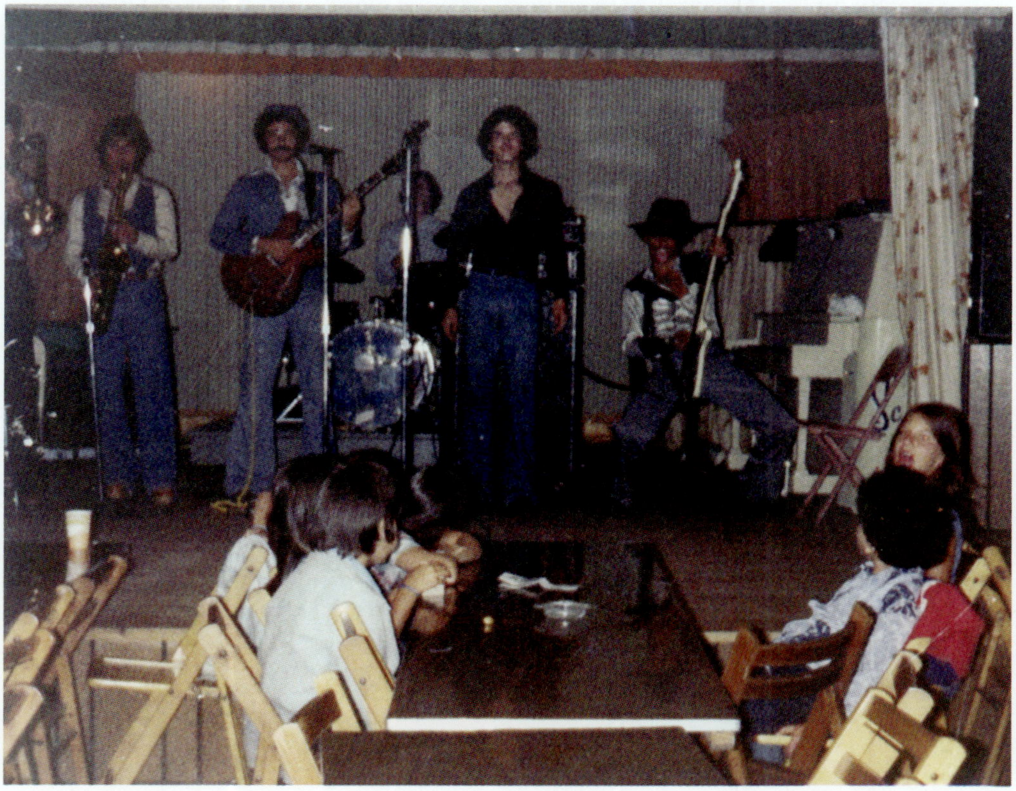

Jody was able to get us a booking at the Tamarack lodge for the summer of 1976. We were to be the house band and to keep the younger kids dancing. The Catskill hotels were just beginning to fade away at the time, and a number of them had already closed by the time we arrived. For years, these hotels were the vacation spot for the New York Jewish community. Traditionally, husbands would pack up the wife and kids and send them to one of the Catskills resorts for the summer. The husband would work all week in the city and then drive up to see the family on the weekends. In the 1960s, low airfares allowed families to go anywhere they wanted for about the same amount of money as the Catskills. That was the beginning of the end.

We were thrilled to be at the Tamarack. We were young men, eighteen to nineteen years old—you had to be 18 because they served liquor—and we were musicians, getting paid to do what we loved. We stayed in our own cabin and slept in bunk beds. When we played our gigs, we had girls following us around like we were rock stars, although I had a girlfriend up there the whole time.

On a normal day, CRACHEE and I would hang around the pool at the hotel, smoking cigarettes and drinking until show time. After our set, we'd head back to our wooden cabin called The Normandy. CRACHEE was seeing two different girls, so I never knew who'd be there when I arrived with my girlfriend, Laurie.

All of these girls were rebelling against their parents—or it's possible they were just bored. We didn't care. We'd party through the night and then the girls would sneak off at sunrise to get back to their parents. In September, it was all going to end anyway. When you know a relationship is going to end, it's amazing how much information you'll reveal to your partner. I knew more about Laurie in two months time than I ever did about Karen. Of course, Karen and I never had the privacy Laurie and I had at the Tamarack, because the Bronx was always crowded.

Opposite page: Advertisement for the Tamarack lodge. Circa 1972.
This page: Bazay Band play at Tamarack lodge. 1976.

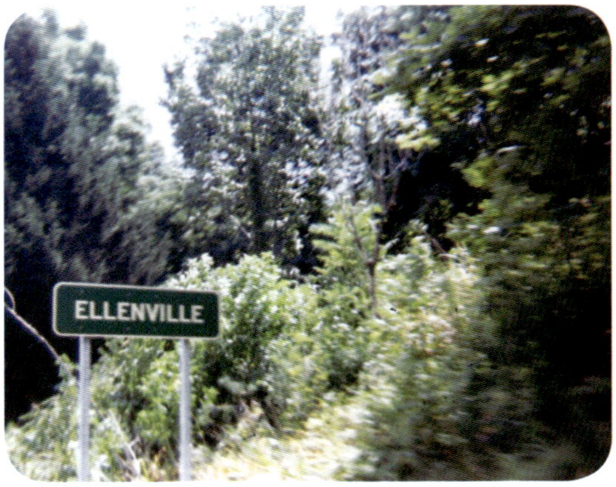

ELLENVILLE N.Y. 1976
ON OUR WAY TO THE
TAMARACK HOTEL

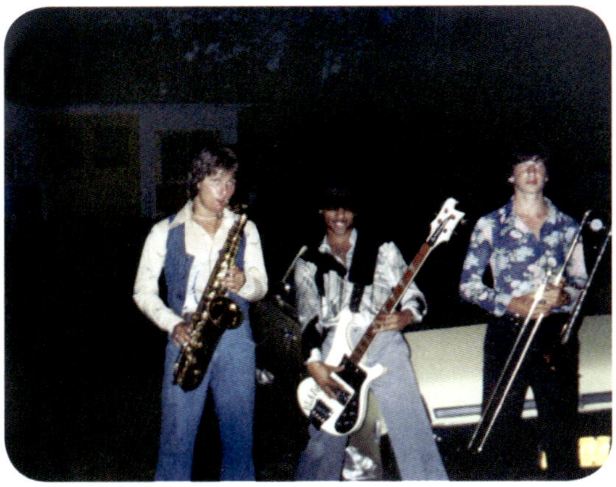

TAMARACK

CRACHEE ON SAX
BLADE ON BASS
I FORGOT
THE TROMBONE
PLAYERS NAME.
HIS PARENTS
WOULD NOT LET
HIM LEAVE ELLENVILLE
AFTER HIS BAMITZVA
AGE - 16 -

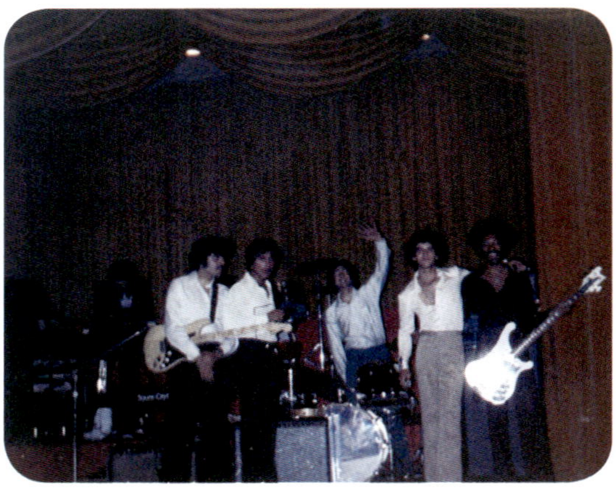

SUMMER AT THE
TAMARACK
1976

Red Room

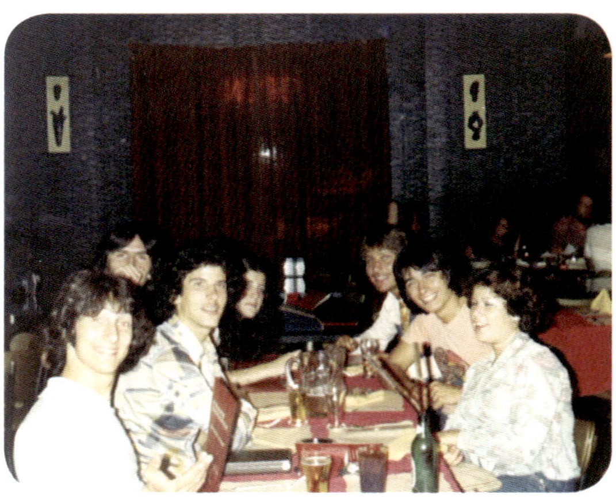

TAMARACK HOTEL 1976

VANN
JODY
CATHY
CRACHEE
JIMMY BIRD
LORI
PAUL COBEL

FREE BEER FOR
THE UNDER AGE TEENAGERS
YESSSSS!

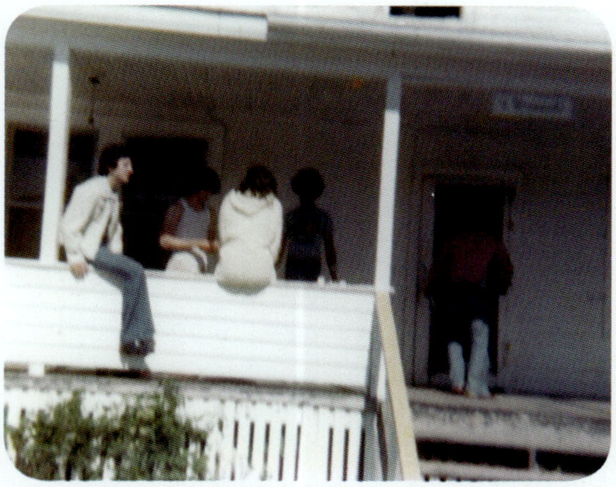

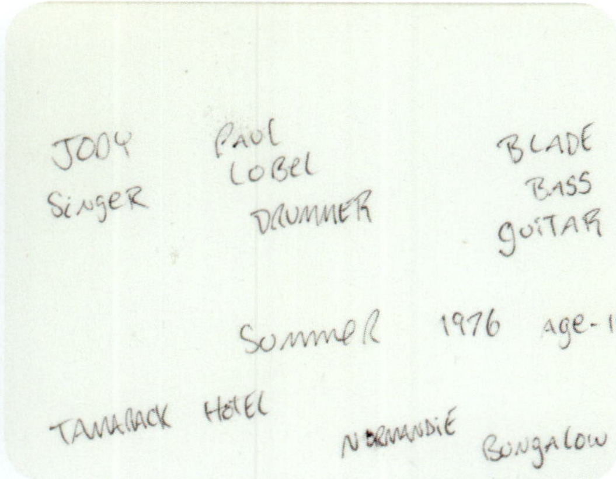
JODY
Singer
Paul
Lobel
Drummer
BLADE
Bass
Guitar
Summer 1976 age-1
TAMARACK HOTEL
NORMANDIE
Bungalow

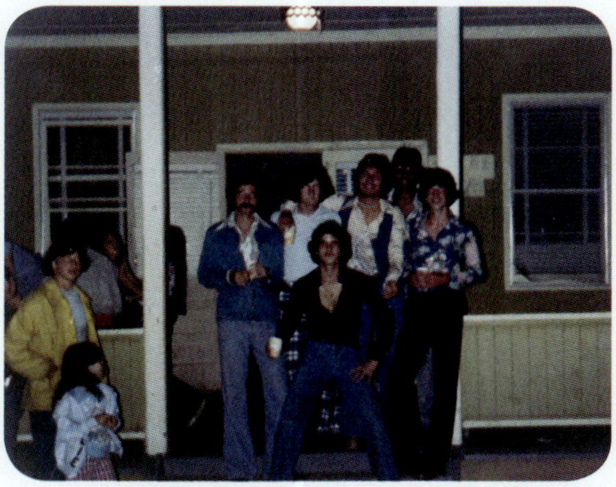

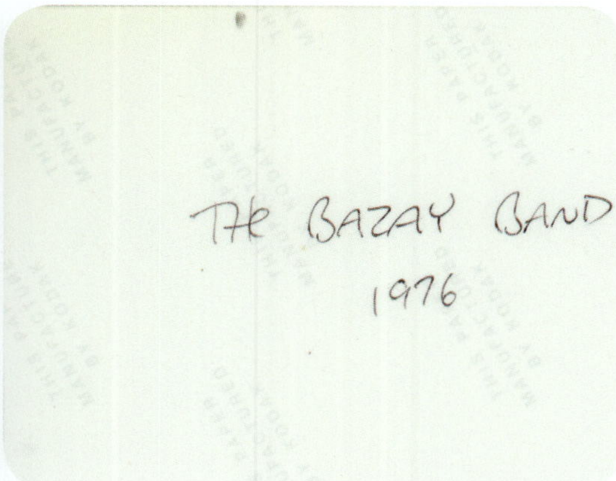
THE BAZAY BAND
1976

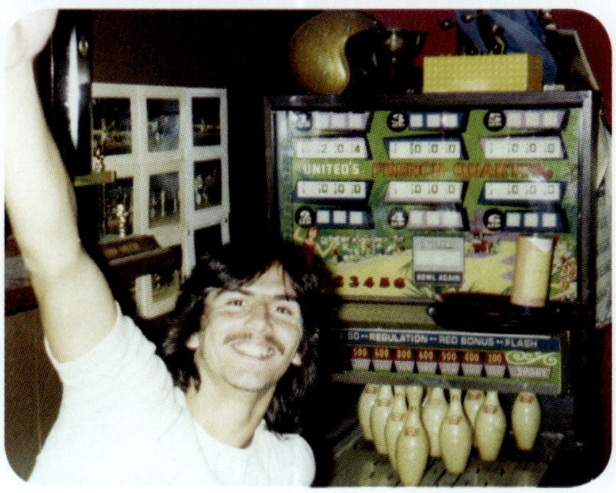
UNITED'S
BOWL AGAIN

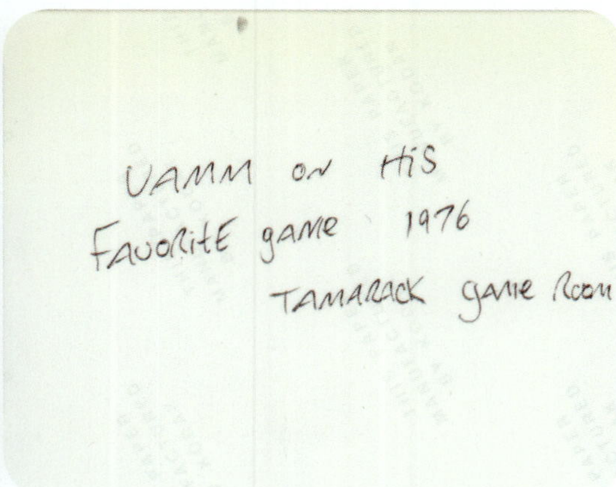
VAMM on his
Favorite game 1976
TAMARACK game Room

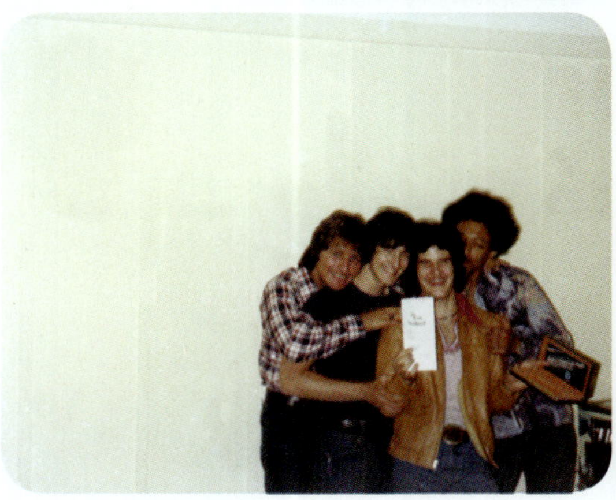

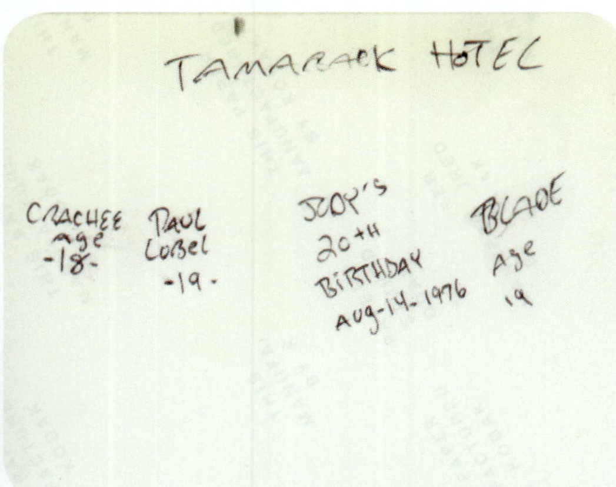
TAMARACK HOTEL
CRACHEE
age
-18-
Paul
Lobel
-19-
JODY'S
20TH
BIRTHDAY
AUG-14-1976
BLADE
Age
19

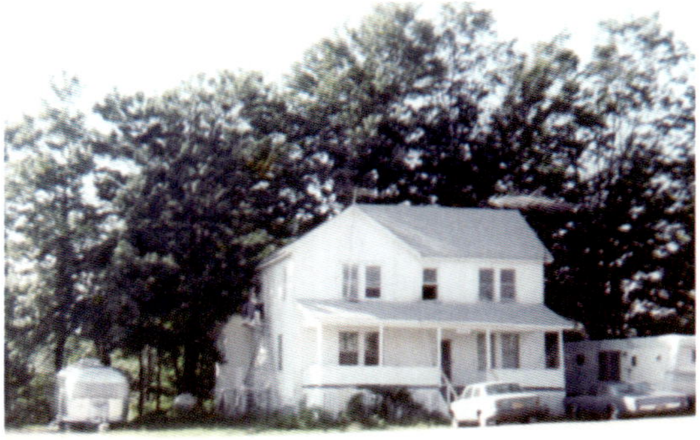

NORMANDIE

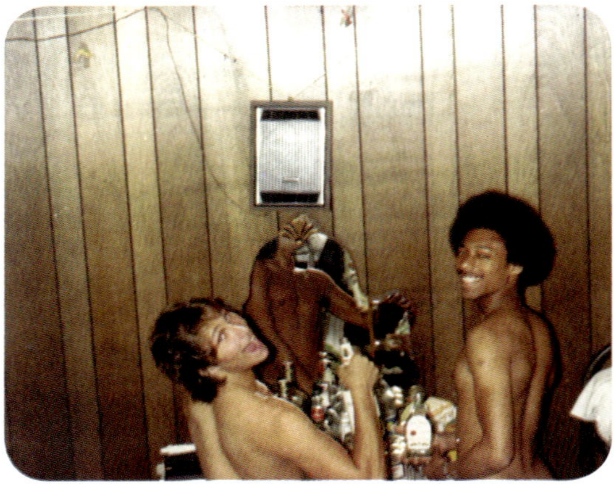

CRACHEE 11   BLADE I

DRINKIN' BACARDI STRAIGHT
TAMARACK 1976 - PHOTO BY
LORI + SUE

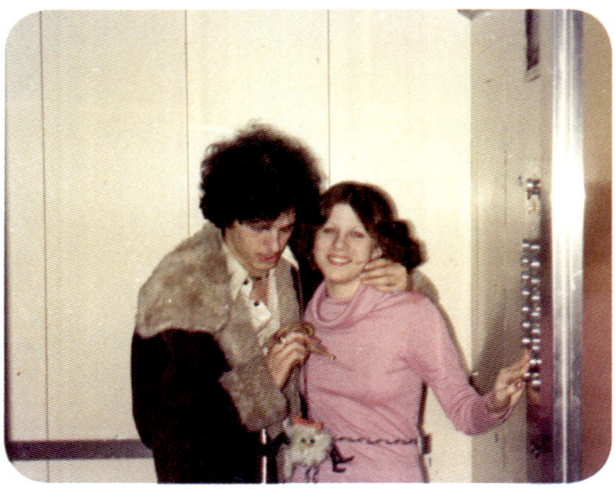

END OF 1976 MET HER AT THE
TAMARACK

JODY HELENE
GLICKMAN

1976

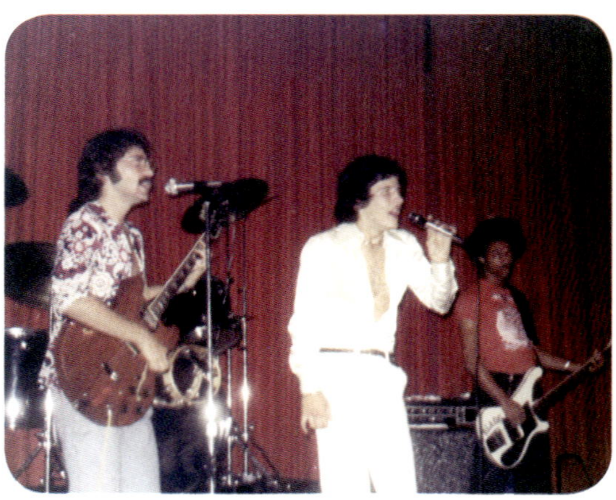

TAMARACK

HARVEY ON GUITAR   JODY   BLADE

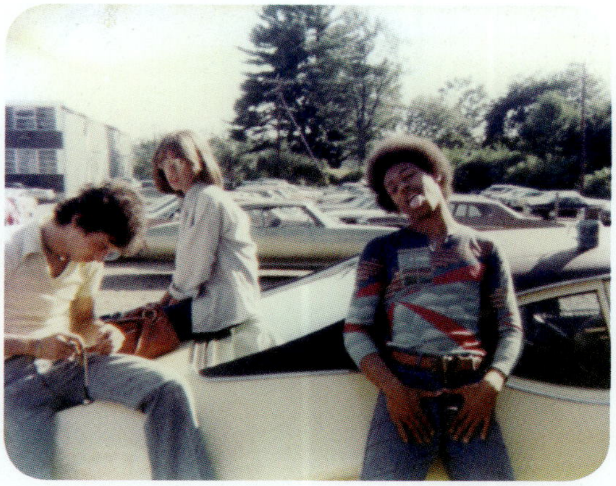

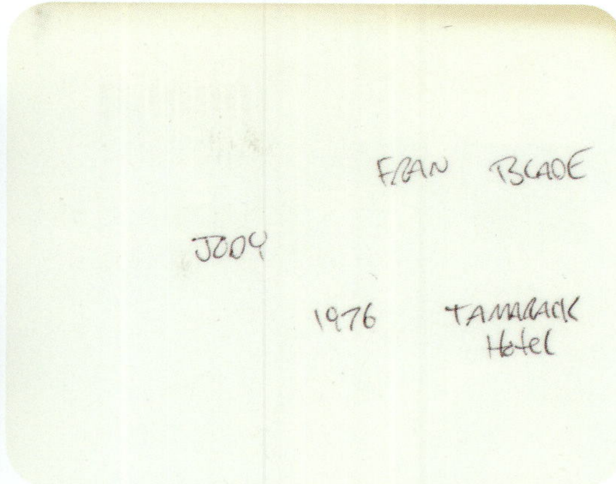
FRAN BLADE
JODY
1976 TAMARACK Hotel

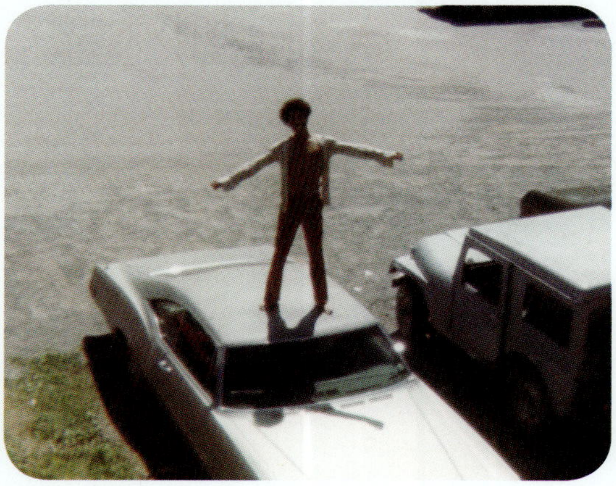

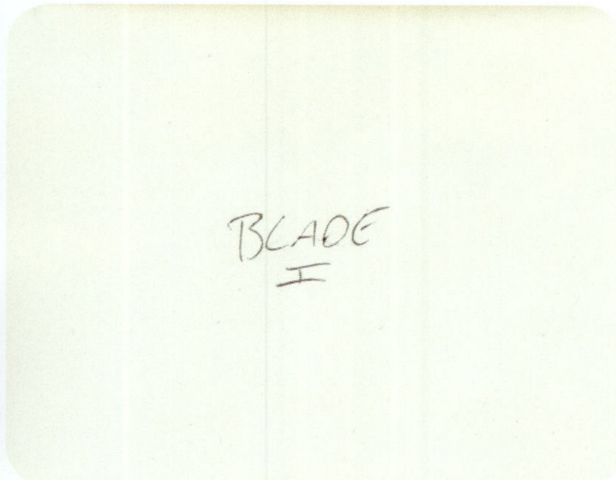
BLADE
I

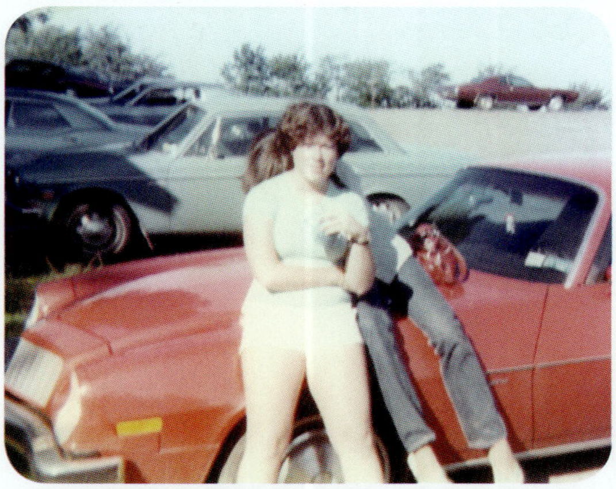

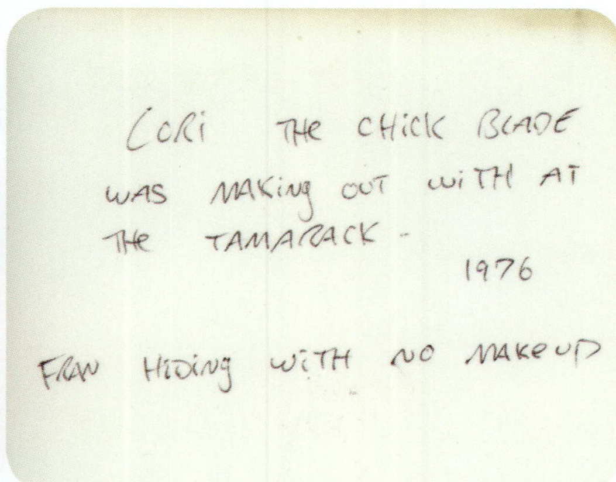
Lori THE CHICK BLADE
WAS MAKING OUT WITH AT
THE TAMARACK -
1976
FRAN HIDING WITH NO MAKEUP

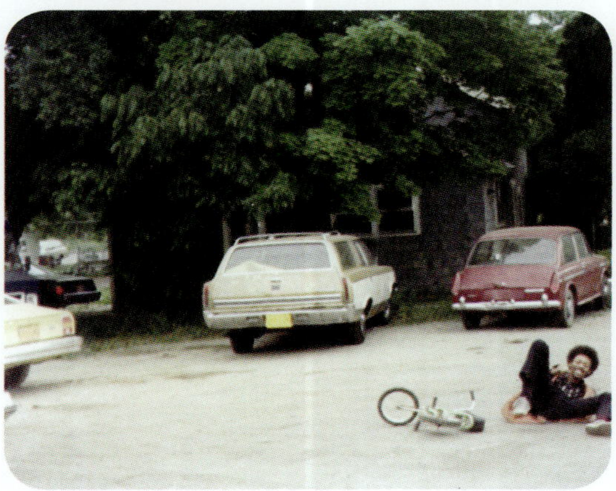

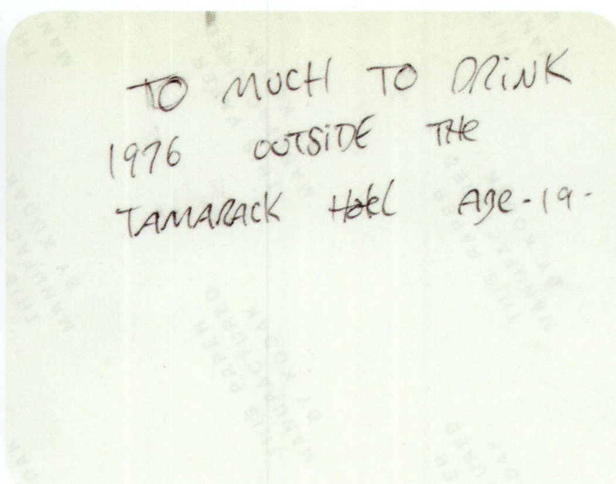
TO MUCH TO DRINK
1976 OUTSIDE THE
TAMARACK Hotel Age-19-

Back in the Bronx, writers were wondering where I had gone. I'd sneak into the city once a month and hit the Burke Avenue lay-up, doing ten pieces in a two-day span, and then we'd drive back to the Catskills. Since CRACHEE was also in the band, we'd go on racking missions in the small towns along the way. The upstate stores were so old that most of them still had real wooden floors. They also continued to display spray paint right on the floor—the way you'd display buckets of house paint. They were the easiest racks in the world, and so we'd drive around the Catskills with hundreds of cans in our trunk.

On September 8th, I said my goodbyes to Laurie and the Tamarack as the band drove back to the Bronx for good. Excited about our future, we talked the whole way home. There were eight of us in two cars with a U-Haul trailer behind us. We listened to music and got high the whole way home.

By the time we reached Co-op City, we were exhausted from talking about our future plans as a band—a band that got paid good money to rock the Catskills. I stepped out of the car and took the elevator upstairs. When I got off the elevator, there were bags of things outside my family's door—my things, all of my belongings. My dad chose this day to tell me it was time to go, turning the best day of my life into one of the worst.

The major battle at home centered on my dad trying to turn me into a robot. He wanted me in a blue-collar job for forty years and unhappy. It was never about what I wanted. And so we'd have these blowouts and I'd leave. Eventually, I'd come back and things would be fine until the next fight. Nothing's changed after all these years. I'm a legitimate artist who's shown around the world and my dad still views me as a vandal.

The next day, my mom and I went to Pelham Parkway where we met with this old Jewish lady and my mom laid out the dough for one month's rent and security, which I paid back within the year. 2505 Olinville Avenue—one hundred and sixty bucks a month and it was mine.

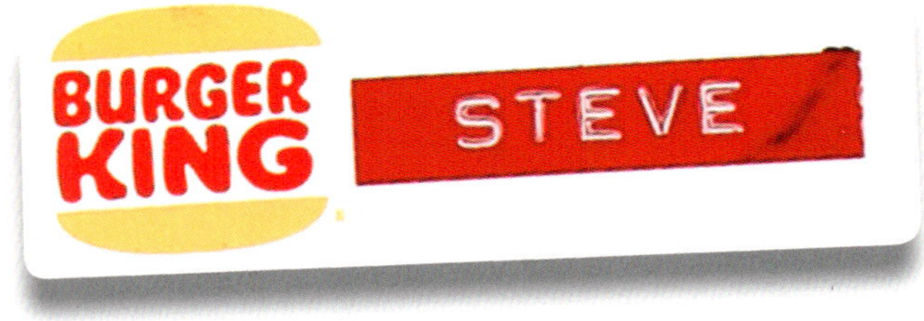

I needed a job right away, so I found one at McDonalds. I made McMuffins for a year and then moved on to Burger King. McDonalds and Burger King were brilliant in how they set their organizations up: everybody had a single job, maybe two if they liked you. One guy did fries and sodas; another person specialized in burgers. If you knew too much, you became valuable and they didn't want that. By keeping you doing one thing, you were replaceable and they could pay you whatever they wanted, which was minimum wage. But I liked the job and I got to eat one meal with my shift. I had a manager named Bob, who staked his whole future on working at Burger King. He was always tense and he would get on you for the stupidest thing. One time we had an argument over an egg.

Bob: Steven, did you drop an egg?

Me: Yes Bob, the egg slipped and fell on the floor.

Bob: Are you fucking kidding me?

Me: No Bob, if you crack a thousand eggs in a week, one of them is going to fall, Bob.

Bob: That's just not true, Steven. I've cracked thousands of eggs and never dropped one on the floor.

Me: That's why you got promoted to manager, Bob.

This page: BLADE's name badge from when he worked at Burger King. 1975.
Opposite page: BLADE on the steps of his first apartment on Olinville Avenue. 1975.

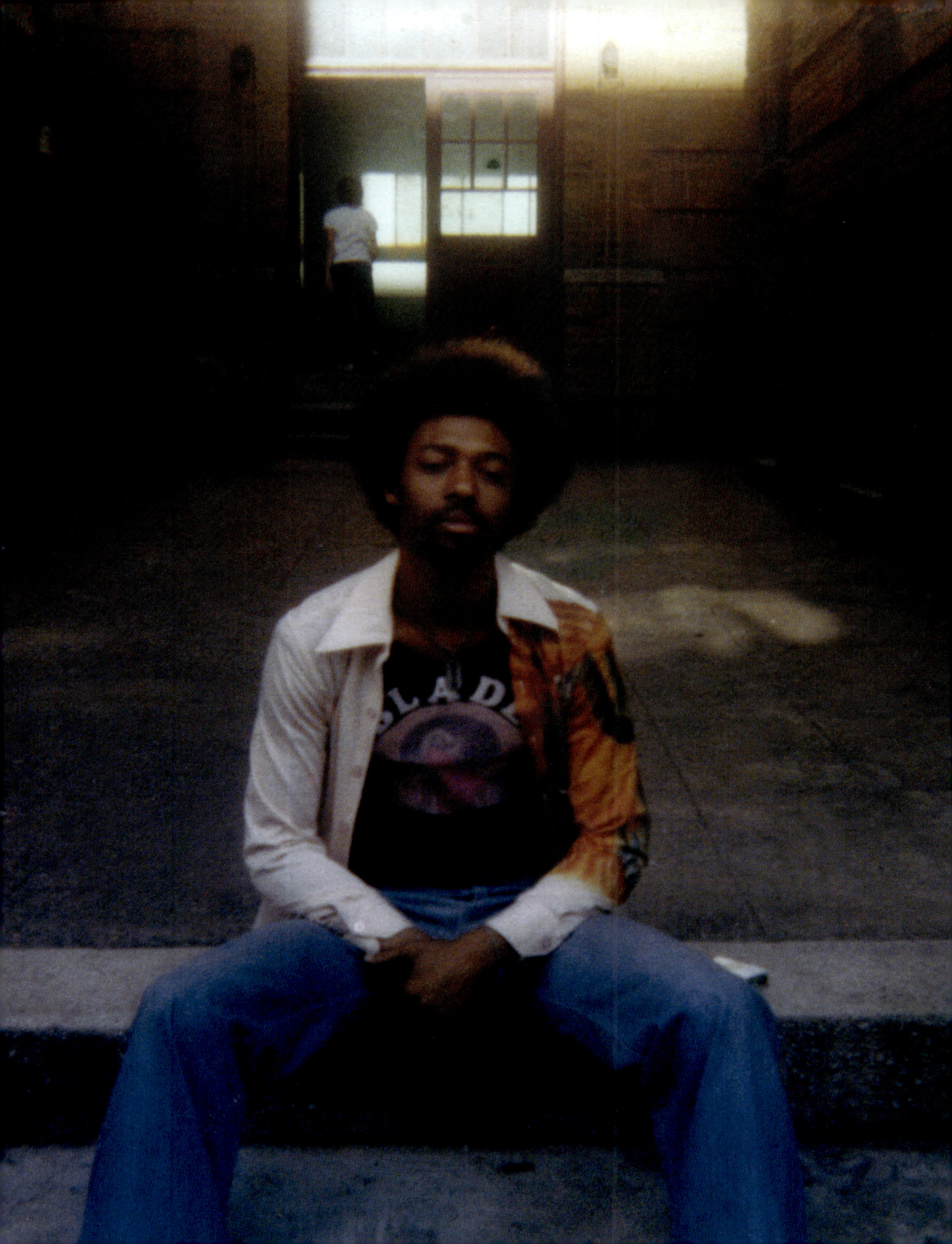

"THERE WERE MONTHS WHEN WE WOULDN'T HAVE THE MONEY FOR THE ELECTRIC BILL SO IT WOULD GET SHUT DOWN."

The job was worth it because I got the apartment and the apartment was great. All of our furniture came from the streets. We stole these giant wooden cable spools from Con Edison and used them as tables. I also found a gold lounge chair on the sidewalk; it was in great shape and it was exclusively mine. People knew not to go near my lounge chair, and there were a lot of people. It seemed like everybody roamed through the doors, sometimes twenty in a day. We'd watch *The Gong Show, Welcome Back Kotter,* and *Happy Days* on our little black-and-white TV with the rabbit ear antenna, while passing a joint around.

KRAM was the first of THE CRAZY 5 to move in. He paid half of the rent and slept in the living room. In the fall of 1976, KRAM had just gotten back from Vietnam and he was trying to move on with his life. He rarely talked about his experience in the army, and we didn't ask. Nor did we think of him as a Vietnam vet. To us, he was a member of THE CRAZY 5 who hung out at Parkside every day—until his lottery number came up and it was time to go. DEATH was also old enough to have a lottery number, but lucky for him, the war ended before he was drafted.

There were months when we wouldn't have the money for the electric bill so it would get shut down. When that happened, we'd run extension cords down the dumbwaiter to tap into the super's outlets. The super of the building was an old-school Italian guy who had a beautiful sixteen-year old daughter named Dolores. She and I met at the local bowling alley and soon she was sneaking up to my place once her parents fell asleep. It didn't take long for our romance to blossom.

Dolores's father wasn't happy to learn that his daughter was spending time with a graffiti artist / musician with a giant Afro. To this day, I don't know which of those three descriptions frightened him more, but if I had to guess I'd say it was the Afro. My parents, on the other hand, liked Dolores and encouraged me to bring her to dinner. I think they felt she would be the one to get me away from writing. While Dolores was a stabilizing force in my life, even she couldn't get me off the trains.

In 1977, DEATH and COMET moved into the apartment and KRAM moved on. DEATH slept in my chair and COMET slept on the couch. The parties got louder and the drug use got harder and more frequent. Our apartment became a huge clubhouse in the winter, when it was too cold to hang out in the playground. Everybody was getting smashed, sniffing glue and playing cards; sometimes fifty people in a day. Writers like BILLY 167 started getting into the drug thing. It was sad, because BILLY 167 was one of those incredibly talented guys, but he was small so guys would steal his paint. SILVERTIPS had the same problem, because he was short. Both were great writers who had to battle twice as hard to get up on the trains.

Opposite page:
Top: BLADE sketch for a piece for Dolores. Bottom: Finished Dolores piece. 1978.

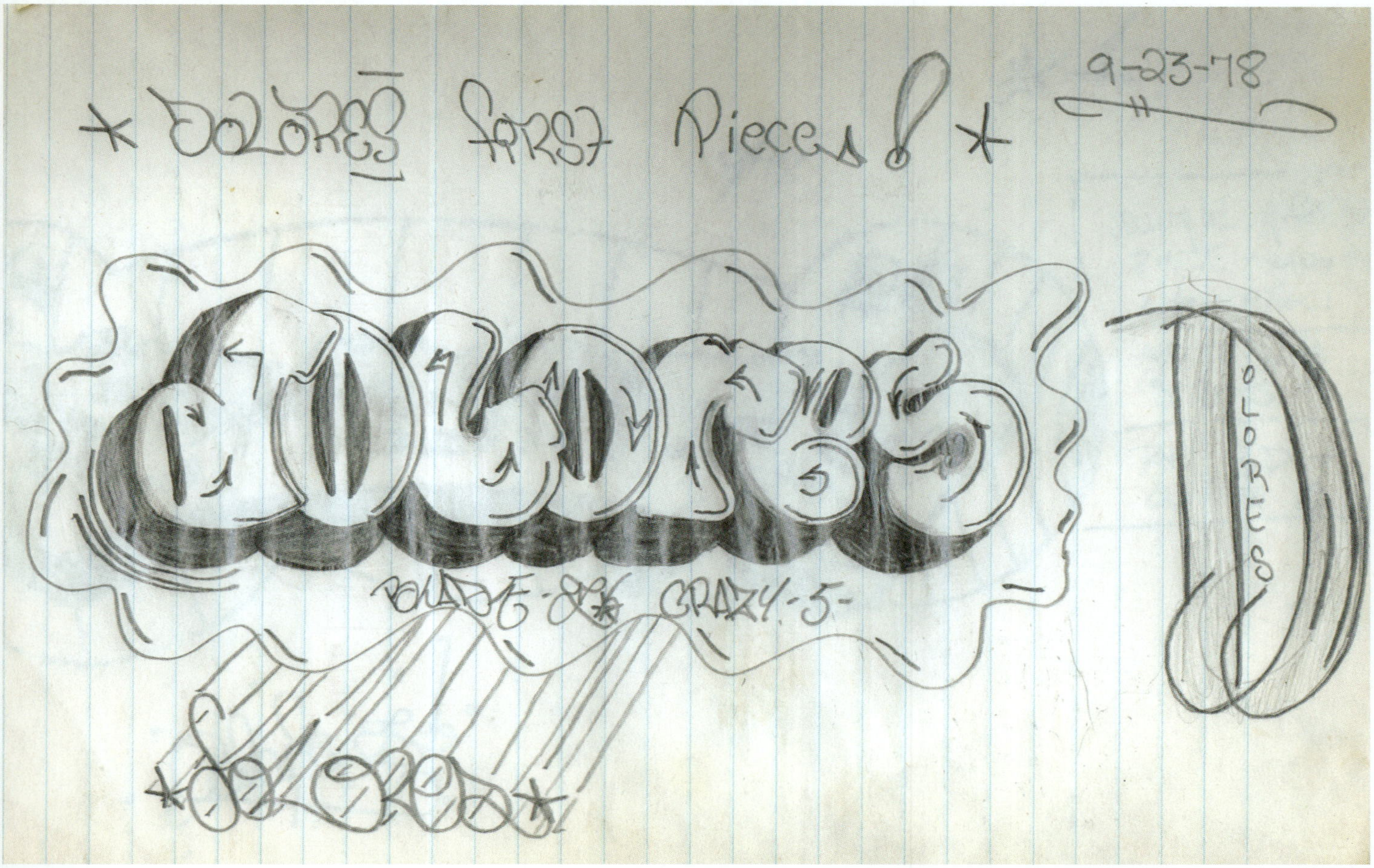
* DOLORES first Pieces! *
9-23-78

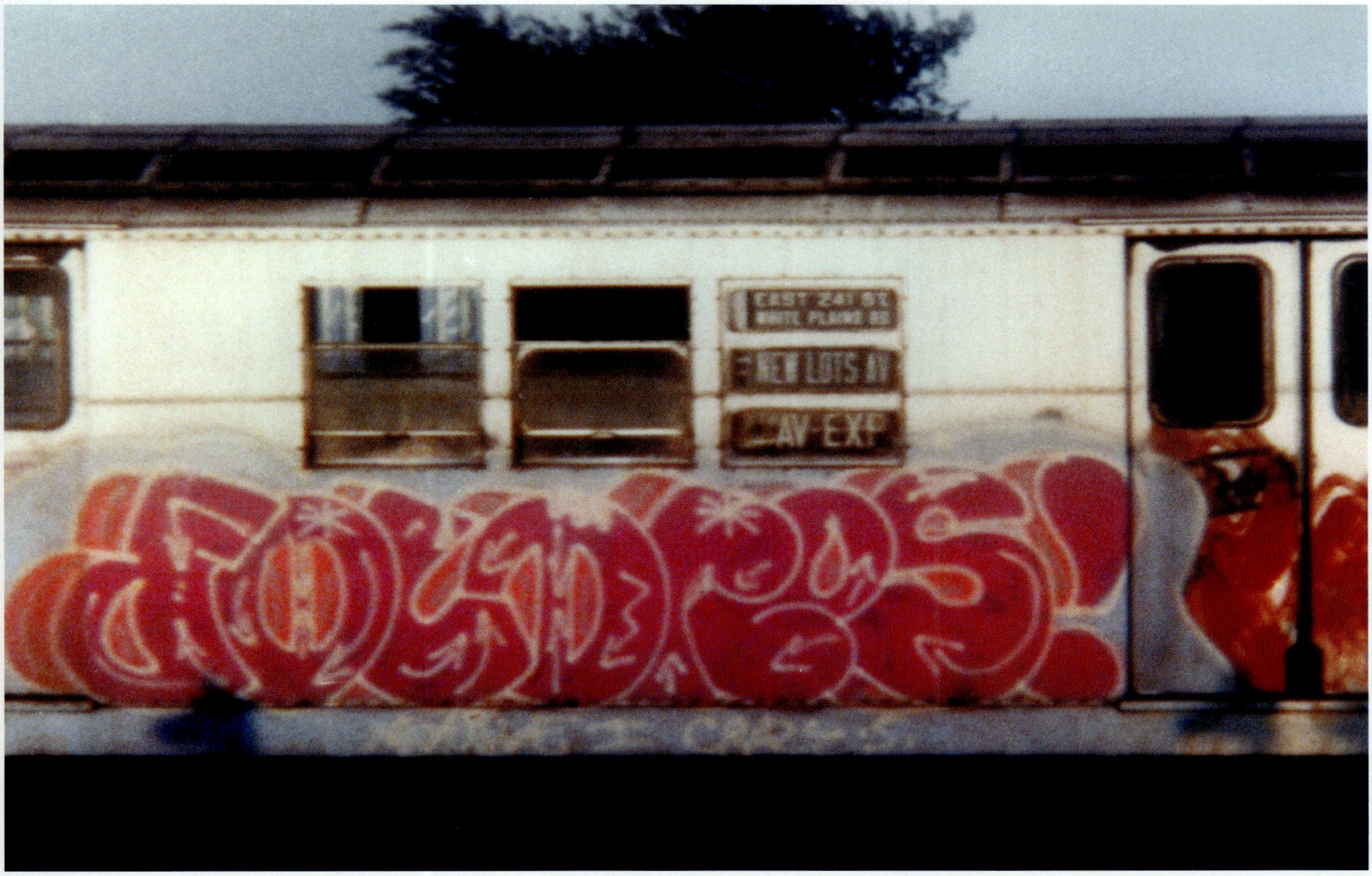
EAST 241 ST
WHITE PLAINS RD
NEW LOTS AV
AV-EXP

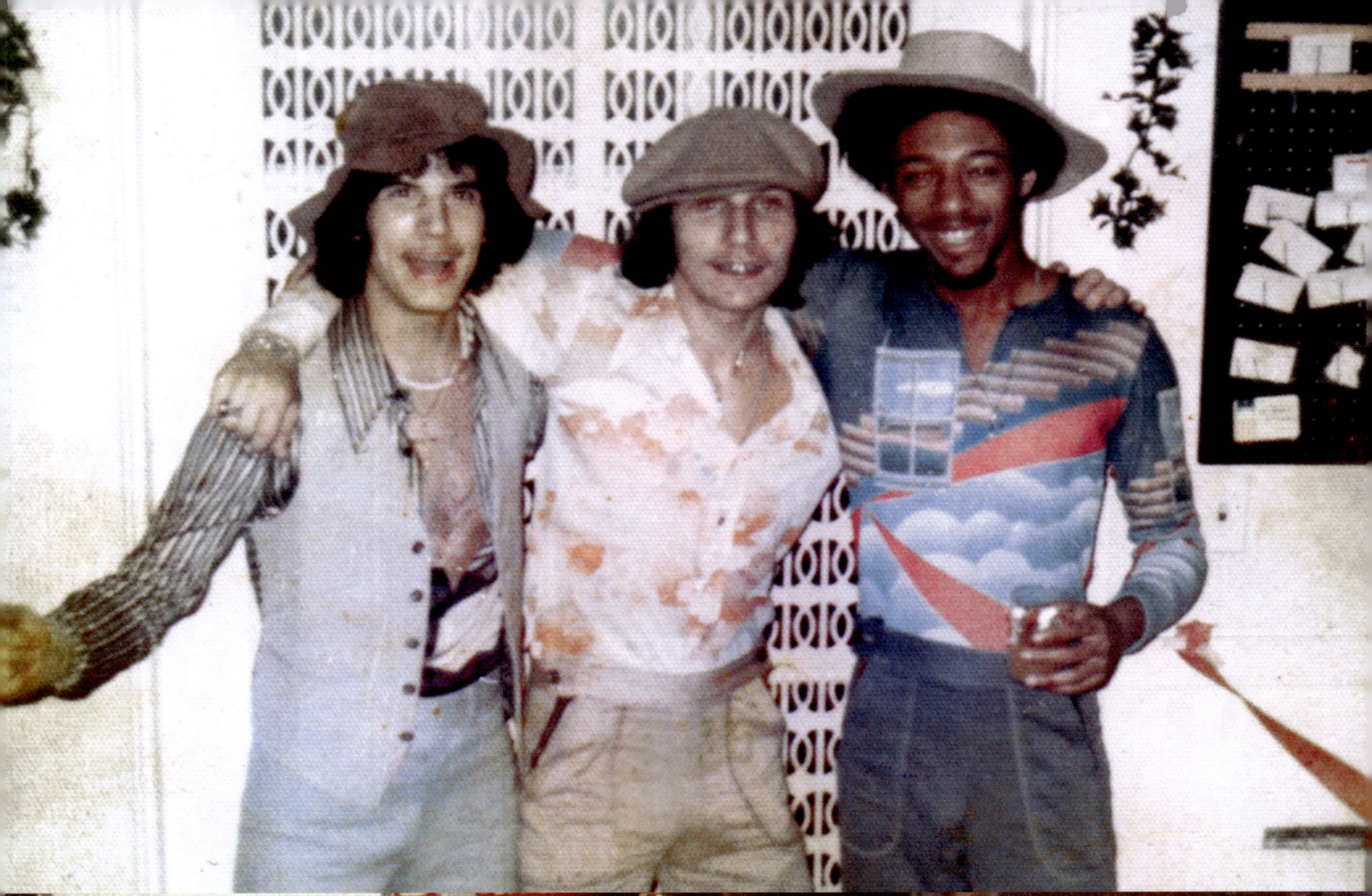

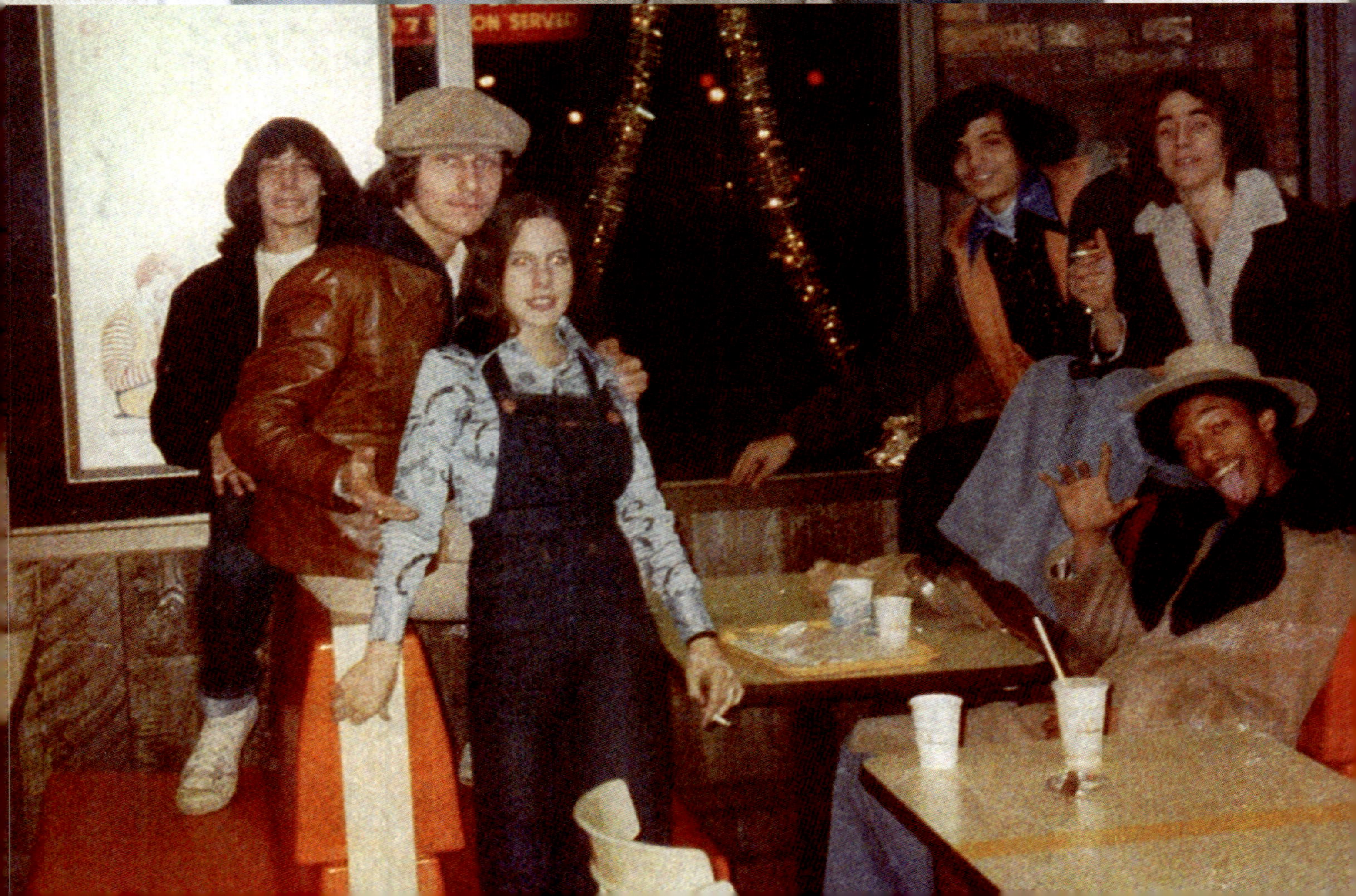

To this day, I don't know how DEATH got his money together for the rent. He wasn't really a drug user, but he was a drinker. Each night, he'd drink himself into a coma or he'd consider the night a failure. Even with a home to go to, DEATH remained crazy. One afternoon, shortly after he moved in, he stepped out of the shower with his hair soaking-wet. He looked around for his blow dryer and couldn't find it, so he threw on a pair of jeans and raced out the front door without a shirt or shoes. I followed him across the street to the Whelan's Drugstore, where he lifted a heavy metal garbage can and launched it through the window. The entire pane of glass shattered at his feet, and then he reached inside and grabbed a blow dryer. The two of us ran home together. Things only got worse.

In order to pay for the drugs, a lot of the guys shoplifted everything they could find, some of them even turned to pulling heists. There was a moment during all of the craziness when it got to be too much for me. I decided to try my own hand at robbery, partly on a dare from COMET and partly because of the stories I had heard about Pete Townsend stealing his guitars after smashing one in a show. There was a music store on Gun Hill Road across the street from Evander. The store had a Fender bass I coveted since my first days in high school. COMET said if I took it he'd stop anybody that ran after me. The plan sounded great on paper, but in 1977, I was smoking two packs of Kools a day. Some of the store employees caught me as I ran out of breath not far from Gun Hill Road. COMET got away and called CRACHEE to tell him what happened. The cops came and took me to the local precinct.

I couldn't believe I was sitting in a squad car with the sirens blaring. This was everything I didn't want in my life. The moment I got to the precinct, the cops were all over me, "What'd you do with the bass?" The same question, over and over again. My answer was the same as well, "I have no idea what you're talking about officer. You've got the wrong guy." This went on for an hour. The longer the questioning took, the more I realized something had broken in my favor and I was going to get away with this. The cops weren't at the scene of the crime. The reality was they knew blacks were picked up all the time based on color and the say-so of a store owner. So, the cops weren't totally convinced I was the culprit, and the fact that nobody could find the bass was turning a small crime into a giant waste of their time and manpower. When the night shift came on, they kicked me loose.

I had the biggest smile on my face as I left the precinct. No more robberies ever again. I was an idiot and still got away with it. When I arrived at home, COMET told me how I came to avoid jail: After I ran out of the store, COMET laid back to see what would happen. He followed the guys chasing me, and when he walked by his mom's house he noticed the bass in the yard. COMET grabbed the bass and quietly walked the other way. He knew I wouldn't talk. And without the bass, there was no crime. COMET presented the instrument to me as he finished the story. He was my hero, but the night was young.

Opposite page: Top: Joel Papelski, Spanish John and BLADE. New Years eve 1976. Bottom: DEATH, CRACHEE, Laura, BLADE and other friends at McDonalds. New Years eve 1976.

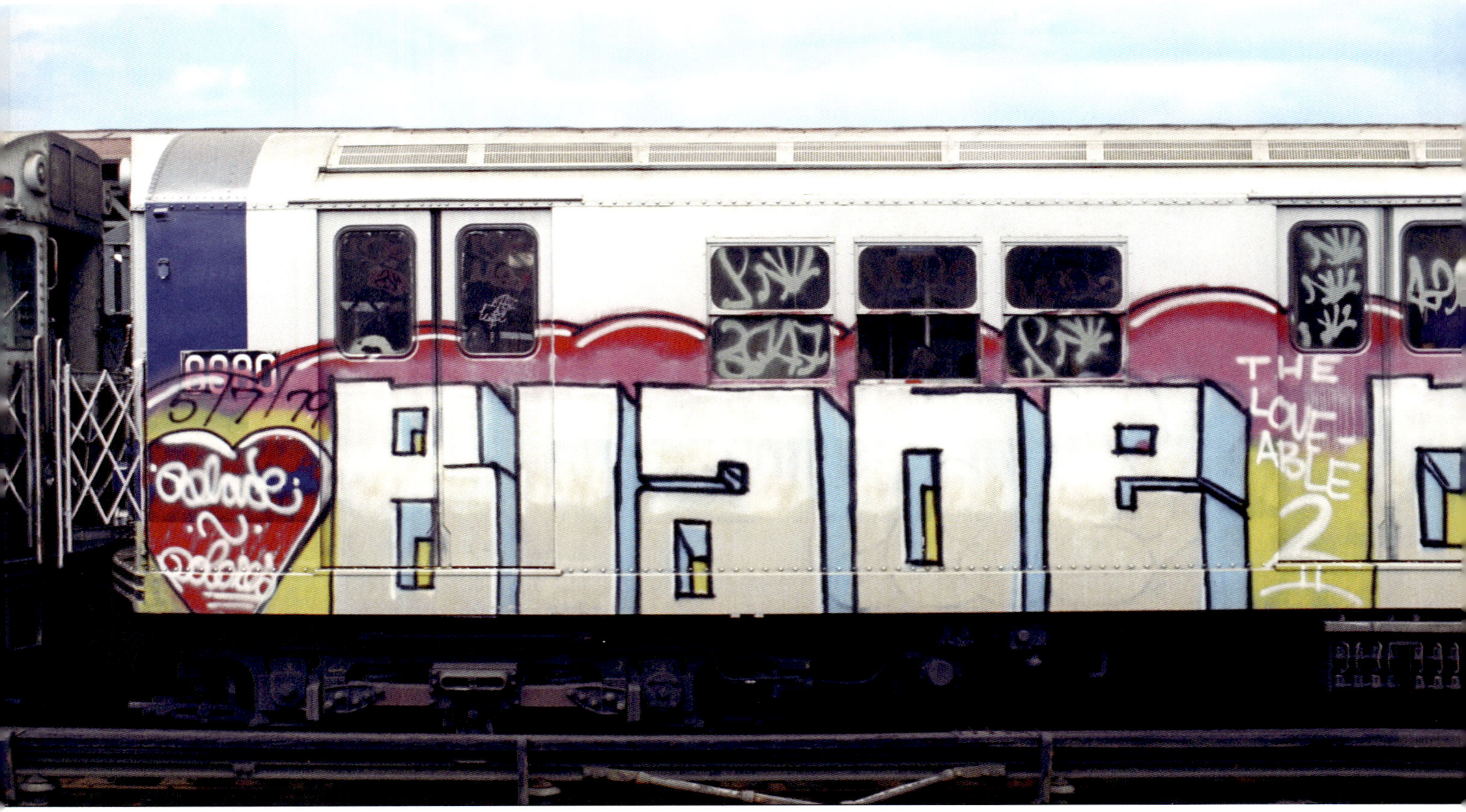

DEATH had just slid past us in the doorway and there was a commotion outside. There was a loud banging on our door—the kind that cops do to get your attention. I opened the door and asked if I could help them. There were two cops standing there and sirens blaring in the background. The first cop said, "Did a white kid just run in here?"

"No officer." I gave my standard response to cops.

"Some punk just pushed an old lady down the stairs. I'm going to ask you again, did a white kid just run in here?"

"No officer." What the fuck had Gillen done? I was pissed off, but refused to give him up to the cops.

The cops stared at me hard, but after the day I just had I wasn't going to back down now. They moved on and they banged on more doors the way cops do. The only information I ever got from DEATH was that it was an accident.

It was time to get out. I moved in with my girlfriend Dolores, partly because of the party atmosphere and crime and partly because of the problem with my first girlfriend Karen. It was sad what happened to her.

Most of the group home people got into drugs hard. And why not? Nobody cared about them. From there they got into prostitution to pay for the drugs. Big Mike and COMET would take Karen and her friends Valerie and Shorty to 42nd Street in Mike's gold Charger and leave them off to make money. It's not like they were pimps; they were just there to make sure the girls were all right. Karen and I were over before I moved into the new apartment, but she was still one of us and she still hung out watching TV all day and

This spread: BLADE and Dolores. 1978. Photo by Henry Chalfant, Subway Art, 25th Anniversary Edition, Thames and Hudson, Ltd. London 2009.

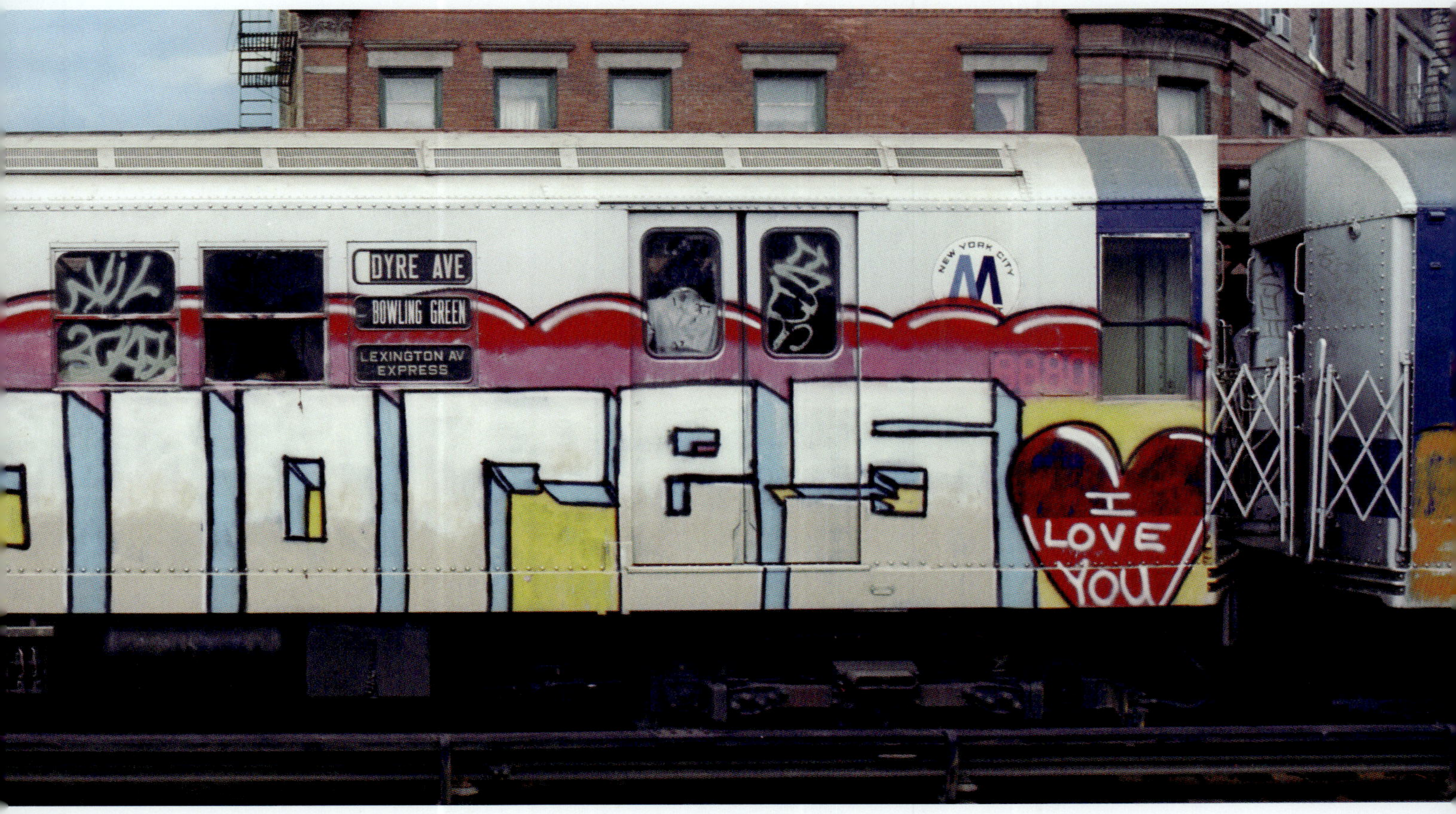

listening to music. By 1977, all Karen wanted was to chain smoke Kools and do drugs all day. In my life with my new girlfriend, Dolores, there were no drugs and there was very little drama, and that's the way I wanted it.

Karen and Shorty stayed at the house sometimes. Karen and I would argue about work. I worked a legit job at McDonalds across the street and I'd have to listen to her say, "Well, I've got to go out and make money tonight." It drove me nuts, so I'd yell at her to get her working papers and get a real job. There's no shame in working at McDonalds—it's honest work—but she wanted the fast money.

When she wasn't staying with us, she'd get high and start kicking in the door. All the while yelling nasty things about Dolores: "Why are you living with a white girl instead of me?" It was definitely time to move.

Now it was Dolores and I against the world. We gathered all of our stuff and moved to 820 east 227th street in the middle of the night. Nobody knew, not even COMET. As it was time to make the break from Parkside, I continued to hold onto the lease to the Olinville Avenue apartment, but I never went back.

COMET and I continued as writing partners, but I wouldn't see DEATH again for thirty years. COMET said that DEATH woke up one morning and left the apartment to interview for a job in Manhattan because he was tired of scrambling and pulling heists and wanted to live a normal life. He got the job, and after that, nobody heard from him.

CHAPTER NINE

THE BLOCKBUSTER

Once in a while, COMET would have problems with his girlfriend Jennifer. She needed more attention, which meant more dating, and that cut into his writing time. Lucky for me, I had my pick of whom I wanted to team up with. JOHN 150 was a great partner and was part of the Eyeball car, done in 1975. JOHN 150 hung out with ALE and DOO 2, but he always wanted to go piecing. We painted together at least thirty times, including a couple of whole-cars and at least four top-to-bottoms.

Another partner who filled in nicely for COMET was GEAR. GEAR was a great guy, but I could never get caught writing with him or there'd be hell to pay to his older brother, DEMON 1, a tough Irish kid that we all liked. DEMON painted from 1973 to 1974. He had a nice, round letter style. DEMON didn't like DEATH and they got into a fight about once a month. I didn't know if DEMON could take me in a fight, but I didn't want to find out. His younger brother Steve started to hang out at Parkside in 1974. He was only fourteen and so he was teased a lot. Hanging out with a lot of older big-time writers, it was to be expected. Slowly, he began to get his name, GEAR, up on the trains, writing with anyone he could. If DEMON caught the writer he was painting with, they'd get a warning: "Do not get my brother busted or I will kill you." I was one of a long line of writers who got that warning.

Much like JOHN 150, GEAR had his own writing career, usually with the Boulevard Boys, COMET, FRITZ, and SHAKE. GEAR and I would go piecing together at Esplanade. Although he was young, he was calm and fun to be around. GEAR didn't like to act crazy, like a lot of the other writers, and I responded to writers who wanted to write and who treated the lay-ups with a sort of reverence. Show up, paint, get out, and don't leave a mess. There was a period where Esplanade got burned because toy writers were showing up and kicking the windows out of the cars. When that happened, we'd go to Burke. One of the more famous trains we painted together had the Rolling Stones tongue in it. That car ran for ages.

In 1976, you really didn't see much of TRACY 168 and the WANTED crew or the INDs anymore. 3YB continued, but it was mostly with lesser-known writers. THE MG BOYS—MARK 198, KIT 17, NIC 707, BOOTS 119, VICTOR, and SIMON—were starting to come into their own.

Opposite page:
JOHN 150 and BLADE. 1975. Photo ©Keith Baugh.

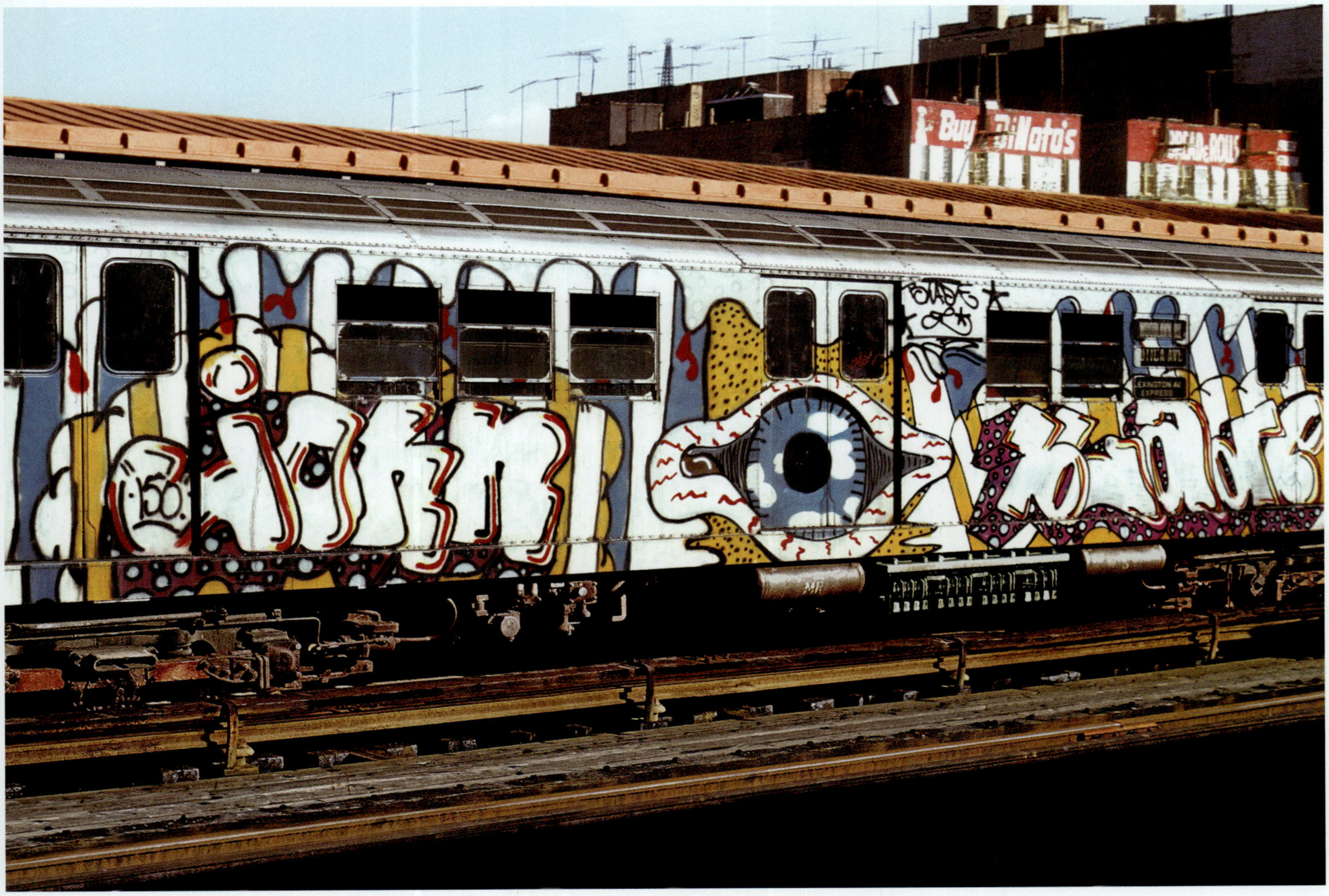
Buy DiNoto's

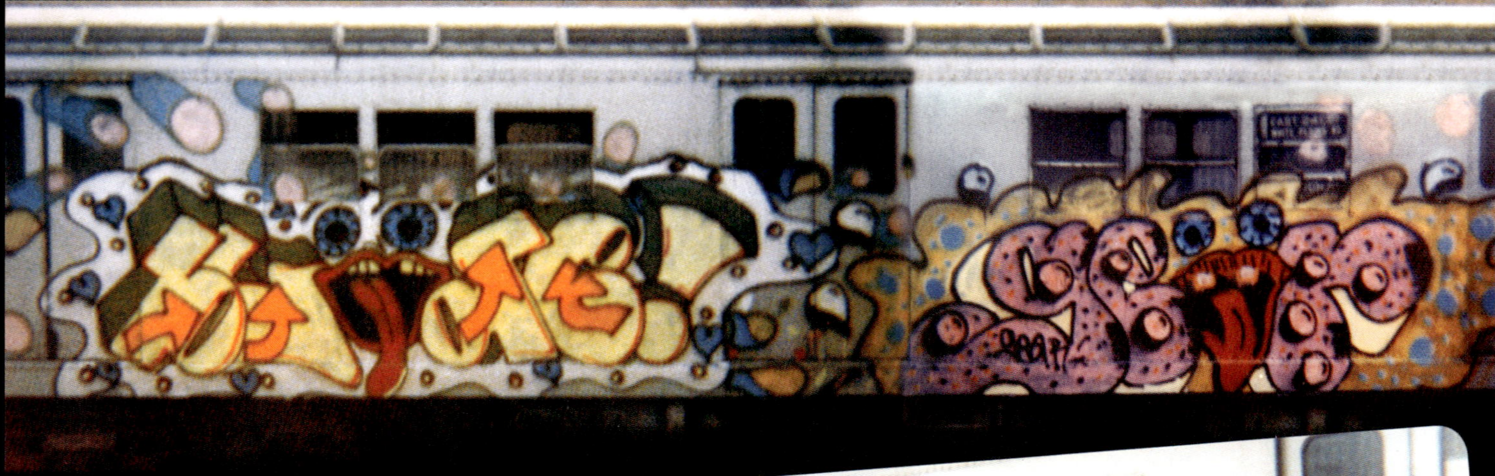

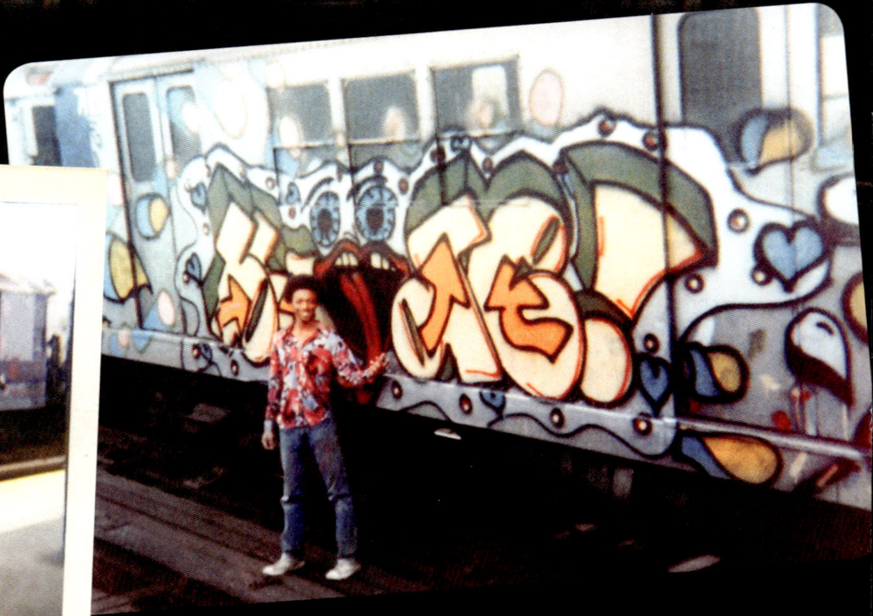

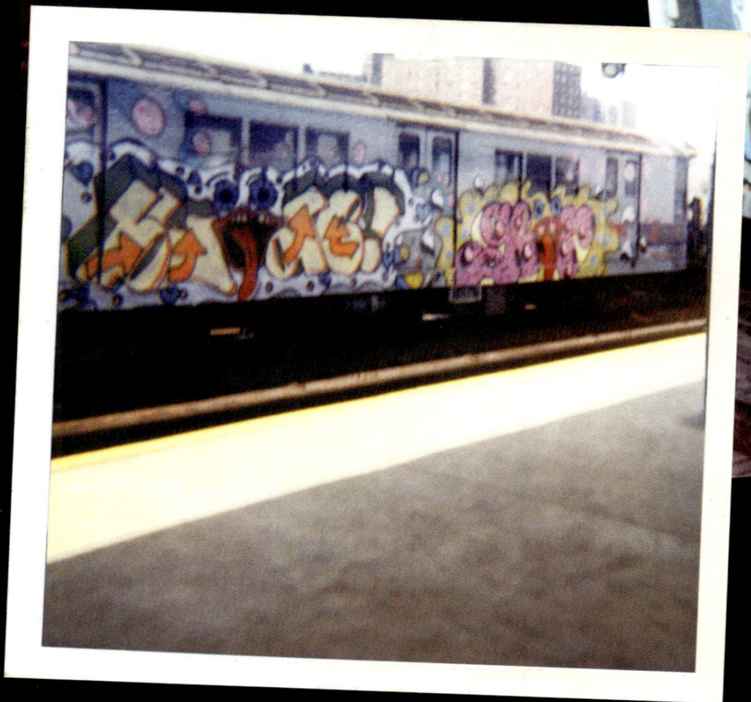

"ONE OF THE MORE FAMOUS TRAINS WE PAINTED TOGETHER HAD THE ROLLING STONES TONGUE IN IT. THAT CAR RAN FOR AGES."

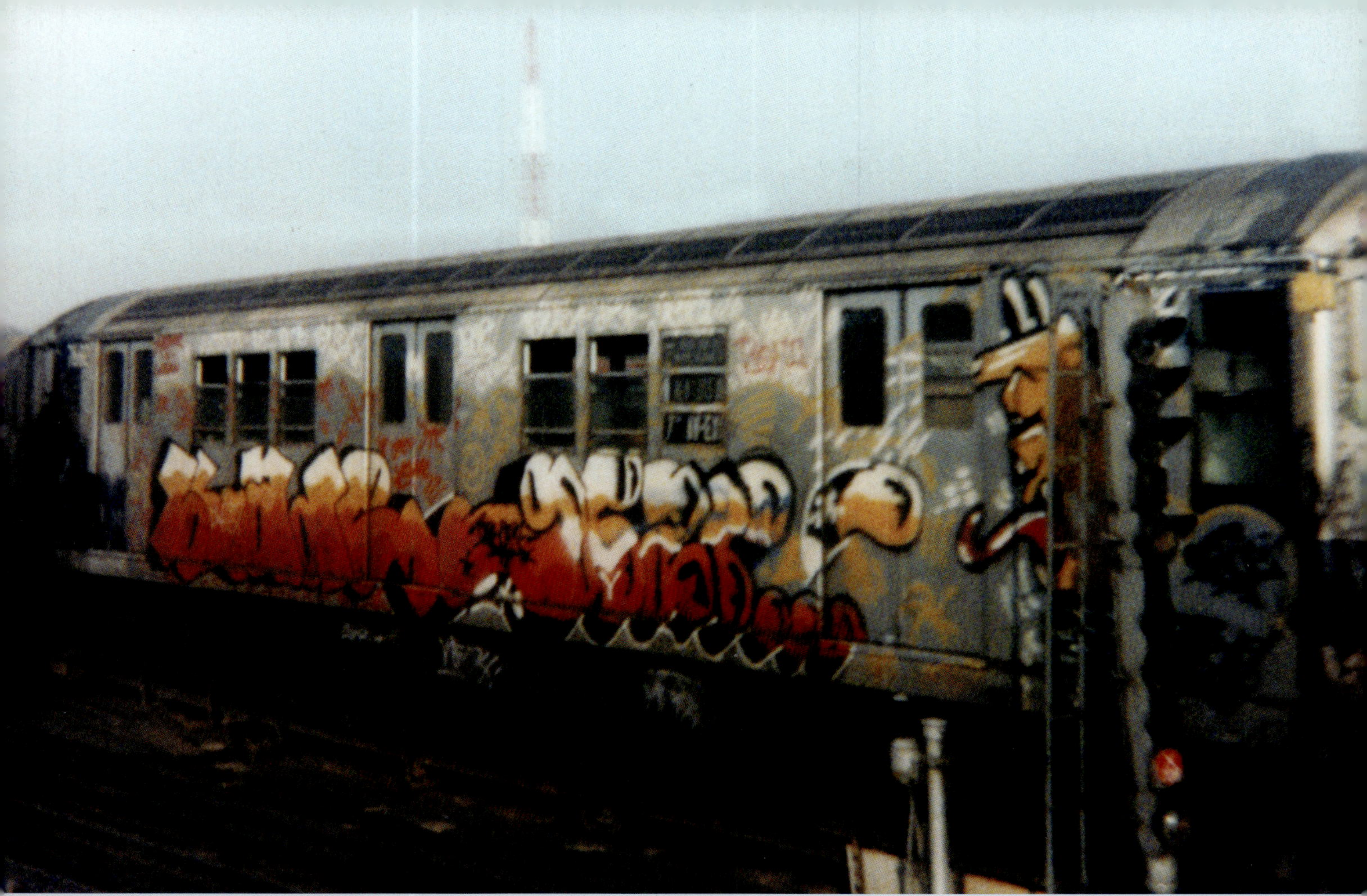

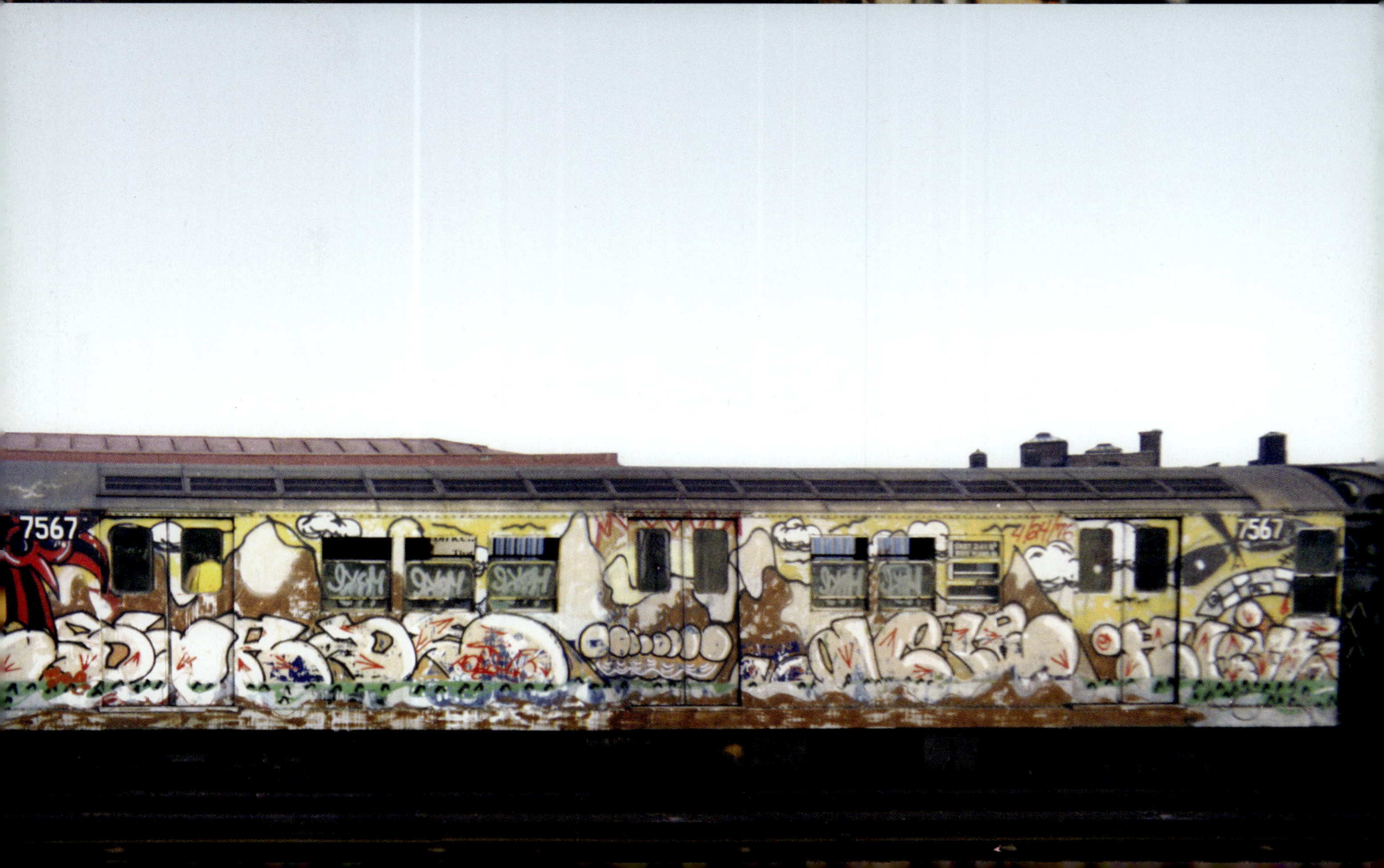
7567

"GOING FROM ONE END OF A NINETY-FOOT LONG TRAIN TO THE OTHER, THEY WERE BILLBOARD PIECES THAT COULD BE SEEN FROM BLOCKS AWAY..."

1977 was a good time to retire, and it was something Dolores wanted me to do. A lot of writers retired then, because of the emergence of "the buff." Basically, the city installed car wash stations in different train yards to clean the trains with a chemical solvent. The stuff was lethal and the MTA workers hated it. Even after a few runs through, the buff it wouldn't take off all of the paint; it just turned the trains into a grey mess. The problem for writers was that the train you worked eight hours on to paint could be buffed the next day, and that was discouraging.

If the buff didn't discourage you, then the emergence of throw-up crews like the TOP crew from Brooklyn could be disheartening. They had a great line-up of writers, but they insisted on doing throw-ups on the IRT lines, including the 2s and 5s. I didn't have a problem going over them with my pieces, but I was concerned with the direction in which graffiti was heading. A lot of good writers quit because of the buff. Some, such as DEAN and JESTER, turned to throw-ups as a way to compete. I didn't want to go that route. I wanted my trains big and colorful. I thought that was what people loved about graffiti.

COMET and I began looking for a new approach, so we began experimenting with a new style that covered more of the cars with paint. I did the A on the middle door first and then spread out from there. Each letter was the same size, covering the train from the windows down. We called the style "blockbuster." It was pretty simple to do and we decided to run with it. One night on the 4 line, I did four of them in six hours.

The blockbuster had an amazing impact. One of the most important aspects of graffiti is to have your name stick out from the others. The blockbuster was a great way to do that. Going from one end of a ninety-foot long train to the other, they were billboard pieces that could be seen from blocks away—wide geometric letters just rolling by, one after another. When a ten-car train rode by, passengers would see hundreds of smaller colorful pieces—most of them illegible—then they'd see BLADE and COMET in bright silver, taking up two cars.

COMET and I did about four hundred of them, all of which were identical in their outlines, but the colors changed depending on what kind of paint we had. The funny thing is, although writers doing smaller pieces sometimes took as long as we did, we were the names you remembered.

Opposite page:
Window-down, end to end blockbusters by BLADE. Circa 1977.

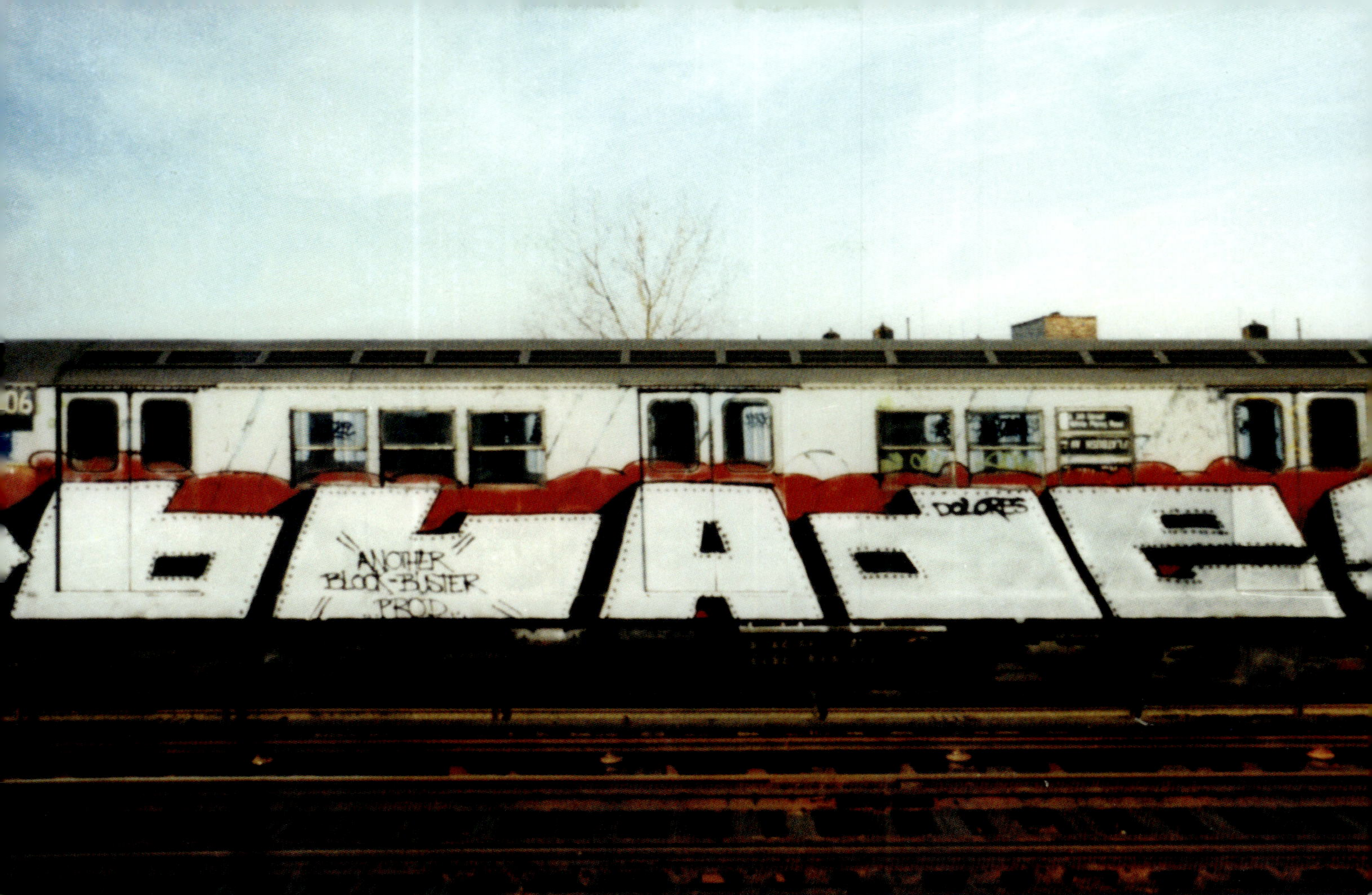
DOLORES
ANOTHER BLOCK-BUSTER PROD.

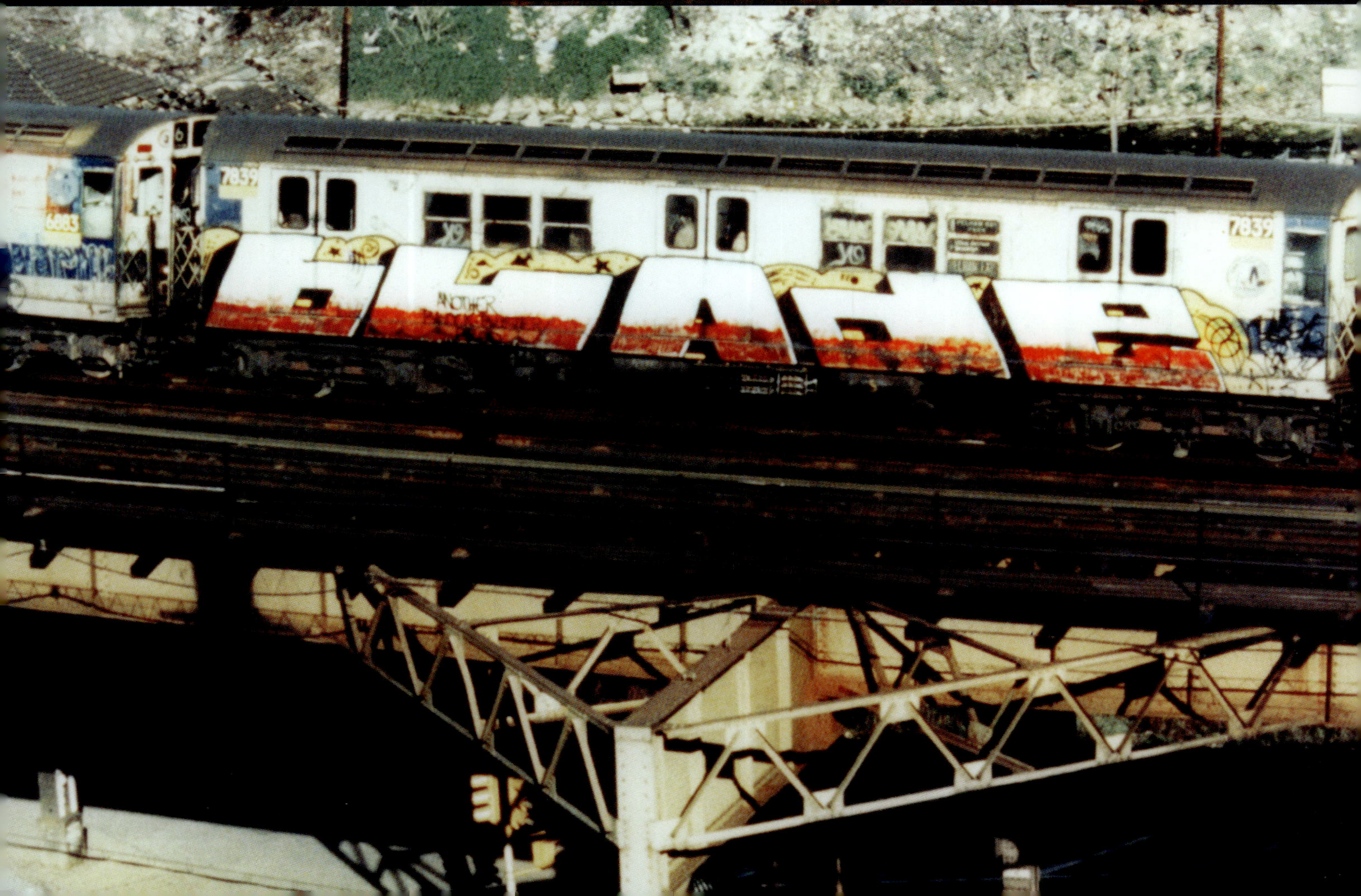
7839
ANOTHER
7839

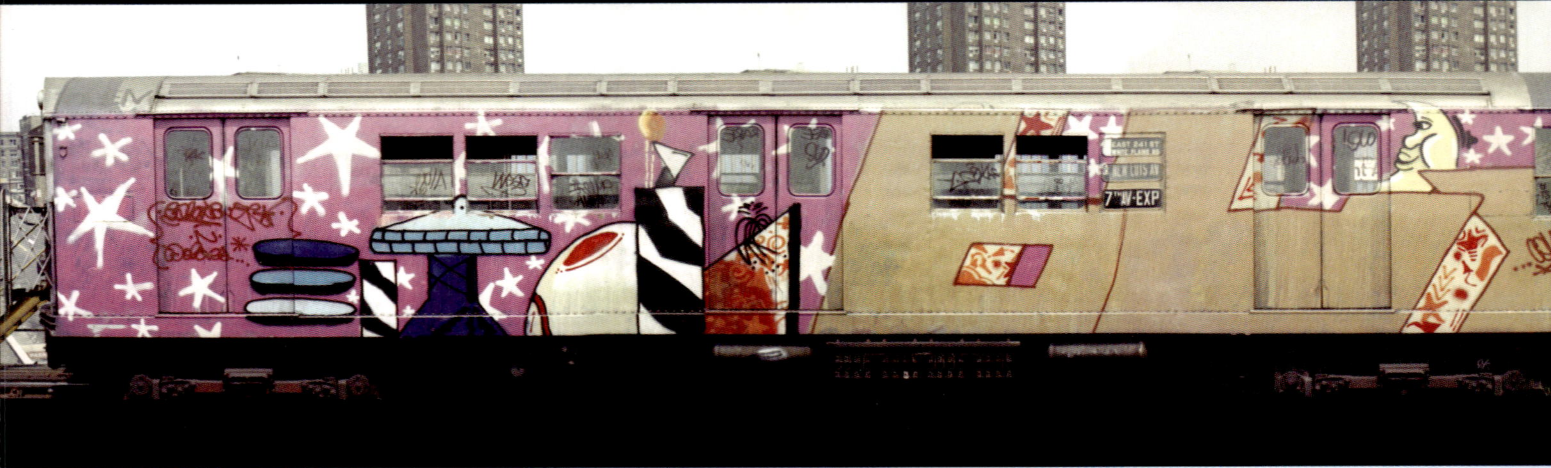

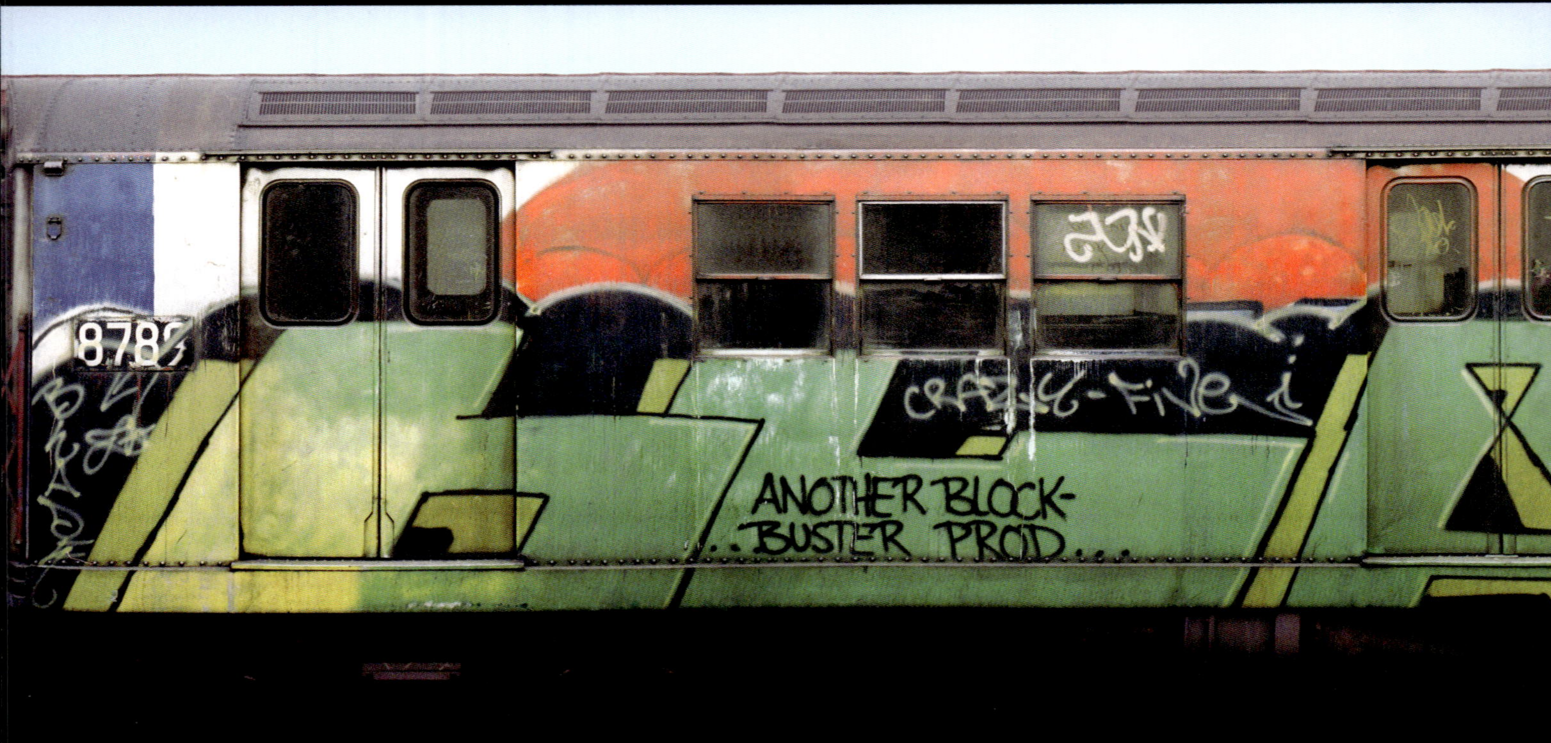

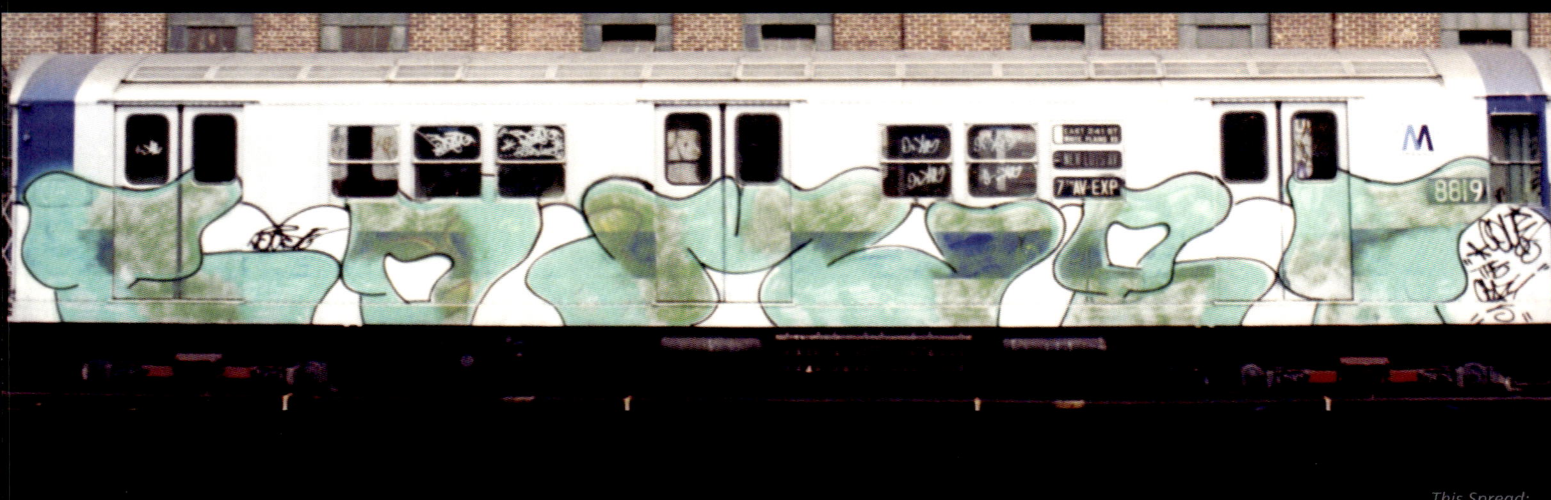

This Spread:
BLADE and BLADE and COMET go BIG! circa 1978. Photo by Henry Chalfant, Subway Art, 25th Anniversary Edition, Thames and Hudson, Ltd. London 2009.

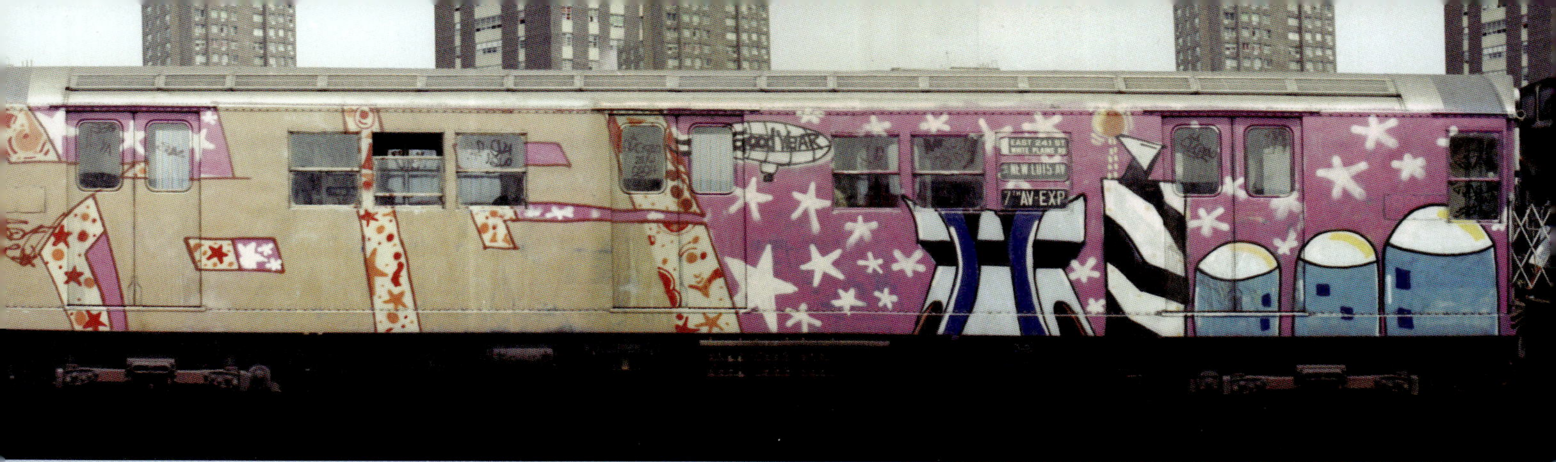
GOOD YEAR
EAST 241 ST
WHITE PLAINS RD
NEW LOTS AV
7TH AV-EXP

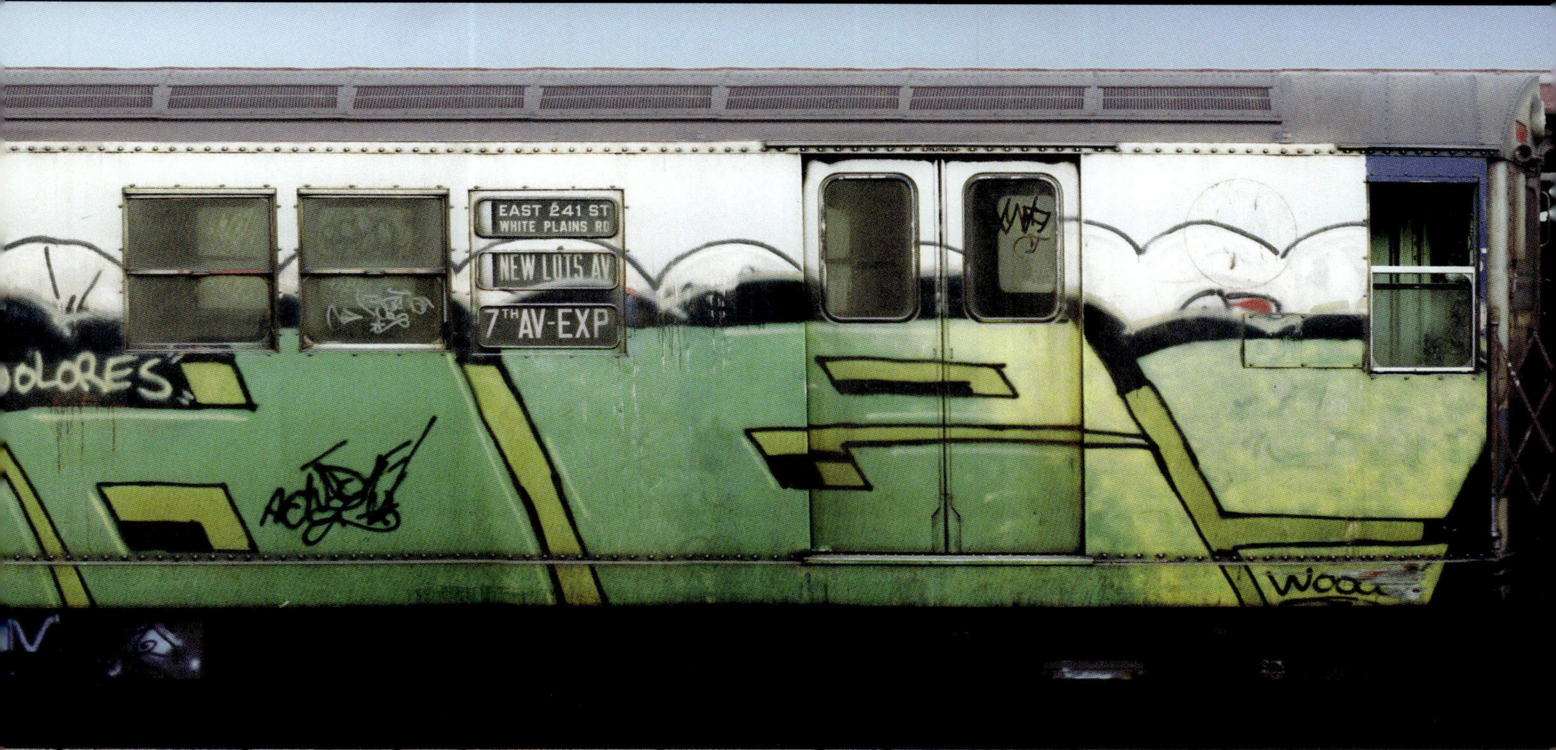
EAST 241 ST
WHITE PLAINS RD
NEW LOTS AV
7TH AV-EXP
DOLORES

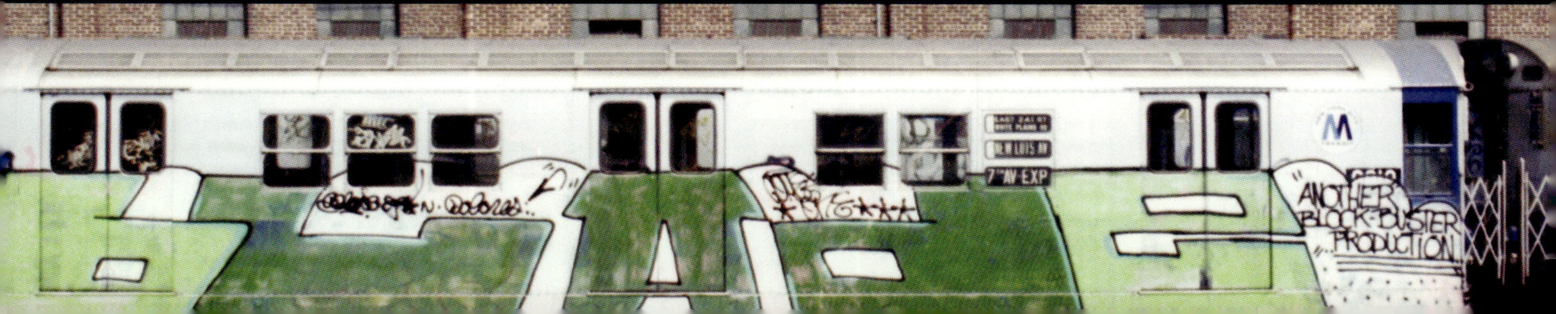
7TH AV-EXP
ANOTHER BLOCK-BUSTER PRODUCTION

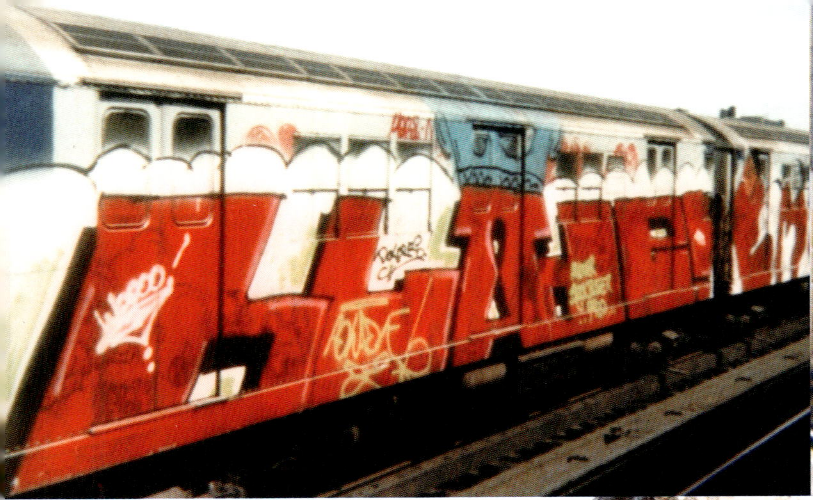
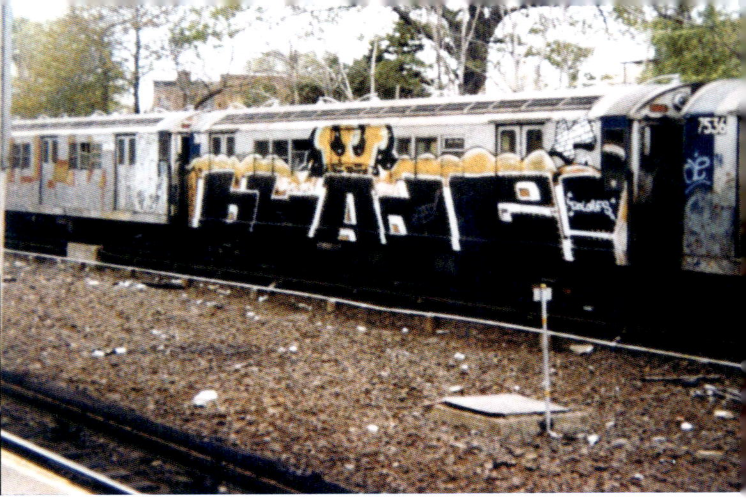
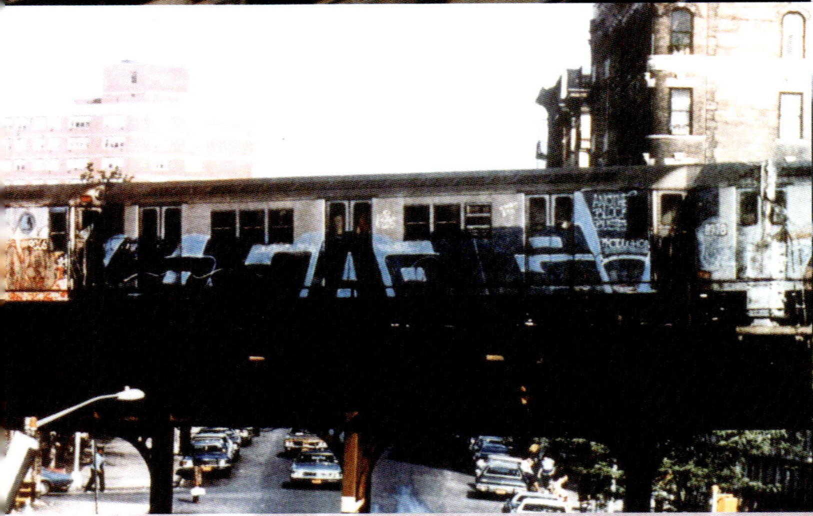
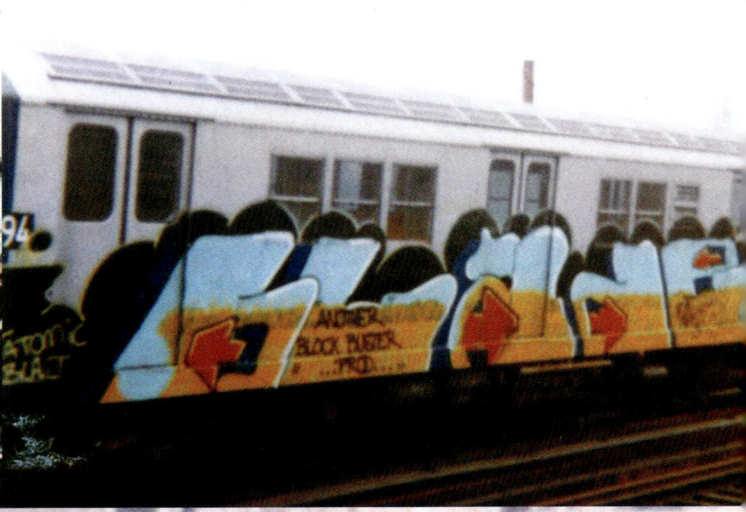
ANOTHER
BLOCK BUSTER
...PROD...
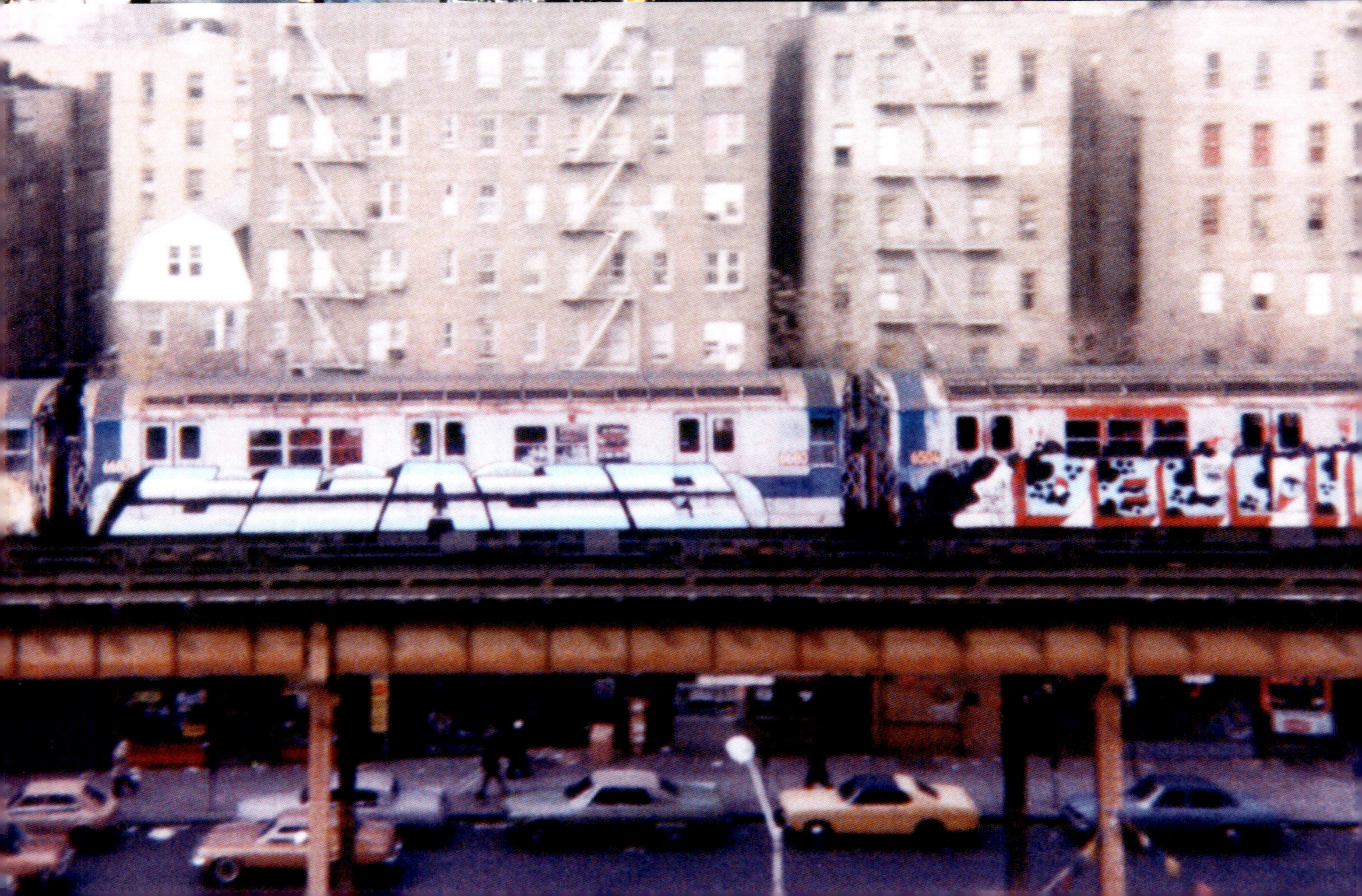

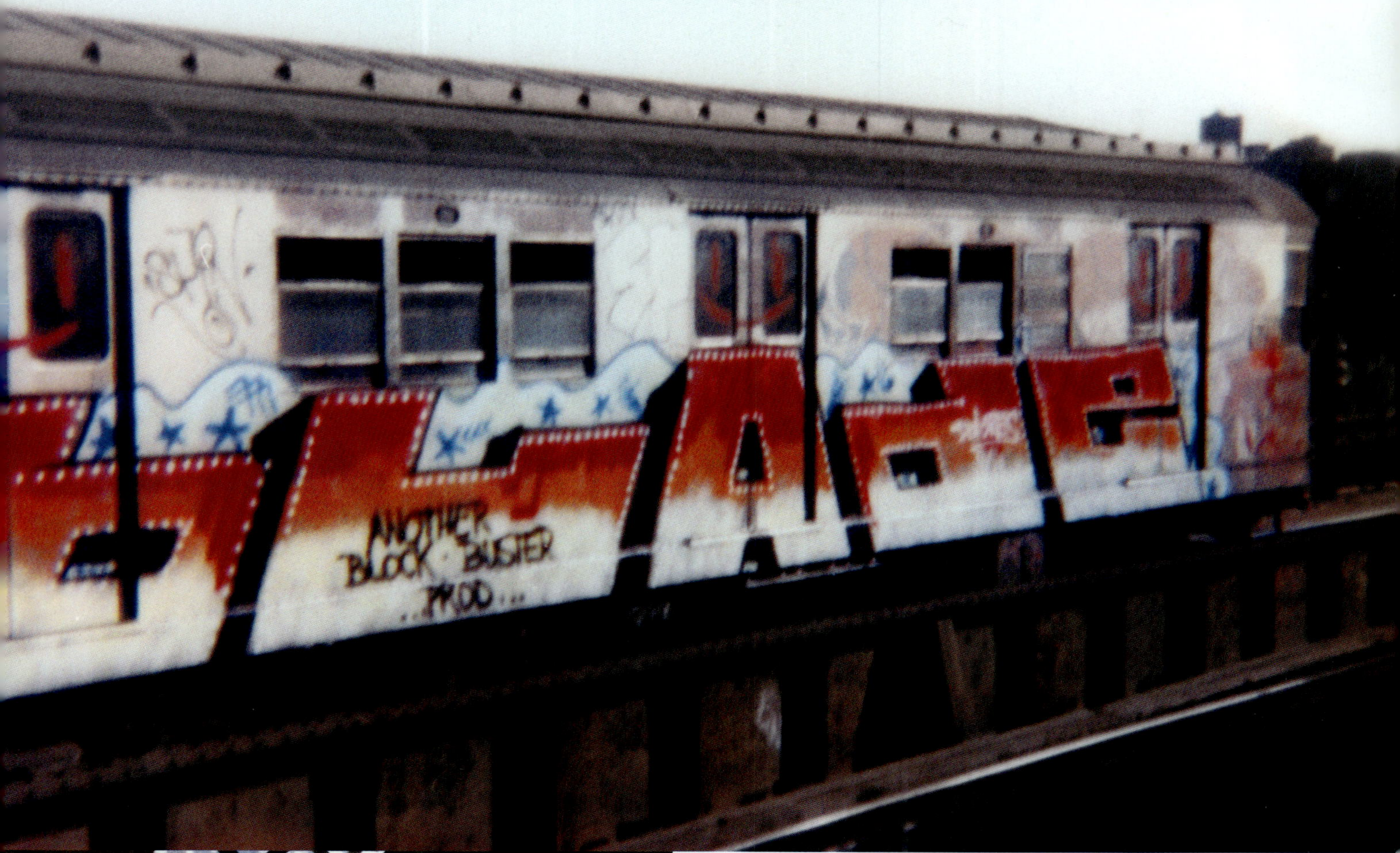
ANOTHER BLOCK BUSTER PROD...

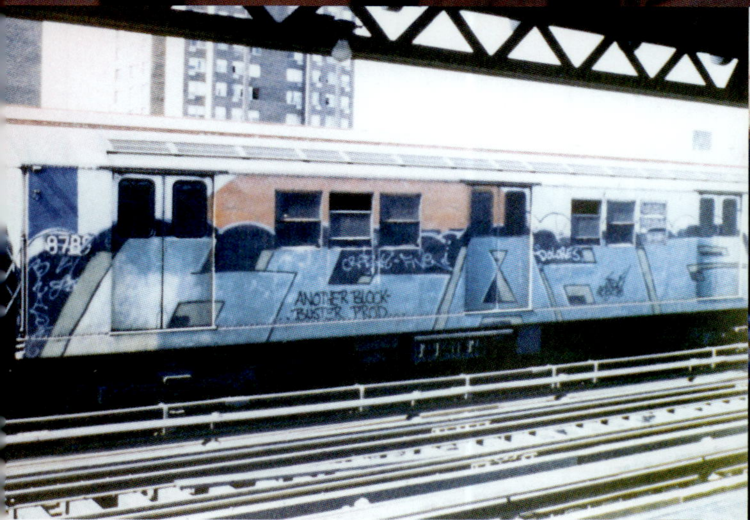
ANOTHER BLOCK BUSTER PROD

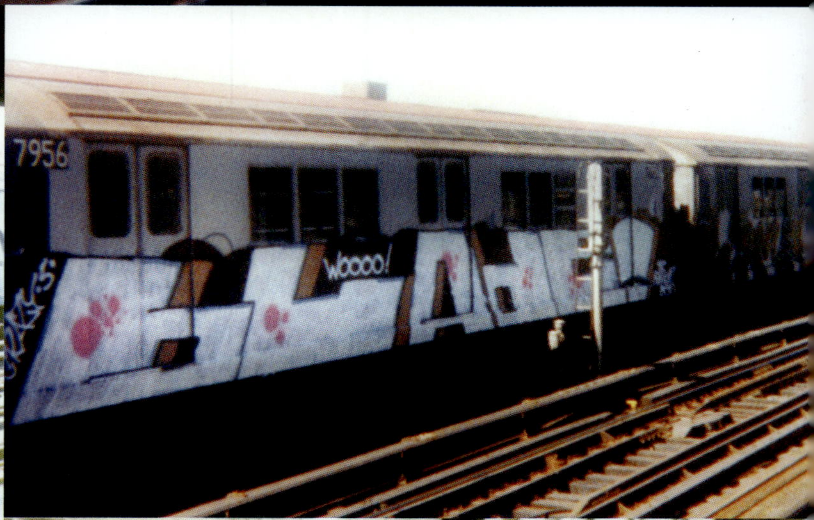
7956
WOOOO!

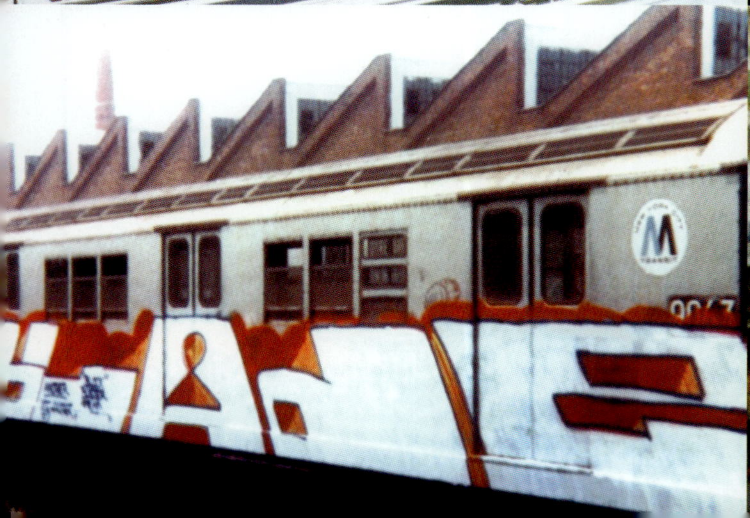

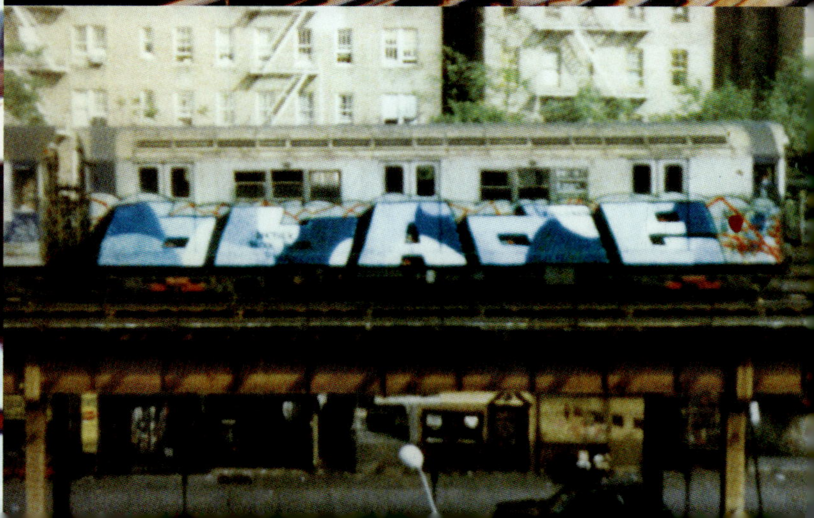

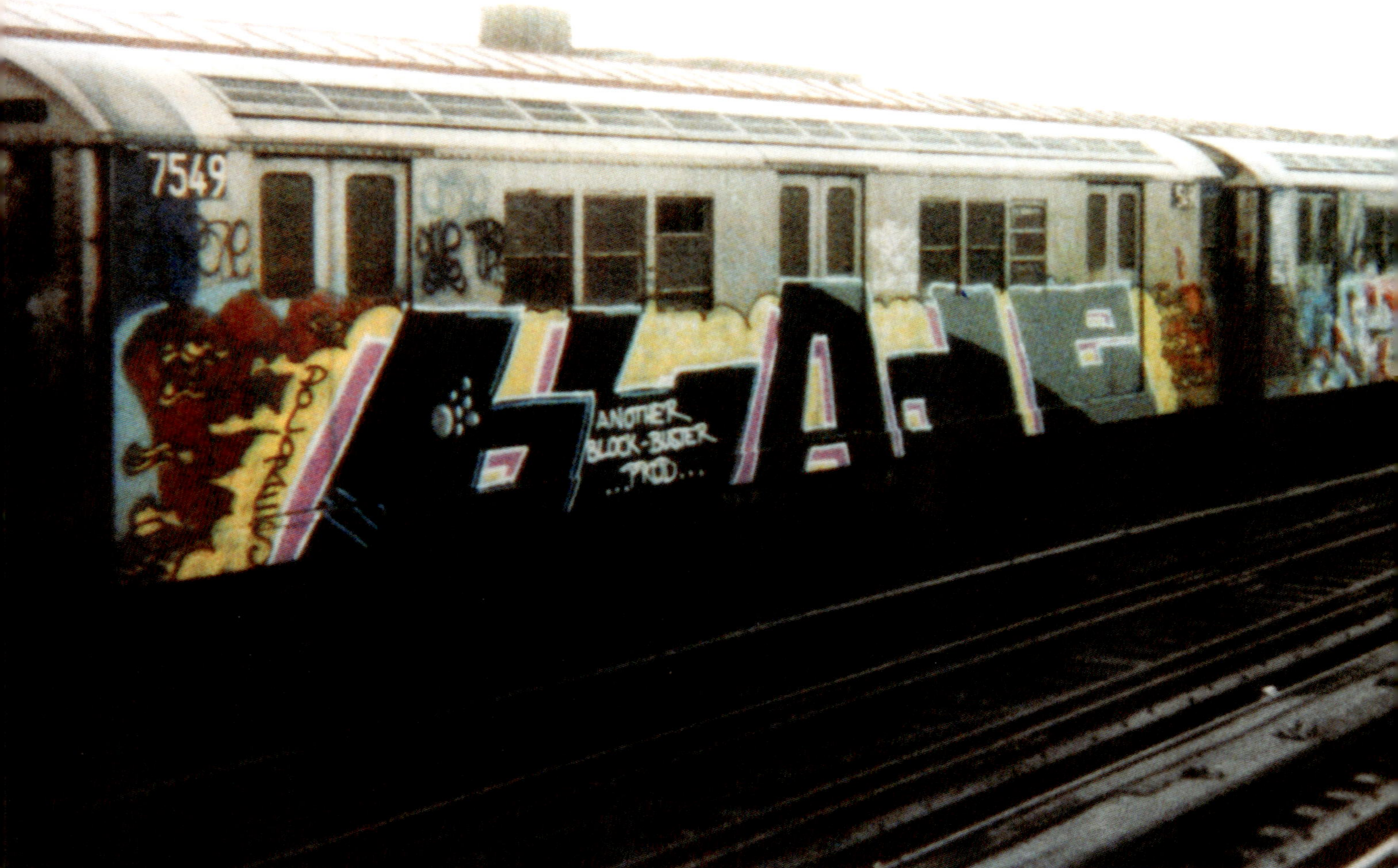
7549
ANOTHER
BLOCK-BUSTER
...PROD...

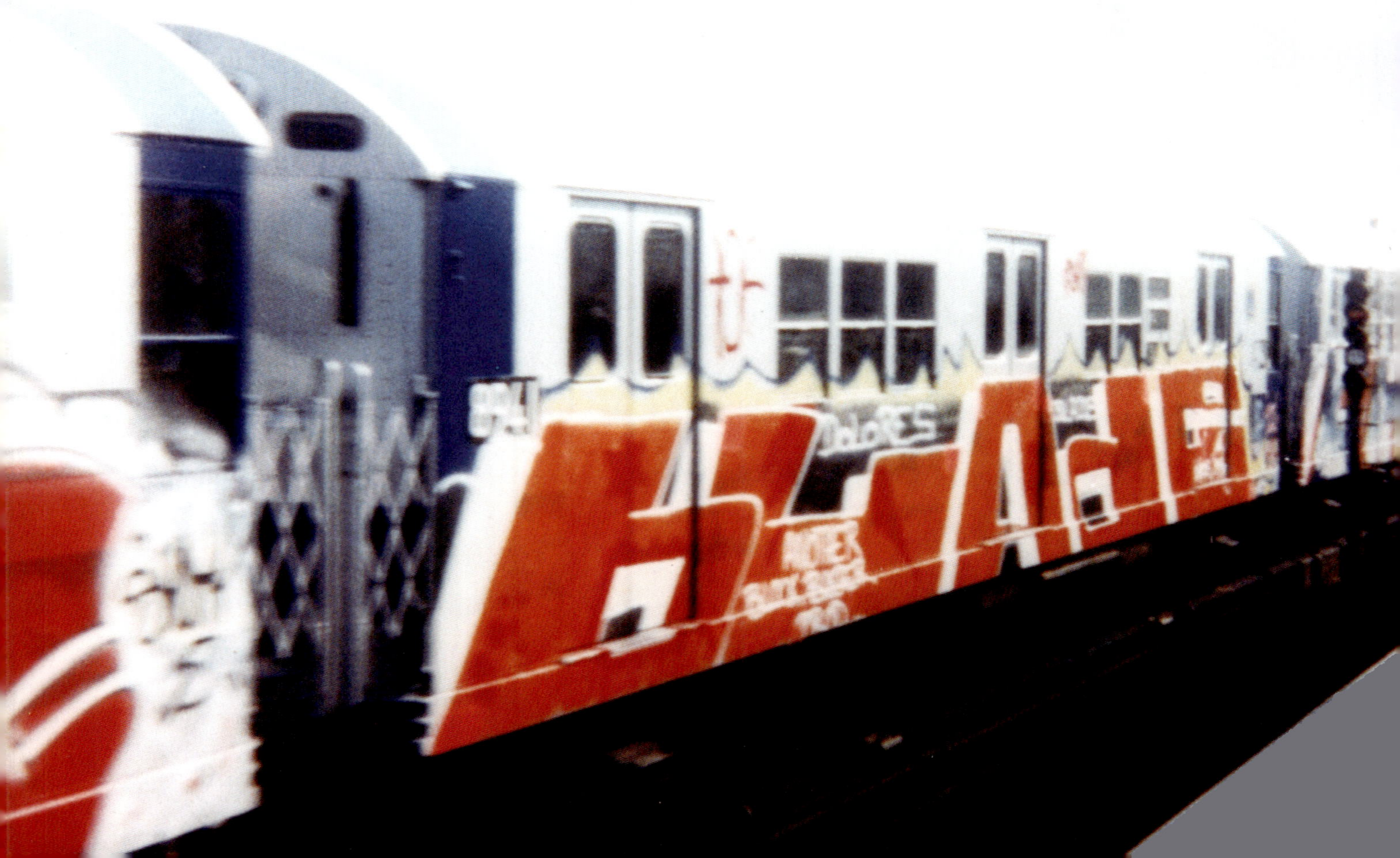
DoloRES

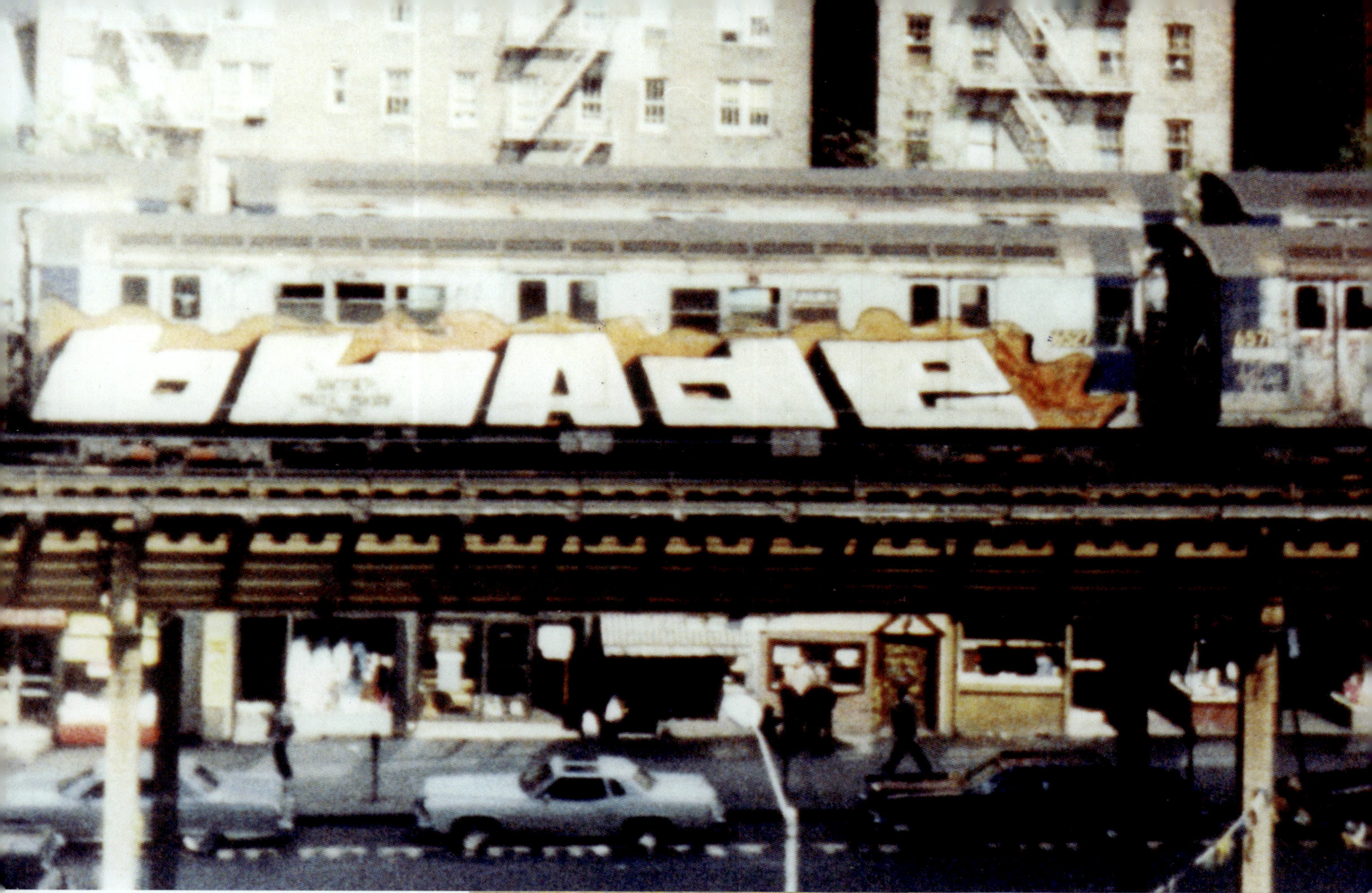

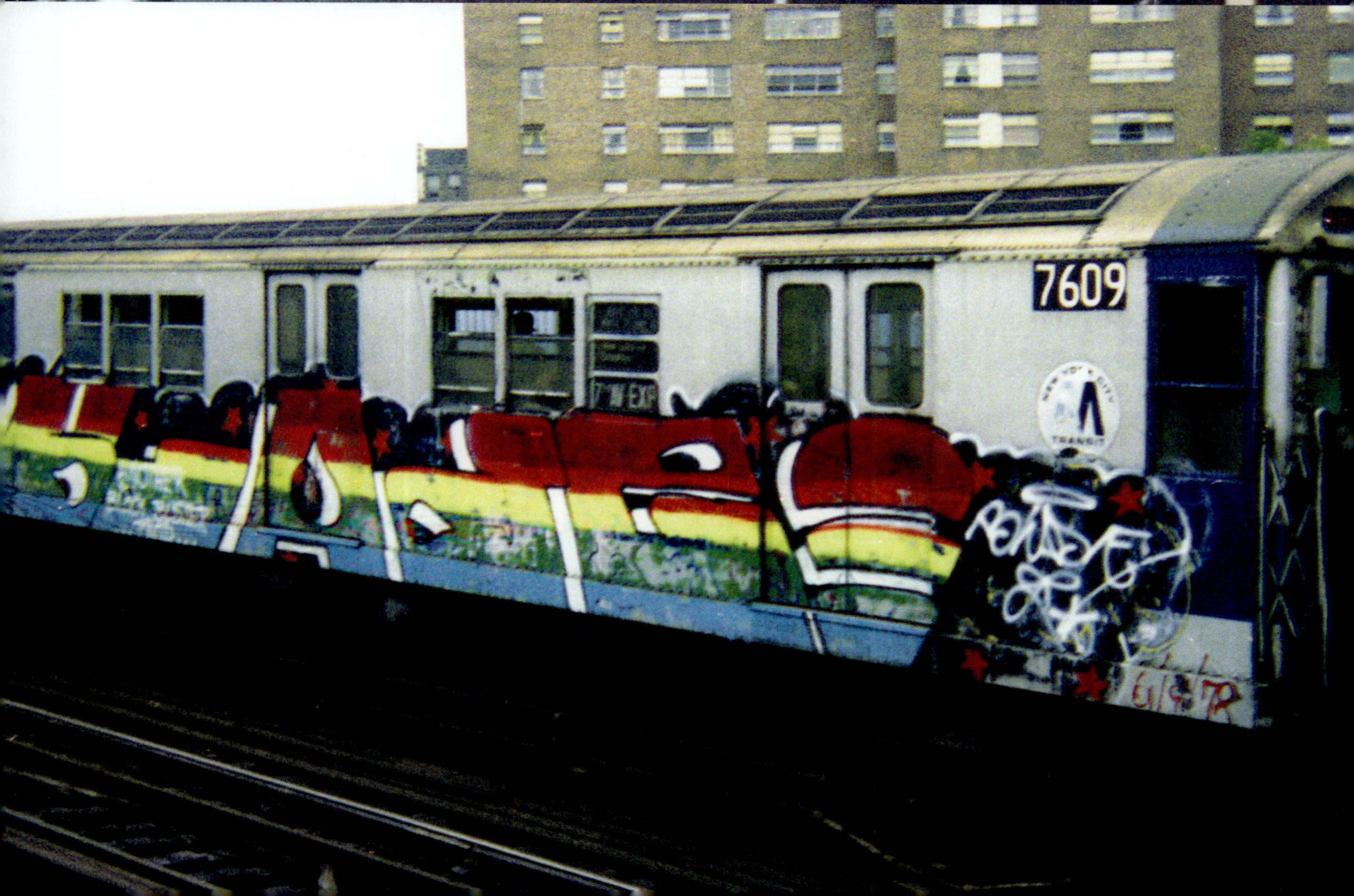
7609

As COMET and I continued to do blockbusters, an unlikely new partner joined us. His name was MAZE. Dolores's little brother was fascinated with graffiti and he took every chance he could to come by the apartment. In 1977, we started to take him to Esplanade, where we'd do outlines for him. MAZE was a great kid, but at twelve years old, he was just that. I was nineteen at the time. He was a big kid with broad shoulders, so at least he looked older than his age. MAZE would join COMET and me for the next three years. We mentored him, urging him to at least go to school. Sometimes when he'd go with us to watch, he'd look up from where he was sitting and say, "Gramps, how many blockbusters are we gonna' do tonight?"

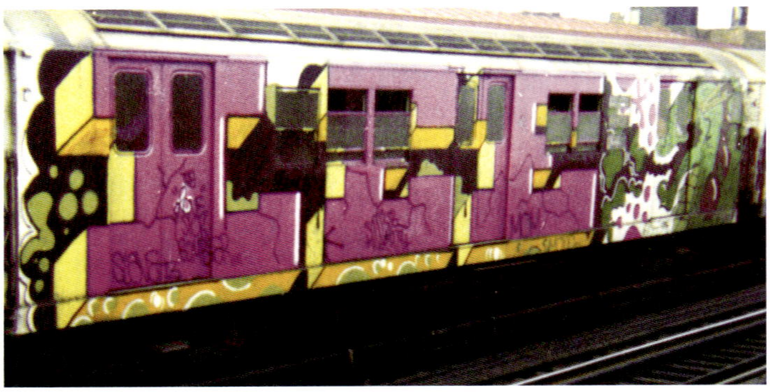

In 1978, Dolores wanted me to grow up. We were living in our second apartment and I was still out bombing—even worse, bombing with her little brother—and she wanted us to do more as a couple. If LEE hadn't come along, I might've quit writing. He inspired me to do some of my best work in that period. No matter how far I would go to take things, there was always this kid LEE pissing me off. One time, on my way to work, the LEE train with the dragon rolled in and there he was photographing it. I couldn't stop talking about it. Dolores responded, "What do you care about this toy?" He was standing right there. I did care. I was twenty-one, he was seventeen, and I had to keep writing because he painted a dragon.

When we moved to De Kalb Avenue in 1980, I took over the 4 line from the MG BOYS. The MISSION GRAFFITI writers were guys I respected because they could do so much with just two colors. They had nice style, but it wasn't wild style, which made them stick out more at that point in graffiti. A train would come by and you'd have a blur of wild style pieces by TEAN and KADE, which would take a while to figure it out. Then you'd see a MARK 198 or KIT 17 piece and you knew exactly what it said. Those were the writers I had to beat.

It was also becoming increasingly more important that I didn't get caught while bombing. I simply couldn't afford it. Dolores was trying to get her degree to work with special needs kids, and so I did my best to save money. Some of the chases that year were incredible and we did our best to remain cautious.

Dolores could see the lay-up from our fire escape, which made things easier, because she was able to signal when something didn't look right. One night, we had an amazing chase up there. The cops came in from both sides. I climbed down the elevated pole, but there was a black-and-white cop car beneath me, so I had to climb right back up. I was about to get busted, so as the cops approached me I started yelling back at them: "Please! Please turn the flashlight off! It's blinding me!! I'm afraid I'll hit the third rail. I'm begging you, turn it off!" Amazingly the cops turned off their flashlights, and I took off. I ran the boards for fifteen cars in the darkness then climbed under the train and waited. That was the scariest chase because I knew I couldn't get caught, since I had to be at work the next day. I was twenty-three at the time.

This page: LEE and his dragon. The train that made BLADE push harder! 1978.
Opposite page: Two cars by MAZE, Dolores's little brother. Circa 1978.

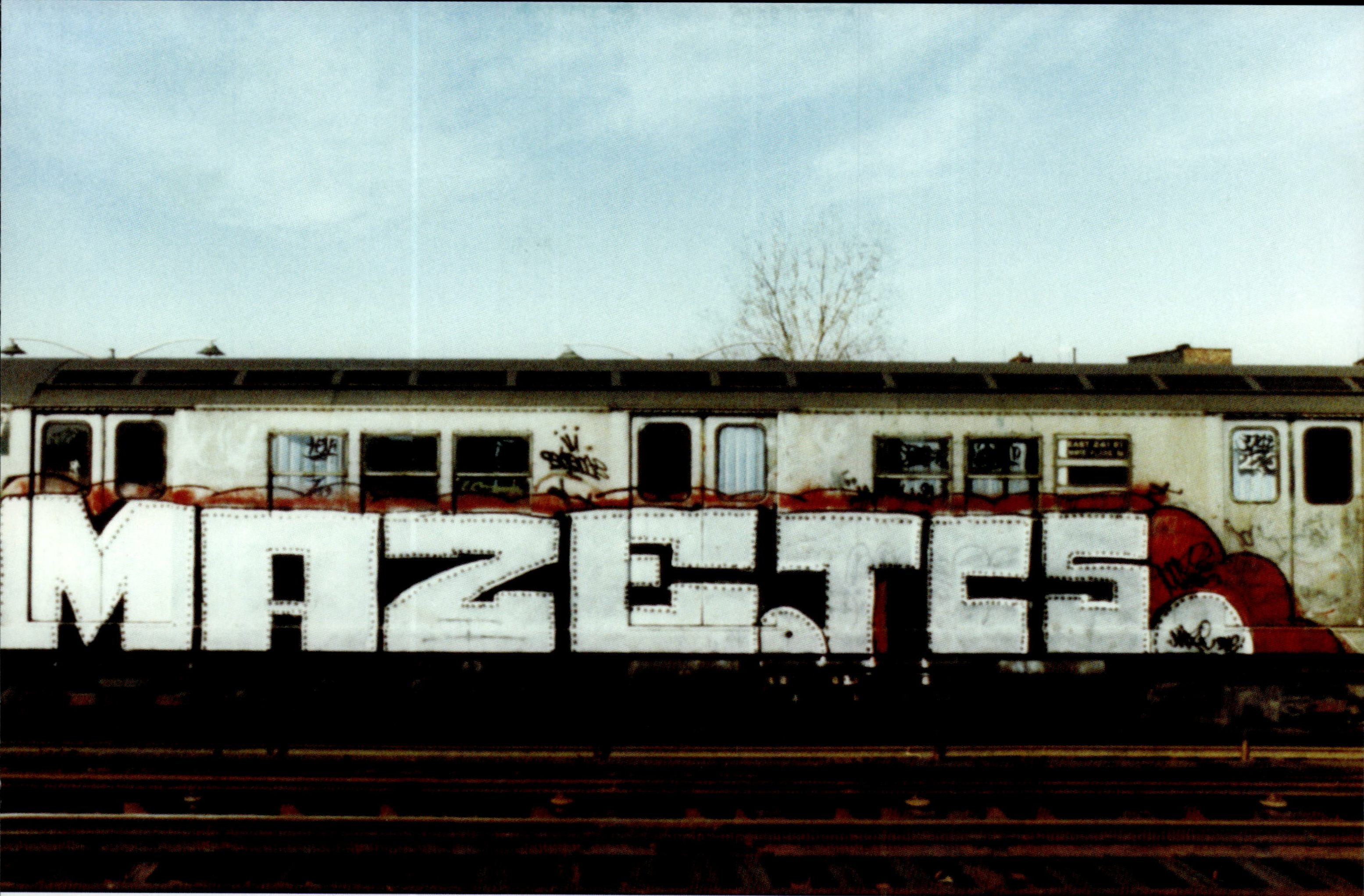
MAZE TC5

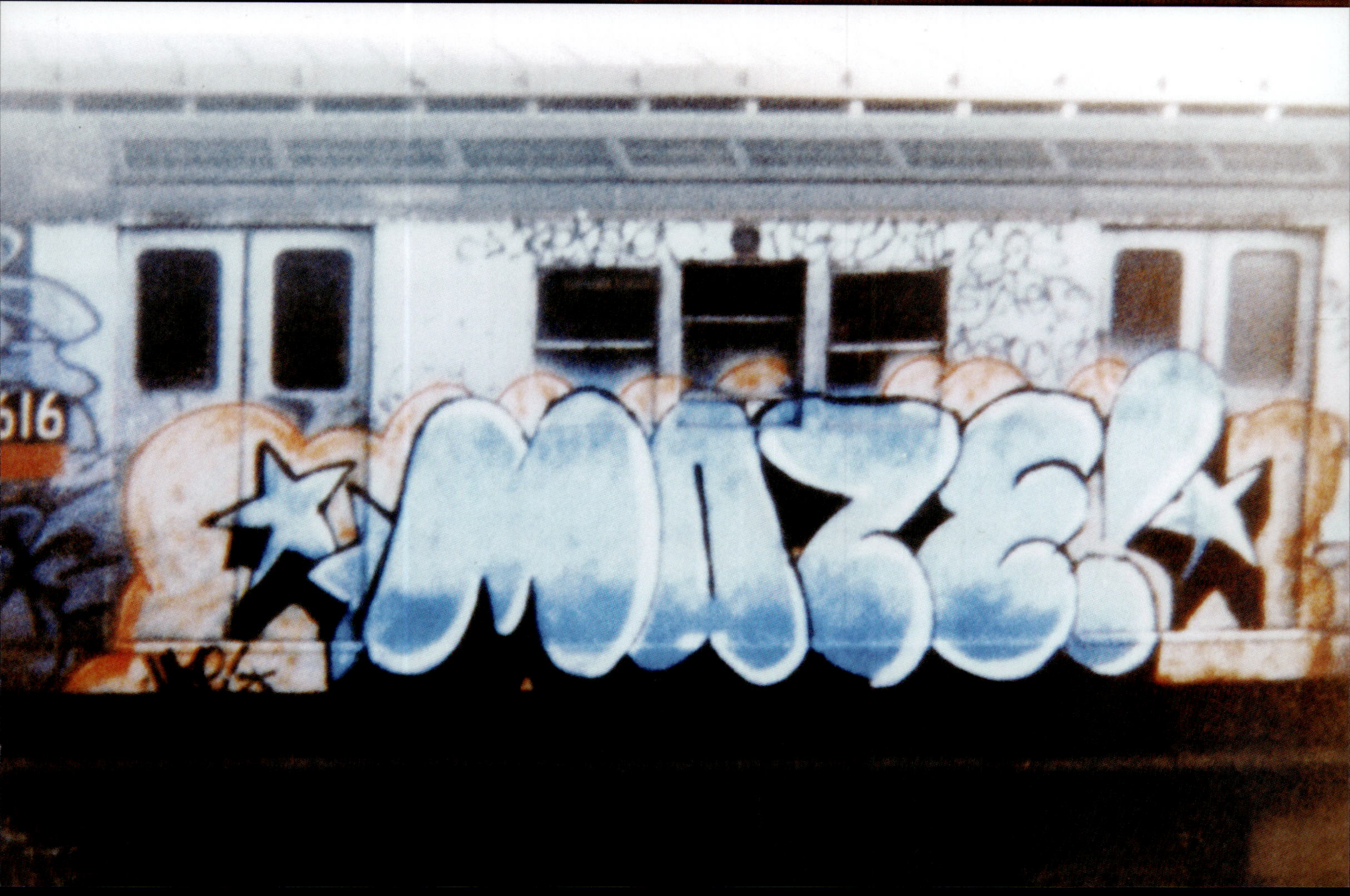
MAZE!

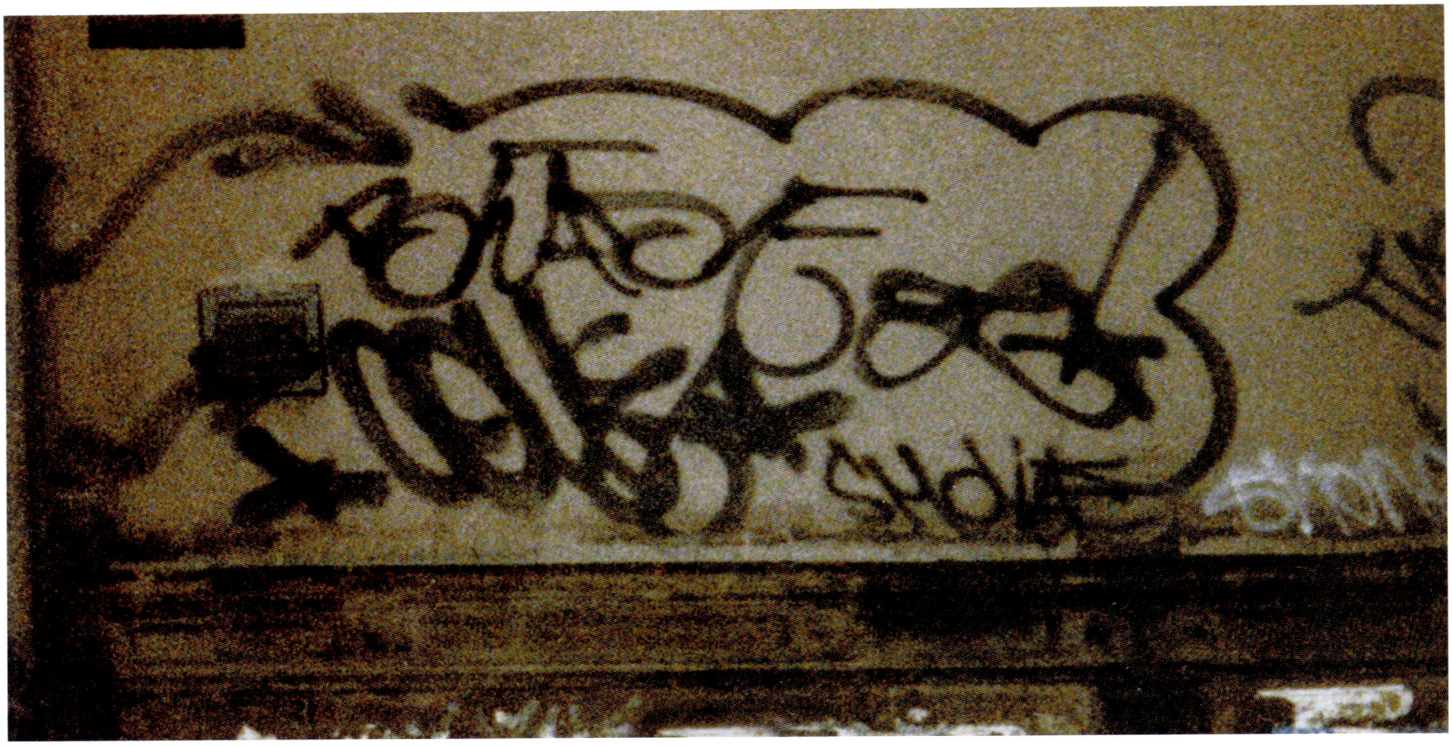

One day, COMET made an amazing discovery as he and I benched trains at Tremont Avenue. He turned to me and said, "Yo, BLADE, check out that train with your blockbuster on it."

"What about it?" I took a closer look. The header said it was car number 7592. I suddenly knew what he wanted me to see. "We're going over ourselves! Oh shit!"

"We must be the only two writers who are up so much that we have to go over ourselves." COMET smacked a pack of Marlboro cigarettes against the meat right under his thumb. He opened the pack and handed me one. While I normally smoked Kools, I was getting desperate. He looked at me and said, "Well now what?"

"I don't really know, what else is there? I don't want to quit writing."

Two more trains pulled through and we examined them both. I had three pieces on one and two on the other, COMET only had two pieces total, but he had a ton of throw-ups. The train that came after was the kicker. We had done blockbusters over ourselves. Now we were both really pissed off, so we got quiet for a while until COMET said, "Let's hit the streets."

"How much scrap paint do you have?" I asked.

"All of my scrap paint goes into throw-ups. I don't keep that shit, but I do have some shitty colors I'm not going to use and a lot of flat blacks."

"So, lets bomb the streets with those cans. We'll use those Flash Gordon fat caps of yours and get giant hits everywhere."

Suddenly, the day was a little brighter as we got excited about hitting the streets.

In the early days of graffiti, street bombing was important, even when the writers found the trains. That ended in 1973, when the focus shifted to doing pieces. By 1978, no one was hitting the streets hard. We spent the rest of that day talking about how we could do it differently. Like with the blockbuster pieces, we were trying to figure out how to get the maximum effect from our hits. We came up with a strategy to hit highways in the different boroughs. Since I didn't have a car yet, there was really no easy way to do this. We had to walk the city streets late into the night, and that's what we did.

This page: BLADE and COMET tags. Circa 1978.
Opposite page: BLADE piece on top of the train platform at Burke Ave and White Plains Road. Circa 1977. Photo © by Martha Cooper. Inset photo by CRACHEE.

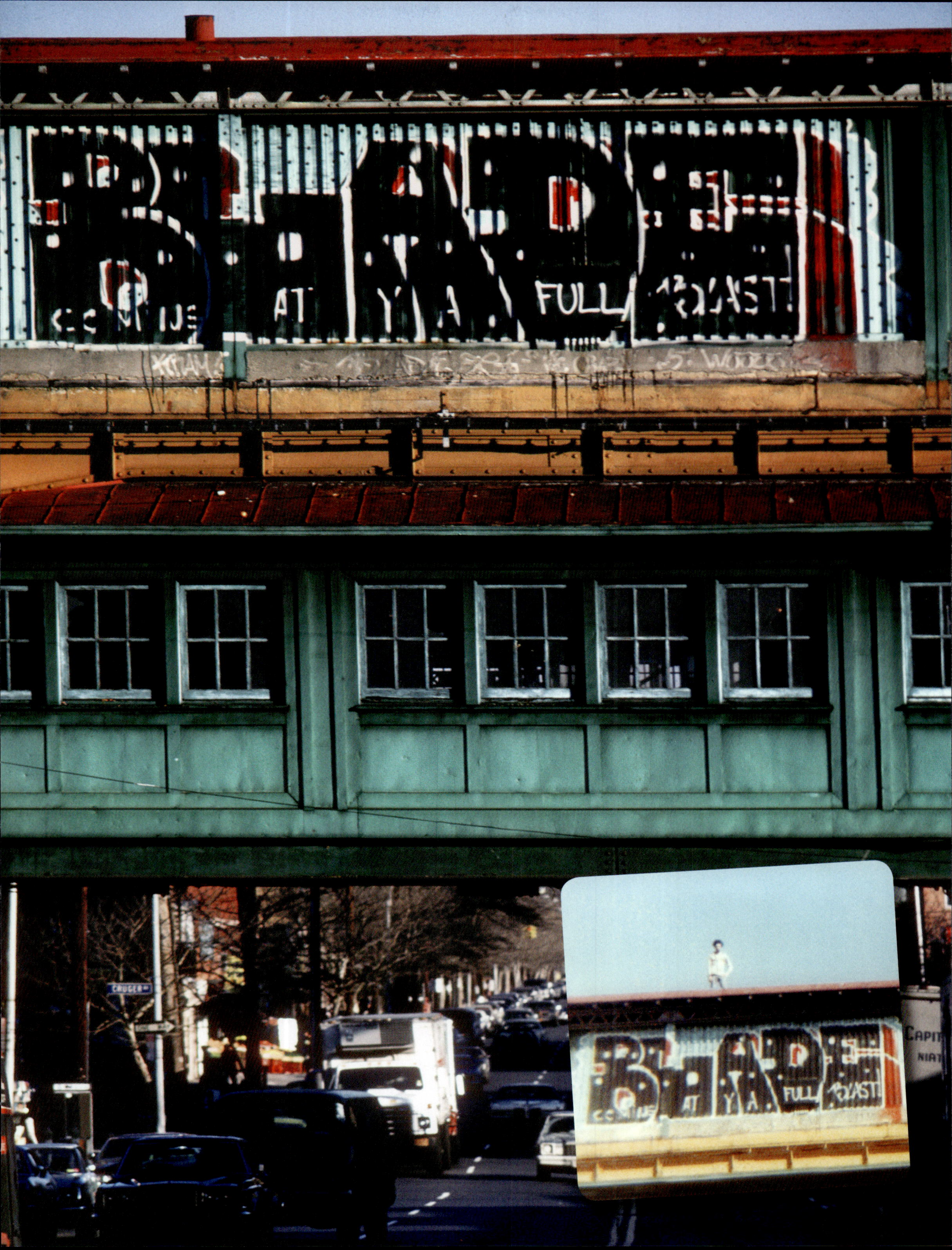
FULL

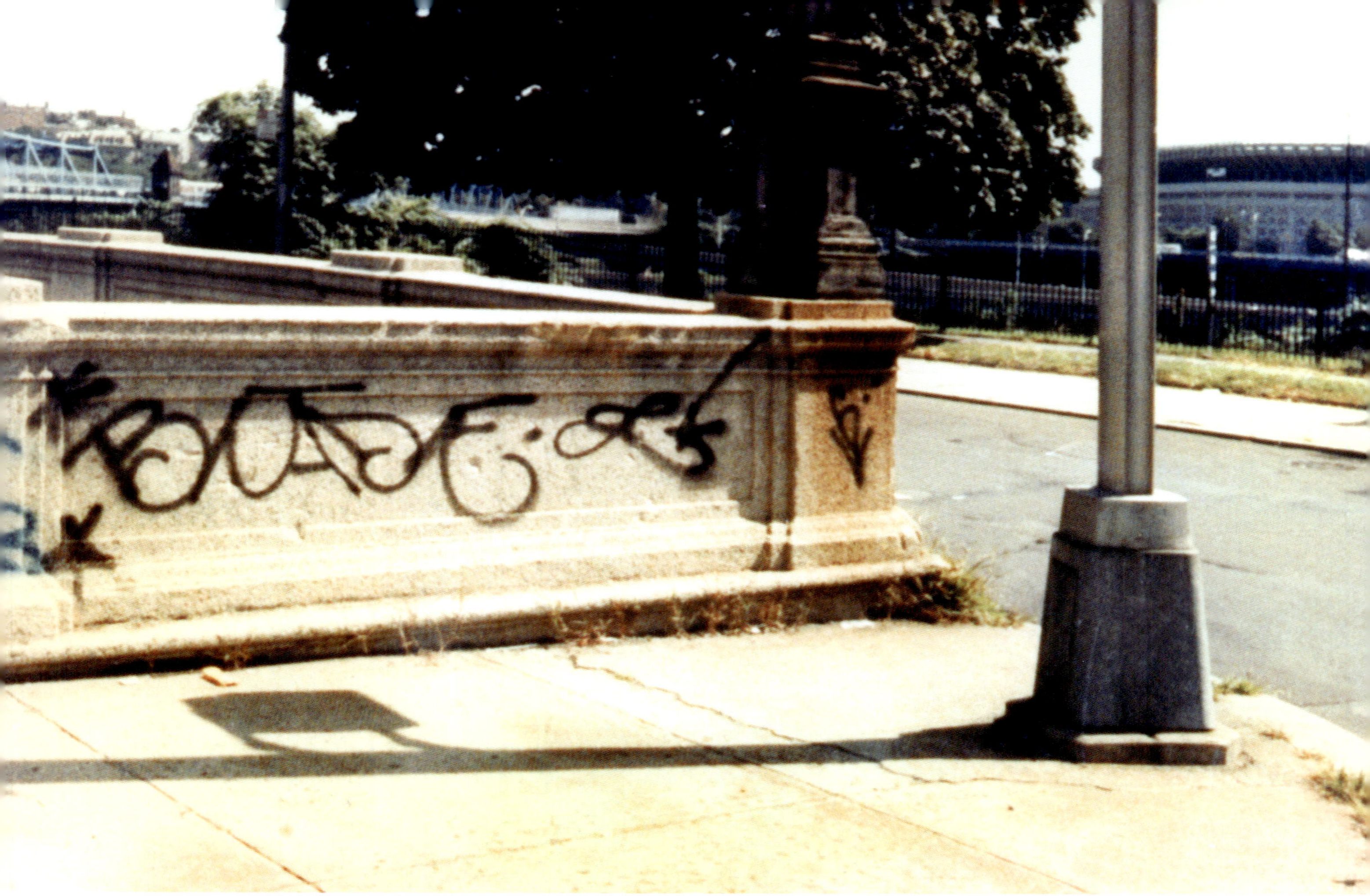

The highways were liberating for us. We'd take the train downtown to 34th Street in Manhattan and hit a bodega, rack up a few Colt 45s, and head over to the highway. One night it would be the FDR on the east side of Manhattan; the next night it might be the West Side Highway. Another trip took us into Queens, where we walked over the triborough bridge hitting everything in sight. I had known COMET since 1973, and he wasn't a big talker. While painting trains, a lot of times we worked in different spots. Finally, in 1978, we had no choice but to talk; otherwise it would be a mighty boring trip.

It turned out that COMET and I were more alike than we thought. We were both in committed relationships at the time, which took a lot of work, and we talked about it endlessly. We also talked about our friends getting into heroin and throwing their lives away, trying to make sense out of something that we could never understand. We talked about our family lives. The one thing it seems that we didn't talk about was our future, because we were living it. Most people our age were going to have to wait a while to live out their dreams, but we were doing it. We wanted to be kings and we were.

We walked through Astoria and got stared down by white people. We walked through the South Bronx where the blacks stared at COMET. And we didn't give a shit. We were in our own little world. We watched as tenements burned to the ground right in front of us so the landlords could collect the insurance money. By the time we were done street hitting, there weren't many walls left in the South Bronx. All through 1978, every time one of our layups got hit, it was back to the streets.

This page: BLADE tag with Shea Stadium in the background. Circa 1978.
Opposite page: BLADE on the streets. Circa 1978.

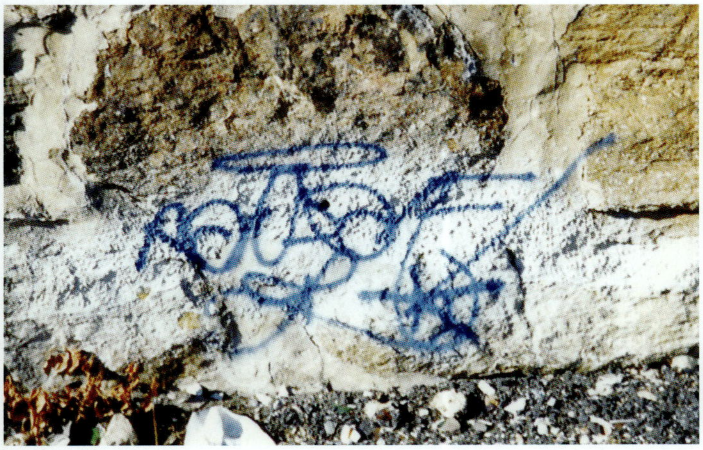

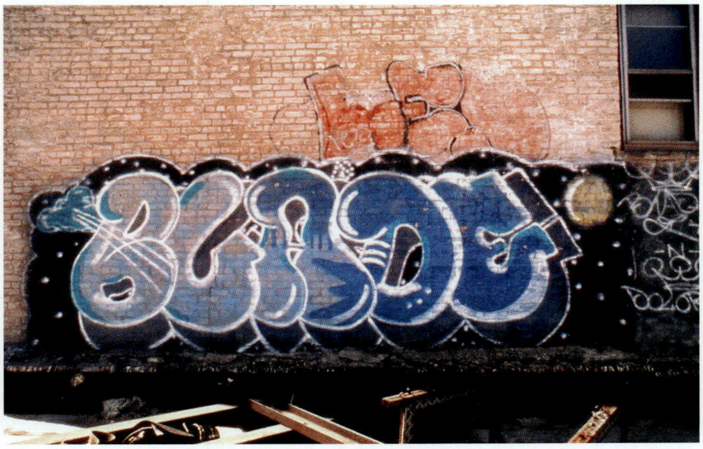

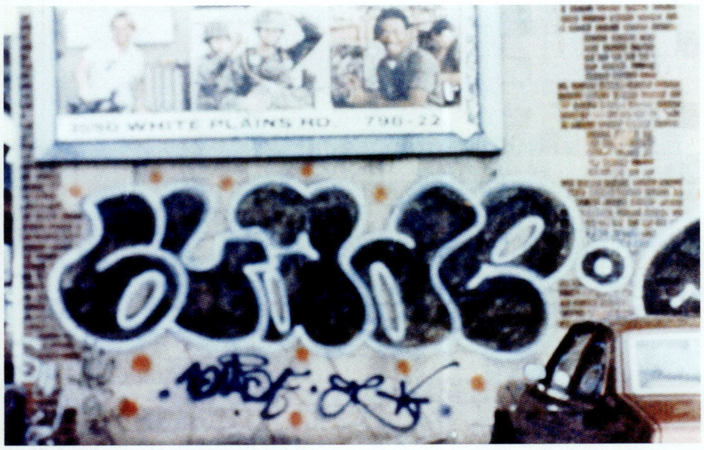
WHITE PLAINS RD.

3977

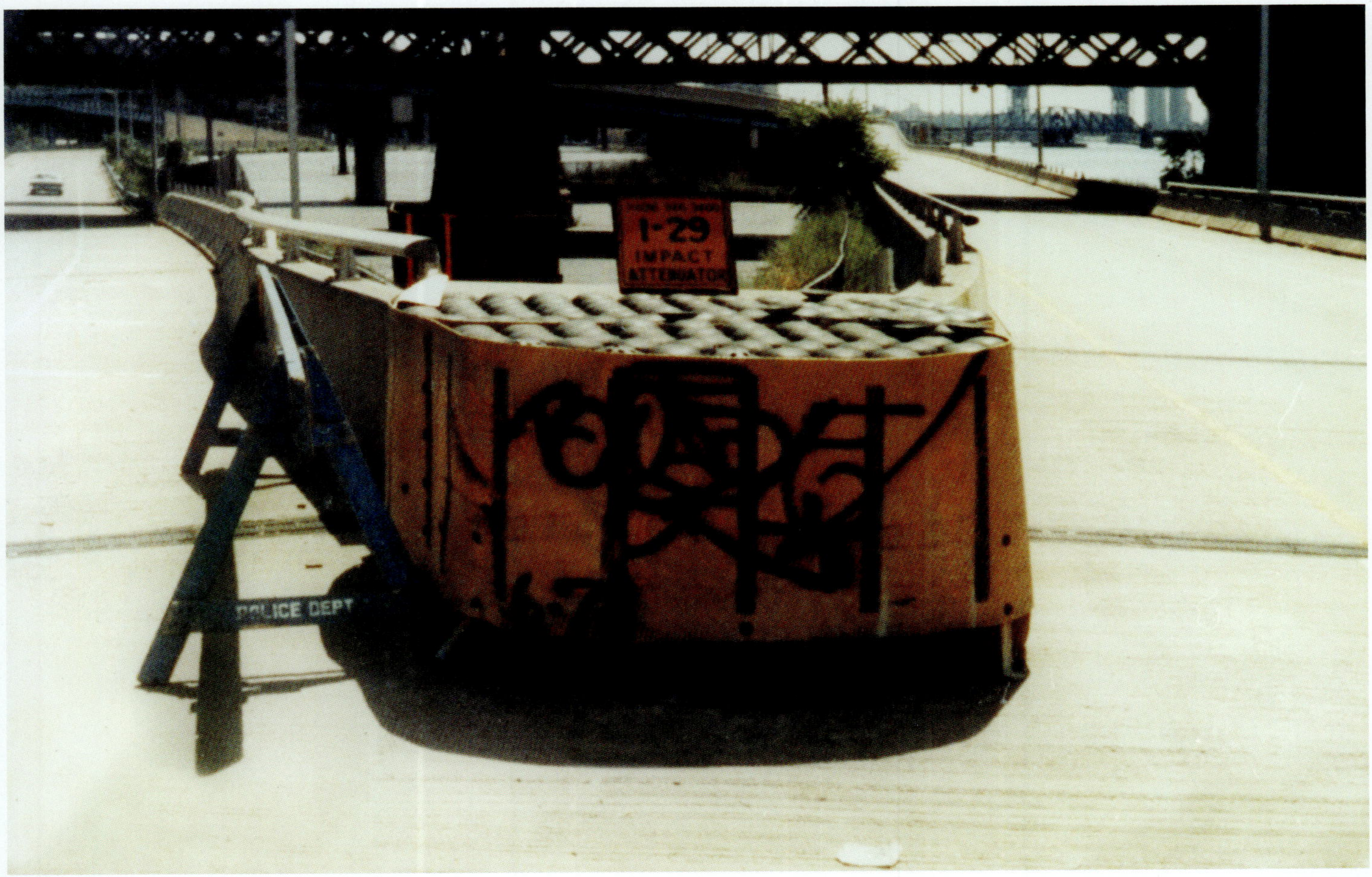
I-29
IMPACT
ATTENUATOR
POLICE DEPT

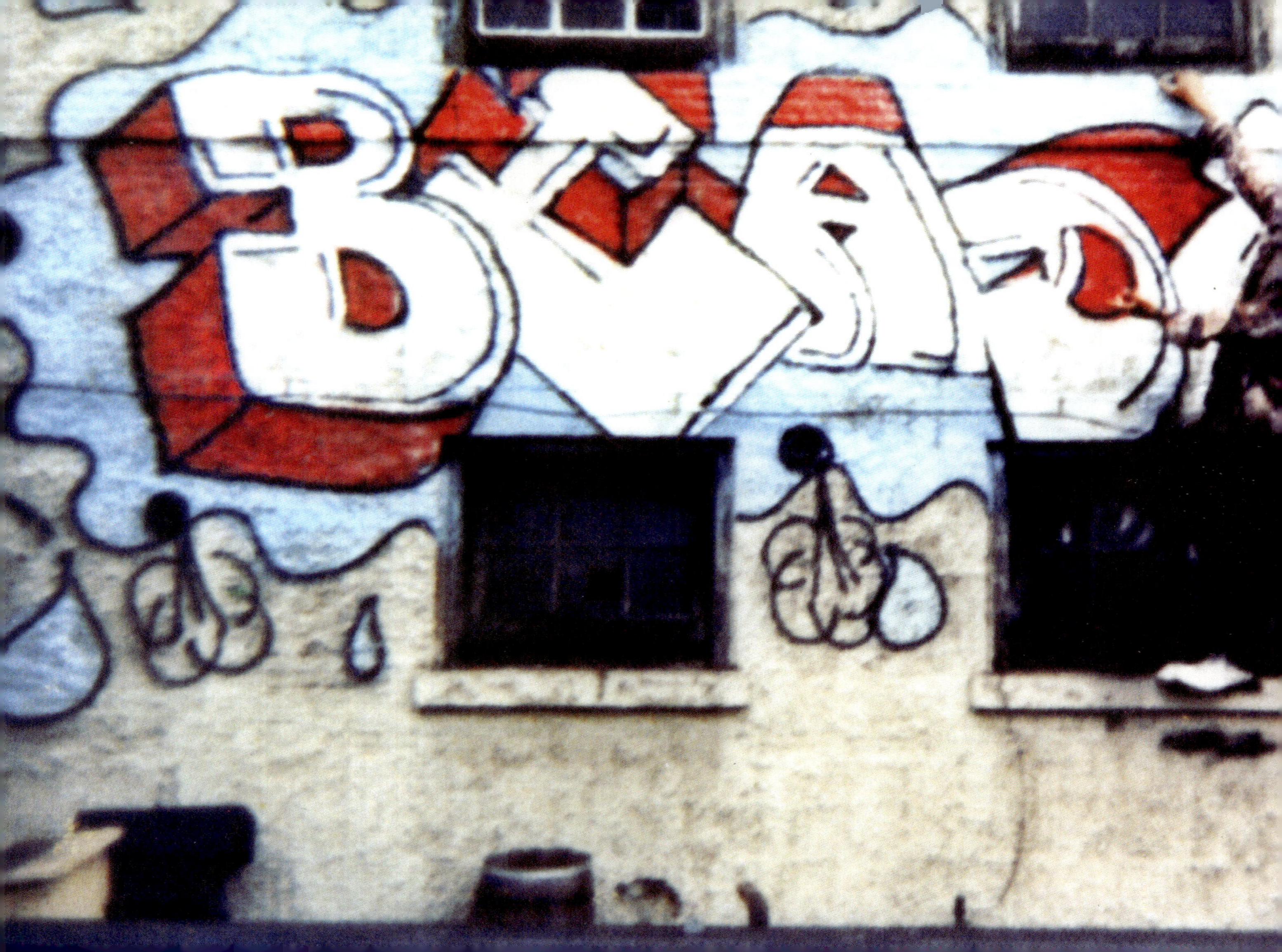

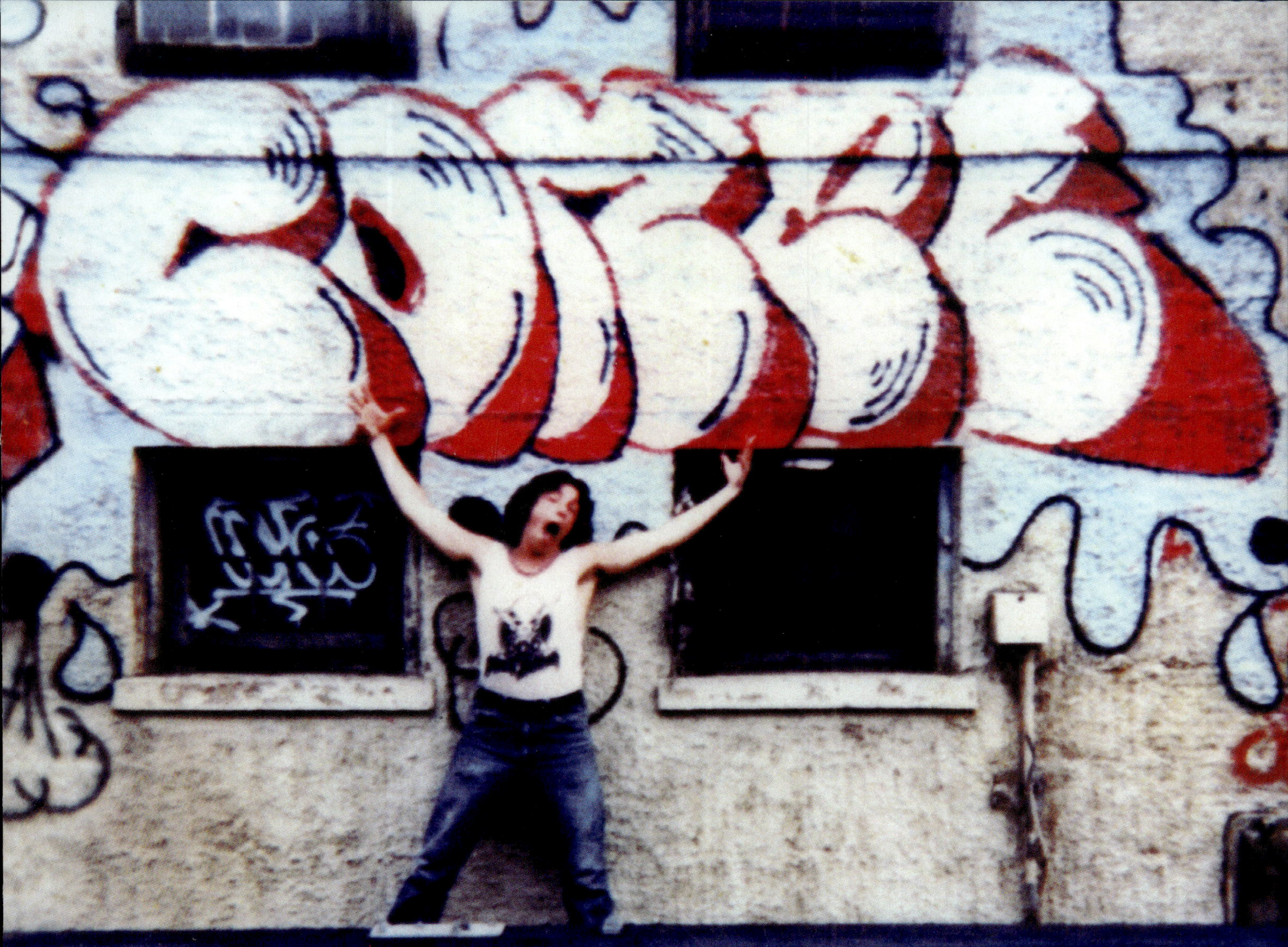

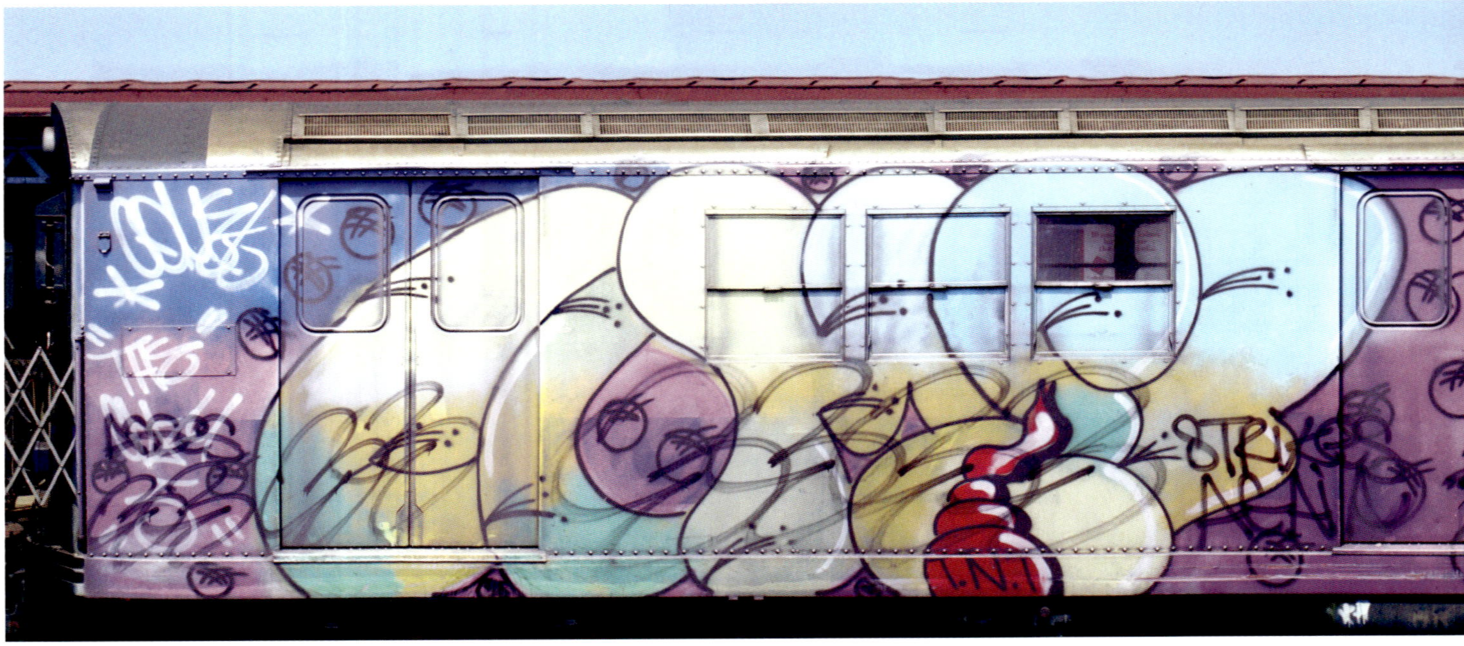

In 1979, Esplanade remained our home turf, but it was different. The kids from the neighborhood started using it as a hangout to get high and they'd cause all sorts of trouble. Some nights, we'd smell smoke while painting; it was one of those stupid kids setting fire to something. Other nights, we'd hear them breaking train windows. We weren't worried about the kids—in fact, they were afraid of us—we were worried about them burning our lay-up. That caused some tension.

To add to the trouble, CAZ and IZ started pulling out whole-cars at Esplanade. We even bumped into them a few times in the tunnel. Everybody was friendly. We'd light a joint, talk about writing, get busy with our work, and then they'd disappear. They was competition on the line, but not much, because their whole-cars would roll by and you wouldn't even notice them. IZ would go on to be a much better painter, but CAZ was bad from day one. When you saw a LEE or SLAVE whole-car, that was amazing! No one felt that way about CAZ and IZ. COMET was so disgusted with CAZ that he went over a few of his pieces. He'd never go over a LEE whole-car, because COMET respected talent. The next thing we knew, COMET was getting crossed out and we were sure it was CAZ doing it.

One night, in the spring of 1979, COMET and I came upon a newly painted train—four perfectly clean cars. It was an amazing sight in 1979, when most cars were still a murky grey after going through the buff. That night, we did four whole-cars, two cars each with our names stretched across them, one hundred and eighty feet long. We hadn't planned it, but you can't pass up an opportunity like that. Great cars like that are a once-in-a-lifetime chance.

A few months later, as spring gave way to summer, COMET and I headed to Esplanade to paint some trains. We paid to get in the station, walked down the stairs quietly, and looked up and down the platforms, finally deciding Esplanade was empty. No people, no kids acting stupid, no cops—our kind of night. I jumped down to the tracks and climbed up the front of the train. COMET stayed down below as we moved forward toward the stump. The only sound was the rattling of the spray cans in our bags. I could hear COMET say that our trains were there—the four whole-cars we had done earlier. I didn't answer him, because I had just noticed two silhouettes on top of the last car. I stayed quiet and ducked down. They weren't cops, and they were too big to be kids, which meant they were probably writers. I quickly moved forward when I heard COMET yelling.

"What the fuck is this? BLADE! Someone went over me!"

"Not the whole-cars?" I replied.

COMET continued reporting, "Yeah, they used a can of forest green and put a line right through my whole-car. Both of them! They left yours alone. The paint's still wet."

This spread: COMET and BLADE dissed. Circa 1978. Photo by Henry Chalfant.
Opposite page: COMET and BLADE solo double whole-cars that were quickly dissed. 1979.

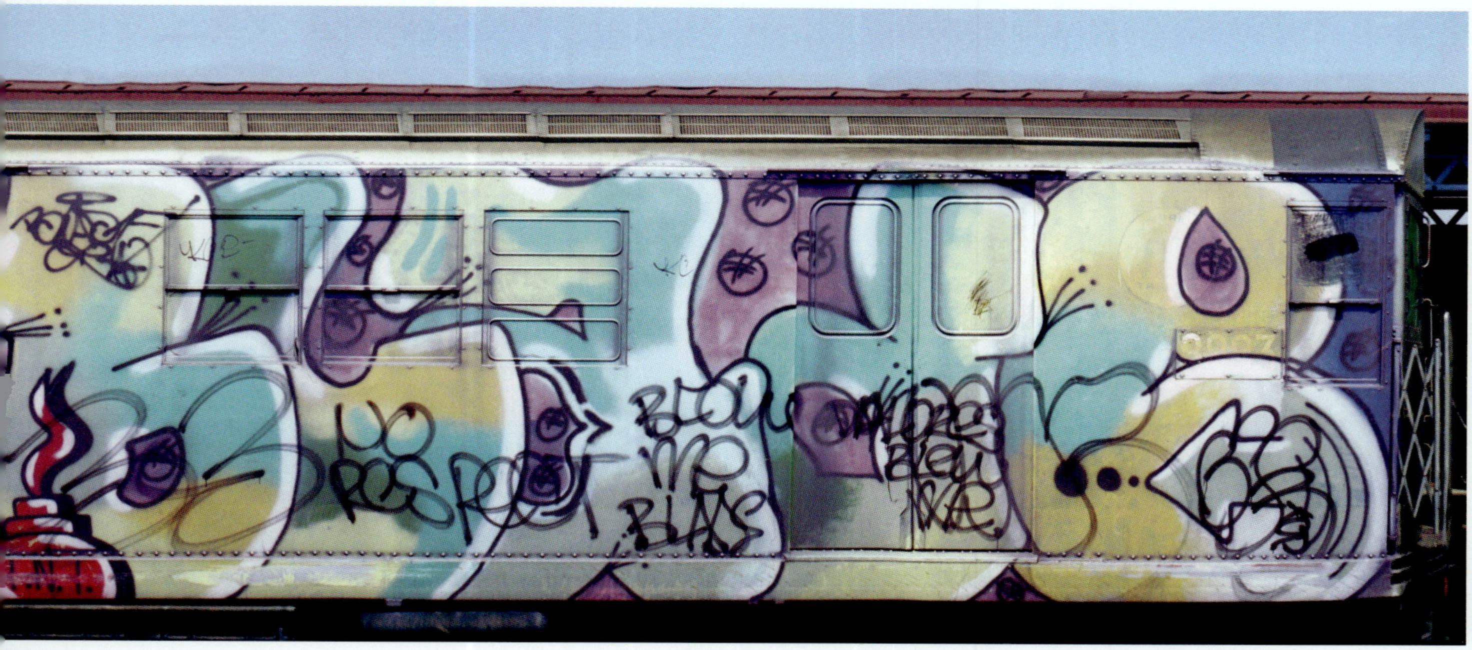

COMET looked up at the top of the train. I looked forward at the shadowy figures. It was eerily quiet, except for low hissing sound, which sounded like an air brake. I heard COMET's footsteps on the gravel rocks below as he strained to see who was above him. Then I heard COMET.

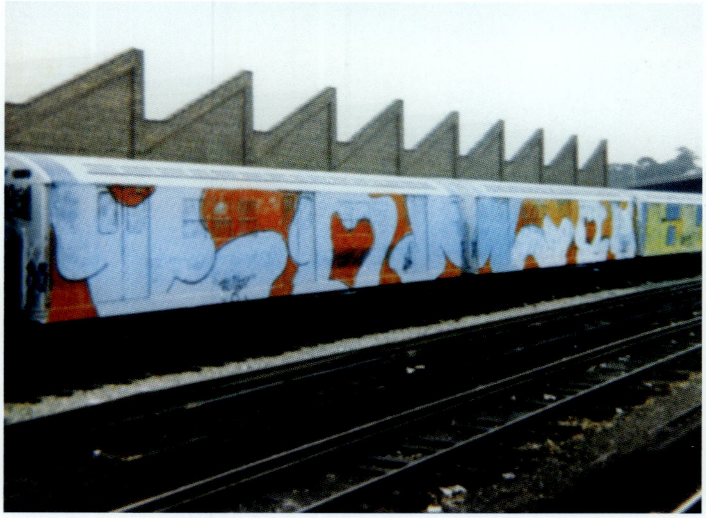

"CAZ, is that you? Did you cross me out? You stupid motherfucker, get your ass down here. I'm gonna' fuck you and IZ up. I'm fighting you both, get the fuck down here!"

COMET exploded. Although he always had a bad temper, in this case it was about CAZ committing the greatest sin there was: nobody crossed out COMET.

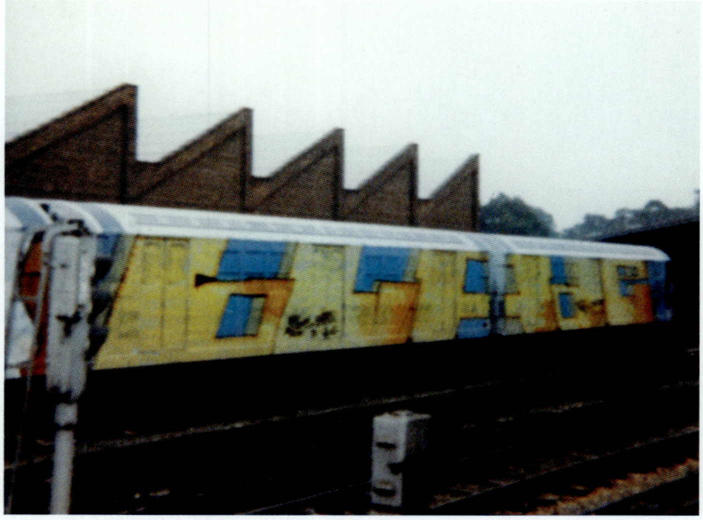

All three of us were on the roof of the last car. CAZ paced back and forth while I stood next to IZ. The fight was lining up to be between CAZ and COMET. It's what they both wanted. My role was to keep IZ out of it, which seemed easy enough because he wasn't a violent guy. IZ and I stood toward the end of the car while CAZ continued to pace. I lit up a cigarette and looked IZ in the eye. I tried hard to read the expression on his face—he looked confused, like he really didn't want to be there. COMET continued to yell.

As I looked at IZ, there was a whipping sound. It was like my dad when he hit me with the belt: you heard the belt before it hit you. Whiiiiiiiiiish. Then everything seemed to happen in slow motion. The 'whiiiiish' sound was followed by a crack. It was the back of my skull. CAZ had hit me from behind with a conductor's baton, which was like getting hit by a baseball bat. I tried desperately to stay up, but I couldn't feel my legs. I tumbled off the train fifteen feet to the ground, landing on the gravel rocks in the embankment. To this day, I still feel only a coward would do that. Everything was quiet again; I was unconscious. When I woke up, I heard COMET yelling and some footsteps running on the top of the train, but I couldn't move. I opened my eyes and looked straight into the third rail. It hissed at me. I shut my eyes to sleep.

More crunching footsteps: I could tell they were COMET's. I asked him not to move me. I heard him say, "Those fucking guys, they do this shit and then just run off." I don't remember much of what happened next. COMET must have helped me up and we headed toward the train. For the next hour or so, I didn't really know who I was. I would say something and COMET would laugh. I guess I sounded drunk. When COMET and I reached Gun Hill Road, I told him I could make it home from there, because Dolores and I were still trying to keep our address a secret. COMET looked at me one last time, right in the eyes like a trainer checking on his boxer. My speech was no longer slurred and I knew who I was, so he headed off into the night.

Dolores looked after me for the next two weeks. I'd lie in bed with ice on my head, wondering what I did to deserve this—I didn't cross anybody out. Graffiti could be a rough game. Or was it? I was involved in three altercations revolving around graffiti in an eight-year span. In the Bronx, you could be involved in three altercations in a night. These were just odds catching up to me.

I was always a high-energy guy, so I hated being in bed. I hated missing work, but mostly I hated thinking about my life. I was the king of the trains. But what did that really mean? I thought I was making art by painting on trains, but was it worth it? Dolores, who took care of my wounds and made love to me late into the night, had parents who hated me. I began to wonder if our love was worth breaking a family apart like that. I answered my own questions: I was the king of graffiti and I'd never really know what that meant until it was over. I was making art, which was the greatest gift there was. Dolores was beautiful and we were in love. I was working a shitty job, trying to put her through school because she deserved that. Her parents would just have to deal with it. To this day, I have a large dent in the back of my head.

Upon moving into the new apartment, I started waking up in the middle of the night after having a vivid dream and then waking up Dolores to tell her about my dream. One night, Dolores asked if I'd just do a drawing of the dream and then explain it to her in the morning. This became a ritual. Some dreams could be drawn on paper, some couldn't. The really good dreams could be stretched horizontally onto a subway. While I was laid up, I started to look through the drawings I had done over the last year. I eventually spread them out on the bed and started to write down the color schemes for each. As fall rolled around, I had a lot more trains to paint.

There was a payback for what CAZ did: he was relegated to the lesser IND and BMT lines. Any time he hit the showcase IRT lines, COMET and I would go over him immediately. Eventually, CAZ quit writing for good. IZ went on to become king of the INDs and BMTs. As 1979 drew to a close, I no longer thought about either of them.

Opposite page: Sketch and finished piece by BLADE. 1978.
Following spread: BLADE whole-car painted on the last car outside Esplanade tunnel in the Bronx. 1980. Photo © by Martha Cooper. Inset sketch by BLADE.

“SOME DREAMS COULD BE DRAWN ON PAPER, SOME COULDN’T. THE REALLY GOOD DREAMS COULD BE STRETCHED HORIZONTALLY ONTO A SUBWAY.”

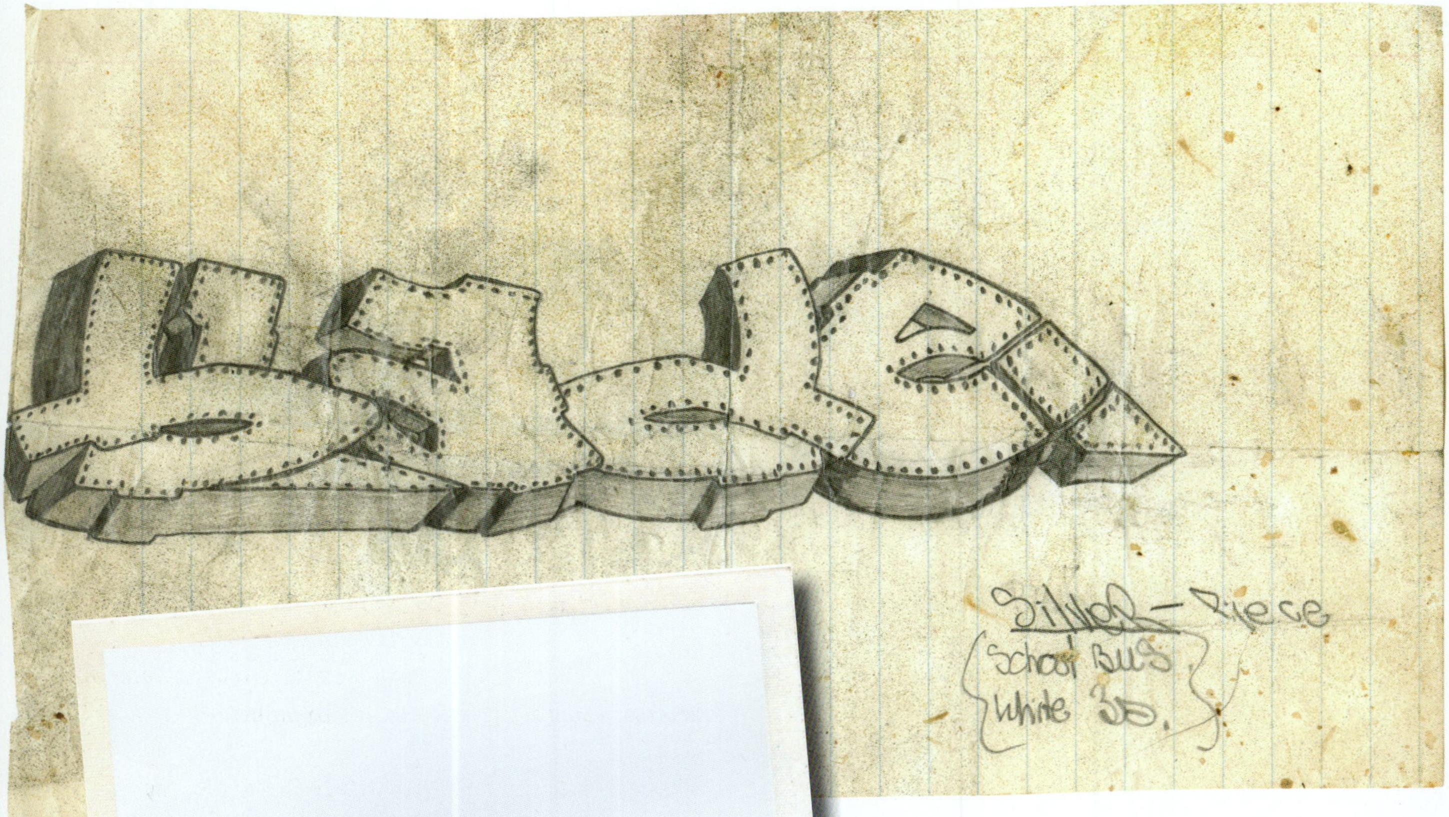

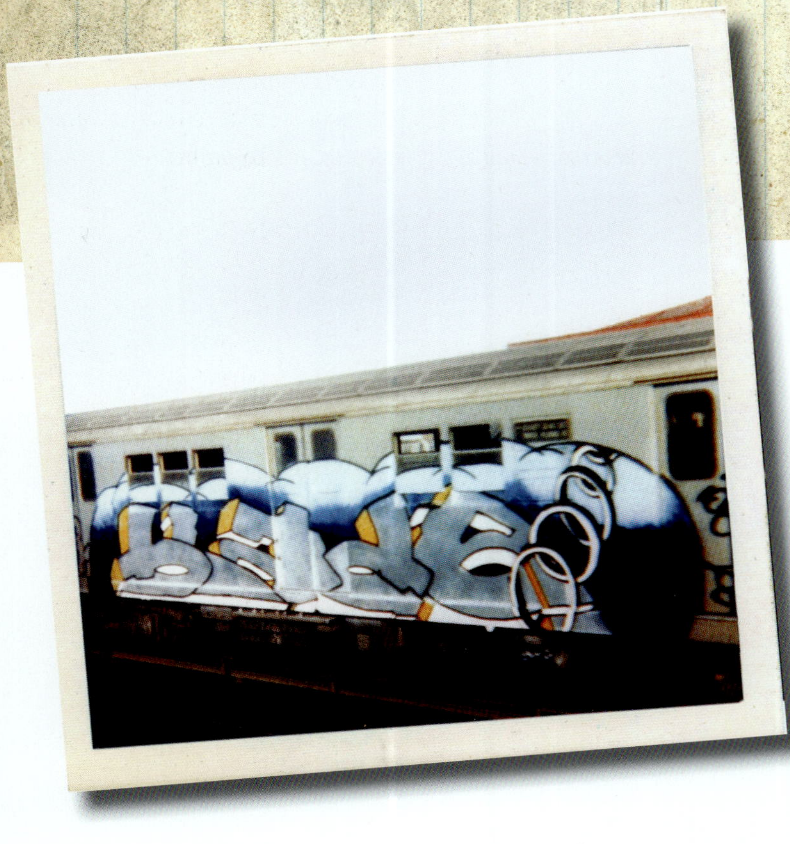

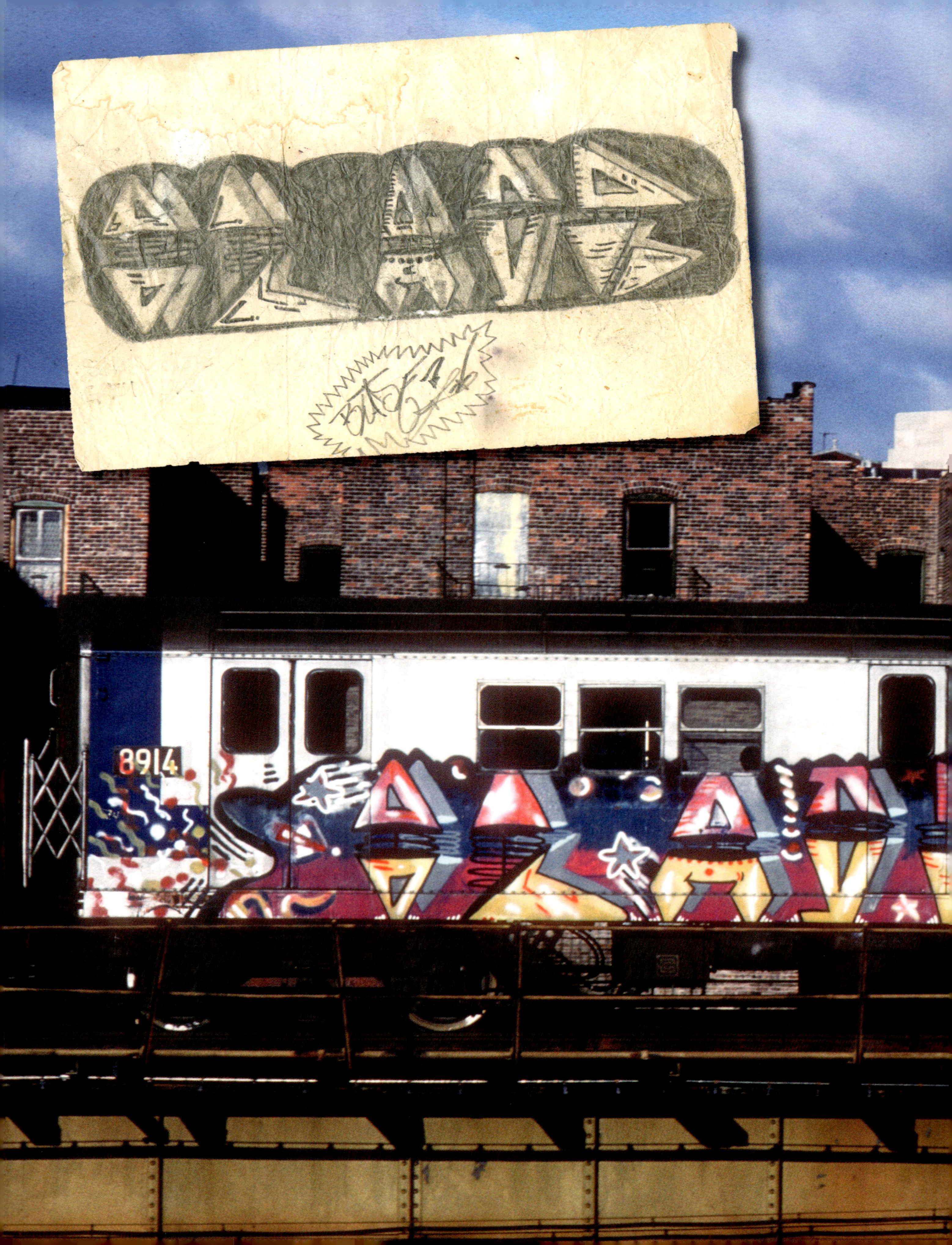
8914

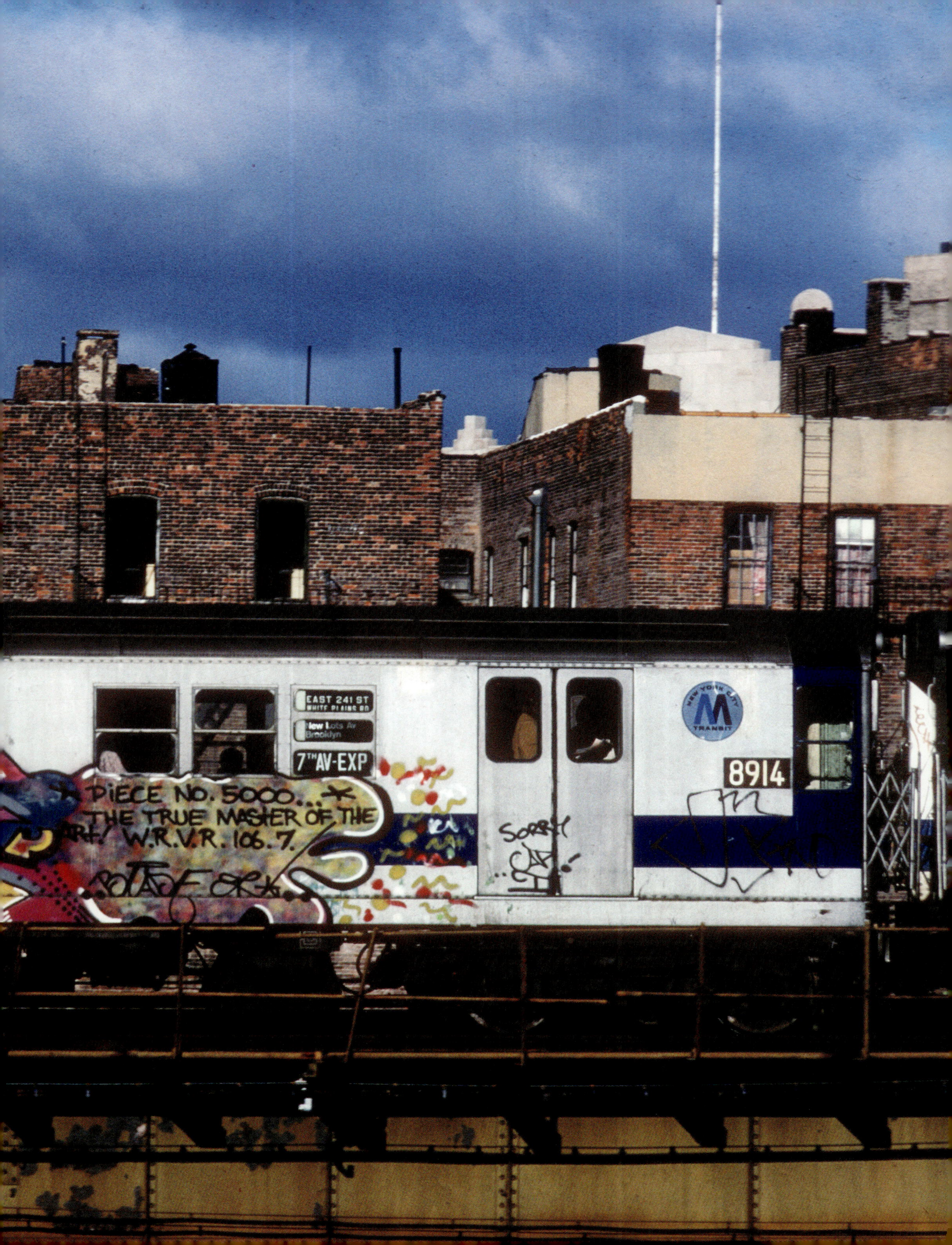
EAST 241 ST
WHITE PLAINS RD
New Lots Av
Brooklyn
7TH AV-EXP
NEW YORK CITY
TRANSIT
8914
PIECE NO. 5000...
THE TRUE MASTER OF THE
ART! W.R.V.R. 106.7

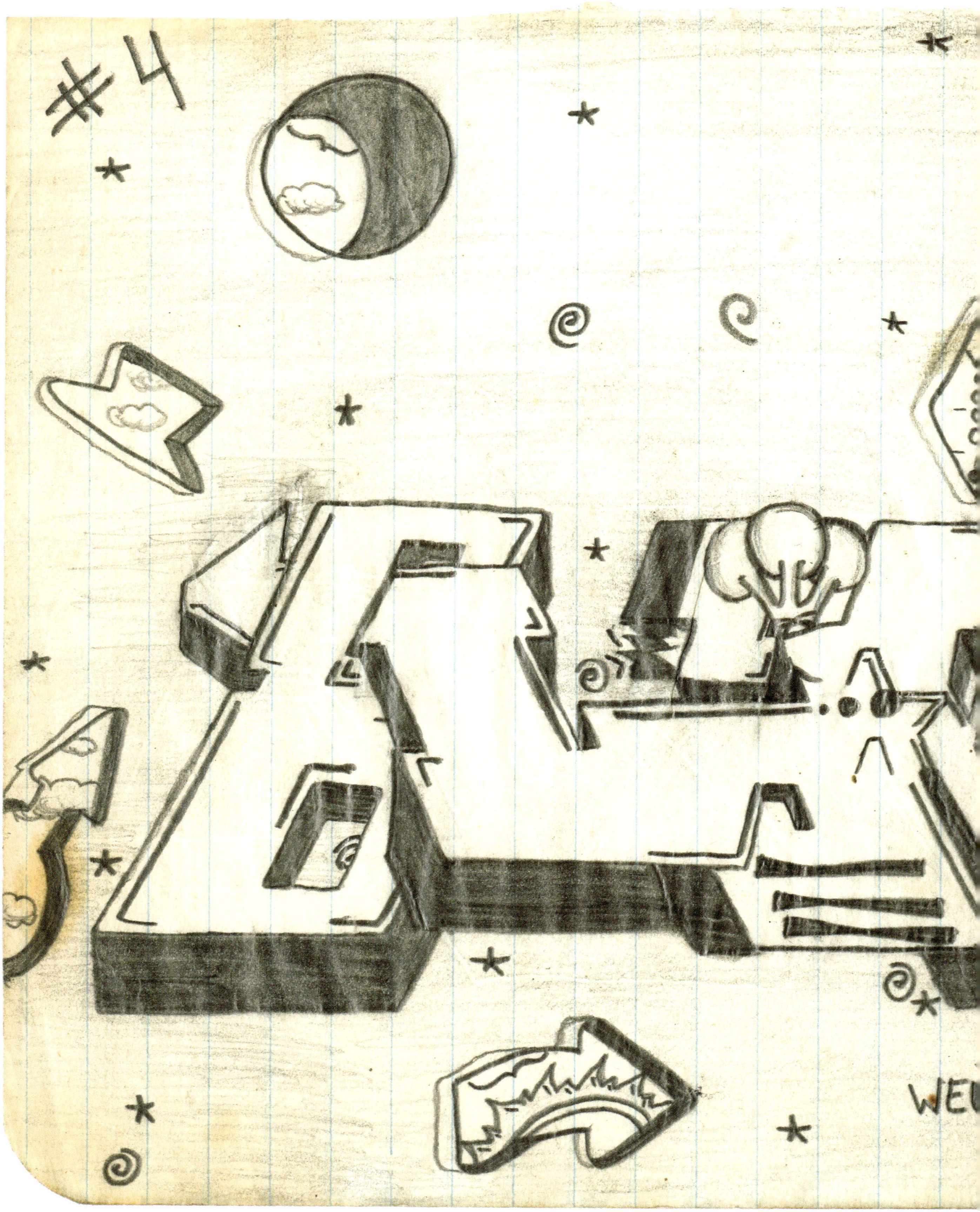

This spread and following 12 spreads:
Sketches and various train pieces by BLADE. Circa 1977–1981.

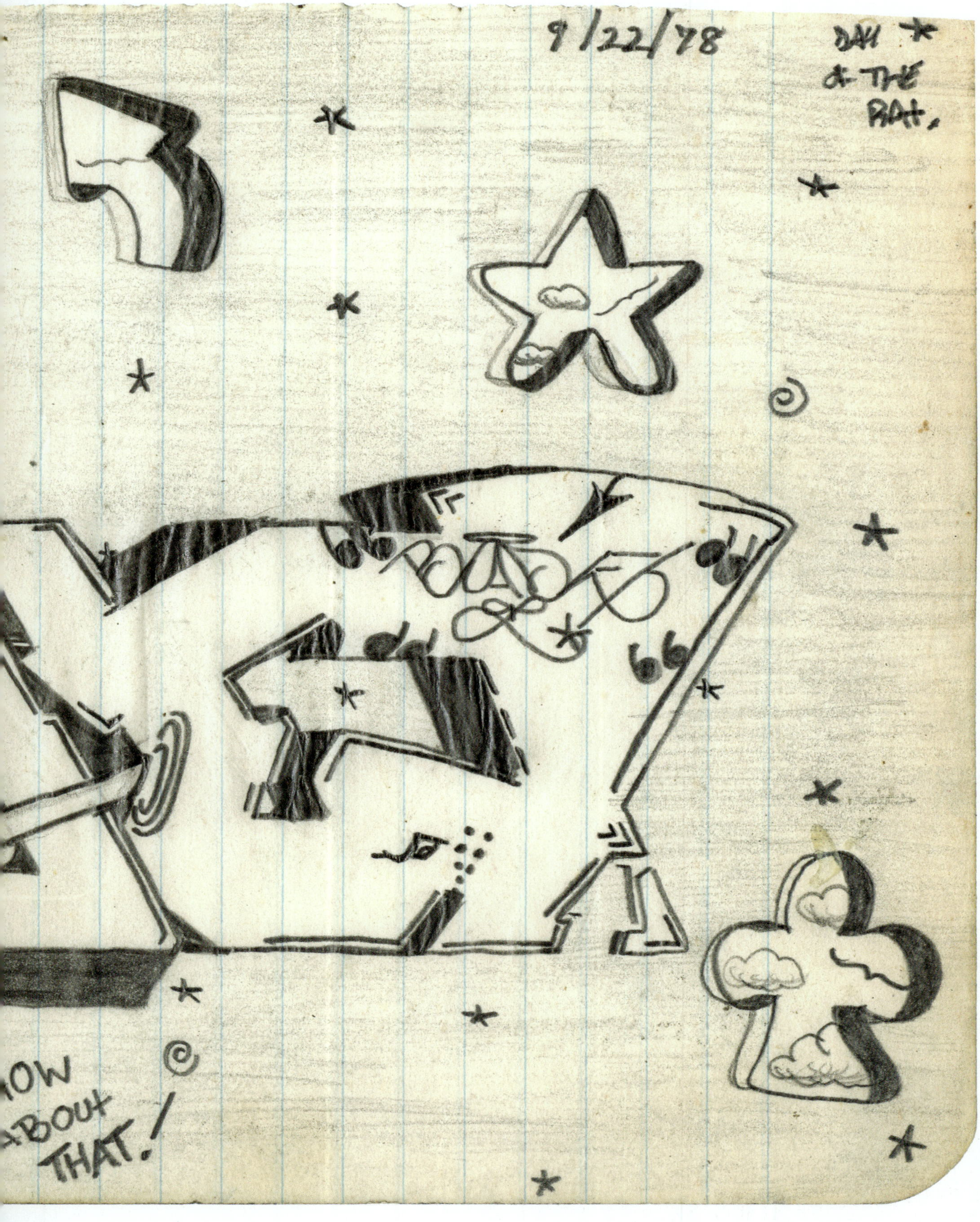
9/22/78
DAY OF THE RAT.
HOW ABOUT THAT!

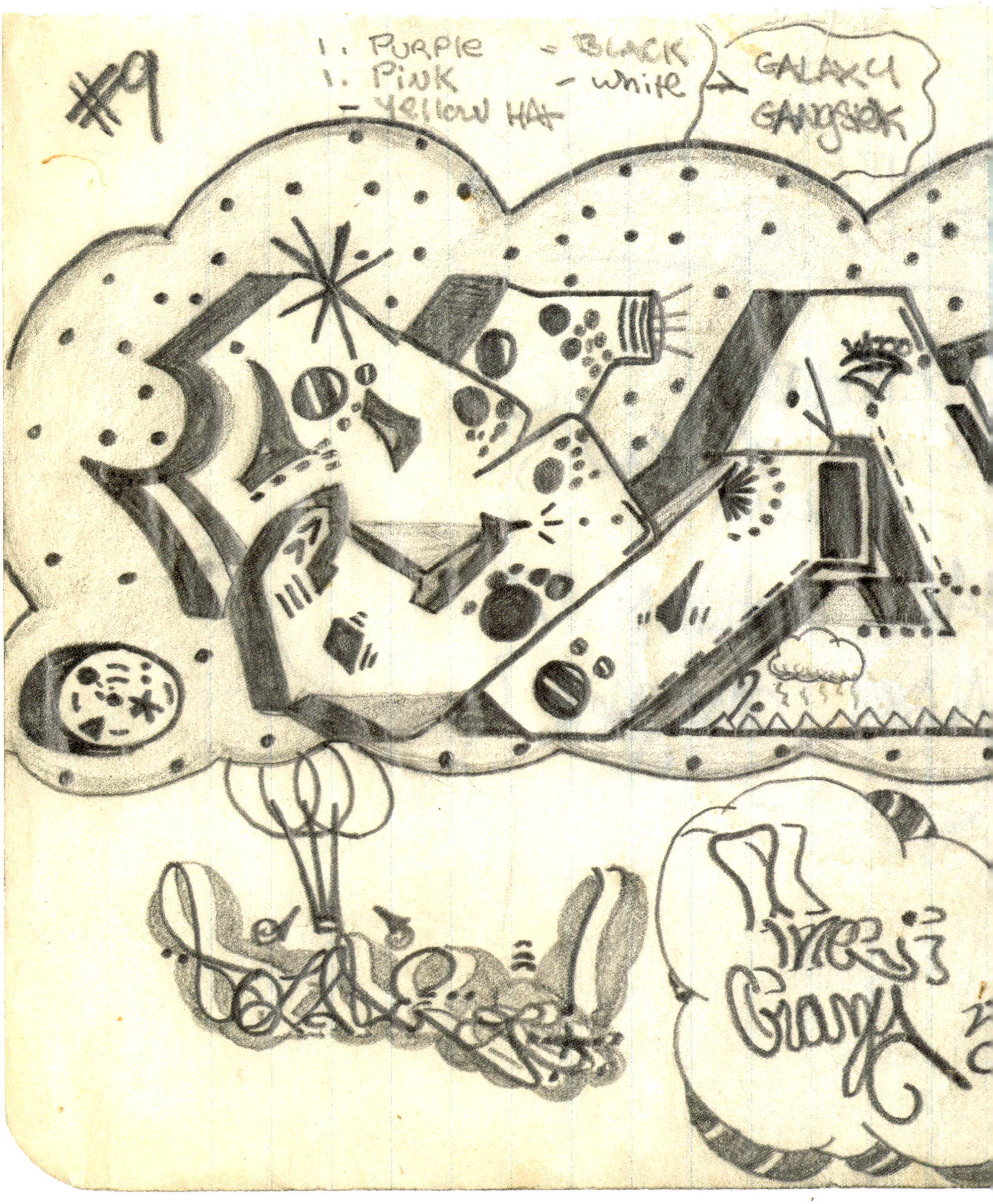
#9
1. Purple - Black
1. Pink - White
- Yellow Hat
GALAXY
GANGSTER

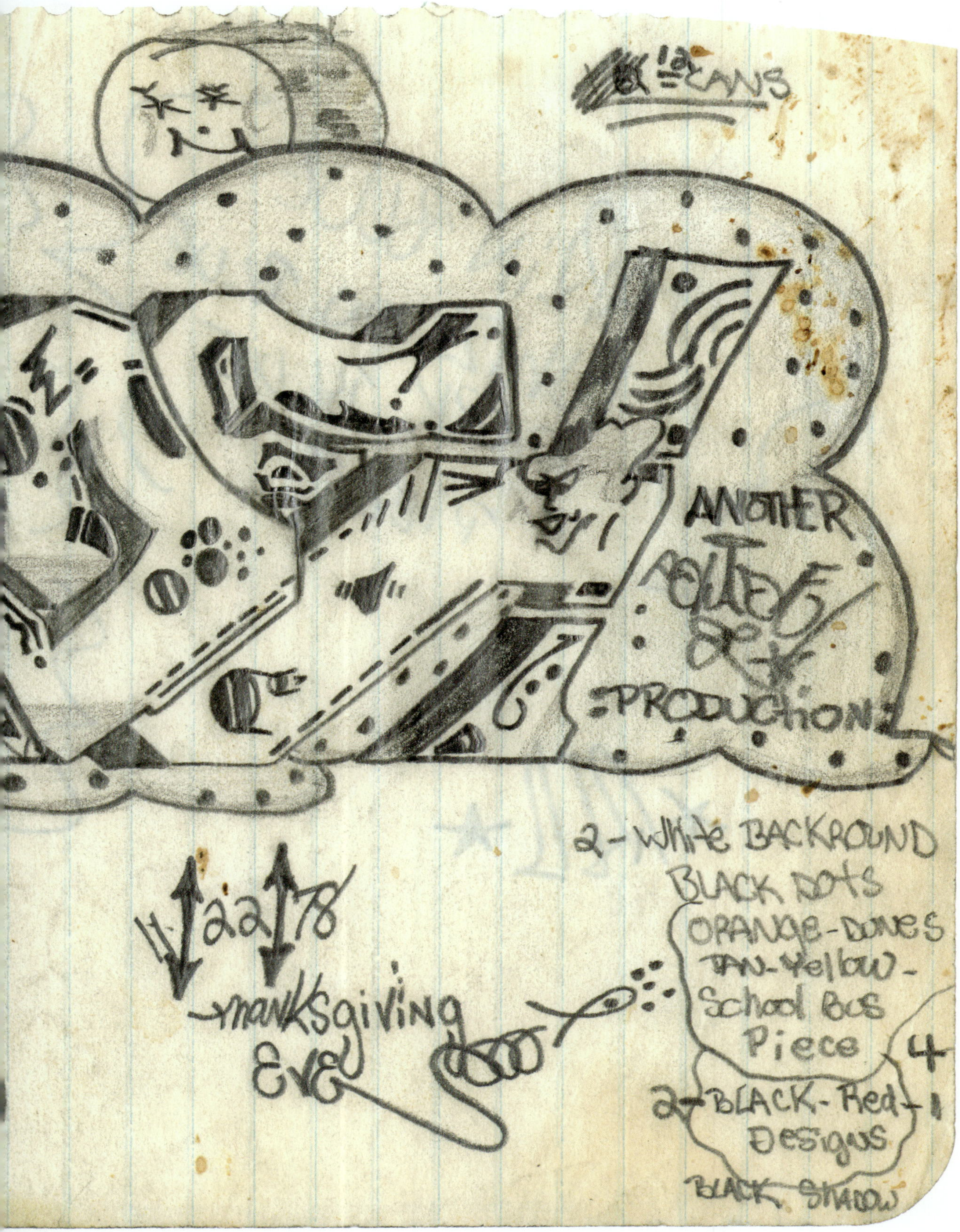
CANS
ANOTHER
PRODUCTION
2- White BACKROUND
BLACK DOTS
TAN-Yellow-
School Bus
Piece
2-BLACK-Red-
Designs
BLACK SHADOW
22 78
Thanksgiving
EVE

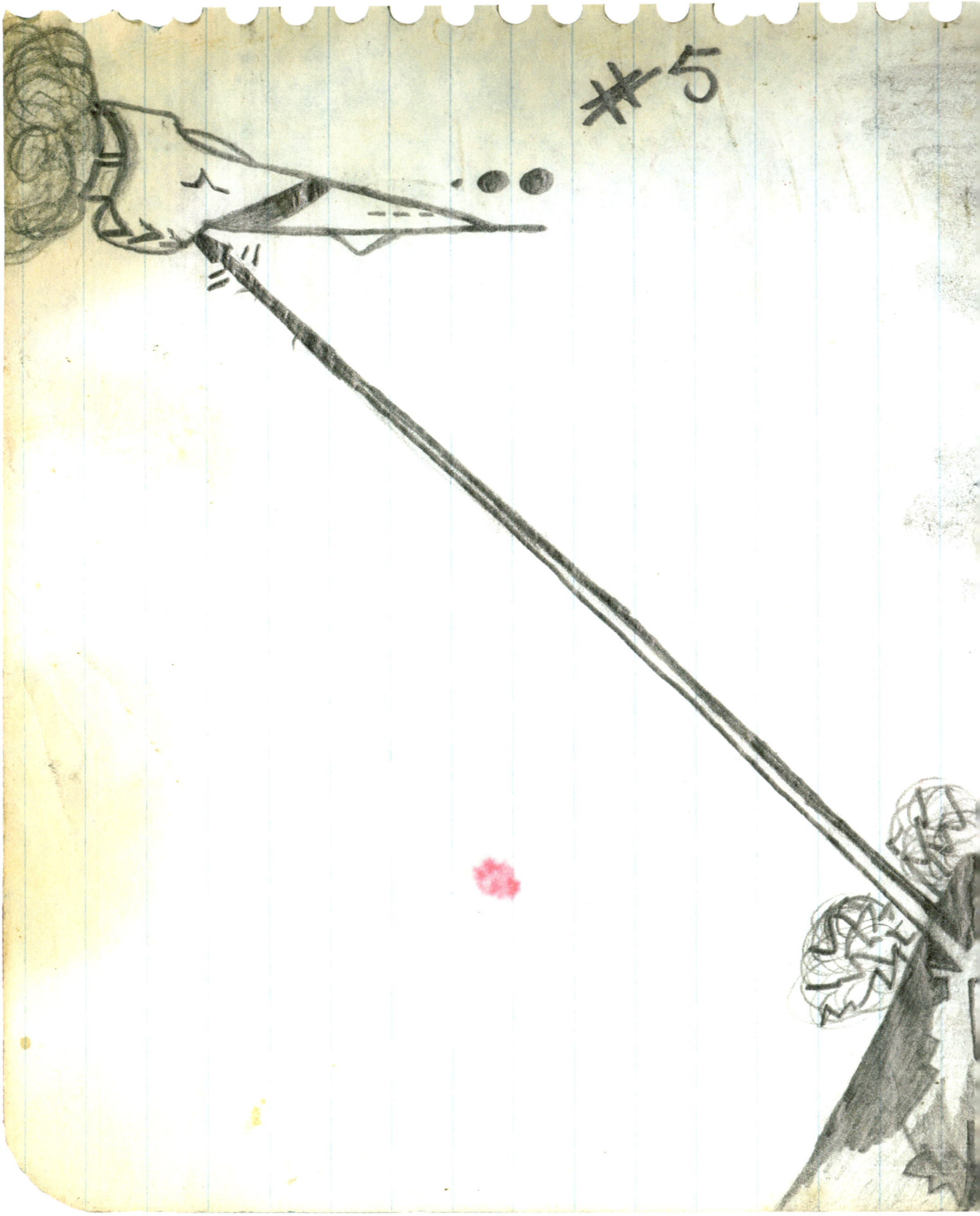
#5

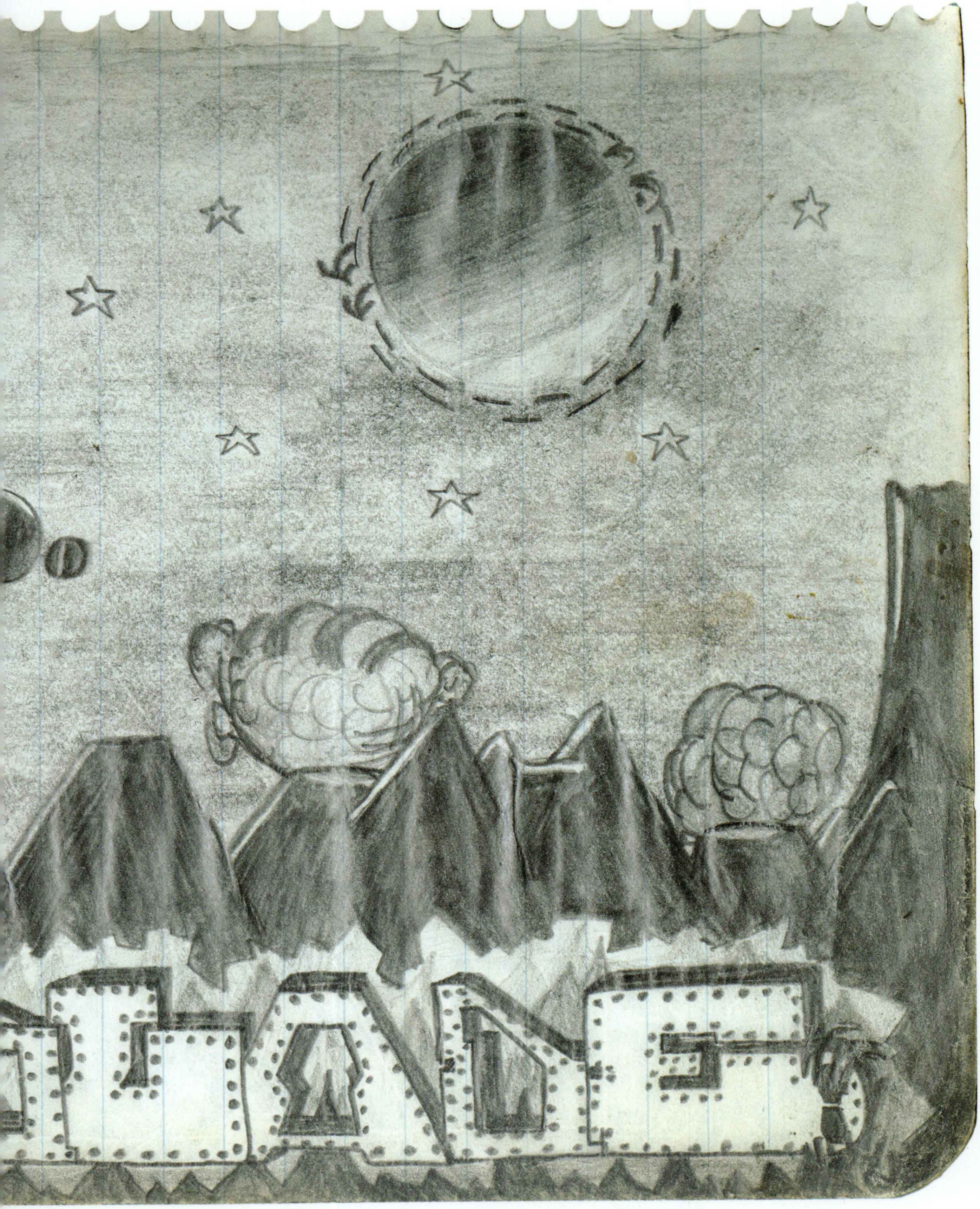

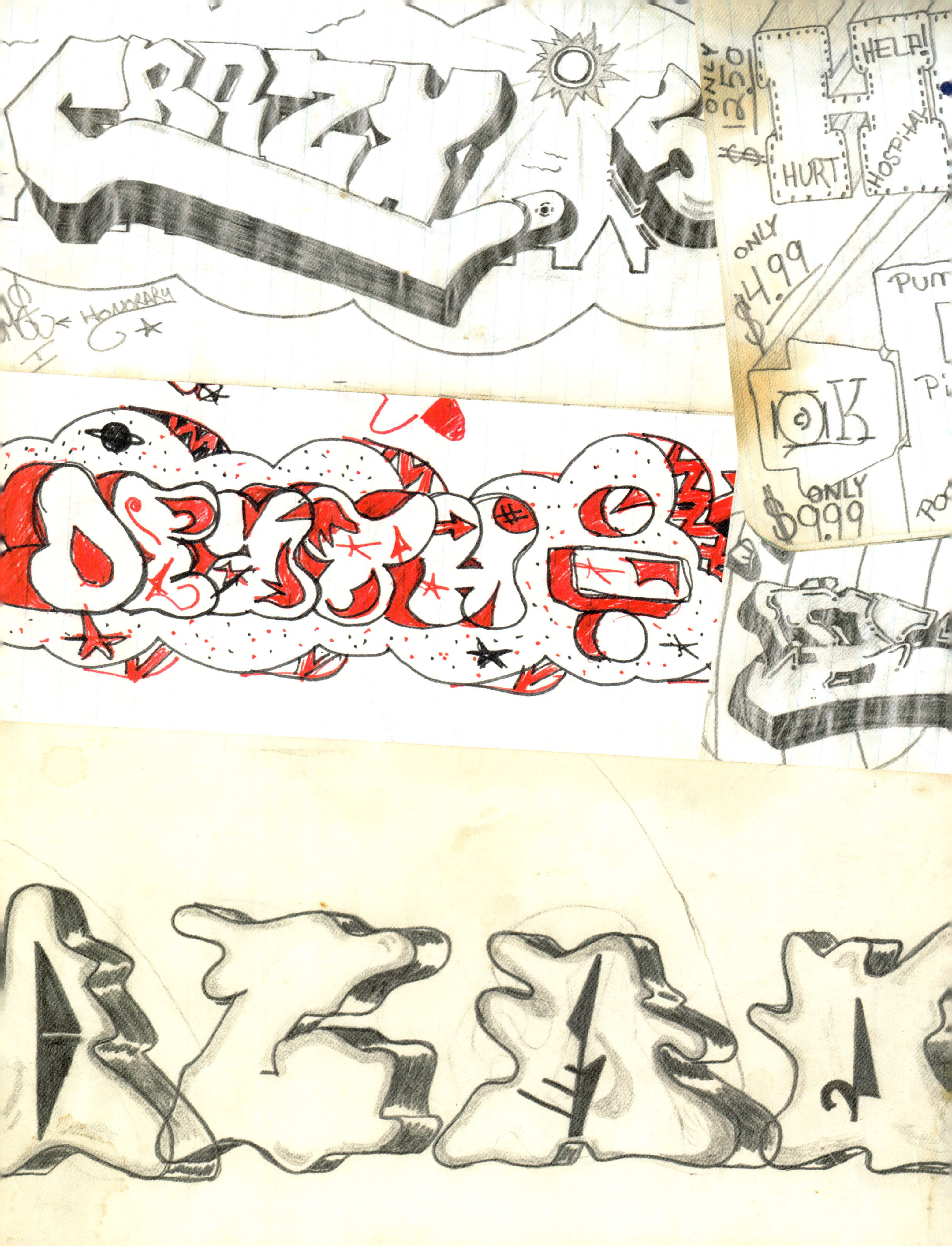
HONORARY
HELP!
HURT
HOSPITAL
ONLY
$4.99
OK
ONLY
$9.99

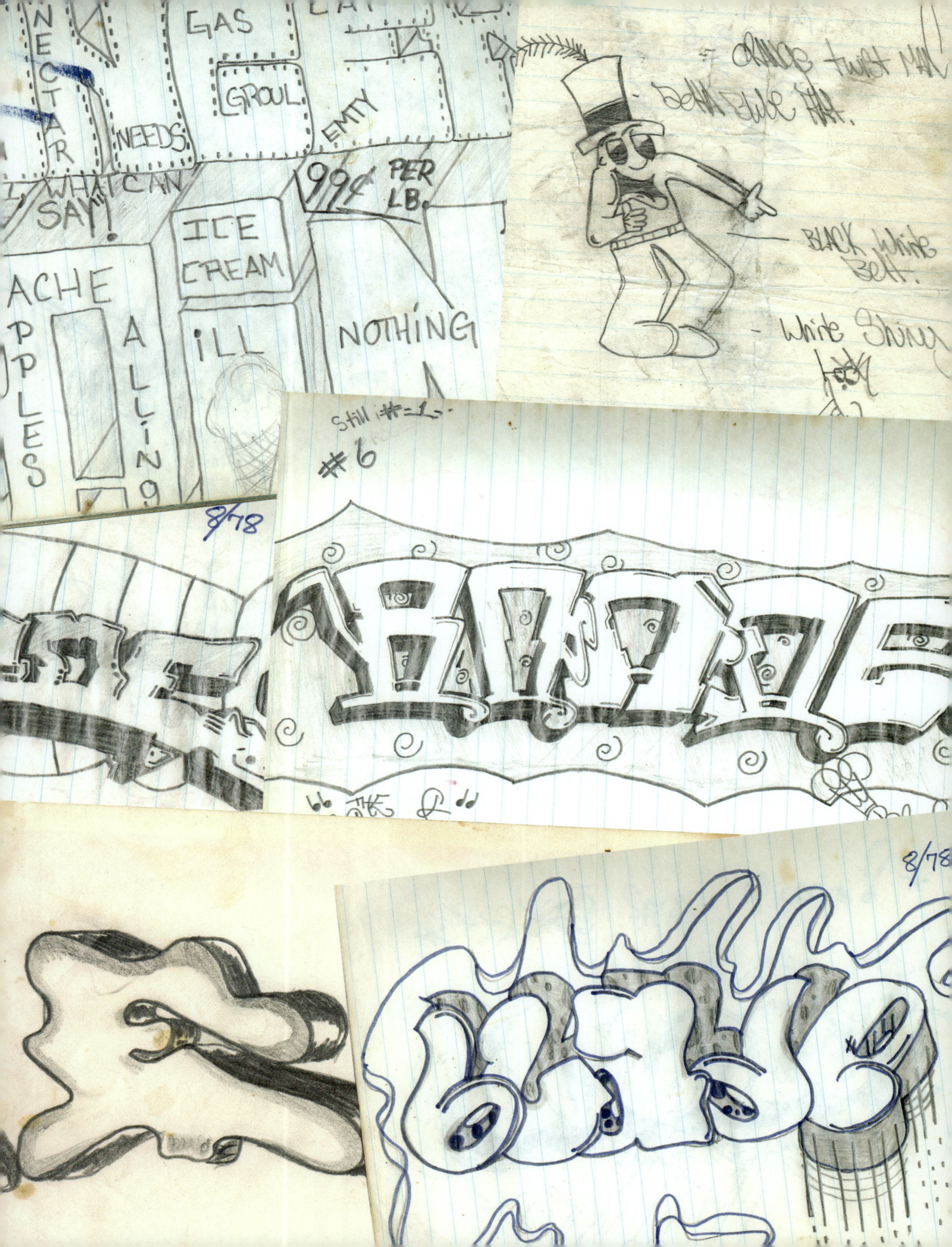

NECTAR
GAS
GROUL
NEEDS
EMTY
WHAT CAN I SAY!
99¢ PER LB.
ICE CREAM
ACHE
APPLES
ALLING
ILL
NOTHING
ORANGE twist MAN
BLACK White Belt.
Still #=1
#6
8/78
8/78

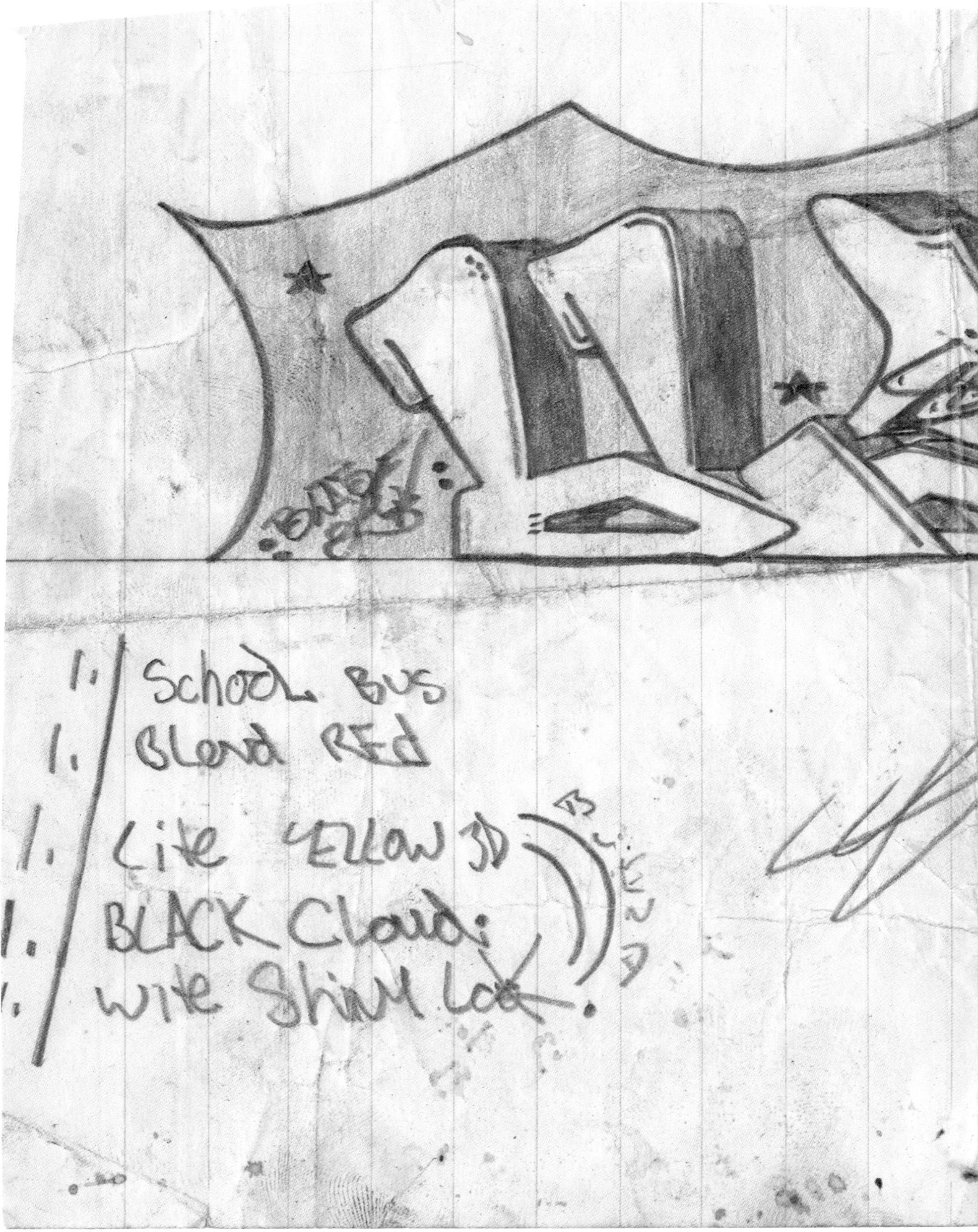
1./ School Bus
1./ Blend Red
1./ Lite Yellow 3D
1./ BLACK Cloud:
1./ Wite Shiny Look

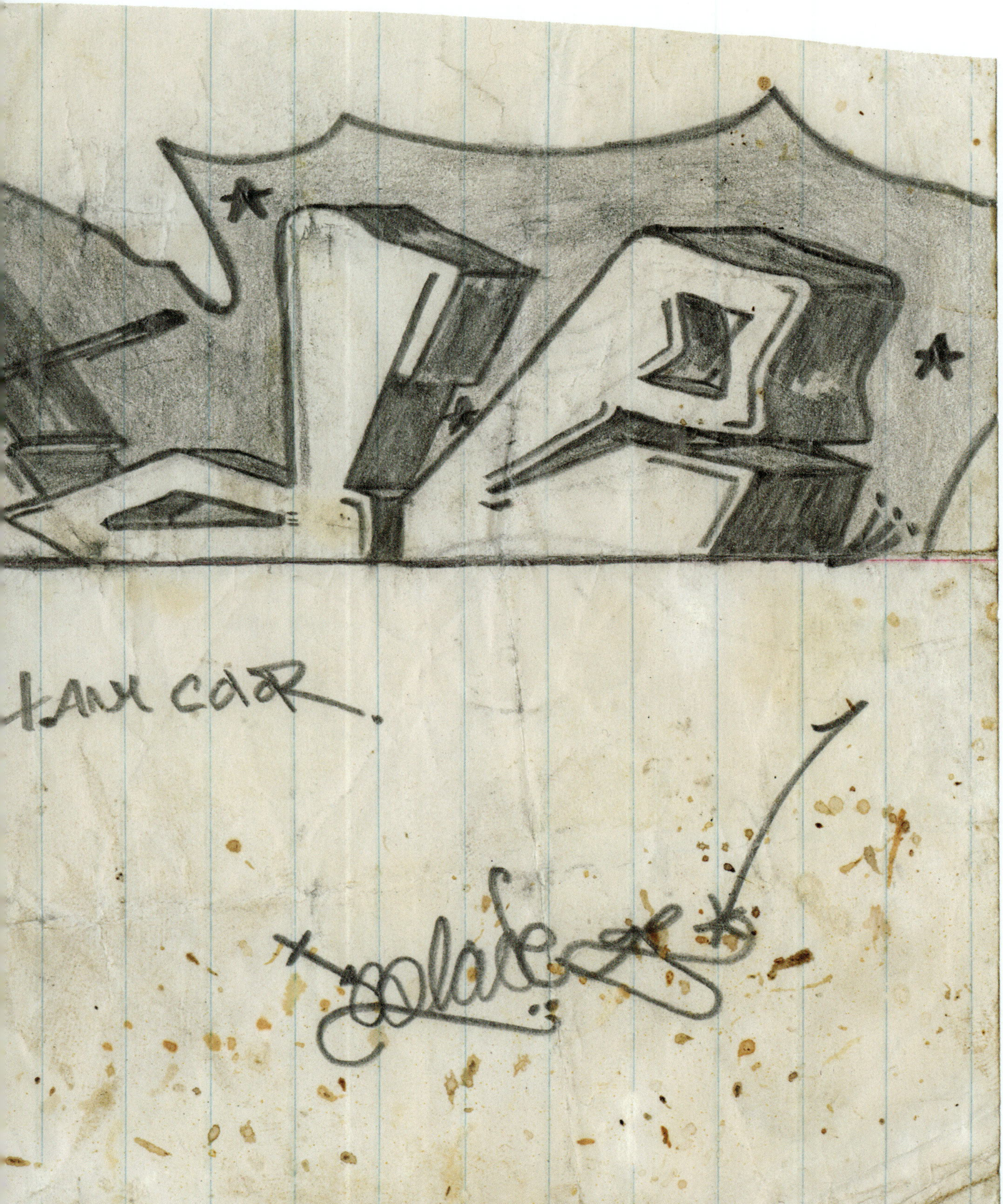
TANK CAR

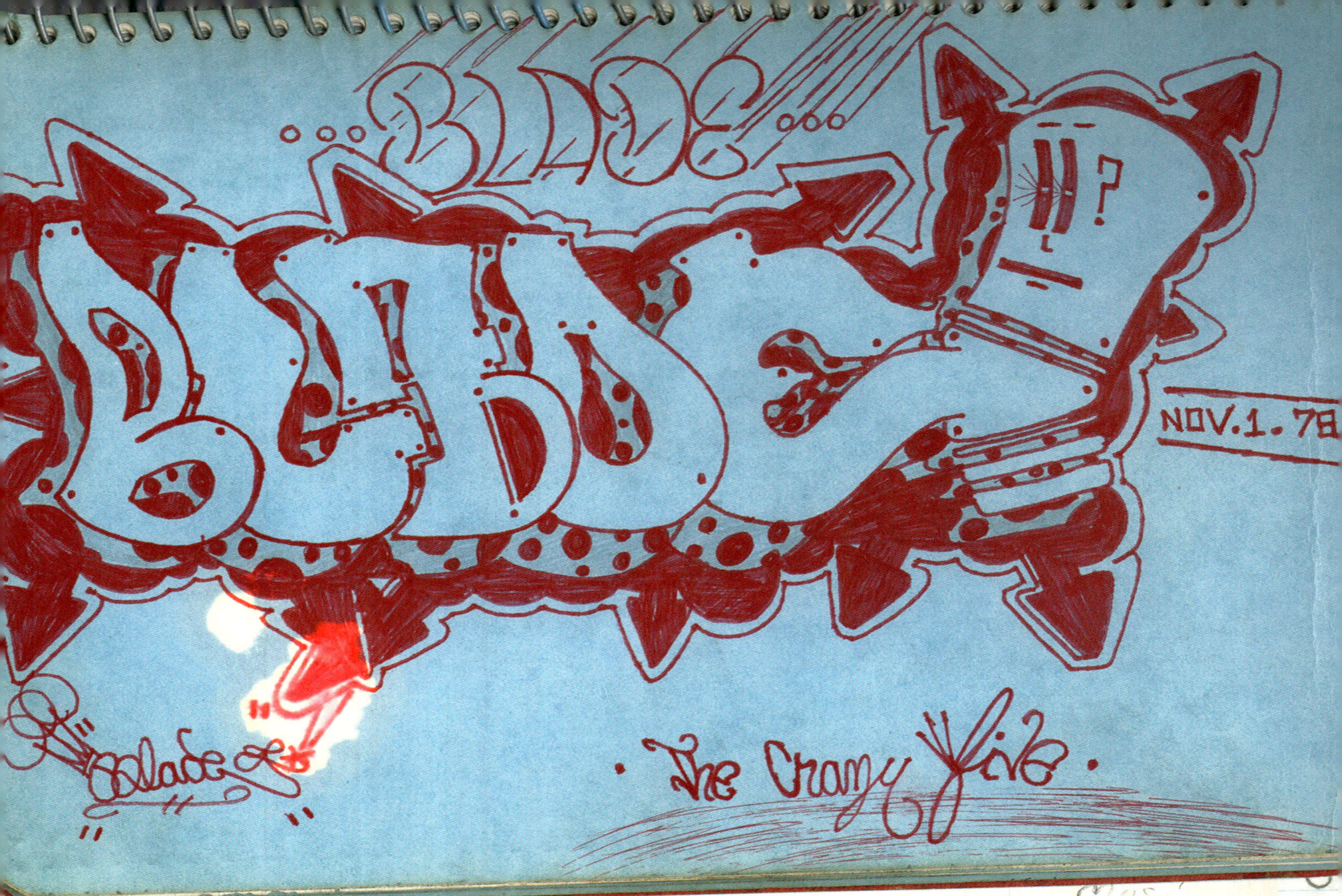
BLADE
NOV. 1. 78
The Crazy Five

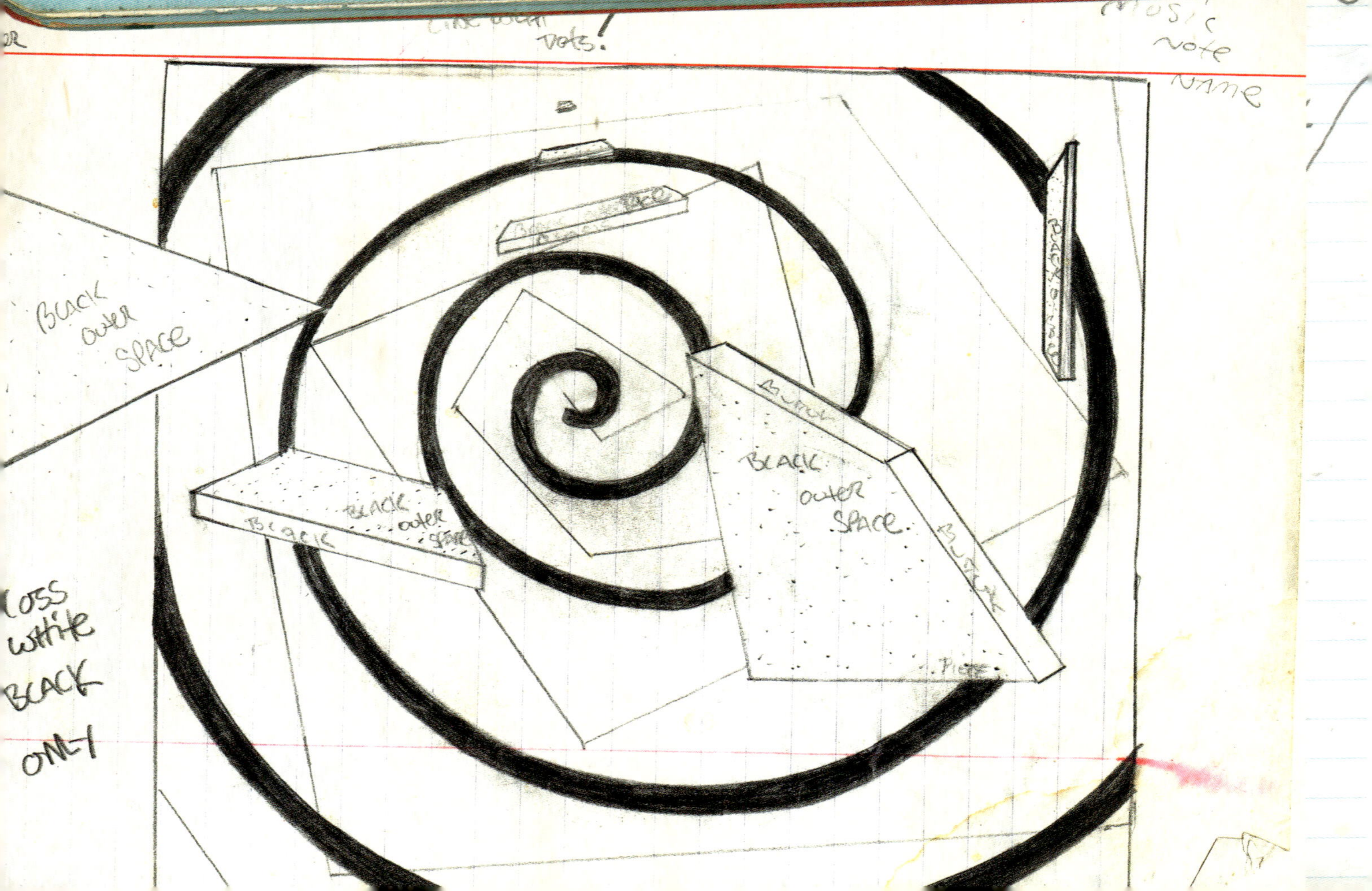
Dots!
Music note name
BLACK OUTER SPACE
BLACK OUTER SPACE
BLACK
BLACK OUTER SPACE
Piece
LOSS WHITE BLACK ONLY

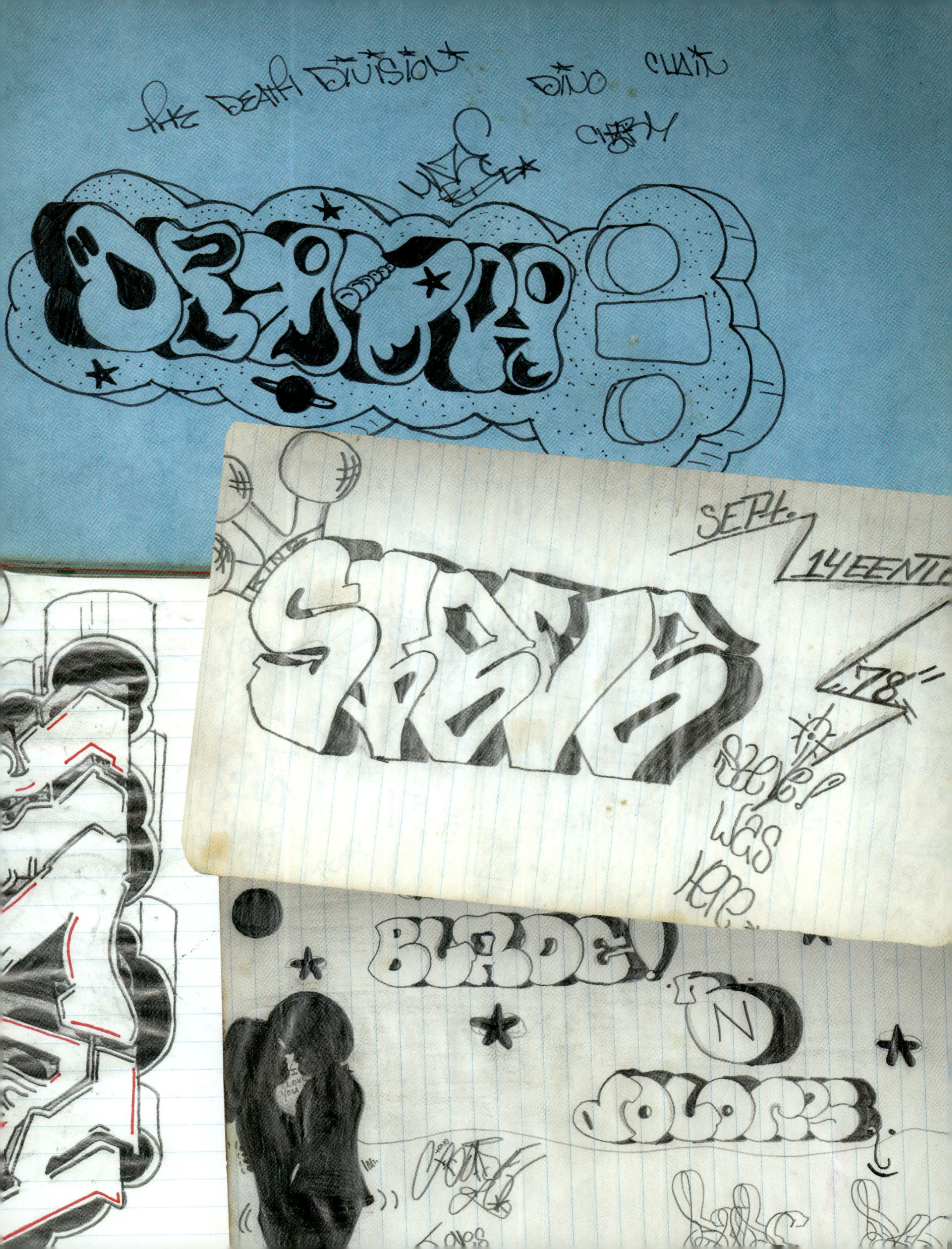

THE DEATH DIVISION
DINO
CHAIN
SEPT.
14EENTH
"78"
STEVE!
WAS
HERE
BLADE!
N
DOLORES
I LOVE YOU

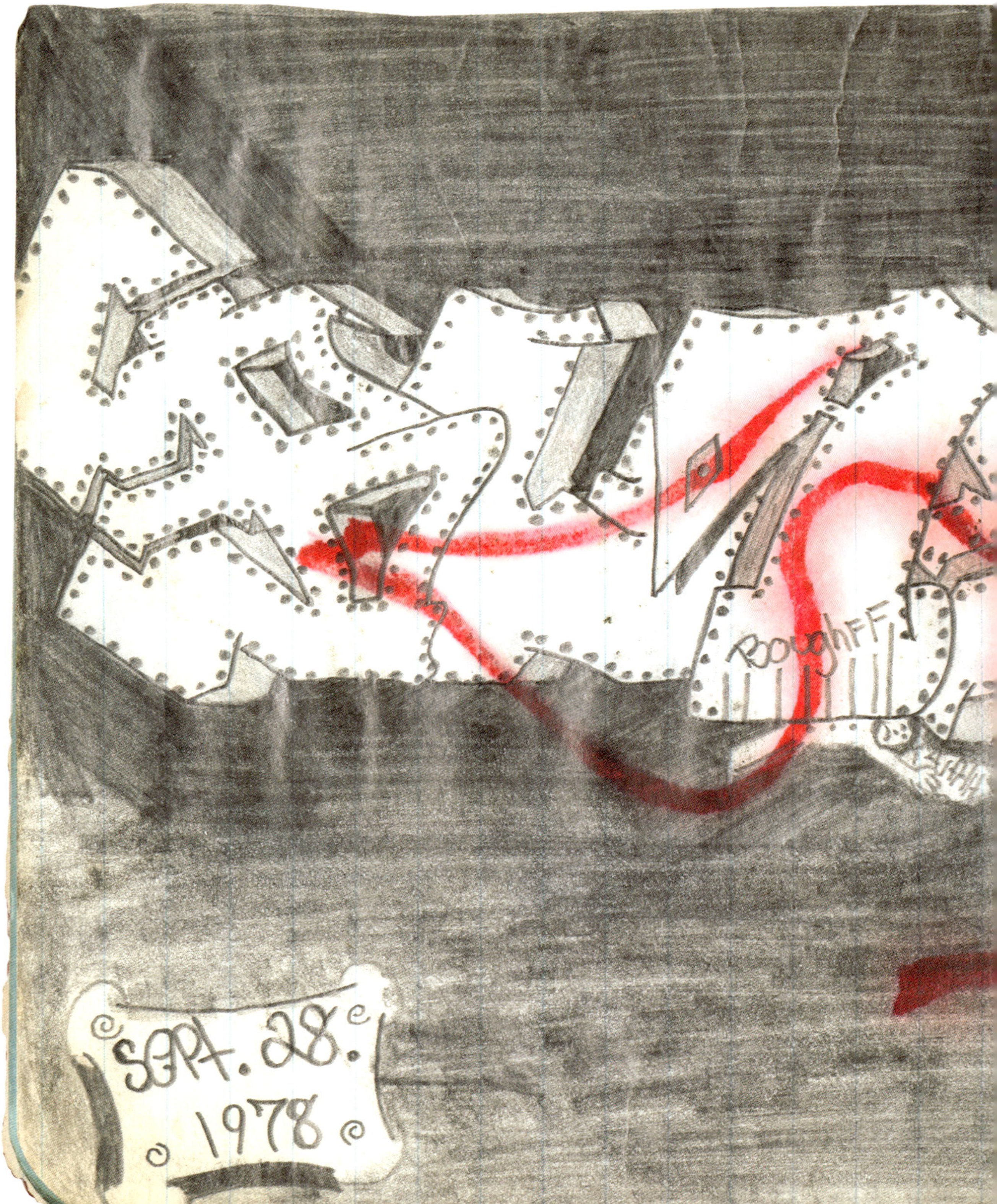
ROUGHFF
SEPT. 28.
1978

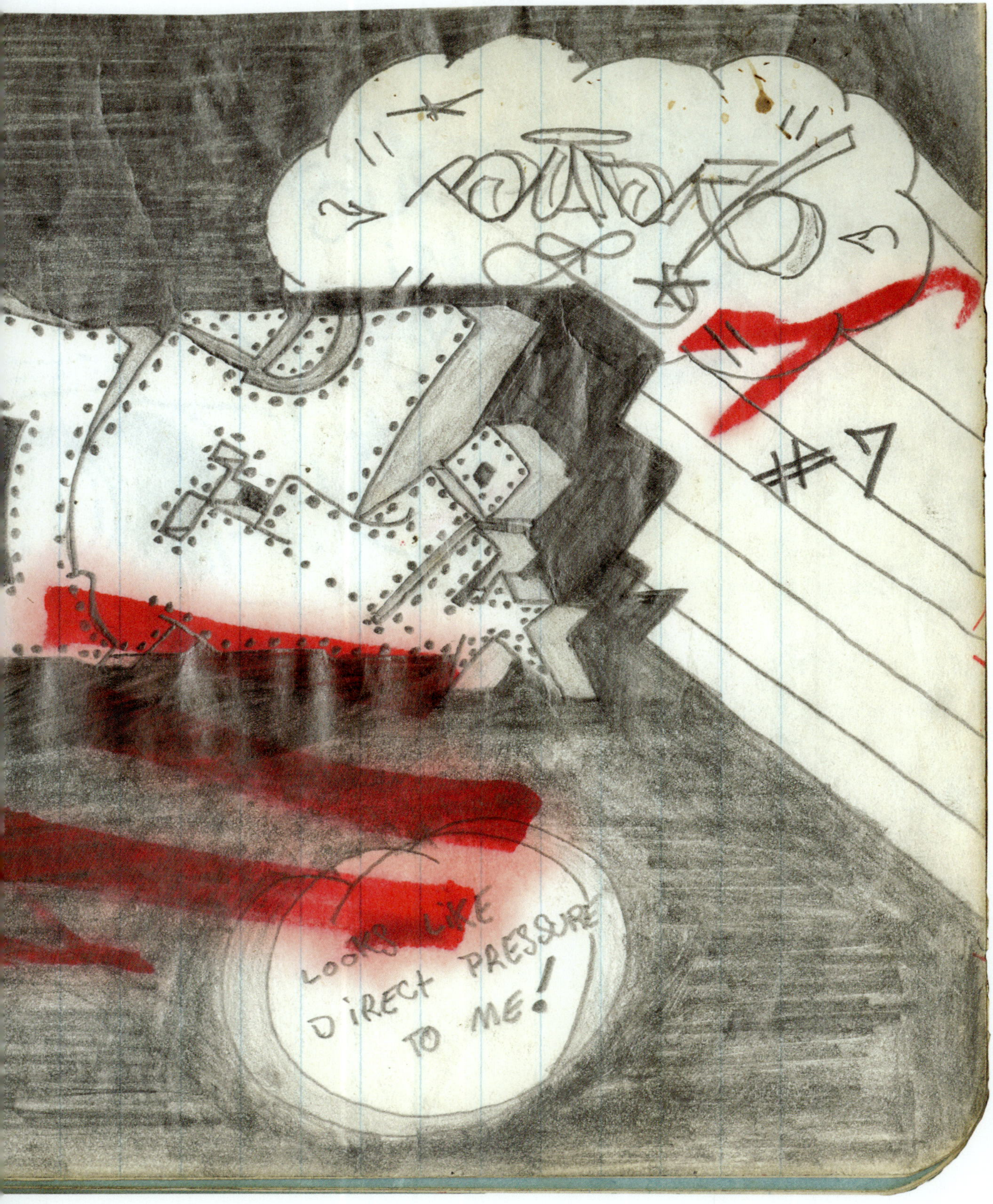
LOOKS LIKE
DIRECT PRESSURE
TO ME!

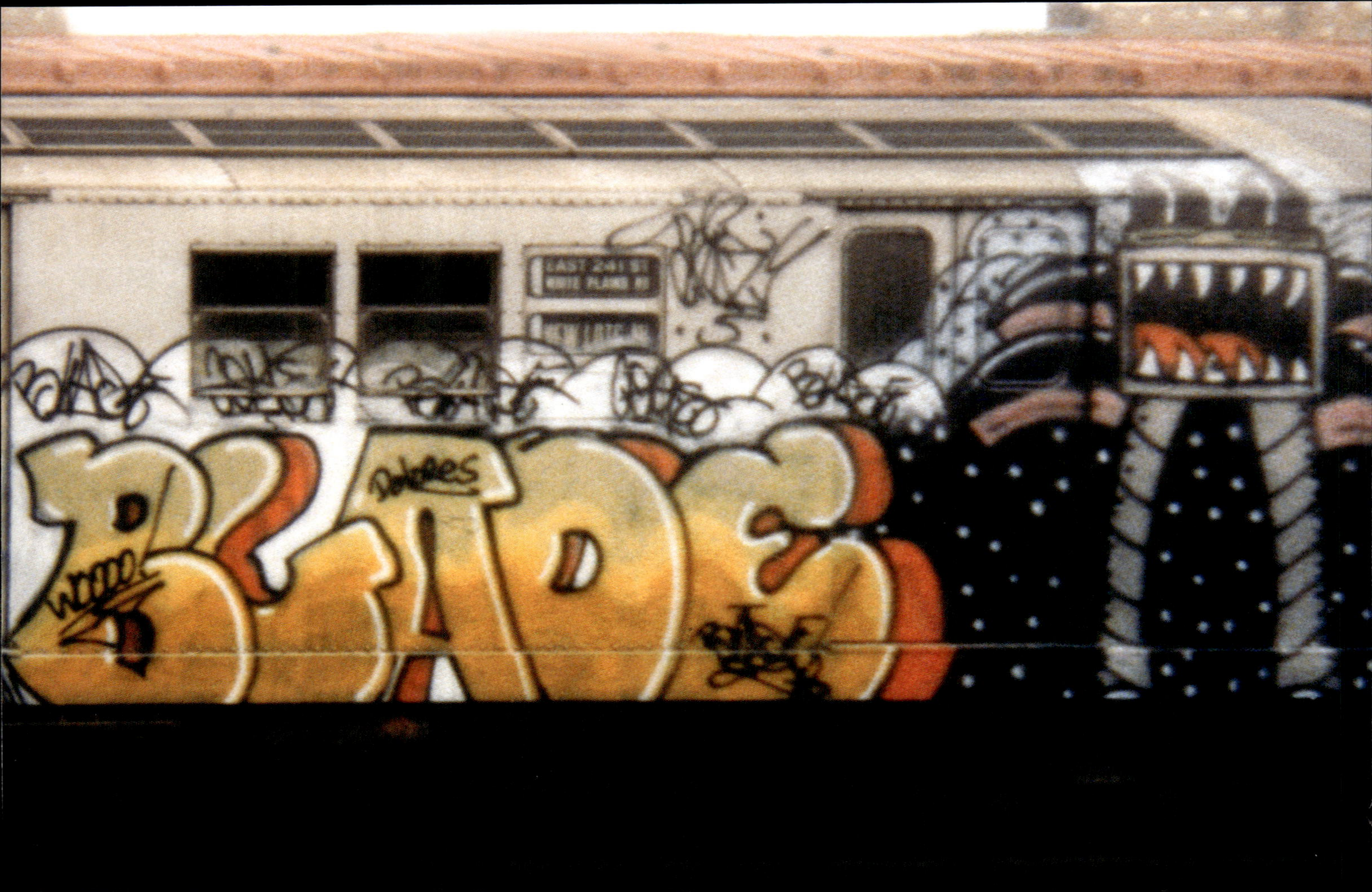

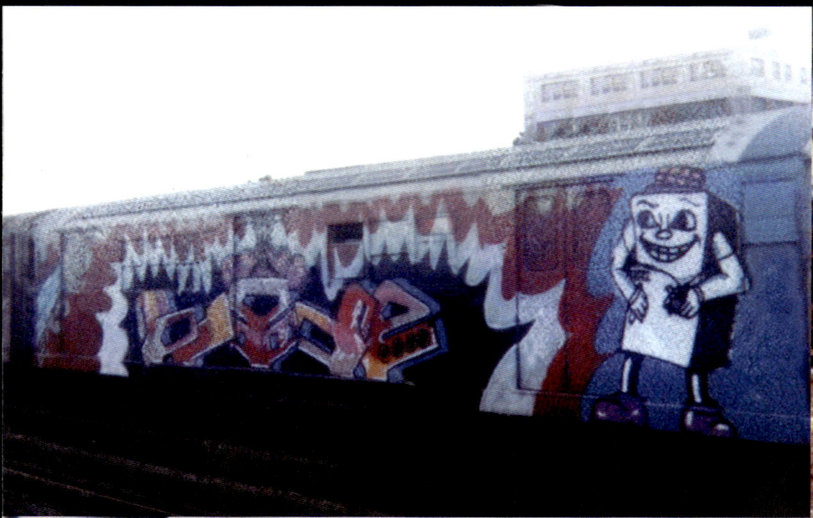

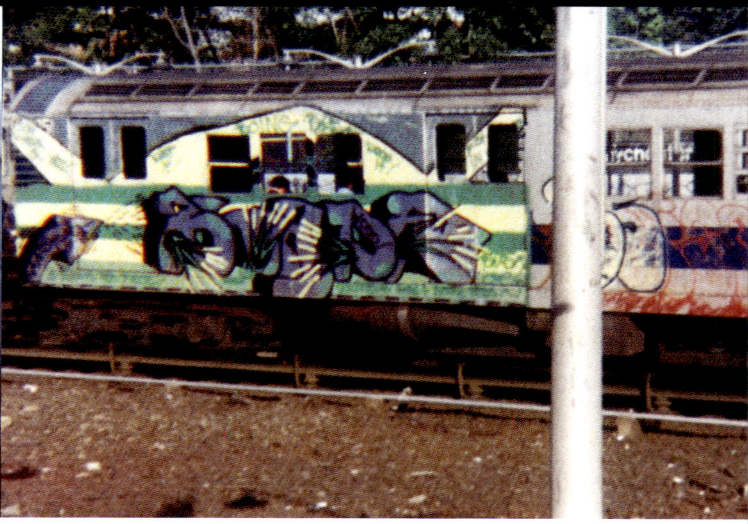

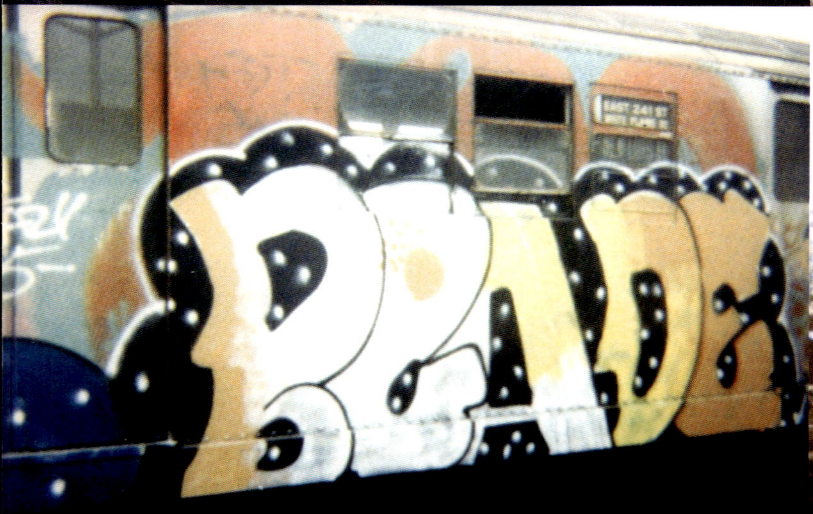

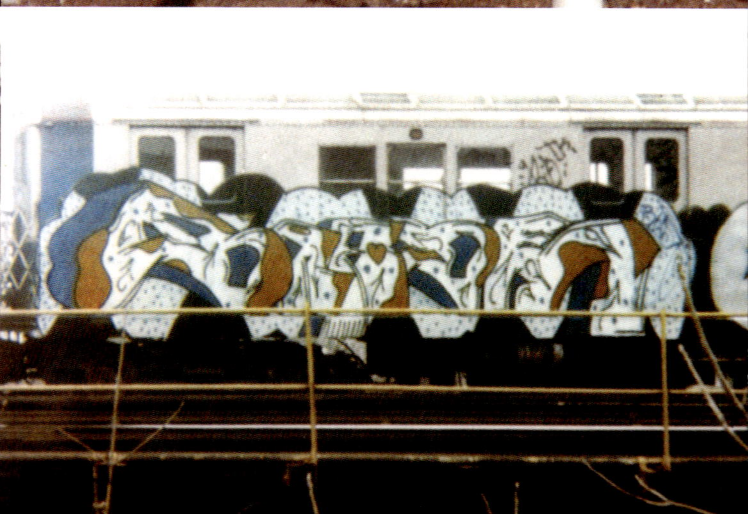

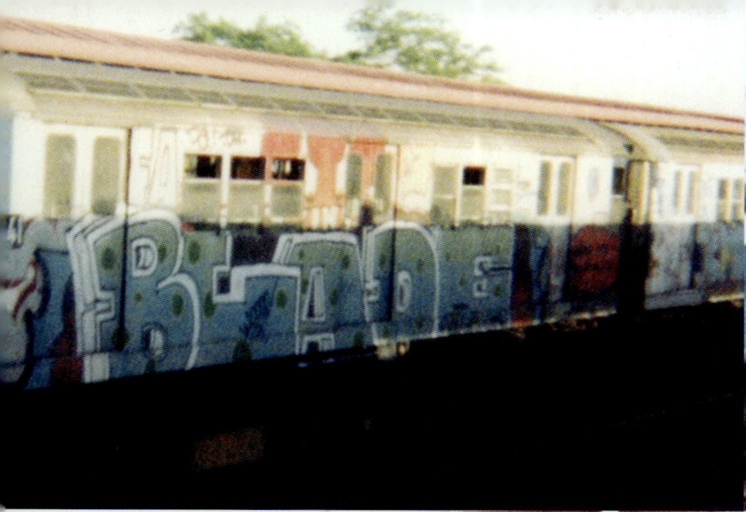

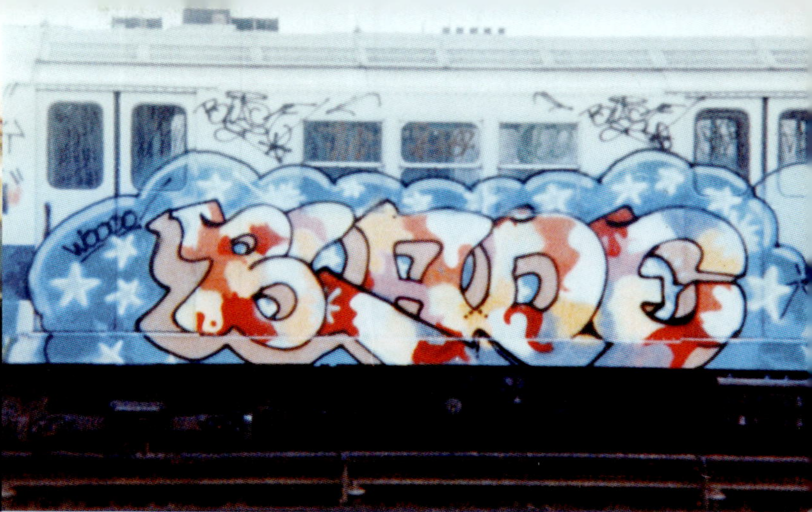

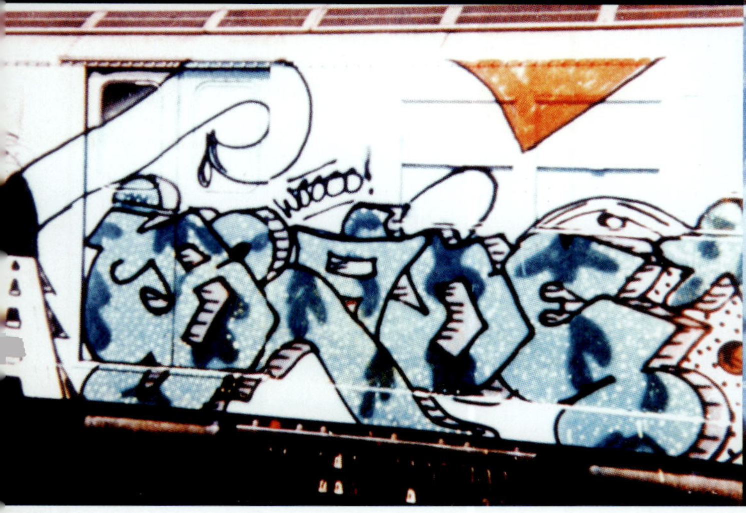

WOOOO!

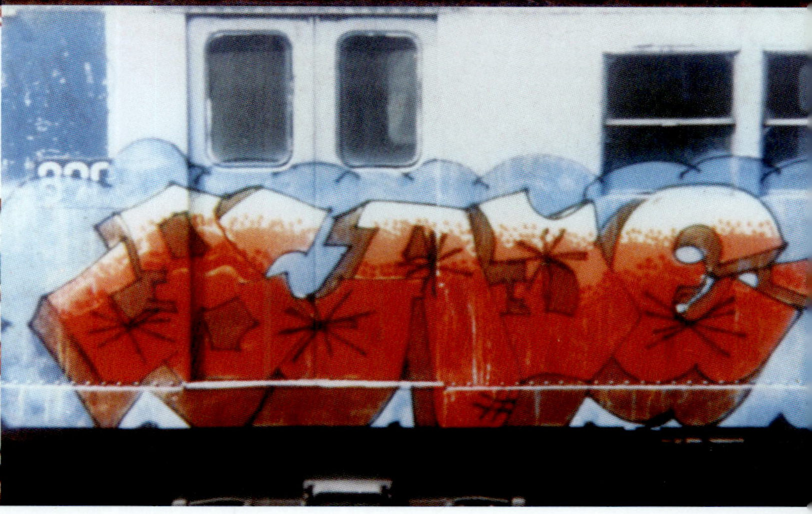

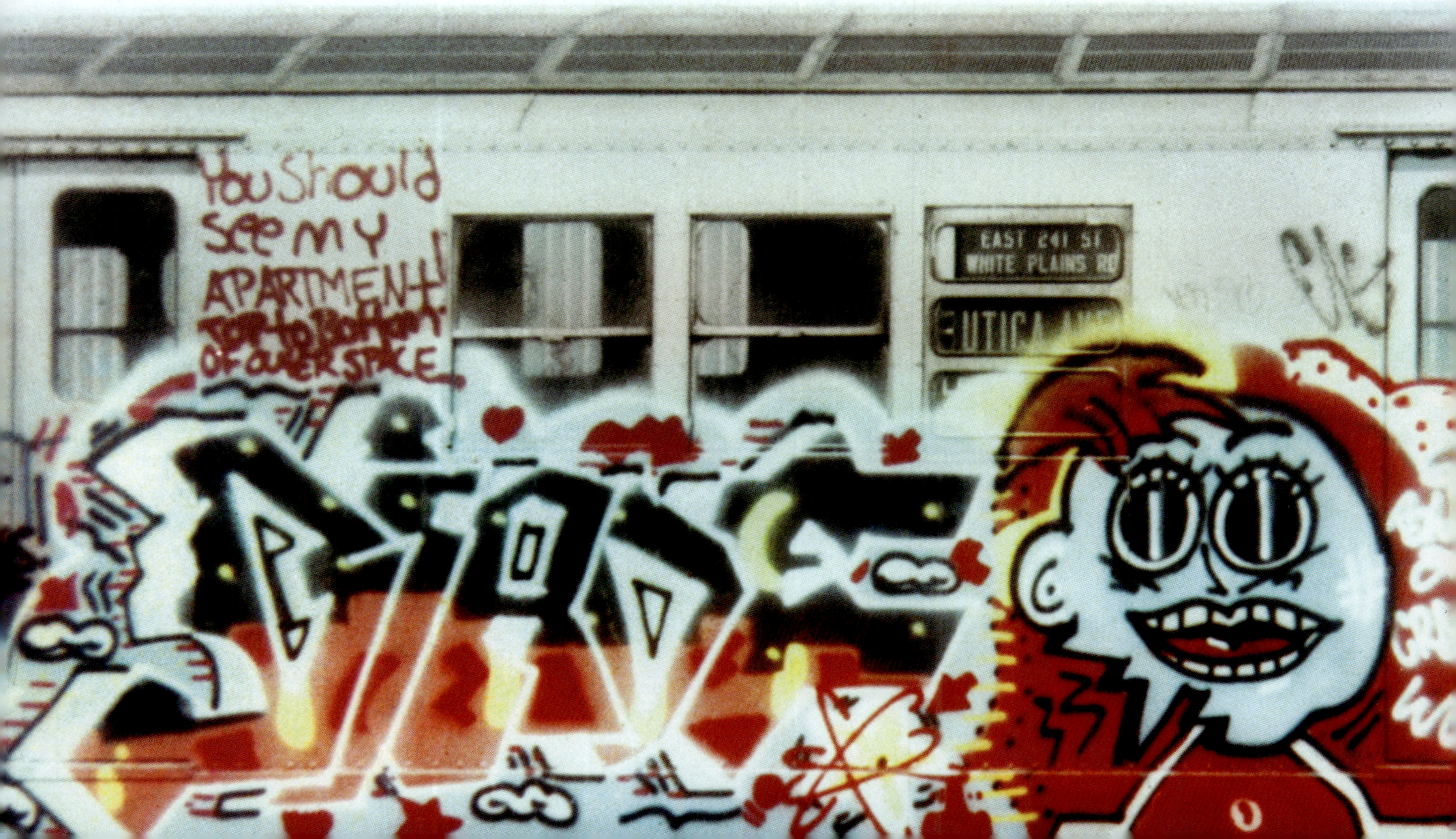

You Should
see my
APARTMENT!
OF OUTER SPACE
EAST 241 ST.
WHITE PLAINS RD
UTICA AV

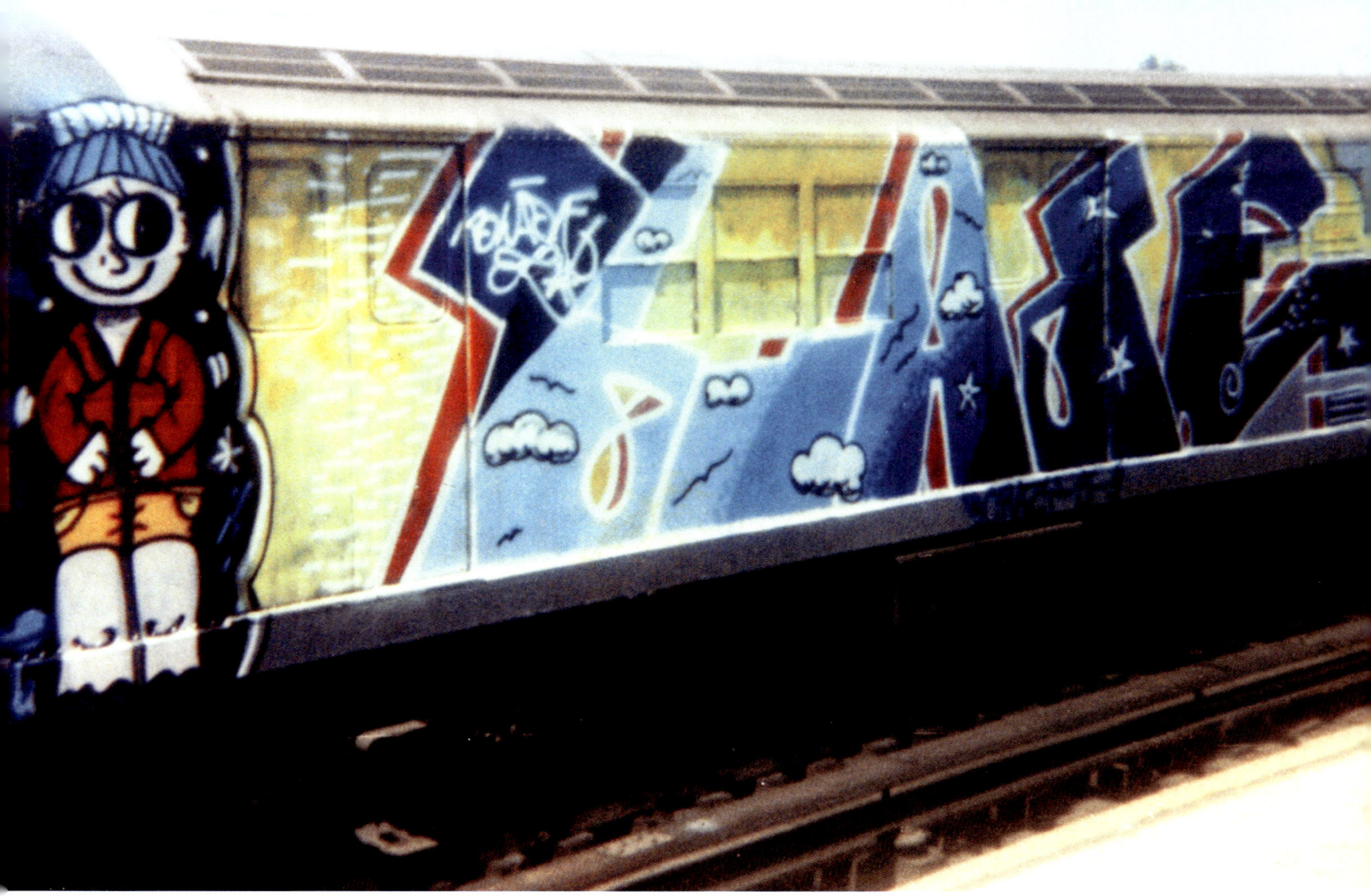

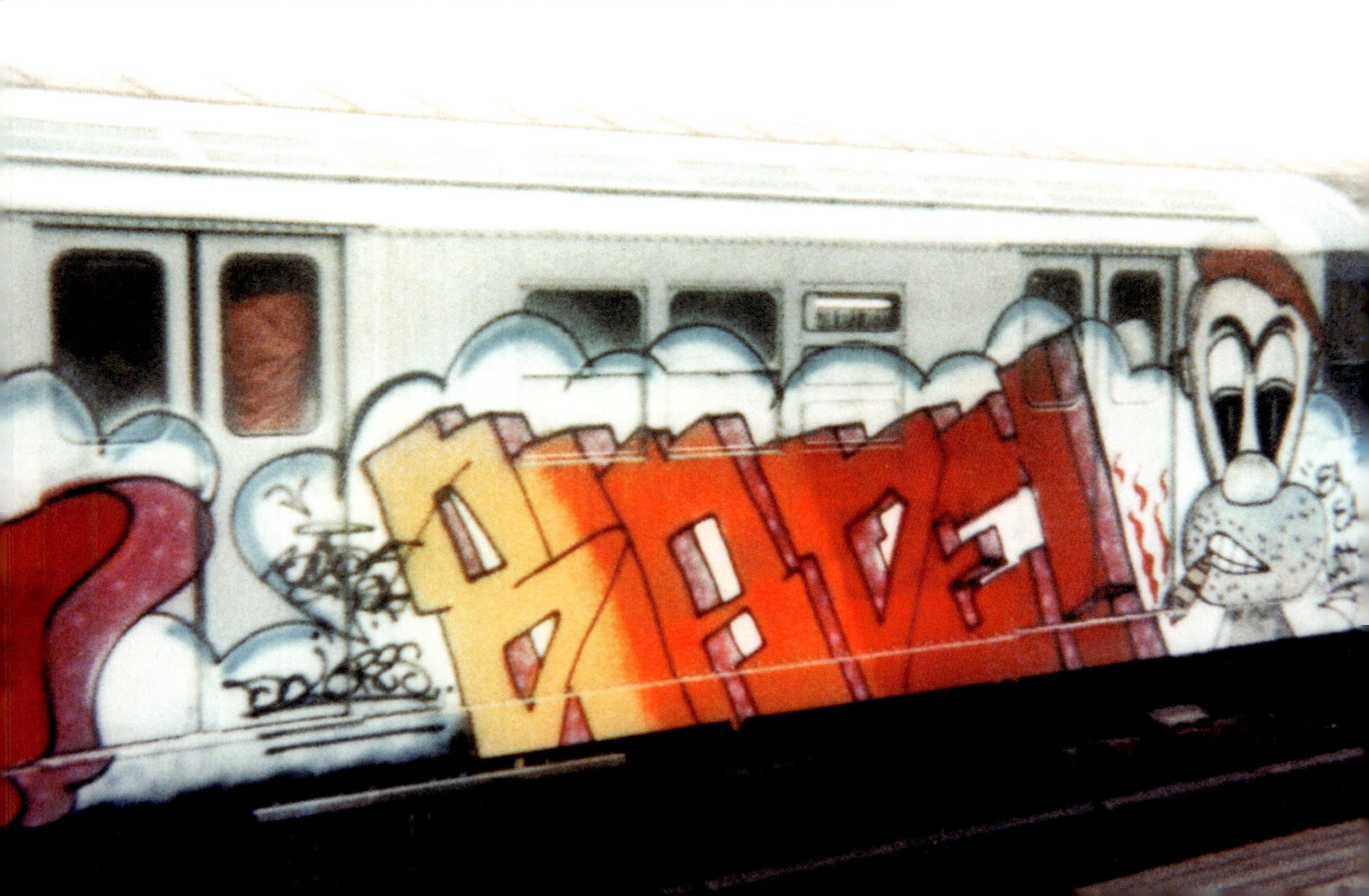

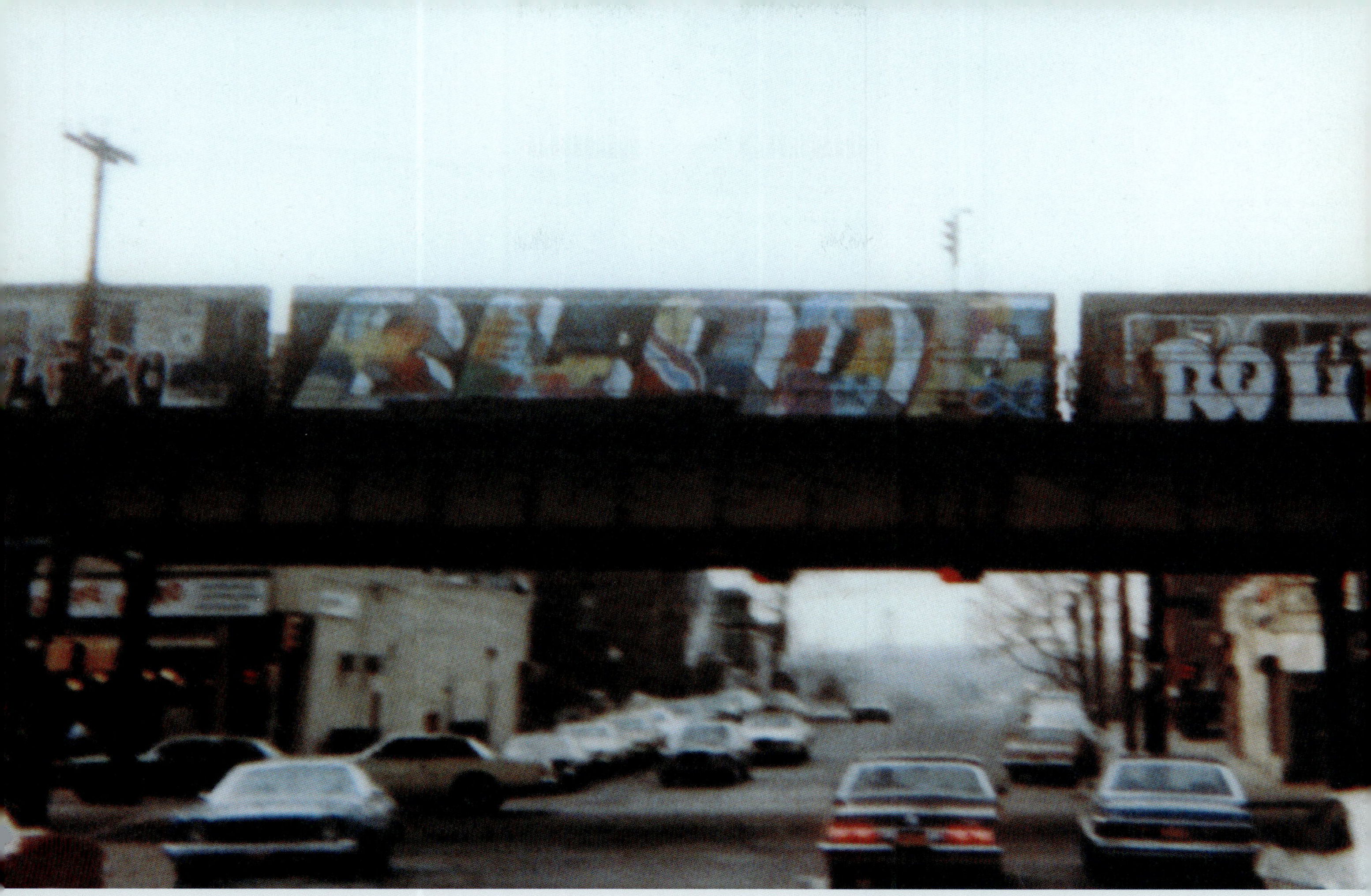

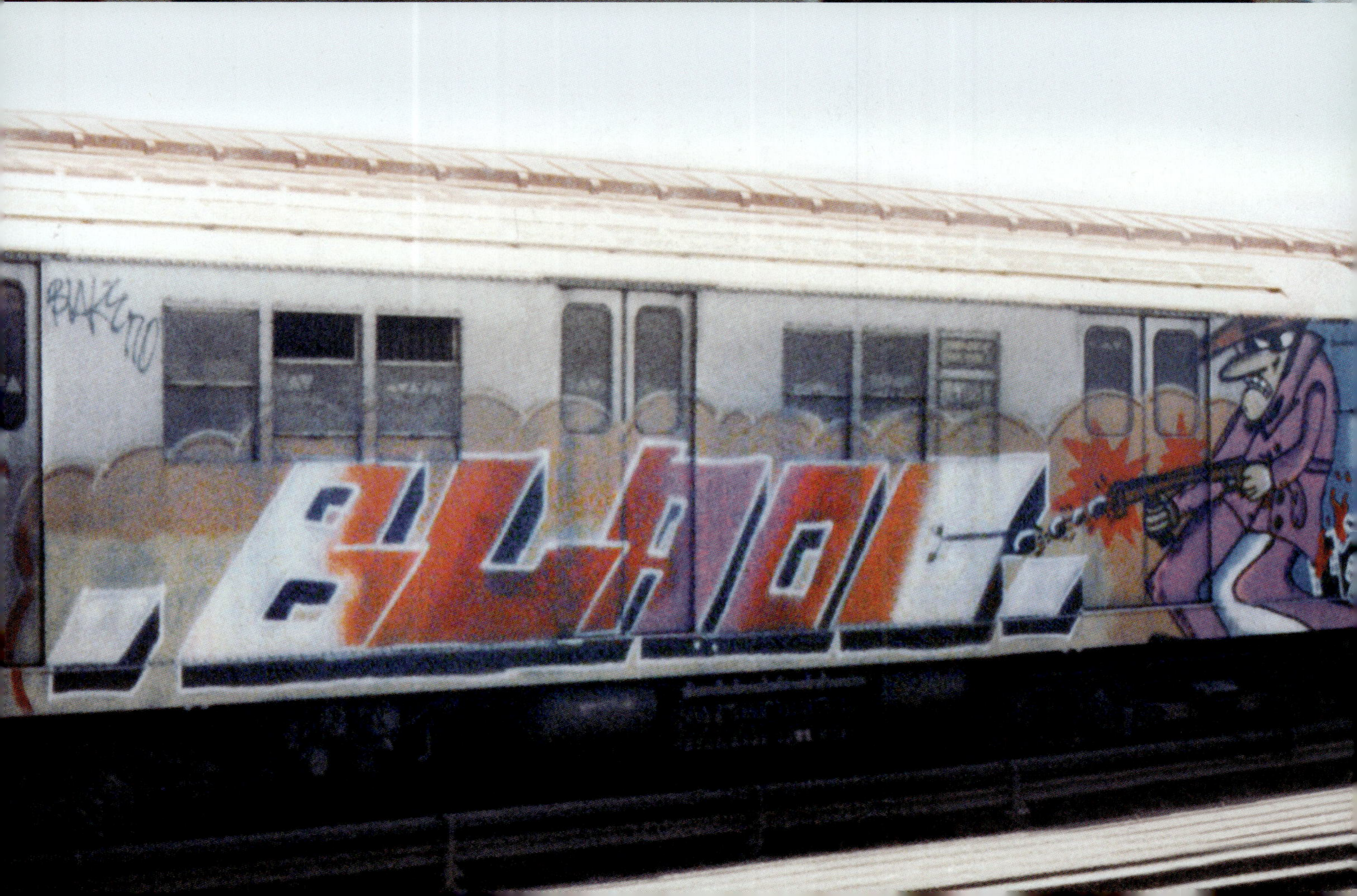

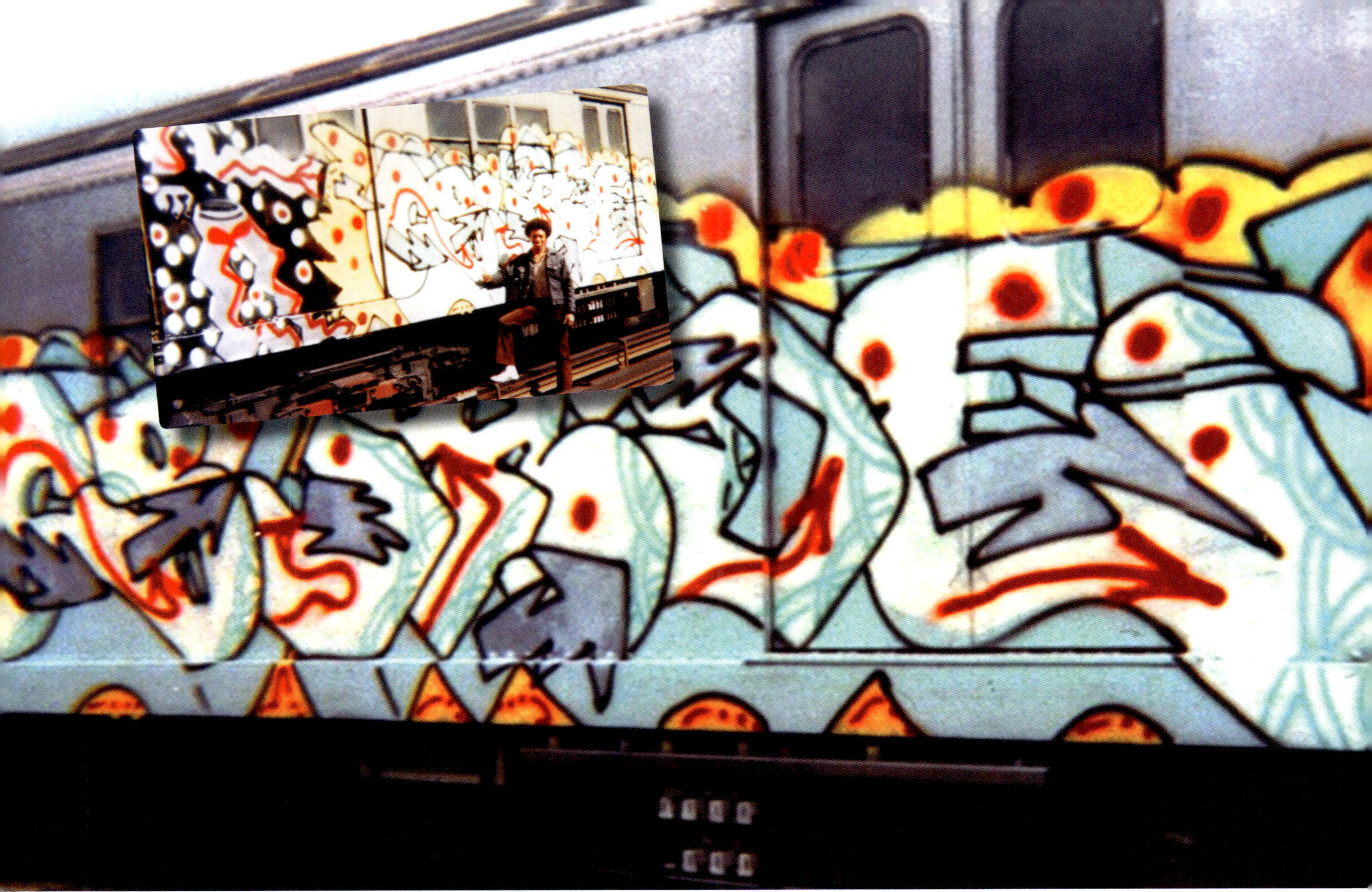

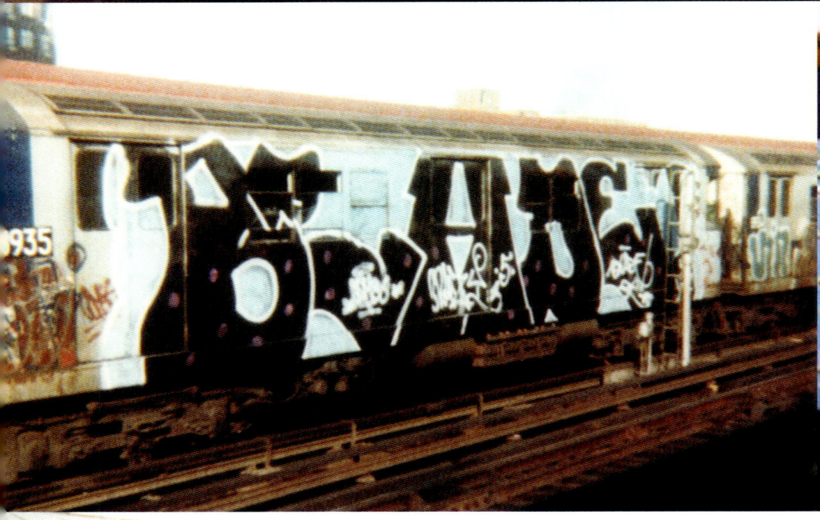

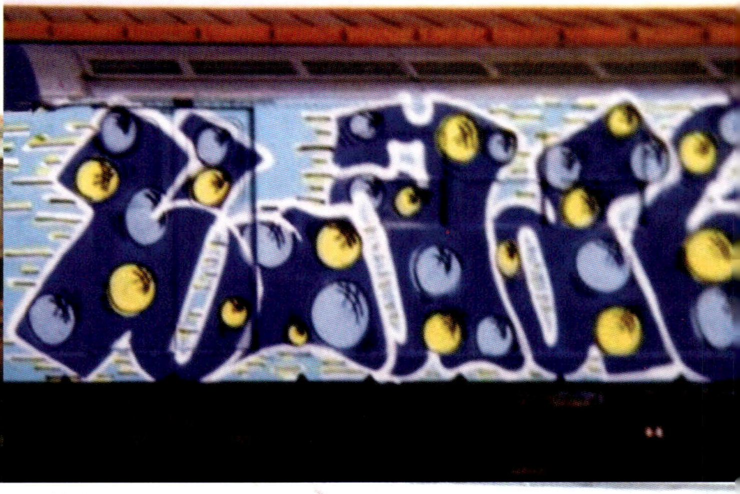

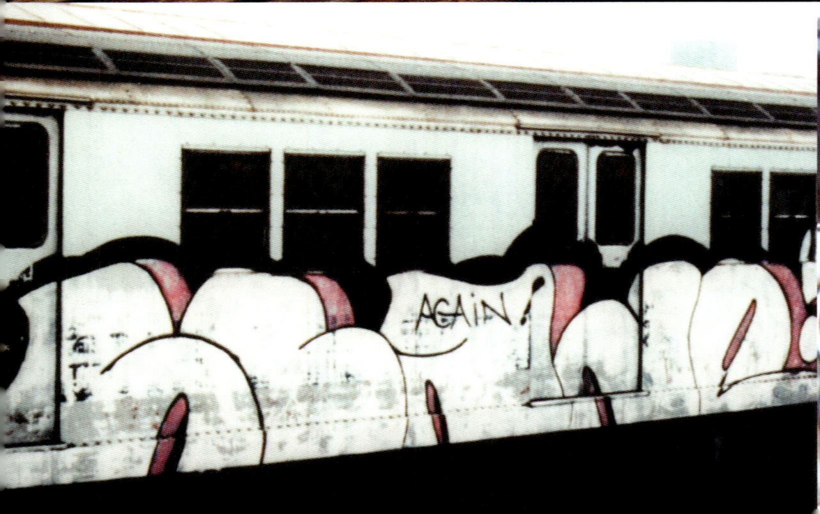
AGAIN

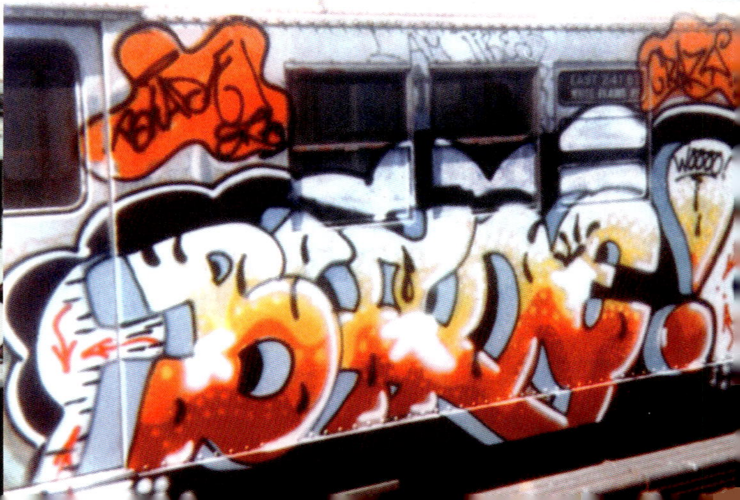

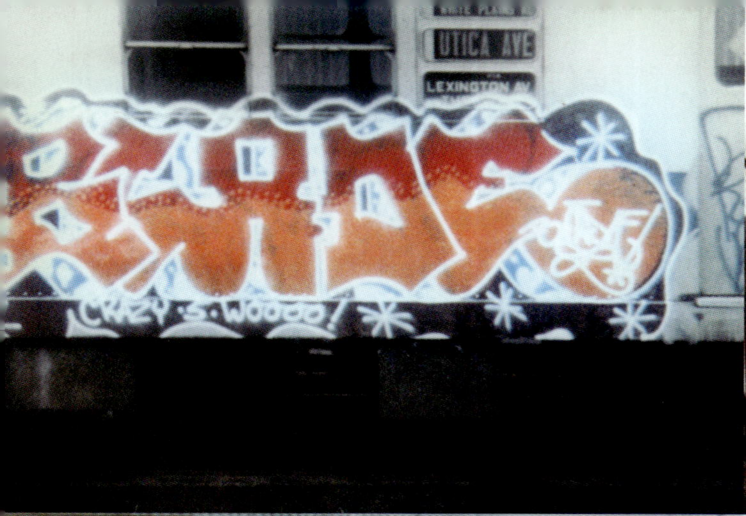

UTICA AVE
LEXINGTON AV

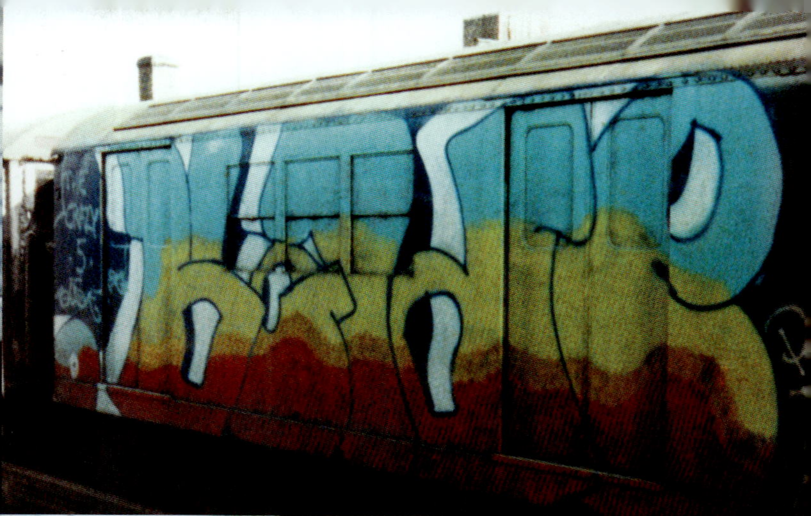

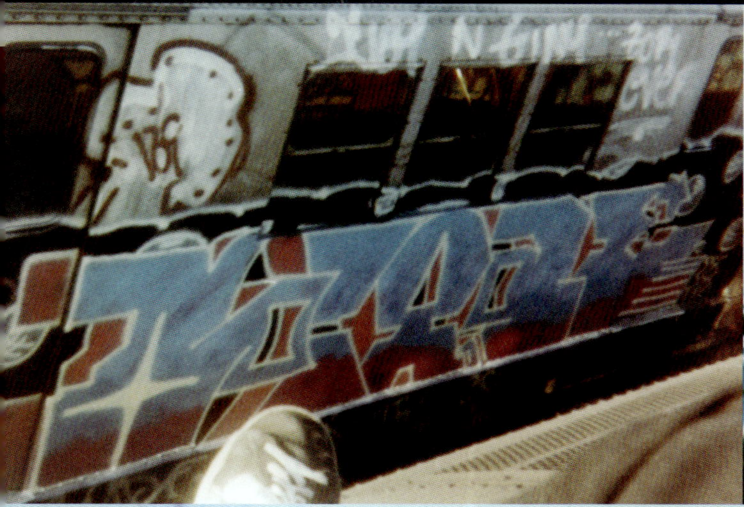

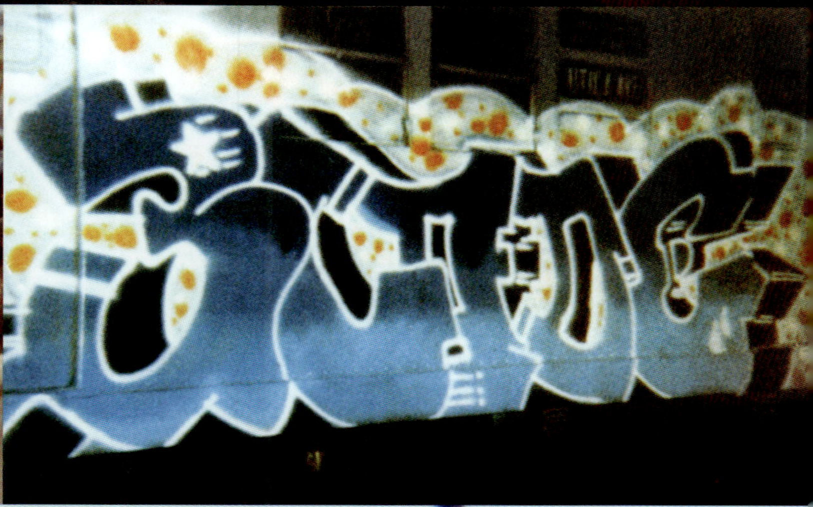

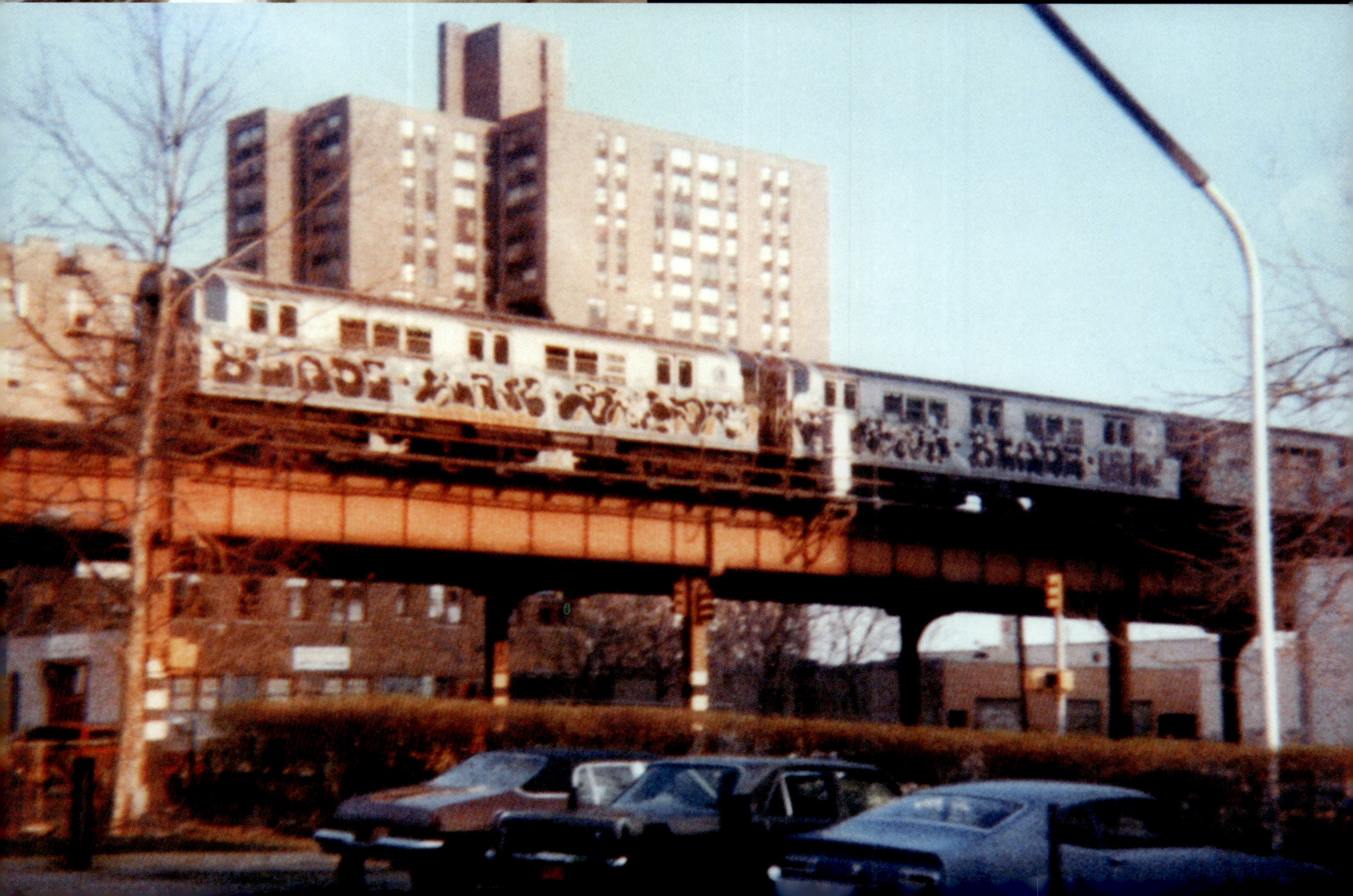

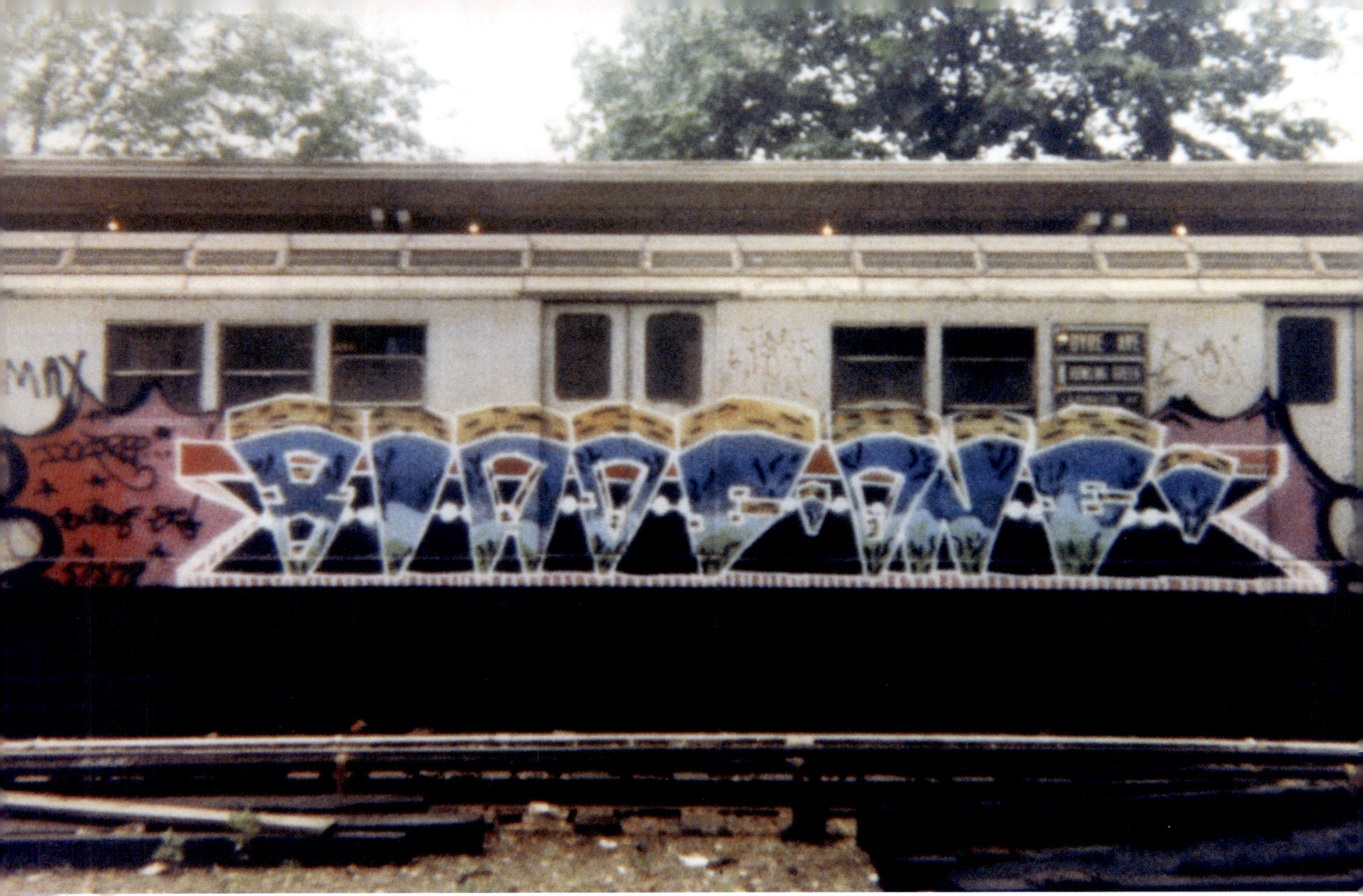
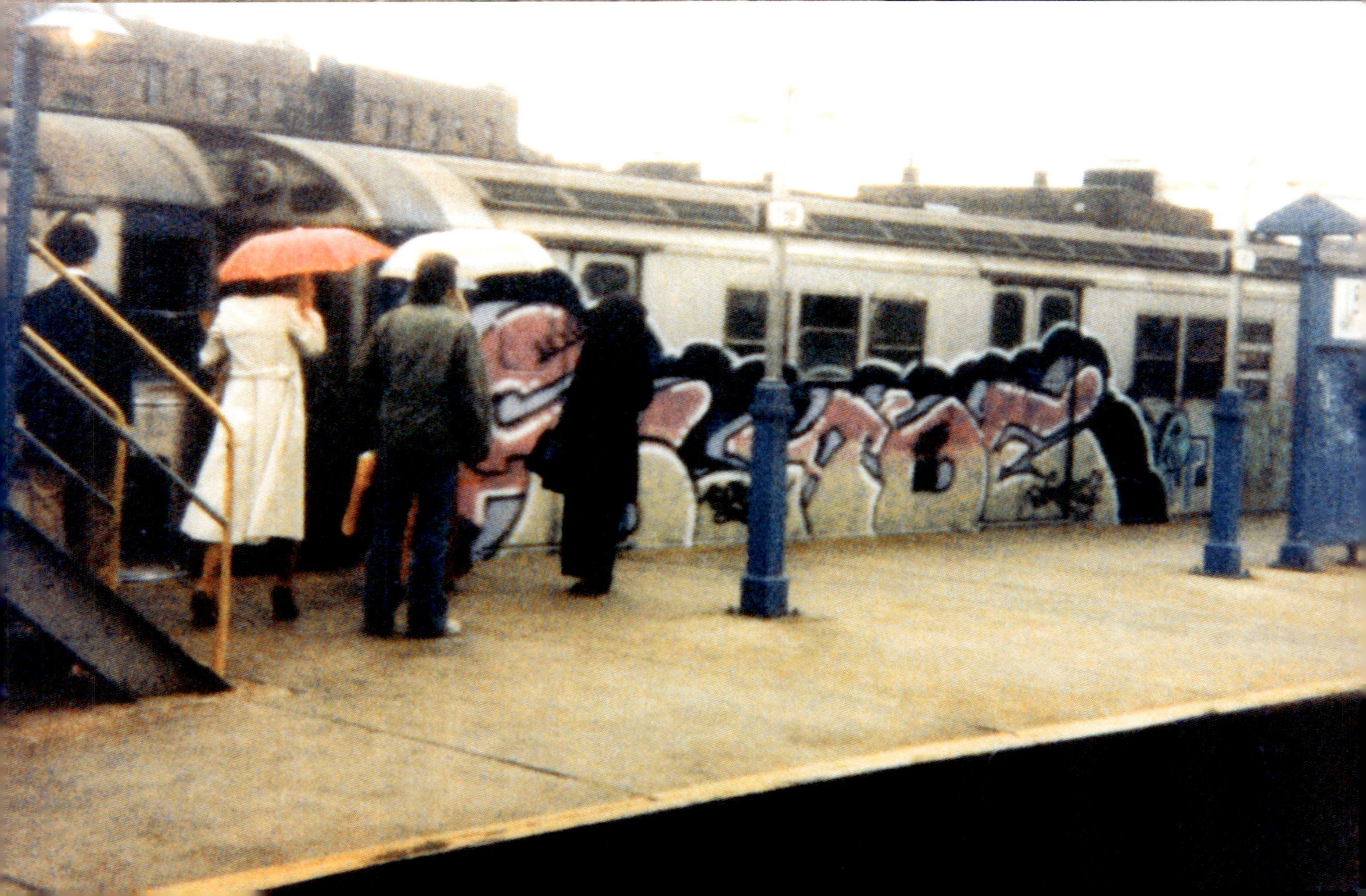

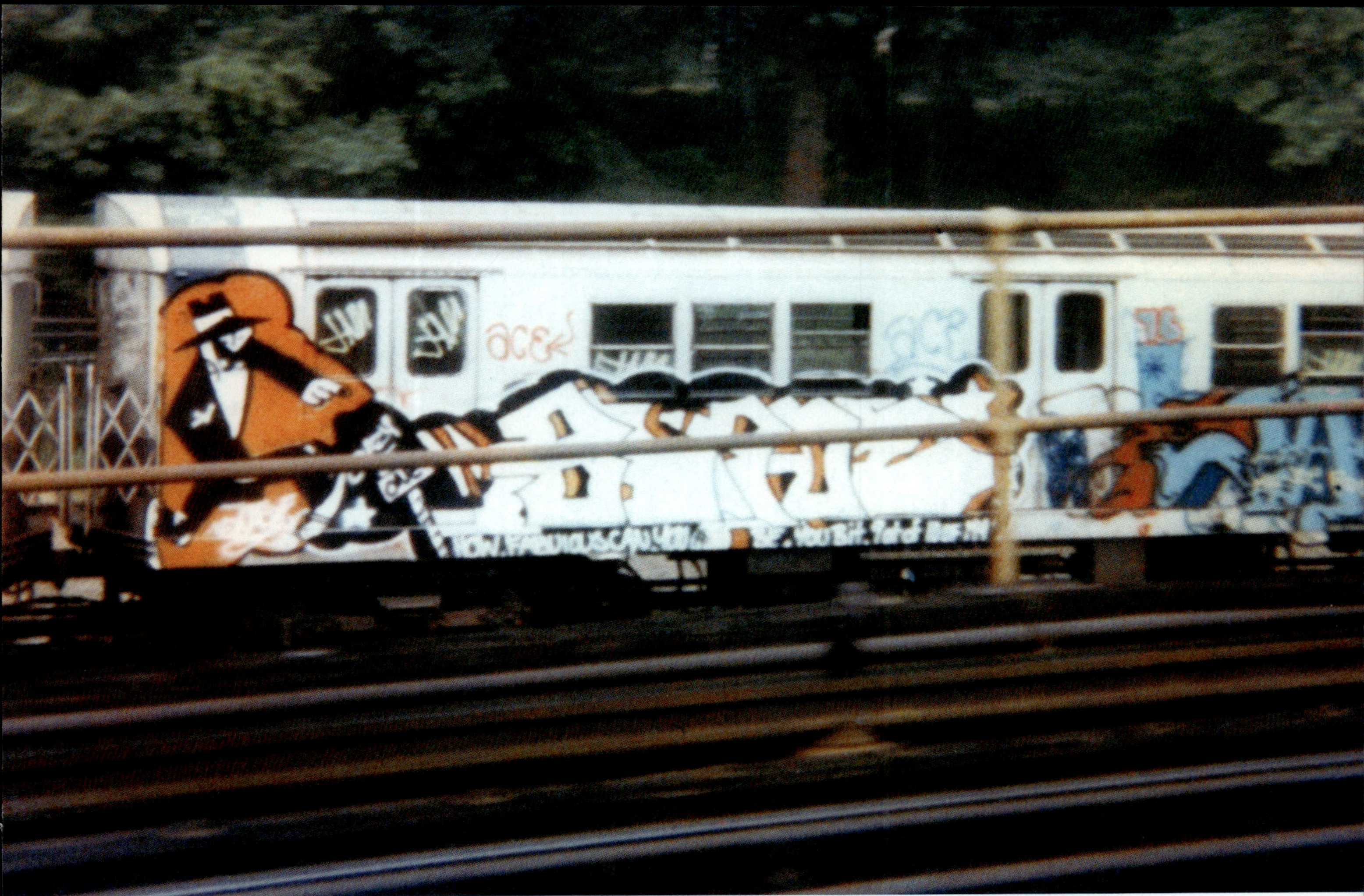

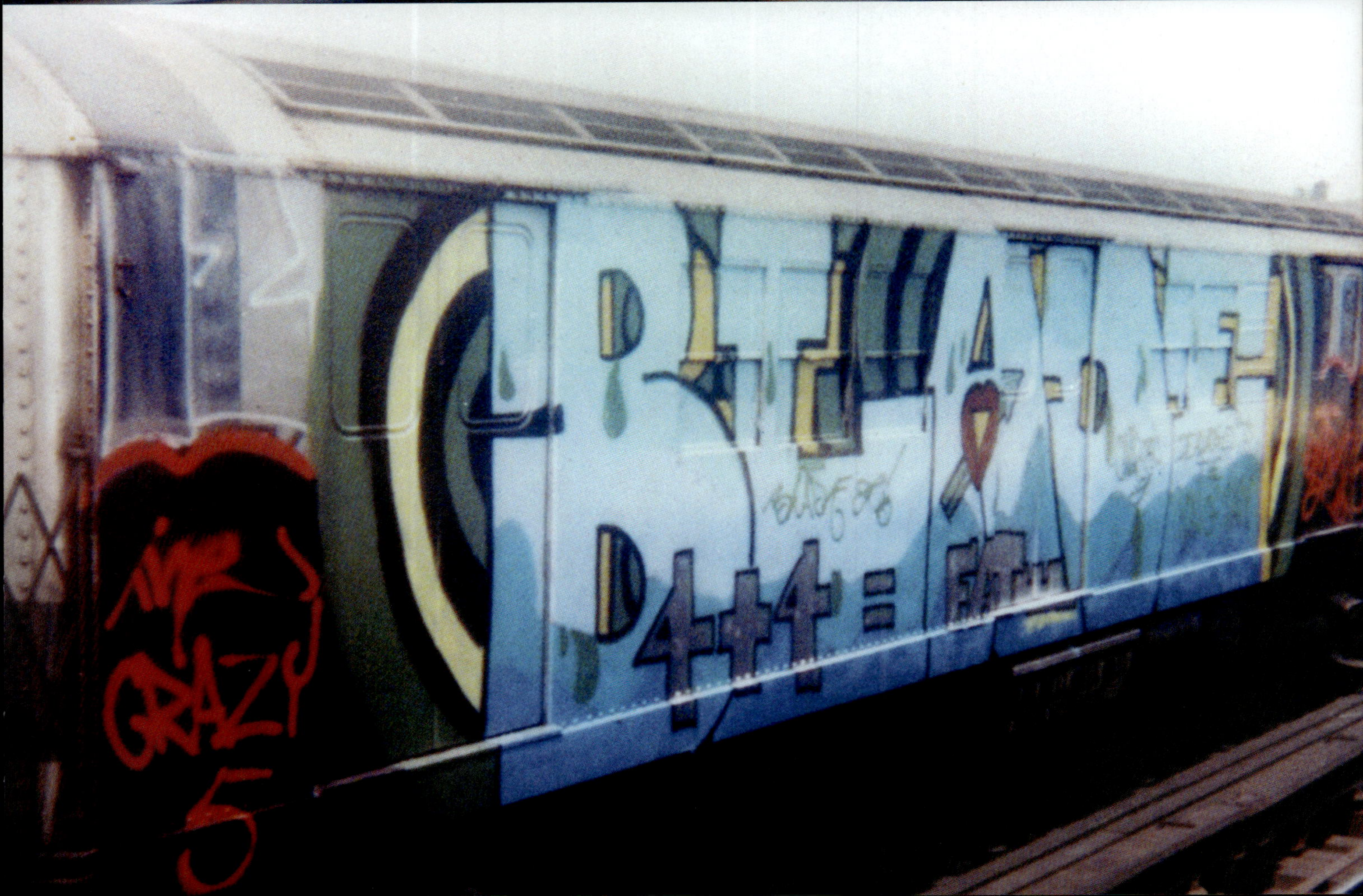

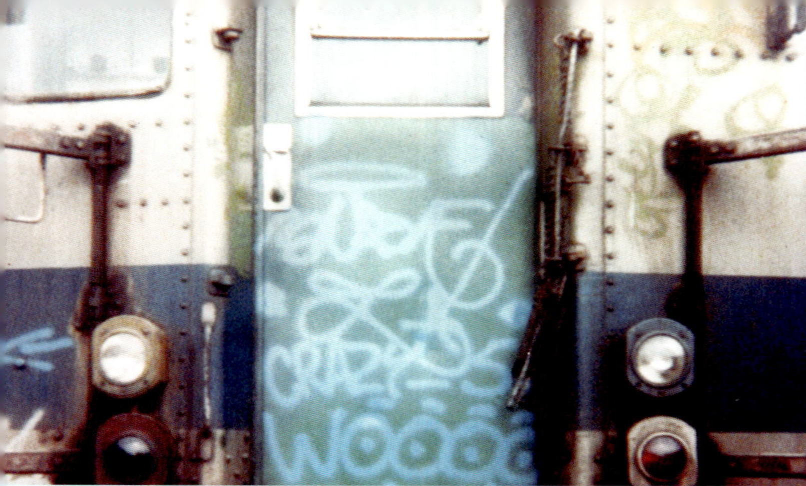

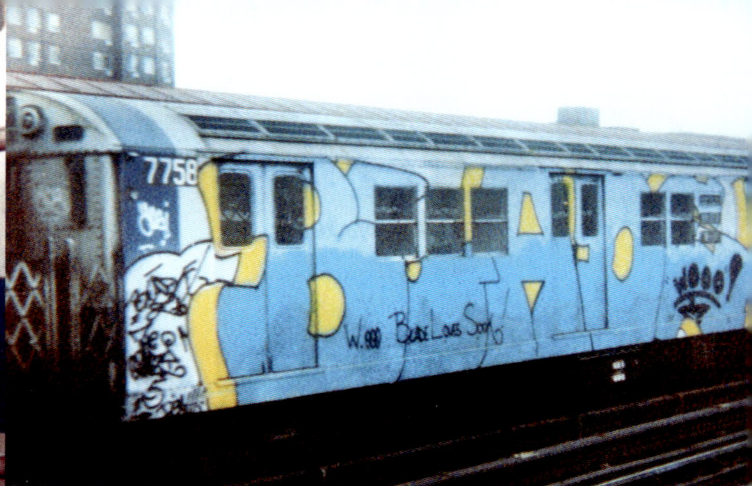
7758

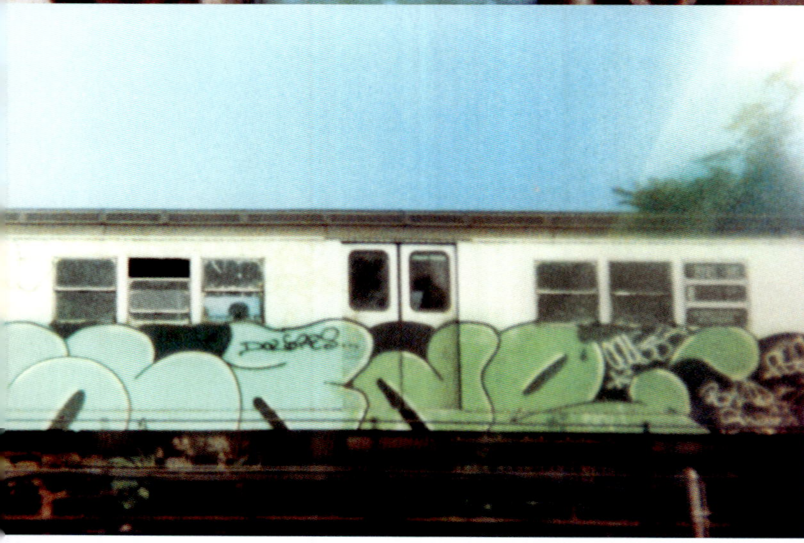

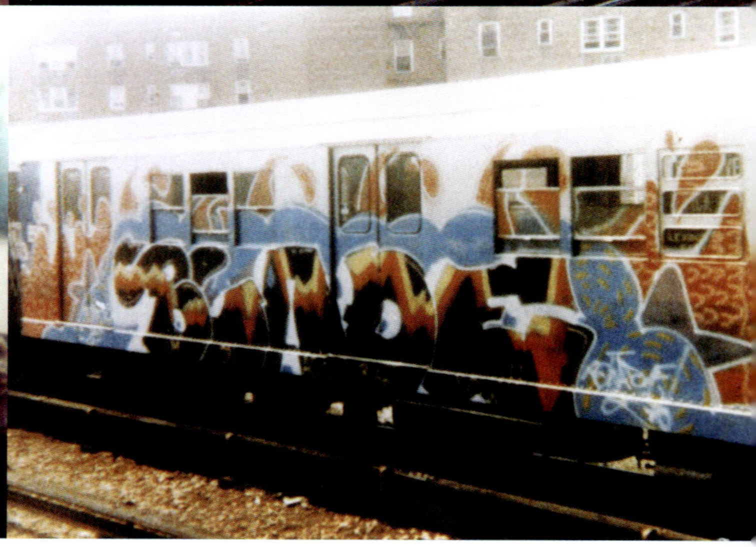

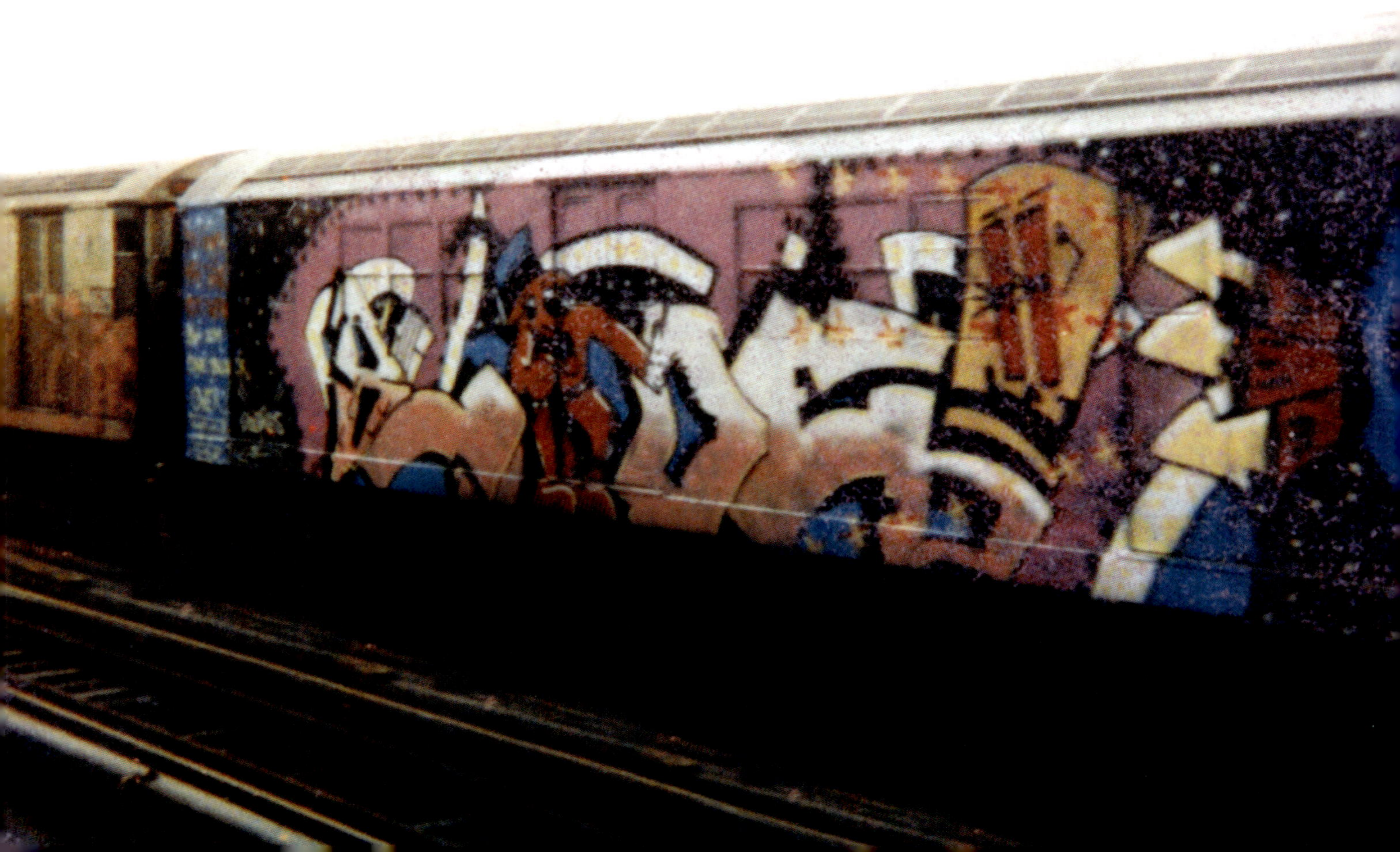

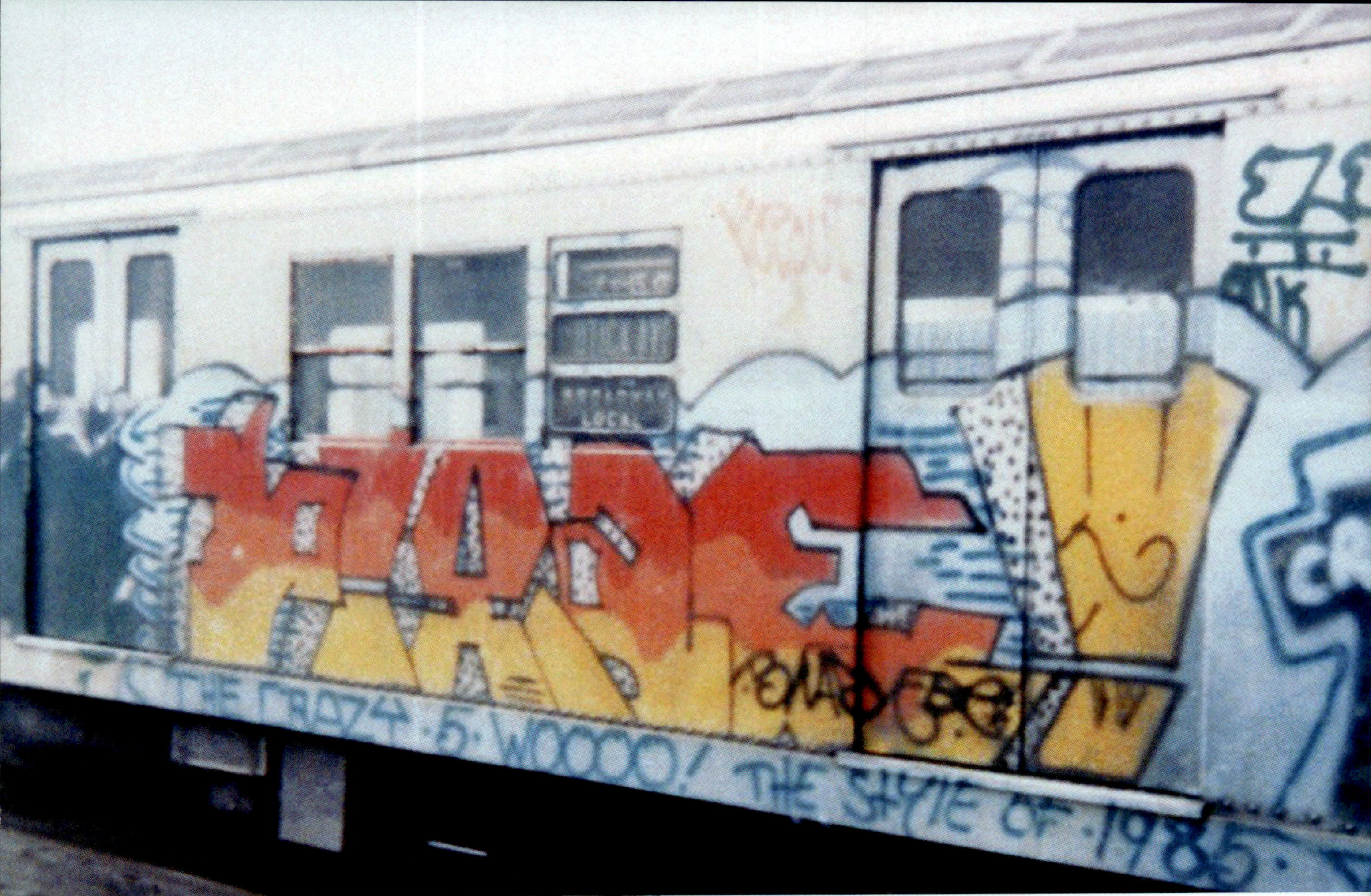
THE CRAZY · 5 · WOOOO! THE STYLE OF · 1985

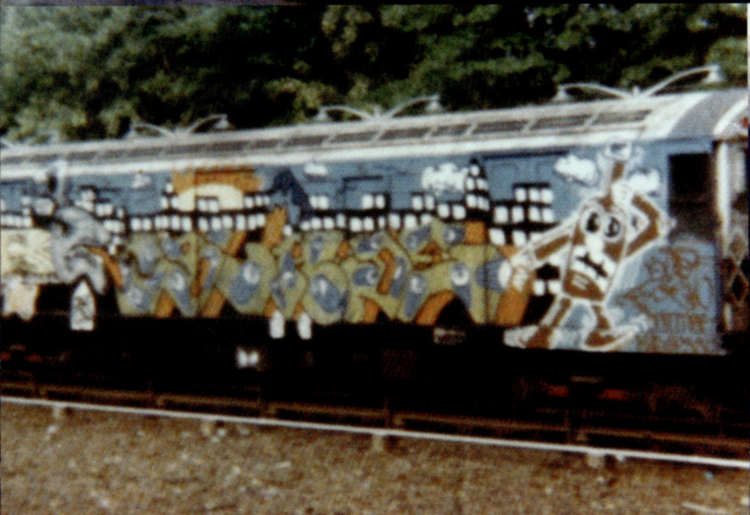

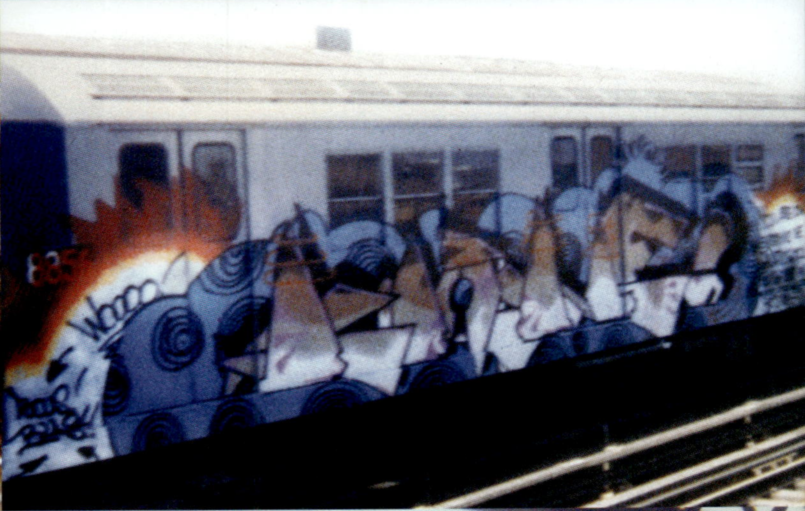

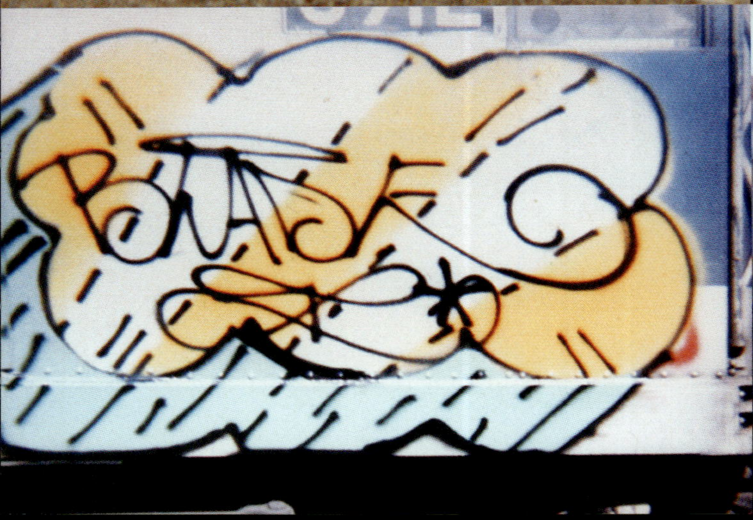

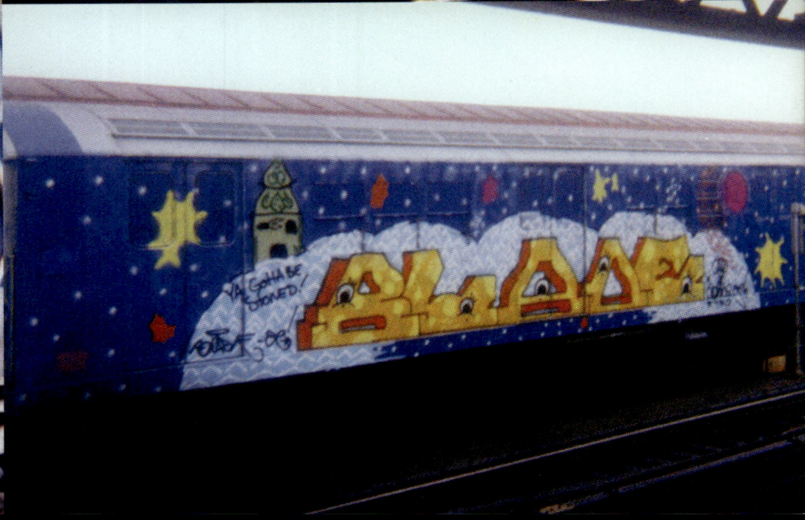

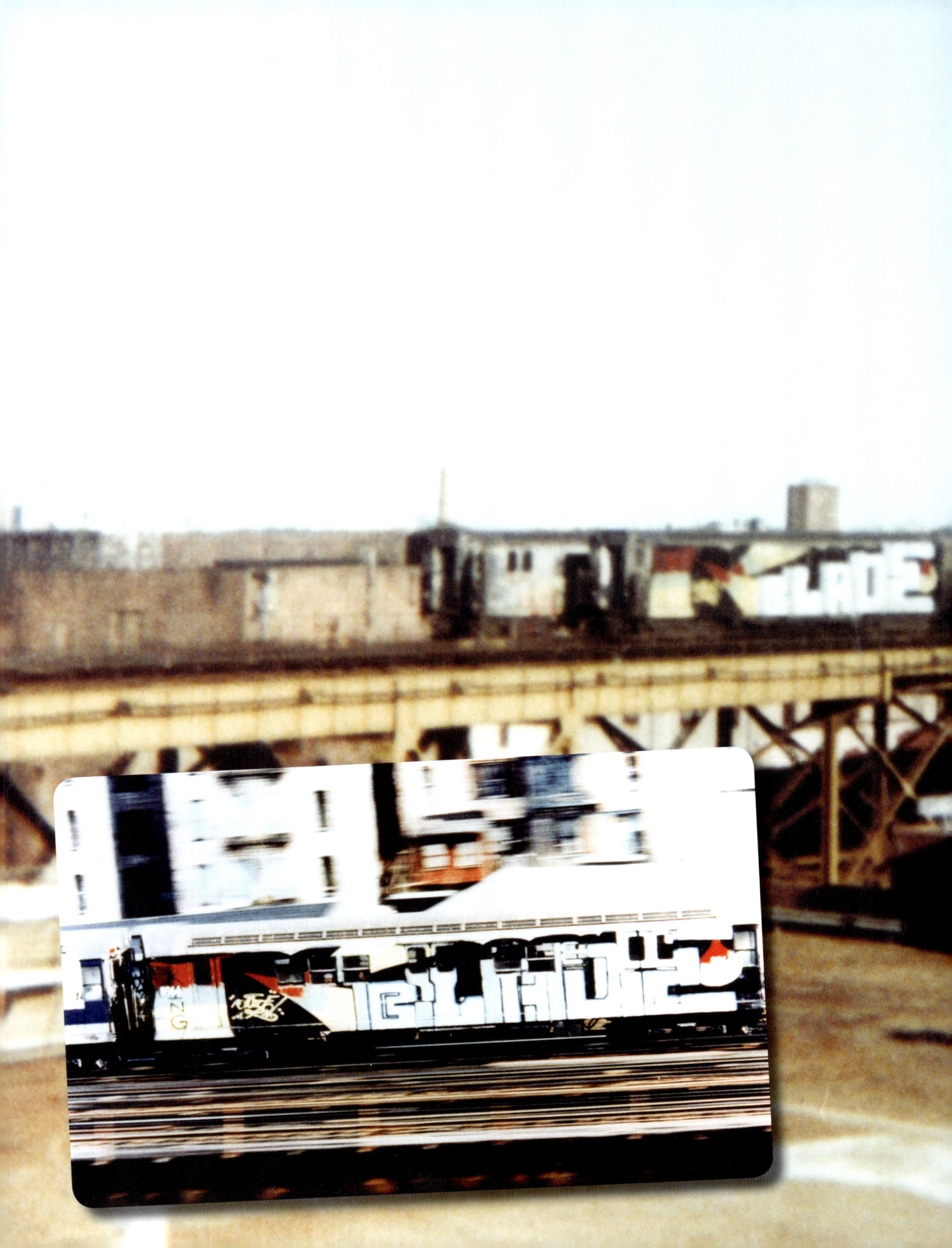
BLADE

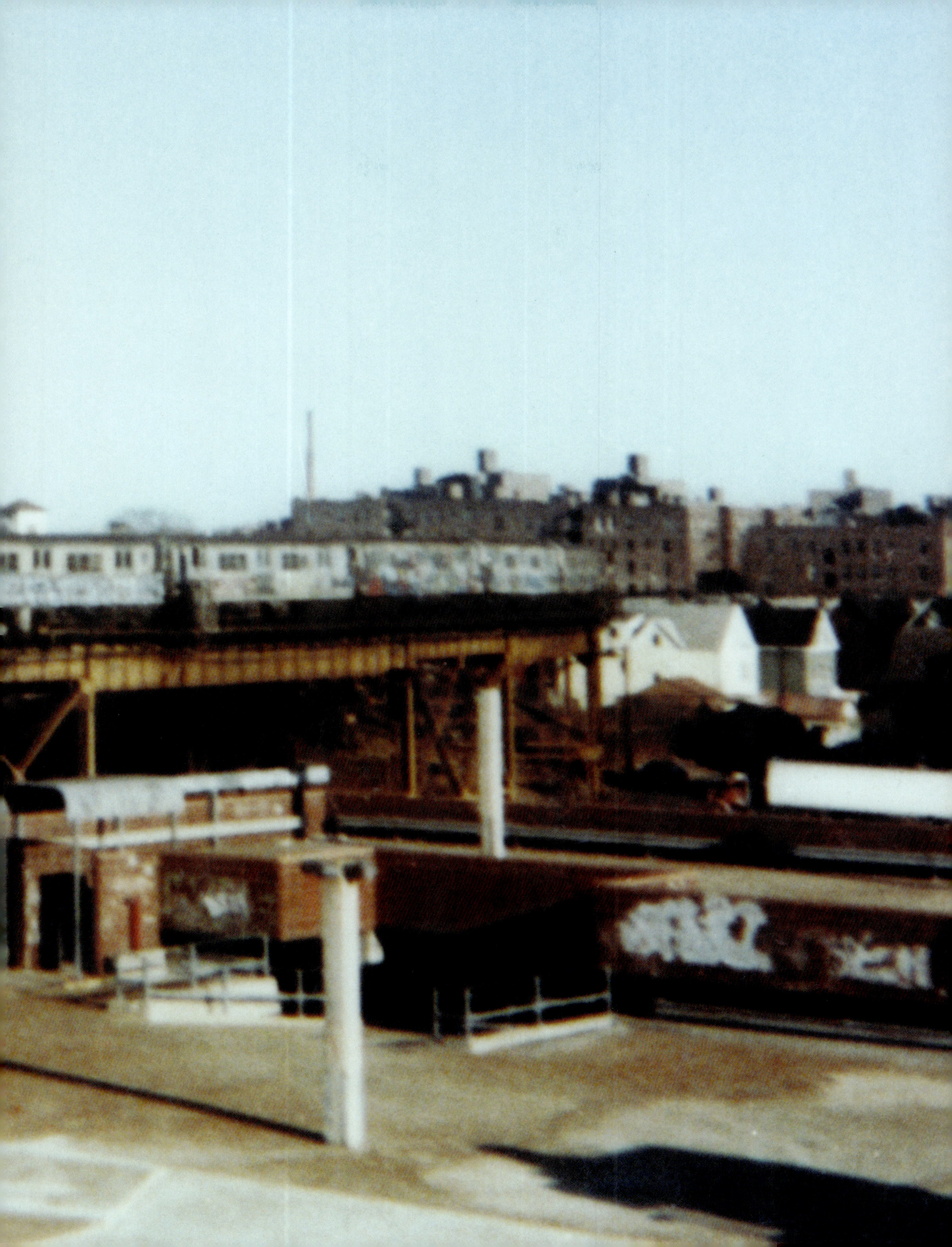

CHAPTER TEN

THE GREAT TRAINS:

1980

For a lot of writers, 1980 seemed like a big year. A lot of people say I did my best work that year—like the Walking Letter piece—even though it didn't begin that way. By then, I had been living with Dolores for several years and we had a great relationship. For the first time as an adult, I felt safe. It was a struggle financially, but that's what life is. Nobody knew where we lived, which helped a lot because there was no drama in my life and I liked it that way. The Walking Letter piece was taken from a dream I had in 1979. While I was laid up, I had a lot of time to refine the drawing.

In 1979, I painted a train with realistic mountains on it. Nobody had done that before; everybody did big cookie cutter images and filled them in. This was important, because, when I did the Walking Letters train in 1980, the background was painted realistically while the letters were painted in a more cartoonish way. The combination of the two really made it work, because it made it seem as though the letters were swinging through the sky.

The Walking Letters train was painted at the stump at Esplanade, at the same spot where I had been knocked off the train. It took all night to paint. I remember finishing it as the sun began to come up. Once COMET finished his bombing mission for the night, he helped me do the marlin blue background. We had a few scrap cans of paint left, so we did some throw-ups before we left. Although I did think it was a great train at the time, I wasn't prepared for what happened next.

Writers at the bench loved the train. But I expected that. At that point in my career, the younger guys were going to love anything I did, and if they didn't, they wouldn't tell me. Then I got some calls from older writers saying they loved the train. This meant a lot to me. SLIP 3 told me I was Picasso and the Walking Letters train would never be surpassed. The next weekend I set out to prove him wrong.

I had done a sketch a year earlier based on a dream about letters walking through portals in space, which I also wanted to put on a train. COMET and I went back to Esplanade and pulled another all-nighter to make that happen. In order for this train—much like the Walking Letters train—to work everything had to be spaced out perfectly. With window-down pieces, even if you were a little off you could paint a design on the other side of the piece to balance it out. With these whole-cars there was no room for error, but the painting conditions were awful, as they were for most writers. As there was no room to back up, I had to trust in my eight years of experience to guide me through it.

Opposite page: BLADE's Walking Letters whole-car. 1980. Photo by Martha Cooper. Following spread: Dreaming of Saratoga whole-car by BLADE. 1978. Inset photo by Henry Chalfant.

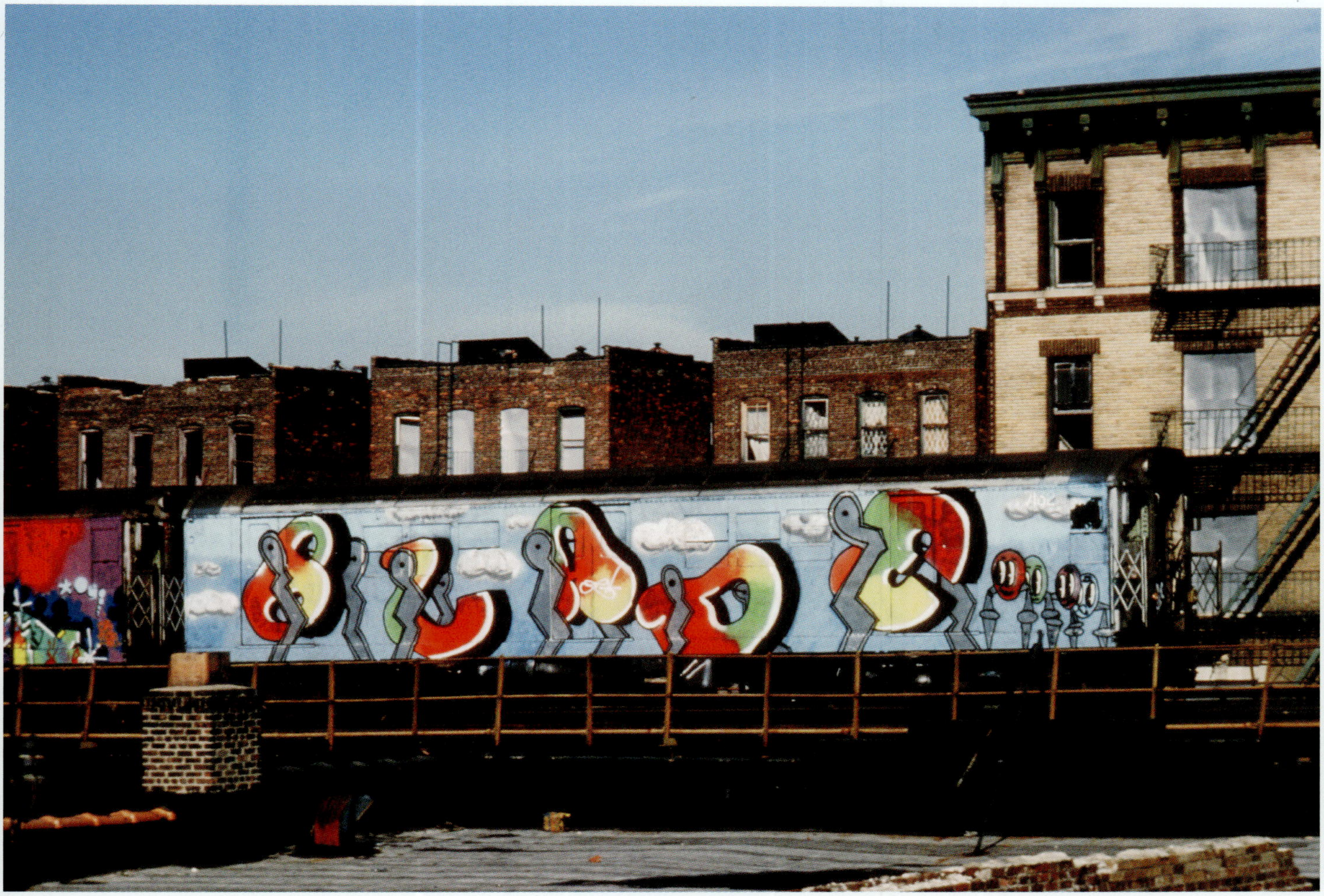

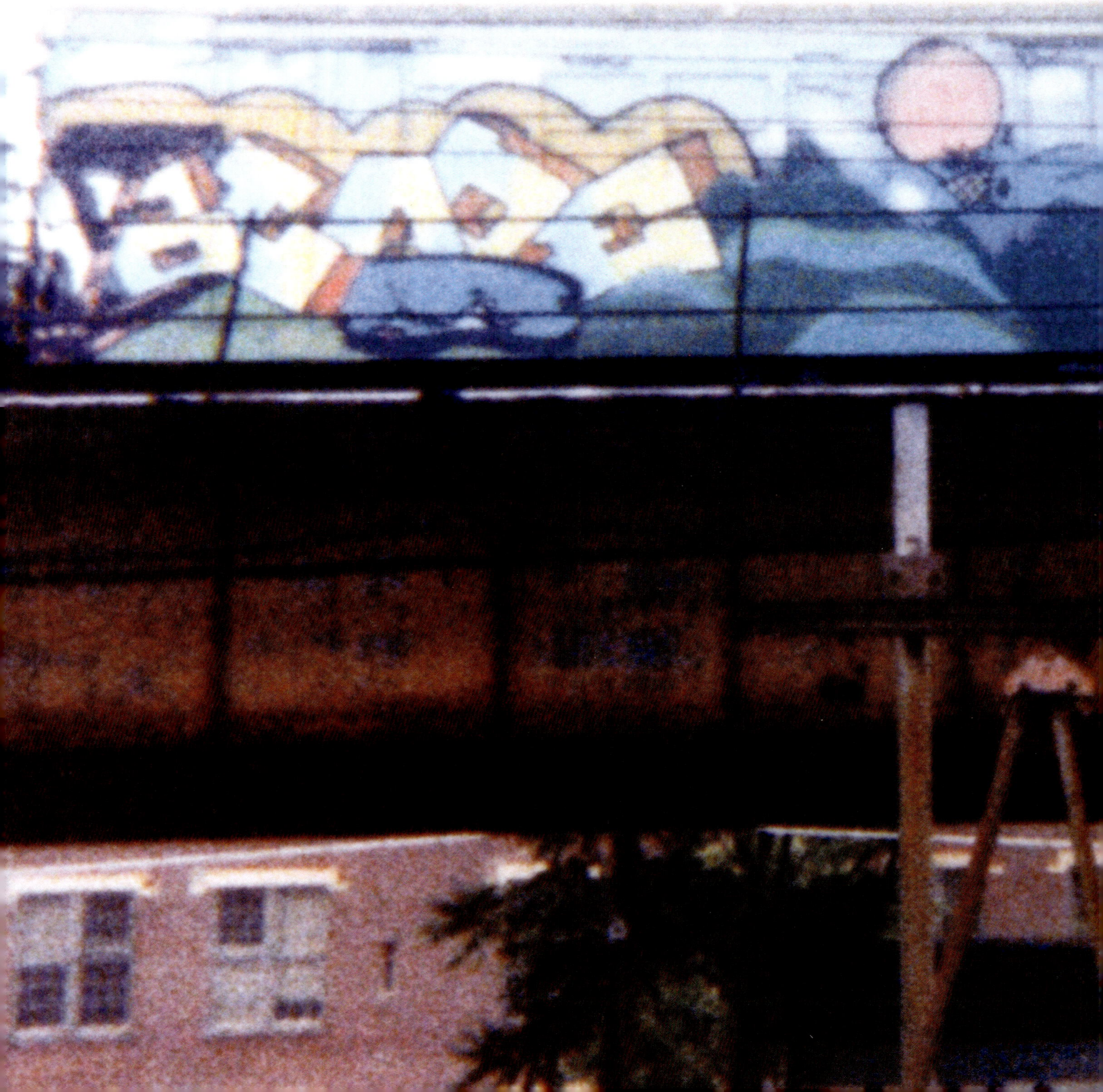

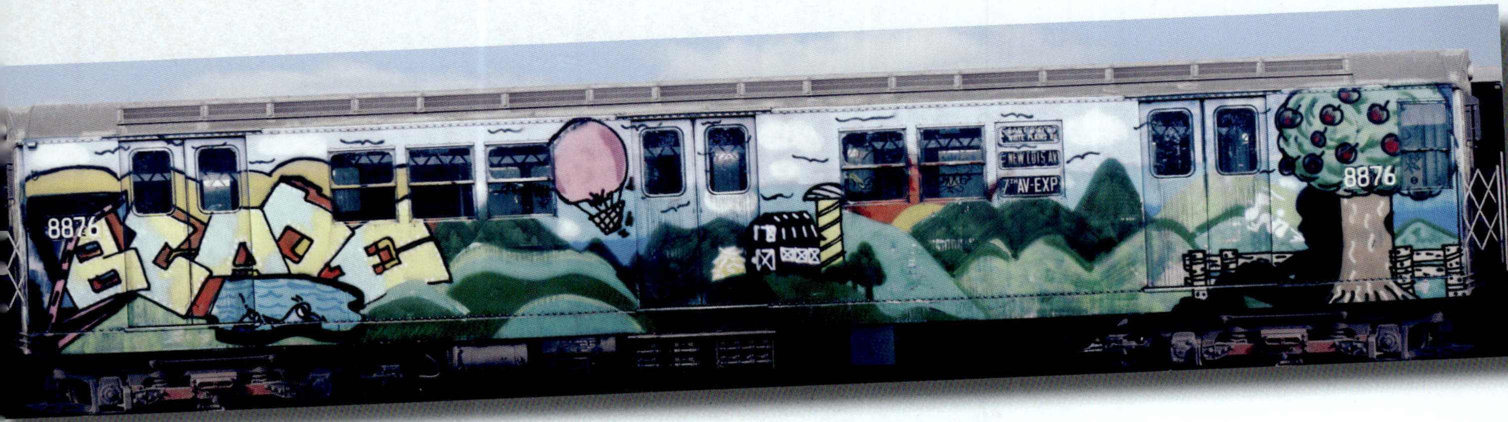
8876
NEW LOTS AV
7TH AV-EXP
8876

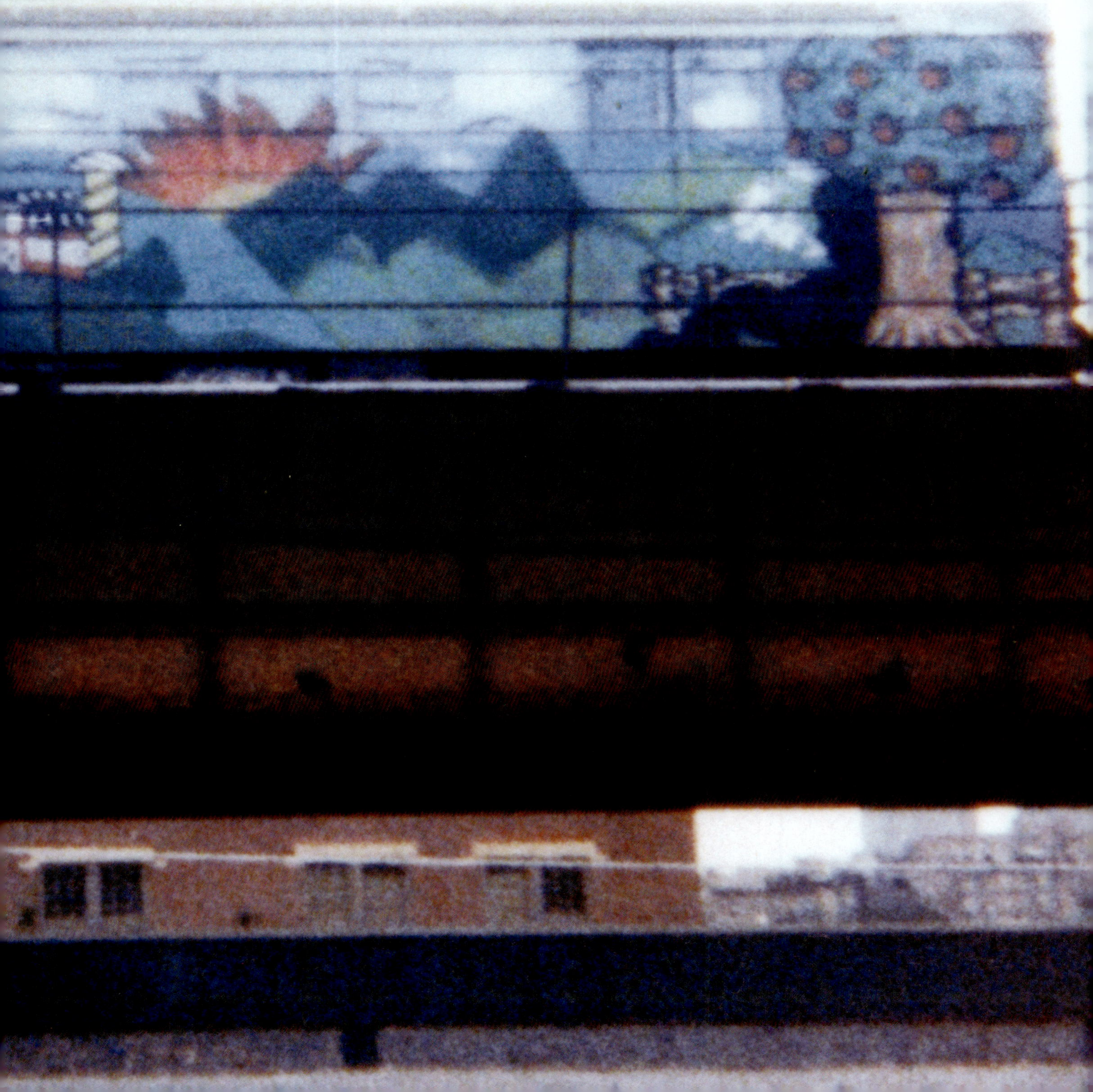

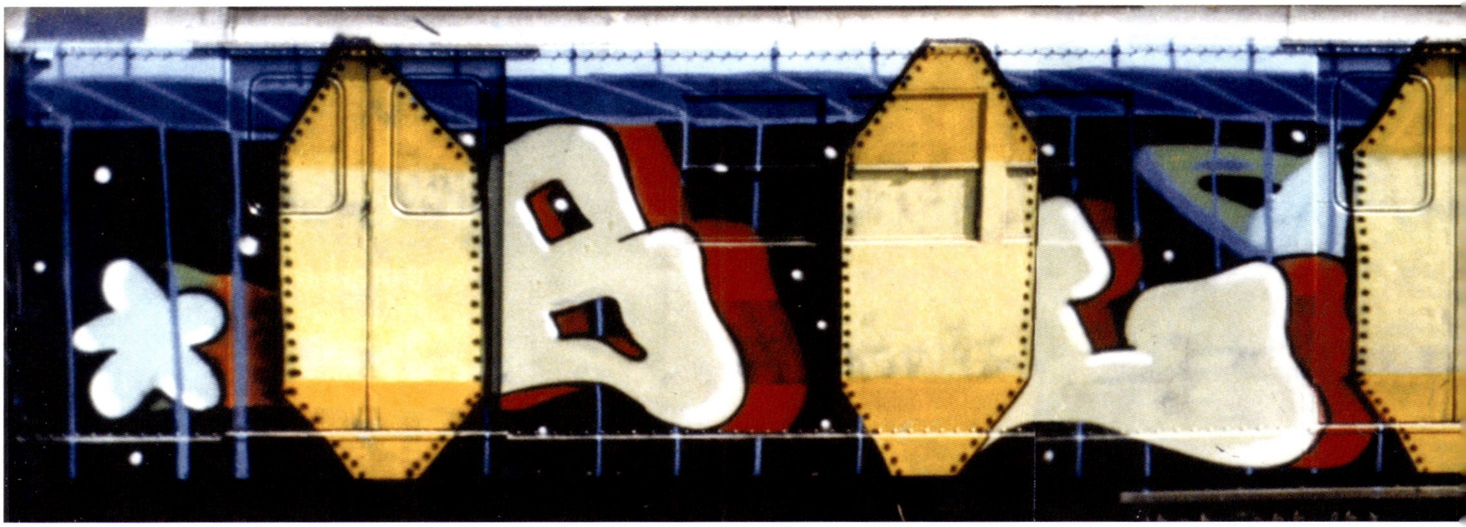

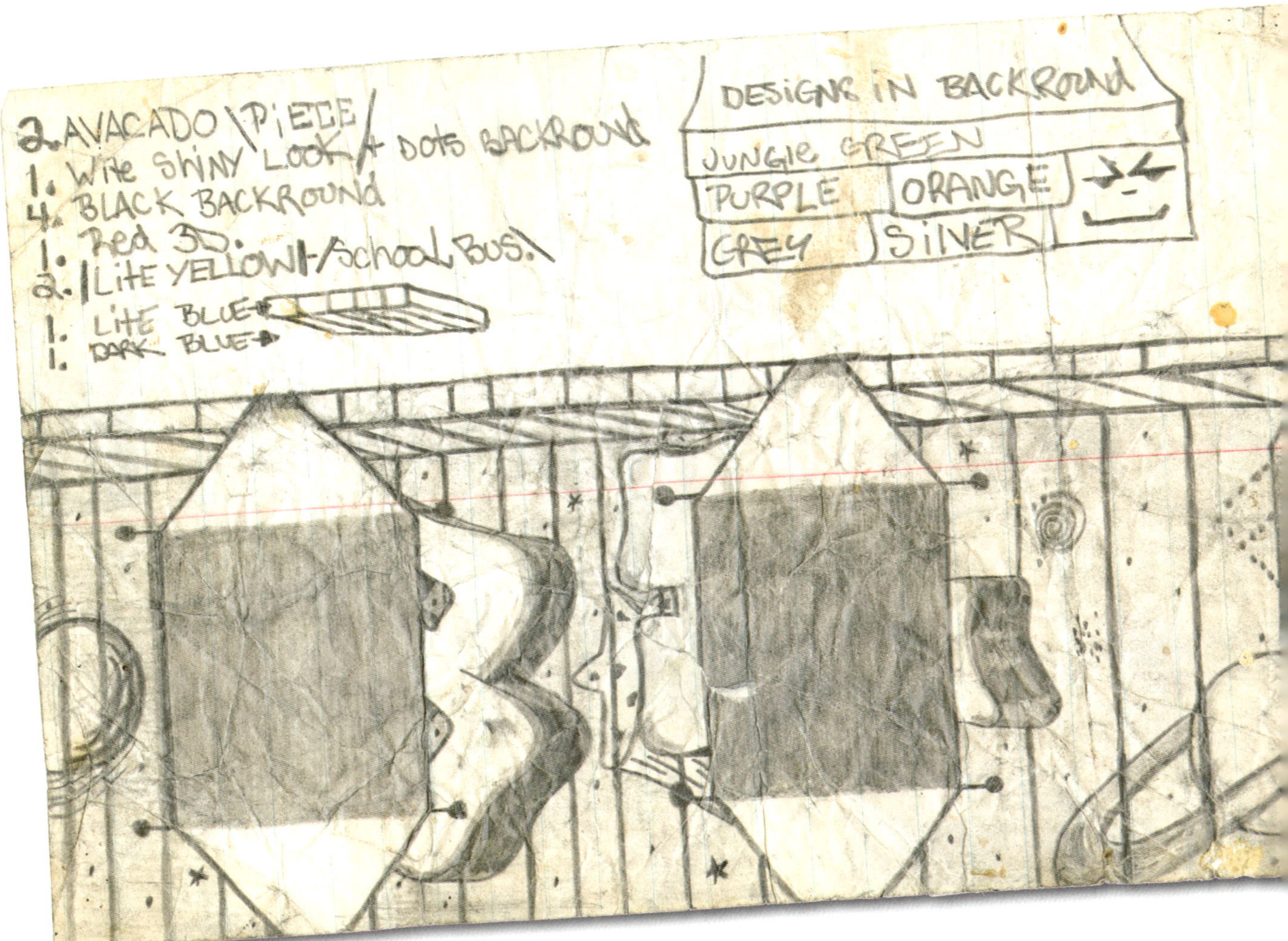

This page:
Across The Universe whole-car and sketch by BLADE. 1980. Photo by Henry Chalfant.

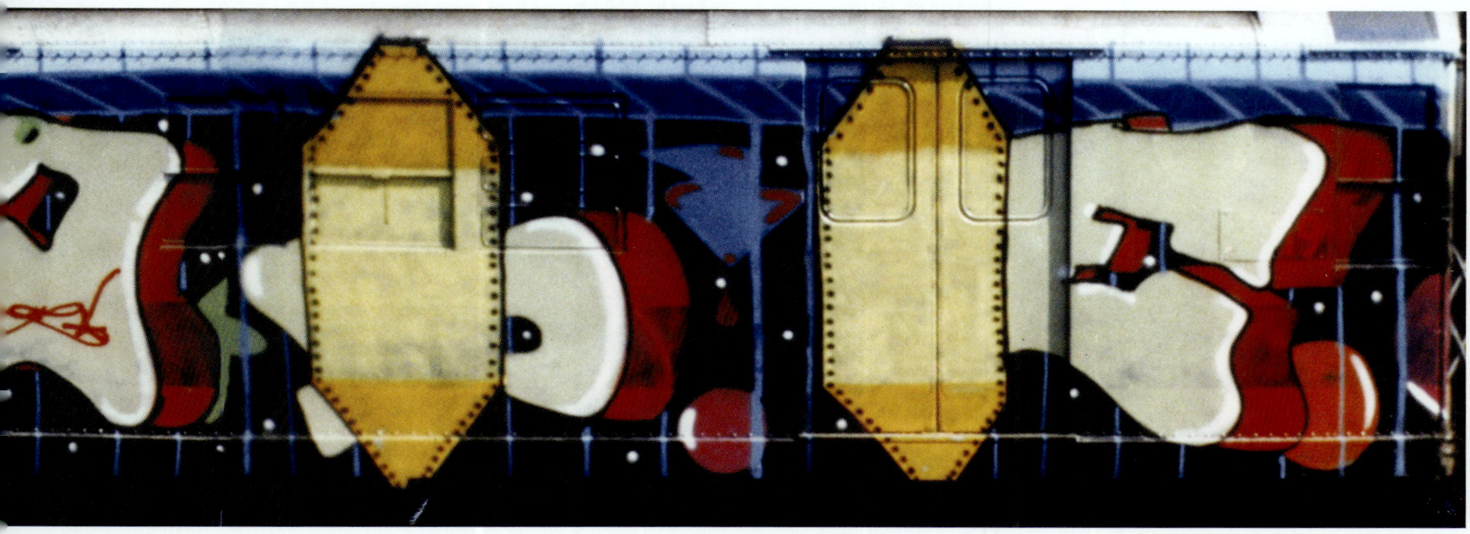

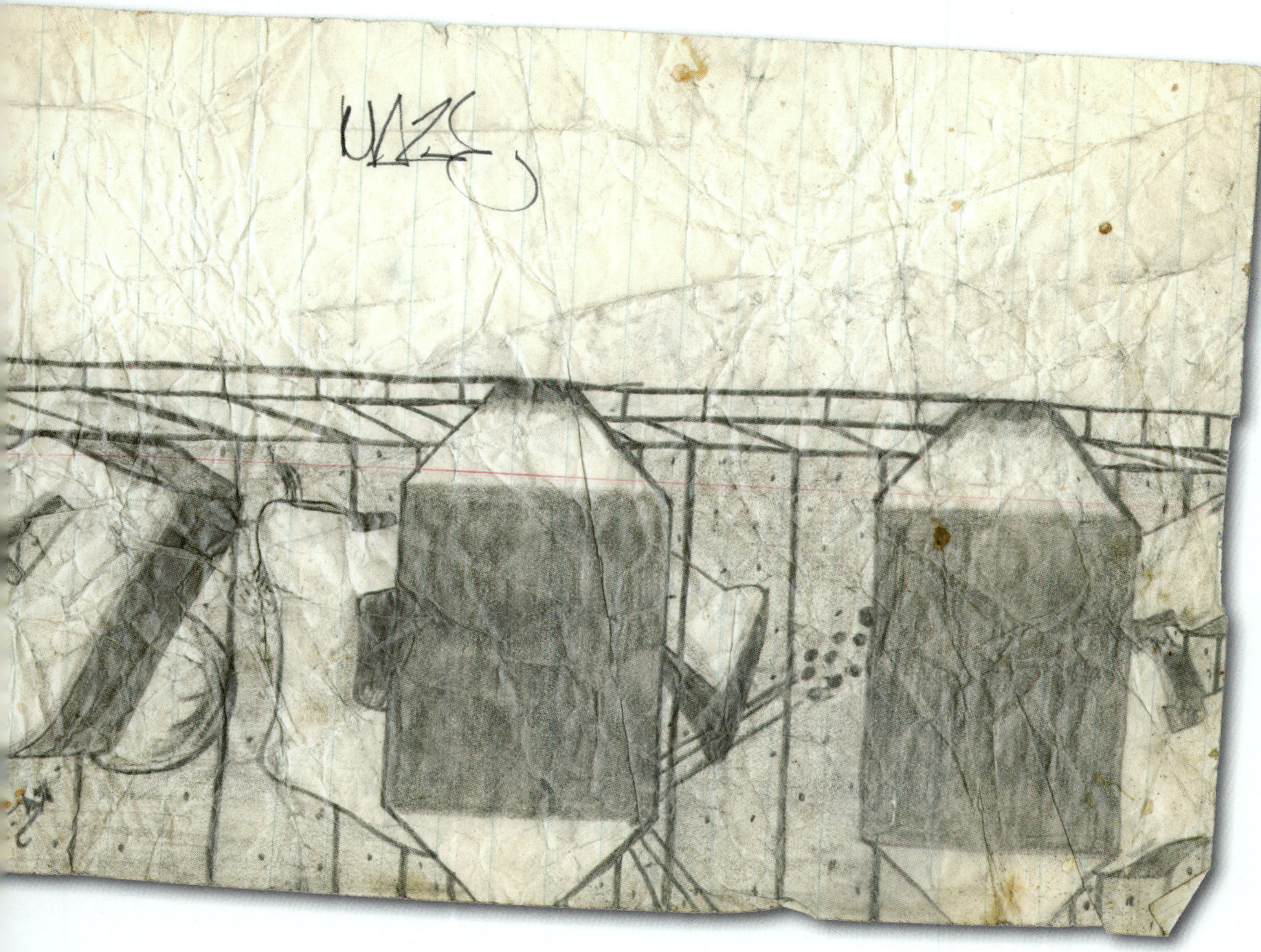

"WHEN WRITERS LIKE THAT REACH OUT TO COMPLIMENT YOU IT MEANS A LOT, AND THAT'S WHAT KEPT ME GOING. I KEPT TRYING TO OUT-DO THE LAST WHOLE-CAR."

Across the Universe also proved to be a big success, but it didn't make it into Subway Art, so it didn't gain the popularity that Walking Letters had. In fact, I was lucky that Henry Chalfant took pictures of it because it was buffed in a week. I painted it the same way I painted the Walking Letters car. The most important part of the car was that it was spaced evenly; I knew no one would care to look at the background imagery if the letters weren't spaced properly. Writers like balance. I think I put as much time into sketching the letters and the portals as I did with the fill-ins.

One of my favorite things about the car was that it could be read on so many different levels. If you were a kid you might just like the giant letters sweeping into the station—like the Walking Letters train. A lot of younger writers were wondering what the portals were. I couldn't really explain it to everybody, you either got it or you didn't. The idea of painting my name with each letter entering a different universe is a pretty layered concept. In 1980, writers like LEE were jumping back and forth between giant blockbuster whole-cars—used to get up—and more thought-provoking cars like Doomsday, or Heaven is Life / Earth is Hell. Those cars you had to study. I wanted people to study my whole-cars—and they did. Writers were taking photos of trains and staring at the pictures, talking about them with friends.

A few days after painting that train, I got a call from my old friend BILLY 167, one of the greatest style writers ever. BILLY had disappeared from the graffiti scene and had developed an addiction to heroin; I rarely heard from him. BILLY 167 complimented me on both cars. When writers like that reach out to compliment you it means a lot, and that's what kept me going. I kept trying to out-do the last whole-car.

Some trains from that year were held up because I didn't have the right color. A famous example of that is the In and Out train—a train that most people refer to as The Scream, because of its seeming resemblance to the painting by Edvard Munch. I needed to rack up a one-pound can of cascade green for that train, and it couldn't be any other color. It took a year to finally get that paint. The moment I did, I was off to Esplanade. MAZE was with me that night, trying to do a top-to-bottom, but he was too drunk to finish. The In and Out train actually had nothing to do with The Scream, rather it was my vision of a passenger doing a double-take as my train pulled in to the station.

Opposite page:
The In and Out whole-car and sketches. 1980. Photo © by Martha Cooper.

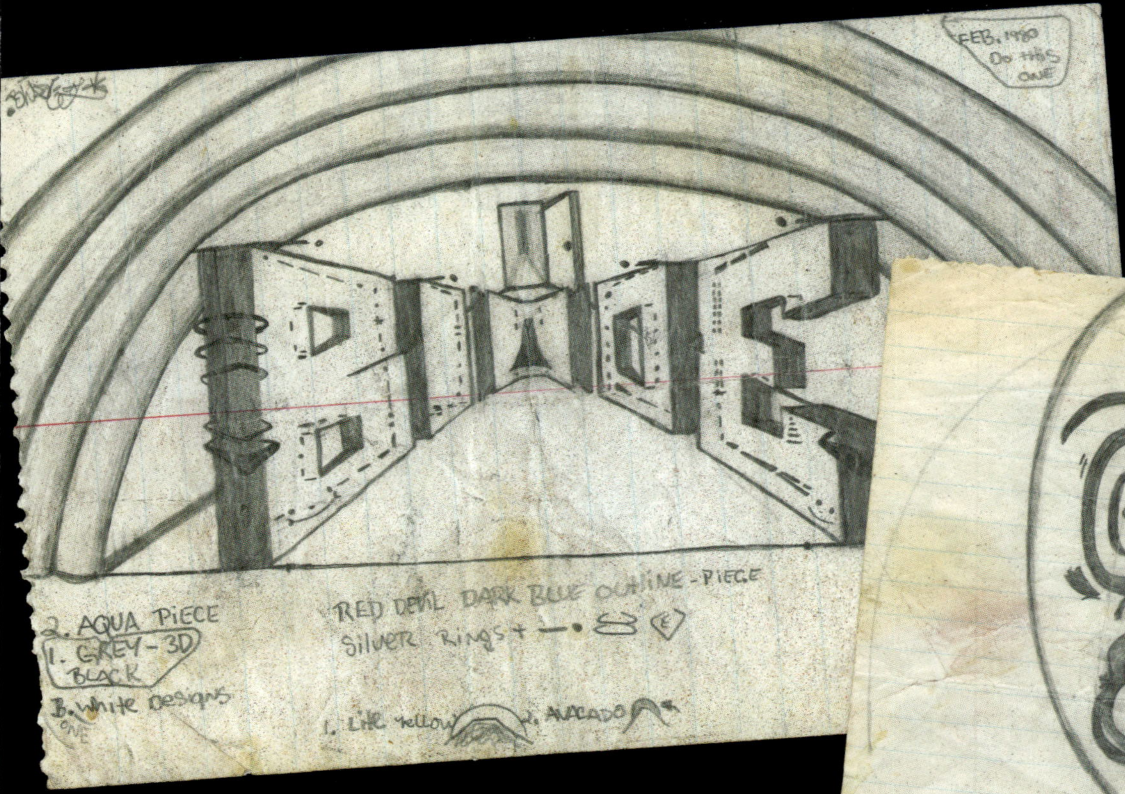
FEB. 1980 Do this one
2. AQUA PIECE
1. GREY-3D BLACK
B. White Designs
RED DEVIL DARK BLUE OUTLINE-PIECE
Silver Rings
1. Lite Yellow
2. AVACADO

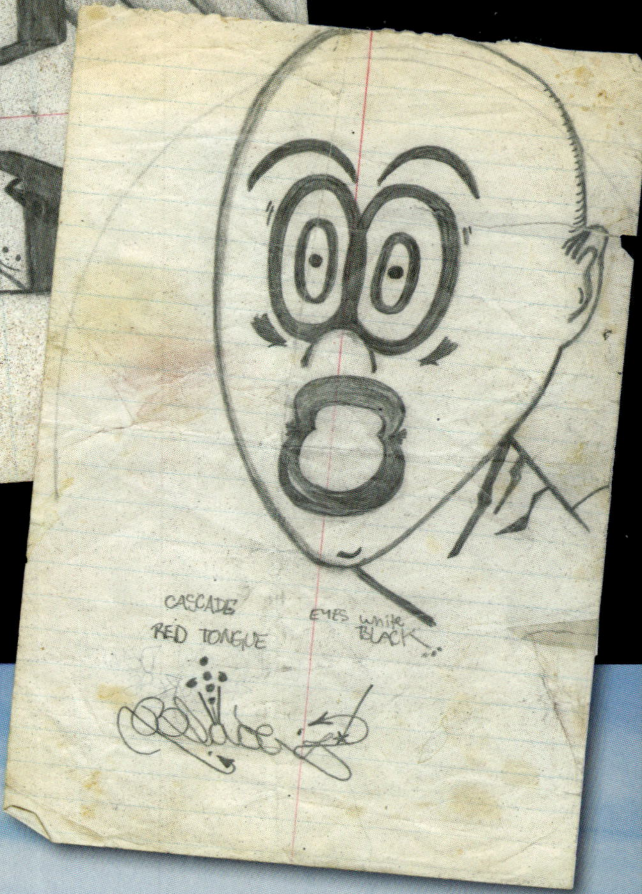
CASCADE
RED TONGUE
EYES White BLACK

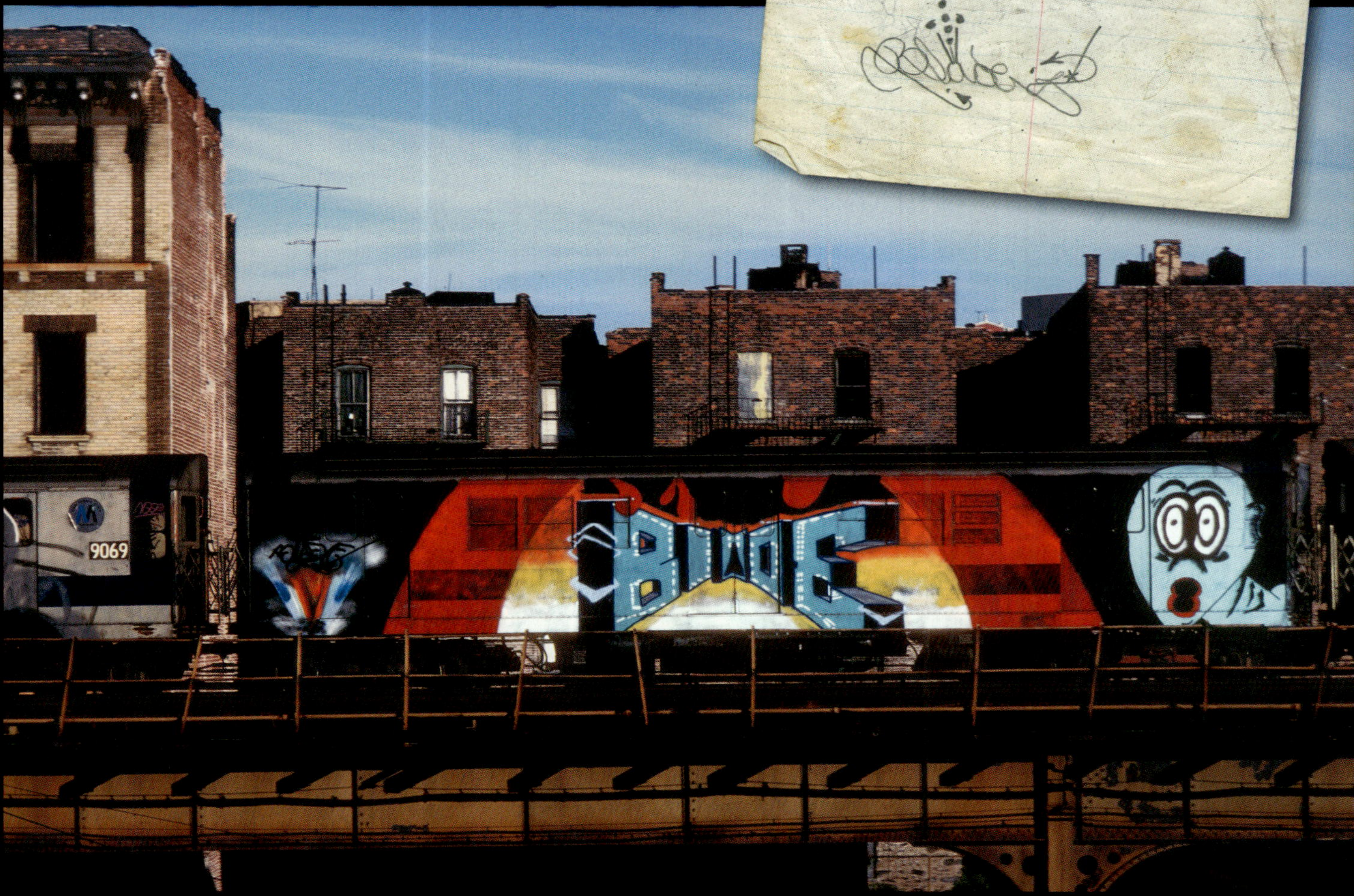
9069

CHAPTER ELEVEN

EXITING GRAFFITI

1981–1982

In 1980, I met Henry Chalfant and Martha Cooper for the first time. Marty was a photojournalist for the *New York Post*, who got hooked on shooting graffiti. The more photographs she took, the more she kept seeing my name up, until finally someone set up a meeting with us. I remember going to her studio on 103rd Street and West End Avenue and viewing some of the slides she took. They were great pictures that showed off the trains the way I wanted them to be seen—with the city as part of the picture. It was inspiring for me to look at my work in this context.

Henry Chalfant worked differently. He'd take eight shots of one car and then put them together so you only saw the art. I liked that as well, although it's harder to hide my mistakes in pictures like these. I also worried his portfolio could land me in jail. I didn't hang out at Henry's studio much, because of all the kids there claiming to be king of the line. They were usually sixteen or seventeen years old. I was ancient at twenty-three. How could you be king of the line with thirty pieces? I had just done my five thousandth car that year, and so it was a bit annoying. There was also a heavy presence of hip-hop at Henry's studio, where break-dancers were often practicing moves. Little did I know that hip-hop and graffiti would become linked, which made no sense then and makes no sense now. I never listened to rap music, and in my opinion graffiti had nothing to do with that scene.

The *Village Voice* ran an article on graffiti in December of 1980. They selected eight of Henry Chalfant's best pictures to put in as a two-page color centerfold, which is something the *Village Voice* had never done before. Of the eight trains published, one of them was mine—not a bad ratio. The article itself was more about the new generation of writers coming up, guys like CRASH and ZEPHYR who deserved the recognition.

CRASH had already been asked to curate a show in the South Bronx at a gallery called Fashion MODA. The artists in that show quickly went on to other gallery shows, and writers started making money from their canvasses. I wasn't a part of those shows because I was twenty-three years old. CRASH was nineteen and he wanted to work with his peers. I knew these things were happening, but I didn't care, I certainly wasn't going to push myself on anybody. I had to go to work, rack paint, and bomb trains.

In 1980, I started parking cars for a garage on the upper east side of Manhattan. After parking cars for one year at Square Parking, I finally got to buy my own. My dad sold me his 1972 Thunderbird for one thousand dollars and life was about to get much easier. COMET and I were still bombing, only now we'd take the car to the lay-ups. I also drove the car to work in Manhattan every day. I had a beautiful girlfriend, a good job, and an apartment.

Opposite page:
BLADE meets Henry Chalfant and Martha Cooper. Circa 1981.

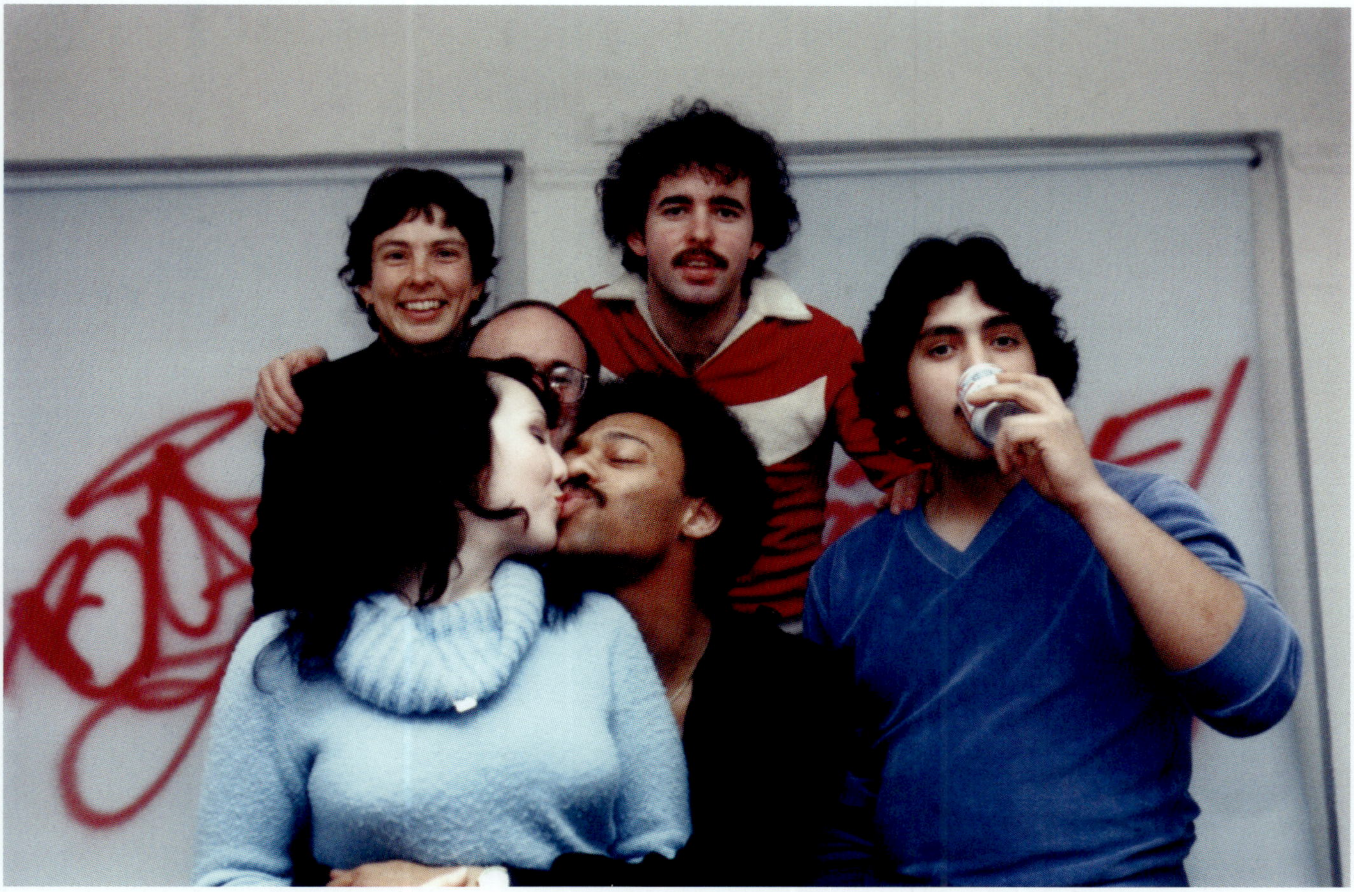

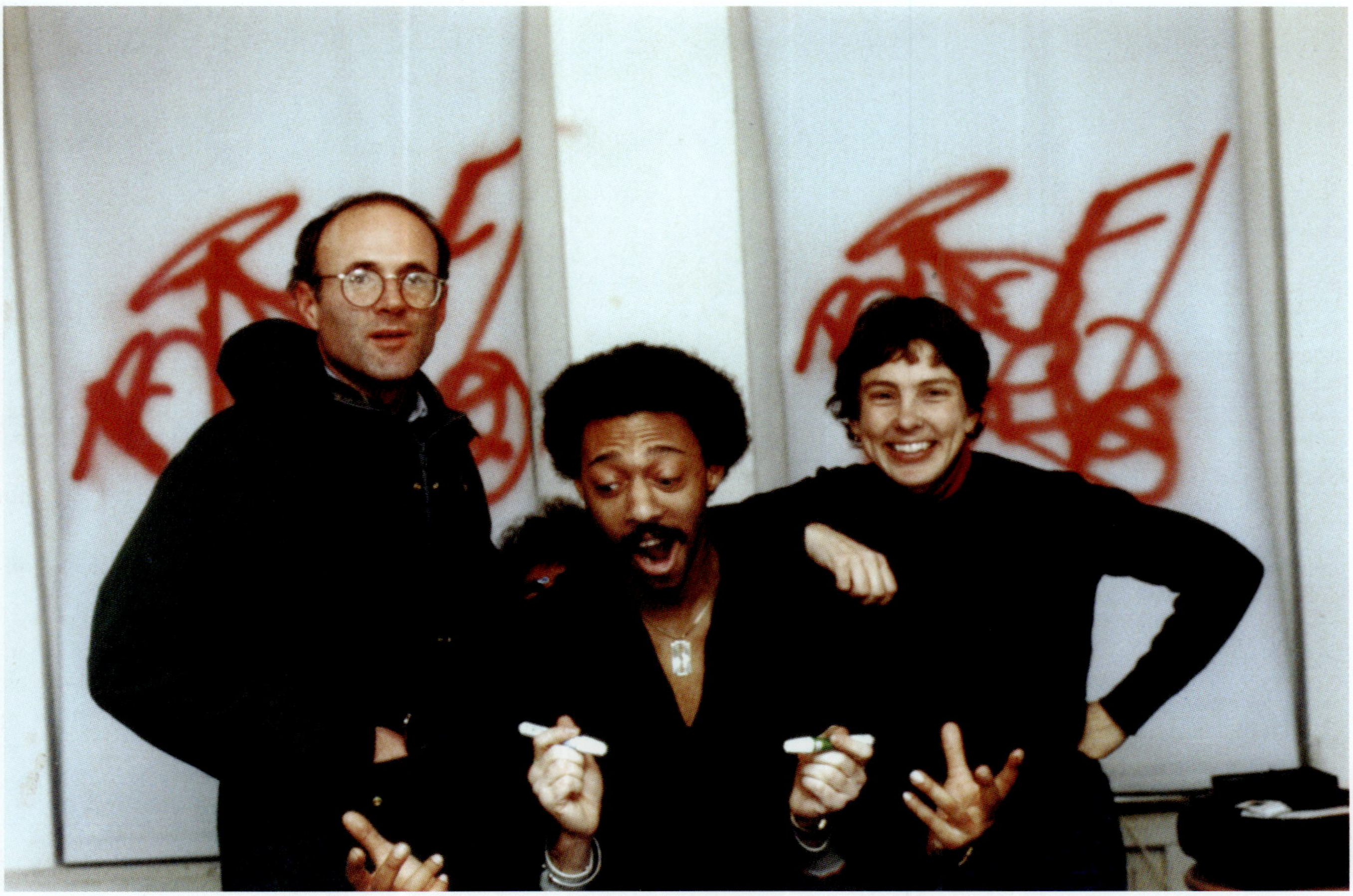

Since I wasn't taking the train to work, I was missing out on who was hitting the insides. One day, while benching trains, I got on one of them and rode it to 180th Street. The interiors were bombed and one name stood out from the others: SEEN TC5.

There were two SEENS back then, LIL SEEN and SEEN UA; LIL SEEN did this tag. I wondered, who put him in the crew? When I asked COMET about it, he said it was him. Not only did COMET put LIL SEEN in the crew, but also he gave him recruiting power. COMET described LIL SEEN to me: a short black kid of fifteen or sixteen years old who hangs out at Parkside, waiting in line for the courts. Originally I was against the idea, probably because I hadn't been consulted. But then I got to know LIL SEEN a bit and I saw how talented he was. Within a short period of time, he put down a number of young writers including LADY PINK, DOC, DOZE, and WEB. Each of the writers SEEN picked was talented and carved out a nice career. Eventually they turned their group into THE COOL 5 in order to differentiate between the two crews.

In the summer of 1982, while cruising around Bronx Park East station, COMET and I saw IZ, MIN, and SACH. COMET leapt out of my car while it was still moving and chased IZ, who dropped his paint while running away, which of course we scooped up. Everyone else stood around, paralyzed with fear. That night, COMET and I used up all of IZ's paint. COMET did a two-man whole-car which we dedicated to IZ.

Years later, in 1992, I met IZ at QUIK's house. He told me his side of the story and I forgave him, because it seems as though he was just put into an unfortunate situation by that toy CAZ. When COMET came over to QUIK's house, IZ got real nervous, but I told COMET what happened; we let it go at that. After all, we were all adults at that point. Years later, when IZ ran the Phun Factory, he'd go out of his way to save the best walls for me to paint on.

I can't remember there ever being a graffiti war before. Sometimes I got crossed out, but that was rare. IN crossed me out once because I went over one of his throw-ups. He had those stupid things on every car, so there was no way to avoid it. I told him that. The cops crossed me out; they even left their badge numbers with the paint. DEATH didn't cross people out, but he went over them, which is the same thing. The one person he loved going over was IN, which was fine with me. I remember some of the TOP crew writers going over the MG BOYS. Some of these things you actually saw and some you just heard about.

One time, in 1977, un-uniformed cops at Esplanade—where we were doing a green top-to-bottom—chased COMET and me. COMET and I ran out of there, and then the cops wrote their badge numbers and the words "bang, bang, bang!" through our names. Once the chase was over, we went to Martin's Paint and racked up a can of gloss white. Later that night, we went back to Esplanade and I outlined our pieces. On it I wrote, "Fuck you, cops!" and "I banged your mothers." Around that same time, THE CROSSOUTS were going over people. We were sure they were cops.

After 1980, a year when some of the best whole-cars were painted, the train lines began to change. There were a lot more throw-ups being done and people started going over each other more and more. I didn't like throw-ups. And this began to change my opinion of the graffiti movement. It seemed as though the trains were starting to look dirty. After a decade of painting, I was finally beginning to slow down.

I started hitting trains in 1972 and I watched as hits turned into masterpieces. The masterpieces developed a 3-D look, with clouds unifying the names. Top-to-bottoms started as early as 1972 and whole-cars started showing up shortly after that. Cartoon whole-cars started in 1974. CAINE and LEE took them to the next level in the next few years. Everything was about moving forward. In 1980 graffiti seemed to reach its peak. And in 1982 it seemed to be going backwards. It was discouraging.

Opposite page: Top: BLADE calling out writers who have dissed him. Circa 1978.
Bottom: COMET and DEATH, with COMET dissed by the Vandal Squad. Circa 1974.

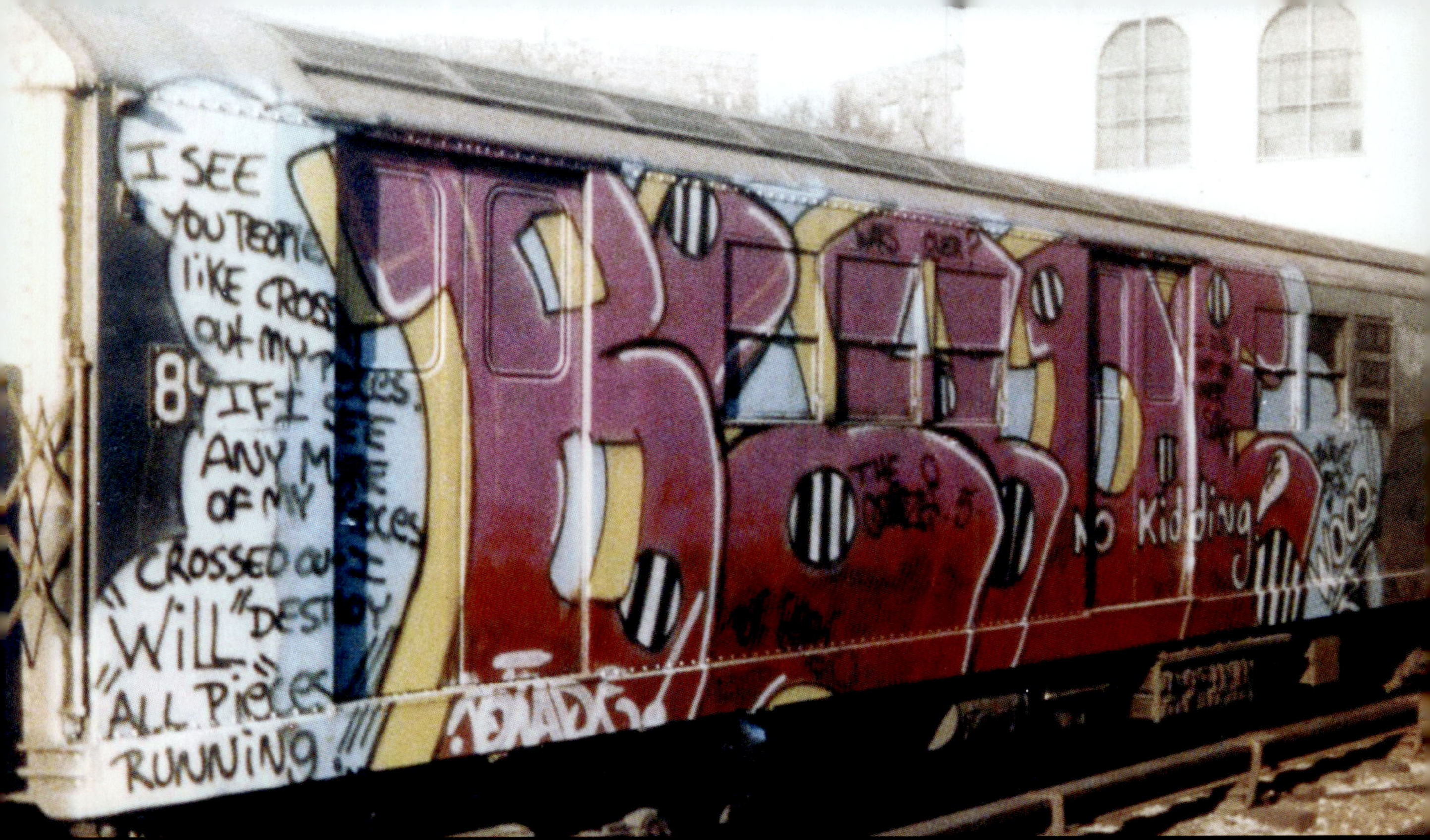
I SEE
YOU PEOPLE
LIKE CROSS
ANY
OF MY
CROSSED
"WILL"
"ALL PIECES
RUNNING
NO Kidding

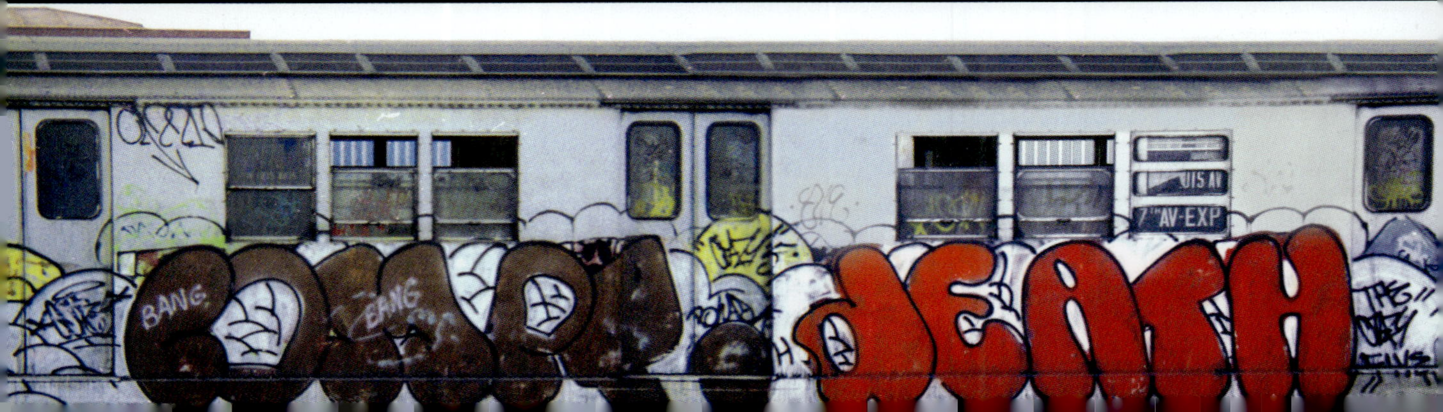
7th AV-EXP
BANG
BANG

CHAPTER TWELVE

THE ART WORLD

1983–1985

In 1980, a number of writers started to enter the art world. Some were truly artists and in it for the long term, whereas others were just out to make a fast buck. I was on the fence, because I wasn't sure if I wanted to paint on canvas—and nobody was asking me to. That changed a few years later, when Yaki Kornblit asked Henry Chalfant who the best writers were and Henry mentioned my name and then to see if I was interested. Yaki was one of the top gallery people in Amsterdam, the Netherlands; he ran a gallery that bore his name. We had an initial meeting at Henry's studio to size each other up, then shortly after we met at SEEN's house, where SEEN's mom cooked us an amazing Italian dinner. We sat around the table talking about our paintings on trains and what we might do on canvas.

Yaki asked us to do a series of paintings for him to show in Europe and he promised us one show per year. This was still more Dolores's dream than mine, because to her it meant I would quit writing and dedicate myself to painting. It was not only bad enough that I had to squeeze my ninety-foot-long concepts into 8-foot canvasses, but also I wasn't ready to quit writing. However, now twenty-five years old, I could make more money from one canvas than I could parking cars for three months.

I spoke to Henry Chalfant and Marty Cooper about the transition to canvas. Their attitude was, "you'll never know until you try it." Marty went so far as to buy me my first roll of canvas. She would eventually buy my first painting. I watched as other writers did this in order to fit into the art world, and the one thing I knew about painting canvasses was that I was not going to abandon my name. It would be a long time before I'd paint a purely abstract work. All of the first paintings had the name BLADE in them. Yaki showed them in his gallery and people bought them. Suddenly I was swept up in the gallery world, shaking hands and signing autographs. With the first five thousand gilders, Dolores and I bought an apartment in Co-op City.

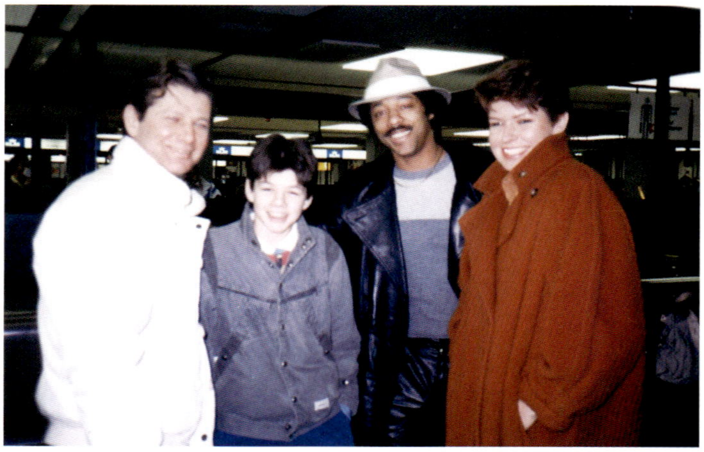

This page: Yaki Kornblitt and family pick BLADE up at the Amsterdam airport. 1986. Opposite page: BLADE, with Dolores, stuffs a canvas bought by Martha Cooper, at Pearl Paint, in his car. 1982. BLADE paints his first canvas. 1982. Photos © by Martha Cooper.

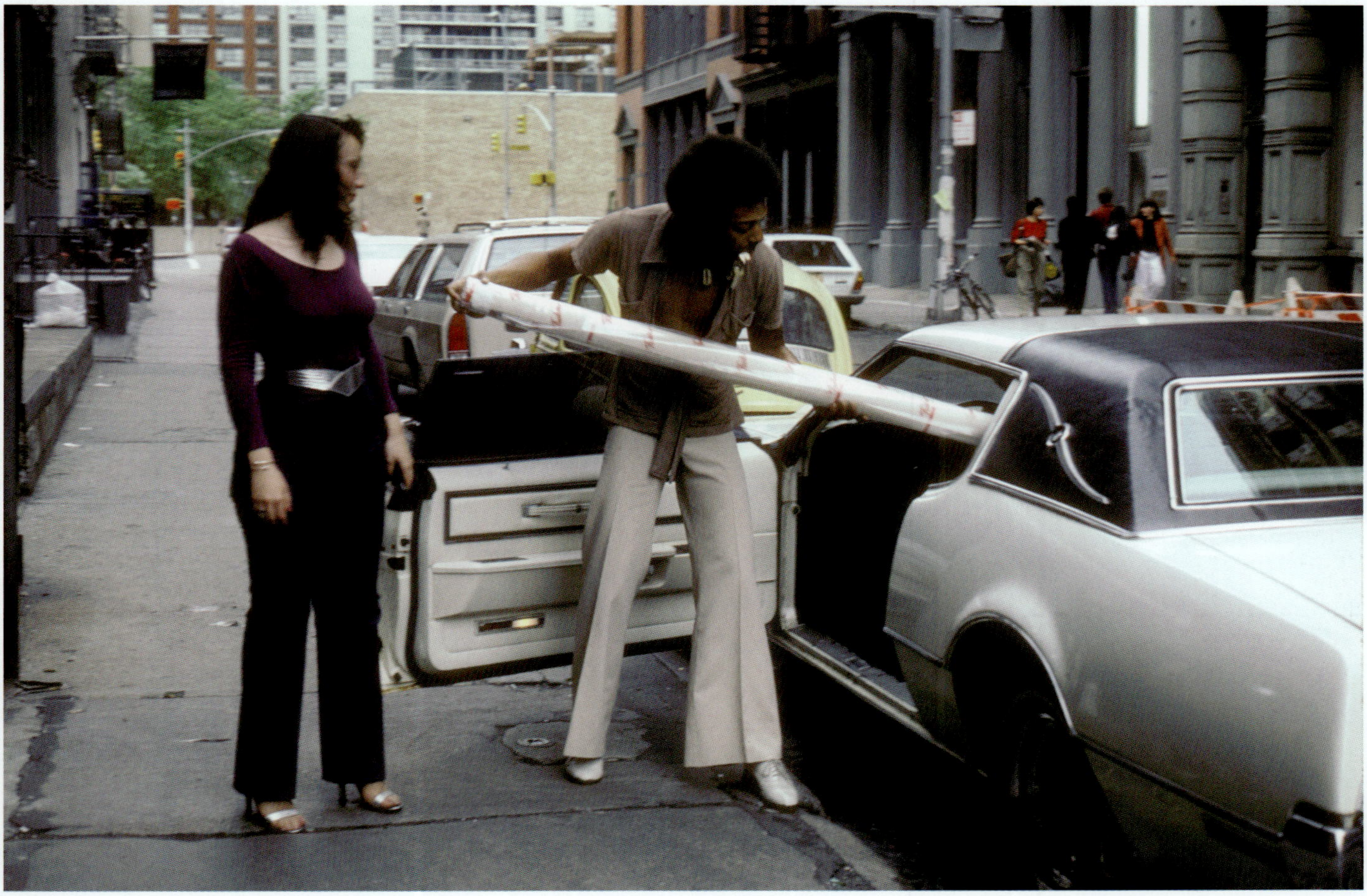

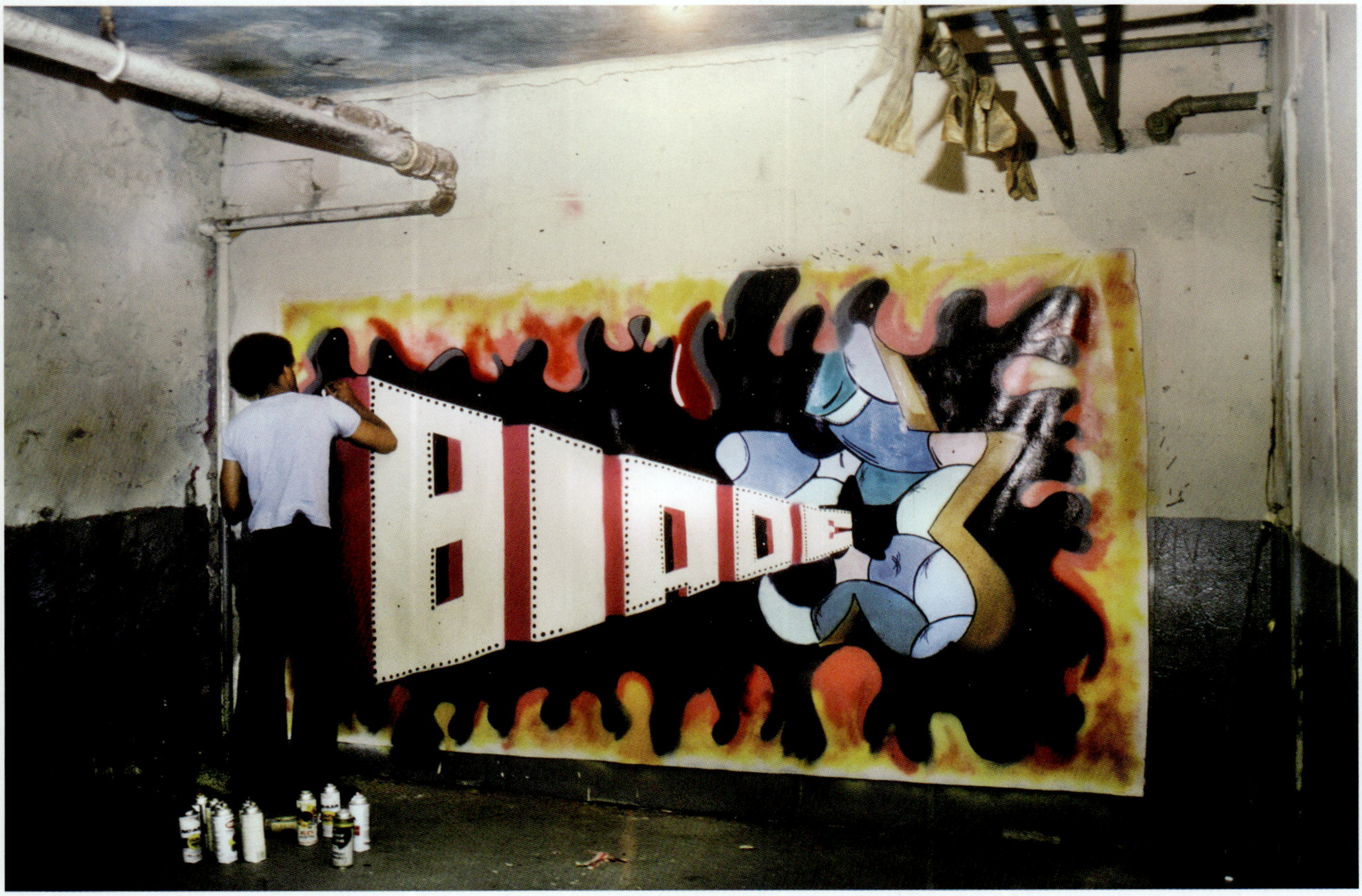

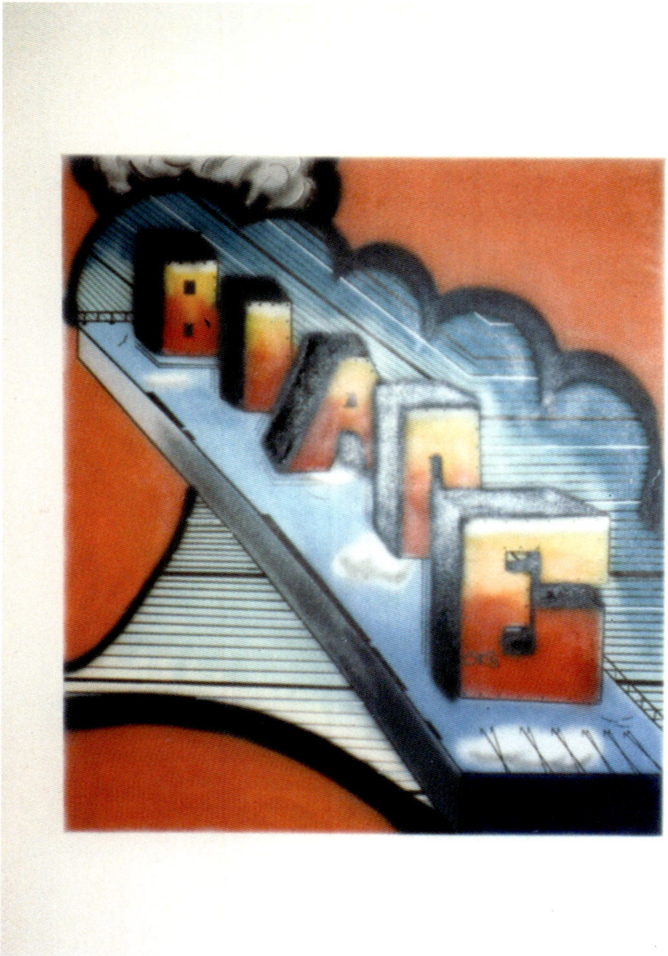

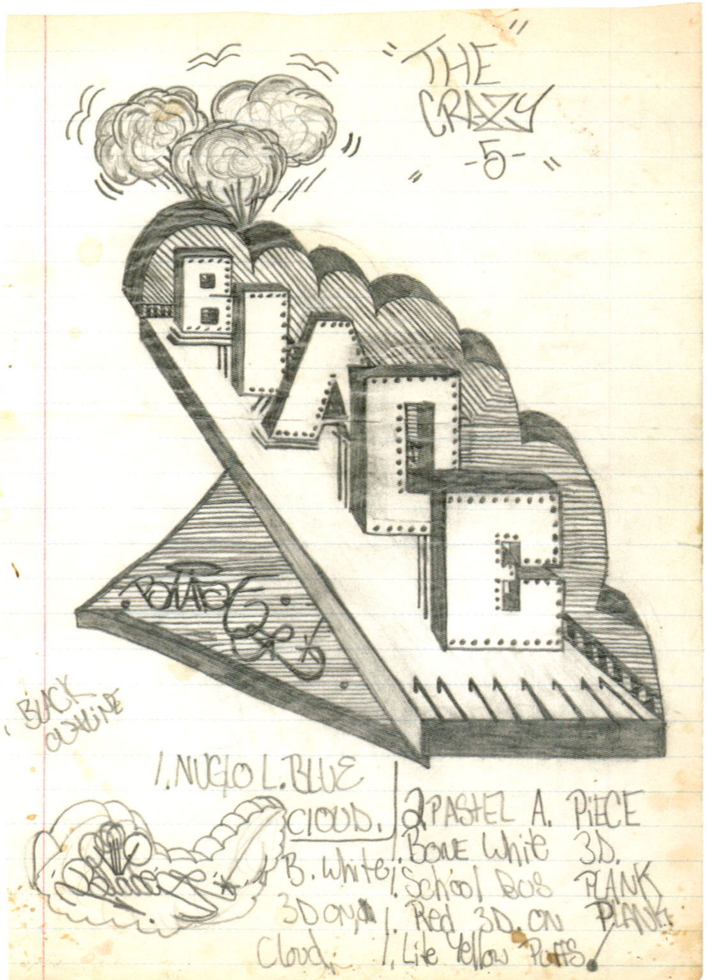

This page: Early BLADE canvas and sketch. Circa 1982.
Opposite page: Top: BLADE at his first solo show in New York City.
Bottom: Sketch for the painting. 1984.

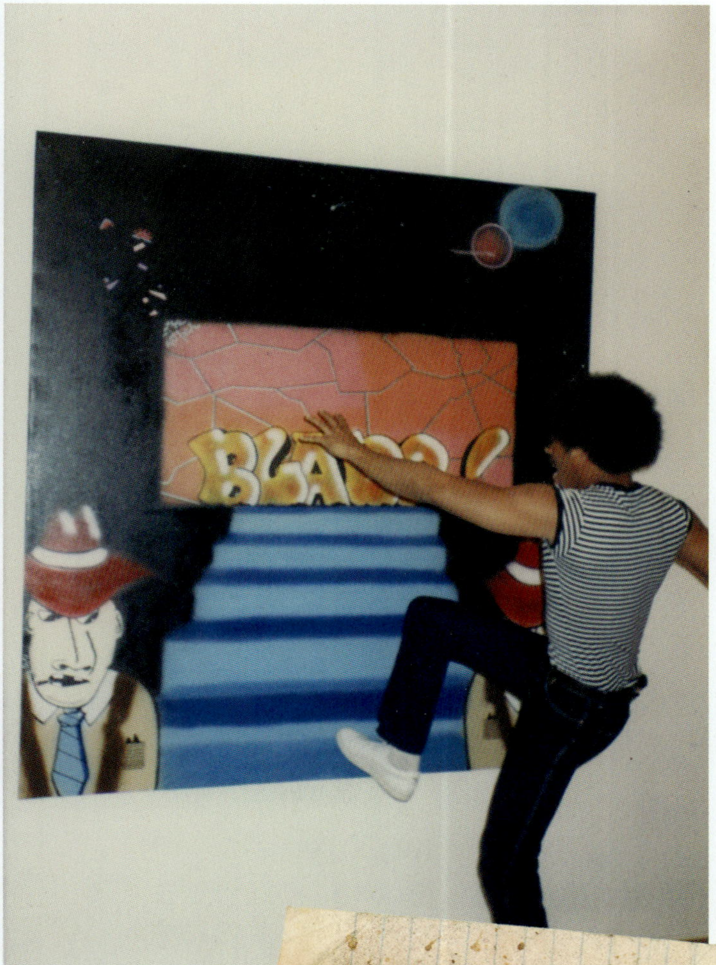

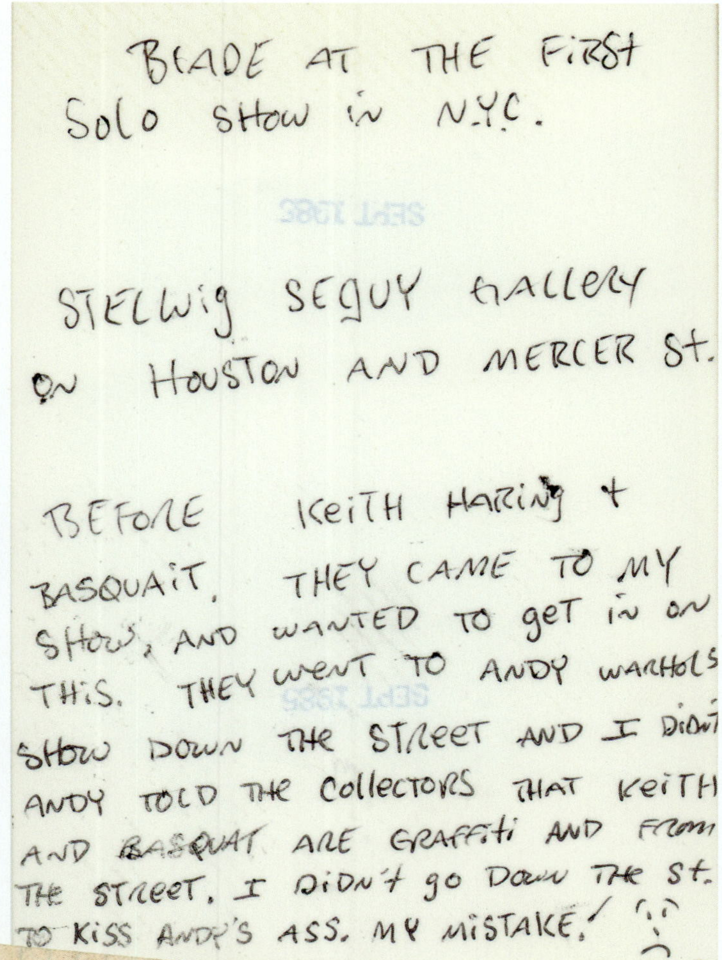

BLADE AT THE FIRST SOLO SHOW IN N.Y.C.

STELWIG SEGUY GALLERY ON HOUSTON AND MERCER ST.

BEFORE KEITH HARING + BASQUAIT. THEY CAME TO MY SHOW, AND WANTED TO GET IN ON THIS. THEY WENT TO ANDY WARHOLS SHOW DOWN THE STREET AND I DIDN'T ANDY TOLD THE COLLECTORS THAT KEITH AND ~~BASQUAT~~ ARE GRAFFITI AND FROM THE STREET. I DIDN'T GO DOWN THE ST. TO KISS ANDY'S ASS. MY MISTAKE!

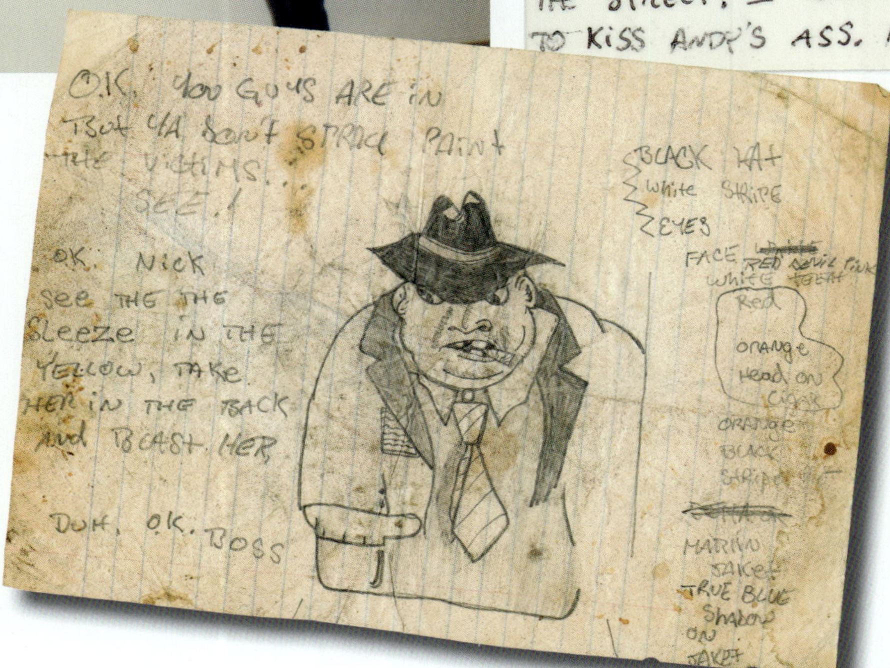

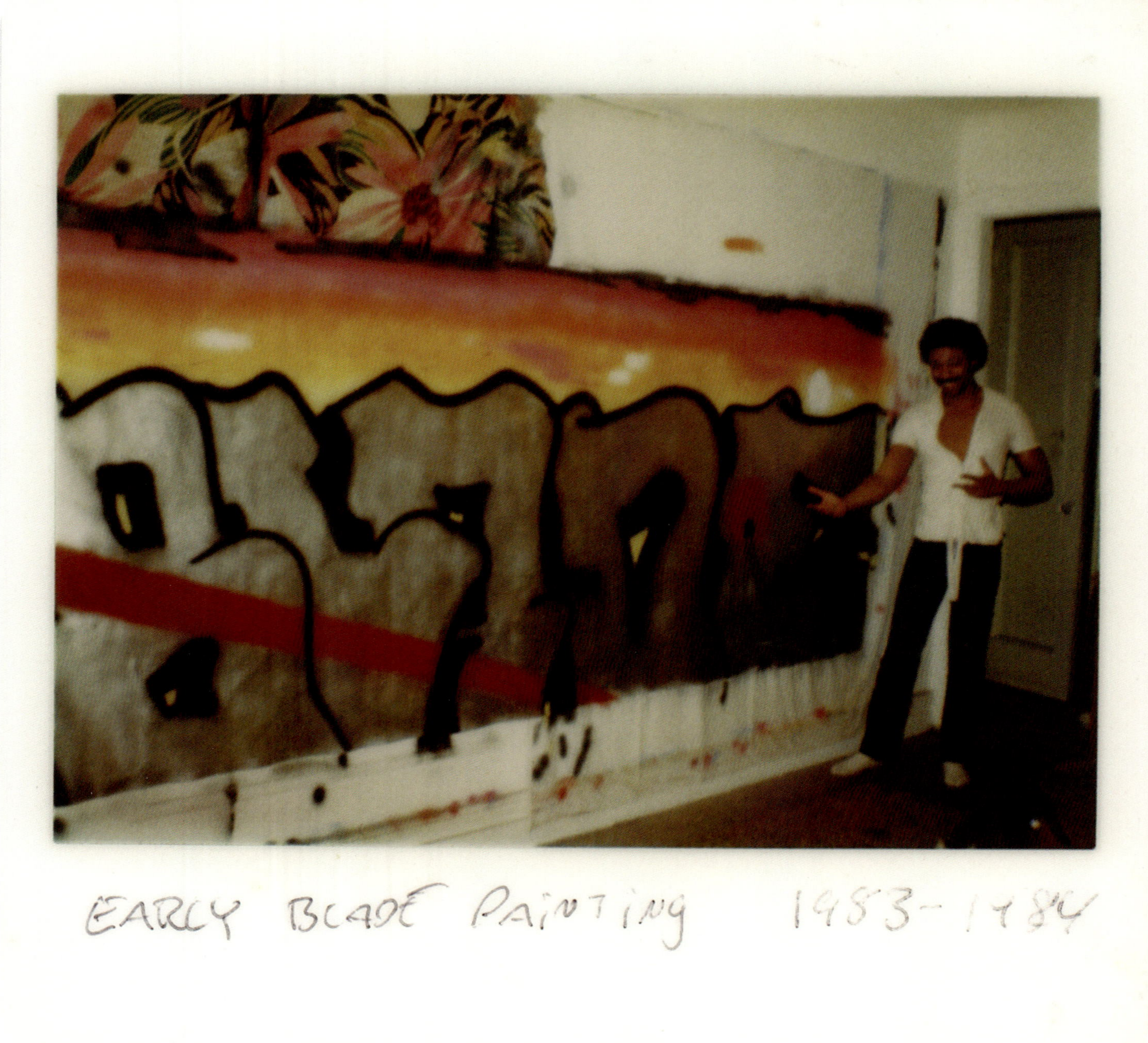

This page: Early BLADE work on canvas. Circa 1983.
Opposite page: BLADE's note to himself about what works he sent Yaki Kornblit in 1988.

Canvases sent to YAKi 8/15/88

1.) Spiritual Enlightment -

(Yin N Yang)

WHitePiece BLACK 3D 2 STATUE MEN

TAN STEPS BLUE Blend SPHERE Yellow

ORANGE PURPLE Blend BACKROUND SPACE BLACK

$6\frac{1}{2}$ long 4 feet High

2) Songs of Light -

DeLtA BLUE PIECE PINK 3D

TRIANGLE letters guitar STRINGS Triangle

PIECE BLACK BACKROUND.

5 Feet long 4 Feet High

3) BLUE PIECE Blend PINK 3D

AQUA TURQUSE BACKROUND BLACK STRIPES

PURPLE ORANGE SPLASH BEHIND. tekool letters (1974)

Colours from a Rainbow

9 Feet Long 4 Feet High

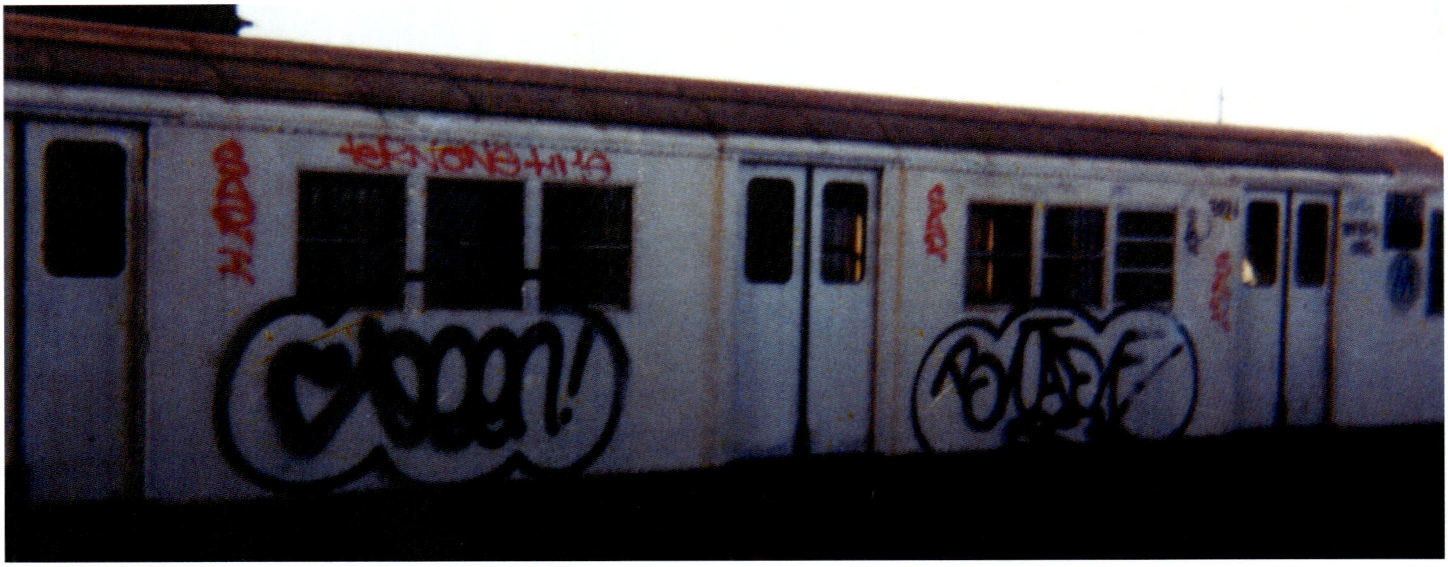

The Dutch people—with a little coaxing from Yaki—had the insight to grab at something and it worked. They've collected all the paintings from the early 1980s: important early works from CRASH, DONDI, TOXIC, QUIK, and me. They have the stuff that all the museums need—all sitting in the homes of about ten different collectors.

In 1983, the MTA painted a lot of the trains white. At first, everybody was excited, because we thought the buses would become giant canvasses. But the white trains didn't work out, partly because a lot of toys were writing on them with black markers—the tags would stick out from under your piece. SEEN and I took to hitting the white trains with hundreds of giant fat cap tags done in flat black; the tags were the size of a window-down burner.

When Yaki came to New York in 1984, it drove him nuts that SEEN and I were still bombing. He took us aside one day and said, "This is a waste! You're gallery artists now. You paint on canvas, not on metal trains! " And he was right. I was almost thirty years old and I had done everything I wanted to do on the trains. It was time to quit. Later that week, I did a pink blockbuster with SEEN, which was my final train.

While Yaki may have wanted us to quit writing on trains, he had no problem with us doing an illegal wall a block from his gallery. I was painting with DELTA, CAT, and MICKEY TFP—all famous European writers—when the cops showed up. None of us were sure if we were painting legally, so we ran way, jumping over a fence to get away. I did not want to get busted in Europe. The one the cops did nab was Yaki, the only one of us not able to clear the fence, but he was able to smooth-talk the cops. He even brought them into the gallery. Yaki was the one responsible for the end of my writing career.

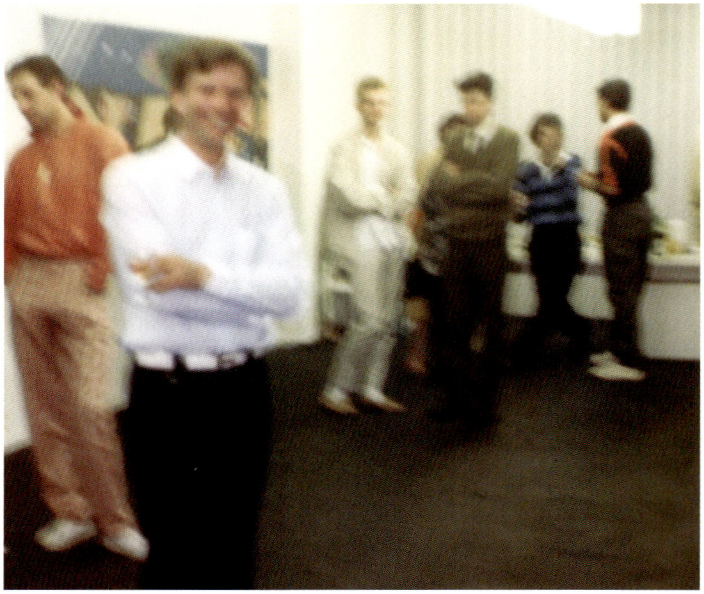

I had my first solo show at the Stellweg Seguy Gallery in New York in 1984. That same night, Andy Warhol had one of his final shows two doors down, and there was a huge amount of media coverage. My show did very well. I think that's when I decided to become a full-time professional artist.

This spread: Top: SEEN and BLADE tags on the 2 line. 1984. Photo by CAVS. Bottom: Yaki in his gallery. Circa 1985. Opposite page: Top: BLADE paints his last car. 1984. Photo by SEEN. Bottom. BLADE's last car. 1984. Following two spreads: BLADE and MAZE paint a handball court. 1986. Photos by Jim Prigoff and Henry Chalfant.

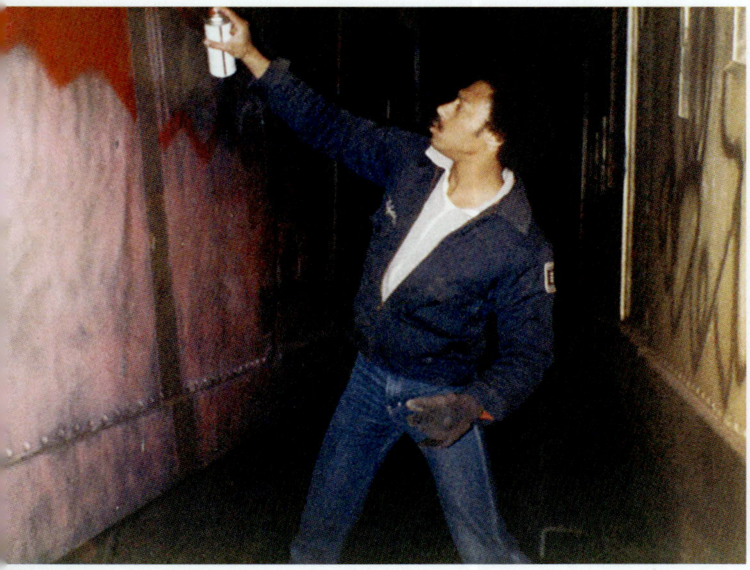

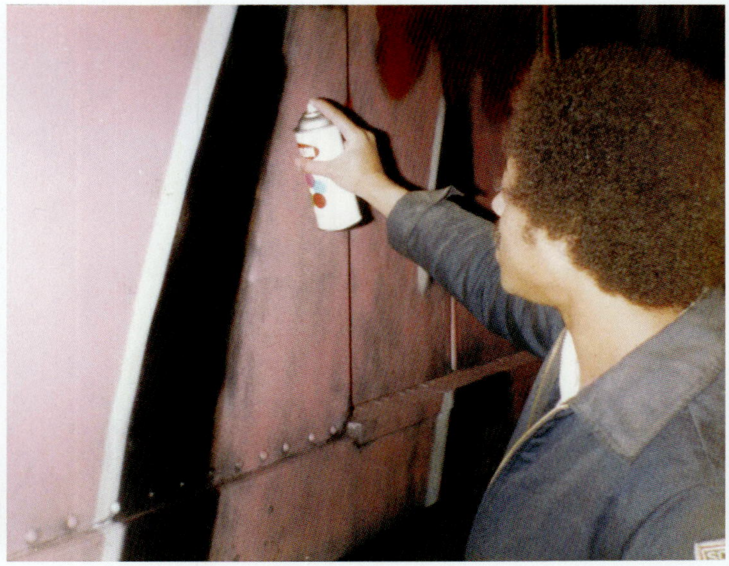

"I WAS ALMOST THIRTY YEARS OLD AND I HAD DONE EVERYTHING I WANTED TO DO ON THE TRAINS. IT WAS TIME TO QUIT...."

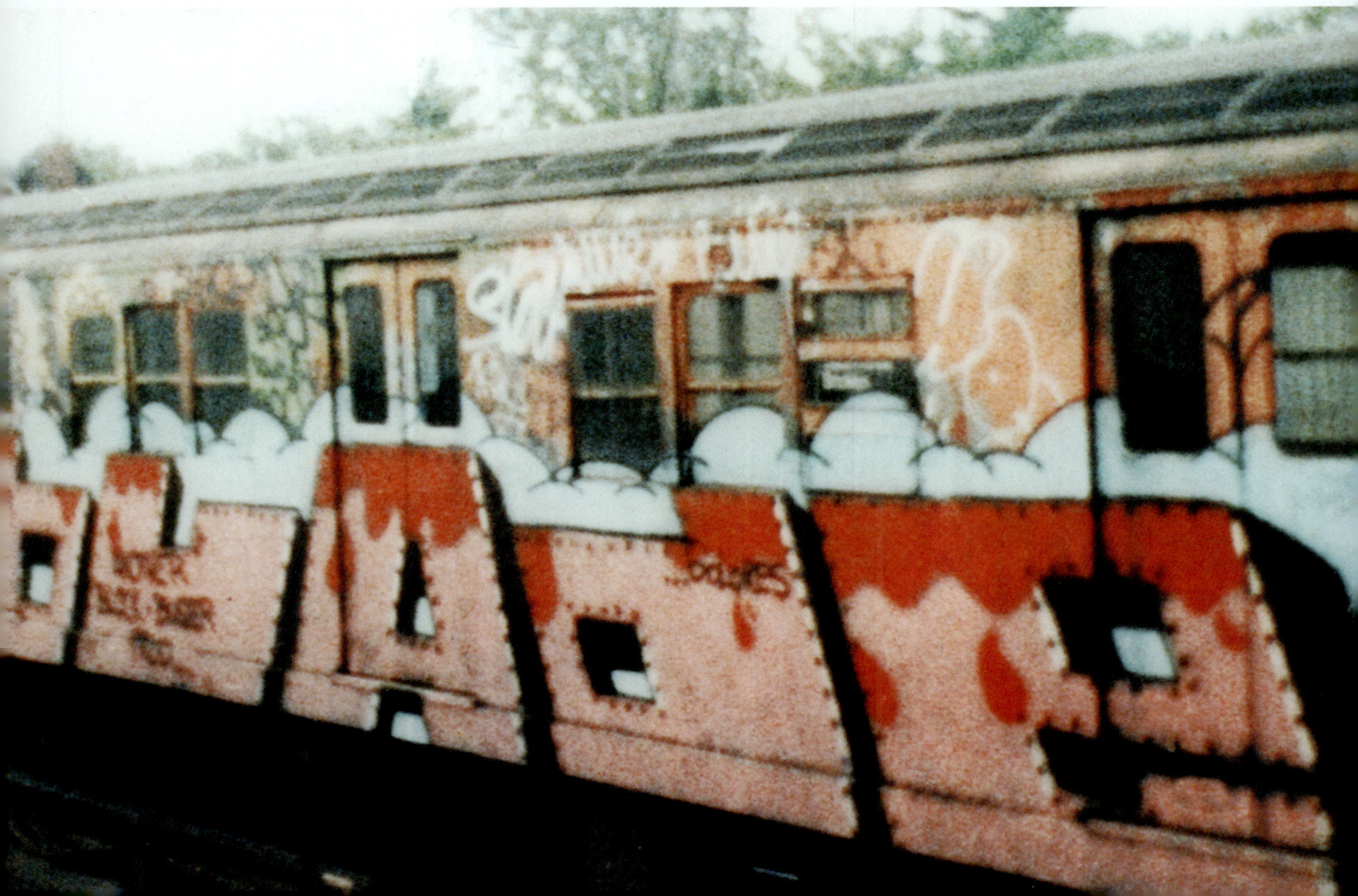

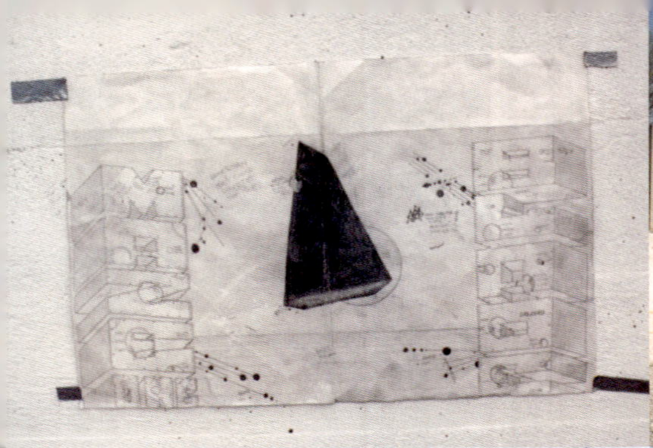
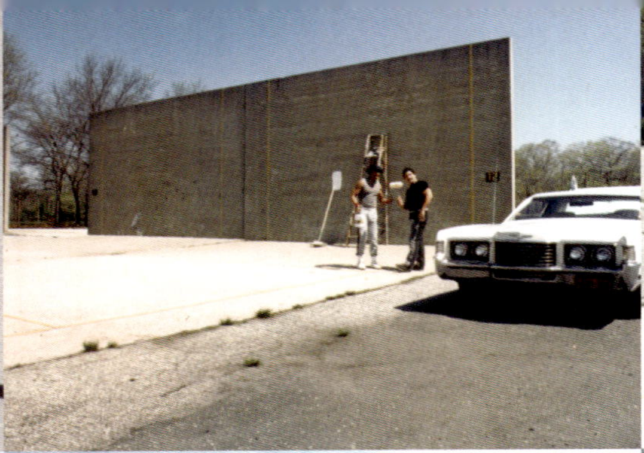
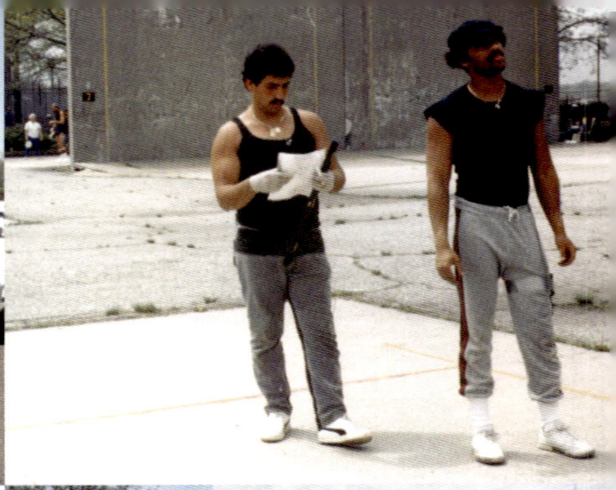
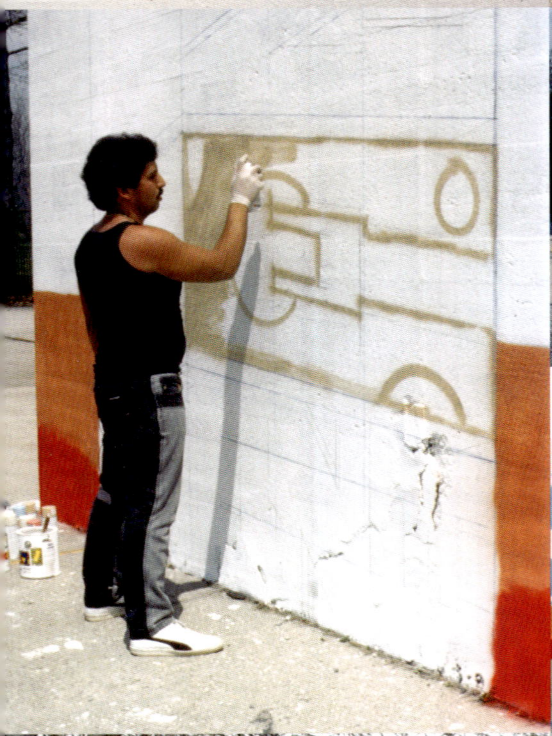
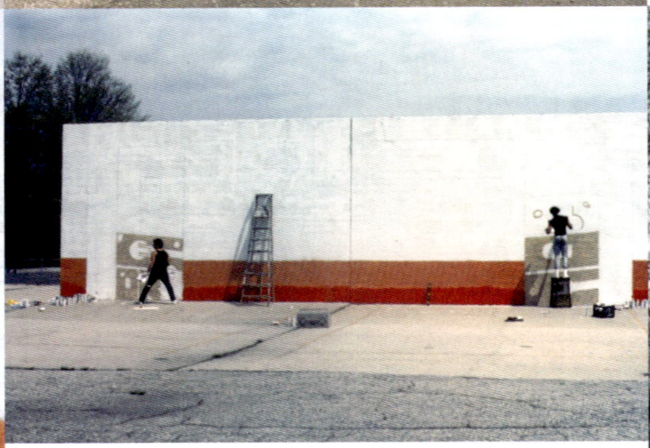
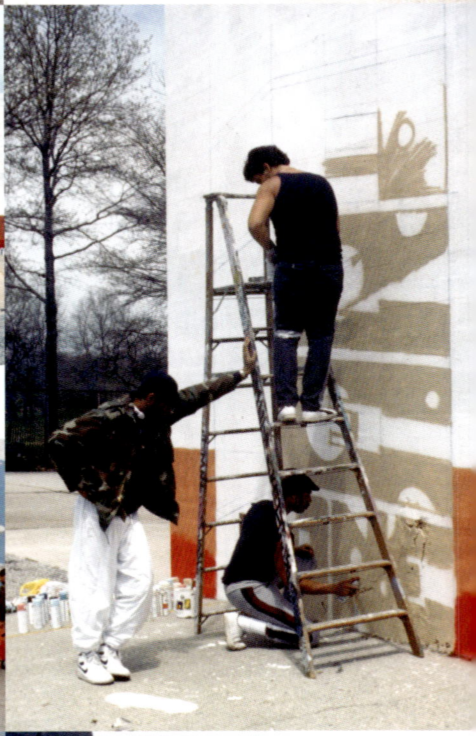
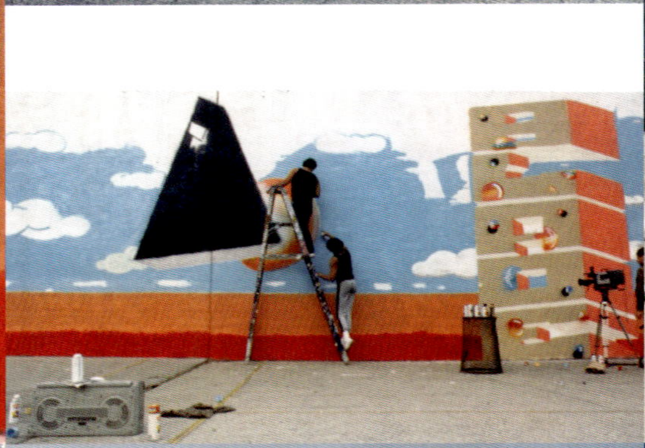
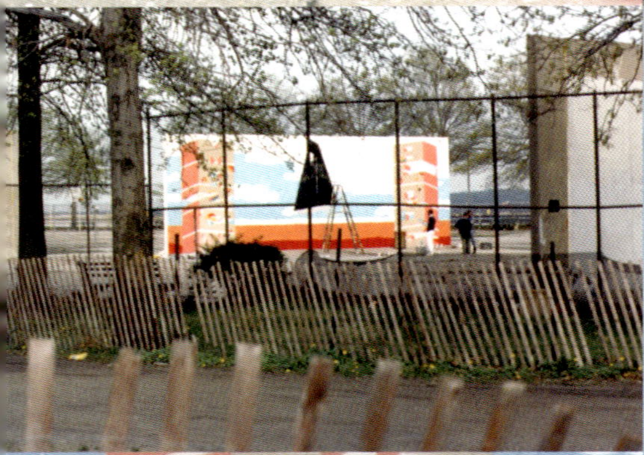
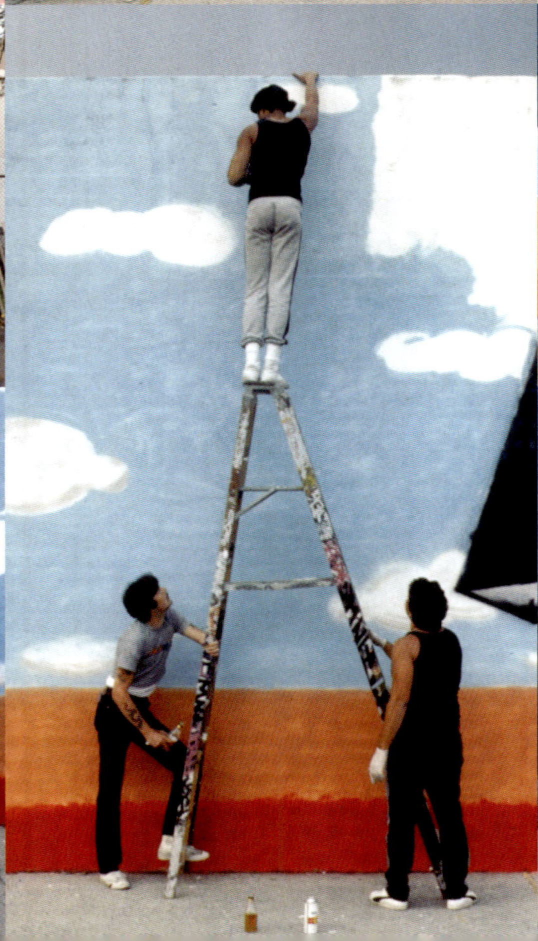
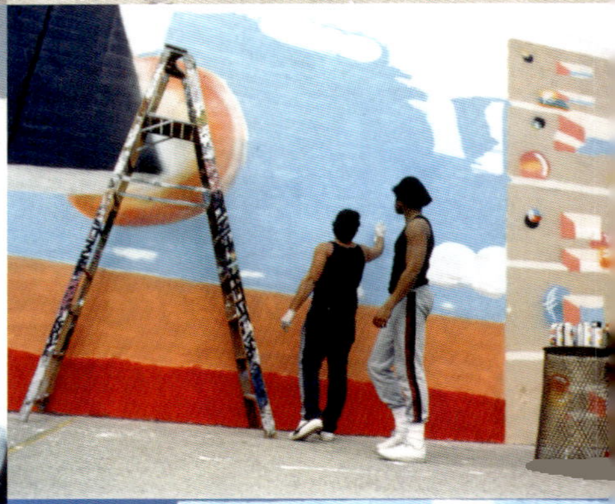
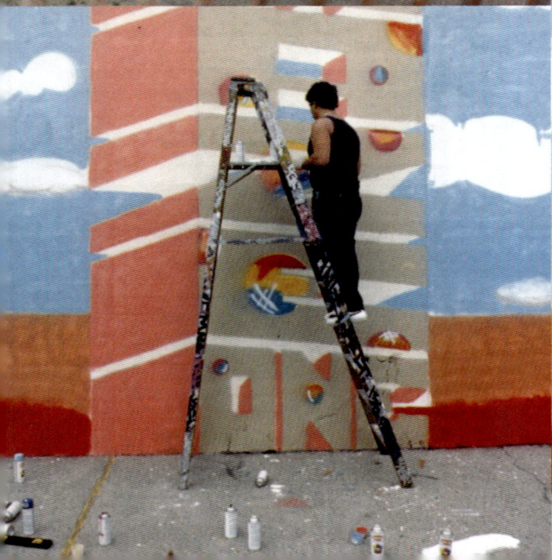
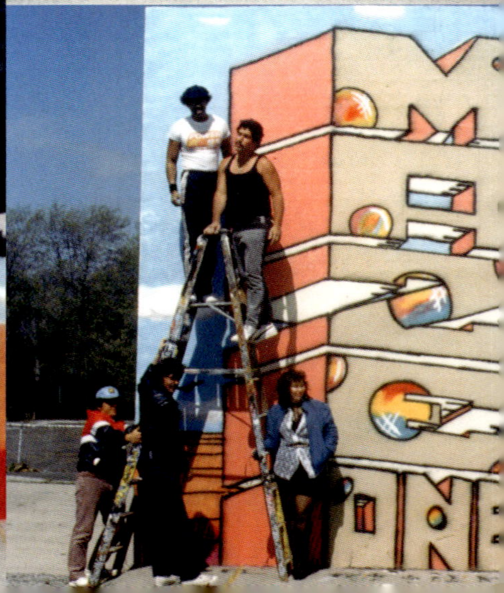

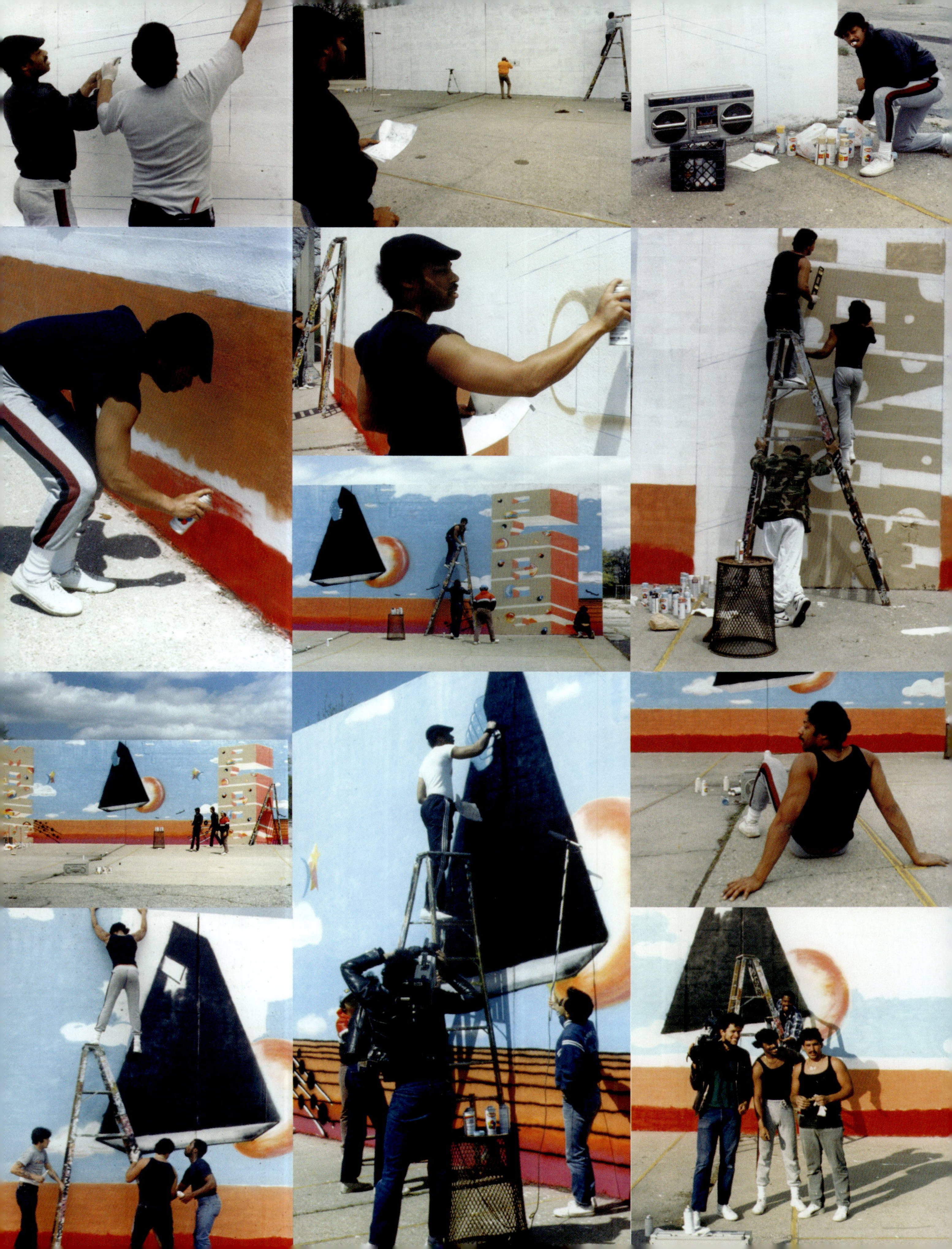

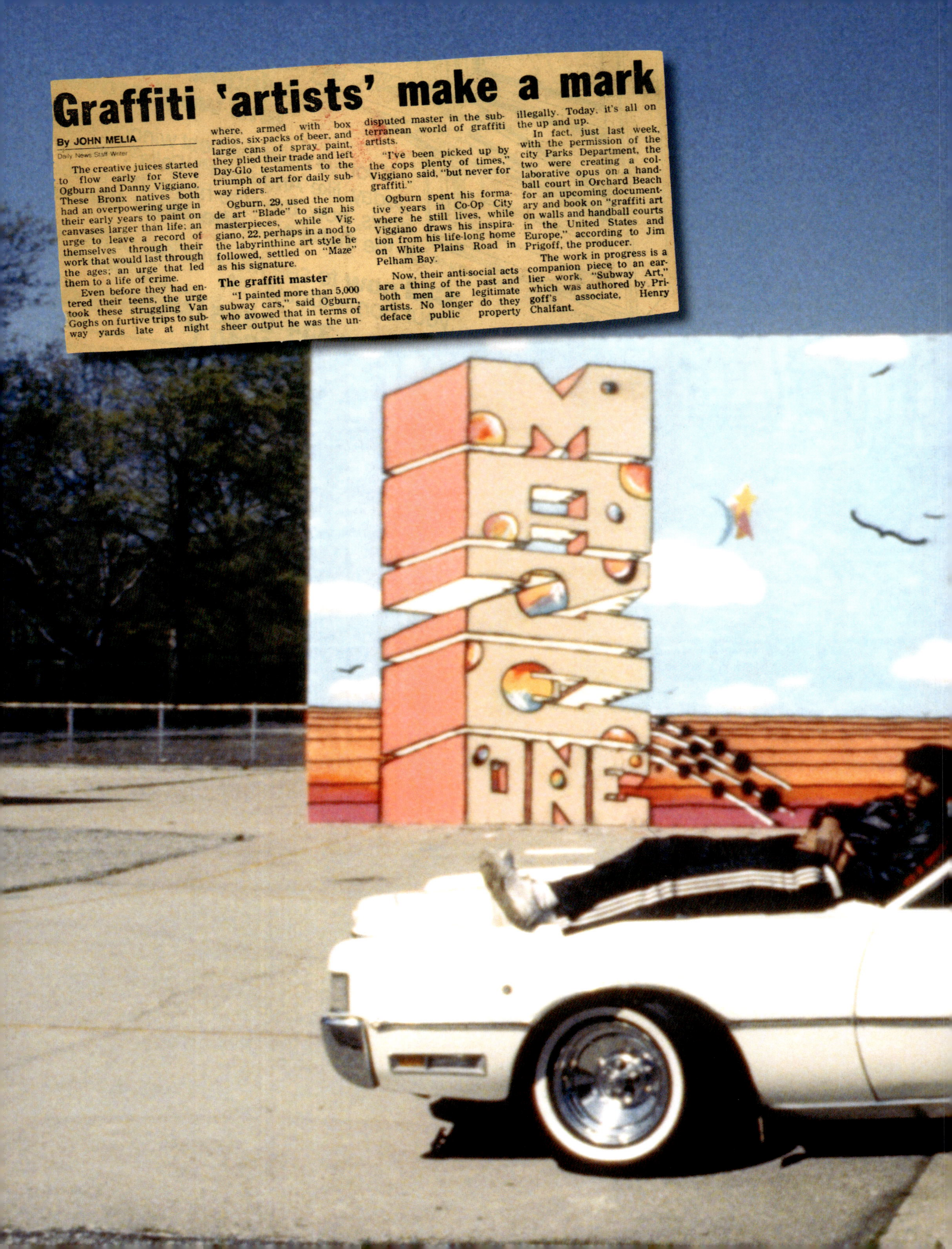

Graffiti 'artists' make a mark

By JOHN MELIA

Daily News Staff Writer

The creative juices started to flow early for Steve Ogburn and Danny Viggiano. These Bronx natives both had an overpowering urge in their early years to paint on canvases larger than life; an urge to leave a record of themselves through their work that would last through the ages; an urge that led them to a life of crime.

Even before they had entered their teens, the urge took these struggling Van Goghs on furtive trips to subway yards late at night where, armed with box radios, six-packs of beer, and large cans of spray paint, they plied their trade and left Day-Glo testaments to the triumph of art for daily subway riders.

Ogburn, 29, used the nom de art "Blade" to sign his masterpieces, while Viggiano, 22, perhaps in a nod to the labyrinthine art style he followed, settled on "Maze" as his signature.

The graffiti master

"I painted more than 5,000 subway cars," said Ogburn, who avowed that in terms of sheer output he was the undisputed master in the subterranean world of graffiti artists.

"I've been picked up by the cops plenty of times," Viggiano said, "but never for graffiti."

Ogburn spent his formative years in Co-Op City where he still lives, while Viggiano draws his inspiration from his life-long home on White Plains Road in Pelham Bay.

Now, their anti-social acts are a thing of the past and both men are legitimate artists. No longer do they deface public property illegally. Today, it's all on the up and up.

In fact, just last week, with the permission of the city Parks Department, the two were creating a collaborative opus on a handball court in Orchard Beach for an upcoming documentary and book on "graffiti art on walls and handball courts in the United States and Europe," according to Jim Prigoff, the producer.

The work in progress is a companion piece to an earlier work, "Subway Art," which was authored by Prigoff's associate, Henry Chalfant.

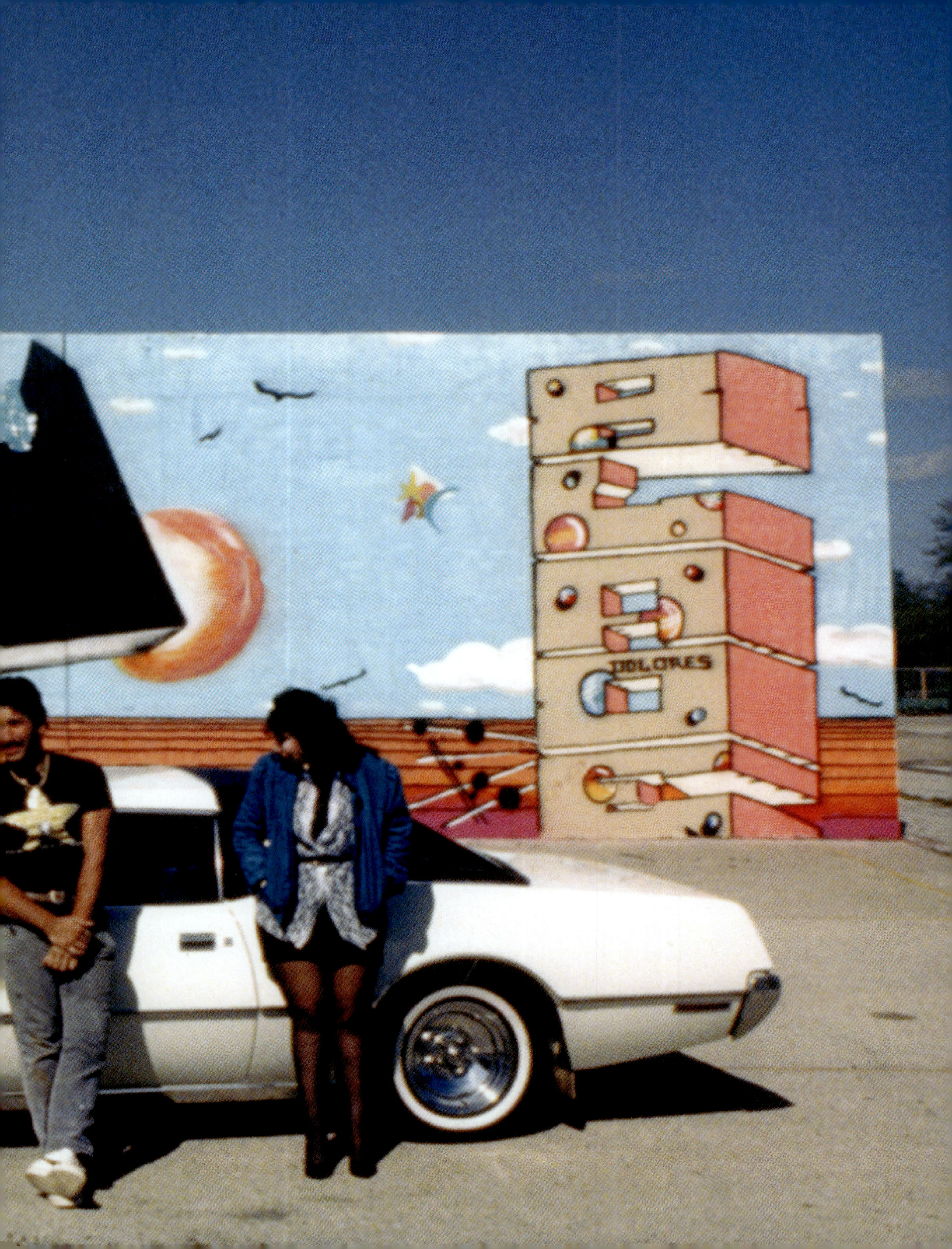
DOLORES

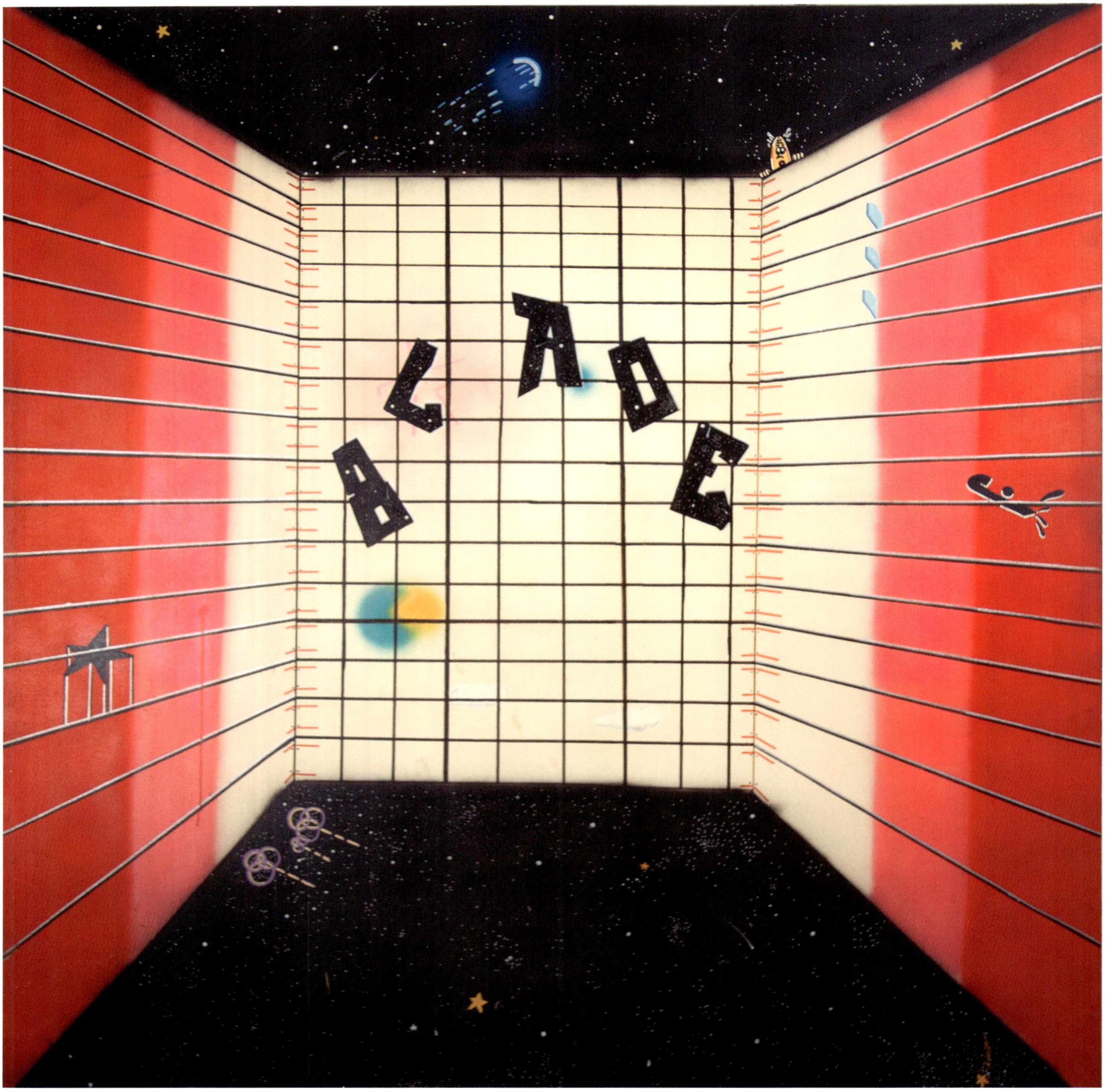

This page: Maniac 2 by BLADE. 1984.
Opposite page: BLADE's Taxi license. 1993. Photo by Adam Wallacavage.

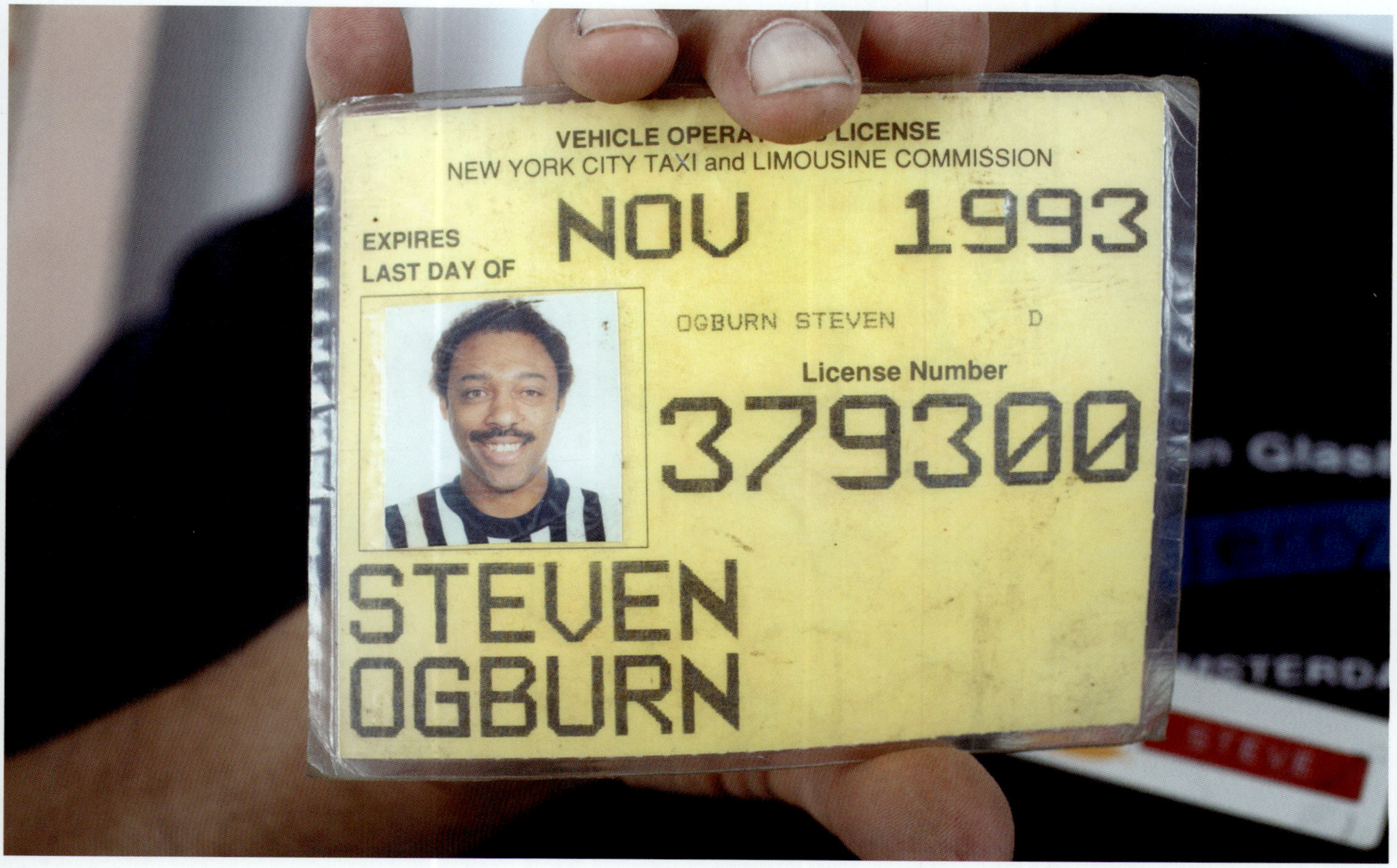

This could not have been better news for Dolores, who felt that painting on trains was a kid's game—meaning it was time for me to grow the fuck up. From an artistic point of view, I never really agreed with her or Yaki, I still think that there were some things left to do on the trains, although I don't know what because my mind started to shift to canvas. My apartment became my art studio; it was on the twentieth floor and had a balcony where I could do my spray painting. I began to learn about the process of art, the different types of canvas and stretchers, newer tools such as paint markers, and what I liked and what I didn't like. It was exciting, but it was also expensive. Graffiti cost me nothing, but painting on canvas meant buying supplies and putting in a lot of time. Some writers gave up on the art scene because of that.

The group of us from New York—CRASH, DAZE, LEE, FUTURA, DONDI, QUIK, TOXIC, A-ONE, and KOOR—all had sold-out shows in the Netherlands, but that was one show a year and there was no guarantee. The most sensible thing for me to do was to take on a new job, something that would give me the flexibility to both paint and leave the country when I needed to. I became a taxi driver, working the daytime shifts in Manhattan on weekends. I liked being a hack, although when I worked at nights, my paranoia jumped into third gear. Working nights was scary: you never knew who was getting into your cab and if and when somebody might put a gun to your head.

With the money I earned from driving on weekends, Dolores and I settled into a domestic routine like any other couple. The only difference was that I liked to work late into the night, seemingly the one time I could focus. Unlike a lot of men I knew, I had no problems making decisions with Dolores. I felt we were a team. For instance, early on she was the one to come up with the idea of buying the apartment, which was a smart move. She was also responsible for my putting away a good percentage of the money I made from painting. I know a lot of writers from that period who made huge amounts of cash and have nothing to show for it. At the after party for the Stellweg Seguy show, there were lines of coke everywhere. I'll never forget it—it was like *Scarface*. That night, Dolores and I went home early and partied with each other.

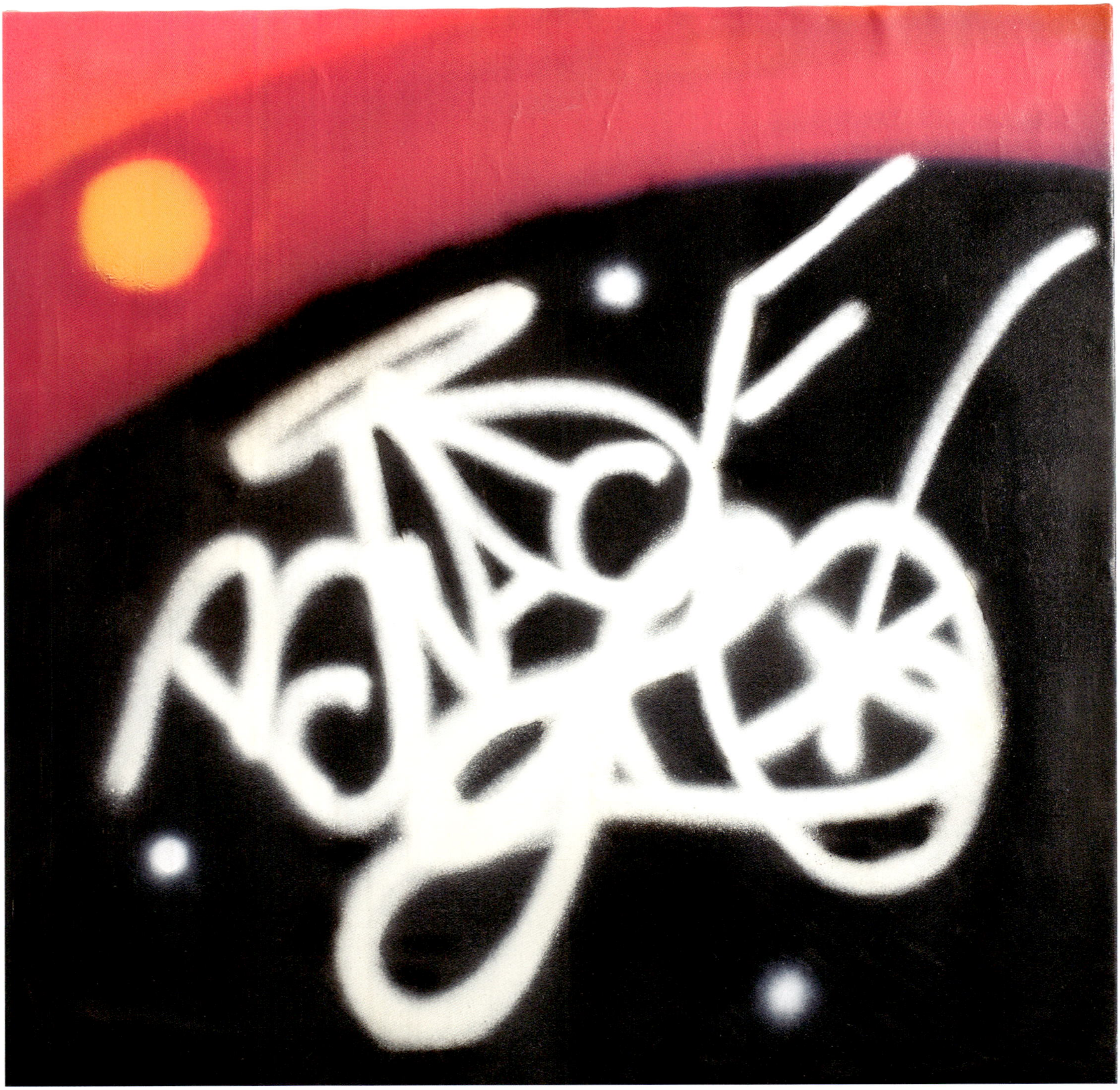

This page: BLADE! painting. 1982.
Opposite page: BLADE abstract painting. 1984.

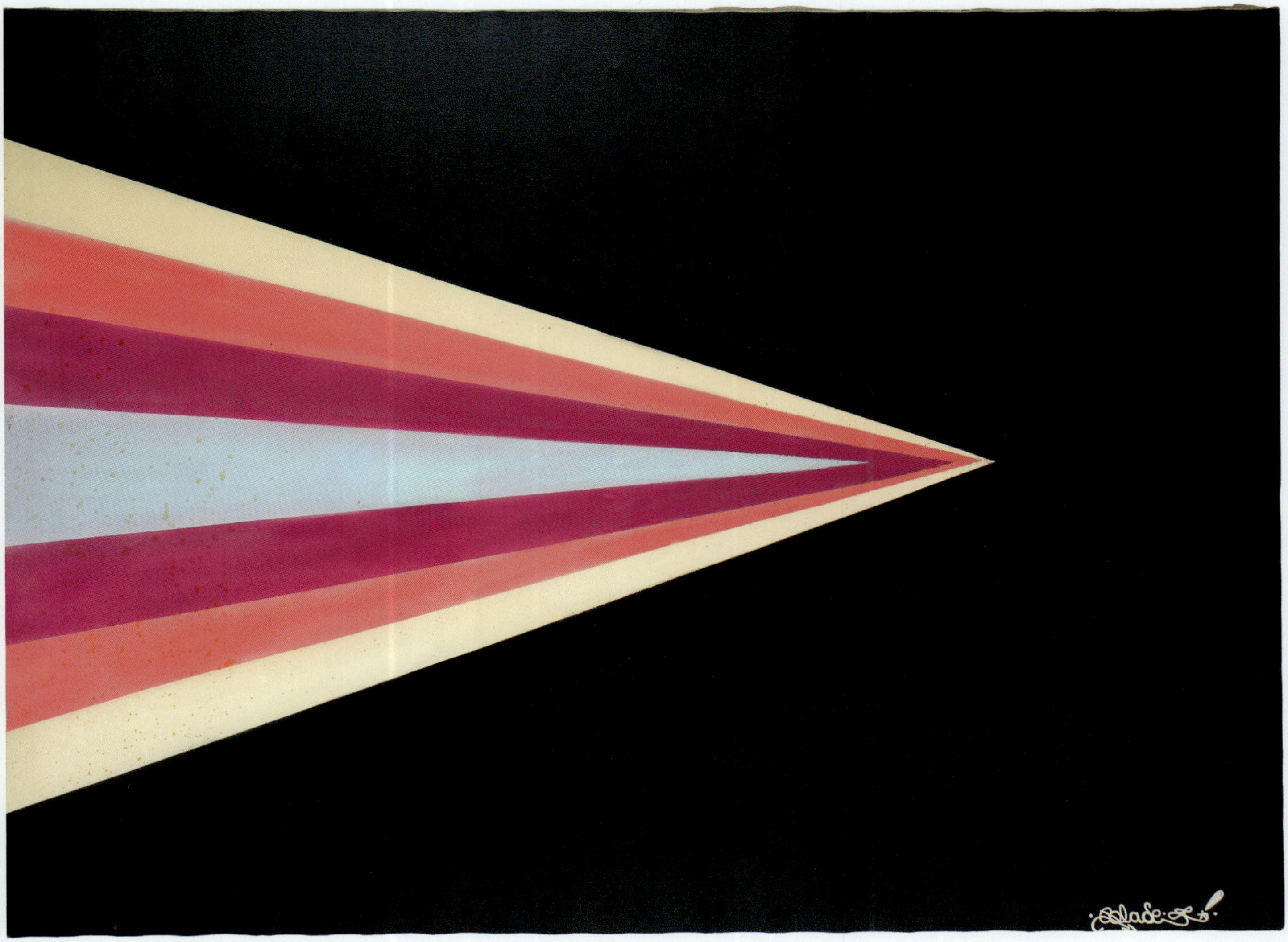

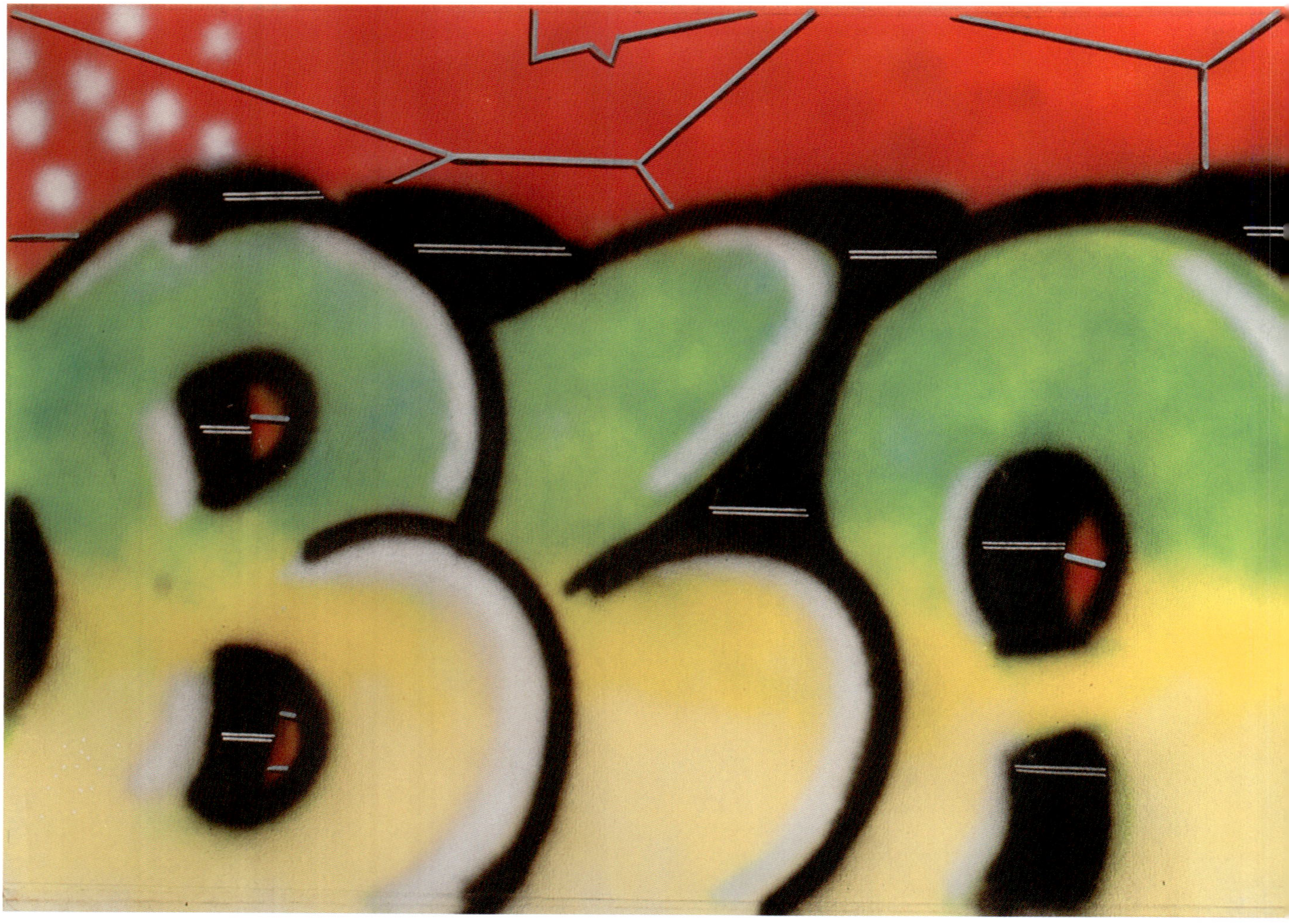

This spread: Express Lane by BLADE. 1984.

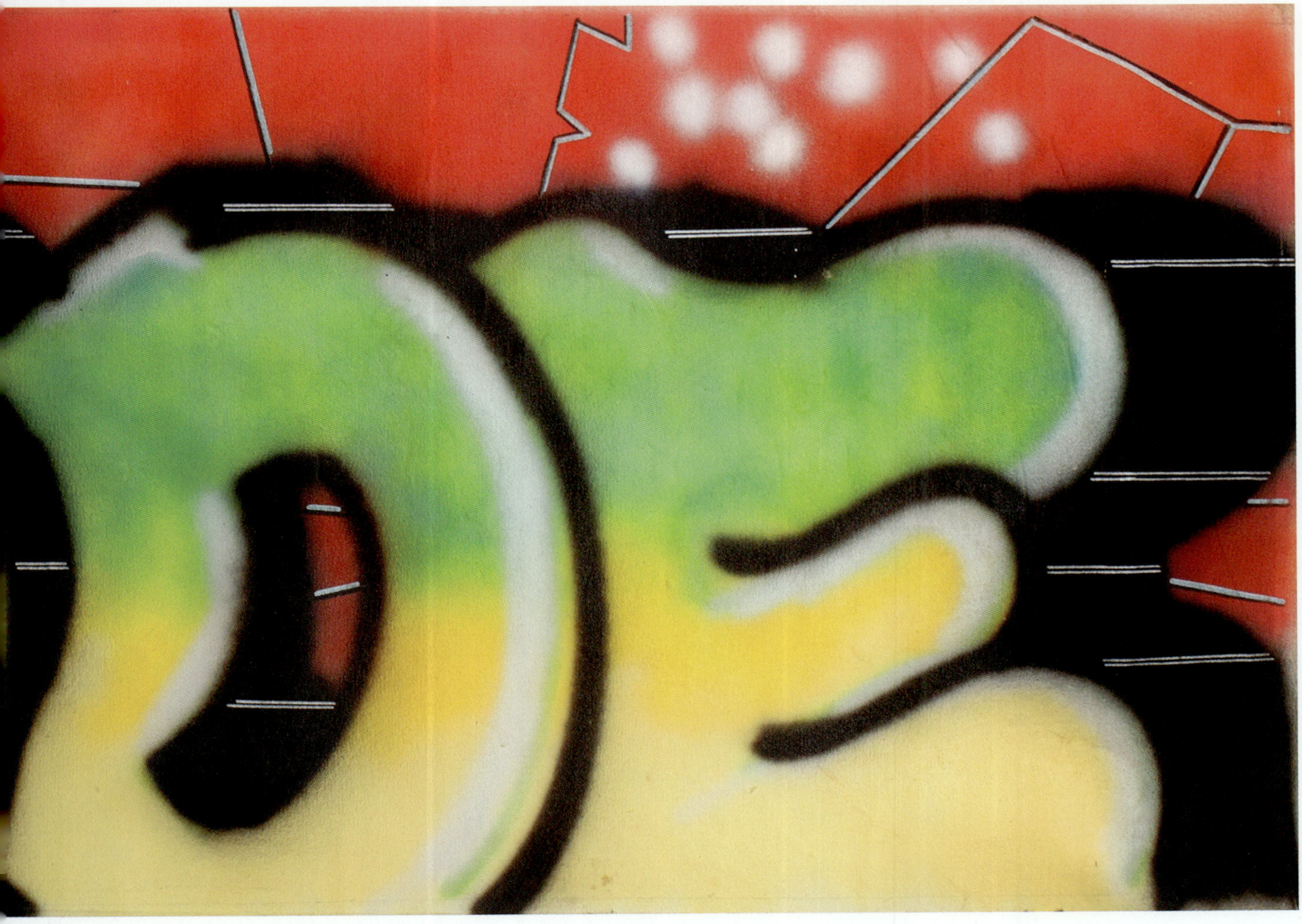

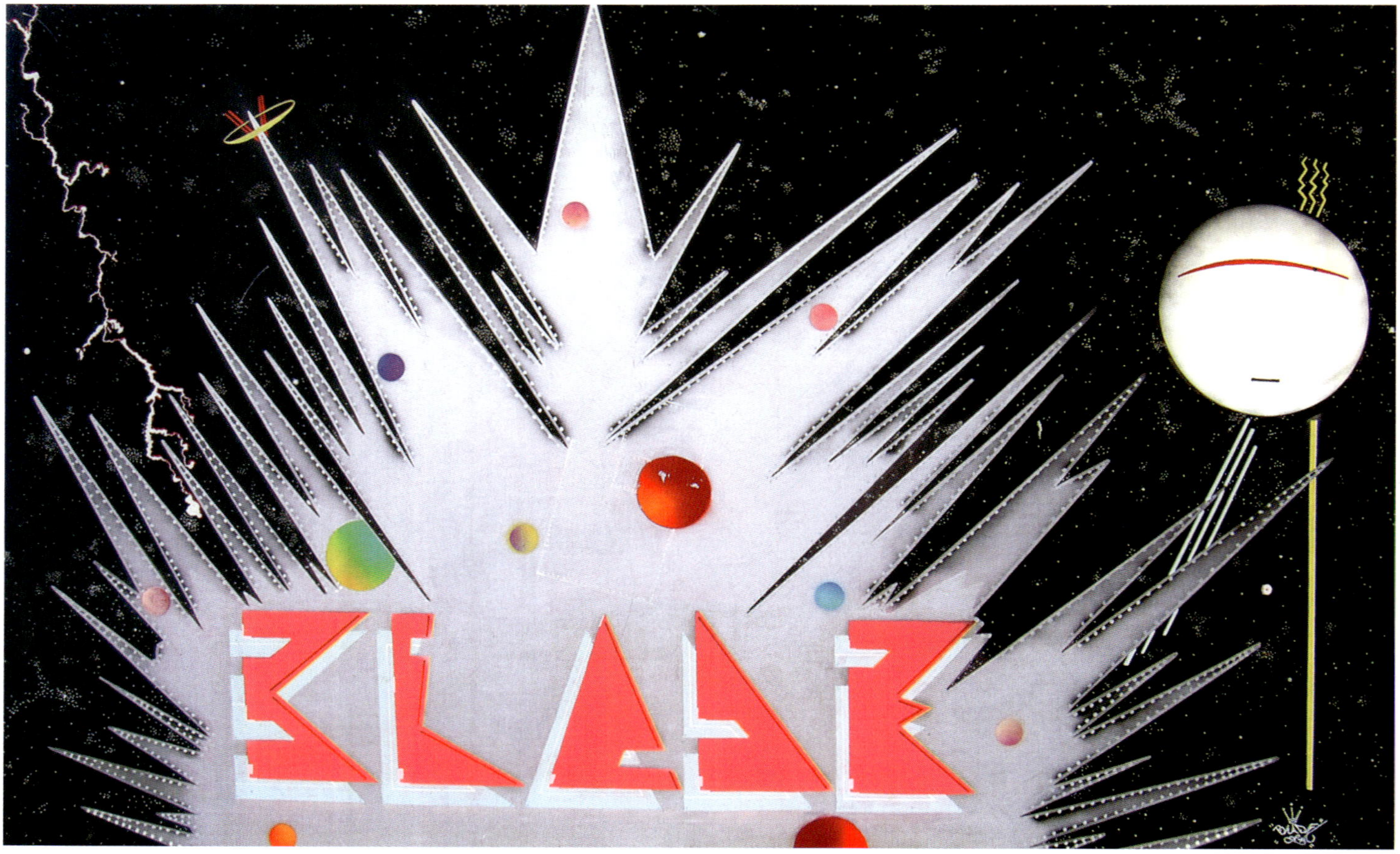
BLADE

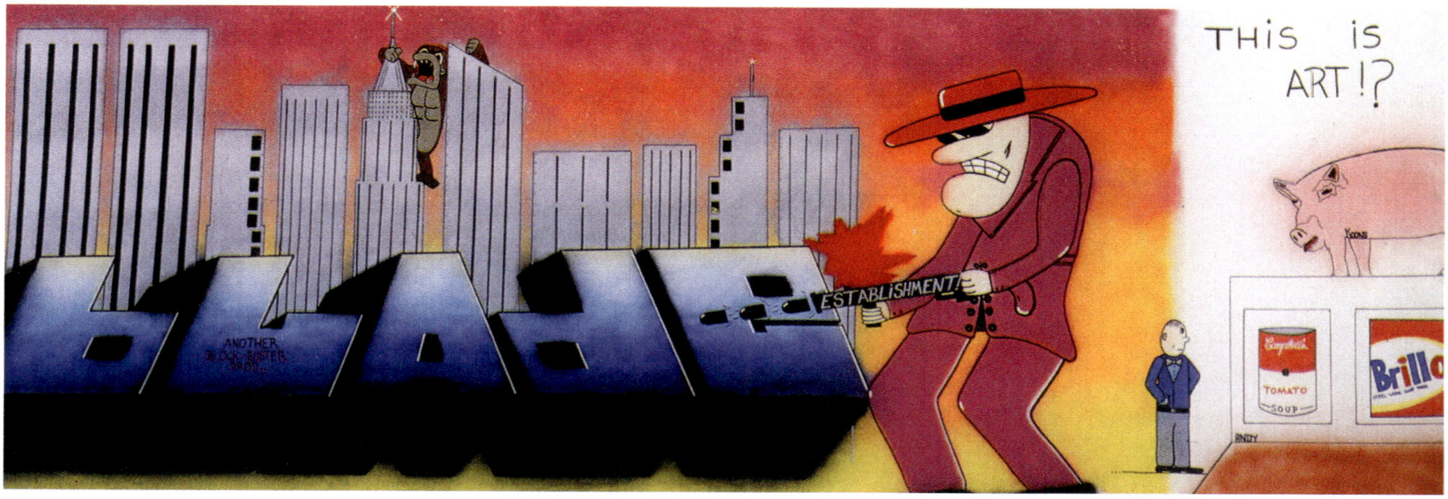
THIS is ART !?
ESTABLISHMENT!
ANOTHER BLOCK BUSTER
TOMATO
SOUP
Brillo

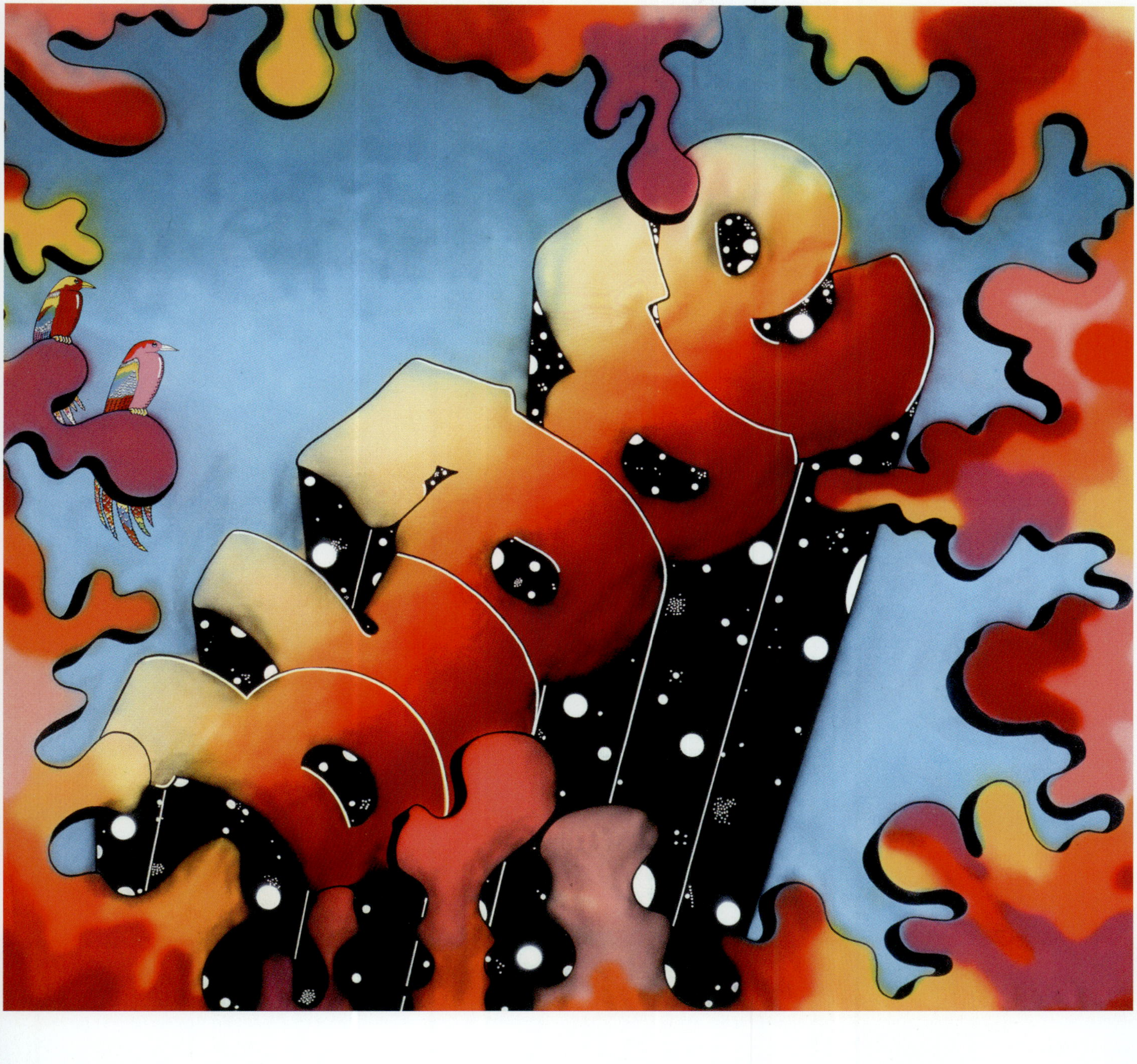

Opposite page: Top: 21st Century Art Today by BLADE. 1989.
Bottom: This is Art? Another Blockbuster Production by BLADE. 1989.
This page: Fantasia by BLADE. 1990.

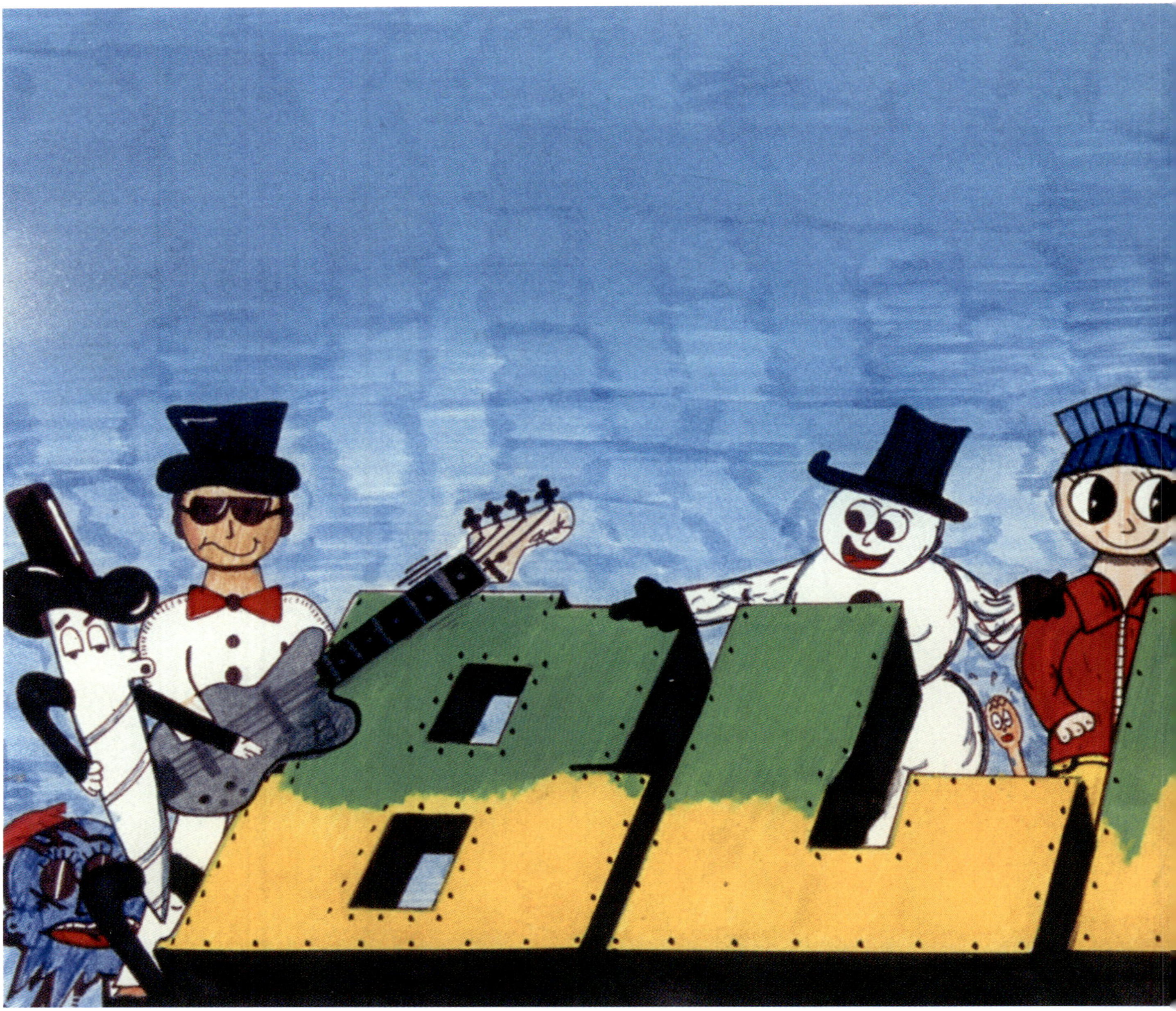

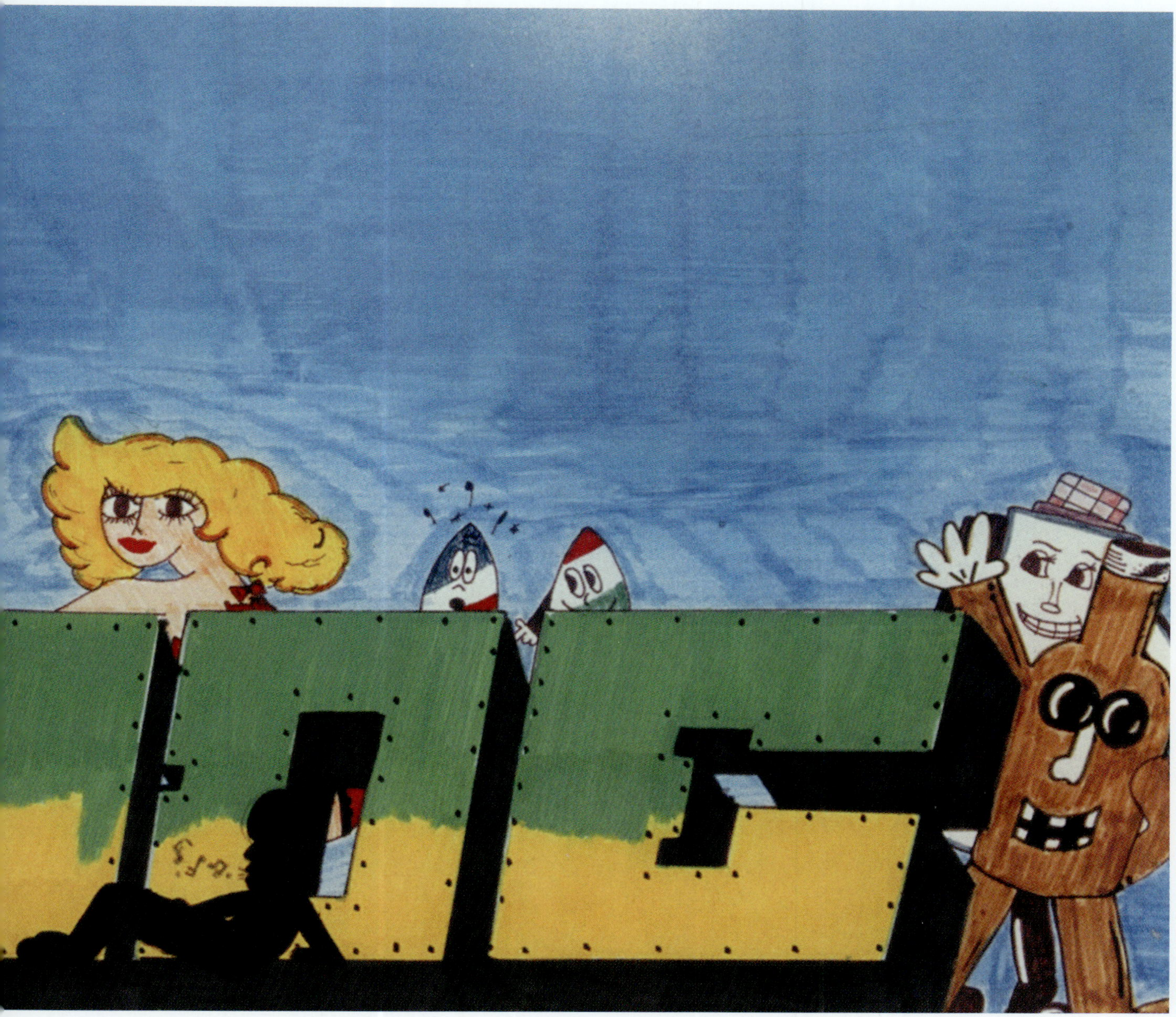

This Spread: Hanging out in 1984 by BLADE. 1984.

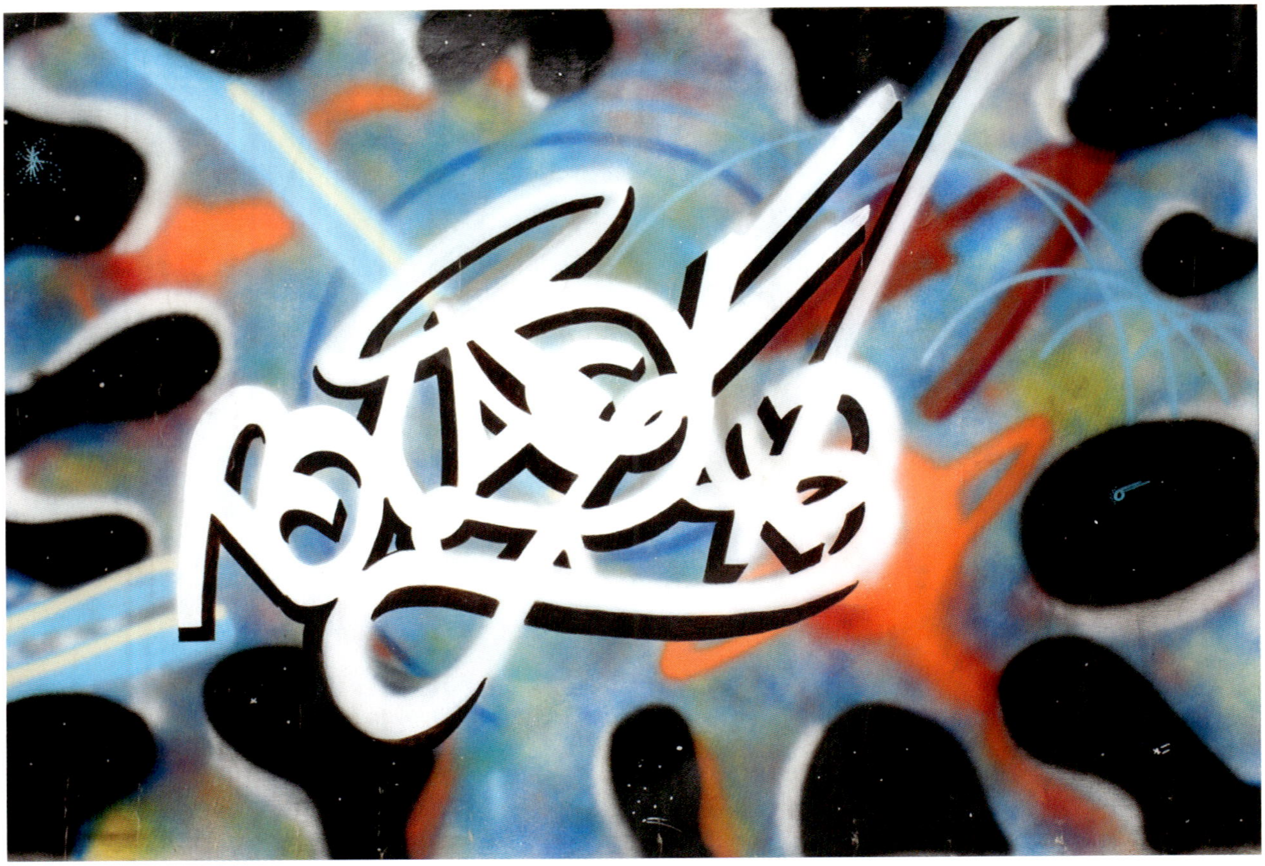

The attitude in the art community was that you should spend it as fast as you made it. And if you spent it on cocaine or heroin, all the better. Jean Michel Basquiat was a perfect example of that mentality. That wasn't going to be me.

In 1987, the art bubble burst. Wall Street crashed and suddenly nobody wanted graffiti art. A lot of writers quit painting, including two of my favorites, LEE and FUTURA. I wasn't impacted by the crash, partly because my collectors were collecting BLADE paintings and not graffiti souvenirs. There was a huge difference between my primitive works of 1983 and my paintings from just a few years later. The early paintings were usually re-workings of my subway works. Although I wanted people to like them, I quickly realized this was limiting. I still had dreams at night to translate to canvas, only now they didn't always center on bubble letter pieces. The works also became sharper as I got used to working in a quiet environment without the wind at my back.

As the art world crumbled, the subway graffiti movement ended. People called to ask my opinion as the last graffitied trains were taken out of service in 1989. The reality is, I didn't care. I was so far removed from the scene that it didn't impact me at all; I was an artist now. Other people cared, particularly the writers in Europe who were starting their own graffiti movement. If there was one thing I learned in 1989, it's that writers around the world knew who I was, and they referred to me as the King of Graffiti—a title I earned the hard way. If you'd told me in the seventies that graffiti would become a world-wide phenomenon and I'd be hanging out with talented European writers like MICKEY TFP and SHOE, I'd have asked you where I could get the weed you were smoking.

Dolores, my partner in all of this, was unhappy. It's not easy living with an artist, particularly one who needed to be alone to do his work. My nights were filled with music and painting—the way I work to this day. I never felt the loneliness, and if I did it probably helped my art. I'm sure Dolores felt it. In 1992, after a successful show in Amsterdam, I came home to find half of the furniture gone. Dolores and I split up after being together for sixteen years. Today, she lives in Florida and she is happily married. We remain friends and I'm grateful for the time we had together.

This page: Time Warp by BLADE. 1984. Photo by Adam Wallacavage.
Opposite page: Top: BLADE paints a bus in Amsterdam. 1992. Photo by CHEA – OMM CREW, The Netherlands. Bottom: Flyer for Coming From The Subway show at The Groniger Museum in Amsterdam. 1992. Courtsey of CHEA – OMM CREW, The Netherlands.

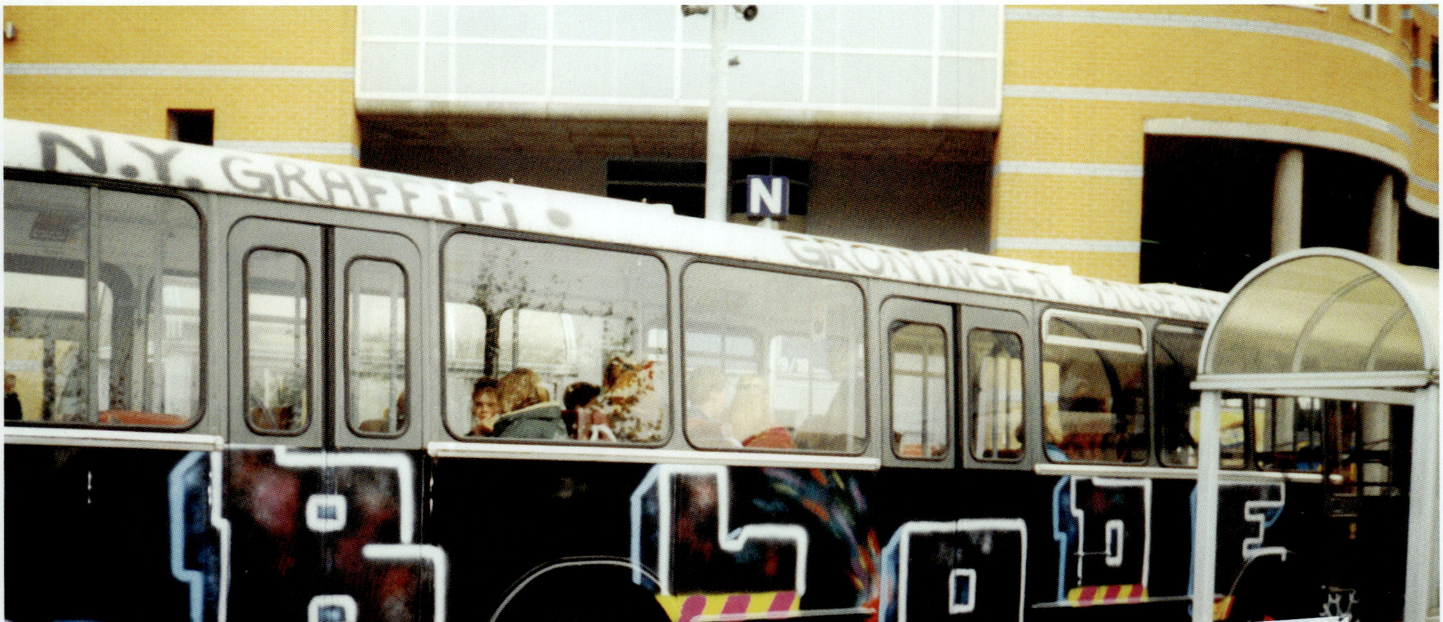

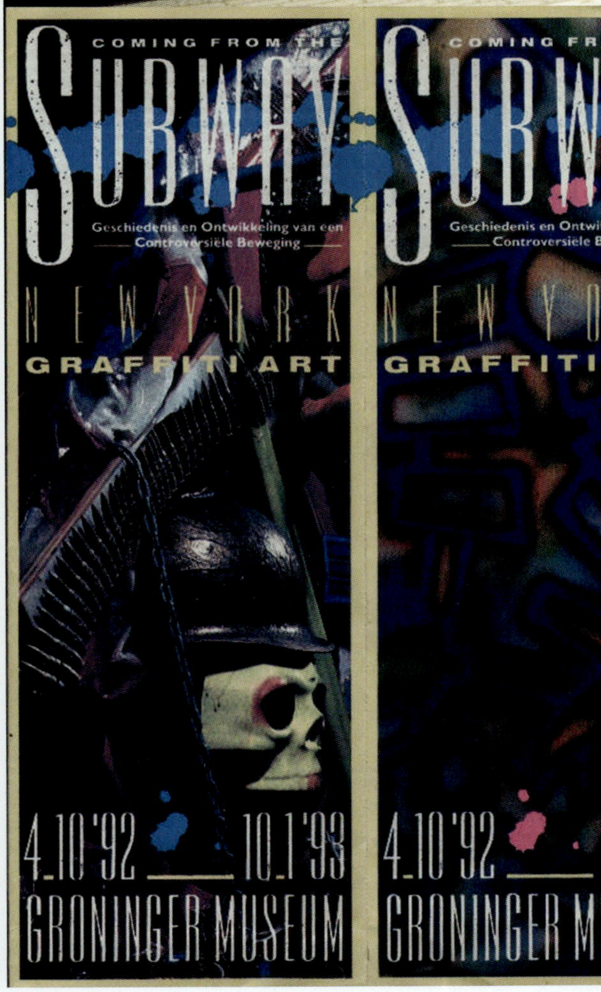

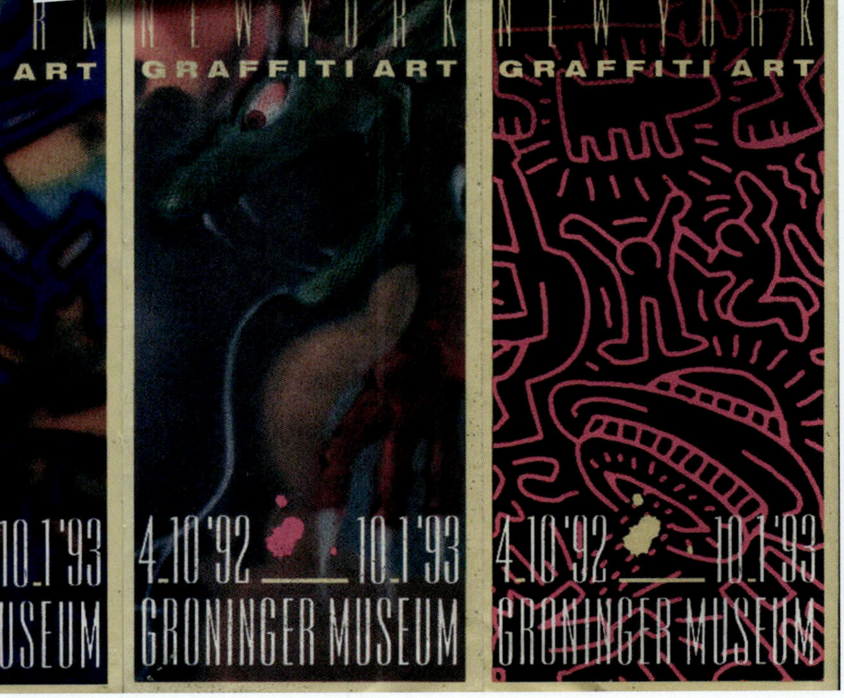

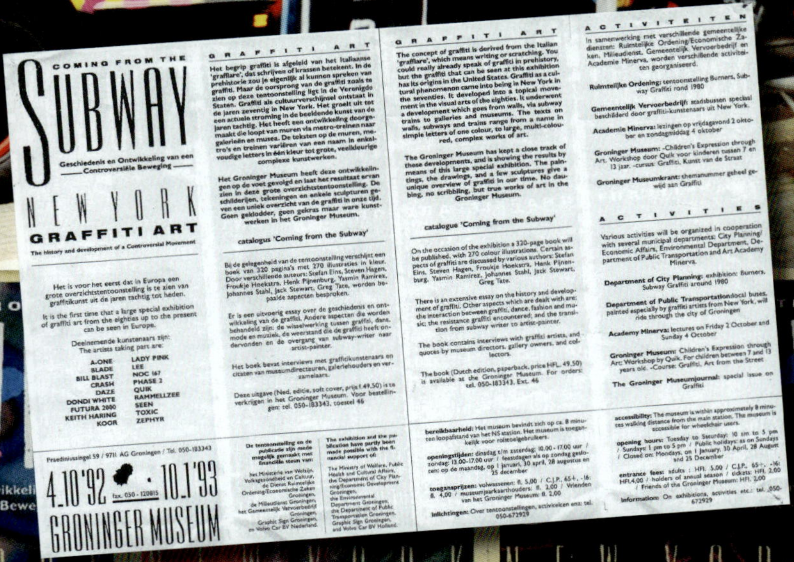
COMING FROM THE

SUBWAY

Geschiedenis en Ontwikkeling van een Controversiële Beweging

NEW YORK

GRAFFITI ART

The history and development of a Controversial Movement

Het is voor het eerst dat in Europa een grote overzichtstentoonstelling is te zien van graffitikunst uit de jaren tachtig tot heden.

It is the first time that a large special exhibition of graffiti art from the eighties up to the present can be seen in Europe.

Deelnemende kunstenaars zijn:
The artists taking part are:

A-ONE, BLADE, BILL BLAST, CRASH, DAZE, DONDI WHITE, FUTURA 2000, KEITH HARING, KOOR, LADY PINK, LEE, NOC 167, PHASE 2, QUIK, RAMMELLZEE, SEEN, TOXIC, ZEPHYR

GRAFFITI ART

Het begrip graffiti is afgeleid van het Italiaanse 'graffiare', dat schrijven of krassen betekent. In de prehistorie zou je eigenlijk al kunnen spreken van graffiti. Maar de oorsprong van de graffiti zoals te zien op deze tentoonstelling ligt in de Verenigde Staten. Graffiti als cultuurverschijnsel ontstaat in de jaren zeventig in New York. Het groeit uit tot een actuele stroming in de beeldende kunst van de jaren tachtig. Het heeft een ontwikkeling doorgemaakt die loopt van muren via metro-treinen naar galerieën en musea. De teksten op de muren, metro's en treinen variëren van een naam in enkelvoudige letters in één kleur tot grote, veelkleurige complexe kunstwerken.

Het Groninger Museum heeft deze ontwikkelingen op de voet gevolgd en laat het resultaat ervan zien in deze grote overzichtstentoonstelling. De schilderijen, tekeningen en enkele sculpturen geven een uniek overzicht van de graffiti in onze tijd. Geen geklodder, geen gekras maar ware kunstwerken in het Groninger Museum.

catalogus 'Coming from the Subway'

Bij de gelegenheid van de tentoonstelling verschijnt een boek van 320 pagina's met 270 illustraties in kleur. Door verschillende auteurs: Stefan Eins, Steven Hagen, Froukje Hoekstra, Henk Pijnenburg, Yasmin Ramirez, Johannes Stahl, Jack Stewart, Greg Tate, worden bepaalde aspecten besproken.

Er is een uitvoerig essay over de geschiedenis en ontwikkeling van de graffiti. Andere aspecten die worden behandeld zijn: de wisselwerking tussen graffiti, dans, mode en muziek, de weerstand die de graffiti heeft ondervonden en de overgang van subway-writer naar artist-painter.

Het boek bevat interviews met graffitikunstenaars en citaten van museumdirecteuren, galeriehouders en verzamelaars.

Deze uitgave (Ned. editie, soft cover, prijs f.49,50) is te verkrijgen in het Groninger Museum. Voor bestellingen: tel. 050-183343, toestel 46

GRAFFITI ART

The concept of graffiti is derived from the Italian 'graffiare', which means writing or scratching. You could really already speak of graffiti in prehistory, but the graffiti that can be seen at this exhibition has its origins in the United States. Graffiti as a cultural phenomenon came into being in New York in the seventies. It developed into a topical movement in the visual arts of the eighties. It underwent a development which goes from walls, via subway trains to galleries and museums. The texts on walls, subways and trains range from a name in simple letters of one colour, to large, multi-coloured, complex works of art.

The Groninger Museum has kept a close track of these developments, and is showing the results by means of this large special exhibition. The paintings, the drawings, and a few sculptures give a unique overview of graffiti in our time. No daubing, no scribbling, but true works of art in the Groninger Museum.

catalogue 'Coming from the Subway'

On the occasion of the exhibition a 320-page book will be published, with 270 colour illustrations. Certain aspects of graffiti are discussed by various authors: Stefan Eins, Steven Hagen, Froukje Hoekstra, Henk Pijnenburg, Yasmin Ramirez, Johannes Stahl, Jack Stewart, Greg Tate.

There is an extensive essay on the history and development of graffiti. Other aspects which are dealt with are: the interaction between graffiti, dance, fashion and music; the resistance graffiti encountered; and the transition from subway writer to artist-painter.

The book contains interviews with graffiti artists, and quotes by museum directors, gallery owners, and collectors.

The book (Dutch edition, paperback, price HFL. 49,50) is available at the Groninger Museum. For orders: tel. 050-183343, Ext. 46

ACTIVITEITEN

In samenwerking met verschillende gemeentelijke diensten: Ruimtelijke Ordening/Economische Zaken, Milieudienst, Gemeentelijk Vervoerbedrijf en Academie Minerva, worden verschillende activiteiten georganiseerd.

Ruimtelijke Ordening: tentoonstelling Burners, Subway Graffiti rond 1980

Gemeentelijk Vervoerbedrijf: stadsbussen speciaal beschilderd door graffiti-kunstenaars uit New York.

Academie Minerva: lezingen op vrijdagavond 2 oktober en zondagmiddag 4 oktober

Groninger Museum: -Children's Expression through Art. Workshop door Quik voor kinderen tussen 7 en 13 jaar. -cursus: Graffiti, Kunst van de Straat

Groninger Museumkrant: themanummer geheel gewijd aan Graffiti

ACTIVITIES

Various activities will be organized in cooperation with several municipal departments: City Planning/Economic Affairs, Environmental Department, Department of Public Transportation and Art Academy Minerva.

Department of City Planning: exhibition: Burners, Subway Graffiti around 1980

Department of Public Transportation: local buses, painted especially by graffiti artists from New York, will ride through the city of Groningen

Academy Minerva: lectures on Friday 2 October and Sunday 4 October

Groninger Museum: Children's Expression through Art: Workshop by Quik. For children between 7 and 13 years old. -Course: Graffiti, Art from the Street

The Groninger Museumjournal: special issue on Graffiti

Praediniussingel 59 / 9711 AG Groningen / Tel. 050-183343

4.10'92 · 10.1'93

fax. 050 - 120815

GRONINGER MUSEUM

De tentoonstelling en de publicatie zijn mede mogelijk gemaakt met financiële steun van:

het Ministerie van Welzijn, Volksgezondheid en Cultuur, de Dienst Ruimtelijke Ordening/Economische Zaken Groningen, de Milieudienst Groningen, het Gemeentelijk Vervoerbedrijf Groningen, Graphic Sign Groningen, en Volvo Car BV Nederland.

The exhibition and the publication have partly been made possible with the financial support of:

The Ministry of Welfare, Public Health and Cultural Affairs, the Department of City Planning/Economic Development Groningen, the Environmental Department Groningen, the Department of Public Transportation Groningen, Graphic Sign Groningen, and Volvo Car BV Holland.

bereikbaarheid: Het museum bevindt zich op ca. 8 minuten loopafstand van het NS station. Het museum is toegankelijk voor rolstoelgebruikers.

openingstijden: dinsdag t/m zaterdag: 10.00 - 17.00 uur / zondag: 13.00-17.00 uur / feestdagen als op zondag gesloten: op de maandag, op 1 januari, 30 april, 28 augustus en 25 december

toegansprijzen: volwassenen: fl. 5,00 / C.J.P., 65+, -16: fl. 4,00 / museumjaarkaarthouders: fl. 2,00 / Vrienden van het Groninger Museum: fl. 2,00

Inlichtingen: Over tentoonstellingen, activiteiten enz: tel. 050-672929

accessibility: The museum is within approximately 8 minutes walking distance from the main station. The museum is accessible for wheelchair users.

opening hours: Tuesday to Saturday: 10 am to 5 pm / Sundays: 1 pm to 5 pm / Public holidays: as on Sundays / Closed on: Mondays, on 1 January, 30 April, 28 August and 25 December

entrance fees: adults : Hfl. 5,00 / C.J.P., 65+, -16: Hfl.4,00 / holders of annual season / tickets: Hfl. 2,00 / Friends of the Groninger Museum: Hfl. 2,00

Information: On exhibitions, activities etc.: tel. 050-672929

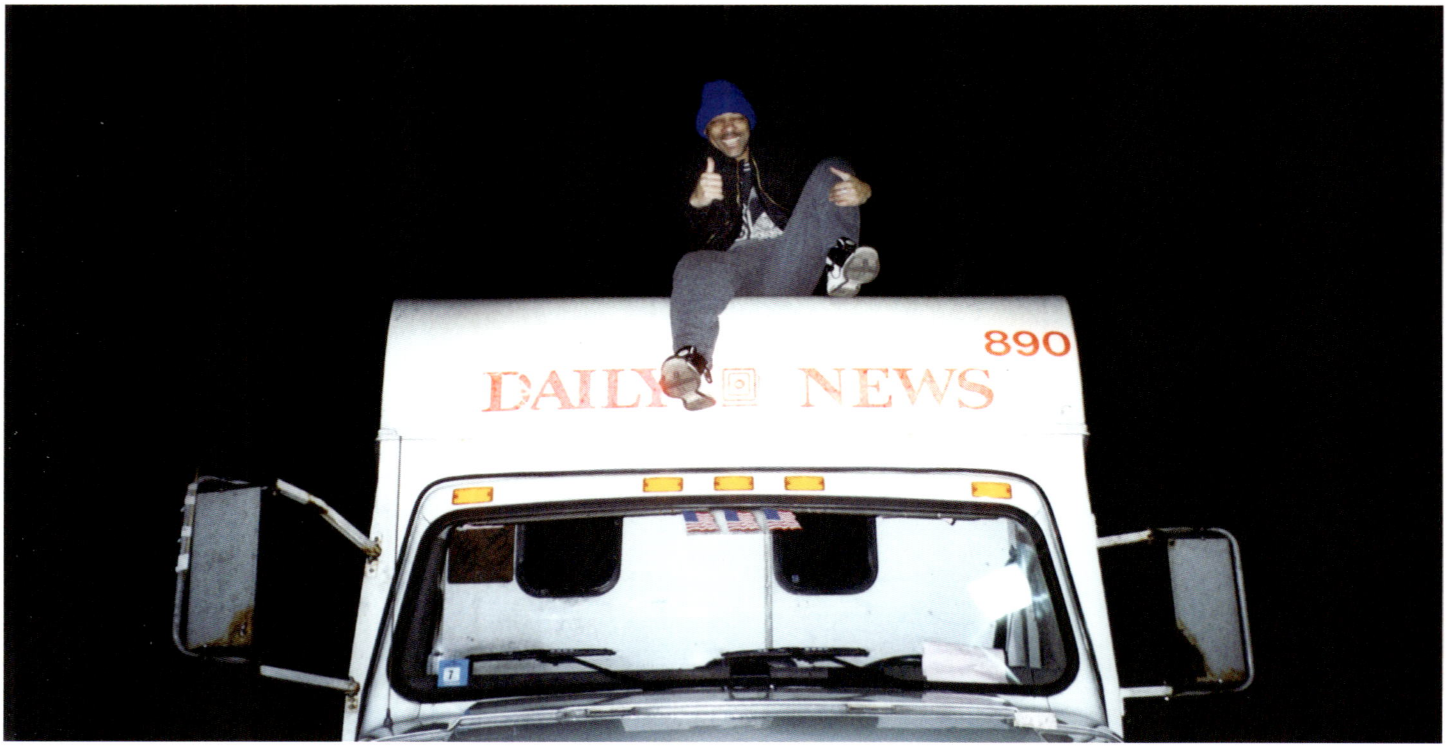

My life was unusual, to say the least. In Europe, graffiti festivals were popping up to celebrate the culture. Promoters would pay to fly me over and I was treated like a celebrity. My gallery career provided more trips to Europe and the works continued to sell. I was building a large body of work for critics to dissect and analyze long after my death. Back in the states, I began working a new job driving a truck for the *Daily News*. I liked the job, because I was my own boss and worked at night and I could take off whenever I wanted to fly to Europe on a whim. I took the job in 1996 with the goal of retiring early and painting full time. If that failed, I knew I'd at least have a pension to fall back on.

The job ended up giving me much more than a pension: it re-introduced me to Parkside Houses and, more importantly, to Portia McHenry. Portia and I grew up together in the 1960s before I was sent to Saratoga. She was my first crush and we each shared our first kiss together. When I came back from Saratoga in 1970, Portia was still there but we always seemed to get sidetracked with other people.

Parkside Houses changed over the years as time hadn't been kind to the projects. The days of selling hash and pot at the basketball courts were replaced with kids who ran drug gangs. Everything changed in the 1980s, when crack cocaine entered Parkside. A thirteen-year-old kid could make more money in one day selling crack than Glazer had made in a year selling pot in the seventies. Of course, with the money came the guns—automatic weapons used by kids to kill other kids. When the crack epidemic slowed down, dealers put their money into crystal meth and the kids didn't miss a beat.

In 1998, I knocked on Portia's old apartment door, wondering if she was still there. Portia opened the door, invited me in, and we talked through the night and into morning. She stayed at Parkside to take care of her grandmother. Although she thought about leaving many times, there always seemed to be something stopping her. We began dating, going to nice restaurants and movies. We were both in our early forties. We'd possibly lived half of our lives already. I wanted Portia with me for the second half.

Portia was both smart and great with people, so she started doing all of the things in my art career I hated. She kept in touch with all of my collectors and dealers via e-mail. I hated the computer and just wanted to paint. I continued to both work at the *Daily News* and show at galleries in Europe. Portia and I continued that way for the next ten years, as it quickly became the BLADE and Portia show—the way it should be.

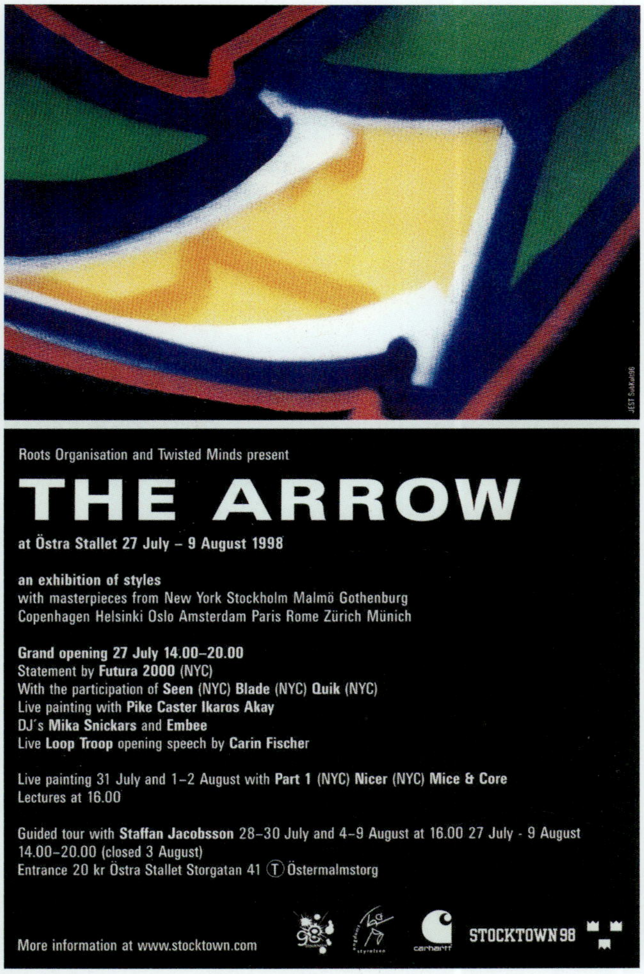

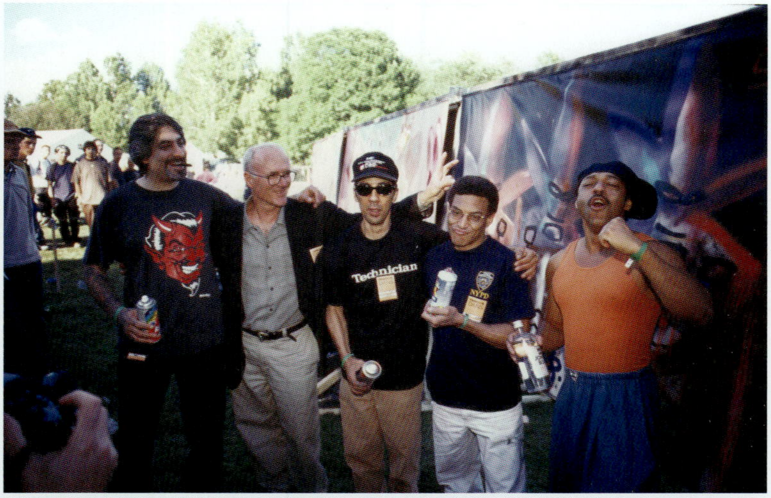

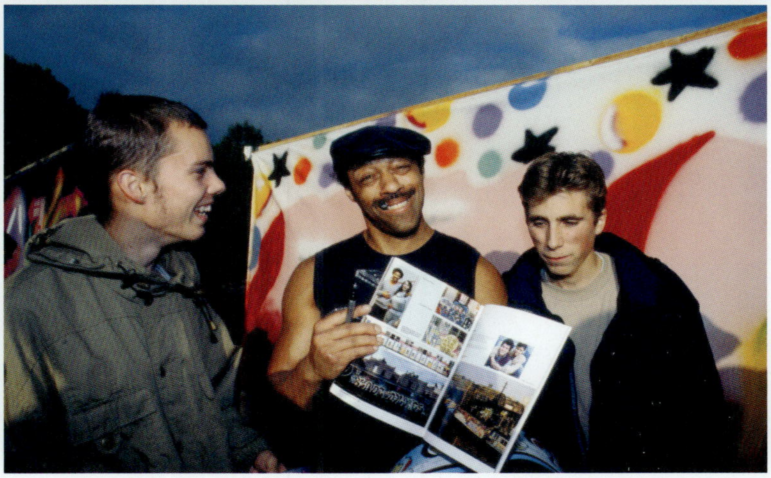

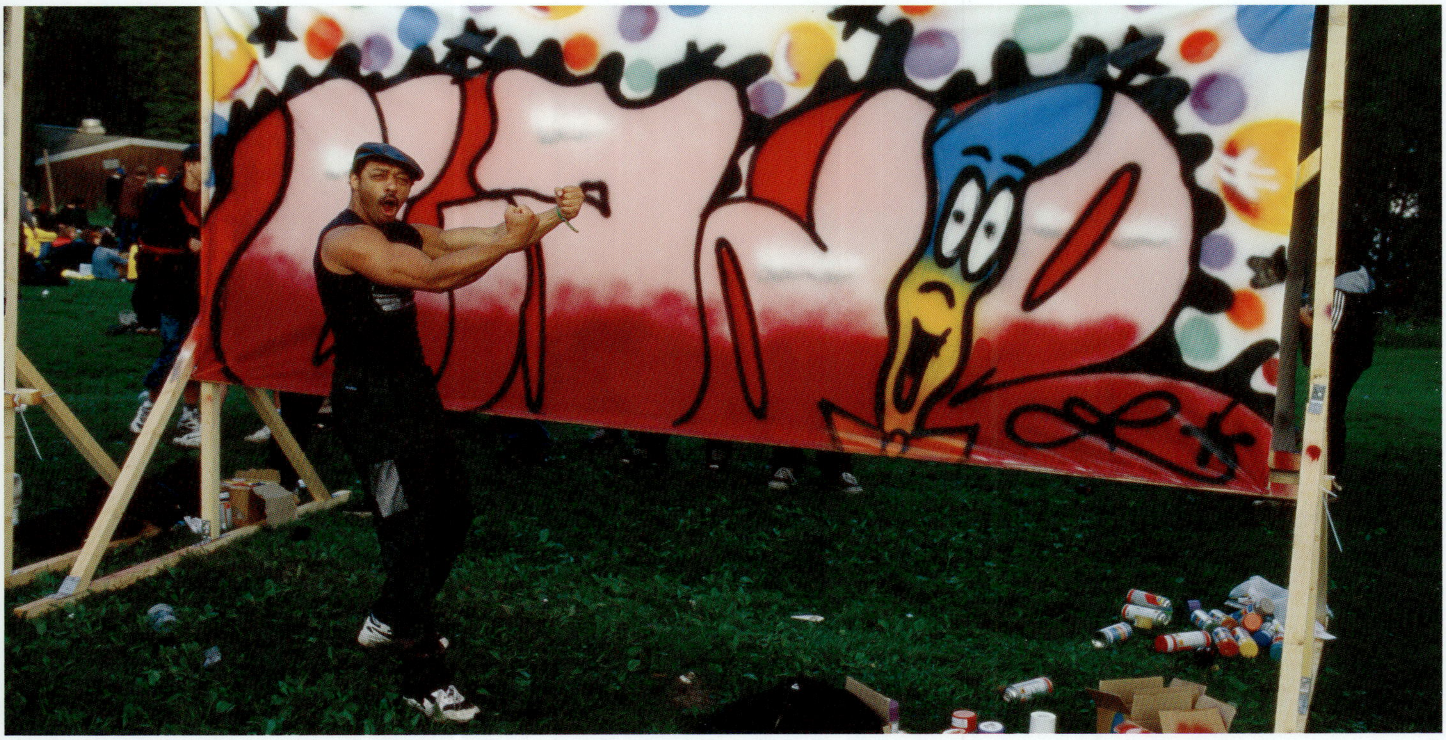

Opposite page: BLADE on top of his Daily News truck. *Circa 1997.*
This Page: Painting for The Arrow exhibit in Stockholm. 1998. Photos by Malcolm Jacobson. Following two spreads: BLADE and friends on various walls around New York City. Circa 1992. Photos by CAVS.

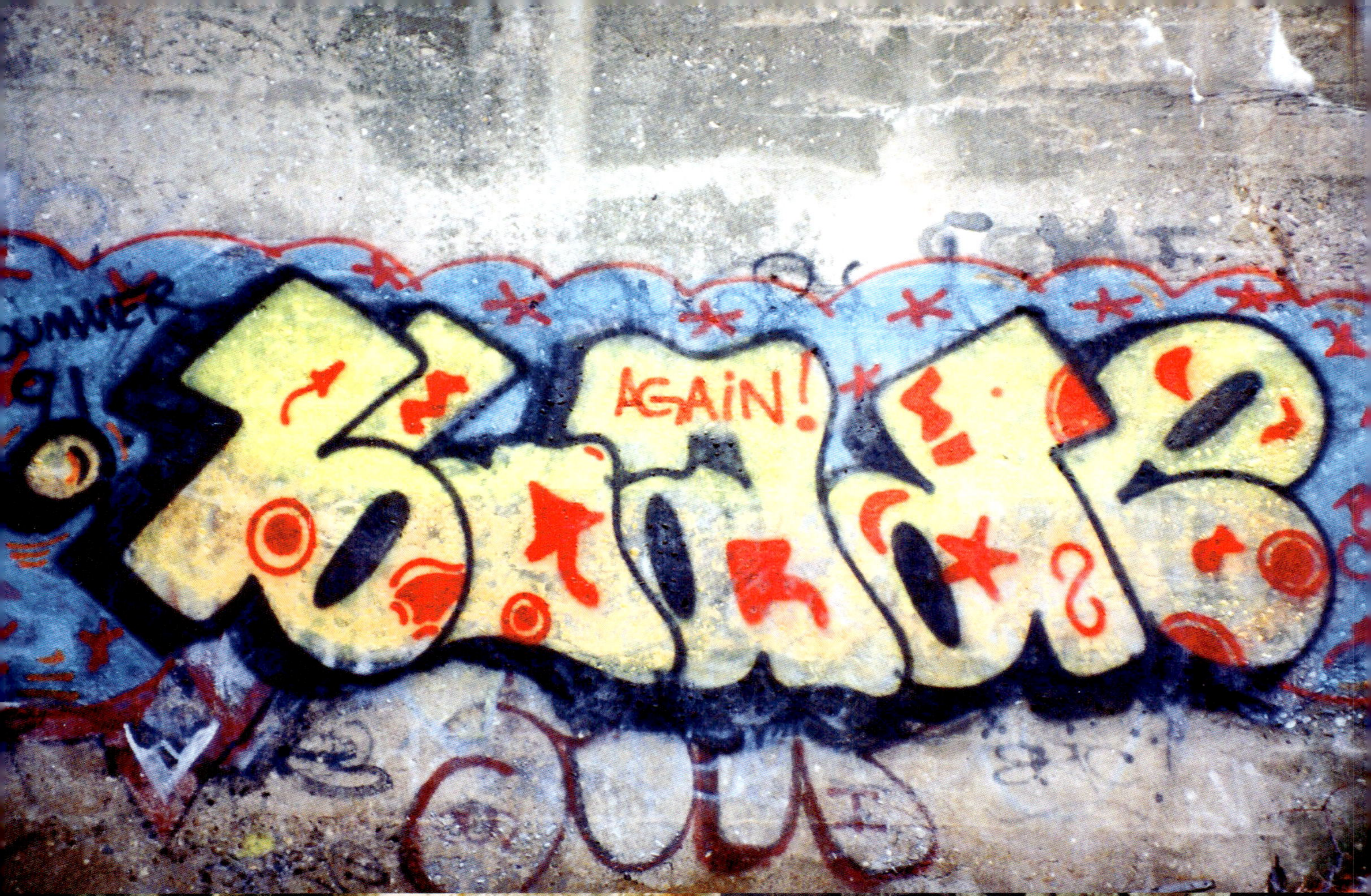
AGAIN!

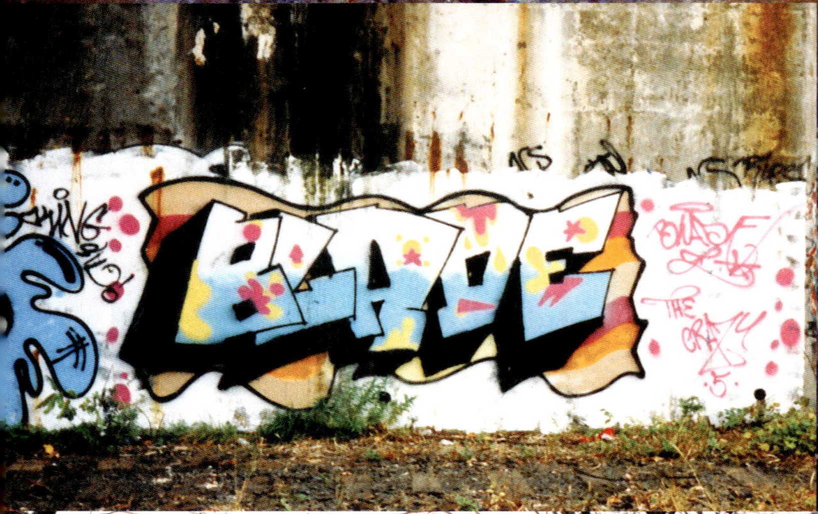

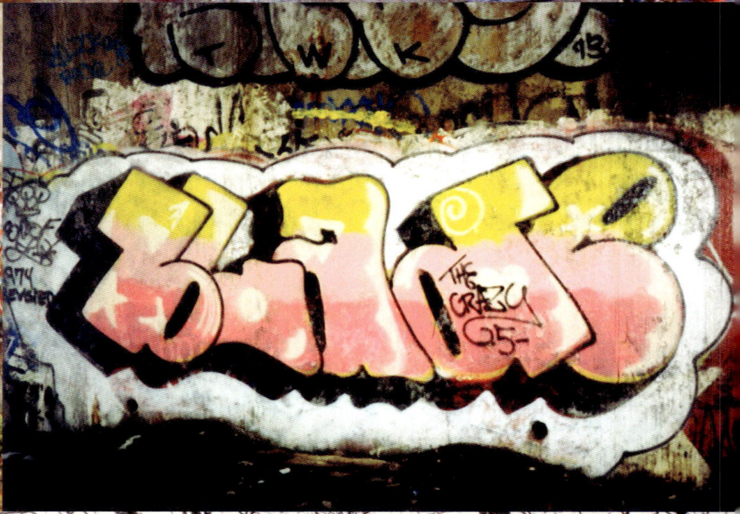

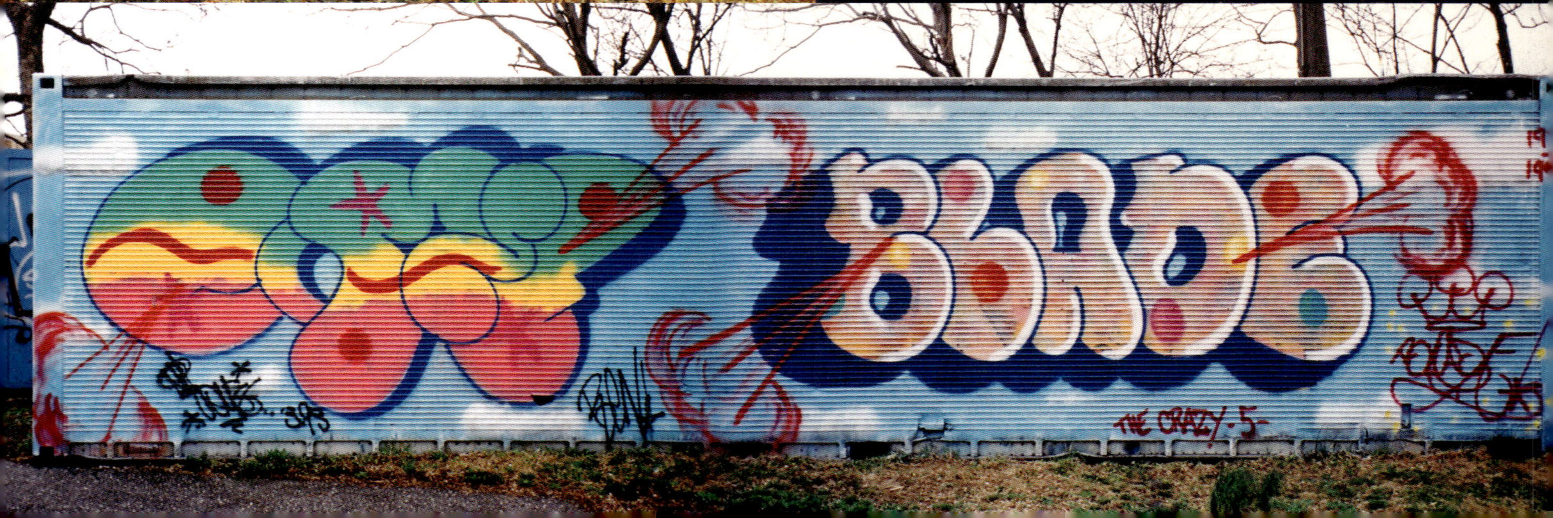
THE CRAZY-5-

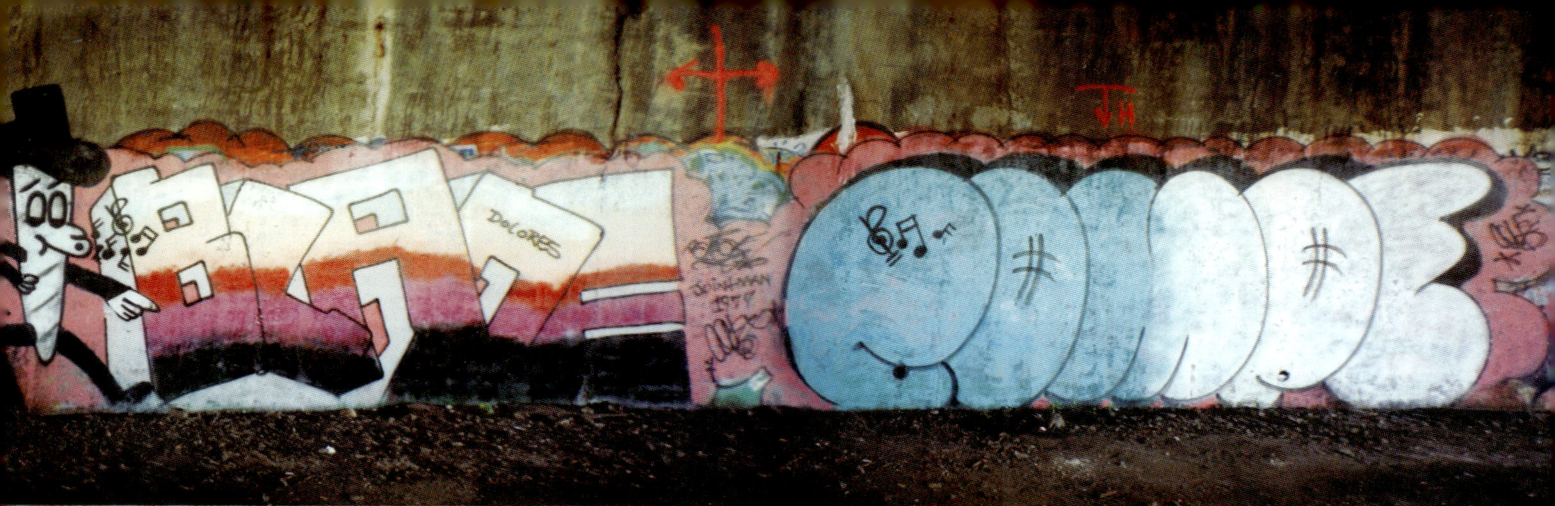
DOLORES

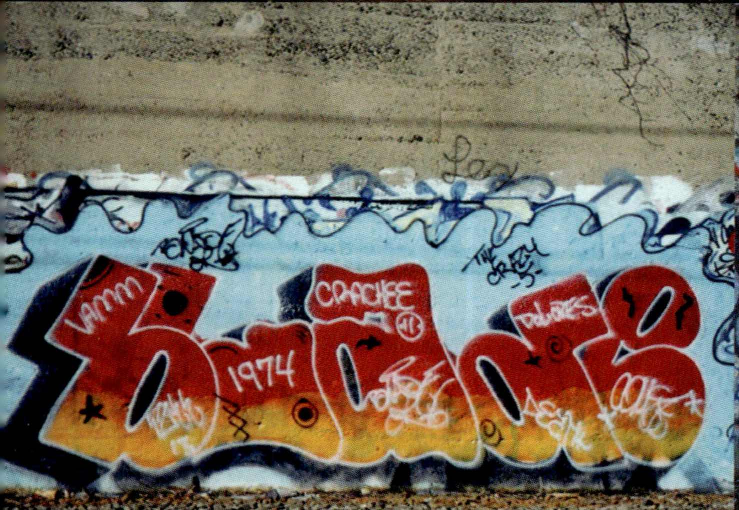
VAMM
CRACHEE
1974
DOLORES

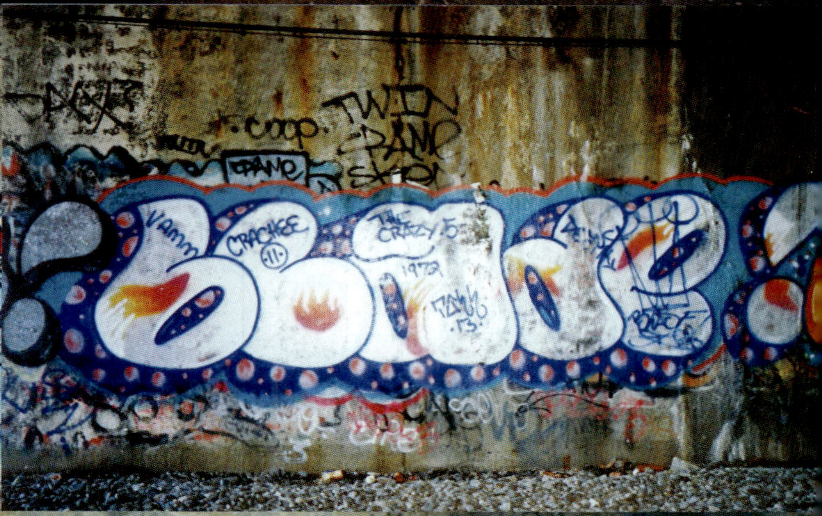
TWIN
VAMM
CRACHEE

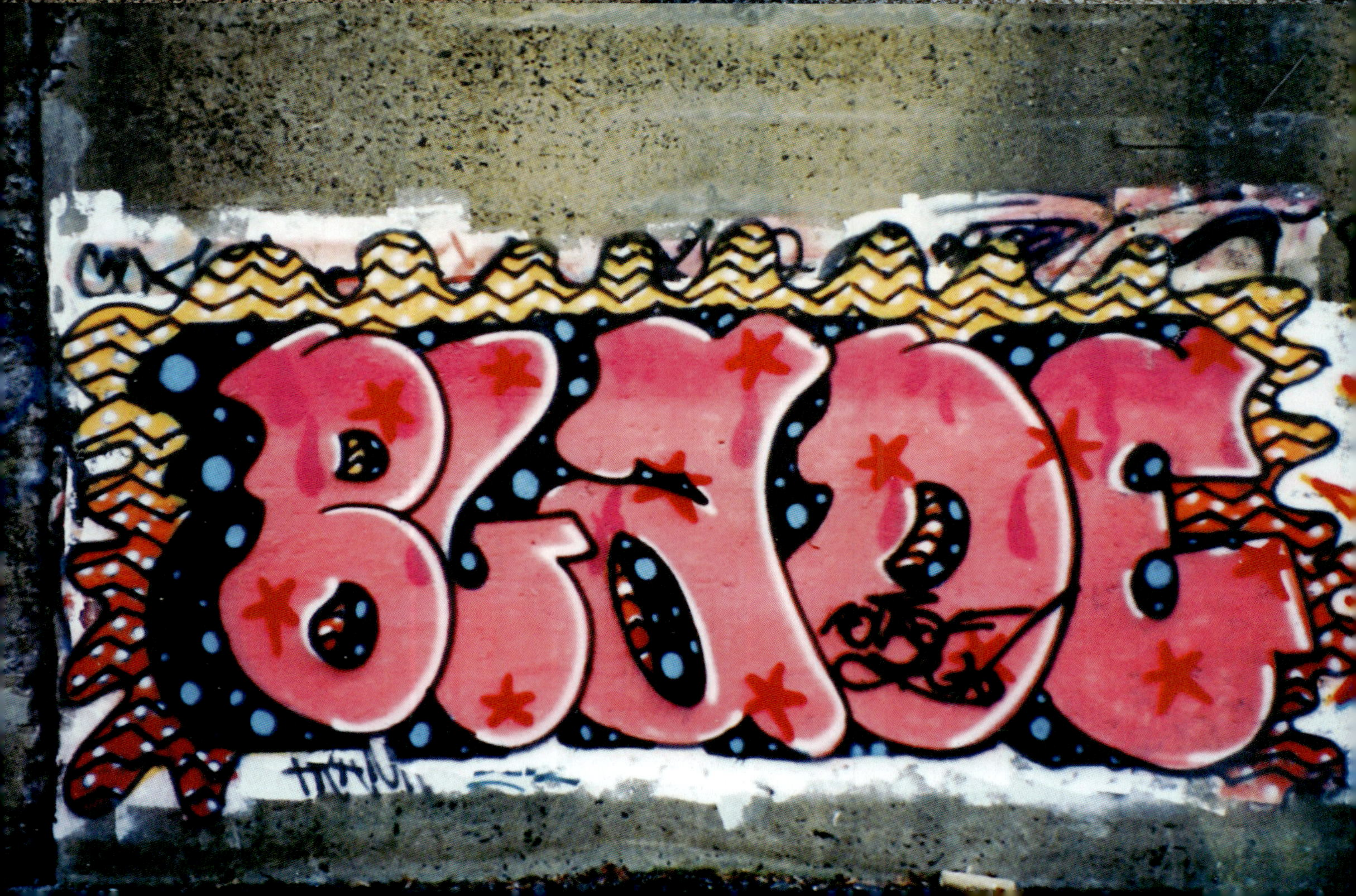

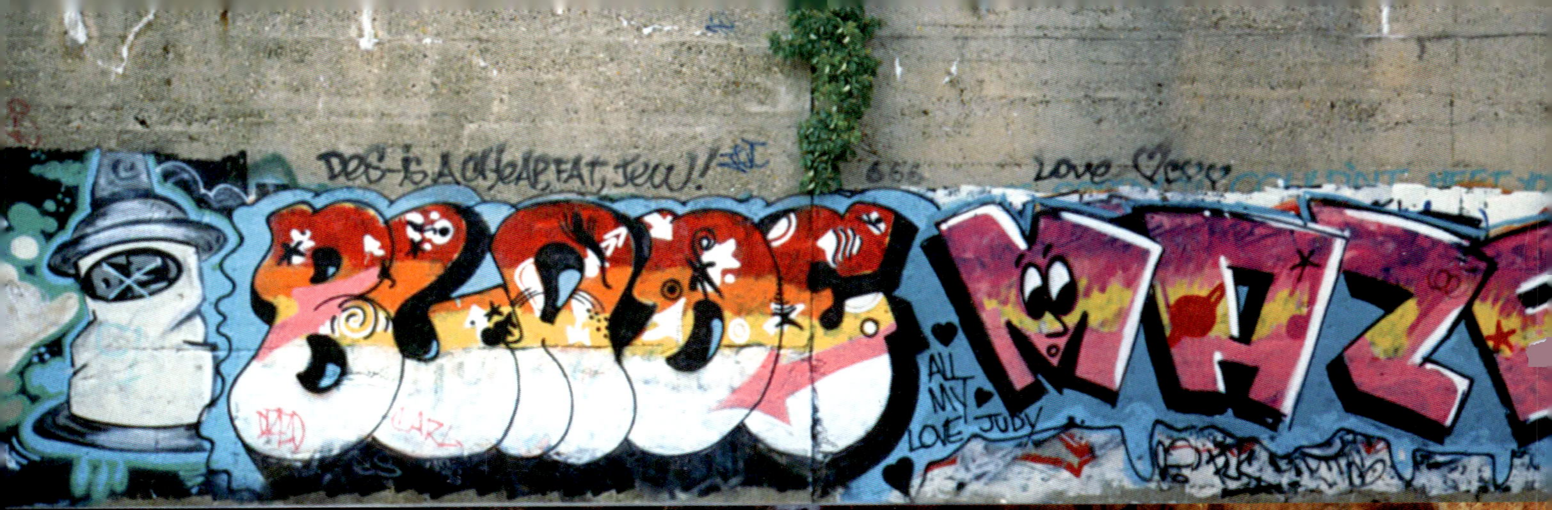
ALL MY LOVE JUDY

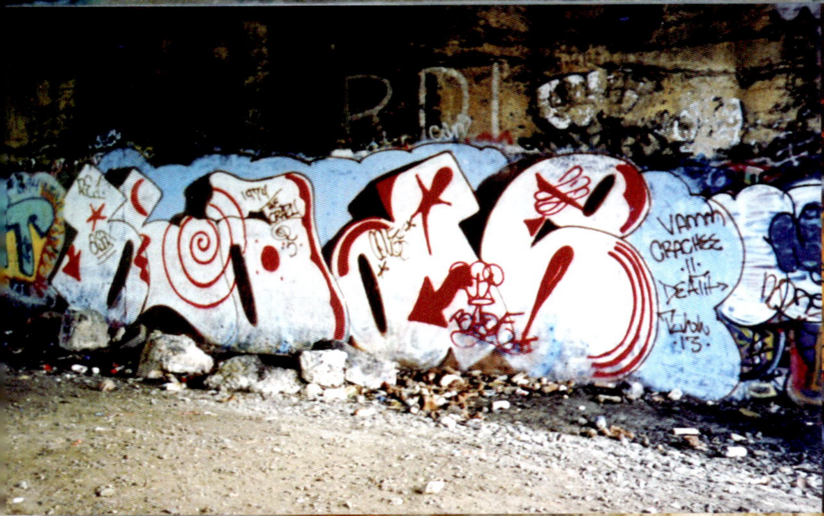

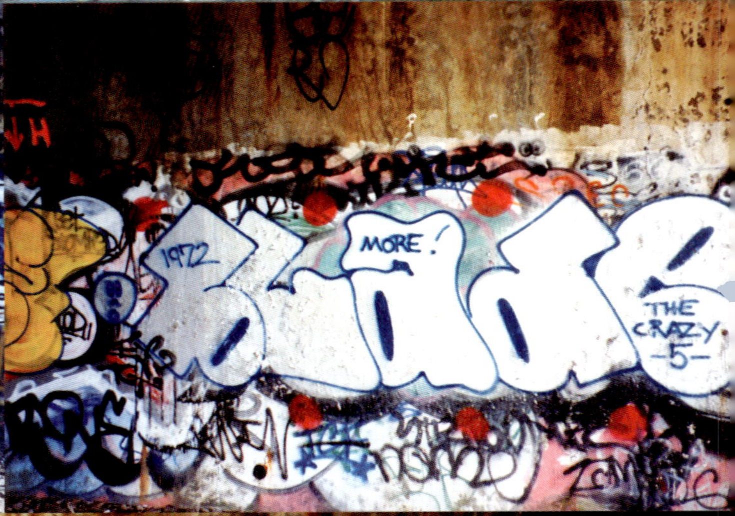
1972
MORE!
THE CRAZY -5-

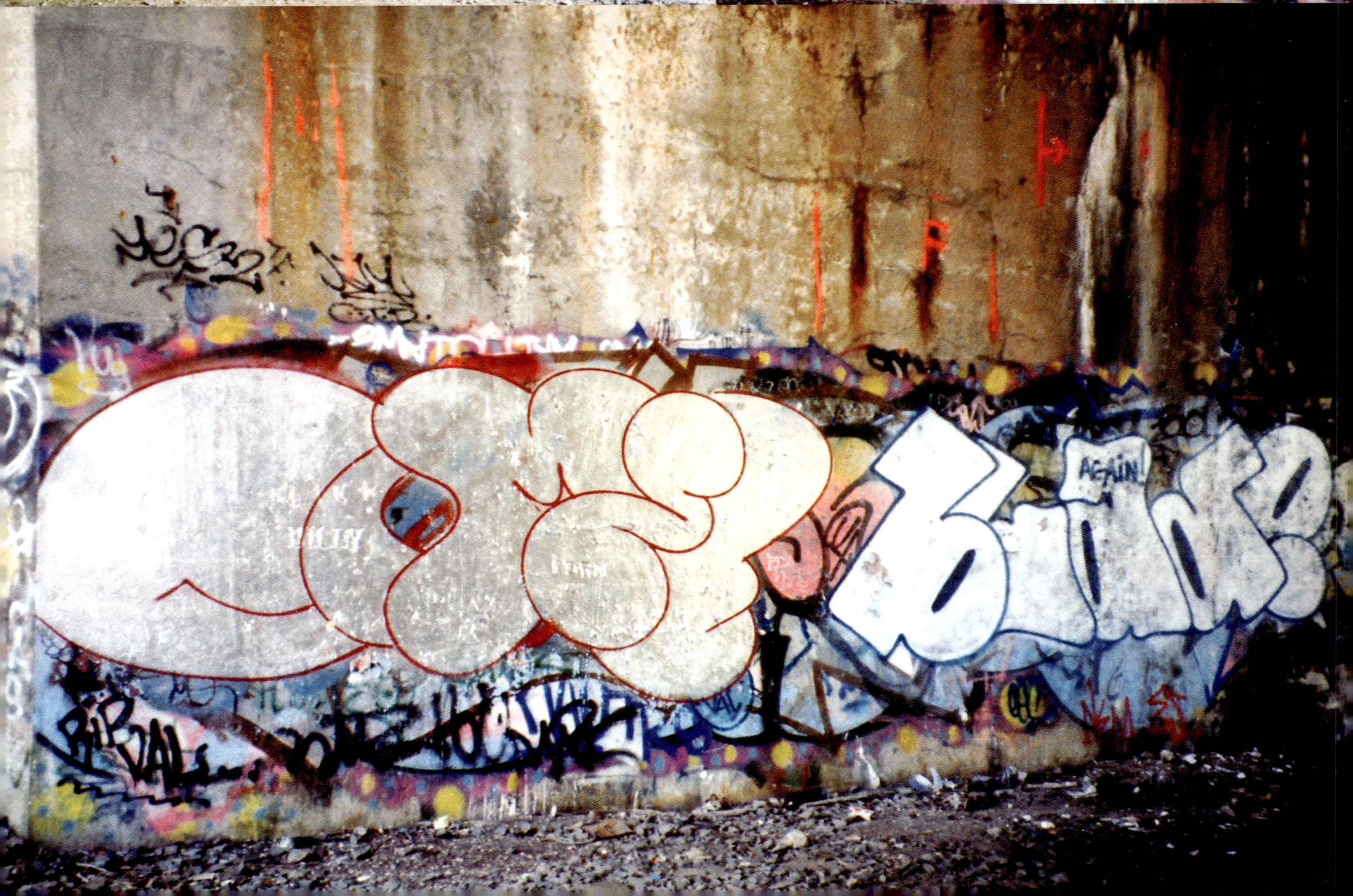
AGAIN!

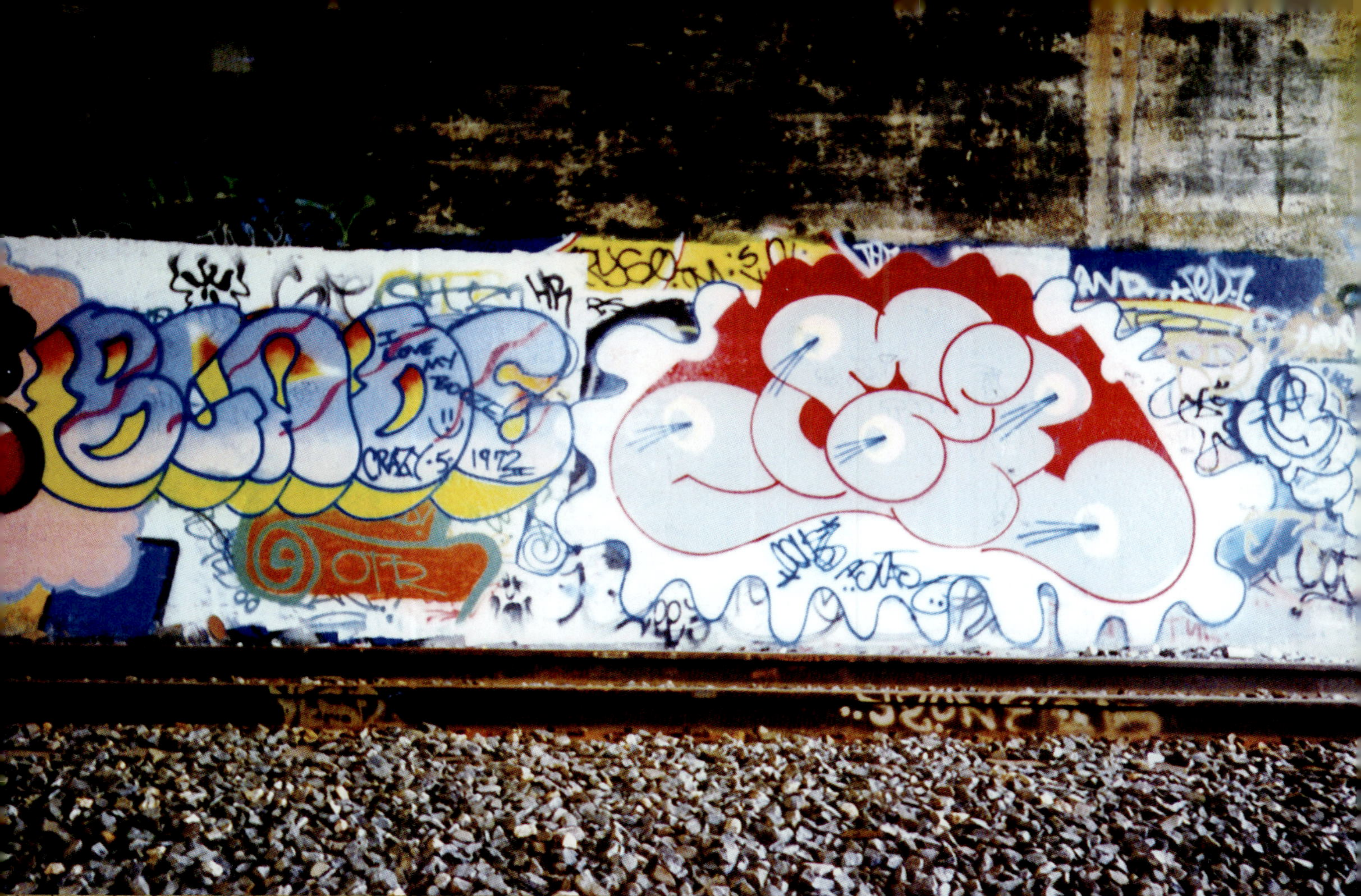

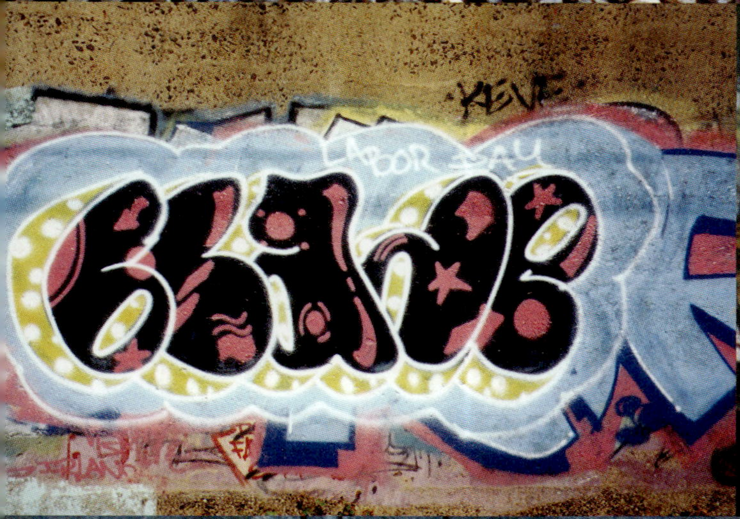
LABOR DAY

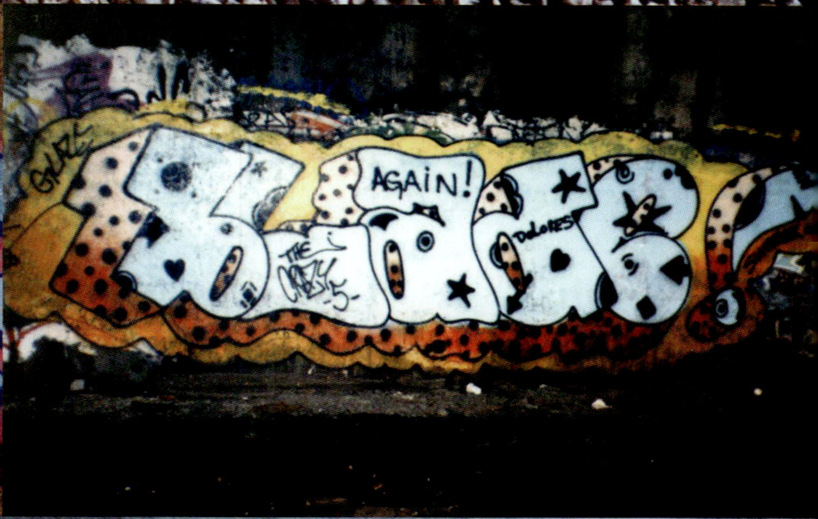
AGAIN!

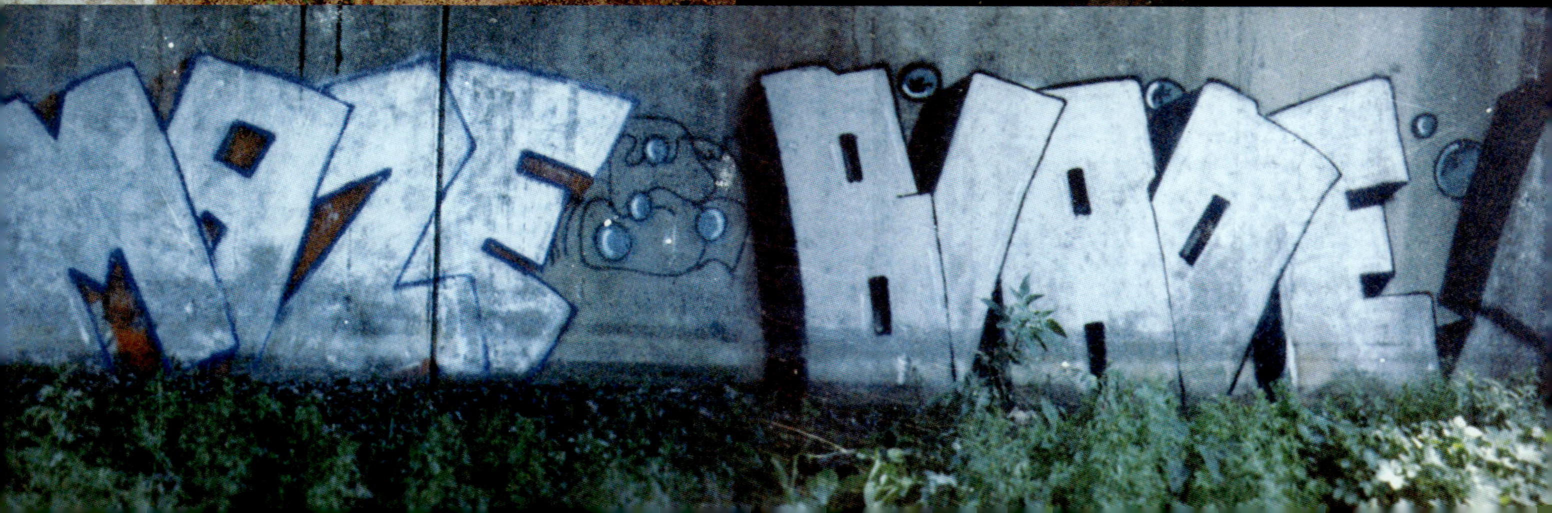

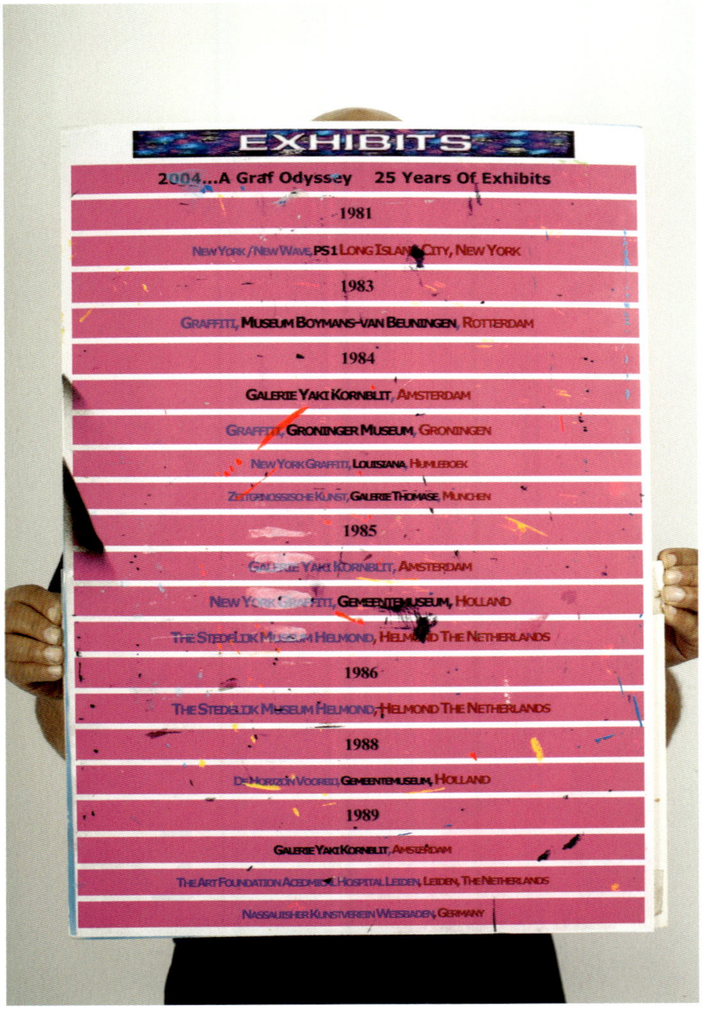

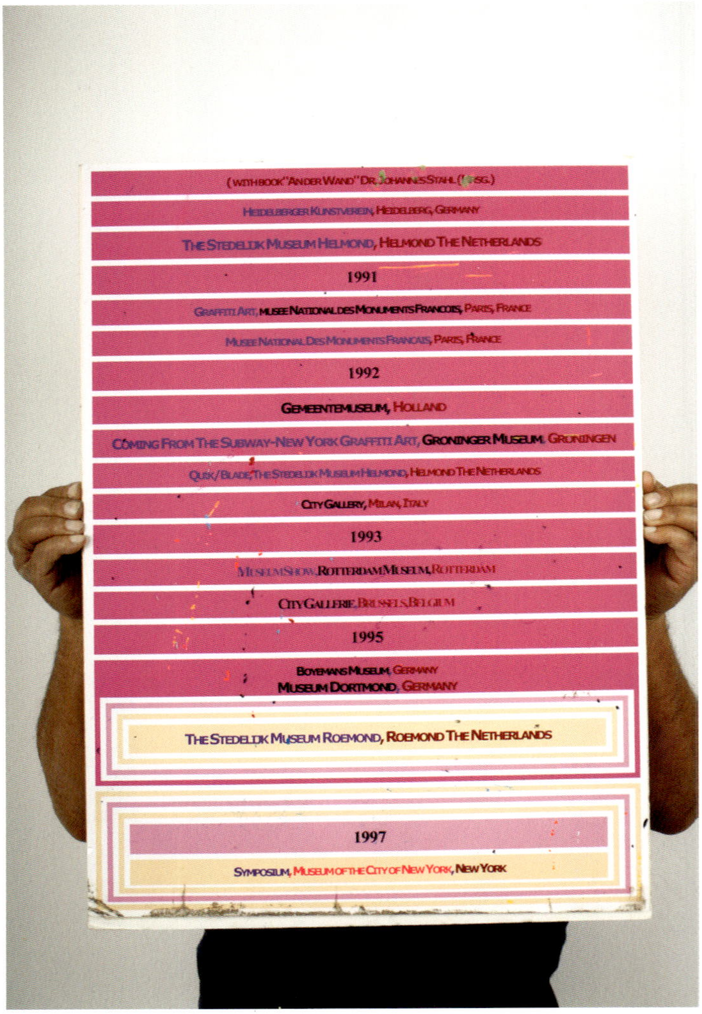

This spread:
BLADE holds up his gallery exhibition history that was used at solo show in 2006 at The Merchantile Stock Exchange (Wall Street). Photos by Adam Wallacavage

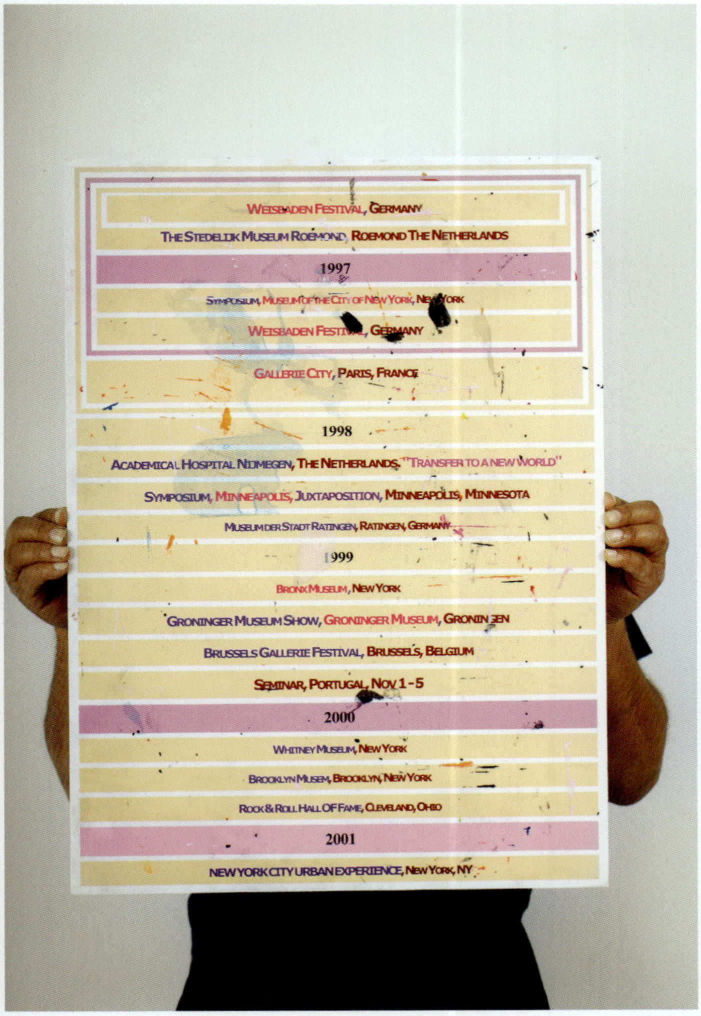
Weisbaden Festival, Germany
The Stedelijk Museum Roemond, Roemond The Netherlands
1997
Symposium, Museum of the City of New York, New York
Weisbaden Festi, Germany
Gallerie City, Paris, France
1998
Academical Hospital Nijmegen, The Netherlands. "Transfer to a new world"
Symposium, Minneapolis, Juxtaposition, Minneapolis, Minnesota
Museum der Stadt Ratingen, Ratingen, Germany
1999
Bronx Museum, New York
Groninger Museum Show, Groninger Museum, Gronin en
Brussels Gallerie Festival, Brussels, Belgium
Seminar, Portugal, Nov 1-5
2000
Whitney Museum, New York
Brooklyn Musem, Brooklyn, New York
Rock & Roll Hall Of Fame, Cleveland, Ohio
2001
New York City Urban Experience, New York, NY

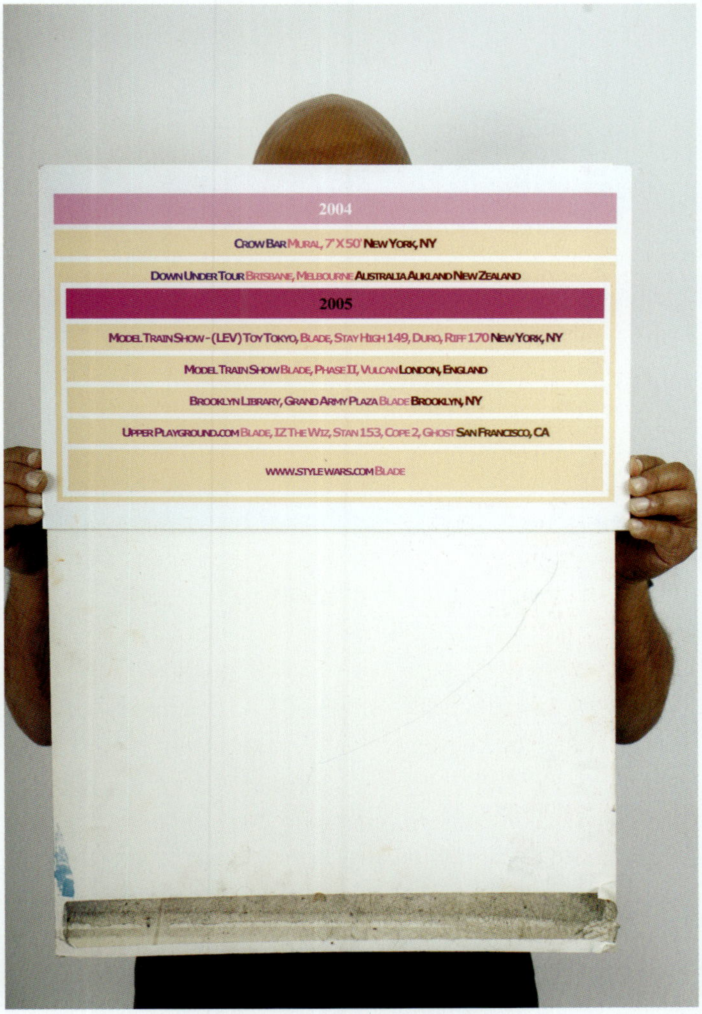
2004
Crow Bar Mural, 7' X 50' New York, NY
Down Under Tour Brisbane, Melbourne Australia Aukland New Zealand
2005
Model Train Show - (LEV) Toy Tokyo, Blade, Stay High 149, Duro, Riff 170 New York, NY
Model Train Show Blade, Phase II, Vulcan London, England
Brooklyn Library, Grand Army Plaza Blade Brooklyn, NY
Upper Playground.com Blade, IZ The Wiz, Stan 153, Cope 2, Ghost San Francisco, CA
www.stylewars.com Blade

In 2008, I had enough money to retire, I had everything I wanted, and I looked forward to the move to Florida. There were rumors surfacing that DEATH was alive and living in Rhode Island. He reached out to VAMM who put him in touch with me. We decided to get together one last time before one of us died. Then we decided we should all get together—the original members of THE CRAZY 5—just the five of us. On a hot summer night in 2011, we met at a bar in Pelham Bay. CRACHEE couldn't make it but sent us his best wishes. Marty Cooper, the graffiti historian, showed up to document the event and to take a group photograph.

We were all middle-aged men; some of us wore it better than the others. We talked a lot about writing, and while I was proud of the accomplishment of kinging the trains, I was also proud of how I lived my life. The rest of THE CRAZY 5 didn't disappoint in their accomplishments. CRACHEE became a newspaper reporter; he's the author of two books and he won a Pulitzer Prize in 2004. VAMM has been working for a bread company since late 1975; he's now one of the top men at the company. He has been married since 1980 and he has two grown children. MARIO is a professor at a college in Texas, where he teaches computer science. He laughed when he found out that Portia answered my e-mails. DEATH, the craziest of THE CRAZY 5, woke up from a drunken stupor in my old apartment one morning and decided to change his life. He went into Manhattan, interviewed for a job, and to his amazement he got it. He worked hard and managed to stay away from the Parkside group. The company moved to Rhode Island in 1983 and he moved with it. When he left the Bronx, he left behind the self-destructive path he had been on. He still works for the same company and he is a family man with grandchildren.

Other names came up, such as COMET. COMET did a bid upstate in the 1980s. When he came back, he turned his life around. He's worked as an electrical engineer for well over twenty years and he has recently started to paint again, showing successfully in Europe. GEAR, another one of my partners, owns a Mercedes Benz dealership in Westchester and has raised a family. One of the final names to come up was MAZE. Everyone jokingly asked about my twelve-year-old partner who never went to school. There was only one job left that MAZE was capable of doing. He became a cop!

The stories at the bar went late into the night, until we began repeating ourselves. After that, new identities emerged for the members of the group as new passions emerged. You want to talk about cars, call VAMM or GEAR. You want to talk about chess, talk to Gillen. Need help with a computer? Contact MARIO, because that's one of the subjects he teaches. As a reporter, CRACHEE can talk about anything at depth, but our conversations usually revolve around music rather than the hazy days of graffiti. We closed the bar and I said goodbye to my childhood friends, knowing I was about to start a new chapter in my life.

Just two months later, as the leaves began to change color in the Bronx, Portia and I packed a lifetime of memories into boxes. The boxes went into a large U-Haul van that we attached to back of the car I've owned for forty years. We said goodbye to our neighbors and took one last look around the neighborhood. The Baychester lay-up was less than a mile away. I stopped the car and got out for a moment. The fence is much taller now, and kids don't paint trains anymore, but I swear as I stood there I could hear the clanking sounds of spray cans. The final stop was Parkside Houses, home to Portia and me for so many years. I watched the kids play basketball and I wondered if they knew that I had once been one of them. From Parkside I turned the car onto the highway and headed south, away from the Bronx—my home for all but two years of my life.

We arrived in Florida two days later and started setting up our new home. I still wake up at 2:00 a.m., put some music on, and start to paint. Some things never change.

Opposite page: BLADE and Portia at their new home in Florida. 2012.
Following two spreads: BLADE and friends.

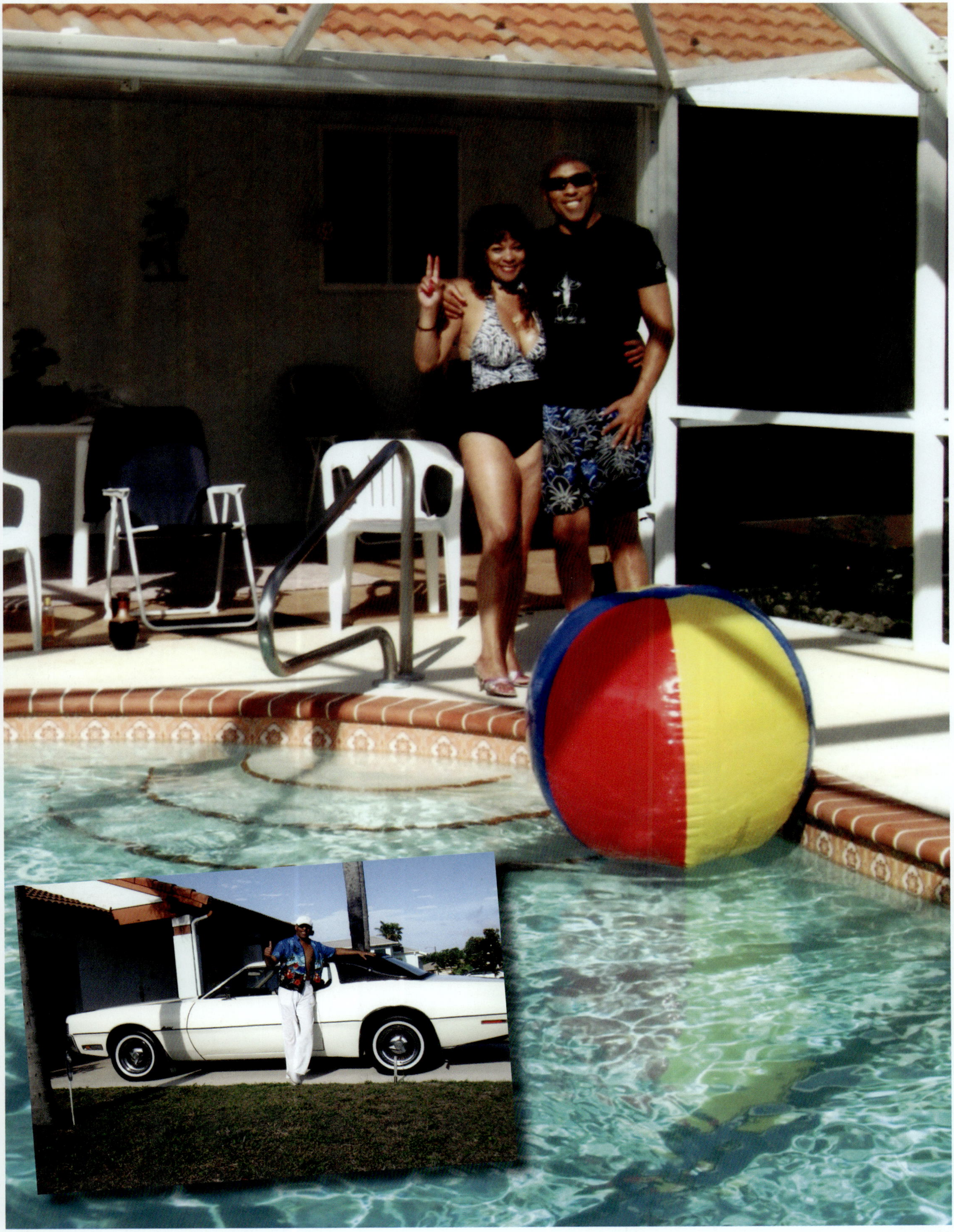

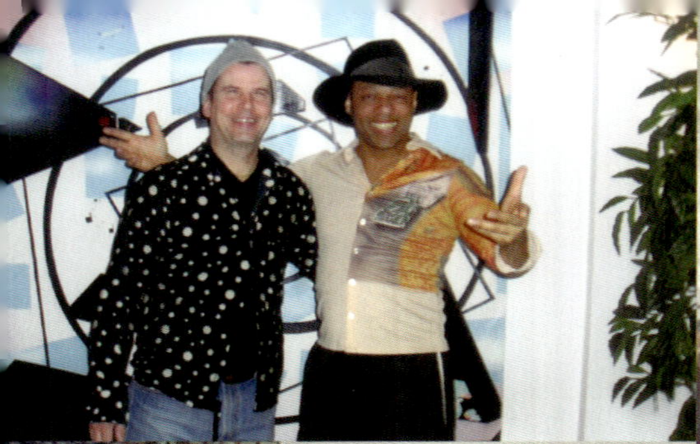
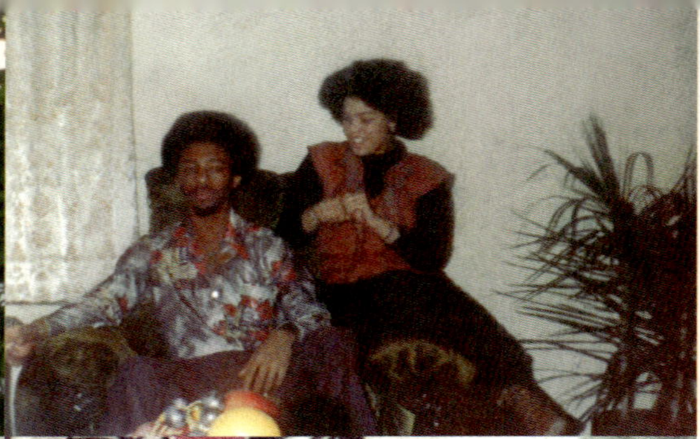
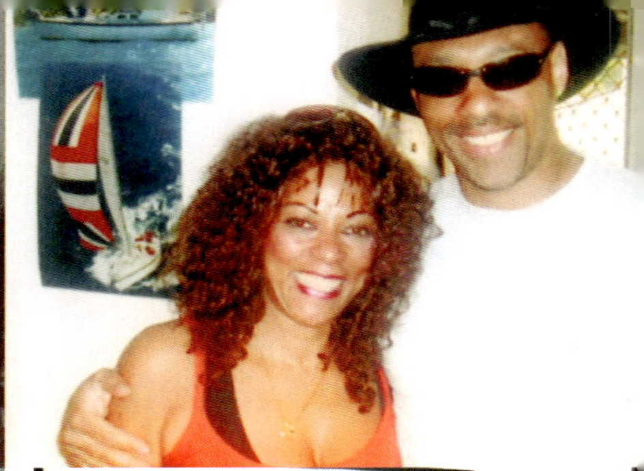
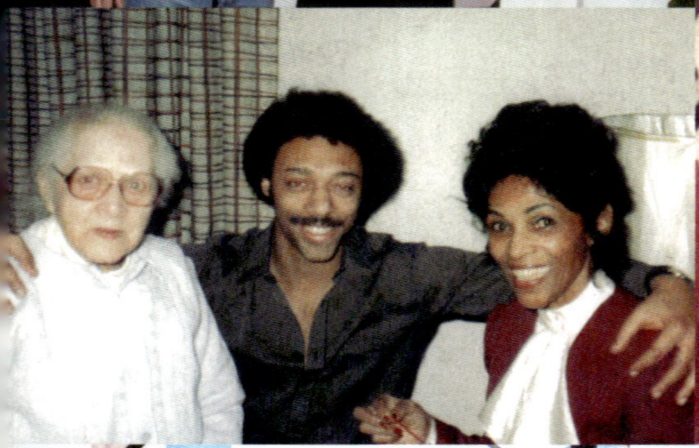
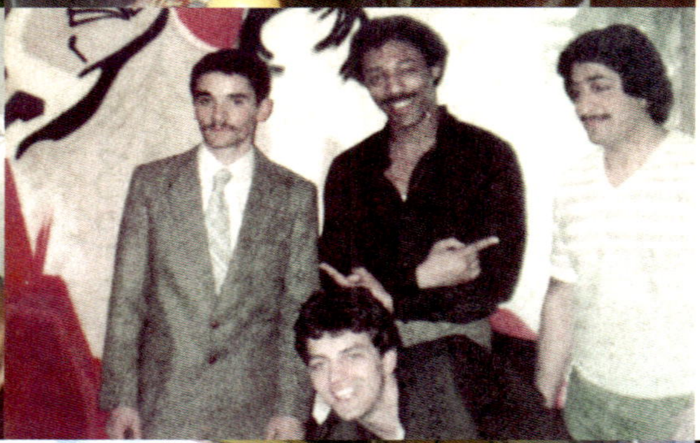
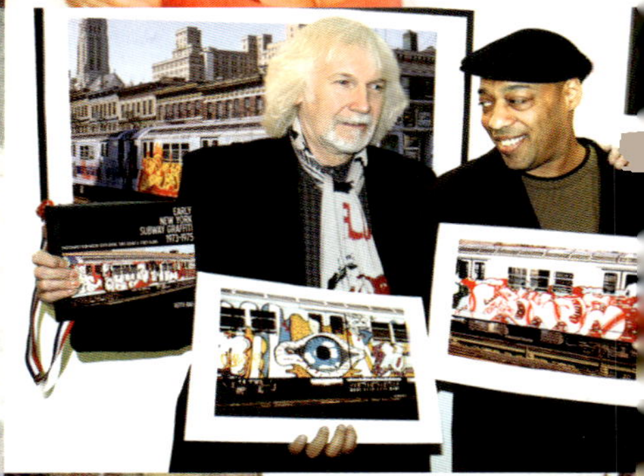
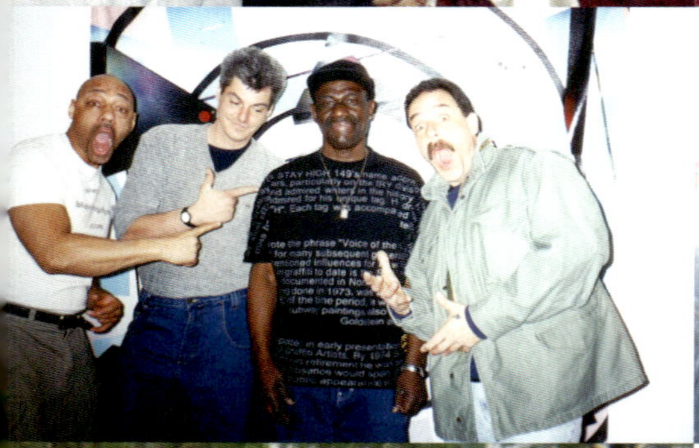
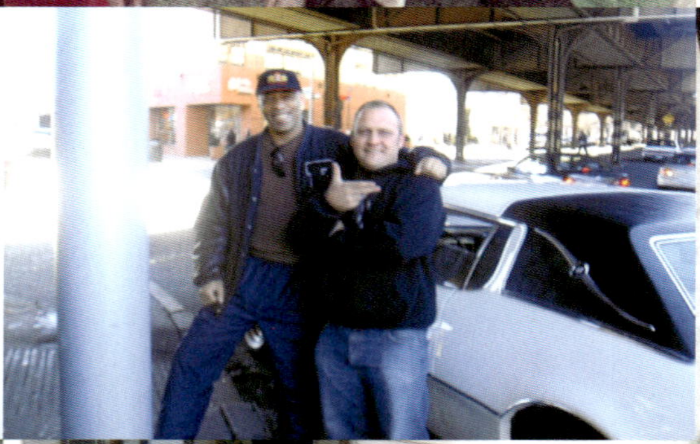
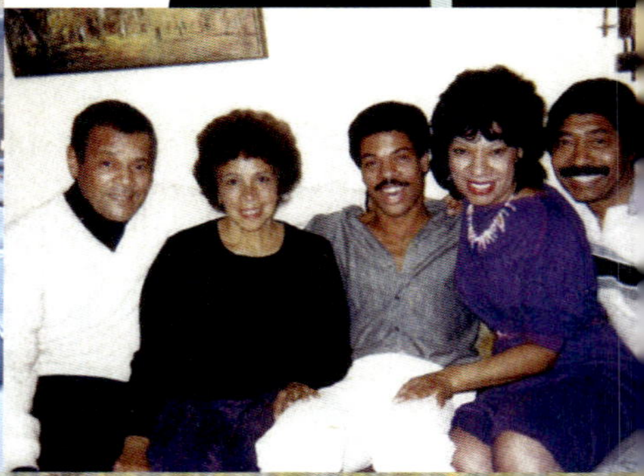
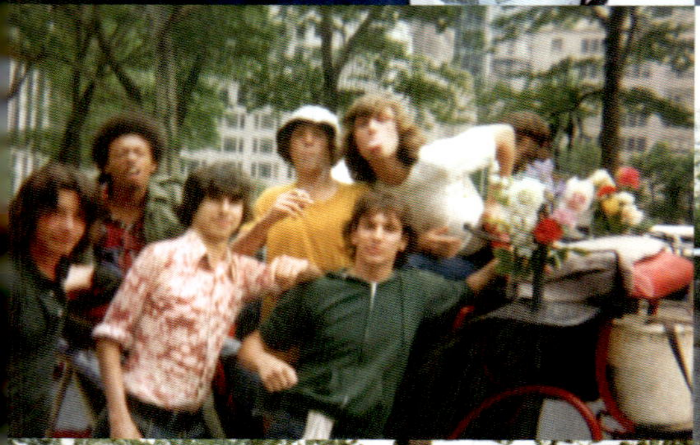
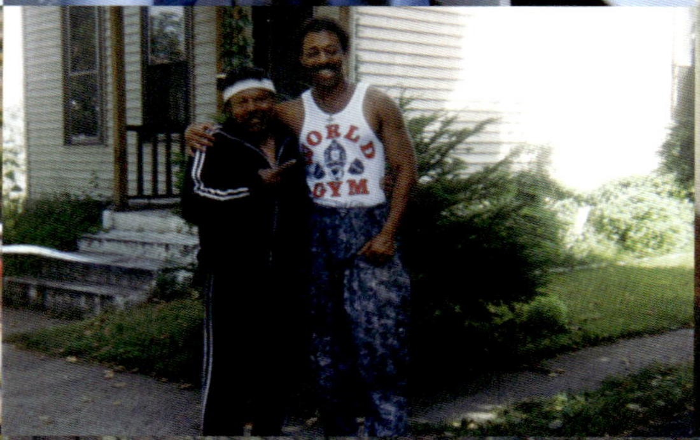
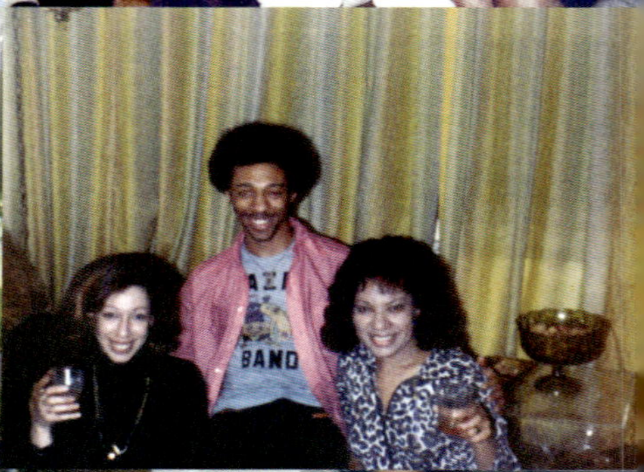
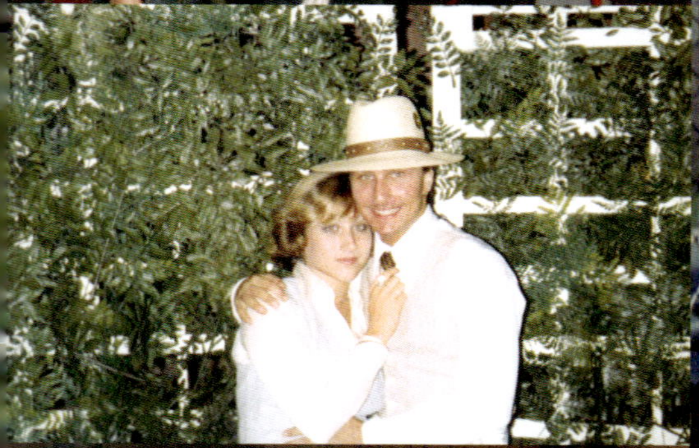
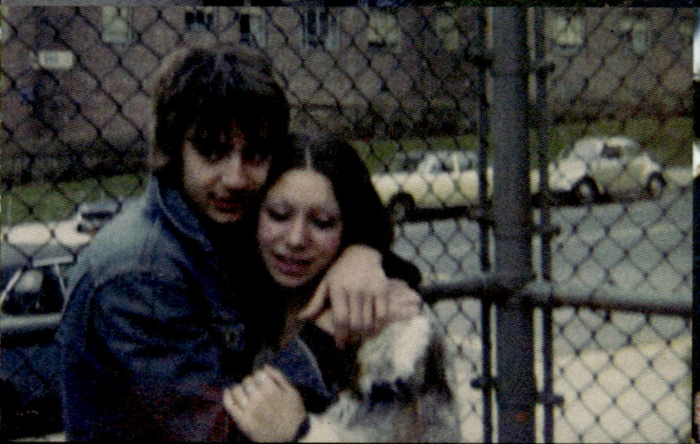
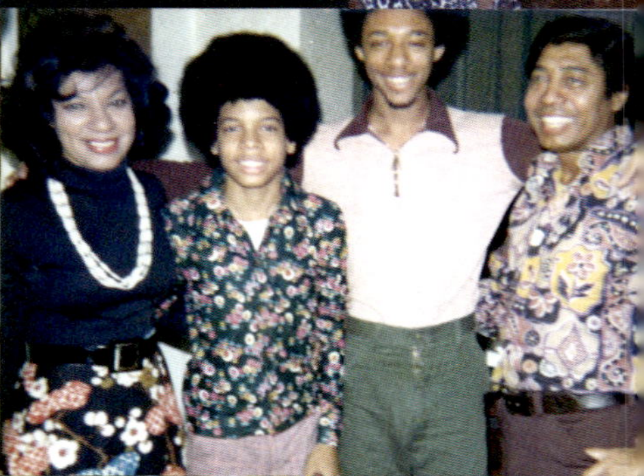
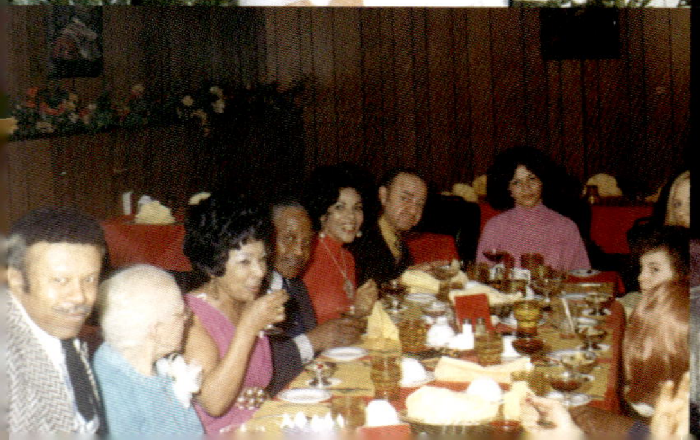
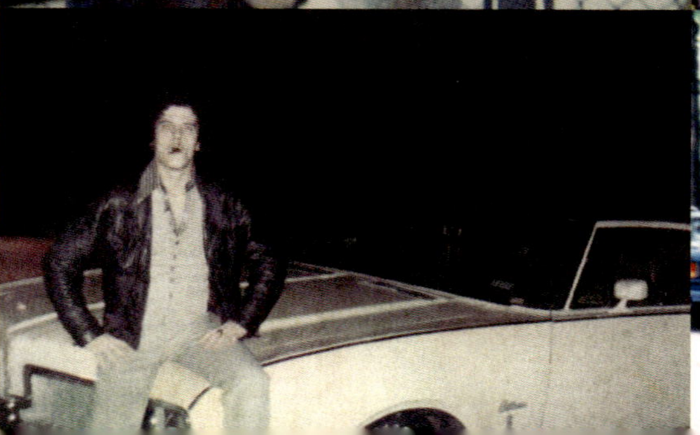
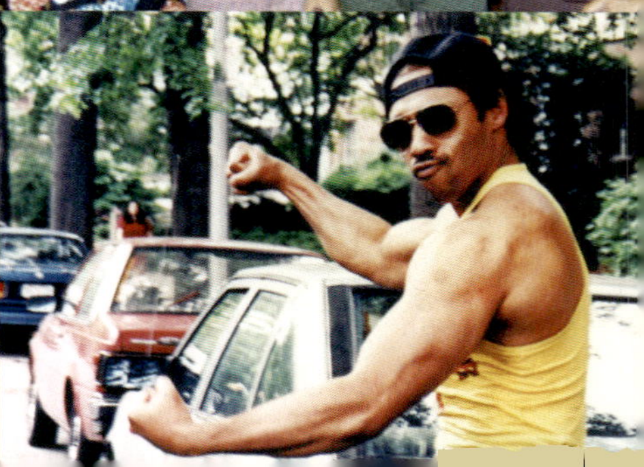

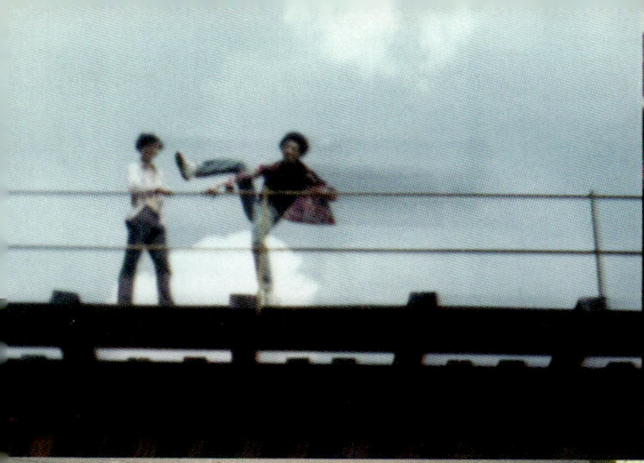
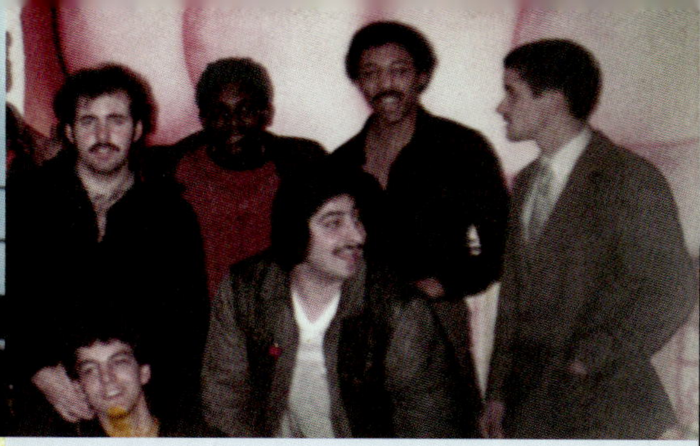
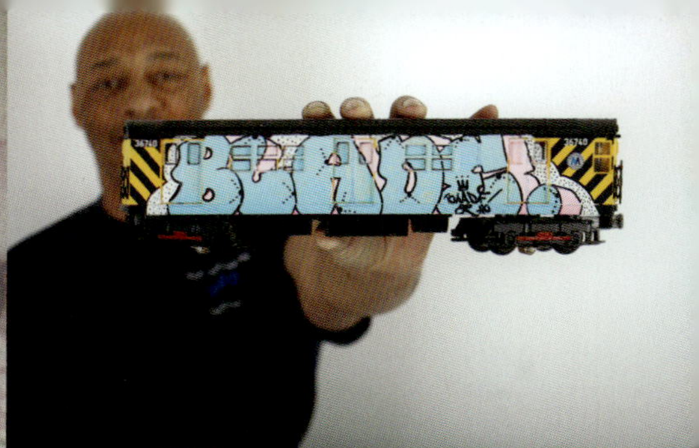
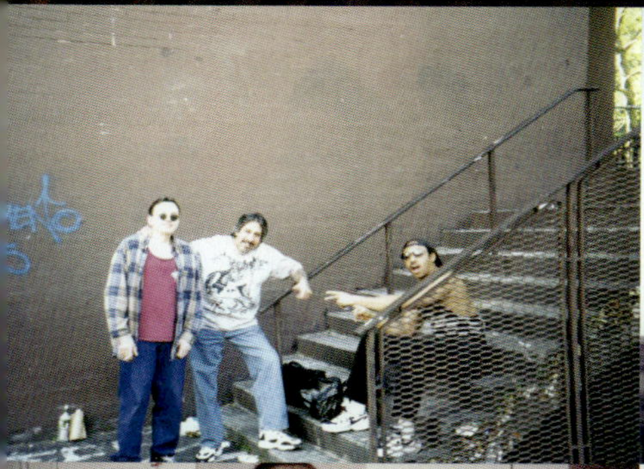
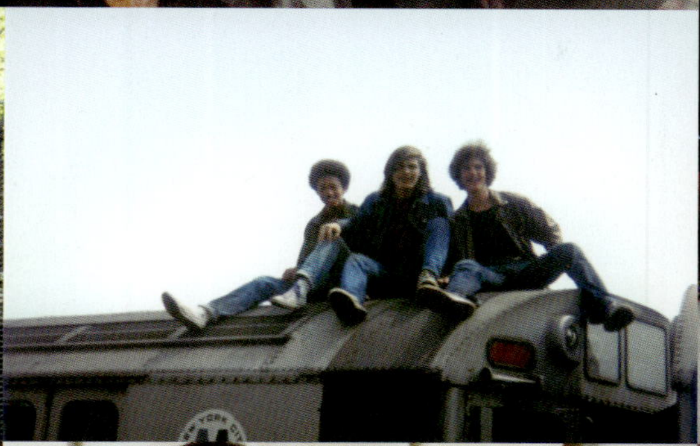
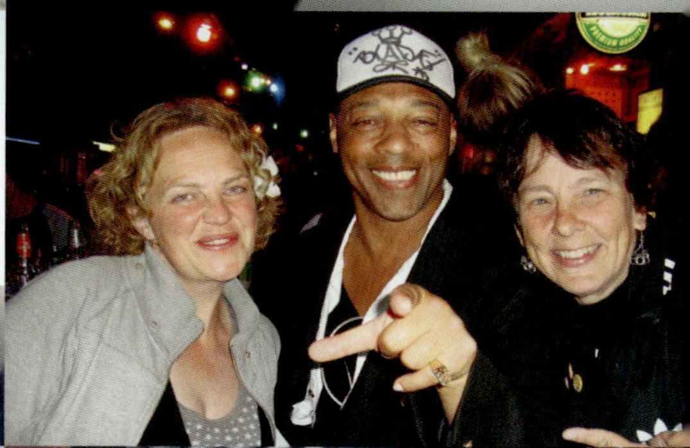
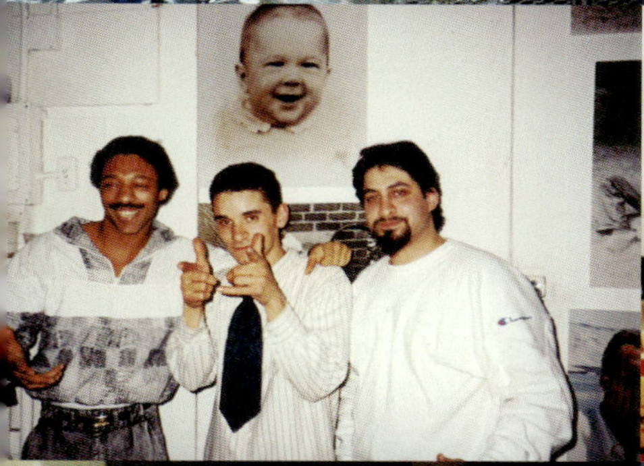
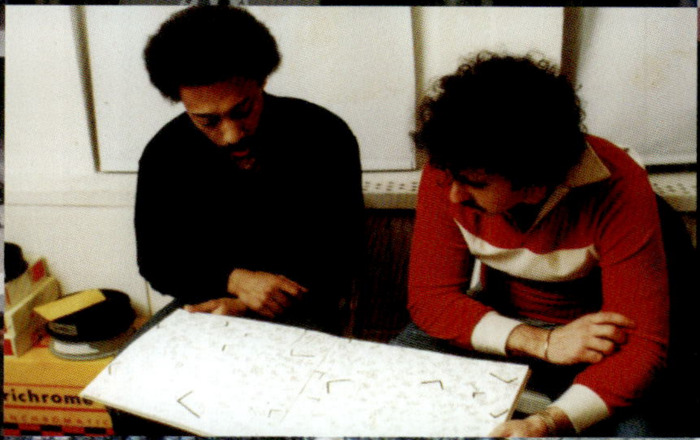
richrome
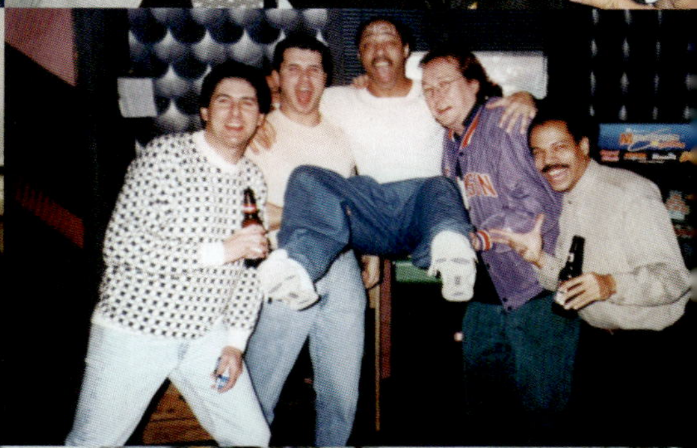
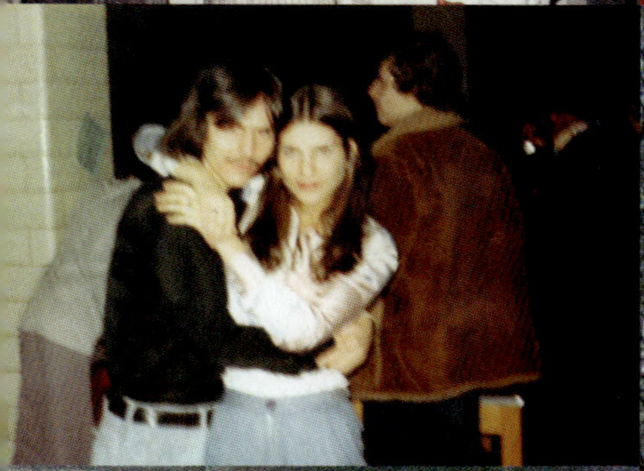
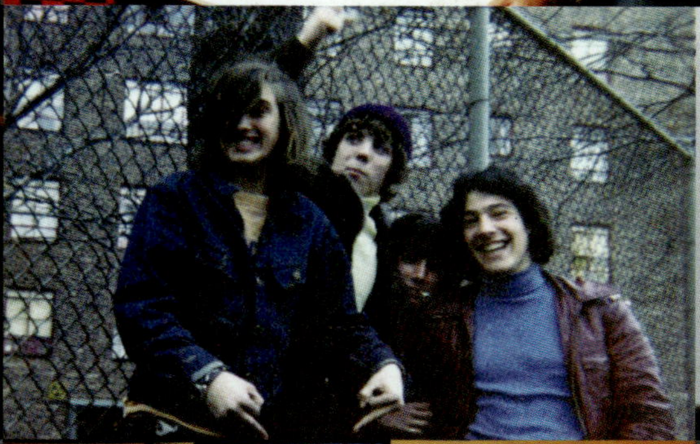
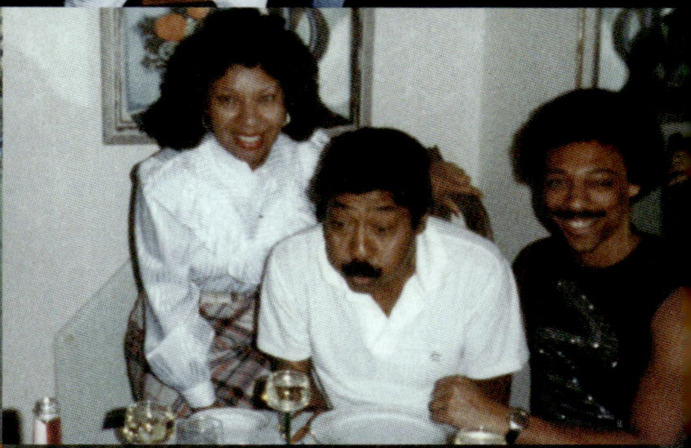
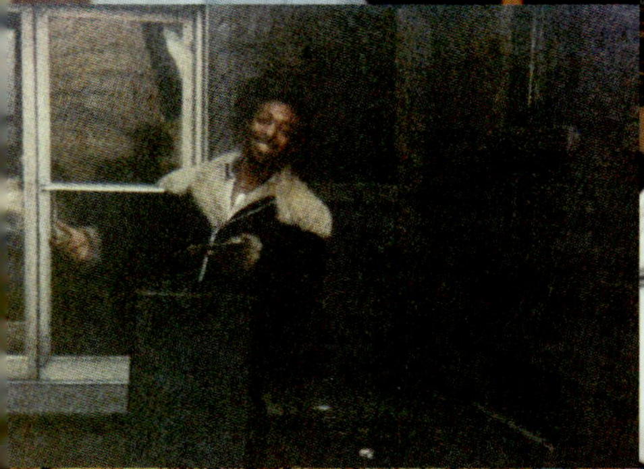
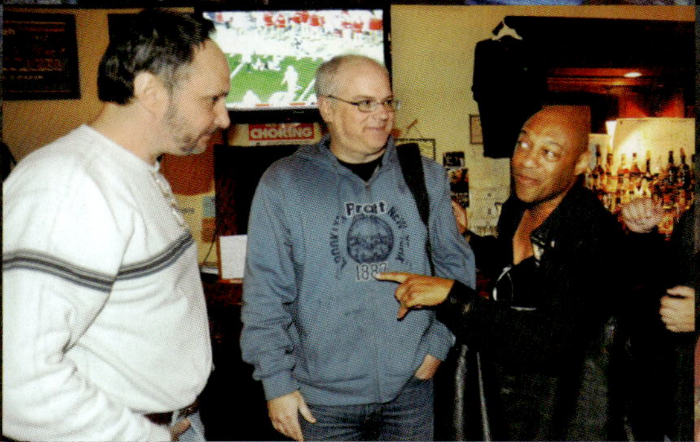
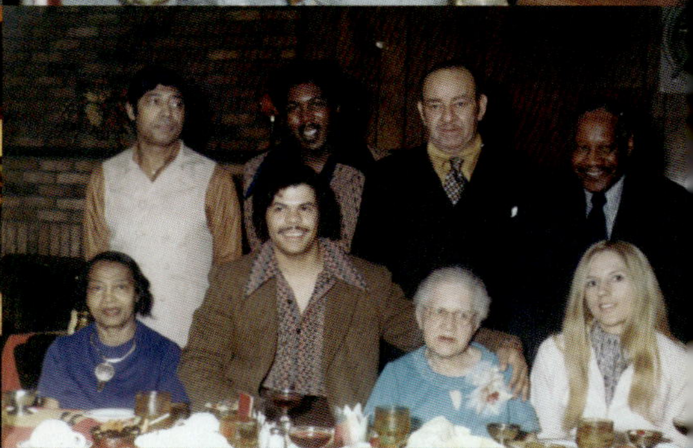
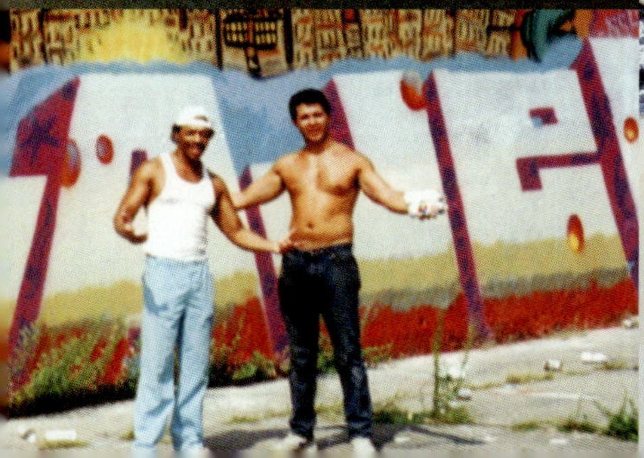

GIOS
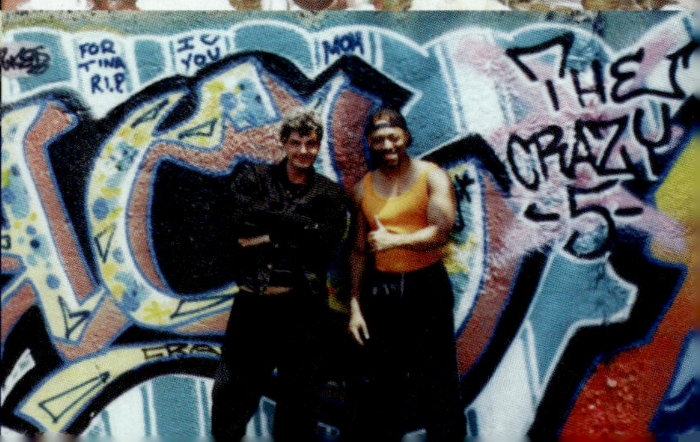
FOR TINA R.I.P.
THE CRAZY 5

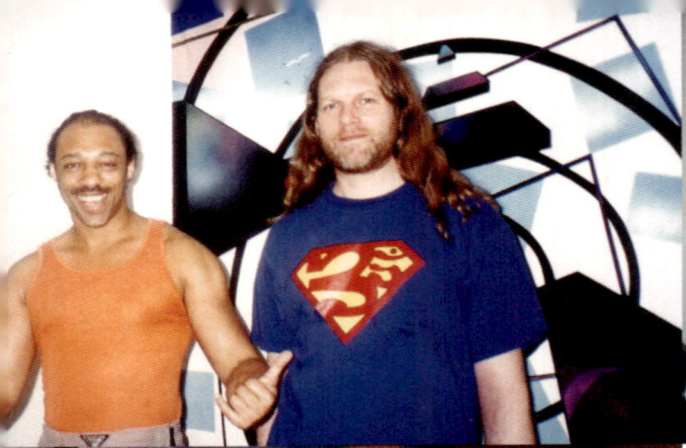
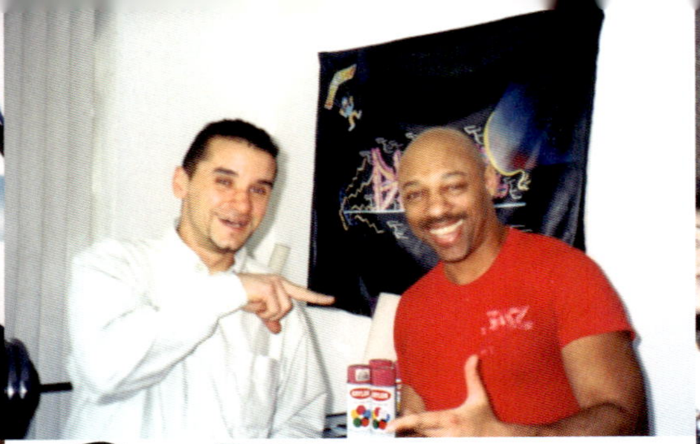
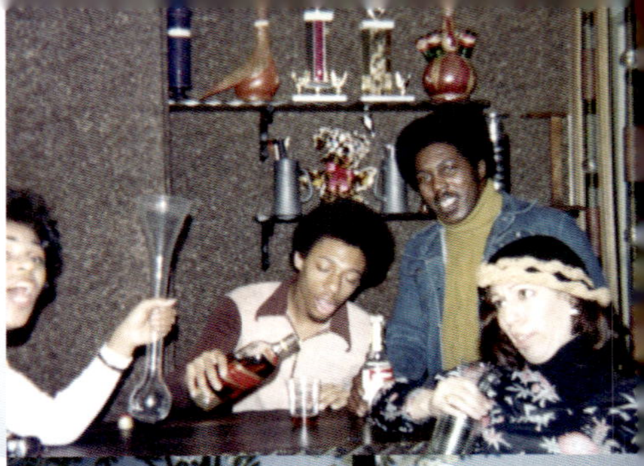
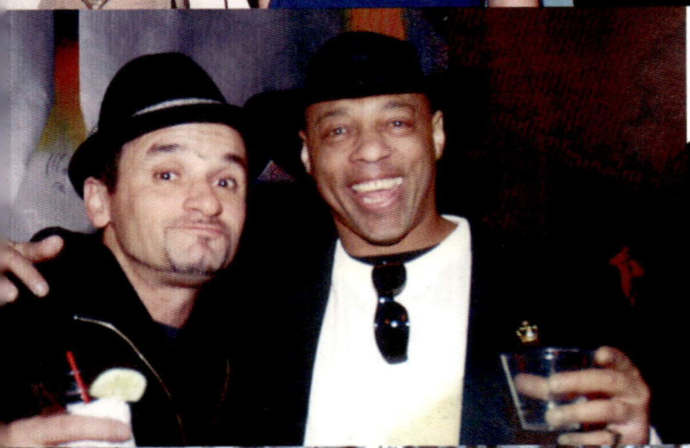
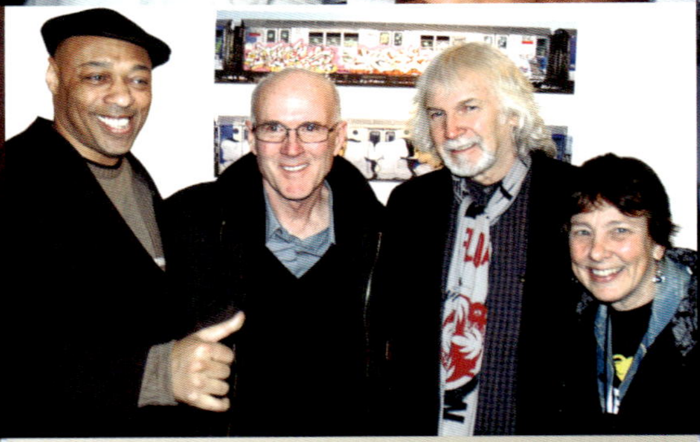
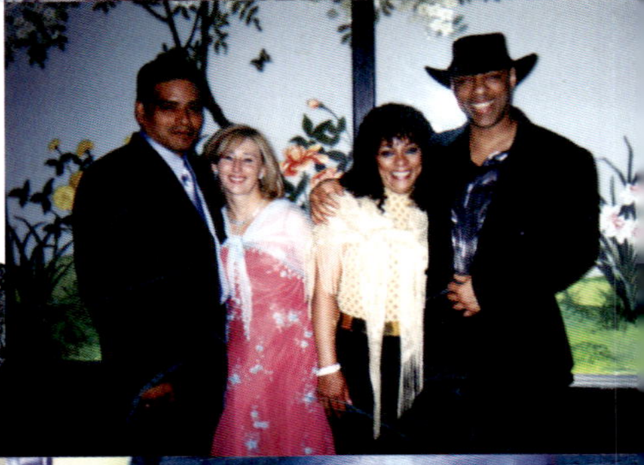
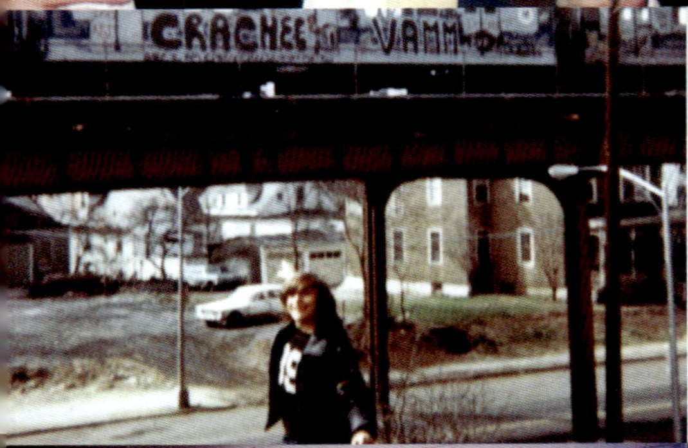
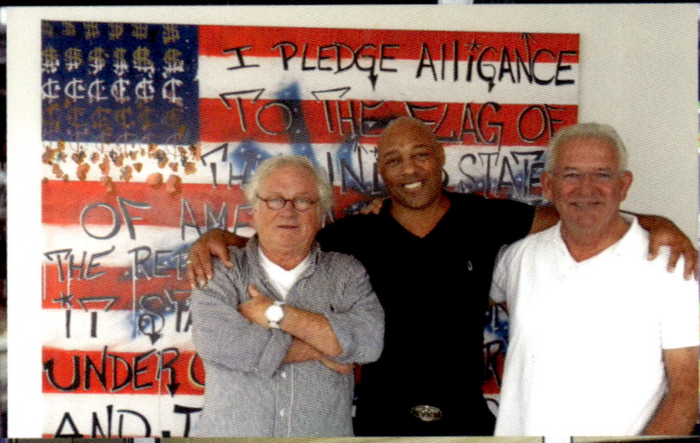
I PLEDGE ALLIGANCE
TO THE FLAG OF
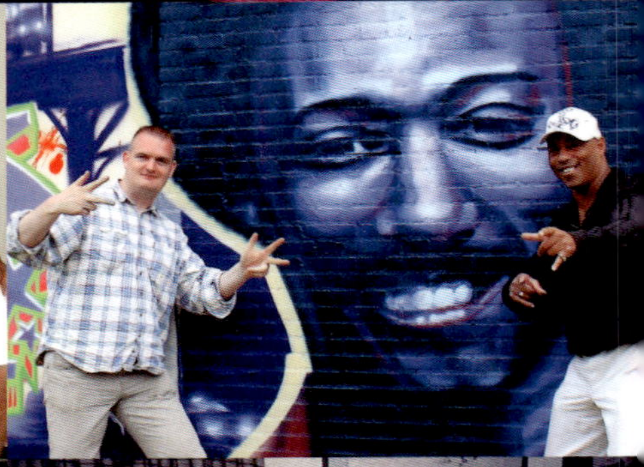
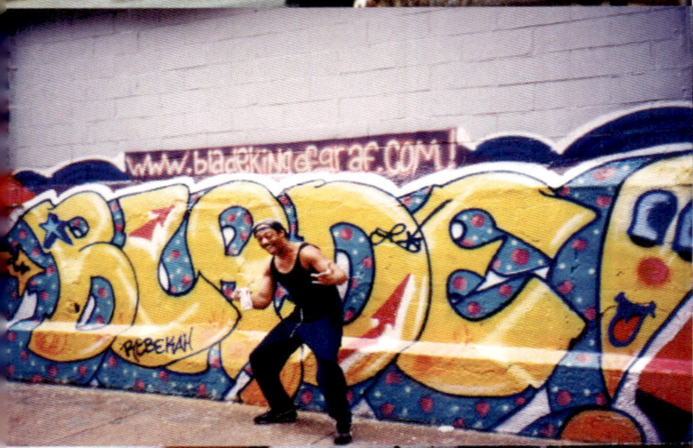
www.bladekingofgraf.com
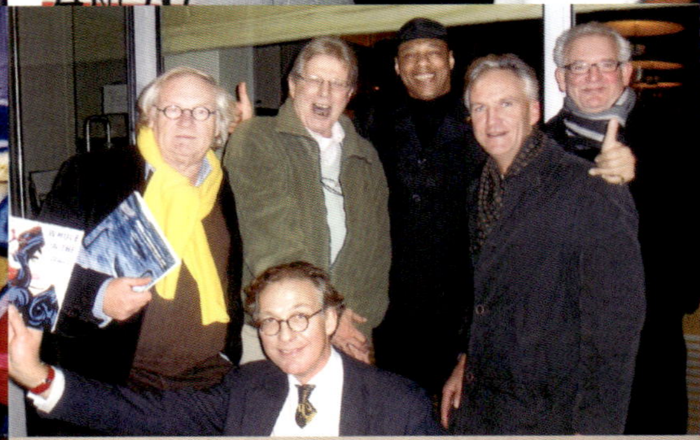
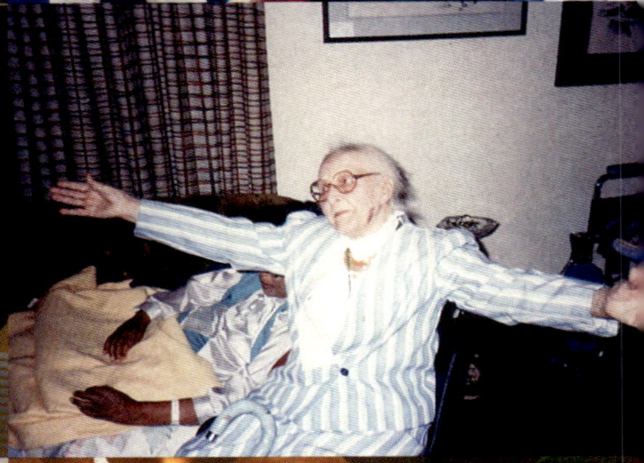
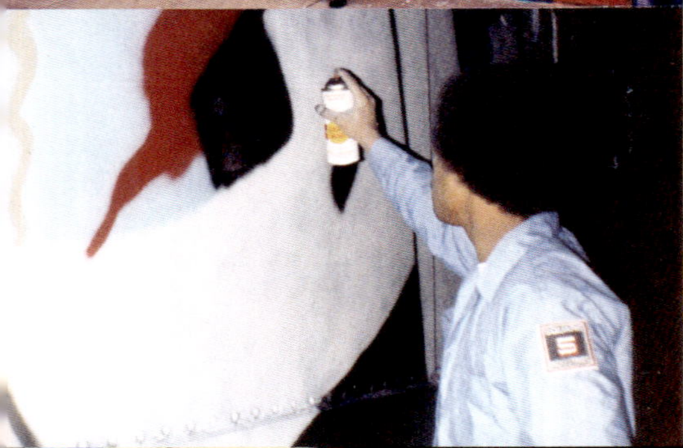
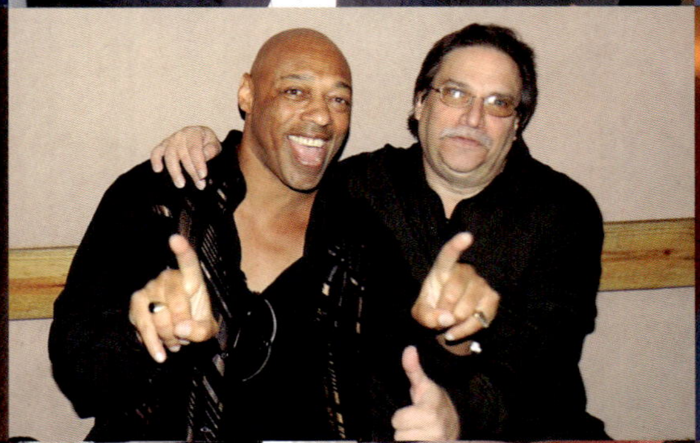
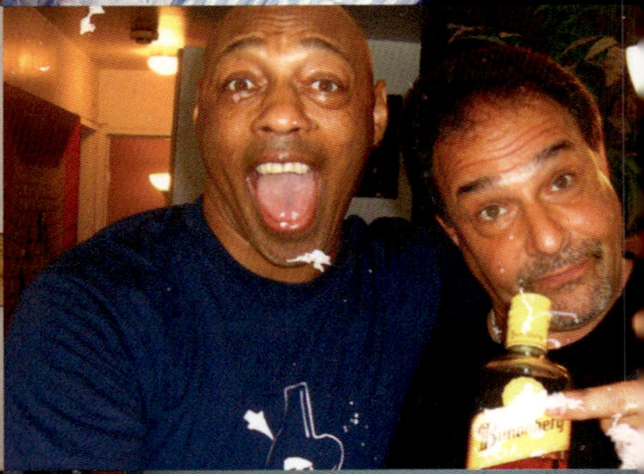
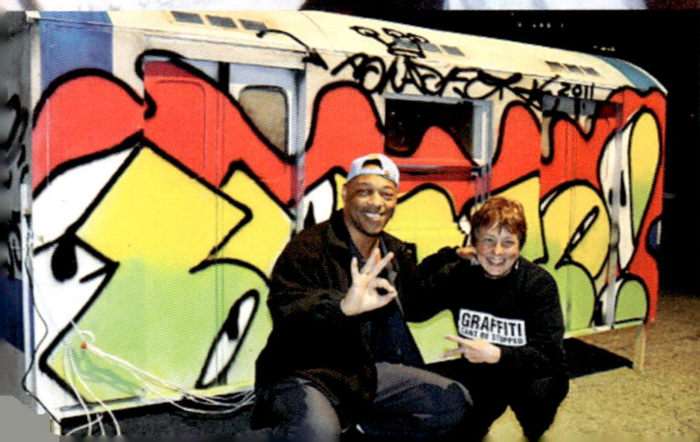
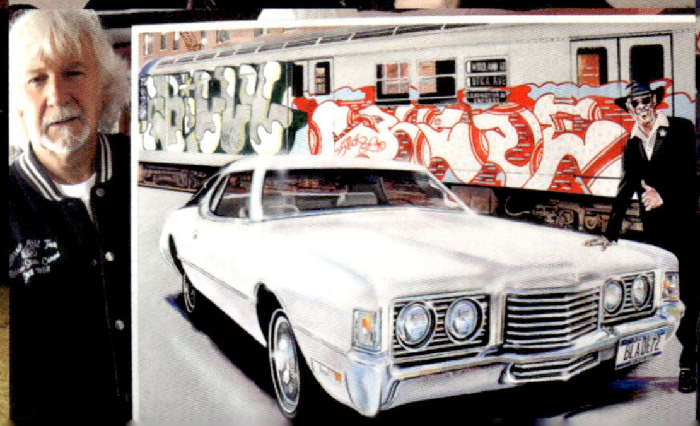
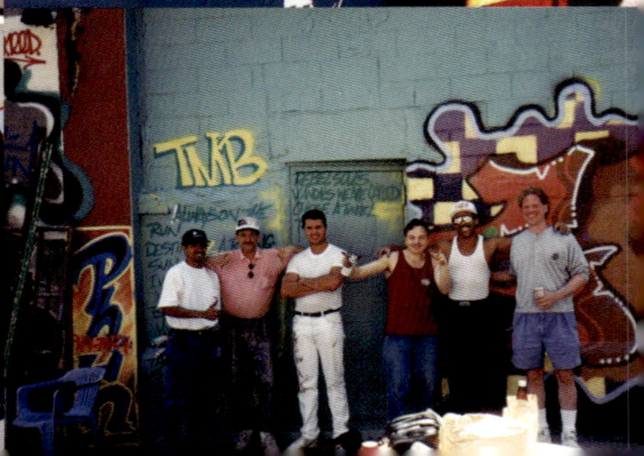
TMB

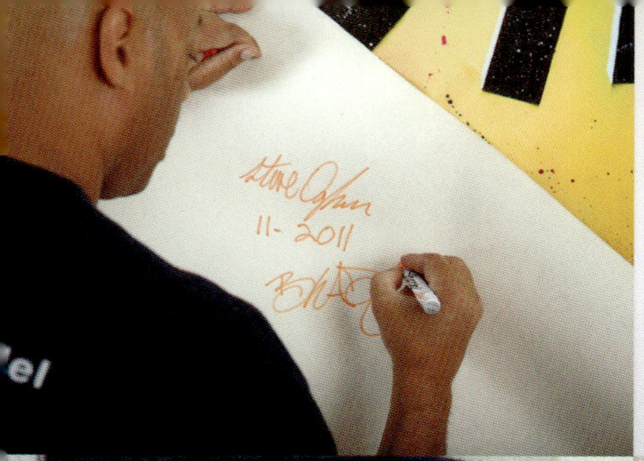
11- 2011
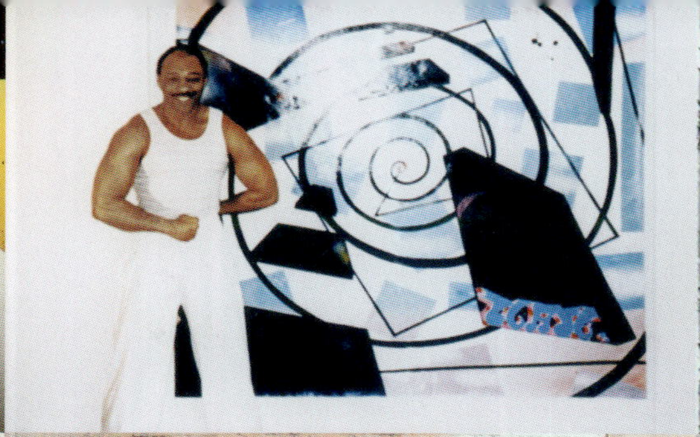
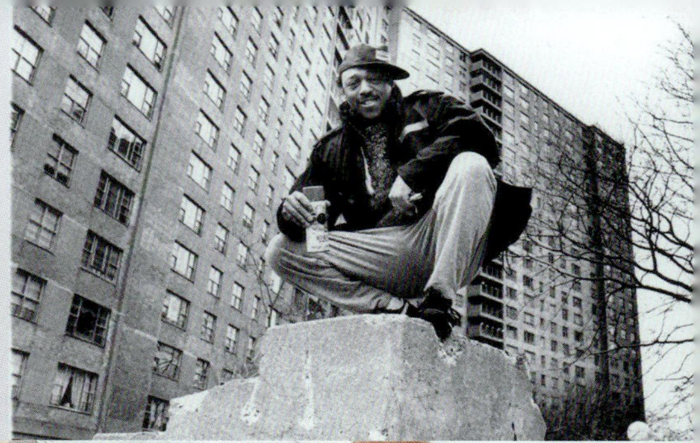
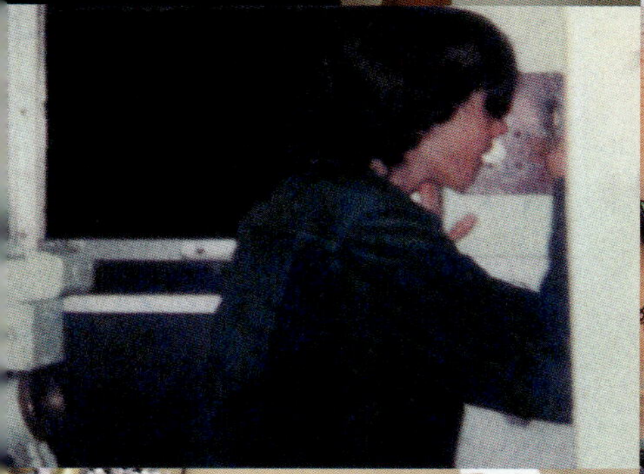
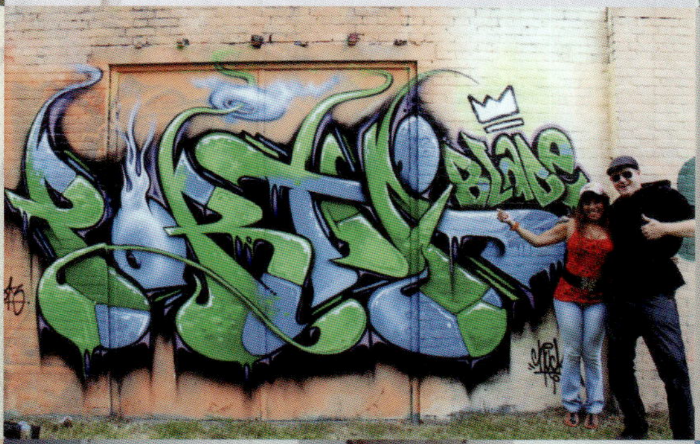
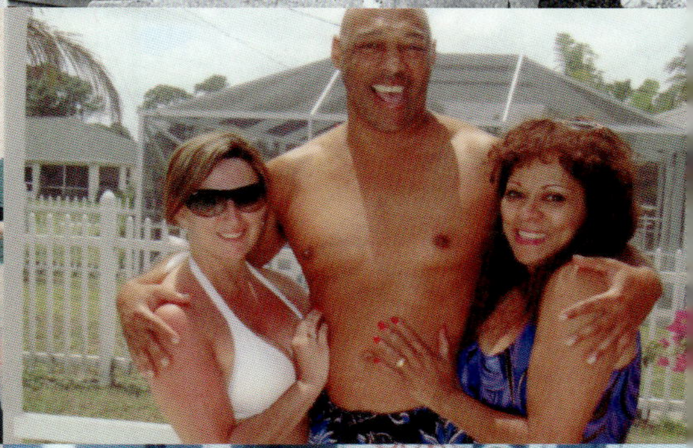
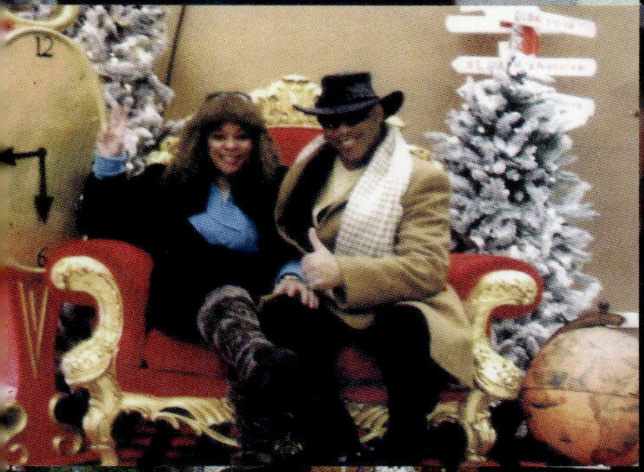
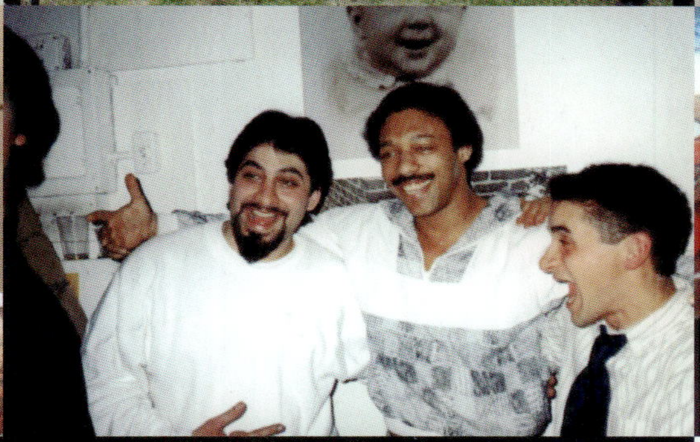
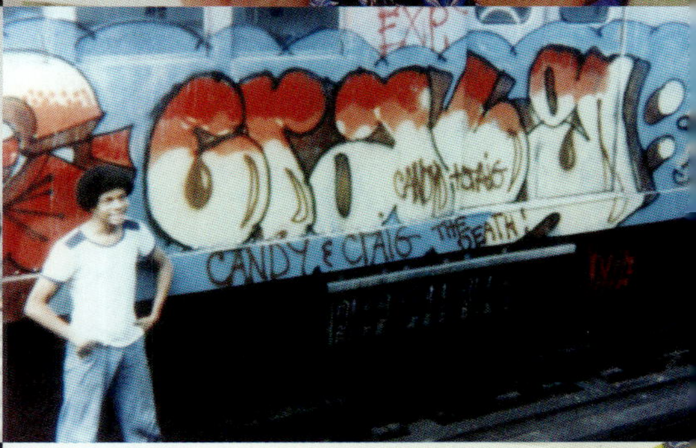
CANDY & CRAIG
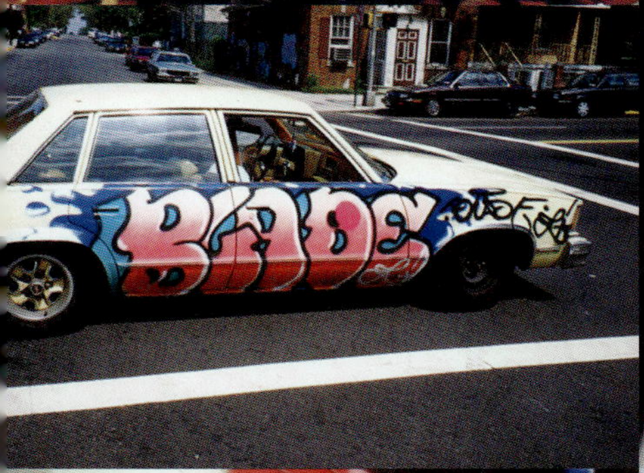
BLADE
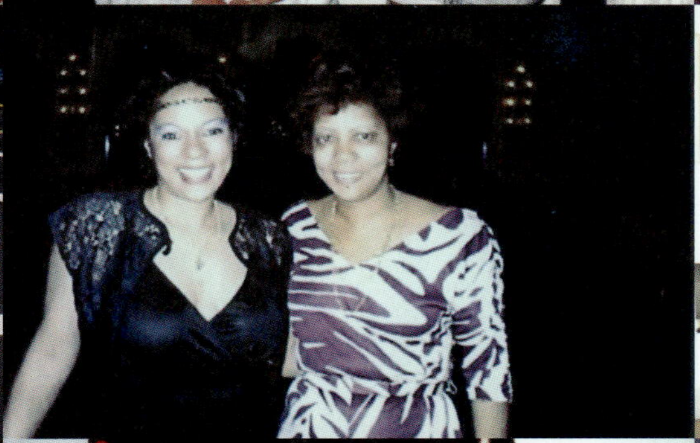
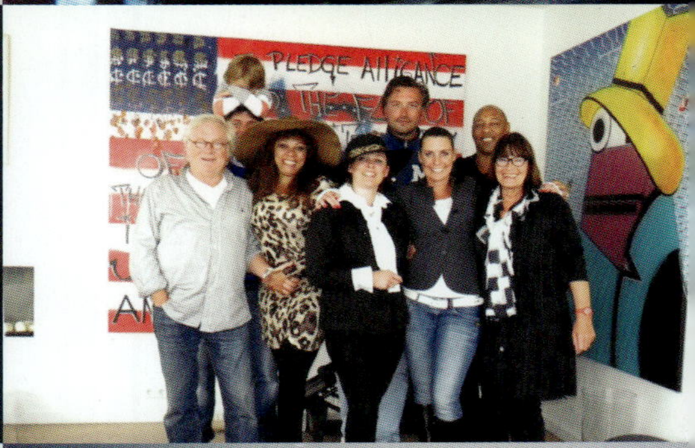
PLEDGE ALLIANCE
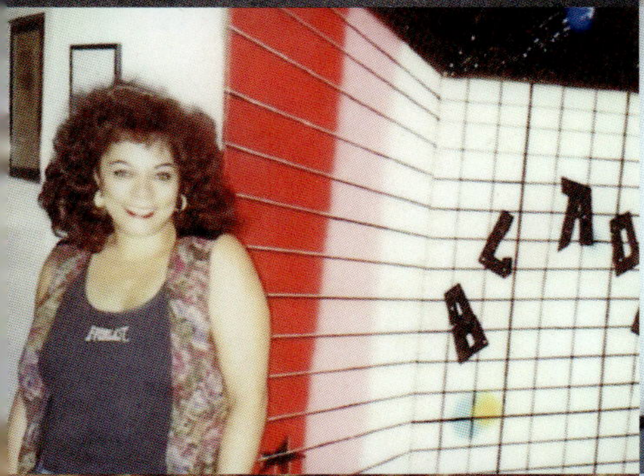
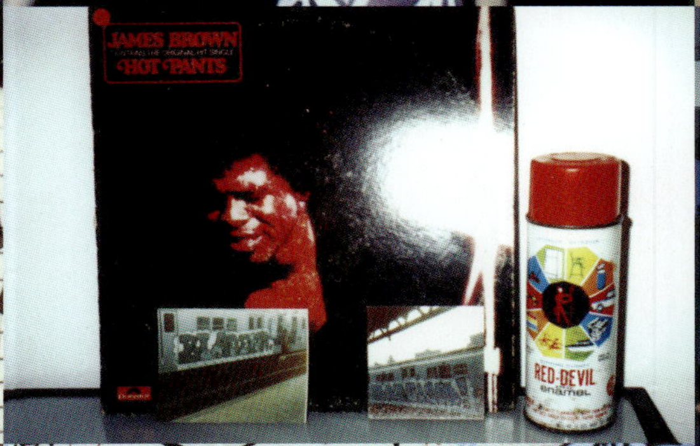
JAMES BROWN
HOT PANTS
RED-DEVIL
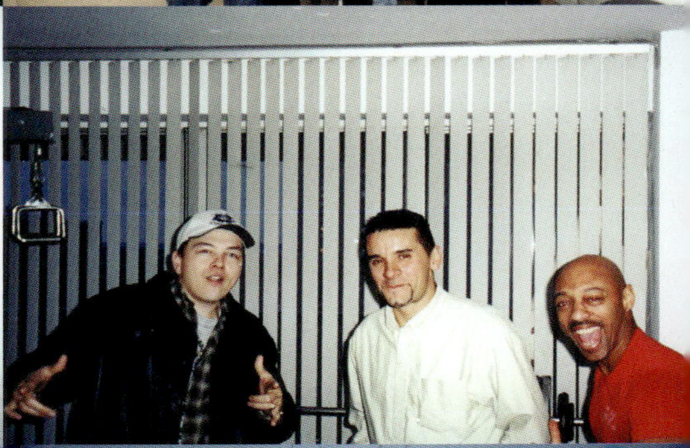
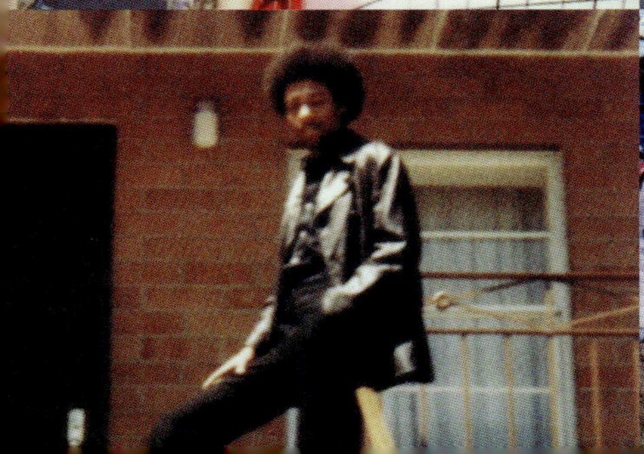
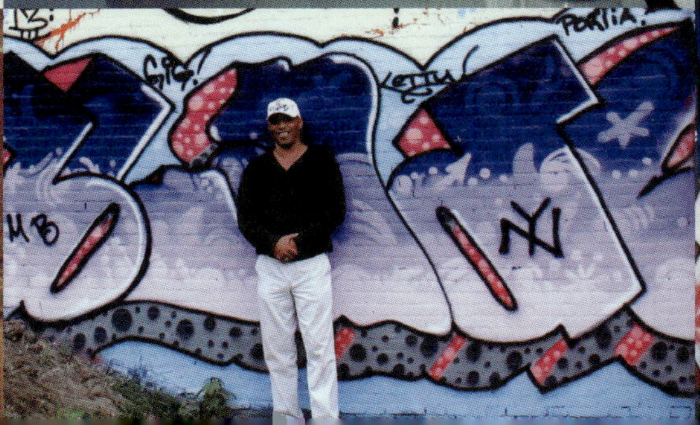
NY
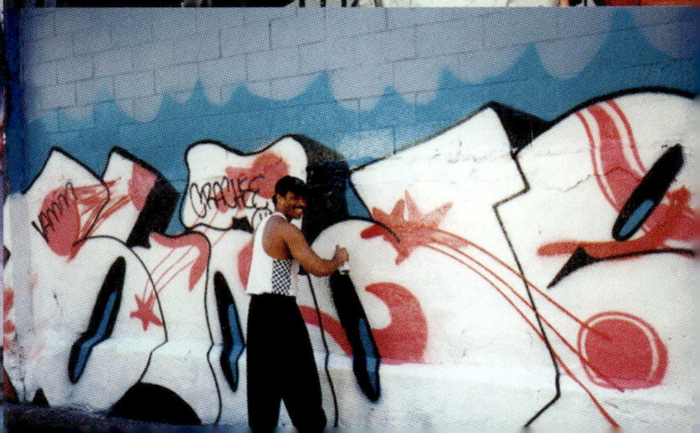

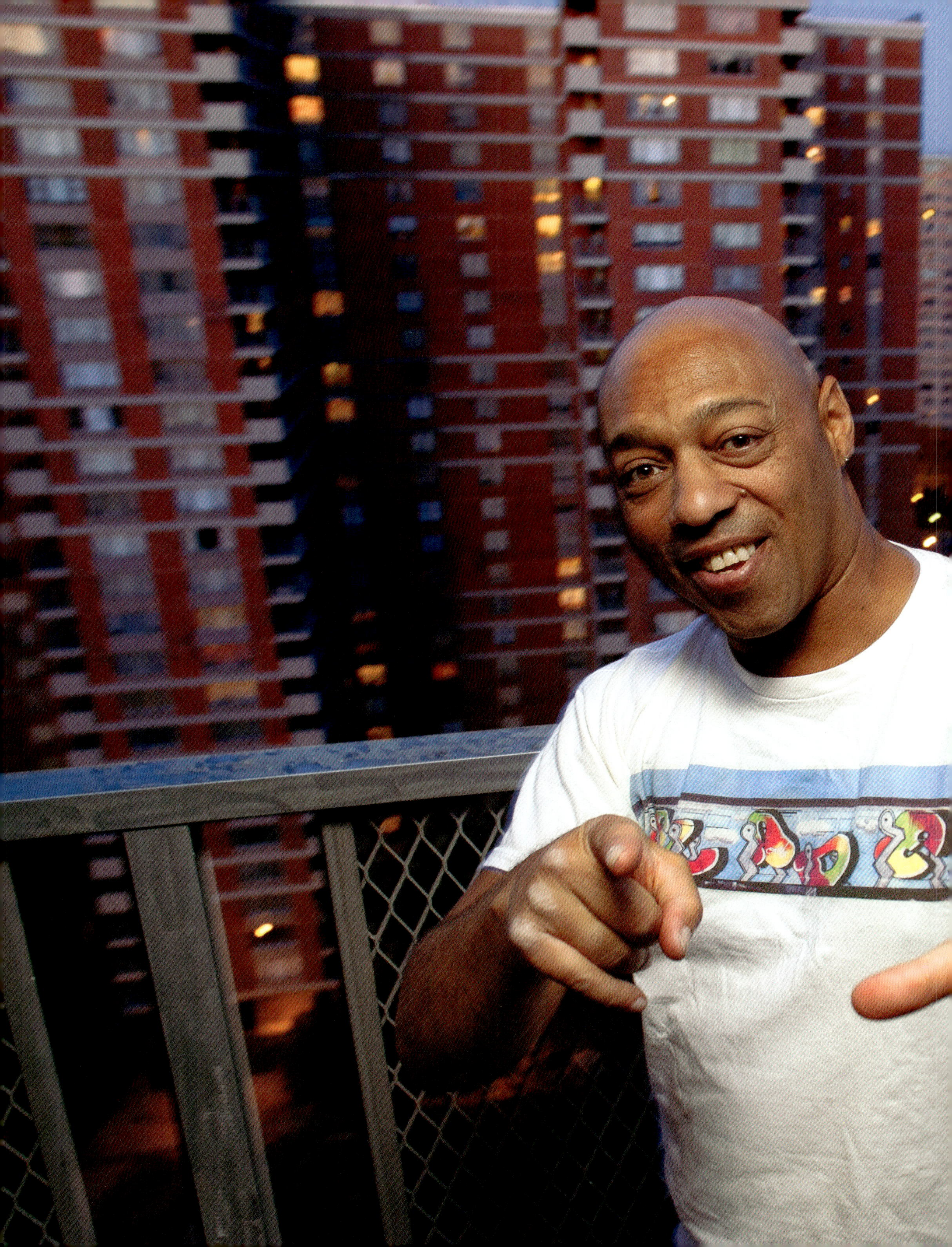

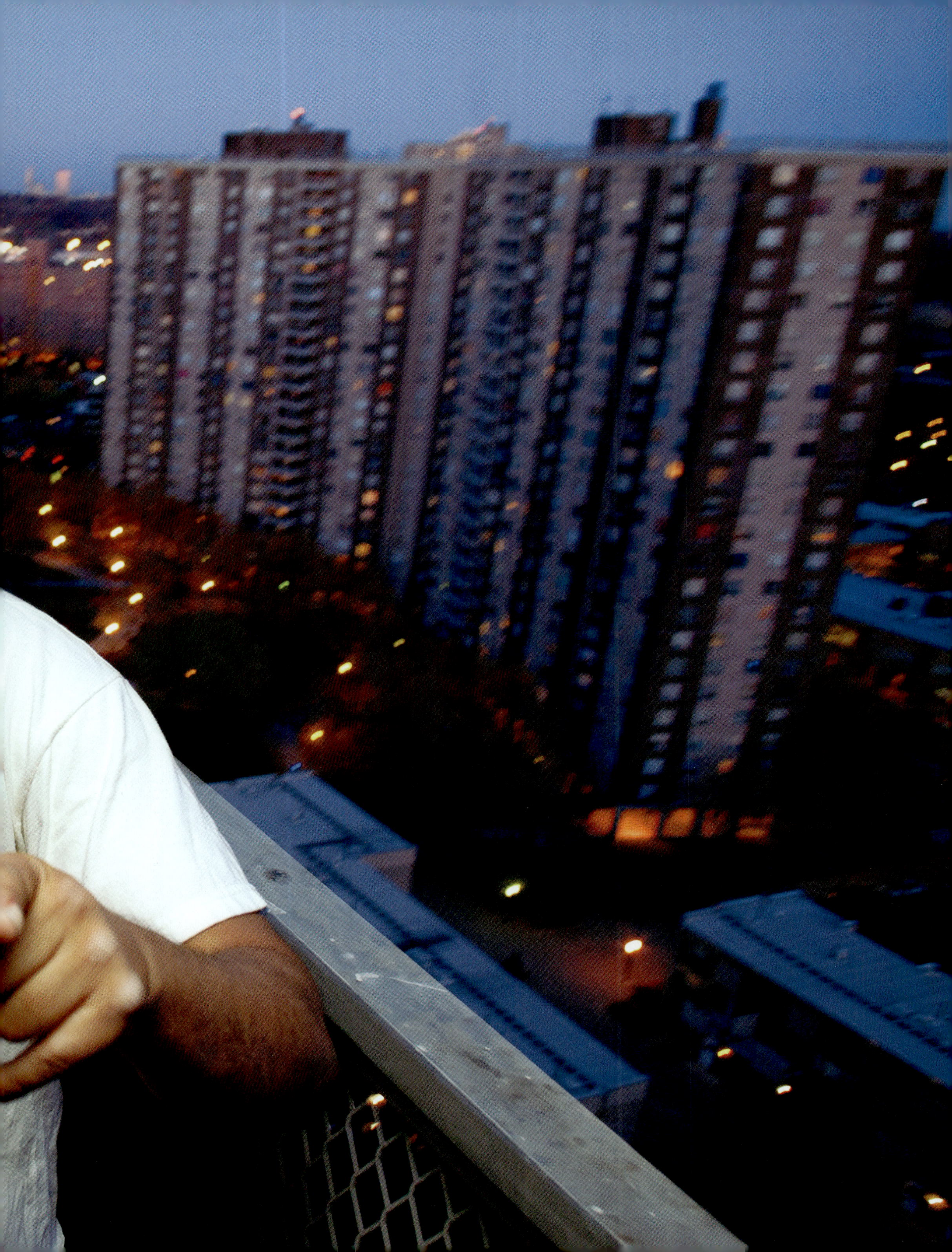

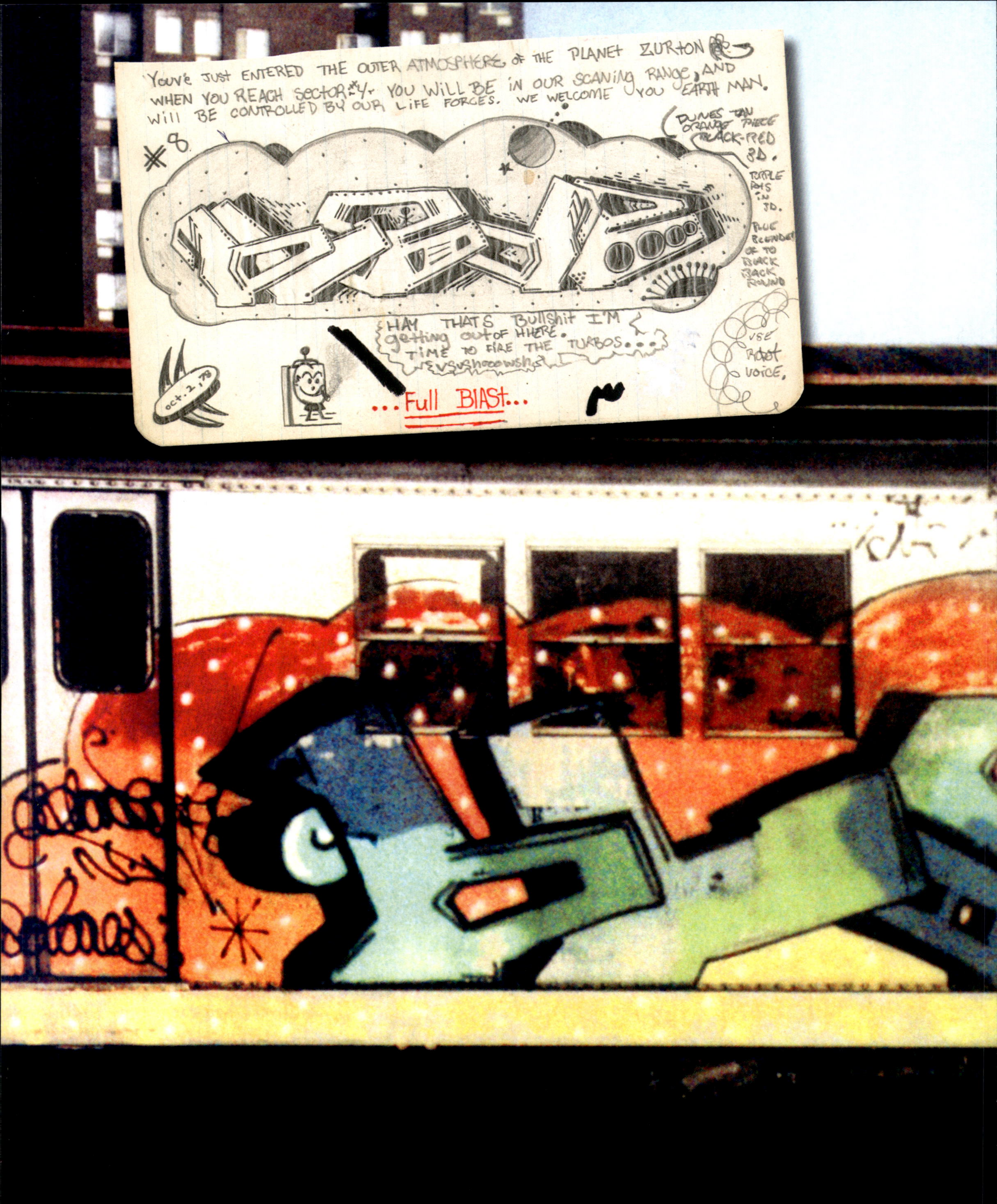

Previous spread: BLADE in the Bronx. 2012. Photo by Adam Wallacavage.

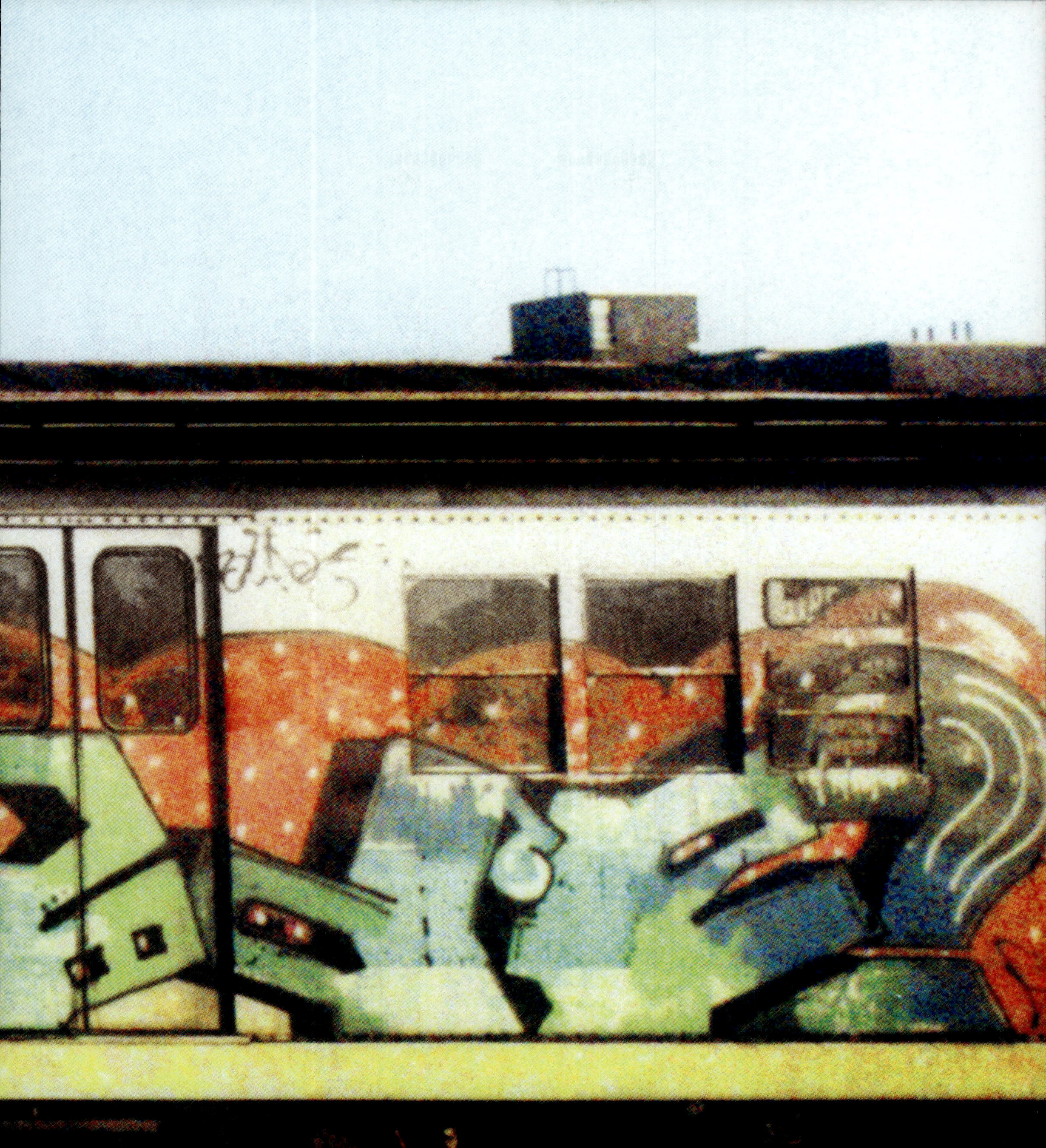

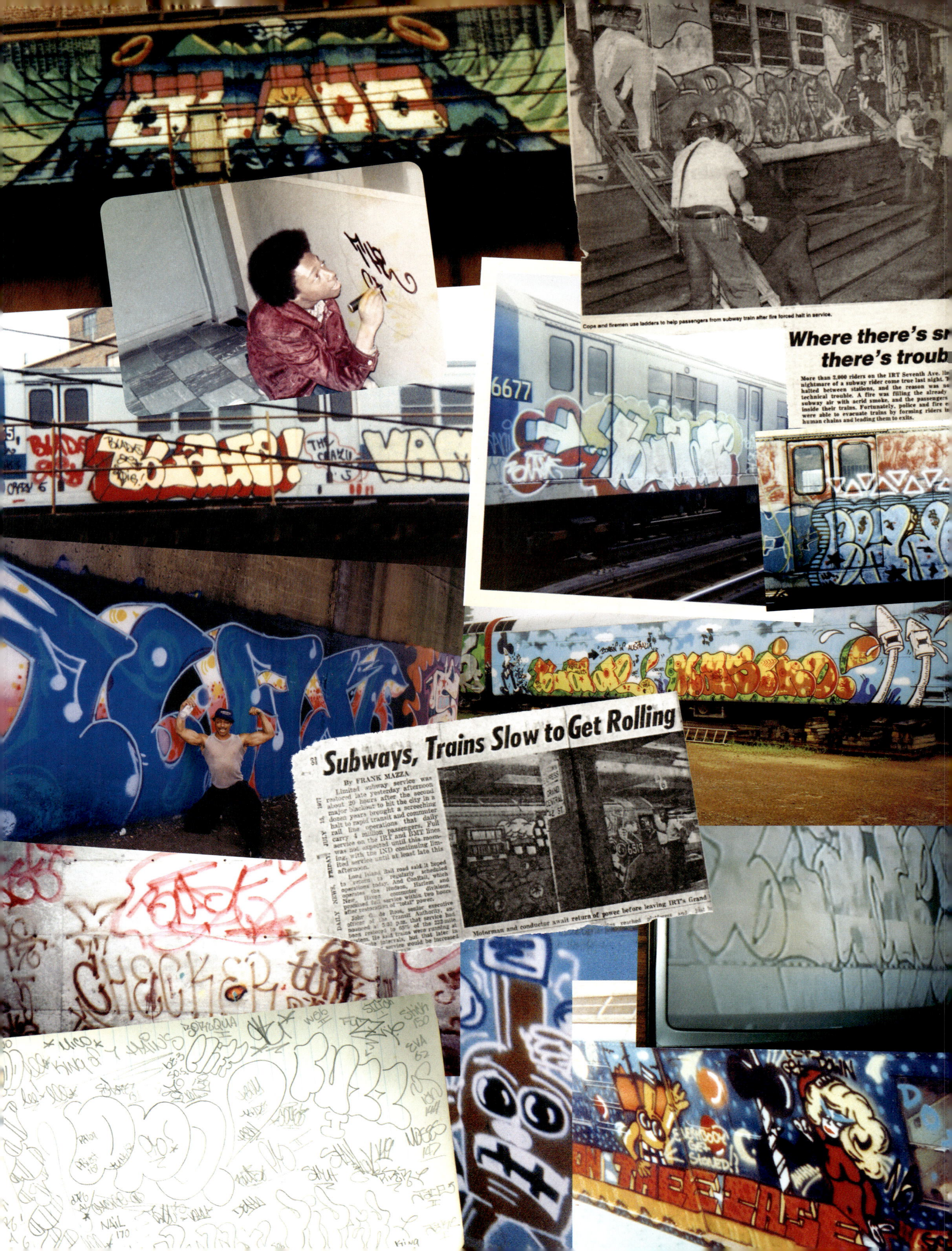

Cops and firemen use ladders to help passengers from subway train after fire forced halt in service.
Where there's sm
there's troub
More than 2,000 riders on the IRT Seventh Ave.
nightmare of a subway rider come true last night.
halted between stations, and the reason was
technical trouble. A fire was filling the already
subway air with acrid smoke, and the passengers
inside their trains. Fortunately, police and fire
were able to evacuate trains by forming riders
human chains and leading them to exits.
Subways, Trains Slow to Get Rolling
DAILY NEWS, FRIDAY, JULY 15, 1977
By FRANK MAZZA
Limited subway service was restored late yesterday afternoon about 20 hours after the second major blackout to hit the city in a dozen years brought a screeching halt to rapid transit and commuter rail line operations that daily carry 4 million passengers. Full service on the IRT and BMT lines was not expected until this morning, with the IND continuing limited service until at least late this afternoon.
Long Island Rail road said it hoped to return to regularly scheduled operations today. And ConRail, which operates the Hudson, Harlem and New Haven commuter divisions, promised full service within two hours after restoration of "total" power.
Motorman and conductor await return of power before leaving IRT's Grand

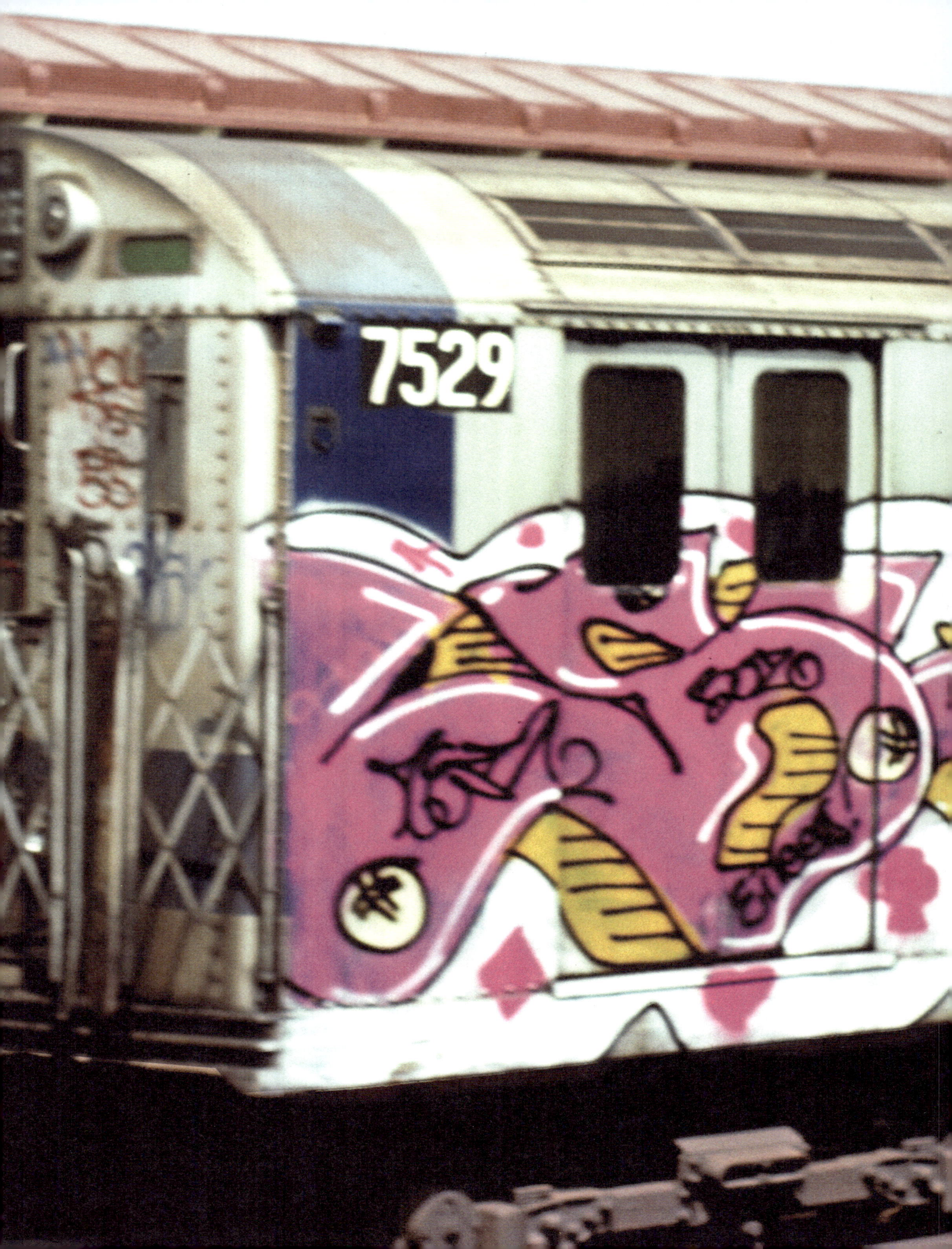
7529